龍眠手寫五馬圖一

Taxing Heaven's Storehouse

HARVARD-YENCHING INSTITUTE MONOGRAPH SERIES
32

TAXING HEAVEN'S STOREHOUSE

Horses, Bureaucrats, and the Destruction of the Sichuan Tea Industry, 1074–1224

PAUL J. SMITH

Published by the COUNCIL ON EAST ASIAN STUDIES, HARVARD UNIVERSITY, and distributed by the HARVARD UNIVERSITY PRESS, Cambridge (Massachusetts) and London   1991

The Harvard-Yenching Institute, founded in 1928 and headquartered at Harvard University, is a foundation dedicated to the advancement of higher education in the humanities and social sciences in East and Southeast Asia. The Institute supports advanced research at Harvard by faculty members of certain Asian universities, and doctoral studies at Harvard and other universities by junior faculty at the same universities. It also supports East Asian studies at Harvard through contributions to the Harvard-Yenching Library and publication of the *Harvard Journal of Asiatic Studies* and books on premodern East Asian history and literature.

Library of Congress Cataloging-in-Publication Data

Smith, Paul J., 1947–
    Taxing heaven's storehouse : horses, bureaucrats, and the
destruction of the Sichuan tea industry, 1074–1224 / Paul J. Smith.
        p.   cm.—(Harvard-Yenching Institute monograph series ; 32)
    Includes bibliographical references and index.
    ISBN 0-674-40641-9
    1. Tea trade—China—Szechwan Province—History.   2. Horse
industry—China—Szechwan Province—History.   3. Tea—Taxation—
China—History.   4. Cavalry horses—China—History.   5. China—
History—Sung dynasty, 960–1279.   I. Title.   II. Series.
HD9198.C5S64   1991
354.51'38008261372—dc20   91-7539
                                                                            CIP

The author wishes to thank Pat McDowell for drawing the maps and John Gates for indexing the text.

Endpaper illustration: Groom leading the horse Fine-Head Red (nine *sui* in age; 13 hands, 3 inches, in height), brought in through the Qinzhou market in 1087. From "Portrait of Five Horses" *(Wuma tu)* by Li Gonglin (1049–1106).

To my father, Barnet Norman Smith,
and the people he watched over and loved

Acknowledgments

In the ten long years it has taken to see this project to completion, I have incurred many debts, but more importantly made many friends. Many sponsors generously supported *Taxing Heaven's Storehouse* in its first phase as a dissertation project at the University of Pennsylvania. The Social Science Research Council funded the basic research for my dissertation at one of the world's great Sinological institutes, the Research Institute for Humanistic Studies of Kyoto University. During my two-year stay in Kyoto I received kind help and advice from Professors Umehara Kaoru and Shiba Yoshinobu, as well as the unstinting friendship and assistance of Sugiyama Masaaki. I remain deeply grateful to them and to the scholars and staff of the Institute and Kyoto University. On returning to the United States, I received continuing support from the University of Pennsylvania, which encouraged me to complete the project as soon as possible by providing a Mellon Dissertation Fellowship. That year taxed more than Heaven's Storehouse, as my manuscript grew increasingly fat and my mentors increasingly nervous. Sue Naquin peppered my margins with impatient queries about why I was telling her so much about so seemingly little, and there is no question she was right; the dissertation did contain a welter of undigested detail. But my chief task at that time was simply to finish, for a post-doctoral fellowship awaited me at the Center for Chinese Studies of the University of Michigan, and so I had no choice but to follow the advice of my advisor, Robert M. Hartwell: There's no fixing the thing now, so just finish it. You're only going to have to rewrite it completely for publication anyway. And of course he was right as well.

It turns out that dissertations are no less easy to unwrite than they are to write. Over time, as other projects and my job at Haverford came between me and the dissertation, I think I became a better historian; thus when I finally got down to the task of cutting a 750-page thesis in half, I was shocked and dismayed at what in my youth I had wrought. But again many friends and institutions came to my assistance. Haverford got the job rolling by transferring the manuscript—perhaps one of the last ever written on a typewriter—to disk. Al Feuerwerker, Bob Hymes, Peter Bol, Valerie Hansen, Hugh Clark, and Bill Rowe looked at all or parts of the manuscript in various stages of revision, as did anonymous peer reviewers at three stages in my career; and all offered comments that were both helpful and encouraging. I especially value a comment by John Chaffee, who, having read both the fat dissertation and the thin book manuscript, expressed regret for the details that had unavoidably been cut.

But three people in particular have helped bring this project to a close. Vasiliki Limberis entered my life as the process of rewriting was under way, and she not only agreed to honeymoon with me in Chengdu, but also to read my revisions as we fought off Sichuan's winter chill. I took it as an expression of affirmation that an historian of early Christianity could read a manuscript on Chinese fiscal sociology without showing too many signs of impatience.

Richard von Glahn has been my friend and colleague since our first seminar together under Bob Hartwell, and it has been a special pleasure to work on northern Sichuan during the Song at the same time that he worked on the south. Richard has read and commented on the entire manuscript, and helped me solve innumerable problems of scholarship, strategy, and morale. Not least, he has helped me formulate responses to the third key player in this publishing process, our mutual editor Katherine Keenum. Katherine has had perhaps the most difficult job of all, for it is she who has had to fight against the impatience and stubbornness of the author to turn a manuscript into a real book. I confess that I was shocked at all the work that remained after naively thinking that the book was finished—editorial details to which this author at least never gave a thought, but that inevitably turn up to haunt the printed page. Katherine has been thorough and patient through this entire process, and has always given me a second chance to fix problems that I refused to acknowledge the first time around. But even so there were suggestions that I resisted, and these will no doubt show up as the remaining flaws in the book.

Finally I must give thanks to our daughter Antigone, who at twenty months of age and armed with only a box of crayons, has discovered just what to do with the huge mountain of manuscript paper this book has spawned.

Contents

Tables

Maps

A Note on Measures

The following measures are used in the book:

Weight

> 1 *liang* = roughly 1.3 ounces
> 1 *jin* (or catty) = 16 *liang*, 1.3 pounds
> 1 *tuo* (of tea) = 100 *jin*
> 1 *liao* (a measure of maritime shipping capacity) = 500 pounds

Capacity

> 1 *sheng* = .86 quarts
> 1 *dou* = 10 *sheng*
> 1 *dan* = 100 *sheng*, or approximately 2.7 bushels

Area

> 1 *mou* = approximately one seventh of an acre
> 1 *qing* = 100 *mou*, or 13.99 acres

Distance

> 1 *li* = approximately one third of a mile

Counters

> 1 *pi* = a roll of silk approximately 40 feet in length
> 1 *guan* or *min* = a unit of account nominally worth 1,000 cash

Taxing Heaven's Storehouse

The one thousand *li* of the fertile lands of Shu are called "the land as productive as the sea." In the dry seasons water is raised to irrigate the soil; in the rainy seasons the sluice gates are shut. Therefore the *History of Yizhou* says:

> Flooding and drought are controlled by man, and there is no knowledge of hunger or dearth. For generations there have been no famine years, and all under heaven call Shu "Heaven's Storehouse."

Chang Ju
Huayang guozhi
Fourth century

Introduction

The fiscal history of a people is above all an essential part of its general history. An enormous influence on the fate of nations emanates from the economic bleeding which the needs of the state necessitates, and from the use to which its results are put . . . [F]iscal measures have created and destroyed industries, industrial forms and industrial regions even where this was not their intent, and have in this manner contributed directly to the construction (and distortion) of the edifice of the modern economy and through it of the modern spirit . . . The spirit of a people, its cultural level, its social structure, the deeds its policy may prepare—all this and more is written in its fiscal history, stripped of all phrases . . . The public finances are one of the best starting points for an investigation of society, especially though not exclusively of its political life. The full fruitfulness of this approach is seen particularly at those turning points, or better epochs, during which existing forms begin to die off and to change into something new, and which always involve a crisis of the old fiscal methods.[1]

Thus did Joseph Schumpeter, surveying the ruins of his own Austrian economy in the aftermath of World War I, outline his goals for a new field of "fiscal sociology." By its very definition fiscal sociology addresses the relationship between the state and the economy. In its fiscal dimension, it includes the study of the formulation, enactment, and consequences of economic policy. But fiscal sociology must also be resolutely sociological. As such it focuses on the relationship between social structure and economic policy, and draws us inevitably to the interaction between the state and society. Moreover, since it seeks to interpret how the state commands and exploits economic resources, fiscal sociology is also—indeed primarily—about power: how the state carves out its power to tax the economy from society at large, the means with which it exercises that power, and the impact of its power to tax on society and the economy. And finally, since the power to tax is shaped by long-term competition among agents of the state, local elites, and (in an agrarian economy) the peasants who supply the goods and services that fuel the economy, fiscal sociology must also be historical. At its broadest, then, fiscal sociology turns the study of a specific fiscal measure into an opportunity to investigate the social and economic prerequisites, as well as the consequences, of the exercise of state power.

The specific focus of my investigation is a state-run economic enterprise during the Song dynasty (960–1279)—the Sichuan Tea and Horse Agency. The Tea and Horse Agency was born in crisis, one facet of the New Policies reform movement spearheaded by Wang Anshi in 1068 that expanded the arena of state power in order to stem impending fiscal and military disaster. As the apogee of a three-century cycle of state activism, the fifteen-year reform campaign cast the relations between society, state, and the economy into sharp relief at a crucial point of transition, and revealed the capacities and limits of the imperial state in domestic and international arenas. As the epitome of New Policies economic activism, the Sichuan Tea and Horse Agency illuminates the distinctive features of the Song political economy, and provides a benchmark for assessing the impact of state economic policy during the Song and identifying key changes in the Chinese political economy between the Song and the late imperial era. The interrelationship between economic activism, China's medieval social and economic transformation, and the crisis of the mid eleventh century forms the background to this study of the establishment, exercise, and impact of bureaucratic control on the regional economy.

THE MEDIEVAL TRANSFORMATION, ECONOMIC ACTIVISM, AND THE CRISIS OF THE MID ELEVENTH CENTURY

Ever since the early twentieth century and the work of Naitō Torajiro, historians have come to view the late Tang and Song—roughly the mid eighth through the mid thirteenth centuries—as a period of fundamental change and a pivotal era in the shaping of early modern China. With each generation Song historians find new ways in which this medieval transformation, preserved for us in relatively rich detail thanks to the spread of woodblock printing in the ninth century, profoundly recast the social, intellectual, and economic life of the Chinese empire.[2]

The primary engine of this medieval transformation was the shift in the demographic center of the empire from the old political heartland of the Wei River valley and the North China plain to the lush frontier south of the Yangzi. Completion of a canal linking the Yellow River with the Yangzi in the early seventh century, widescale political disruption in the mid eighth and late ninth centuries, and gradual mastery of the techniques of rice cultivation drew migrants from the dry cereal-growing plains of the north to the paddy fields of the south. By mid Tang the five macroregions of South China (the Lower, Middle, and Upper Yangzi, the Southeast, and Lingnan), which in total held only 21 percent of the empire's population in A.D. 2 and 25 percent in 609, had grown to contain 46 percent of the entire population; the proportion climbed to 65 percent in 1080 and 71 percent by 1200.[3]

The expansion of irrigation works, new rice strains, and the spread of double cropping fostered what one scholar has referred to as a medieval "Green Revolution" in South China during the Song, providing grain surpluses that freed regions and producers to specialize in market-oriented tea and fiber-crop cultivation, timber and livestock husbandry, mining and salt production, textile, pottery, and metalurgical handicrafts and industries, and ship-building.[4] During the transition from Tang to Song, commodities entering the market expanded from luxury goods for the rich to daily necessities for much of the population. Economic self-sufficiency broke down as farmers in various regions of China were drawn into a network of internal trade, and trade itself spilled out of the confines of urban and quasi-urban regulated markets to encompass an articulated hierarchy linking rural periodic markets with great urban centers of distribution and consumption long distances away.[5]

Demographic change and economic growth intersected with the dynastic cycle of disintegration and reunification to produce a metamorphosis of the Chinese elite, a second essential feature of the medieval transformation. Over the long run, that metamorphosis can be described as the collapse of the medieval aristocracy and its replacement as China's dominant class by the local gentry. Here I would like to emphasize an intermediate stage in the transformation, the "bureaucratization of the Chinese elite" during the late Tang and especially the Northern Song.[6]

During the early Tang (618–907), high office and social prominence were monopolized by a small number of powerful lineages, descendants of the hereditary aristocracy that emerged in North China during the political fragmentation of the third through the sixth centuries.[7] Though the prestige of these great clans was checked by the abolutist aspirations of the Tang ruling house, the first persistent challenge to their political power came from the rise of regional military governorships in the eighth century, which fostered political mobility by recruiting members of prominent local lineages for key positions in provincial government. Aristocratic power succumbed completely to the social and military upheavals that engulfed the Tang in the late ninth and early tenth centuries, which drove the great clans south to seek safety and employment with the warlords who ruled South China during the period of the Five Dynasties (907–960). The local elites of South China, on the other hand, prospered from political fragmentation, especially the abundant opportunities it provided to turn wealth and military prowess into political power.

After the empire was reestablished by Song Taizu in 960, the last vestiges of the Tang great clans were able to survive as a coherent status group only by becoming what Robert Hartwell has termed a "professional elite"—families claiming pre-Song great-clan ancestry who, among other things, "placed most of their sons in the higher offices of the bureaucracy generation after generation, and . . . periodically controlled [Song] government between 980 and 1100."[8] For them, government service was the sine qua non of a distinctive social existence. At the same time the Song founders used a vastly expanded examination system to transform "local magnates" *(tuhao)* and "influential families" *(xingshihu)* into "official families" *(guanhu)*, or servants of the state.[9] As civil administration replaced the military institutions of the Five dynasties era and the authority of the central government grew, prominent families found ample reason to switch from local landlord to imperial civil servant. In addition to the immense prestige that came from membership in the most prominent status group in a new and vigorous dynasty, official service offered such substantial material rewards as relatively generous salaries, exemptions from labor service, and valuable legal privileges.[10] Perhaps most importantly, middle- and high-level officials could use the yin privilege to obtain official rank for their relatives, providing a way to perpetuate office-holding that was more reliable—and eventually statistically more significant—than the examination system.[11] The size of the civil service grew from around 10,000 individuals in the early eleventh century to over 34,000 individuals in 1080, at the height of the New Policies. Although the civil service roster never amounted to more than 0.25 percent of all Chinese households during this period, for wealthy families with good connections and the means to educate a son the chances of entering the civil service must have still appeared quite good.[12] By the twelfth century over-recruitment and factionalism, among other factors, would erode the predictability of office holding: The professional elite would merge indistinguishably into the local gentry, who would in turn pursue office-holding as just one facet of a local-oriented diversified mobility strategy that also included land-owning, commerce, and a variety of learned professions.[13] But during the eleventh century the aspirations of ambitious men were focused on the capital and the state, as the best minds of the empire left their native ties behind to join in common interest with their fellow scholar-officials.[14] The ideological coherence and ésprit de corps of the eleventh-century civil service insulated the Northern Song state to some extent from the importunate demands of specific social groups and classes, and contributed to a high level of what some sociologists term "state autonomy."[15] Autonomy in turn promoted an expansive view of the appropriate spheres of state power, and an activist orientation to the burgeoning commercial economy. By economic activism I mean, first, the propensity of the state to participate in the commercial economy both directly, through monopolies and government enterprises, and indirectly through commercial taxation; and second, a commitment to using state power both to promote economic activity and to increase the government's share of the economy's total resources. Many scholars agree that in terms of its theoretical orientation, its dependence on the extraction of revenues from commerce, and very probably the share of total economic activity that it commanded, the Song state—and in particular the statist reforms of the New Policies—represents the apex of economic activism in the imperial era.[16]

Economic activism was directly fostered by the increasing importance of government service in the lives of the Chinese elite. Following the rebellion of An Lushan in the mid eighth century, the channels of political mobility were expanded by the creation of new specialized financial institutions dedicated to exploring the rapidly growing commercial economy to replace revenues lost from direct taxation. By the rise of the Song in the tenth and eleventh centuries, this Tang nucleus of financial specialists had developed into a functionally integrated financial administration, disproportionately staffed by members and associates of the professional bureaucratic elite.[17] By the mid eleventh century these financial specialists, jealously perceived by the rest of the civil service to have the best chances for professional success,[18] had created a dense network of state monopolies and commercial tax stations dedicated to economic regulation, a network that drew half the state's revenues from commerce and industry.[19] This commercialization of the fisc, an extraordinary phenomenon in an agrarian pre-modern society, was not again repeated until the last century of the Qing, when political crisis and

y created by the Tea and Horse Agency subjected the Si-
a industry to centralized control for the first time and served
ening wedge for state penetration of the entire regional
. Moreover, the Agency survived both the reversal of the
in 1086 and the Jurchen conquest of North China in 1127
me a permanent fixture of regional government, generating
of administrative records that extends from the founding of
ncy in 1074 through the first quarter of the thirteenth cen-
is therefore possible to analyze the methods by which bu-
tic power was implanted and maintained, to evaluate the
rm capacity of bureaucratic power to secure goods and ser-
rom actors within and outside its territorial domain, and to
he impact of bureaucratic control on the Sichuan tea industry
e wider economy. These questions form the focus of Part
a case study of the Tea and Horse Agency in terms of the
ure, exercise, and limits of bureaucratic power. But in order
derstand why Song policy-makers thought a tea and horse trade
ecessary, and to appreciate the obstacles that had to be sur-
ted before the trade could be established, we have to examine
istorical background. Therefore in the three chapters of Part
I trace the evolution of Song horse procurement and the Si-
n tea industry, and analyse the sociological key to the creation
e Sichuan Tea and Horse Agency: the transformation of Si-
n's rural barons and local magnates—men who for centuries
ted the exercise of state power in their region—into imperial
servants eager to foster the tax power of the state.

the exhortation of foreign financial advisors once again heightened
the state's interest in taxing commerce.[20]

An elite whose wealth and power is directly linked to government service can be expected to formulate an activist and expansive
role for the state. But economic activism was reenforced by the
geopolitical context of the medieval transformation. As shown in
Map 1, the Song was coeval with the rise of the great steppes empires, products of a cumulative process of political maturing that
began with the Tibetan, Turkish, and Uighur empires during the
Tang, continued with the Khitan Liao (907–1125), Tangut Xi Xia
(c. 990–1227), and Jurchen Jin (1115–1234) empires during the
Song, and culminated in the world-conquering Mongol empire of
the Yuan (1260–1368). These steppes polities were able to fuse
their native mastery of mobile mounted warfare to increasingly
complex and disciplined forms of political and strategic organization, and to arm themselves with advanced military technology
bought, borrowed, and stolen from the Chinese. The lessons learned
by one nomad state were taken over by the next, each occupying a
larger portion of the steppe and agrarian China and presenting a
graver threat to the survival of the Song state until, by overthrow-
ing Song in 1279, the Mongols became the first nomad power to
conquer all of China.[21] Just as the unique relationship of the Song
state to the commercial economy was manifested in the structure of
taxation, so, too, the dynasty's unique relationship to its neighbors
was objectified in the structure of diplomatic intercourse. Alone
among the major ruling houses, the Song court was obliged to acknowledge the long-term diplomatic equality of its counterparts,
Xi Xia, the Liao, and Liao's conquerors the Jin, in a multi-state
Asian system.[22] In more practical terms, the rise of the steppes
empires left even the Northern Song with the smallest sovereign
territory of any major ruling house.

Song policy makers were constantly aware of their vulnerability
to the hostile empires of the steppe, and this sense of vulnerability
helped foster an innovative and interventionist approach to the
economy. The Song's precocious development of mining, iron and

steel, armaments, and naval technologies all derived in part from the need to repel sophisticated steppes cavalries. At the same time the Song state's unusually active involvement in domestic and international commerce was prompted by an endless search for new methods of generating revenues to finance these expensive technological and logistical solutions to military vulnerability.[23] State involvement could help stimulate the economy: Through its investment in mining and metallurgy, transportation and irrigation, its expansion of the money supply, and its dissemination of new knowledge and techniques, the Song financial administration initially helped promote China's medieval economic revolution.[24] But the transformation of the Song fisc into what Sogabe Shizuo has referred to as a perpetual "wartime economy" placed an escalating burden on producers, merchants, and consumers. By 1065, for example, defense expenditures alone consumed 83 percent of the government's cash and 43 percent of its total yearly income, surpassing by 35 percent the entire Ming budget of 1502.[25] Entire sectors of the economy, in particular salt and southeastern tea, were linked to the government's provisioning policies, making them especially vulnerable to panic-induced policy shifts. The government's tendency to flood the market with inflated salt and tea vouchers periodically threw both industries into depression, and by 1059 the southeastern industry had almost ground to a halt.[26]

Even as taxation dug ever more deeply into the economy of the mid eleventh century, the specter of military disaster began to loom. In the late 1050s and early 1060s the Tangut Xi Xia, already in possession of the entire Gansu corridor and the Central Asian trade routes leading through it, threatened to engulf the Tibetan tribes of Qinghai and Gansu, on the Song's northwest frontier. A Tangut-dominated Qinghai would have severed the court's last links with Central Asia, opened the Song to invasion from the steppe, and cut off the dynasty's only source of cavalry horses, the most critical component of defense along the northern frontier and the sole element of its defensive arsenal that the Song had exclusively to import.

Crises fuel the growth of the state. As historians, sociologists,

and political scientists have shown
in Europe and the Third World, "
tivities of state officials, especially
relatively insulated from ties to cur
interests, are likely to launch distinct
of crisis . . . [or to] elaborate already
distinctive ways, acting relatively co
of time."[27] When Emperor Yingzong
ran deep indeed: not only had fiscal a
but the nation had lost two emperors
Heaven's displeasure and a crushing
fers.[28] With the accession to the thro
nineteen-year-old son Shenzong, the w
political leadership and a renewal of imp
as his advisor Wang Anshi, who in 1
"Myriad Word Memorial" a blueprint f
ciety and the state. From 1068 until W
councillor in 1076, and thereafter until S
Wang and the emperor embroiled the na
known as the New Policies *(xinfa)*. New P
built on the cumulative apparatus and tech
financial service by mobilizing an expand
technicians to extend state control to new
and directly challenge private commercial i
foreign and domestic trade, in order to fin
policy of territorial expansion and national d

In Sichuan, the chief vehicle of state exp
Policies was the Tea and Horse Agency, crea
olize a hitherto untaxed industry—Sichuanese
ical component of defense—Tibetan war hor
and horse trade highlights the theory, practi
of New Policies activism with exceptional cla
omy had been highly impervious to centralize
tion from Tang through the early eleventh ce
protected its tea industry from regulation even
tea economy was coming under increasing gove

monopo
chuan te
as an o
econom
reforms
to beco
a body
the age
tury. I
reaucra
long-te
vices f
assess
and t
Two,
struct
to un
was
mou
the
One
chua
of t
chua
resis
civi

Part One

Linking Tea and Horses: Geopolitics and Horse Supply during the Northern Song

From the rise of the mounted archer around the fourth century B.C. until the incursion of European imperlialism in the eighteenth century A.D., the chief external threat to sedentary China issued from the nomad warriors of Inner Asia. Throughout these two millennia the predominant strategic goal of Chinese rulers was defense. Only rarely were armies sent out from agrarian China to conquer mobile warriors of the steppe; and until the Manchu-Qing conquest of Inner Asia in the eighteenth century paved the way for Han colonization, the results of expansion were always unstable.[1]

Preeminent among China's arts of defense were political strategies that aimed at neutralizing Inner Asian adversaries without lifting a sword, such as "controlling barbarians with barbarians" (*Yi Yi zhi Yi*), "halter and bridle" (*jimi*), and above all mutual trade (*hushi*).[2] But political management alone was insufficient to assure a stable frontier, and in the course of many centuries Chinese strategists evolved a military system calculated to hold back the nomad hordes when diplomacy and trade broke down.

Five components of what was at its best an integrated defensive network stand out. Visually the most prominent was the wall, ranging from the 1,400-mile Great Wall, begun in the third century B.C. and expanded throughout the imperial era in an effort to barricade China proper from the hostile steppe, to the rammed earthen walls that surrounded most towns and cities in the empire. Second, both walls and exposed frontier were defended by huge standing armies that by the eleventh century exceeded 1,000,000 men, supplied with provisions by elaborate systems of private merchant contracting and public works. Third, Chinese soldiers were armed and Chinese walls fortified by an armaments industry that by Song times turned out mass-produced weapons of iron and steel, and incendiary devices and projectiles employing gunpowder. Fourth, China's coast and its southern rivers and lakes were patrolled between the twelfth and the fifteenth centuries by the world's first permanently stationed navy. And finally, to provide mobility on the open plains and project imperial power outward in preemptive raids and expansionist campaigns, Chinese rulers from the third century B.C. on sought to put their own soldiers on horseback.[3]

Horses and Defense

The specific role of the cavalry within this integrated defensive system varied according to the circumstances and topography of battle. In a post-mortem assessment of the Jurchen Jin conquest of North China in 1127, the equestrian and imperial adviser Lü Yihao offered a formula on the subject: "A level plain covered by shallow grass, on which horses can advance and withdraw with ease, is the perfect terrain for the use of cavalry. There one soldier on horseback can oppose ten soldiers on foot. But mountain forests and streams and marshes, which endanger and impede the forward and backward movement of horses, is just the right terrain for the use of foot soldiers. There one soldier on foot can defend against ten soldiers on horseback."[4]

An anecdote from the end of the Sino-Jurchen war suggests that even Lü Yihao underestimated the advantage that well-drilled cavalrymen enjoyed on the open plains. Following the conclusion of a peace treaty, the Jurchen sent seventeen horsemen from Kaifeng to report to their government in Hebei. Along the way they encountered a Chinese military commander and his 2,000 foot soldiers, who refused to let the Jurchen messengers pass. The seventeen cavalrymen divided into three groups, and "seven of them came to the front and five each were disposed on the left and right wings. As they approached the government forces, the seven horsemen charged and the government soldiers retreated a little. The wings took advantage of the retreat and rode into the government forces, shooting arrows. The government forces were dispersed, and almost half the troops were lost."[5] Because almost all of China's northern frontier was composed of plains suited to the deployment of mounted soldiers, the possession of an adequate cavalry adequately supplied with horses must be counted as an important part of China's front line of defense.

But despite a basic mastery of the technique of cavalry warfare by the second century B.C., the sedentary Chinese could never compete with nomads whose way of life was founded on breeding horses and riding them in war and the hunt.[6] Moreover, warhorses were the only component of the Chinese defensive system that could not be domestically supplied. Perhaps because Chinese strategists were so keenly aware of their disadvantages in cavalry warfare, they accorded the horse the paramount role in the preservation of the state. The Han general Ma Yuan (14 B.C.–A.D. 49), for example, had inscribed in bronze his conviction that "[h]orses are the foundation of military might, the great resource of the state."[7] Men of Tang believed that "horses are the military preparedness of the state; if Heaven takes this preparedness away, the state will totter to a fall."[8] And virtually identical sentiments were expressed during the Song and after.

Although no nomad federation could conquer and rule China without learning complex lessons of political organization and military technology, Chinese statesmen had convincing evidence that through their abundance of horses and mastery of cavalry warfare the nations of the steppes could topple Chinese states. The *Yuan History* boasted, for example, that "the Yuan . . . conquered all under Heaven with the power of the bow and the horse."[9] Similarly, although dynasties crumbled as much from internal decay as from a shortage of horses, dynastic collapse and crises of horse supply often occurred together. Several years before the Jurchen conquest of North China, the Song horse supply system had fallen into disarray, inspiring the Song patriot and defender Li Gang to write that "the Jin were victorious only because they used iron-shielded cavalry, while we opposed them with foot soldiers. It is only to be expected that [our soldiers] were scattered and dispersed."[10] A century later, when the Jin in turn succumbed to the Mongols, Jurchen soldiers were themselves unable to obtain horses.[11]

Because every ruling house of China, whether native or foreign, needed to create and maintain an adequate supply of horses, equine administration developed into a special field of military administration. Horse procurement required more elaborate policies in some periods than in others, but it is probable that no dynasty created more elaborate mechanisms or devoted greater effort to obtaining sufficient horses than the Song. As a rough comparison of dynastic herd sizes reveals, it is certain that no dynasty met with less success.

Among the native dynasties, for example, the early Han possessed a herd of 300,000 head, grazed in thirty-six pastures located on its northern and western borders. The early Tang had a herd over twice that size, numbering 760,000 head, pastured in North China and out through the Gansu corridor. And the Ming (1368–1644) state had access to an estimated 800,000 horses for civil, postal, and military use, 395,000 head of which were deployed for frontier defense. Herd sizes for the great Yuan and Qing (1644–1911) conquest dynasties are not known, but there are some figures available for the smaller steppes empires, occupying only a fraction of the Yuan and Qing pasture lands. The fifth-century Northern Wei claimed a total population of 2,000,000 horses; the Khitan Liao may have had 1,800,000 battle-ready mounts, if a statutory allotment of three horses for each soldier was strictly followed; and the Jurchen Jin had 470,000 horses in government pastures in 1188.[12]

How many horses did the Song state possess? Starting from a maximum of 200,000 head in 1008, the number of horses of all ages and sizes held in government pastures or distributed among the armies dropped to about 153,000 in 1069, when the government was forced to abandon the policy of keeping reserve horses in favor of buying replacements as they were needed.[13] Moreover as numbers declined, so, too, did horse quality, forcing Song cavalrymen to ride animals that were much smaller and less hardy than the steppes ponies that carried their opponents into battle.[14] Thus, even as Song iron, armaments, and naval technologies were leaking out to the steppes through trade and the migration or capture of Chinese artisans, depriving the government of its major strategic advantages, the dynasty's ability to field a cavalry was also deteriorating.[15]

Understandably, both Northern and Southern Song policy makers and critics were possessed by the vision of an irreparable horse gap. In 1061, when no more than a fifth of the nation's's 60,000 cavalrymen could count on finding a mount, Director of Herds and Pastures Song Qi lamented that "[t]he northern [Liao] and western [Xi Xia] enemies are able to oppose China only because they have many horses and practice riding; this is their strength. China has few horses, and its men do not practice riding; this is China's weakness. Whenever the enemy transgresses against us, the court confronts strength with weakness. Thus in ten battles there are ten defeats, and the principle of victory is rare. These days memorialists wish only to increase our army in order to destroy the enemy. They do not realize that without horses we cannot even create an army."[16] A century later the Viceroy of Sichuan, Yu Yunwen, put the matter more succinctly: "The [Jurchen] enemy is strong because it has many horses, and we are weak because we have none. Any three-foot-high toddler knows the difference between strength and weakness."[17]

GEOGRAPHY AND HORSE SUPPLY

But why was the Song, whose financial administrators could harness the productivity of the great medieval economic revolution and whose foundries, arsenals, and shipyards fostered the industrialization of war, so unable to supply itself with horses? The primary factor was geopolitical. As part of a multi-state Asian system (see Map 1), the Song was coeval with the rise of the great steppes empires: the Xi Xia and Liao states that dominated the Great Wall frontier of the Northern Song, and the Jin and Mongol empires that first drove the Song southward and then eradicated it completely. Represent-

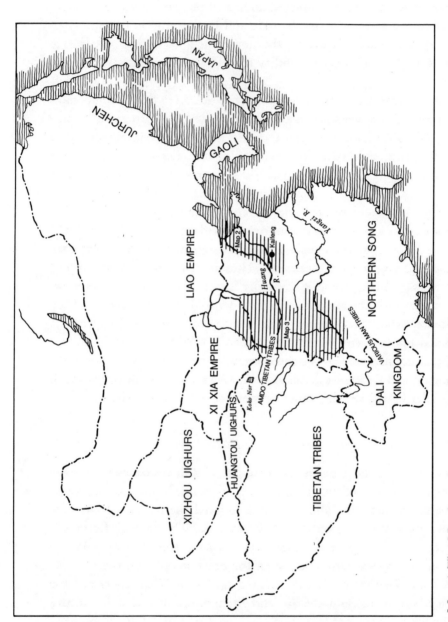

Map 1 The Northern Song in a Multi-State Asia

Source: Zhongguo lishi dituji, vol. 6 (Shanghai, Ditu chubanshe, 1982), plates 3–4.

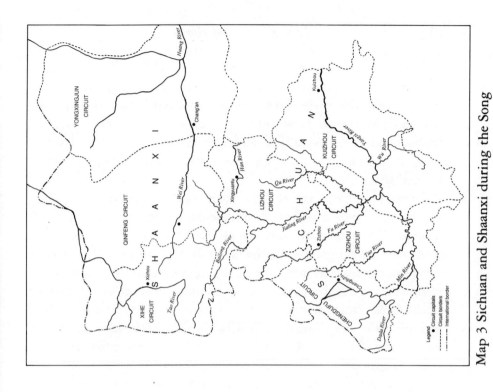

Map 3 Sichuan and Shaanxi during the Song

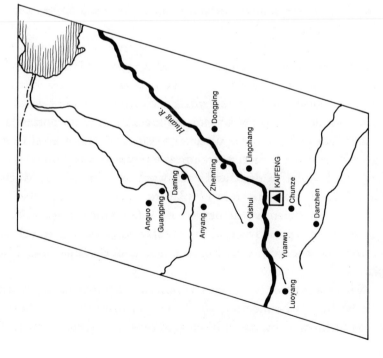

Map 2 The Northern Song Pasturage Inspectorates,
ca. 1005

Sources: SHY bing 21/4a–5b; *SS* 198/4928

ing the political zenith of the nomad way of life, these steppes empires not only enjoyed abundant supplies of horses of their own, but were also able to deny the Song access to Asia's most productive pastures and foreign horse supplies. This created a vicious circle: without horses the Song was unable to defend the lands and suppliers it had, and thus its sources of cavalry mounts became more limited still.

Geography, then, trapped the Song state in an ever tighter dilemma that fused together the problems of horse acquisition and defense. One important casualty of the Song's strategic encirclement was its program of national herds and pastures. The Song occupied the smallest territory of any of the major dynasties. The territories inherited by the Northern Song fell short of the traditional Great Wall border of China proper by sixteen prefectures, including the site of modern Beijing, which remained under Liao sovereignty.[18] Even in the northwest, the border was at first as close as the Liupan Shan, east of the modern province of Gansu;[19] and in the southwest, the frontier began at the Yunnan and Guizhou plateau. The Southern Song, driven south of the Huai River, was even more tightly confined.

The horse was native to only a very few pockets within the boundaries of the Song empire, including parts of Huainan; Fujian, and the aboriginal territories of Hunan and Lingnan, but these southern horses were all too small and fragile to be ridden by armored soldiers.[20] Nor was there any pressing need for horses in the Chinese economy, since population pressure and the nature of Chinese agriculture made it more economical to employ water buffalo, donkeys, and mules in draft and pack work and for riding. With no fundamental economic role to play in agrarian China, the horse remained an expensive luxury whose sole civilian users were men requiring an especially rapid or ostentatious means of travel, such as officials, the very wealthy, doctors, and Buddhist and Daoist priests.[21]

With such strict limits on the number of horses naturally available within its boundaries, the Song had to meet its replacement needs (estimated by one mid-eleventh-century observer as 22,000 head annually) by building up herds in its own state pastures or buying horses from foreign suppliers.[22] Herd-building could be costly, but it freed Chinese dynasties from too great a dependence on unreliable nomad horse traders. In the early seventh century, Zhang Wansui, Lesser Lord of the Tang Imperial Stables, had built 5,000 horses into a national herd of 700,000 head, bred and pastured in the northern grasslands of Shaanxi, Ningxia, and the Gansu corridor. Song officials longed to imitate the Tang system; but in the intervening centuries, most of the lands used by Tang had been lost to the Tanguts, Uighurs, and Tibetans, had been ploughed under by a land-hungry local populace, or were now too close to the militarized frontier for the safe pasturing of horses.[23] Song administrators turned instead to the North China plain and the Wei River valley, where by 1005 they had located fourteen pasturage inspectorates (*jianmu*) occupying 690,000 acres in an arc radiating out from the capital city of Kaifeng (see Map 2).[24]

Great official optimism accompanied creation of the stock-raising program: in 979, one impassioned advocate of domestic breeding anticipated producing 10,000 foals annually from 20,000 mares, which he predicted would free the Song from all dependence on foreign suppliers within a decade.[25] But geography and an agrarian regime that resisted the intrusion of the horse placed two insurmountable obstacles in the way of a reliable pasturage system. First was the inexperience of the Song Chinese population in all matters hippological. Roughly 16,000 military pasture hands (*bingxiao*) were needed to staff the pasturage system; but because horses were marginal to the Chinese economy, the pool of men knowledgeable about breeding and horse management was inadequate. The incompetence of the handlers kept birth and foal survival rates well below target and produced horses that were worthless as cavalry mounts. By the early 1070s, when the pasturage system was dismantled, stock farms produced an average of only 1,600 foals annually, of which few more than 250 head on average could be judged battle-worthy.[26]

The second obstacle was the need to locate pastures in a region of low economic productivity and high population density. By the late tenth and eleventh centuries warfare and the consumption needs

of the capital and the frontier armies had turned all of North China
into a deficit region. In order to supply the capital and the frontier
with grain, the government had to import 6,000,000 *dan* (ca.
16,150,000 bushels) of tribute rice yearly from the southeast, and
negotiate expensive provisioning contracts, paid for out of the public monopolies, with northern grain merchants.[27] North China's
low agricultural productivity affected the pasturage inspectorates as
well, for despite an allotment of 50 *mou* (ca. 7 acres) per horse, the
system was still far from self-sufficient. Hay, cereals, and sugar and
medicines had to be imported for the animals, at a cost of "several
million strings of cash yearly" by 1026.[28] But if 50 *mou* of land
were needed to support a single horse, only about eighteen *mou* (2.5
acres) were necessary to feed a family of five during the eleventh
century.[29] The inhabitants of the North China plain, the most populous and third most densely populated region of Northern Song
China, were naturally quick to chip away at the fringes of the government's grasslands; and from the 990s to the mid 1070s some
320,000 acres of government grasslands were lost to farm families.[30]

The pasturage system succumbed to the reforming zeal of the
New Policies. One hallmark of the New Policies administrators was
their propensity to invest every possible state resource in productive, or at least profit-making, ventures. Greatly dissatisfied with
the useless breeding program and expense of maintaining a reserve
herd, the reform government chose not to fight the squatters, but
rather to close down the inspectorates and rent out the pasture lands
to the farmers that had coveted them for decades. By 1075 all but
one of the original fourteen inspectorates had been abolished, their
good horses distributed to the armies and the rest sold off *(chimai)*
to private buyers.[31] This reform-era disestablishment marked the
end of an active Song commitment to creating and maintaining a
national herd. Through the *baoma* (baojia horse), *huma* (household
horse), and *jidi muma* (land in return for pasturing a horse) measures, the New Policies and successive administrations attempted
to stable a small number of government-owned horses among the
populace in return for tax exemptions, incentives in cash and land

use, and limited use of the animals themselves.[32] The three policies were designed primarily to keep a small number of animals within reach of the capital at no, or only modest, cost to the government, and in practice at least did not contribute to building a national herd. During the 1130s and 1140s the Southern Song government attempted to breed and build up herds in various prefectures along the Yangzi River, but the results were predictably dismal. As Li Xinchuan, the main chronicler for the Southern Song, remarked of the effort, "[T]he entire nation's supply of horses depended upon [foreign horses bought at] the three frontiers of Sichuan, [Gansu], and Guangxi."[33]

It should be noted, however, that the Song was not unique in its failure to build a national herd within the confines of agrarian China. In the mid eighth century, when Tang lost its pastures in the Gansu corridor to the unified kingdom of Tibet, it, too, was forced to rely on foreign suppliers, mostly Uighurs, for war horses.[34] Similarly in Ming, despite territorial control that encompassed the entirety of China proper, the policy of private stock-farming that at first provided the foundation of the dynasty's horse supply was transformed in about a century into a monetary tax used to buy horses from the Mongols.[35] And even the Mongol founders of the Yuan, deprived of access to the horses and breeding grounds of the steppes by the princely rebellions that lasted until the early fourteenth century, "were unable, from the imperial center in China, to acquire enough horses to back a regular and realistic horse policy which would have given them the mobility always to act successfully against rebels and retain the unity of the empire."[36]

Thus ultimately any dynasty that did not possess substantial tracts of steppe land was forced to buy horses from the pastoralists who did. In this sense, the Song was confined by geopolitical constraints that were shared in some measure by all native dynasties, and in some circumstances by conquest dynasties as well. But because of its strategic encirclement, the Song was doubly constrained. For while the Han, Tang, and Ming all enjoyed the advantage of a disunited steppe, filled with nomad tribes eager to sell China their horses, the Song faced a steppe dominated by united empires, willing to withhold their own horses from trade, and able to block the horse trade of others. And as the steppes empires grew stronger, the Song's range of suppliers grew increasingly narrow, making it almost as difficult for the Chinese state to buy foreign horses as it was to breed its own.

A broad survey of China's horse suppliers over time reveals the dimensions of the problem faced by the Song. Most Chinese dynasties could purchase war horses from a wide range of Inner Asian suppliers; but of the nine major pasture regions shown on Map 4, the Song could obtain reliable cavalry horses from just one. Transoxania (Region I) and Dzungaria, Tianshan, and the Tarim Basin (Region II) sent extremely valuable horses to the Han and Tang; and the Tianshan grasslands also served as a major pasturing region for the Qing.[37] The Tarim Basin oases of Kucha and Khotan and the Turfan oasis of Karakhojo maintained continuous trade relations with China all through the Northern Song; but though these kingdoms were all skilled horse breeders, their contributions to the Song herds were limited to occasional presentations of a few exceptional mounts. Even Khotan, which in the nineteenth century was a major seller of horses to India, sent only a few of its horses to the Song, although five of these are portrayed in a series of paintings by the Northern Song artist Li Gonglin.[38]

Region III, the Mongolian steppe, traditionally provided sedentary China with both its fiercest enemies and its greatest numbers of foreign horses. But Xi Xia and Liao dominion over the Ordos Desert and the Inner Mongolian plateau effectively blocked the Song's access to Mongolian ponies. Liao rulers also interdicted the horse trade from modern Manchuria (Region IV), an important source of horses for the Tang and Ming. At first the Song bought Manchurian horses from the Jurchen; but by the late tenth century the trade was permanently severed by the Liao, despite an effort by the Song in 1081 to reroute the trade through Korea.[39]

Perhaps most damaging of all was the Song's exclusion from the pastures of Inner Mongolia (Region V) and Hexi (Region VI). The Ming fairs set up to buy horses from the Tumed and Ordos Mongols attracted more animals than the government could use, demonstrat-

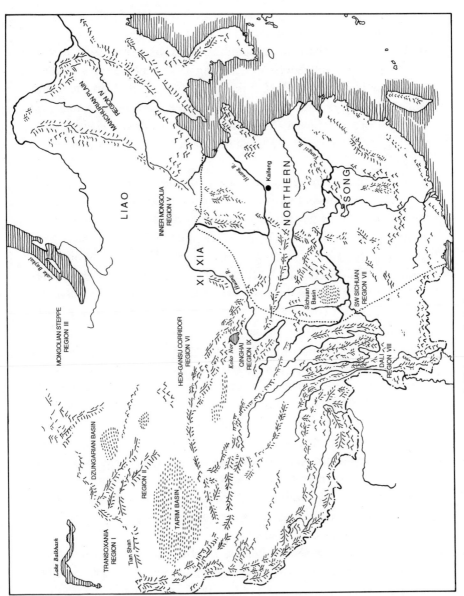

Map 4 Major Pasture Regions of China and Asia

Lake Baikal

MONGOLIAN STEPPE
REGION III

LIAO

MANCHURIAN PLAIN
REGION IV

INNER MONGOLIA
REGION V

XI XIA

Huang R.

Kaifeng

NORTHERN

SONG

Yangzi R.

TRANSOXANIA
REGION I

Tian Shan

DZUNGARIAN BASIN

REGION II

TARIM BASIN

HEXI-GANSU CORRIDOR
REGION VI

Etsin R.

Koko Nor

QINGHAI
REGION IX

Sichuan
Basin

SW SICHUAN
REGION VII

DALI
REGION VIII

ing how unnecessary it was to exercise sovereignty over a pastoral region in order to benefit from its bounty. But during Song times these lands were directly occupied by the Liao and Xi Xia, neither of whom would sell horses to the Song.[40] Initially the government could buy horses from Hexi, a major supplier to the Han and Tang. But the Tanguts effectively shut down the Hexi horse trade, first by expelling the Liugu (Six Valleys) Tibetans from Liangzhou in 1011 and then driving the Uighurs out of Ganzhou, Guazhou, and Shazhou in 1028.[41]

Where then could Song military planners buy horses? Three alternatives were available, but two of these were severely restricted. Song purchasing agents could buy horses from the *Man* pastoralists of southwestern Sichuan (Region VII); but Sichuanese horses were in general too small and fragile to survive the trip to the northern front, let alone serve in battle. Even during the Southern Song, when the roughly 5,000 horses purchased annually in Sichuan had become a critical component of the government's horse supply, these undersized ponies were disparaged as "halter-and-bridle horses," (*jimima*), in reference to the court's largesse in accepting them and in contradistinction to the "war horses" (*zhanma*) bought in the northern markets.[42] Usable horses were bred in the highlands of Dali (Region VIII), successor of the Yunnanese kingdom of Nan-zhao. The Southern Song government, its capital and militarized borders pushed far south, opened markets in Guangxi to buy 1,500–3,000 Yunnanese horses annually; but given the mortality rates for convoying horses through China, sectioned by mountains and river valleys and lacking forage along the way, it would have done little good for the Northern Song state to buy horses in Guangxi for battles along the Great Wall.[43]

Thus for Northern Song the only reliable source of cavalry mounts came to be the high grasslands of northeastern Tibet (Region IX, the modern Chinese province of Qinghai), particularly the rich valleys of the Yellow River tributaries east of Lake Koko Nor (Lake Qinghai) that even today send some 20,000 horses yearly to the Tibetan interior.[44] The Tibetan tribes of Amdo were grouped into three territorial and political clusters during the early Song. The northernmost territory, centered around the town of Liangzhou (Ningxia, Wuweixian), gateway to the Gansu corridor, had been dominated since the early tenth century by the Liugu (Six Valleys) tribal federation. The Six Valleys federation was the Song's most powerful ally from the last decade of the tenth century until its expulsion from Liangzhou by the Tanguts in 1011.[45]

South of the Six Valleys federation, the Qingtang Tibetan tribes occupied the Huanghe and Huangshui valleys east of Lake Koko Nor and Xining. From 1008 on the region gradually came under the leadership of Juesiluo (Tib. rGyal-sras, "Son of Buddha"), a scion of royal Tibetan stock imported from Gaochang to unite the fractious tribes of Qinghai. By 1015 the Qingtang Tibetans under Juesiluo had replaced the Liugu federation in the Song diplomatic alliance, and they remained Song's chief ally through the eleventh century.[46] A third cluster of Tibetan tribes occupied the Longxi basin of Gansu, bounded to the south and east by the Wei River and the Liupan Shan. Termed *shuhu,* meaning "cooked" tribes who acknowledged Chinese suzerainty, these tent-dwelling pastoralists never attained the political autonomy of the two larger Amdo federations (see Map 5).[47]

With good grasslands, a surplus of horses, and armies of 60,000–100,000 troops, the military strength of the two major Tibetan federations was impressive.[48] But the main source of their wealth and power was the profits they accrued as participants and middlemen in the Inner Asian trade. Because of their position at the eastern terminus of the Gansu corridor, virtually all of the trade routes linking Turkestan and Song China passed through Tibetan domains and depended on the Tibetans for protection against raids by Xi Xia and the smaller steppes tribes.[49] In fact the Qingtang Tibetans derived enormous advantage from Tangut expansion through Liangzhou into the Gansu corridor, which drove more and more traders through their domains. By 1028 Juesiluo's monopoly over the Central Asian trade routes into Song China was complete, and "because the merchants of all the countries of Gaochang had to pass through Qingtang," wrote the authors of the *Song History,* "Juesiluo became wealthy and powerful."[50]

In addition to profiting from the trade of other nations, the Qinghai Tibetans controlled profitable mineral resources of their own and derived various animal products from oxen, sheep, and camels.[51] But unquestionably their most important economic asset was the horse.[52]

Song officials brought two perspectives to the Tibetan horse trade. On the one hand, they saw in its great profitability a powerful instrument for binding Tibetan interests to the Song—the "halter-and-bridle policy"—and for persuading Tibetan tribes to fight the Xi Xia—the equally classic policy of "using barbarians to fight barbarians."[53] The frontier expert Zhang Qixian stressed this perspective when he reflected on the consequences of the Tangut conquest of Lingzhou in 1001. A strategically located town on the Yellow River that communicated directly with Liangzhou, Lingzhou had been the Song's only outpost in the Ordos (see Map 5).[54] In a memorial submitted in 1002, Zhang worried that the Xi Xia leader Li Jiqian planned to augment his conquest by luring the Liangzhou Tibetans to his side, which would alienate the Song court from the only group strong enough to serve as a buffer between themselves and the Tanguts. Echoing contemporary opinion, Zhang wrote that although Tibetan loyalty could not be counted on, their greed at least was reliable. Therefore, "in order to bind their hearts, we must entice them with great profits." And the key to successful enticement was to "pay the Tibetans a much more generous price than usual for horses, and to regale them with drink and food, in order to enrich and gratify them." By enhancing the profitability of the horse trade, Zhang hoped not only to guarantee Tibetan loyalty to the Song but to encourage their animosity to the Xi Xia as well. For as Zhang saw it, "[Liangzhou] and the smaller local western Tibetan tribes depend exclusively on selling horses for their profits, and receive thereby the Court's grace and trust. If Bandit Li Jiqian cuts their trade routes, this must certainly bind [the Tibetan tribes together in feelings of] vengeance and hate, which will inspire them to fight on their own. The principle is quite clear."[55]

But if officials sought to bind Tibetans to the Song through the horse trade, they also recognized that the horse trade bound the

Song to the Tibetans. It was this perspective that Zhang Qixian's colleague He Liang had emphasized in 999, as the Song court debated whether to defend its precarious position in Lingzhou:

> Horses flourish in the lands north of Qi [the Inner Mongolian pasturelands north of Hebei and Shanxi], but since the [Liao] became wild and intractable, no horses have come south . . . Nor have the Tangut bandits ever sold horses in our frontier commanderies. Therefore cavalry horses for punitive expeditions can be obtained only from the western [Six Valleys] Tibetans. But if we abandon [our bridgehead at] Lingzhou, then the cruel and clever Tangut bandits . . . will bring [the smaller eastern Tibetan tribes of the Longxi Basin] under submission and blockade the sale of horses from the west. Should that happen, I do not know where war horses for the Middle Kingdom will come from.[56]

Xi Xia did indeed attempt to woo away the Liangzhou and Longxi basin tribes, but Zhang Qixian was proved right in his prediction that the Tibetans would fight to preserve the profits of their horse trade with the Song rather than submit to the blandishments of the Tanguts.[57] Though alliances with the Tanguts or Khitan against the Song could serve as a powerful lever during internal tribal power struggles, in the long run stable relations between steppes dwellers were limited by the similarity of their pastoral economies.[58] The Qinghai Tibetans and Xi Xia both produced livestock and salt, and thus had little basis for trade with each other. Sedentary China was the only source of the agricultural and manufactured goods, in particular metalware, textiles, and tea, that the pastoralists desired. Liao and Xi Xia were imposing enough to use war or the threat of war to force Song to give them many of the goods they desired as tribute or appeasement payments.[59] But the fragmented Tibetan tribes of the Song era did not possess that power, and therefore it was in their interests to preserve their access to the products of agrarian China through an alliance based on trade.

Thus on a foundation of mutual interest a military and economic alliance developed between the Song and the Tibetan federations. From the Tibetan perspective this alliance was based on their need for Chinese products and the profits of international trade. For the Song the alliance was founded on the need for open routes to the far west, for a stable buffer zone between itself and the powerful and ambitious Xi Xia, and for the absolutely irreplaceable Tibetan horses.

But these mutually interlocking concerns were confronted by a twofold set of problems, both related to the expansion of the Xi Xia empire. The first set was strategic in nature: On the Tibetan side, the tribes in Qinghai gradually lost territory and trade routes, and their always fragile political unity fragmented. At the same time, the number and geographic range of Song horse markets steadily diminished, the supply of horses fell short, and by the 1060s the Song border itself was threatened.

The second cluster of problems involved finance. Once the horse trade was regularized, the government had to find an acceptable way of financing it. Because of the fiscal crises of the mid eleventh century, this meant devising a method of paying for horses that did not require disbursements from the central government. Moreover, since classical Chinese monetary analysis held that the export of copper bullion and bronze coins through foreign trade would depress the price of grain and hence harm the farmer, it was necessary to pay for horses with commodities rather than currency.[60] But because the Shaanxi-Gansu frontier was a deficit region of low productivity, countertrade commodities had to be transported in; and because it was a region of poor transportation facilities, the movement of goods was very costly. The problem was thus one of linking horse purchases to some regional industry in a way that would relieve the central government of the financing burden, and provide countertrade commodities that could be commanded by the government, transported economically, and accepted by the Tibetan traders.

The Sino-Tibetan alliance of trade and mutual defense was the Song answer to the broad structural challenge of procuring horses. The strategic and financial problems associated with horse procurement for the Song eventually found their most stable solution in the reform policy of expanding the frontier, forcibly annexing the Tibetan tribal lands of the northwest, and subsequently establishing a state-run enterprise that nestled markets in the new territories and paid for Tibetan horses with Sichuanese tea. Behind this strategy lay a series of policies in response to crises brought on fundamentally by Tangut expansion. The reform policy can be understood, therefore, only in the context of events and the particularities of the frontier marketing system on the eve of the New Policies and the creation of the Tea and Horse Agency.

THE FRONTIER MARKETING SYSTEM

Horse procurement during the first three decades of the Song was relatively unspecialized, with responsibility shared between local prefectural officials on the one hand, and emissaries despatched on ad hoc procurement missions from the capital on the other.[61] In 991 one such envoy, Palace Auxiliary Ding Weiqing, was sent to buy horses in Liangzhou, setting off a chain of events that culminated in regularization of the trade. At the Tibetans' request Ding helped escort their horse caravans past Tangut raiding parties through Lingzhou and on to Kaifeng, and henceforth the pace of the horse trade quickened. Horse tributes from the Liangzhou Tibetans are recorded regularly from 994 on, and in 996 Ding was permanently assigned to Liangzhou to help counter Tangut efforts to interdict the trade.[62] At the end of 998 the Liangzhou ruler Yulongben personally accompanied a tribute of 2,000 horses to Kaifeng, the first of four generations of Six Valleys chieftains given the privilege by the Song of going to court.[63] The Song-Tibetan economic and defensive alliance was now firmly established.

In 998 the government also institutionalized the marketing system, in order to accommodate the accelerating flow of horses. At the center the government set up a Horse Pricing Agency (*gumasi*) in Kaifeng to evaluate and set a price on foreign horses, and to distribute the animals to appropriate pastorage inspectorates. Horses were in turn funneled to the capital and regional armies through a system of permanent prefectural horse markets (*shima zhi chu*), supplemented by a network of "horse summoning centers" (*zhaoma zhi chu*). Native horse traders were encouraged to bring their animals to the permanently staffed market bureaus opened in each of nineteen prefectures, arrayed in an arc extending from the northeast loop of the Yellow River through Gansu and down to the southwest corner of Sichuan (see Map 5). But for additional territorial range

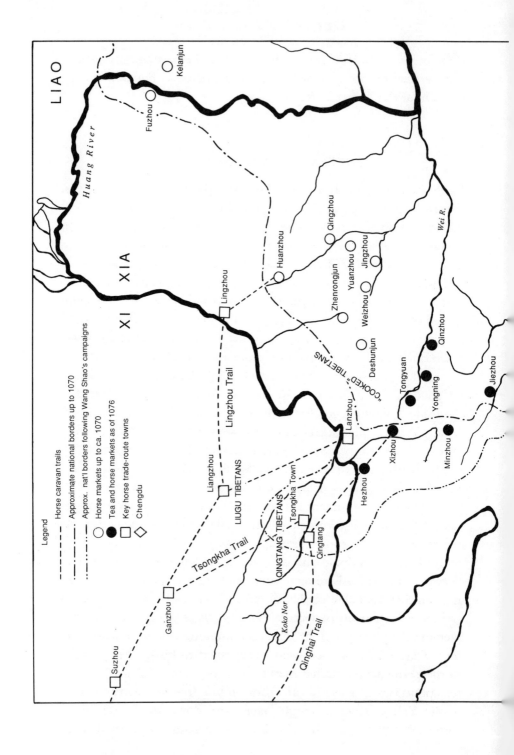

LIAO

XI XIA

Huang River

Kelanjun

Fuzhou

Lingzhou

Huanzhou

Qingzhou

Yuanzhou

Zhenrongjun

Jingzhou

Weizhou

Deshunjun

"COOKED" TIBETANS

Wei R.

Qinzhou

Tongyuan

Yongning

Jiezhou

Lanzhou

Xizhou

Minzhou

Liangzhou

Lingzhou Trail

Hezhou

LIUGU TIBETANS

Tsongkha Town

QINGTANG TIBETANS

Qingtang

Tsongkha Trail

Ganzhou

Koko Nor

Qinghai Trail

Suzhou

Legend

Horse caravan trails

Approximate national borders up to 1070

Approx. nat'l borders following Wang Shao's campaigns

○ Horse markets up to ca. 1070

● Tea and horse markets as of 1076

□ Key horse trade-route towns

◇ Chengdu

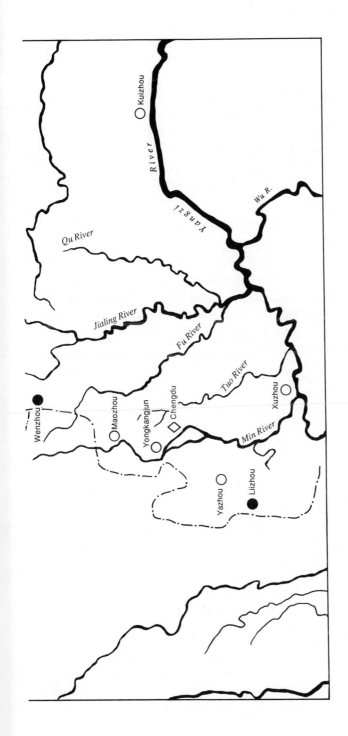

Map 5 Horse Markets in the Northern Song

and marketing flexibility seventeen prefectures and sub-prefectures along the far northwest frontier were designated as "horse-summoning centers," from which local military personal were sent to drum up trade with, among others, the local Tibetan, Uighur, and Tangut tribes. The horse-summoning policy was also intended to encourage native dealers to drive their herds all the way to the capital, for which they were issued travel vouchers that facilitated their passage along Chinese roads, and probably got them food, lodging, and provender along the way.[64]

This basic marketing structure was altered only slightly over the next half century. In 1007 the previously autonomous Horse Pricing Agency was subordinated to a stronger, more centralized Directorate of Herds and Pastures.[65] Around the same time the horse-summoning system was transformed into the "traders' caravan" (*quanma*) policy (the permanent frontier markets policy, which was now called the *shengma* or field-administered horse policy, was unchanged). Under the "traders' caravan" system, native horse sellers brought animals to the prefectural markets, where they were given a partial payment per head. The sellers then assembled their horses into caravans of ten to one hundred head, called a *quan,* and drove them to the capital.[66] The system as it operated in 1060 was described by Xue Xiang, who was at that time charged with reforming it:

Each Tibetan or Han merchant assembles in the frontier prefectural markets 50, 70, or 100 horses, which are called a *quan.* For each horse driven to the market 1,000 cash is given. Thereafter at each staging point *(cheng)* straw and grain is provided, as is food for the leaders up to the capital. There the Bureau of Diplomatic Protocol also provides funds for fifteen days of entertainment and the provision of wine and food. Only then do the convoyers go to the Horse Pricing Agency, which appraises the horses, and then the Office of Funds, which pays the price in money and silks. Then on departing from the court there are also such gifts as brocade robes and silver girdles to consider. The horse sellers are given a receipt for the value of the goods and money obtained, exempting them from paying taxes en route to the border. When the total cost is considered, each horse comes to not less than 50,000 or 60,000 cash.[67]

Xue's description makes it clear that with horses no less than with other commodities the government paid stiff premiums for contracting out the burdensome task of transportation. But the premiums must have attracted sellers, for the 1006 quota for "traders' caravan" horses convoyed out of northwestern markets came to 24,351 head, as opposed to 3,234 head bought through the field-administered system.[68]

By around 1007, then, a working market structure had been erected, and the government's main task for the next half century was to preserve the vulnerable system against rising Tangut national ambitions. Three phases in the Tangut ascent to empire most directly impinged on the horse trade. In 1001 Li Jiqian captured Lingzhou and in 1003 made it his capital, giving him control of the principal Central Asian trade route.[69] The disastrous impact on Song horse supply that frontier advisors had long predicted was averted by the availability of alternative horse-convoy routes (principally the one from Liangzhou to Lanzhou), and by the international repercussions of Li Jiqian's death in 1003 and the Song peace with Liao in 1005. All major players on the northern frontier, including Li Jiqian's son and successor Li Deming (r. 1004–1031), saw domestic advantages in maintaining peace; and the Tangut leader even swore an oath of allegiance—and sold horses—to the Song court.[70] Thus the consequences of Lingzhou's fall for horse supply were offset by temporary international cooperation. As a purchase quota of 24,000 head and a national herd of 200,000 head suggest, for some years after 1005 foreign horses streamed into Kaifeng and government pastures were, in the eyes of some, over-full.[71]

Peace with the Tanguts proved ephemeral, however. In 1009 drought and famine at home drove Li Deming into a series of campaigns against the Ganzhou Uighurs, Qingtang Tibetans, local Qinzhou tribes, and in 1011 against Liangzhou. Liangzhou fell in 1015; and although it was subsequently recaptured by the Ganzhou Uighurs, the region and its horses were henceforth lost to the Song.[72] Again, however, the dynasty was spared the worst possible consequences of a major strategic defeat, this time by the eagerness of the

Qingtang tribes under Juesiluo to take over the diplomatic and commercial roles vacated by the dispossessed Six Valleys Tibetans. As Song gifts and stipends were rerouted from Liangzhou to the successive Tibetan capitals of Tsongkha (Zongge), Miaochuan, and Qingtang (Xining), Qingtang troops (swelled by Liangzhou refugees) provided a precarious buffer against the Tanguts and Qingtang horses replaced those of Liangzhou.[73] Tangut military activity did paralyze horse purchasing in the northeast quadrant of the Yellow River loop, and by 1026 thirteen northeasterly markets and horse-summoning centers had fallen into disuse.[74] Yet even with this truncated market structure there was still an abundance of horses: the Qinghai-Gansu pastures were able to provide the nine remaining Shaanxi markets with as many as 34,000 head around 1026; and in the absence of protracted hostilities, mortality rates among the Song herds were probably low. Again the government was buying too many horses for its pastures, and 1026 witnessed the first wide-scale closing of pasturage inspectorates. At the same time private subjects were allowed to buy the surplus Tibetan horses, thereby turning private grasslands into the state's "outer stable."[75]

Alternatives were dwindling, however, and the Song was less able to avert disaster in the final Tangut drive to empire. In 1028 Li Deming's son, the reformer and opponent of Sinification Li Yuanhao, initiated a sixteen-year campaign of conquest and high diplomacy that engulfed the Gansu corridor and threatened to destroy the Qingtang state, while humiliating the Song army and destroying its horses more rapidly than they could be replaced.

In the first year of his campaign Yuanhao captured Liang and Ganzhou from the Uighurs, and by 1036 (according to traditional dating) he was in permanent possession of all the oasis cities of the Gansu corridor.[76] Yuanhao's second objective was the Qingtang kingdom, against which he personally led a protracted assault in 1035. Juesiluo successfully resisted the Tangut invasion, but his resources were so drained by the campaign that the Tibetan chief was unable (or unwilling) to aid Song in their own war with the Tanguts.[77] In 1038 Yuanhao proclaimed himself emperor of the state of Great Xia; the Song court responded by severing diplomatic and commercial relations and putting a price on Yuanhao's head. War broke out in 1040; and after four years marked by three stunning victories and no important defeats, Xi Xia bowed to Liao pressure and sued for peace with the Song in 1044.[78]

During the war the Song's need for cavalry mounts far outstripped the capacity of its embattled Tibetan suppliers, and the government was forced to enact emergency requisitions, known generically as "all-embracing" *(kuomai)* or "harmonious" *(hemai)* purchases. Requisitioning began in 1037, but became widespread in 1040 when the government sought to buy or register all privately owned horses in Kaifeng and North China.[79] Requisitioning was successful in Kaifeng and Hebei but foundered in Shaanxi, where proximity to the war zone quickly exhausted the region's herds and forced the government to turn instead to donkeys.[80] In the end, domestic horse and donkey supply had just barely kept the bloated and inefficient Song armies on the move until diplomacy and appeasement payments could come to their rescue.

Nor did settlement of the war bring an end to the horse-supply crisis. Short-term stratagems were employed to get horses to the armies of the northern frontier, which were dangerously short of mounts. Most interesting of these was the "horse cooperative" *(mashe)*, which encouraged companies of soldiers to pool their funds to buy horses locally in expectation of a refund from the government.[81] In addition county and prefectural officials in Hebei were ordered to stimulate local horse sales in 1050; and two "harmonious trade" *(heshi)* markets that had opened as part of the Song–Xi Xia settlement were directed to buy horses from the Tanguts.[82]

But no short-term solutions could compensate for the fundamental damage done to the Sino-Tibetan horse trade by Tangut expansion and war. Envoys were sent out in 1046 and 1047 to revive the horse trade with Juesiluo and with the closer Longxi Basin Tibetans, but they had been as deeply involved in the fighting as the Song, and their pastures appear to have been emptied.[83] And a series of reports from the early 1050s indicates that on the Chinese side the marketing system was in a shambles. Of the nine Shaanxi markets operating in 1026, only Qinzhou survived the war; and

Qinzhou was buying only 3,000–4,000 head a year—almost 17,000 head less than the annual replacement needs. Nor could the horses be distributed very easily, since the horse-convoy relay stations had fallen into disrepair.[84] Major reforms were in order.

RESHAPING HORSE PROCUREMENT

XUE XIANG'S FISCAL REFORMS. The Song at mid century was heading for a crisis. Despite a standing army of 1,250,000 men, the nation had lost all major battles in its war with the Tanguts; and distrust and factionalism had aborted the Qingli reform effort that a losing war had spawned.[85] Throughout the 1050s and 1060s the inflationary aftermath of the Tangut war and the progressive ossification of fiscal institutions erected during the reigns of Emperors Zhenzong (998–1022) and Renzong (1023–1063) prompted one financial crisis after another. The nation's tea and salt monopolies staggered under the burden of the military provisioning policies they were intended to fund, and revenues declined steadily until, in 1065, they fell 12 percent below expenditures.[86] At the same time, Song and Xi Xia engaged in a contest for power and influence in the Qinghai-Gansu borderlands, where Juesiluo's eroding control threatened Song horse supply and its very borders.

The New Policies reform campaign launched in 1068 by Emperor Shenzong and his chief minister Wang Anshi aimed at providing a comprehensive solution to the converging economic and strategic crises; but the reforms were anticipated by at least a decade of questioning and hesitant experimentation, as statesmen reevaluated and in some cases dismantled policies that no longer worked. As a critical component of national defense, horse procurement was an inevitable candidate for high-level scrutiny, and in 1060 a high-level committee was convened to investigate all aspects of the nation's horse policy. Included on the committee were the Director of Herds and Pastures, Ouyang Xiu, who provided the major statement on pasturing and herd-building, and the thirty-nine-year-old Wang Anshi, who as Supervisor of Funds in the Finance Commission crafted the prevailing policy on foreign horse purchases.[87]

Wang Anshi traced the collapse of the horse-procurement program to the government's failure to combine the right man with the appropriate post, but this seemingly conventional view masked Wang's desire to fundamentally restructure the procurement system. Up to this point horse policy had been decided by the Directorate of Herds and Pastures and other agencies in the capital and implemented in the prefectural markets and inspectorates, with no intervening level of administration. But Wang proposed the appointment of an Intendant for Horse Purchases and Pastures to assume control of all aspects of horse procurement in Shaanxi, interposing a new regional level of coordination and decision-making between the capital and the local markets and inspectorates. Wang specifically recommended that the post be given concurrently to the financial virtuoso Xue Xiang, who as Assistant Fiscal Intendant and Regulator of Jiezhou Salt was already the most powerful fiscal official in Shaanxi. And in order to enhance Xue's effectiveness, Wang urged that he be given a long term in office, wide latitude in the selection of assisting officials, and a broad mandate to experiment in the organization and financing of markets and pastures. This proposal to solve a specific cluster of problems by appointing a proven innovator to an experimental office rehearsed a theory of bureaucratic enterpreneurship that Wang had first enunciated in his "Myriad Word Memorial" of 1058 and that he would put to widespread application in the New Policies.[88]

Xue Xiang was expected to rebuild the battered marketing system, and he promptly pushed new markets out to the very edge of the Sino-Tibetan frontier, along the Qinghai-Gansu borderlands.[89] His most significant reform, however, was to transfer the responsibility of capitalizing the horse trade from the court to regional industries in Shaanxi and Sichuan. Up through the 1050s horse purchases were financed primarily by the central government, either through direct payments to foreign merchants by the Office of Funds in Kaifeng or by subventions of silver and silk to prefectural markets by the Finance Commission or the Inner Treasury. As recently as 1055, for example, the government had been forced to allocate 100,000 *liang* of silver a year—half its yearly production—to revi-

talize the horse trade in Shaanxi.[90] Caught between rising costs and
declining revenues, mid-century policy-makers were anxious to divert whatever financial burdens they could from the central government to new or as yet untapped regional industries; and in his original recommendation Wang Anshi invited Xue to experiment with
regional sources of financing:

> Up until now horses have been paid for primarily with the profits of the
> Jiezhou salt ponds, by disbursements of silver and silk from the Finance
> Commission, and also by cash gotten by exchanging these goods on the
> market through the Shaanxi Fiscal Intendant. Now, since Xue Xiang man-
> ages Jiezhou salt and also directs Shaanxi finances, he can depart from
> standard practices and shift and change with the circumstances *(tongrong
> bianzhuan)*, which will be of great advantage in his management of af-
> fairs.[91]

In his first financial experiment, Xue sought to replace the costly
"traders' caravan," paid for directly in the capital, with a transaction that paid Tibetan merchants with Jiezhou salt certificates, which
they could in turn redeem in Shaanxi for government salt.[92] The
policy was intended to preclude all need for subventions of silver or
silk. But probably because the Tibetans controlled sufficient salt
reserves of their own, the policy foundered; and in 1062 the central
government was again forced to disburse its own silver and silk to
the horse markets.[93] Shaanxi produced little other than salt that
could be traded for horses; but in a second attempt to buy horses
with salt certificates in 1064, Xue Xiang offered them not as claims
on salt, but as negotiable instruments that horse merchants could
exchange for goods produced in Sichuan. In this new policy the
Tibetans would take their certificates to the commercial center of
Qinzhou, trade them with Sichuanese merchants for commodities
from their home province, and return to their tribal domains. The
Sichuanese merchants, in turn, would take their salt certificates to
government offices in Fengxiangfu or Chang'an, cash them in for
silver, and return to Sichuan to buy more trade goods.[94]

Sichuanese merchants had long been accustomed to selling their
textiles in the northwest for silver or for government reserves of
Sichuanese iron-cash exchange notes *(jiaozi)*, and to serving as pro-

curement contractors for Shaanxi government agencies.[95] Therefore, Xue's proposal fit in with a pattern of movement of goods and services that had become fairly commonplace. But Xue was the first to introduce Sichuanese commodities directly into the horse trade. These goods must have proved attractive to Tibetan horse traders; for in a short time the government deepened Sichuan's involvement by assigning increasing amounts of the region's taxable silk to the trade, while simultaneously decreasing its own contribution. In 1067 Sichuan was allotted a quota of 30,000 rolls a year, almost one-third the total procurement subvention of 100,000 rolls.[96] This Sichuanese silk was said to have lured Tibetan horse sellers to market in great numbers, and three years later Sichuan's share was doubled.[97] The central government's subventions had been reduced to a minority role.

WANG SHAO'S FRONTIER MANAGEMENT. From his perspective as financial chief of an entire macroregion, Xue Xiang could harness the immediate requirements of local horse markets to the resources and commodity flows of Shaanxi and its trading partner Sichuan. The bond he fostered between the Sichuanese economy and the Qinghai horse trade can be understood as the outcome of a series of explicitly mandated financial experiments, carried out through the relatively more responsive mechanism of a regional rather than a central agency. The reforms Xue Xiang initiated nonetheless provided only a partial solution to the problems that beset horse procurement. On the one hand, though Sichuan as a whole had been relatively lightly taxed in the seventy years since the rebellion of Wang Xiaobo and Li Shun had wracked the province, the region's silk industry had been driven by tax quotas and government requisitions into clothing the armies of the northern frontier. In the decades following the Sino-Tangut war, the government was forced to reduce the burden on Sichuan's silk producers; and it is doubtful whether by the late 1060s the industry had recovered enough to sustain the increased taxes and requisitions that would inevitably accompany linkage to the horse trade.[98]

In addition, Xue Xiang's reforms were limited to issues of marketing and finance. Because they did not address the strategic threat posed by the waning influence of Juesiluo and his line, they offered only a transitional solution to the problems of horse supply. But the trend initiated by Xue Xiang was incorporated into a more comprehensive approach to frontier management by the soldier-of-fortune Wang Shao, a *jinshi* degree-holder who had abandoned the early stages of a typical bureaucratic career to investigate Shaanxi border affairs on his own. Though very much a political unknown up to this point, Wang Shao's policies of frontier annexation and state-run trade appear to have played a central role in shaping the New Policies agenda of state-sponsored expansion and economic activism. Wang was catapulted into the national political arena in late 1067, when he responded to Shenzong's inaugural summons for memorials on the national crisis with a proposal to reconquer Qinghai—once the Tang territory of Hehuang—for the Song, and to finance the conquest with a state monopoly on the lucrative frontier trade. Wang Shao's ambitious plan was especially appealing to a young ruler chafing under the military weakness of his empire, and in 1068 Wang was named chief secretary of the Military Affairs Commission in Western Shaanxi and charged with putting his proposal into action.[99] As one by-product of his overall scheme, Wang's annexation of the Qinghai-Gansu borderlands created a stable location for Song horse markets for the next fifty years. At the same time, his frontier marketing and exchange bureau yoked the horse trade to the vigorous Sichuanese tea industry, paving the way for a horse-procurement policy that was profitable as well as self-financing.

The frontier problems that Wang Shao now confronted were generated in part by power struggles within the Tibetan oligarchy. Some decades earlier Juesiluo had banished his first two wives, daughters of his chief rival Li Lizun, and disinherited the sons they bore him in favor of Dongzhan, his son by a third woman. Resentment smoldered in the Li clan, and a Li grandson, Muzheng, set up a regime in Hezhou that was implacably hostile to Juesiluo and the Song. When Dongzhan inherited Juesiluo's position in 1065, Muzheng and his allies began openly to defy Qingtang and the Song, for a time blocking the tribute traffic from Khotan that passed over the last stages of the Qingtang highway.[100]

Discord prompted defections, as Tibetan tribes began deserting to the Xi Xia side from the late 1050s on, culminating in 1066 when Muzheng submitted to the Tanguts.[101] Moreover, defections and instability emboldened the Tanguts into undertaking direct military actions throughout the troubled border region. Xi Xia sent 200,000 troops against Guwei in 1063, attacked "cooked" border tribes and military colonists in 1064, engaged Juesiluo's troops just east of Qingtang in 1065, and despatched large-scale forces against Chinese commanderies on the Sino-Tangut border in 1066.[102] By the end of the decade border unrest was again choking off the horse trade. The major Shaanxi markets were getting only about 5,700 horses a year, and skittish military commanders had begun to block Tibetan horse caravans coming into Song even as Tibetan horse traders slowed down their caravans in fear of bandit raids.[103]

In his analysis of the unstable frontier situation, Wang Shao argued that although divisiveness in the Tibetan ranks could enable the Tanguts to march unopposed into China, that same fragmentation offered an opportunity to annex the borderlands as a stepping-stone from which Song could itself conquer the Tanguts.[104] Wang predicted that if the Tibetan towns were turned into Chinese prefectures (as they had been under Han and Tang) and the fractious inhabitants transformed into submissive Chinese subjects, then Song would have the Xi Xia state "in the palm of their hands."

Wang Shao personally directed the pacification campaigns. In Qingtang, Juesiluo's heir Dongzhan had much to gain from Song sponsorship, and he remained a loyalist to his death in 1086. No military actions were directed against Qingtang and the other northeastern Qinghai strongholds until 1099, when the court exhausted its supply of reliable Tibetan surrogates.[105] But in the Qinghai-Gansu borderlands, a hard campaign had to be fought against the intractable Muzheng, who did not submit to accepting the imperial surname until 1074. The towns he and his allies had controlled, in the rich Tao River valley separating Song and Qingtang, were reorganized into the Song prefectures of He, Xi, and Min and placed under the new military sub-circuit of Xihe Lu.[106]

The value of Wang Shao's irredentist policy was a matter of contemporary and historical controversy, and the entire New Policies thrust towards military confrontation and frontier expansion was denounced by conservatives as dangerous and destabilizing adventurism.[107] But Wang Shao's projection of Song sovereignty into the new Xihe Circuit did provide a stable location for the Shaanxi horse markets for the remaining fifty years of the Northern Song, close to the centers of Tibetan horse production yet fairly secure against immediate Xi Xia threats. For the first several years of Wang Shao's campaign, Tibetan horse merchants practiced a disciplined embargo against selling horses to Song, forcing the government hurriedly to reactivate markets in Sichuan and to promote private trade missions deep into Yunnan.[108] But gradually the horse traders returned to sell their animals; and by 1075 a new system of seven horse markets had been created around the new prefectures of He, Xi, and Min and the older frontier markets in Qinzhou, Tongyuan (Guwei), Yongning, and Jiezhou.[109] The first of the issues left pending by Xue Xiang had been resolved.

WANG SHAO'S STATE TRADE BUREAU AND THE TEA AND HORSE TRADE. We may imagine that one reason Tibetan horse merchants lifted their embargo was the attraction exerted by the Sichuanese trade goods brought in to stock Wang Shao's state trade bureaus *(shiyiwu)*. Much as Wang Shao's frontier campaigns signaled the New Policies commitment to an aggressive and expansionist approach to national defense, his state trade measure advanced the reformers' resolution to expand the powers of the state in order to challenge private economic actors for the control of commerce and agricultural credit. The market and exchange policy Wang Shao enacted in Shaanxi in 1070 served as the prototype for the empire-wide measure of 1072, and consummated the link between Qinghai horses and Sichuanese tea.

By the time the state trade act was adopted in Kaifeng in 1072, revenue gathering had been joined to more populist goals. At that time the measure was touted as a way of breaking up the commercial monopolies erected by the great guild merchants in order to stabilize commodity prices and free up markets and goods for the small merchant and consumer as well as generating new revenues for the state.[110] In 1070, however, Wang Shao was more narrowly concerned with capturing trade away from private merchants in order to subsidize his frontier campaigns:

> Of all the frontier prefectures and commanderies only those in Qinfeng Circuit are contiguous with the various western Tibetan nations. I do not know how many hundreds, thousands, and ten-thousands of strings' worth of goods flow from all four corners of the Tibetan lands to us every year, yet the profits created by these merchant travelers all revert back to the people. [I] wish to set up a state trade agency in this circuit, and to borrow government funds to use as capital [with which to buy commodities to trade to the foreign merchants in order to] capture [for the state] the profits that otherwise flow to merchants and traders. One year's income [from this state-run trade] will not be less than one- to two-hundred-thousand strings of cash.[111]

The first bureau was soon opened in Qinzhou, then moved in the middle of the year to Tongyuan where foreign merchants could more easily congregate and reside.[112]

Wang Anshi actively promoted Wang Shao's proposal, which he valued both for its revenue potential and as a useful complement to military conquest. Indeed just after Wang Shao captured Xizhou in 1072, Wang Anshi reminded him that just as soon as the town was walled, Wang Shao should open a state trade bureau and "lend government capital to Tibetan and Chinese persons of means to assist them in establishing wards and commercial districts. In this way Tibetans and Chinese, government and private interests will all benefit, and holding the region will be easy and gaining submission of the Tibetans swift."[113]

By 1070, when the first bureau was established, the idea of using Sichuan's surplus to subsidize government operations in Shaanxi was very much in the air; and from the beginning, the state trade bureaus were kept stocked with Sichuanese commodities.[114] One early tactic for obtaining these goods was to send agents down to Sichuan well supplied with *jiaozi* exchange notes that had accumulated in the office of the Qinfeng Military Affairs Commission, and authorizing the purchasers to buy up commercial goods in Chengdu for shipment to the frontier markets in Shaanxi.[115] Although silk no doubt constituted the major trade item, some tea was also included; and in 1073 the main tea market was transferred from Qinzhou to Xizhou to accommodate the commercial interests of "the recently submitted Tibetan tribes."[116]

Not long after opening its metropolitan State Trade Bureau in Kaifeng in 1072, the government began to extend the state trade measure throughout the country.[117] Wang Shao's frontier markets were proving gratifyingly profitable, and by late 1073 Sichuan's prominence as a supplier for the frontier trade had begun to stimulate interest in establishing a state trade bureau in Chengdu as well.[118] Between the last month of 1073 and the first month of 1074 three separate investigators converged on Chengdu, despatched by the Finance Commission, the Superintendancy for Markets and Exchange, and Wang Anshi himself.[119] Gradually the initial concern, planning a market and exchange bureau in Chengdu, shifted to buying large stocks of Sichuanese tea for the frontier bureaus in the northwest.[120] Then in mid 1074 the direction of events was altered. As Wang Shao's pacification campaign wound down, Tibetan horse merchants began returning to trade in great number. In an urgent request from the field, Wang Shao observed that these merchants were most interested in trading for tea: "The Westerners have begun to bring good horses to the frontier. All they desire is tea, but there is not enough tea to trade to them. [I] request that the tea-purchase office buy tea in all haste."[121]

The planning investigation for the Chengdu bureau was abruptly canceled, and henceforth all activity was directed to buying large volumes of tea in Sichuan, shipping it to Shaanxi, and setting up six markets in Xihe and Qinfeng to trade the tea for horses.[122] Finally in the eleventh month of 1074, two of the original field investigators, Li Qi and the Sichuanese native Pu Zongmin, were named the first Intendant and Co-Intendant for Tea Purchasing in western Sichuan and the Hanzhong Basin. [123] The bridge between Sichuanese tea and Tibetan horses had now been built. Henceforth the organization that Li, Pu, and their successors were about to create, the Superintendancy for Tea and Horses, would thrust the state directly into the center of the Sichuanese economy, and completely transform the nature of the Sichuanese tea industry.

TWO

Market Segregation and the Structure of the Sichuanese Tea Industry on the Eve of the Tea and Horse Trade

The rich region that was commanding such intense official attention in 1074 was first called Sichuan—literally "Four Rivers," in reference to the four great tributaries that swelled the Yangzi River—early in the Song.[1] Spatially the region encompassed the Hanzhong Basin, in modern Shaanxi; the mountains and valleys of the Upper Jialing River and its tributary the Bailong River, in modern Gansu; and the Sichuan Basin itself, the core of the modern province. Administered during Song times through the four circuits of Chengdu, Lizhou, Zizhou, and Kuizhou, the entire territory comprised an historically integrated region coinciding with the classical conception and territorial administration of "Greater Shu"—that is, the eponymous territory of Shu itself in the west, the territory of Ba in the east, and the Hanzhong Basin in the north. Except for the inclusion of Hanzhong, the dimensions of Song Sichuan were almost identical with what modern researchers, following Skinner, have come to call the Upper Yangzi macroregion.[2]

An alternative Song designation for Sichuan—Chuanxia, or "Rivers and Gorges"—might better describe the region's topography. The Sichuan Basin was originally a great inland sea, drained off as the

Yangzi River carved its twisting gorges deep through the Dabashan
Mountains and east to the plains of Hubei. In Hanzhong the process
was replicated in miniature, as the Han River cut through the
Wudang Mountains to attain the plains northeast of Xiangyang.
Girdling the macroregion is a massive belt of mountains, the easternmost promontory of the Tibetan highlands jutting into the heart
of agrarian China: to the west the region is walled by the 7,500- to
18,000-foot peaks and ranges of the Daxue and Qionglai ranges of
the Tibetan fringe; to the north, it is separated from the cold and
dry continental air masses of Northwest China by the 7,500- to
11,000-foot Qinlingshan range; to the east, the Sichuan Basin is
cut off from the central lakes plains by the 7,500-foot Dabashan
range; and on the south, the basin is rimmed by the 3,500- to
6,000-foot Guizhou and Yunnan plateaus. These mountains have,
of course, defined the region's relationship to the rest of the Chinese
world and imposed an enormous obstacle to communication and
political and economic integration.

Sichuan's interior is almost as hilly as its mountainous rim. Although the Chengdu Plain is level, well-watered, and covered with
a thick mantle of fertile alluvial soil, farmers outside the Chengdu
Plain have had to adapt to an extremely inhospitable terrain. Eastern Sichuan (Song Kuizhou Circuit) is dominated by steep, high
parallel anticlinal ridges, with very restricted plains or gentler hills,
and covered with a shallow and unproductive limestone soil. Soils
in the middle third of the Sichuan Basin, roughly equivalent to
Zizhou Circuit, are better; but though the area looks flat on most
maps, it is in fact so craggy and precipitous that here alone Song
surveyors were unable to estimate the lands under cultivation.[3] Further to the north, only the narrow Han River valley near Hanzhong
is suitable for intensive agriculture.

Despite its uninviting topography, however, the Upper Yangzi
is extremely lush. The same mountains that have cut Sichuan off
from the rest of China have endowed it with a warm, moist climate,
enjoying ample rainfall and a long growing season. As one modern
geographer has put it, Sichuan "is a large rice-bowl, containing
within its rim virtually all the ingredients of the varied topography,

climates, vegetation, crops, and human activities that are found in South China, with the exception of a coastline."[4] Sichuan was in fact one of China's earliest rice-growing regions and had attained a reputation for wealth and abundance well before the imperial era. As one of four centers of intensive agriculture during the Han dynasty, Sichuan developed a number of industries, including silk, lacquerware, paper, and later printing, that dominated imperial markets until the explosive rise of South China in the eighth to twelfth centuries. One of the most important of these industries was tea.

SICHUAN AND THE DISSEMINATION OF TEA CULTURE

Scholars are divided over whether tea spread to China from the hill country of Assam or the forests of Yunnan, Burma, and Laos.[5] Whichever its ultimate origin, however, there is scholarly agreement that the introduction of tea into Sichuan marked the plant's first appearance in Chinese culture.[6] Texts dating from the Han dynasty (202 B.C.–A.D. 9) point to the early rise of tea as a beverage and item of trade in the commercialized districts of western Sichuan, followed by the gradual spread of tea consumption and cultivation east down the Yangzi, and north across the Qinling mountains. The earliest generally accepted piece of evidence for both the consumption and commercial sale of tea is Wang Bao's "Contract for a Slave." Written in 59 B.C., when Wang was passing through Chengdu, the "Contract" specifies in great and droll detail the new duties to be required of the obstinate slave he had just bought from his hostess. Among the responsibilities forced on the slave were to "boil tea and fill the utensils" when guests were present and to "buy tea in Wuyang."[7] The fact that tea was not only consumed but also bought and sold in an apparently unexceptional fashion indicates that it was already well established in Sichuan, although we can only guess at the social and ethnic layers through which it must have filtered before becoming an item of trade in Wuyang and a beverage served to the guests of the well-to-do.

Other historical sources, brought together in the eighth century by Lu Yu in his *Classic of Tea (Chajing)*, indicate the presence of tea in Hunan and Lingnan as well as Sichuan during the Han.[8] But although references to tea in the south and southwest continue to increase from the Three Kingdoms (220–265) on, the radiation outward was surprisingly slow, and Sichuan remained the center of commercial production through the fifth century. Fu Xian's late-fourth-century "Report of the Chief Administrator of the Capital" suggests Sichuan's range as a supplier of tea for popular consumption: "I have heard that [in the Southern Market of Luoyang] old women of Sichuan make a gruel of tea and sell it. [Following] an investigation, their utensils and implements were smashed and destroyed. They also sell cakes in the market. What is the reason for prohibiting the sale of tea gruel and troubling these old women of Sichuan?"[9] Fu Xian's report provides the earliest evidence for the sale of Sichuanese tea outside the region, as well as the first instance of the public control of tea sales.

During the political division of the Northern and Southern Dynasties (420–589) tea began to assume a more important role in the diet and culture of the southeast, as reflected in the greater attention given southeastern tea in contemporary botanical and pharmacological notices.[10] There is little evidence that tea made any serious inroads into the northern diet at this time, however, and the main beverage of the north continued to be wine and milk-products, expecially kumiss—fermented milk.[11] And as late as the sixth and seventh centuries, long after tea bushes had begun to carpet the hills of southeast China, private observers and official pharmacologists both continued to identify tea as a generic product of Sichuan. In the latter half of the sixth century, for example, Lu Deming, a resident of what was to become the tea-producing center of Suzhou, could still gloss tea by writing that "today people from Shu use it to make a beverage."[12] About half a century later the authors of the *New Pharmacopoeia (Xinxiu bencao)* described tea as a product of Chengdu and the upper Han River valley—the two regions that would fall under the Sichuan Tea Monopoly—but omitted any mention of tea in the southeast, where cultivation and consumption were no longer a novelty.[13]

During the eighth century, however, tea was to become firmly established as a southeastern crop, as well as the staple beverage of Chinese in the north and south. By the rebellion of An Lushan the demographic filling-in of the tea regions of the southeast, combined with the growth of national markets as a consequence of political unification and the economic integration provided by canal-building and interregional taxation,[14] fostered the emergence of a well-developed southeastern tea economy, linked by river and canal to new markets in the north. One by-product of this confluence of trends was the gradual displacement of Sichuan's tea, along with its lacquerware and paper, from the main imperial markets.[15] Gradually a distinct Upper Yangzi tea economy emerged, oriented towards intraregional and non-Han markets and subject to separate structures of fiscal control.

Feng Yan (*jinshi* 756), a rough contemporary of *Classic of Tea* author Lu Yu, has documented the entry of southeastern tea into the monasteries and markets of North China:

> Tea: Picked early, it is called *cha;* picked late, it is called *ming.* The *Pharmacopoeia* says, "It quenches thirst and causes people not to sleep." Southerners like to drink it, but at first northerners did not. In the mid Kaiyuan period [ca. 726], teachers in the Lingyan Monastery of Taishan sat cross-legged and raised high the teaching of Chan Buddhism. They pursued their study of Chan without going to bed or eating in the evening, relying only on their drinking of tea. Soon people naturally came to hold and embrace this habit, everywhere boiling and drinking tea, and before long the northerners also followed suit. Thereafter tea-drinking became a habit, and in [Shandong, Hebei . . .], and gradually even in the capital city of Chang'an, many walled markets opened up shops that brewed tea and sold it. All people regardless of their religious beliefs or customs just threw down their cash and picked up [their tea] to drink. Their tea came from the regions of the Yangzi and Huai Rivers, with boat and cart following in succession. The tea grown in the mountains of the southeast was plentiful, and the varieties exceedingly numerous.[16]

We also learn from Feng Yan that around this time tea "began to spread from the interior to the lands outside the fortifications. In recent years the Uighurs have come to pay court, driving their famous horses before them in great number to trade for tea."[17] Thus from an item of the monastic diet, where it replaced the forbidden wine and kept the monks awake for their religious studies, tea gradually entered into the culinary life of North China and the steppe. But the tea that supplied the shops and frontier trading posts of the north came not from Sichuan, but from centers of cultivation in the Lower and Middle Yangzi regions, carried up the Bian canal, then northeast along the Yellow river and the Yongji Canal to the major cities of the North China plain, or west along the canal, river, and land-carriage system that linked Chang'an and Luoyang with the Bian Canal.[18] Nor was it only the processed leaf that was transported up the new canals to the capital: among the low-bulk high-value goods sent to Chang'an on the new canal spurs constructed in 743 were tea cauldrons, firing pans, and bowls from Yuchang, the manufacturing center west of Poyang Lake.[19]

The newly elevated status of tea in Han culture and the Han diet was celebrated by a flurry of treatises and poems. Most prominent among the treatises was Lu Yu's own *Classic of Tea*. Written around 760, it surveyed the eighth-century corpus of wisdom on the cultivation, manufacture, and consumption of tea; gathered in one place the basic sources on the history of the plant; and provided a comprehensive geography of the distribution of tea, with notes on comparative qualities.[20] Lu himself wrote other works, now lost, extolling the virtues of tea; and tea treatises by at least nine other Tang authors can be traced.[21] Sichuan produced one important work on tea in the early tenth century, the *Tea Anthology (Chapu)* by Mao Wenxi of the state of Former Shu, only fragments of which now survive.[22] And of course from the mid eighth century on, tea began to vie with wine as a topic for Chinese poets, and gifts of tea to give rise to a special genre, the "thank you" poem.[23]

The eighth-century southeastern tea industry stood at the center of China's transition from localized natural economies to a national monetized market network. Bo Juyi eulogized the rising commercial spirit of the wholesale tea merchants of Chang'an in a poem, writing that "merchants value profits and think nothing of separations [from home]; last year they went to Fuliang [just east of Poyang Lake] to buy tea."[24] Because of the great distances they traveled and the value of their trade, eighth-century tea merchants played a key role in the development of "flying money" *(feiqian),* bills of exchange that allowed tea merchants to sell their tea and other goods in Chang'an, deposit their cash with one of the chancelleries maintained by each province in the capital, and be reimbursed an equivalent sum on presentation of their receipt in the issuing province itself.[25] Important secondary industries were likewise founded on China's growing thirst for tea, and employed sophisticated commercial devices to heighten demand for their wares. The potters of Luoyang, for example, invented the Hongjian doll, a plaster statuette of Lu Yu presented to any customer buying a certain minimum quantity of tea utensils. Ultimately the dolls took on religious significance, and market people whose tea was not selling well began to offer libations to them, a practice that Ouyang Xiu saw practiced in the Song as well.[26]

Certainly by the eighth century, then, tea had shed its reputation as an exotic product of distant Sichuan and had become fully integrated into the southeastern agrarian regime. And as tea consumption and the tea trade assumed prominence and visibility in the economic life of the empire, the state naturally sought ways to tax it, especially when, following the deterioration of Tang political control as a result of An Lushan's rebellion and the loss of revenues that had previously come from the direct taxation of agriculture, the state was forced to obtain an increasing share of its funds by indirectly taxing commerce.[27] Moreover, even after problems of political control had been solved, during this period of commercial expansion the indirect taxation of trade offered a more elastic and verifiable source of income than did the direct taxation of agriculture. Consequently from the mid eighth century through the Song, state monopolies and commercial taxation provided an increasingly larger share of the government's cash income, reaching 50 percent by the mid eleventh century.[28] Thus the taxation of tea represents not only a short-term response to fiscal crisis, but also part of the long-term adaptation of the state's fiscal structure to the commercial transformation of the Chinese economy.

But fiscal policies shape as well as take shape from the economies they seek to tax. As I will discuss in greater detail in Chapter Three, neither the Tang nor early Song state was able to tax Sichuan's economy effectively. In the case of the budding tea industry, therefore, fiscal administrators devoted far greater effort to nurturing the revenue potential of the southeastern tea economy. By early Song, this came to mean excluding Sichuanese tea from circulation in extraregional markets, where it could compete with the monopolized, and hence state-owned, southeastern tea. Thus, in addition to its loss of comparative advantage to southeastern tea, as a result of the creaton of a canal link to the consuming capital of the empire and the demographic and economic explosion of the south, the tea industry of the Upper Yangzi was also gradually encircled by administrative barriers against trade in Chinese markets.

The policy of regional segregation was not originally intended. The first tax on tea was proposed in 782 as part of a general levy of 10 percent on the mountain products of tea, bamboo, wood, and lacquer, but died the following year when rebels drove the court into temporary exile.[29] The government was more successful in imposing a 10 percent ad valorem tax on tea merchants at or near the point of purchase from the cultivator in 793. Administration of the new tax was divided between the Commissioner for Salt and Iron, which controlled the southeastern tea lands of Huainan and Jiangnan, and the Board of Finance, which gained control over the tax in Sichuan after a successful effort to neutralize Salt and Iron authority in the Upper Yangzi. From the perspective of tea revenues the Board of Finance enjoyed something of a pyrrhic victory; for after an abortive attempt to monopolize rather than merely tax tea production in 835, all tea regulation reverted to the Salt and Iron Commission. From this point on, all significant efforts to tax tea and to monitor tea production were concentrated in the southeast.[30]

The fiscal segregation of Sichuan's tea that began during the Tang by default was perpetuated under the early Song by design. The Song government imposed strict controls over the southeastern lands as soon as they came under its control. By 965 Song administrators had established a state monopoly over all the tea produced in Huainan, buying the tea from the garden households (*yuanhu*) and selling it to merchants and consumers in adjoining regions through a distribution network called the Thirteen Mountain Markets *(shanchang shisan)*. In 975 the state of Southern Tang capitulated, and two years later the Song extended monopoly controls to all the tea lands south of the Yangzi (excluding Guangnan, whose output was insignificant) and as far west as Guizhou, just downriver of the Yangzi Gorges and Sichuan. These tea lands it administered through the six Yangzi River Monopoly Goods Bureaus *(quehuowu)*.[31] But the political turmoil caused by the Song conquest of Later Shu, exacerbated by its policy of confiscation, made any form of systematic monopoly taxation impossible. And even after Sichuan had recovered from the Wang Xiaobo rebellion, the state remained wary of extending to the region the monopoly policies being followed on the other side of the Gorges.[32]

Yet if the state could not tax Sichuan's tea, it at least had to prevent it from competing in the markets set aside for southeastern tea. In an effort to cut the cost of transporting grain and fodder to its frontier armies, the Song government enlisted merchants to supply the necessary provisions and paid them with vouchers for its monopolized commodities, principally salt, spices, and the tea it obtained from its Huainan and Yangzi River markets. In order for this so-called *ruzhong* provisioning policy to elicit enthusiastic participation, the government had to guarantee that merchants would receive a high resale price for their monopolized commodities. Therefore it designated the profitable northern and northwestern markets exclusively for southeastern tea, and confined Sichuanese tea to the borders of its own four circuits. This proscription effectively barricaded Sichuanese tea from its natural, and very lucrative, market in the northwest frontier. From the time the prohibition was imposed around 980 to its suspension in 1059, the only significant buyers of Sichuanese tea otuside the province were the localized Tibetan, Man, and Yi tribes occupying Sichuan's western and southwestern borders.[33] Thus, while from the eighth century on southeastern tea was carried along river and canal, by boat and cart, to ever-widening markets in North China and beyond, Sichuan's tea flowed in increasingly more constricted, land-based markets.

Fiscal regulation, in conjunction with geographic isolation, had drawn an impenetrable curtain around Sichuanese tea.

THE STRUCTURE OF THE SICHUAN TEA INDUSTRY ON THE EVE OF THE TEA MONOPOLY

The displacement of Sichuanese tea from all but intraregional or localized overland markets held back both methods of tea manufacture in Sichuan and the commercial structure of the industry. Much less is known about the manufacture of tea during late Tang and Song in Sichuan than in the southeast, a probable consequence of the diminishing role played by Sichuanese tea in the lives of the literate elite that wrote tea treatises.[34] Moreover, despite the abundance of administrative detail preserved in the records of the Tea and Horse Agency, very little is said there about the production process. But in many cases we do have information about the finished states—that is, loose or compressed, powder or leaf—in which tea circulated; and this information can be employed to locate Sichuan's place in the history of tea manufacturing.[35] Along with the plant itself, Sichuan provided the basic compressed-cake technique that was standard for all teas during the Tang. By Song times, however, southeastern producers had left the Sichuanese technique far behind.

Song administrative records at first categorized tea as *pian* (literally "wafer," but with a generic meaning of compressed) and *san* (loose).[36] Official price lists preserved in the *Song Administrative Digest (Song huiyao)* reveal that solid teas, with a government-purchase price range of about 50 cash per catty to a top of 275 cash per catty, were far more expensive by weight than loose teas, with a comparable range of 16 to 38.5 cash.[37]

Some regions specialized in the manufacture of loose tea only, but many districts that produced solid tea also manufactured a commercial grade of loose tea at a much lower price. A typical example is Huzhou, whose tea was classified into three grades of "wafer," from 132 cash to 187 cash per catty; and one grade of "loose," at 17.6 cash per catty.[38] In such cases the loose tea was no doubt made

up of prunings and late pickings that were not worth the effort of
further manufacture into cake or wafer form, but that were still
good enough to be marketed, probably locally.

Each of the categories of solid and loose could be composed of tea
in its leafy state (including buds and shoots) or of tea that had been
pulverized into powder. Typical examples of solid leaf teas were the
cakes of Sichuan and the wafers of Jiangnan. The classic example of
powdered tea in solid form was the molded tea *(tuan* or *kua)* produced in government gardens and manufactories in Fujian.[39]

Tea could also be ground fine and left uncompressed, as was the
case with *mocha,* "powder tea." When ground in water mills, the
tea was called "water-mill powder tea" *(shuimo mocha).* Water-milled
powder tea enjoyed a great vogue in Kaifeng during the 1070s and
1080s, from which the government sought to profit by controlling
all tea milling in the vicinity of the capital.[40] Early in the Southern
Song mill households in Fujian began to grind leaf tea and pack it
in sacks for sale to merchants, who in turn exported it to Huainan.[41]
Subsequently the two circuits of Jiangnan East and West began to
produce loose powder tea, although it is not clear whether the tea
was ground in water mills.[42] The Jiangnan circuits continued to
produce leaf tea as well.

Tea fashions through the eleventh and twelfth centuries show a
clear trend in the southeast towards loose teas, both powder and
leaf. In the year 1112, for example, a new comprehensive piece of
tea legislation promulgated strict regulations for the contruction,
size, and surveillance of the bamboo baskets used to transport tea
leaves, and implied that similar rules already existed for sacks and
small-holed baskets.[43] A second piece of evidence for this trend is
the gradual replacement of the term *sancha*—loose tea—by the term
caocha—grass or leaf tea. By the second half of the twelfth century,
leaf tea *(caocha)* and powder tea *(mocha)* became the two major des-
ignations on the tea permits *(chayin)* that were used by the government to regulate and tax the southeastern tea trade.[44] It seems clear
that, since both were loose teas, the term *sancha* no longer served as
a fiscal designation and was replaced. Moreover, from the frequency
with which permits for both leaf tea and powder tea were issued to

regional financial agencies from the 1160s on, to be sold to merchants as a means of raising provincial revenues, we can conclude that *pian,* or solid, tea was no longer a major fiscal category, and therefore no longer a significant item of commerce.[45] At some point powder tea dropped out of competition as well, and by the Ming the predominant mode of tea manufacture in the southeast was as uncompressed leaf tea. By this time also the manufacture of compressed cake tea was declared to be a lost art, although cakes were still produced in Sichuan, and the cake tea of the Puer district of Yunnan was just making its appearance.[46]

TEA MANUFACTURE IN SICHUAN. In Sichuan, manufacturers remained wedded to the technique of compressing cake tea long after its abandonment in the southeast. In fact, they appear to have invented it. The method of manufacturing tea and preparing it for consumption that is described as typical of eastern Sichuan and western Hubei in a text attributed to the third-century *Guangya* is almost surely the prototype for the cake-tea technique described by Lu Yu in the *Classic of Tea.* The *Guangya* text says:

> In the region between Jing and Ba the people pick the leaves and make a cake. If the leaves are old, rice paste is used in forming the cake. [People who] wish to brew tea first roast [the cake] until it is a reddish color, pound it into a powder, put it into a porcelain container, and cover it with boiling water. They stew onion, ginger, and orange with it. Drinking it can induce sobriety (from the effects of) wine and cause people not to sleep.[47]

Although the text presents problems of dating and authentication, it can safely be accepted as describing a manufacturing technique practiced between the Han and the fifth century. Other than a curious saliva-induced process of fermentation attributed to the aboriginal Liao tribesmen of Luzhou in southwestern Sichuan, there is no other description of the full manufacturing process until Lu Yu's own prescription for the production and consumption of cake tea.[48]

The seven-step process recommended by Lu Yu may be summarized as follows:[49]

1. Pick tea shoots, buds, and leaves.
2. Steam the tea in an earthenware or wooden steamer.

3. Pound tea leaves in a mortar.
4. Pat and shape the pulped compress in a mold.
5. Dry the molded cake in a rack placed over a drying pit.
6. String the cakes by piercing them in the middle and tying them with bamboo or bark stringers.[50]
7. Seal the tea in paper wrappers.[51]

Lu Yu alludes to other manufacturing techniques, but describes fully only the seven-step process. Thus by the 760s either the technique was standard, or Lu wished to make it so.

In the roughly four centuries separating the *Guangya* text from the *Classic of Tea,* the only essential addition to the manufacturing process was the steaming of the leaves prior to forming the cake, which by interrupting the natural process of fermentation would have facilitated the long-term storage and transportation of the tea. Lu Yu's prescription for preparing the cake tea for consumption also appears to derive from the earlier Sichuanese method. Lu recommends roasting the cake, cooling it in a paper envelope, pulverizing a portion of it into a powder, and stirring the powder into a cauldron of boiled water.[52] The only significant departure from the method attributed to the *Guangya* is the use of paper envelopes. Therefore, we can reasonably conclude that the compressed cake-tea process spread down the Yangzi along with the plant itself, to become established as the favored mode of manufacture for all of Tang China.

But while southeastern tea producers began diversifying into molded powder, loose powder, and loose leaf teas, Sichuanese producers remained attached to the basic cake-tea process.[53] There was to be sure a certain amount of variety. Mengding tea could be had in "small block" or "loose bud" forms; Mei and Da prefectures also produced both compressed and loose teas;[54] and Shuzhou's Qingcheng County manufactured loose leaf and loose powder.[55] But most of the prefectures for which there is information produced only compressed teas, including the "thin wafer" of Quzhou, the "small cake" of Pengzhou, and the "small brick" of Meizhou.[56] And even in those prefectures that are known to have produced both loose and compressed teas, often only the latter were of commercial value. For

example, although Dazhou's Dongxiang County manufactured loose
leaf tea as well as its twenty-five-catty cake pack, itinerant merchants traded only in the cake packs. When, in 1160, monopoly
taxation made trade in the cake tea unprofitable, merchants stopped
dealing in Dongxiang tea altogether rather than switch to the loose
tea.[57] By this same time in the southeast compressed tea had virtually disappeared as a major item of trade and taxation.

Nor did the dominance of compressed tea in Sichuan end with
the Song. During the Ming the basic fiscal unit for Sichuanese tea
was the *bi*—a six- or seven-catty package composed of freshly steamed
tea that was placed inside a bamboo wrapper, further enclosed in a
rope mesh, and set out to dry in the sun.[58] And in the Qing, when
Sichuan sold about 12,000,000 catties of tea annually to Tibet, the
characteristic form of manufacture was the brick.[59] According to
Colborne Baber and other English travelers, Sichuanese tea was typically steamed, pounded into rectangular molds to make bricks of
about four by ten inches weighing four to five catties, and then
dried over a fire.[60] Clearly, little had changed in Sichuan since Lu
Yu wrote his own description in the year 760.

Two factors in particular underlie the remarkable changelessness
of Sichuanese tea manufacturing through the twentieth century.
First, in the centuries following the establishment of the tea and
horse trade in the 1070s, Tibet became not only the Sichuan tea
industry's most active customer, but very nearly its only one. Even
during the Ming Sichuan's best teas went not to Chinese consumers
but to the Tibetans and other non-Han groups in the west, while
during the Qing 90 percent of all Sichuanese tea was sold to Tibet.[61] The Sichuan-Tibetan tea trade was a relatively closed system:
Tibet had no other suppliers of tea, and Sichuan no other buyers.
And in the absence of external competition, there would have been
little reason for either habits of consumption or production to change.

The second factor, more obvious and possibly more significant,
is that the requirements of overland transport were best served by
the manufacture of low-volume high-density compressed tea. Even
in the modern era, teas destined for overland commerce have generally been processed into compressed forms. For example, in the

late nineteenth century, the teas manufactured by Russians in Hankou, Jiujiang, and elsewhere for caravan transport to their own country were processed into bricks, as are teas currently produced in Hunan, Hubei, and Guangxi for overland markets in Xinjiang, Qinghai, and Gansu.[62] Thus with all but a fraction of Sichuan's commercial tea crop traveling over steep mountain paths to Inner Asia, compressed tea, produced by methods quite similar to those of the eighth century or earlier, remained the most logical mode of production long after riverine transport, interregional competition, and new foreign and domestic markets had stimulated the development of diverse methods of manufacture in the southeast.[63]

TEA CULTIVATORS AND LOCAL DISTRIBUTION. Chinese fiscal documents rarely probe those aspects of an industry that lay outside direct state administration, and the state only very rarely administered tea production. Where it did, as in the state-run plantations of Fujian, we have full and straightforward accounts of the organization of tea cultivation and manufacture.[64] But usually administrators were inclined to leave production to the garden households, and either buy the tea crop from them (as in Huainan under the southeastern monopoly of the eleventh century and Sichuan after 1074), or regulate the commerce between cultivator and merchant (for example, the point-of-first-sale taxes levied in the Tang, and the contract markets of the twelfth century). In these, the majority of the cases, official documents merely categorize the fiscal relationships between cultivator, state, and merchant, and preserve little of the information needed to reconstruct the micro-structure of the tea industry. Private observers and public policy critics fill in some of the gaps; but even with their help, the economic organization of the garden households during the Tang and Song remains the most obscure aspect of the tea trade in both Sichuan and the southeast.

Because the household economy of the southeastern and Sichuanese tea cultivators are equally poorly documented, it is impossible to evaluate the specific consequences of market contraction with the same confidence that we can assess its impact on manufacturing techniques or merchant structure. But in 1077 Lü Tao, the

Sichuanese notable and opponent of the New Policies who was then Administrator of Pengzhou, recorded in great detail the process and impact of monopolization on the Qionglai Shan tea regions, and especially in the Jiulong County marketing region of Pengzhou. Based on his own observations, the reports of subordinate officials, and the petitions of local tea cultivators, Lü Tao's three memorials of 1077 shed important light on the nature of individual tea businesses prior to the monopoly. When paired with a second set of memorials Lü wrote in 1086, it becomes possible to draw broad conclusions about the impact of the monopoly on the small tea cultivator, as I will do in Chapter Six. When joined to scattered sources from the pre-monopoly era, Lü's 1077 memorials enable us to speculate about the organization of the tea industry during the Tang-Song transition.[65]

Although the range of markets supplied by Sichuanese tea dwindled between the mid eighth and late eleventh centuries, the intraregional market for tea continued to grow. Total population in the four Song circuits of the Upper Yangzi increased 73 percent from 742 to 1080;[66] and people of all classes drank tea at temple fairs, in urban gathering places, and as an item of daily consumption in their homes.[67] Similarly, the border tribes of Tibet bought tea regularly. Tea growers were assured of a steady market for their product, and commercial cultivation assumed an important economic role in the hill lands west of the Chengdu plain.

The Pengzhou marketing district that Lü Tao investigated was probably one of the most commercially specialized in Sichuan. Scattered through the eastern piedmont of a 12,000-foot mountain barrier dividing the Chengdu plain from the Min River towns of Weizhou and Maozhou, the cultivators of Jiulong County had been acclaimed in Lu Yu's *Classic of Tea* as the producers of Sichuan's finest teas; by 1077 they had been producing for the market for well over three centuries.[68]

In some cases commercial cultivation had fostered the development of large plantations. Lü Tao estimated that tea gardens in Sichuan ranged in yearly output from 100 or 200 catties to a maximum of 50,000 catties.[69] The only plantation I have found in the historical records that might have conceivably approached the upper range was indeed in Jiulong County, owned by Zhang Shougui in the early tenth century and worked by over one hundred hired male and female laborers.[70]

Most commercial cultivation appears to have taken place in small family-run gardens, employing a few hired laborers at critical points in the season to produce between 200 and 500 catties of tea annually. Small garden households certainly predominated in the old Jiulong County market of Pengkouzhen, located nine miles northwest of the county seat where the Mengyang River debouches from the mountains. Lü Tao's attention was drawn to the Pengkou market cultivators when 300 tea households demonstrated against the monopoly early in 1077.[71] Three named cultivators, Dang Yuanji, Mou Yuanji, and Shi Guangyi, presented petitions documenting the nature of their tea businesses and portraying a local upland economy in which tea cultivation for the market constituted the primary household occupation.

The tea gardens of the three petitioners were all situated deep in the mountains, on lands too steep to grow grains and vegetables. Dang Yuanji had inherited a mountain-embankment tea garden and associated businesses located about seventy-five *li* from the Pengkou market. Mou Yuanji rented tea lands on a steep mountain side, and Shi Guangyi occupied tea lands in the remote mountains. These men had "only their small tea gardens" with which to support their families, relying on the profits from tea to buy food and clothing, and to pay their twice-yearly taxes, labor-exemption fees, and debts.[72]

Pengzhou was famous for its small fancy cake teas, described early in the tenth century by Mao Wenxi: "Pengzhou's [tea districts] include Pucun, Pengkou, and Guankou. Its tea gardens are named "Immortal's Cliff," "Stone Flower," and so forth. Pengzhou's tea cakes are small, and those with tender shoots spread through them like a gardenia are extremely fine."[73]

Producing tea fine enough for these cakes required constant care, acclerating to frenetic activity at pruning and harvest time, when extra labor might be required. Both Dang Yuanji and Mou Yuanji, for example, hired laborers in the late fall and winter (lunar winter and spring) to help with the weeding and pruning, stages in the production process eschewed by many late imperial Chinese cultivators.[74] The laborers were rehired in the spring, in time for picking and processing the tea leaves. The date of the first flush of the season, when the young leaves and shoots are ready to be picked, could vary not only between subregions within Sichuan, but also from one part of a district to another.[75] The earliest tea was brought to the Pengkou market by the cultivators of Zhide Mountain, producers of famous tea since the Tang.[76] The Zhide cultivators brought their tea to market during the last ten days of the third lunar month (around late April), which is now the average time for the first flush for the northwestern subregion as a whole.[77] But Dang Yuanji rehired his laborers for picking and processing between "Summer Begins" (May 5) and "Grain Fills" (May 21), while Mou Yuanji and Shi Guangyi did not hire harvest workers until late May. Shi Guangyi employed four laborers to harvest and finish the leaves, a number that was probably average for the Pengkou cultivators.[78]

In order to evaluate the level of specialization in Pengzhou, it would be useful to know where along the chain of production and distribution the tea was processed into cakes. Neither Lü Tao nor other contemporary observers of the Sichuan tea industry address the question directly; but from the information Lü provides, it appears that the cakes were manufactured by shop households *(puhu)* in the market towns. All we are told of the three petitioners is that they engaged in "picking and processing." But we are told that when the cultivators of Zhide Mountain brought their new tea to the market, it had already been roasted over charcoal.[79] Since Lü frequently notes that cultivators brought their tea to market in eighteen-catty sacks, it is probable that they were transporting dried but still uncompressed leaves.[80]

At the market the tea was transferred to the shop households, "who took it in and stored it, processed it, and mixed it with white earth *(baitu)*."[81] White earth, at other times a designation for siliceous clay, may here be an idiomatic reference to an adhesive substance used in forming the cake.[82] It seems, then, that there were two stages to the manufacturing process: The Pengzhou cultivators applied a preliminary steaming or firing to the freshly harvested leaves to fix them chemically and reduce their water content, a stage now technically referred to as *maocha;*[83] then the market-town shop households manufactured the semi-finished leaves into cakes. A similar division of labor was followed in Yazhou in the nineteenth century by cultivators and the brick-tea manufacturers.[84]

In some cases it is clear that the shop households entered into the manufacturing process after buying the crop from the cultivators. In such instances, the shop then acted as distributor to local Han consumers and to non-Han tribesmen who came into the district to trade. In the local Han trade, according to Lü Tao, cultivators, shop households, and by implication the hired laborers all earned modest profits, making tea broadly available to consumers at low cost. For example, on each catty of medium-grade tea (worth about 90 cash) the cultivator earned a net profit of 20 cash, a hired worker earned 13 cash, and the shop owner made a net profit of 10 cash on his sale to Han consumers. "As a result," Lü claimed, "the price of tea in [Sichuan] did not soar to great expense, and the people had enough tea for daily use."[85]

Shops also traded tea to tribesmen from across the Qionglai Mountains in return for native products. Lü portrays the marketing in Daojiang County, a strategic town on the river system just below Yongkang Commandery through which Tibetan tribes passed onto and out of the Chengdu plain. By 1077 the tribes had a long history of bartering in the walled town of Daojiang, exchanging their peppers, wax, straw, and herbals with the shop households for tea. The tribesmen apparently regarded the tea as an essential element of their diet and pharmacopoeia. Lü Tao wrote that "they call it tea-rice *(chami).* Those who have ailments use it as a curative, and [the tribes] cannot be without it."[86]

The shops did not always act as distributor, however. Where they did not, we have no information on whether the shops continued to complete the manufacturing process or served as middlemen. For example, there were at least three types of transaction in which the cultivator sold or bartered his own tea directly: to non-Han traders at the frontier, as in the barter trade between Chinese agriculturalists and native pastoralists in Liizhou;[87] to traveling merchants who went directly to the tea lands in search of tea; and to traveling merchants in the market towns.

Lü Tao describes only the third instance, the direct sale of tea by Pengzhou cultivators to itinerant or "guest" merchants (*keshang*) in the market towns. The relationship between cultivator and merchant involved credit and the purchase of future crops, and must therefore have been a stable and long-standing one. The guest merchants left cash deposits (*dingqian*) for the following year's harvest, which cultivators used to secure tea shoots, probably for garden improvement; or to pay debts, purchase provisions and rice, or hire laborers.[88] Unfortunately Lü Tao probes no further into the transactions between cultivators and merchants prior to the monopoly; and we can only wonder about the possible involvement of the shop households, brokers, or the large private speculators (*jizhu chajia*) who stockpiled tea in anticipation of high prices.[89]

In summary, Lü Tao's memorials attest to a highly commercialized tea economy, in which cultivation and manufacture of fancy teas provided the primary occupation for garden households who either occupied hill lands too steep to farm, or who found commercial tea cultivation preferable to farming. As far as we can tell, most of Sichuan's tea came from small tracts, worked by family members with the addition of a few laborers. It is probable that entire mountain villages were devoted to tea cultivation, but there is no evidence that cultivators sold their tea cooperatively. Rather each garden household seems to have made its own arrangements with the guest merchants, and to have sold its eighteen-catty sacks of half-processed leaves to shop households individually. Because it is not yet possible to compare the garden households of Sichuan with those of the southeast in any systematic fashion, no specific effects of the eighth- to eleventh-century market devolution on the Sichuanese tea cultivators can be perceived. Instead, we can see how the steady growth of intraregional Han and local Tibetan tea consumption fostered the development of tea cultivation as a primary occupation.

TEA MERCHANTS AND INTRAREGIONAL COMMERCE. It is possible to specify with some precision the impact of market devolution on the organizational structure of Sichuan's tea merchants. As Sichuanese tea became confined by competition and government regulation to a purely intraregional commerce in the direction of Han consumers and a largely passive trade in the direction of Tibetan and Man tribes that came into the region to buy tea for themselves, Sichuanese tea traders shed (or never acquired) those forms of organization appropriate to long-distance commerce. The same provincialism that tied Sichuan's tea producers to conservative modes of manufacture made it unnecessary for the region's tea merchants to adopt complex commercial practices and structures. Thus, whereas the regional, national, and international traders in southeastern tea were characterized by great diversity of scales of operation and a highly differentiated corporate structure, the tea merchants of Sichuan were primarily small-scale itinerant peddlers who worked individually and entered into no prominent associations or guilds.

If we assume that a state attempts to maximize revenues by shaping its tax strategies to levy the broadest range of commercial actors, then the methods of taxation used once the tea monopoly was imposed can serve as an indication of the commercial structure of the pre-monopoly economy as well. By such a measure, the tea merchants of Sichuan operated on much the same scale, and that scale was fairly small. For despite the large volume of tea produced in Sichuan and the Hanzhong basin relative to the southeast, from the establishment of the Sichuan tea monopoly in 1074 to the end of our records in 1204, the Tea and Horse Agency was able to regulate the commercial circulation of over 30,000,000 pounds of tea annually with a single denomination of tea license (*changyin,* or "long license"), based on a unit of 100 catties (130 pounds).[90] There was apparently no need to make available licenses for larger transactions. In the southeast during the twelfth century, on the other hand (to take a comparable and well-documented period), the state found it expedient to print licenses in a wide range of denominations and a variety of types in order to accommodate the great range of merchants, and hence maximize its ability to tax them. For example, in 1113 the provincial tea intendancies of the southeast issued "long licenses" costing 50 guan to carry 1,500 catties of tea outside the circuit (or 30 guan to carry 900 catties), along with "short licenses" *(duanyin)* for transactions within the circuit, at 20 guan for 600 catties of tea traded or 10 guan for 300 catties.[91] In the 1190s a 4-guan "small license" in both inter- and intra-circuit forms was printed to facilitate taxing the small-scale rural trade in leaf tea in Liangzhe (Zhejiang and southern Jiangsu provinces) and Jiangdong (southeastern Anhui and northern Jiangxi provinces) and thereby counteract smuggling.[92] In addition large merchants were permitted to buy licenses and then resell the purchased tea to small local merchants who would otherwise be locked out of the trade by their shortage of capital.[93] And government policy also left it up to the merchants to decide whether to sell tea through a registered broker, to negotiate directly with and sell to the shop households, or to make use of "local familiars" *(shoufen zhi ren)* as their agents.[94] None of these stratagems was necessary in the Upper Yangzi.

Our evidence for the absence of joint activity by the tea merchants of Sichuan is especially imperfect, since it is almost wholly negative. Lü Tao tells us of merchants dealing individually and on their own behalf with tea cultivators in Pengkou, and his contemporary and fellow Sichuanese Wen Tong describes a similar but more intensified phenomenon in Yangzhou (on which more below). Before they were made integral functionaries of the monopoly markets in 1074, apparently no use was made of brokers, nor was tea passed along a hierarchy of merchants operating at different marketing levels. For example, until the Tea Market Agency set one up in 1083, there was no wholesale distribution center in Chengdu.[95] It is probable that a single itinerant merchant carried tea from a market in the producing region to retail shops at the prefectural, county, and market-town levels to which more outlying consumers came to buy. A description of what appears to be this type of interlocal trade in goods including tea is provided by Wen Tong in a 1064 commemorative to the rebuilding of a commercially important bridge north of modern Yanting County, on the road between

Zizhou on the Fu River and Langzhou on the Jialing River.[96] Through this strategic pass "guest travelers" "came and went day and night without end," carrying to Langzhou and the central and hinterland districts of Bazhou such products of the industries and agriculture of the Chengdu plain as silk goods and brocades, nettle-hemp, linens, embroidery, engraved-ware, lacquerware, and tea. On their return they carried back the products of northeastern Sichuan's cattle, mule, sheep, and swine herding, and its silkworm cocoons, peppers, and honey. Whether or not each good had its specialist traders, Wen does not say; but the impression he gives is that they did not, and that at this level of commerce merchants transported tea in combination with a variety of other goods as they came on the market.

Finally, as far as we can tell from the sources, the tea merchants of Sichuan had no guild.[97] Only two possible indications of any collective action by Sichuanese tea merchants have been preserved: Wang Xiaobo's rebellion in 993, which Su Che alone linked to the tea trade; and the depredations of "private traders" who are said to have led bands of defeated soldiers in raids on government tea stocks during the Jurchen invasion of northwest China in 1127.[98]

The southeastern tea economy, on the other hand, exhibited some of the most advanced forms of same-trade associations of the period, aimed at maximizing the power of capital, minimizing risk, limiting access to markets, providing for mutual defense, and in the Northern Song at least consolidating political influence. The cartel-like tea *hang* of Kaifeng, for example, was one of the most powerful guilds of the eleventh century. From a famous description by Wang Anshi, who in 1072 used the State Trade Act to break up the cartel, we know that the leaders of the Kaifeng guild played a powerful role in setting the prices received by itinerant merchants bringing up tea from the southeast and paid by the lesser guild merchants who redistributed it in the north.[99] Moreover, the oligopolistic powers of the tea guild were sanctioned by the state, since this expedited the administration of the state's own monopoly regulations. Indeed, to keep state and guild-merchant interests congruent, the most powerful of the tea merchants were formally invited to give their opinions in the debates over tea policy in the early Song.[100] But even the less influential southern tea merchants could act collectively to protect their interests against the government and the large guilds of the capital: In 1048, for example, when the state used tea vouchers redeemable from government markets in the southeast for tea to pay for military provisions bought from grain merchants in the northwest (one facet of the *ruzhong* provisioning policy), it paid so great a nominal value in tea for each grain transaction that the claims on tea could not be collected for years. As a result, the southern tea merchants who bought the tea vouchers from the grain merchants in the Kaifeng note markets refused to pay more than 3,000 cash for vouchers with a nominal value of 100,000 cash; this brought the provisioning trade to one of its periodic halts, instigating reforms that ultimately led to the suspension of the southeastern tea monopoly in 1059.[101]

Information from the twelfth century is especially rich in examples of mutual association for the sake of licit and illicit trade and mutual defense. Shiba Yoshinobu, in his encyclopedic study of commerce during the Song, found that combinations of tea merchants of equal standing in traveling bands of as many as thirty peddlers,[102] and the formation of such same-trade partnerships as "associations of partners" (*jiuhe huoban*), "joint-capital partnerships" (*liancai heben*), and "associations of members without joint capital" (*fei liancai heben er jiuji tonghang*) were common.[103] We also know that tea merchants formed what may have been single-transaction associations with captains of ocean-going vessels and guarantors in order to smuggle Fujianese camphorated tea.[104]

Similarly tea merchants in the southeast were quick to organize for banditry and defense. Tea-bandit gangs (*chakou*) formed by or under the leadership of tea merchants were endemic in the latter half of the twelfth century, when regulations against the free sale of tea in the northern regions controlled by the Jin depressed the tea industry. Such bands rose up in the Middle Yangzi tea lands of Hunan in 1154 and then again in Hubei in 1160, when 11,000 men were sent to quell them.[105] The luxuriant tea country surrounding Poyang Lake in Jiangxi was especially liable to trouble from tea merchants turned to banditry or hooliganism, as occurred in 1159 when traders were thrown out of work by an unspecified depression in the tea economy;[106] and again in 1171 when "tens of hundreds" of "tea guests" were idled by drought and a ruined tea crop.[107] The most notorious of these bandit armies was formed by the tea middleman *(chazang)* Lai Wenzhong in 1175, whose rebel army arose in Hubei and spread to Hunan, Jiangxi, and Guangdong.[108] But these same martial and organizational skills could also be used in the service of the local population: the Righteous and Brave Tea-Merchant Army that was mustered in De'an (Hubei), and the Daring and Brave Army in Xiangyang played critical roles in defending their cities against the Jurchen sieges of 1206–1207.[109]

It seems clear then that compared to their southeastern counterparts the tea merchants of Sichuan were relatively underdeveloped as a corporate group. To be sure, our information about Sichuanese tea merchants is incomparably less rich than what we have for the southeast. But that same gap applies to all our information about Sichuan, and yet we know of other regional trades that showed great entrepreneurial sophistication. For example, the sixteen banking households of Chengdu that created the *jiaozi* exchange medium, one of the earliest true paper monies and soon to become a basic part of Sichuan's currency stock, evidenced great innovativeness in credit techniques and modes of cooperation, and for awhile stood in the same privileged relationship to the Chengdu and regional officiary as the guilds of Kaifeng. The silk and brocade traders of Sichuan also engaged in complex ventures involving elaborate credit and commodity flows, especially when they also served as agents for the government either as provisioners in Shaanxi or silver vendors in Sichuan. During the twelfth century, rich Sichuanese merchants dominated the brocade-and-aromatics trade along the Guangxi border of Vietnam, setting up dependent petty merchants in self-sufficient colonies to trade with the Vietnamese in small amounts of paper, writing brushes, rice, and hempen cloth, while they themselves made one trip yearly for exchanges of brocades and aromatics worth thousands of strings of cash.[110]

Like the tea merchants of the southeast or Kaifeng, the Chengdu banking houses (at least as bankers to the silk industry) and the Sichuanese silk merchants participated in interregional commerce and developed the specialized forms of association such trade required. But Sichuan's tea merchants were confined by competition and government fiat to a relatively localized intraregional commerce, and consequently had no need for a complex and differentiated organizational structure. The Sichuan tea merchant was fixed, as it were, at the first of what Max Weber identified as the four stages in the development of the resident trader: an itinerant peddler, who has acquired a fixed residence and (this we can only assume) who travels periodically in order to market products at a distance or to secure products from a distance. None of his traveling devolved upon an employee or servant or partner, as in the second stage; nor did he found independent settlements or maintain employees at a distance, as in the third; nor had he become fixed in his location, to deal with distant locations by correspondence only, as in the fourth.[111] The itinerant tea merchants of Kaifeng matched in whole or in part the characteristics at the more developed end of the spectrum; and compared to them, the tea merchants of Sichuan were fixed in a stage of comparative backwardness. Because of their backwardness, moreover, when new commercial opportunities appeared, Sichuanese tea merchants were slow to respond; and when a state monopoly was imposed, they were easy to control.

The administrative wall encircling the tea of Sichuan and the Hanzhong Basin was dismantled in the latter half of the eleventh century by two successive but ideologically antithetical acts of government policy. The first was laissez faire in nature: In 1059 the eighty-year southeastern tea monopoly was suspended on all but the camphorated "wax" (*la*) tea of Fujian, and "all other teas allowed to circulate freely everywhere under Heaven."[112] For the next fifteen years, the only such period in the three-hundred-year span of Song history, there were free markets in both the Upper Yangzi and southeastern tea economies.

The monopoly suspension stimulated great interest among the salt merchants of Shaanxi, who began to transport salt from Jiezhou, medicinals probably obtained from Central Asian traders in

Qinzhou, and other goods into Sichuan and the Hanzhong Basin to trade for tea, "which they sold in the prefectures and commanderies of Shaanxi at great profit."[113] This new triangular trade released the long bottled-up productive capacity of the Sichuan tea industry, as cultivators shifted resources to meet the new demand. The resulting surge in production was nowhere more evident than in the Hanzhong Basin, where production stood at 7,400,000 catties in 1074, a level that could only have been achieved in response to extra-regional demand. From Wen Tong again, who was prefect of Yangzhou in 1076 when both the tea and salt trade had fallen under government restriction, we have a picture of this new and vigorous commerce: "Households in the tea-producing hamlets were free to sell tea as they pleased, [while] guest travelers from all the prefectures of Shaanxi came to buy tea, however old or modest in amount it might be. They traveled back and forth on the roads, interlaced like weaving, bearing salt goods into the mountains, and everyone in the markets of the prefecture, districts, villages, hamlets, and market towns engaged in household trade."[114]

From the perspective of production it is apparent that in the producing districts of Yangzhou, where tea shrubs would probably have been ubiquitous as boundary markers, hedgerows, and simply growing wild, households began to tend previously uncultivated trees and to throw their resources into the raising of new shrubs for the market. What is especially noteworthy from the perspective of distribution, however, is that from all available accounts—the Sichuanese observers Lü Tao, Su Che, and Wen Tong, and the Tea and Horse Intendant Liu Zuo—the merchants who took advantage of this new commercial opportunity were the traveling salt merchants of Shaanxi and not the tea merchants of Sichuan. As participants in the state-contracted and regulated Jiezhou salt and frontier provisioning trades, the Shaanxi merchants had had long experience in the movement of large volumes of goods over long distances and could respond quickly to the opportunities provided by a change in government regulations; in fact, this same set of entrepreneurial skills was to keep them prominent into the Qing.[115] But the tea merchants of Sichuan had neither the long-distance commercial experience nor the trading networks to respond with equal speed, and therefore lost their opportunity to move into the export trade.

The second act of government policy to reverse the devolutionary trend in the Upper Yangzi tea industry has already been alluded to: the establishment in 1074 of a government agency to procure Sichuanese tea for the newly revived Qinghai horse trade. Government agents displaced Shaanxi's tea and salt merchants to carve out an exclusive marketing region for Sichuan's tea that exceeded in geographic range and demographic density anything that the region had enjoyed before. Under the aegis of bureaucratic entrepreneurship the three-century process of market contraction was aggressively reversed; and within a decade of the monopoly's establishment, Sichuan's localized high-quality tea industry had been transformed into a bulk producer of low-quality tea for long-distance state-run markets. But government control of the Sichuan tea industry was predicated on a major realliance between Sichuanese elites and the state. The story of that transformation is the subject of the next chapter.

THREE

Bureaucracy, Social Mobilization and the Political Integration of Sichuan

I have claimed that because the Sichuanese economy lay beyond the regulatory reach of the late-Tang and early-Song states, Sichuanese tea was barricaded from extraregional Chinese markets that were earmarked for state-controlled tea from the southeast. But what put the Sichuanese economy beyond the pale of direct state control? The intuitive answer is distance, and Sichuan's distance and isolation from imperial centers naturally increased the costs of centralized control and amplified any tendencies towards regional autonomy. But from the perspective of state economic control, the single most significant gap separating center and region during the Tang and early Song was political: up through the end of the tenth century Sichuanese elites repelled the advance of state power in the region, whereas from the eleventh century on they embraced it. By promoting a transformation in the structure of elite power in Sichuan, the eleventh-century state was able to bridge the administrative distance between center and region to commandeer the Sichuanese tea industry and penetrate to the heart of the Sichuanese economy.

At the broadest level, what are the requirements for effective state intervention in the economy? Dietrich Rueschemeyer and Peter B. Evans, in a 1985 synthesis of the literature on the state and economic transformation, conclude that the best answer is still the one provided by Max Weber: bureaucratic organization. As

Rueschemeyer and Evans point out, in his ideal type Weber identified a number of features of bureaucracy that are crucial for effective economic control, including "corporate cohesion of the organization, differentiation and insulation from its social environment,
unambiguous location of decision making and channels of authority, and internal features fostering instrumental rationality and activism (in particular suitable hiring and promotion practices as well
as organizational designs that minimize obstacles to personnel replacement and to the restructuring of roles and bureaus as needed."[1]
But building a bureaucratic apparatus goes well beyond the simple
creation of a formal organizational structure. One of Rueschemeyer
and Evans' chief contributions is to remind us that constructing an
effective bureaucracy entails a long-term process of institution
building, a process that is in turn predicated on major changes of
attitude and behavior:

> Any institution building requires transcending individual rational-instru-
> mental behavior . . . An effective process of institution building must re-
> shape the goals, priorities, and commitments of core participants and in-
> culcate shared assumptions and expectations on which a common rationality
> can be based. The growth of a distinctive esprit de corps among pivotal
> civil servants is an essential aspect of this process, which in turn is often
> coupled with the emergence of (higher) civil servants as a "status group"
> distinguished by a particular social prestige as well as privileged association
> and exclusiveness. Such institutional constructions are likely to require de-
> cades, if not generations, to become established.[2]

Implanting bureaucracy, then, demands not only that state-builders
extend the tendrils of formal organization into society, but also that
social elites reorient their goals and activities to include participation in the new bureaucratic institutions: state and society must be
made to fit. Thus bureaucratization comprises a social as well as an
organizational metamorphosis, as bureaucratic values and behavior
become a significant component of the political culture.

It is now accepted that in China as a whole, changes in the structure of provincial and financial administration, the demographic
and economic emergence of the south, and the rise of the examination system all promoted an unprecedented role for bureaucratic

methods of governance and for bureaucratic careers as the focus of mobility strategies between the eighth and eleventh centuries. More than at any other time in China's imperial era, government was structured according to the principles of functional specialization characteristic of modern bureaucracies, and participation in government service came to typify elite activity.[3] But Sichuanese were relatively slow to respond to this process of "bureaucratization." From the Sui reunification of the empire in 581 through the late tenth century, the imperatives of political control forced the state to cede civil and military authority to Sichuan's "local magnates and great lineages" *(tuhao dazu)*, who absorbed these new institutions of government authority into the patrimonial structure of magnate society. Government became the captive of local elites, who tolerated the presence of the state but withheld from it their region's wealth.

Sichuan's metamorphosis from a magnate to a bureaucratic society was facilitated by a major political blunder. Following its conquest of the Sichuanese state of Later Shu in 965, Song efforts to confiscate the region's wealth in advance of political consolidation ignited a decade of shattering rebellions at the end of the tenth century. These regionwide upheavals ruptured the socio-economic fabric of magnate power, for the first time opening Sichuanese elites to political recruitment by the centralized state. In the aftermath of the rebellions bureaucratic careers emerged as the primary path to elite power, enabling the Song state to embed centralized structures of bureaucratic government in Sichuan and to mobilize the support of powerful members of the local populace for centrally defined fiscal goals. It was only by transforming magnates into bureaucrats that the Song state could reverse the Tang legacy of fiscal isolation to extend control over the Sichuanese economy. The establishment of the tea and horse trade in 1074, ostensibly just a new fiscal policy launched in response to the military and financial needs of the central government in Kaifeng, was in fact the consummation of a fundamental change in the structure of the Sichuanese elite. The fiscal dimension of the tea and horse trade can be fully understood only against the background of this sociological metamorphosis, the transformation of Sichuan's rural barons and hermit scholars into imperial civil servants, willing and eager to tax their home region for the state.

SICHUAN'S MAGNATE SOCIETY

Historians of Sichuan during the Sui and Tang portray a common trajectory in the relationship between Sichuanese elites and the state. Unlike the politically more sophisticated aristocratic houses (*menfa*) of the north, Sichuan's powerful families entered the period of re-unification firmly wedded to habits of local domination and contemptuous of government service.[4] The *Sui History* provides a classic description of the sullen independence of Sichuanese elites in the late sixth century:

> The people [of Sichuan] are clever and rash, and in appearance many are small and ugly. But they admire literary studies, in which at times they excel. Many indulge in lives of leisure, and very few of them become government officials. There are those who become old and white-haired without ever having left their villages and towns . . . In the frontier wilderness the wealthy have secured control of the profits of "the mountains and the marshes." By means of their wealth and power they have made themselves masters over the native peoples and exact labor services from them. Thus they act with complete impunity in illegally harboring natives within their households. Their influence subverts the authority of the prefectural and county officials. But is this not the age-old custom of the region?[5]

Sichuanese aversion to government service was reenforced during the early Tang, when the region's elites were rewarded for their early capitulation to the new dynasty by a purely nominal application of the *juntian* land equalization policy that left magnate control of land and labor largely untouched.[6] Spurning Tang efforts at political recruitment and largely unthreatened by the thin overlay of civil government that the early Tang was able to field in the region, these powerful lineages were content to expand their wealth and power at the local level and to fold into their network of patron-client bonds the many commoners dispossessed by the government's policies of taxation and labor service.

Matsui Shuichi has argued that the paucity of Sichuanese biographies in the two Tang histories (a total of seven) is itself evidence of the political insularity of Sichuanese elites.[7] Much of our information about Sichuan's magnate society during the Tang must be gleaned from the handful of exceptions. The family of Chen Zi'ang (661–702) of Zizhou probably typifies the relationship between prominent local families and the early Tang state. The Chens owned extensive lands in their region, partly built up by Zi'ang's great uncle Chen Si (d. 632?), who was part of a lineage that had been in Zizhou since the period of the Three Kingdoms. Chen Si spurned the world of officialdom in favor of amassing wealth, which he accomplished by artfully managing the resources of his forests and marshes and by reclaiming good agricultural lands—endeavors which in this period of repopulation brought him great benefits.[8] Zi'ang's father enjoyed a reputation as a champion of justice and was sought out as a mediator in legal disputes. He earned titular official rank for distributing great amounts of grain during a famine, but Zi'ang himself was apparently the first member of the lineage in six generations to leave home for an official post, arriving in Chang'an in 683.

Random anecdotes suggest that early Tang officials were frustrated in their efforts to recruit Sichuanese for the government, and it appears that the early Tang court was forced to fill the region's governorships, prefectures, and county magistracies with outsiders.[9] The chief duty of these outside administrators was to harness Sichuan's riches to the needs of imperial expansion, and at first they were quite successful. But irresponsible officials threatened to undermine Sichuan's productivity and Tang fiscal control. In 648, for example, cash contributions exacted in Sichuan to finance construction of a naval armada aimed at Koguryo forced large numbers of households into vagrancy, caused grain prices to soar, and incited uprisings by Liao tribesmen.[10] Fifty years later the conscription of 160,000 men annually (out of a total regional population of about 880,000 households) to transport grain to the Songpan borderlands of northwestern Sichuan again inflated rice prices and swelled the region's vagrant population.[11] Sichuan's powerful families were no doubt sheltered from most of these exactions. They in fact became the beneficiaries of Tang misrule, as households forced from their lands and livelihoods by wildly fluctuating grain prices and insufferable labor exactions sought the protection of local magnates.

With the aid of Tang's heavy-handed taxation of commoners as well as its relatively slack restraints on estate-building and bondage, Sichuan's powerful landowners extended an ever-widening net over the region's Han and non-Han population alike.[12] Under these circumstances local power-holders were little tempted to participate in government, and Chen Zi'ang's emergence out of magnate society into the world of officialdom at this time was very nearly unique. Nor is it clear that Chen was fully accepted by the official society he sought to join, for he died in prison in his home district, incarcerated by a district magistrate who resented the family's wealth.[13] But not long after Chen's death the situation began to change.

Elite society throughout Tang China was profoundly reshaped by the growth of provincial governments in the course of the eighth century, and ultimately this political change brought even Sichuanese into closer involvement with the state.[14] The foundations of provincial administration were laid in 710, with the establishment of frontier commands *(fanzhen)* headed by permanent military governors *(jiedushi)*.[15] The military governors were allowed large staffs; and given the extensive problems of procurement and transport that attended the maintenance of large standing armies, it can be assumed that they would have valued the services of knowledgeable and powerful locals in key staff positions. A frontier command was first set up in Sichuan in 717, to defend against and control the Tibetans and smaller border tribes of the southwest.[16] By mid century, Sichuanese had begun to participate in provincial and even court politics, as eminent provincial families added official patronage to their inventory of mobility strategies.

Xianyu Zhongtong, for instance, the first of his lineage to accept office in the Tang, was eventually appointed to the Jiannan governorship in 749; and despite his cashiering from that post in 751 for leading 60,000 soldiers to their deaths against the Yunnanese kingdom of Nanzhao, his younger brother Shuming was appointed gov-

ernor of Jiannan East in 768. In a somewhat parallel case, the wealthy
Yan clan (which was related to the Xianyus by marriage), produced
its first politically prominent member in Yan Zhen, who climbed
the ranks from chief secretary of Hezhou, to prefect of Yuzhou (mod.
Chongqing), to the key governorship of Shannan West, a post that
passed at his death in 799 to his chief assistant and security officer,
his cousin Yan Li.[17]

Despite this new willingness to engage in local and regional government, however, for Sichuan's new stratum of officials government service enhanced rather than supplanted old habits of local
domination. From 755 to 762 An Lushan's rebellion rocked the
Tang state; and tremors periodically shook Sichuan as well, particularly in 756 and 757 when Emperor Xuanzong fled to Chengdu
with his armies and his court. In 757 there were a number of local
rebellions that in two instances involved professional soldiers and
the men who had been pressed into military duty in Chengdu, and
in one case a local magnate in Guozhou.[18] Then in 761 the Prefect
of Zizhou, Duan Zizhang, bridled at an attempt by the court to
replace him and, in the course of short but dramatic rebellion, managed to take the prefectural cities of Mian, Sui, and Jian and pro-
claim himself King of Liang.[19] And magnate society profited from
the disruptions of the mid eighth century much as it had gained
from the unrest of the century before.

One of our chief sources on magnate society at this time is the
poet Du Fu. In a memorial of 763 Du Fu, who was then serving as
an official in Sichuan, described how military requisitions for the
frontier campaigns were forcing commoners to mortgage their lands
and bond their persons to the "engrossing magnate families." To
this point Du's theme echoes the laments of Chen Zi'ang to the
Empress Wu half a century earlier, but Du introduces a new charge
that would have been foreign to Chen: "These days the wealth [of
these engrossing magnates] comes from the fact that their sons and
brothers all hold administrative positions in the military governors'
offices and under the chiefs of the prefectural and county offices."[20]

The events documented by Du Fu became increasingly routine
during the eighth and ninth centuries, as higher-order elites in im-

portant prefectural cities and lower-order local magnates continued
to enfold the institutions of provincial administration into their
social and economic bases of power. The most notorious misuse of
public authority for private ends was charged to Yan Zhen's cousin
Yan Li, who around the year 806 used his power as governor of
Jiannan East, whose capital lay in his home prefecture of Zizhou,
to confiscate numerous estates and slaves. As Charles Peterson points
out in his study of the affair, Yan Li's corruption was the unavoid-
able consequence of the dwindling power of the central government
following An Lushan's rebellion.[21] Provincial government and provincial governorships afforded Sichuanese a powerful new lever of
patronage and authority, without imposing any new restraints. For
half a century following the rebellion, the state was too weak to
discipline its provincial governors, who enjoyed increasing autonomy from the center.

Under Emperor Xianzong (r. 806–820) the court did reassert a
measure of authority over its provincial governors in Sichuan. But
this reassertion of central control at the level of the provincial command was accompanied by an even greater devolution of local administrative authority to the region's social and economic elites.
The Tang state was increasingly forced to rely on local personnel to
fill county magistrate and other local bureaucratic posts, and on
local elites to form militia organizations for defense. High-ranking
officials were reluctant to serve in Sichuan or to return there for
subsequent terms of duty, a problem later faced by the Song as well.
Tang policy-makers were forced to reduce the number of regional
posts that had to be filled each year and to assign an ever-greater
number of county magistrates' posts to subaltern officials drawn
from the local populace.[22]

The devolution of public authority to private elites gradually
crystallized around the formation of local defense organizations, which
emerged to provide the public security functions forfeited by an
increasingly weak Tang state. As Tibet and Nanzhao learned of the
Tang state's growing impotence, they stepped up their attacks on
Sichuan; and in early 830 Nanzhao armies even occupied and sacked
Chengdu.[23] Security was finally restored; but Tibetan and Nanzhao
encroachments persisted throughout the century, leaving disorder

and banditry in their wake.[24] During the late 870s the formation
of militia units became especially widespread, possibly in anticipation of a spillover into the region of Huang Chao's rebellion. The
already noticeable unrest in the region was sharply exacerbated when
Xizong's chief eunuch and head of the Palace Armies, Tian Lingzi,
led the emperor in flight to Tian's home in Chengdu, then set up
his brother (Chen Jingxuan) as governor.[25] The ruthlessly oppressive Chen-Tian regime provoked widespread unrest and rebellious-
ness, particularly among military commanders outside the ruling
clique. One such officer, Qian Neng, led his own troops and other
bandit gangs against Chen Jingxuan for most of 882; the prefect of
Fuzhou, Han Xiusheng, revolted at the end of the year; and banditry was endemic throughout the province.[26]

As Tang military capacity dwindled, powerful local figures moved
in to organize their own defense organizations, to whom the state
in turn divested the remainder of their civil authority. The best-
documented example of this devolution of military and civil authority to local elites is the case of Wei Junqing.[27] A powerful
member of the elite of Changzhou, the mountainous prefecture just
west of modern Chongqing, Wei began to organize local defense
units in the late 870s. In 882 he led a "righteous army" *(yijun)*
against Han Xiusheng, and in return was made prefect of Puzhou.
After this Wei's power grew dramatically. By 892, when he built
his massive Yongchang Fortress, Wei was concurrently prefect of
Changzhou and commanding general of the four prefectures of Chang,
Pu, Yu, and He. In sum, Wei commanded thirty-four militia units
comprising 40,000 to 50,000 men, many of whom were his relatives or personal dependents.[28] Of the 149 names listed on the
Yongchang commemorative stele twenty-six were surnamed Wei:
ten shared the generational name Jun, and another ten shared the
generational name Zhu.[29] Moreover it was precisely these relatives,
in particular members of Junqing's generation, that held the most
important local and prefectural-level posts (for example, the bandit-
suppression commissionerships), as well as the leadership positions
in strategically critical garrison towns that either already were or by
Song would become important market centers.[30]

Thus from its origins as a local militia unit, Wei Junqing's organization expanded to include all of the military and much of the civil apparatus of four prefectures, with authority over the region located securely in the Wei clan and its associates, and all with the sanction and even encouragement of the central government. Moreover, this was a phenomenon widespread throughout Sichuan—Qian Neng's uncle headed a similar although probably much smaller lineage-based organization[31]—and the empire as a whole. And while the extreme devolution of public authority to powerful private interests that provincial militarization represented was surely exacerbated by the disintegration of social and political institutions at the end of the Tang, the process itself reflected a long-term transformation of the structure of provincial government in which, as Kurihara puts it, locally powerful elites recombined and absorbed the power of the provincial commands even as they dismantled its structure.[32] For Sichuanese during the latter half of the Tang, office-holding did not represent a transition to bureaucratic values and modes of behavior, but rather the extension of patrimonial forms of authority based on personal loyalty, patron-client relations, and the use of office to expropriate property income, fees, and taxes.[33] The opportunities for enrichment and self-aggrandizement this process offered to the local power-holders was probably one reason the region remained essentially loyal to the dynasty, but in the end it was symptomatic as well of the Tang's failure to penetrate the protective shell of magnate society to link center, region, and locale.

What were the fiscal consequences of the Tang state's weak control of Sichuan? The limited evidence indicates that the court was forced to relinquish Sichuan's wealth in order to retain its political loyalty. One key measure of fiscal control, for instance, is provided by the size of provincial grain revenues available to the central government: In 749, Hebei held 21.9 percent of the state's 96,000,000-*dan* reserve and Henan 23.4 percent, figures that Denis Twitchett uses to demonstrate the importance of those provinces before An Lushan's rebellion. In contrast, Jiannan province, the most populous and intensively cultivated core region of the Upper Yangzi, held but 2 percent; and its half a *dan* per head was the lowest in the empire.[34] Possibly more grain was collected by the powerful governors after the rebellions; but if so, the state had little access to it, and financial administrators keenly felt the loss of Sichuan's resources.

Around 780 the Great Minister Yang Yan, architect of the "two-tax system" *(liangshuifa)*, complained to Emperor Dezong that ever since Cui Ning had usurped the military governorship of Jiannan West fourteen years before, the court had been without its "outer storehouse" and that "the tribute and taxes sent to the court [from Sichuan] are the same as if that land did not exist."[35] Even after instituting Yang's *liangshui* reform, which recognized the taxing powers of the provincial governors and attempted merely to obtain a quota of what was taxed, it appears that funds collected in Sichuan tended to remain there. Governor Wei Gao, for example, a man whose loyalty to the throne was never in question, retained complete fiscal autonomy over his domain. Although he contributed large sums to the court, he did so irregularly and as tribute rather than as tax revenue.[36] Moreover, it appears that very little of the revenues from the tea and salt monopolies that were set up universally to meet the great demand for funds following An Lushan's rebellion came from Sichuan, as we saw in Chapter Two.[37] Viewed in isolation, the Tang's forfeiture of Sichuan's tea revenues looks like the incidental consequence of an interagency squabble; but when put in the context of the court's overall revenue flows, it seems clear that Sichuan's contributions from tea as well as its other taxable resources were irregular and at the discretion of the provincial governors. In order to retain nominal control over Sichuan's magnate society, the Tang court had to forgo taxing the region's wealth.

MAGNATE SOCIETY UNDER FORMER AND LATER SHU

The Tang "imperial coalition" of emperor, personal supporters, provincial allies, and foreign mercenaries did not finally collapse until 907, although the empire had already fallen under the de facto control of a ragtag assortment of provincial governors, warlords, and military adventurers.[38] In 903 the entire Upper Yangzi region came under the domination of Wang Jian, a former mule thief and

Henanese soldier in a provincial army that had joined Xizong in Sichuan. The Shu imperial crown passed to Wang's eleventh son Wang Yan in 918, who lost it eight years later to a Later Tang (923–936) general named Meng Zhixiang. Meng declared his own independence just before dying in 934, and his son Meng Chang ruled the state of Later Shu until its conquest by the Song in 965.[39]

Political power under the two Shu regimes coalesced into two strata. Sichuan had played a unique role during the collapse of the Tang as a comparatively safe haven not only for Emperor Xizong but also for many members of the old Tang elite, and these courtiers flowed naturally into the upper echelons of the two Shu regimes.[40] But most prefectural and local government offices were probably filled by Sichuanese. Long-time residents of the region seem to have reached an easy accommodation with the two Shu states and willingly to have accepted offices at all levels of government, although among late-Tang refugee families who stayed on in Sichuan it later became fashionable to deny having cooperated with the Wang or Meng rulers. Of the nine out of forty-five lineages in Fei Zhu's *Genealogy of {Chengdu} Lineages* about whom the appropriate data is supplied, six families accepted positions under the Shu regimes while three—all refugees with Xizong—claimed to have declined.[41]

Sichuanese office-holding under the two Shu regimes continued the patrimonial patterns of the Tang, with traditionally dominant clans using public office to augment their opportunities for patronage and income. Office-holders typically acquired their posts on the basis of wealth, influence, or connections. In the early 920s, for example, the queen mother and her sister, of the Xu lineage of Chengdu, conspired to auction off all the offices from prefect on down as they became vacant, while placing their relatives in all the highest positions.[42] A less transparent transformation of wealth into office occurred when the local magnate Shi Chuwen of Wanzhou was made head of his home prefecture for contributing large amounts of money and provisions to Meng Zhixian during Meng's campaign in eastern Sichuan.[43] In the eyes of the Song conquerors of Later Shu, local government in Sichuan had become so thoroughly ensnared by patronage and private interests that all incumbent personnel had to be dismissed. A memorial from 965 declares, "Ever since the start of the Five Dynasties the heads of prefectures have mostly been military men and their violent lackeys. But because these men are illiterate, they must arrange for relatives or clerks to manage prefectural affairs for them; and by making use of this delegated power, [these relatives and clerks] have usurped authority illegally."[44]

Patrimonial office benefitted its incumbents in predictable ways. Highly placed sojourner officials amassed large estates through intimidation and outright confiscation. Many of these properties were presented to Song Taizu in 965.[45] The most famous of these estates, built up by Governor Tian Qinquan and presented as "lands for perpetual dwelling" (*changzhutian*) to the Correct Dharma Monastery (Zhengfayuan) of Chengdu, encompassed almost 1,400 acres in Chengdu and Huayang counties.[46] Of greater political significance are the native Sichuanese; and here, too, office-holding and prosperity went hand in hand. We know of at least two lineages—the Feis of Shuangliu County and the Wens of Mianzhou—in which official service coincided with the establishment of branch lineages in neighboring prefectures, a probable sign of enhanced corporate success.[47] And in eastern Sichuan Shi Chuwen, the Wanzhou prefect noted above, opened new lands on a vast scale from which he regularly received enormous amounts of grain.[48]

We possess the richest information about men who held office during the two Shu regimes, and about lineages that eventually made the transition into the civil service status group—that is, the *shidafu*. The histories of these men and families have been preserved in funerary inscriptions, biographies, and genealogies for individual lineages, such as Su Xun's history of the Su clan, his *Sushi zupu,* or collective genealogies such as Fei Zhu's history of the Chengdu elite, the *Shizupu.*[49] It is more difficult to reconstruct the impact of political autonomy on the elite substratum of Sichuanese society that did not make the transition into the bureaucratic class; for our information about them is almost wholly impersonal and categorical in nature, supplied by Song officials who were desperately trying to impose centralized control over a hostile population.

In the very broadest terms, it is clear that in the more developed subregions of western Sichuan the absolute dominance of the "local magnates and great families" began to diminish in the face of economic expansion. The Chengdu Plain, the Tuo River prefectures of Jiannzhou and Lingjingjian, and Ziizhou, commanding the intersection of the riverine routes south and the land routes north, were centers of a flourishing economy based on intensive rice and tea cultivation, sericulture and textile manufacture, and salt.[50] This economic vitality, which enriched the coffers of the two Shu states,[51] found its liveliest manifestation in the spring silkworm markets and autumn herbal markets that proliferated in the Chengdu vicinity. Often located on the grounds of a temple, these markets served as wholesale distribution centers for tea, silks, Chengdu's famous peonies and crab apples; as suppliers of silkworm frames and cocoons and other agricultural implements; and as gathering places for great throngs of local sellers, consumers and itinerant merchants.[52]

Sichuan's economic centers were inhabited by dense or rapidly swelling populations that sought to free themselves from dependency and patrimonial restraints. In Meizhou, Su Shi recorded that peasants organized cooperative labor brigades that spanned the planting season, allocating fines and bonuses on the basis of performance, all without the coercion or intervention of rich landowners.[53] In Chengdu, former tenant-farmers *(dianmeng)* chipped away at the lands of Tian Qinquan's old estate and tried, in the end unsuccessfully, to establish claims for themselves as masters.[54] And in western and northern Sichuan commoners even sought to free themselves from patriarchal restraints by setting up separate households during their parents' lifetimes, although the Song court quickly (969) declared the practice a capital crime.[55] But population growth was probably the most important factor eroding magnate control over labor.[56] As Richard von Glahn shows in his study of state and society on the Sichuan frontier during the Song, gradual crowding of the Chengdu Plain and other core centers in western Sichuan reversed the relative values of land and labor. In the old Shu heartland of western and northern Sichuan guest households (*kehu*—in Sichuan at least an accurate indicator of bondage) constituted only

31 percent of the population in 980. In the labor-poor Ba region of southern and eastern Sichuan, by contrast, they accounted for 76.2 percent of the population.[57] As land became more costly in relation to labor in western Sichuan, magnate domination of the agrarian population declined.

But Sichuan's local barons still emerged from sixty years of independence with sufficient power to interpose themselves between Song centralizers and the local populace. In those regions where magnate influence was most problematic, Song officials painted a composite picture made up of magnates, dependents, and an intermediate stratum of wealthy villagers. At the top, the most powerful families inserted themselves into the political gap between bureaucratic government and the populace at large, commanding enormous leverage to distort government policies to their own ends. In 971, for example, the assistant prefect of Langzhou, Lu Zhong, discovered that "families of substance" (*xingshihu*) regularly conspired with local families conscripted into official service (*zhiyihu*) to conceal tax-paying households, thereby causing delays in tax payments. In order to subject these refractory notables to greater scrutiny, Lu devised a separate "register of families of substance" (*xingshi banbu*), which officials were to use as a basis for regular personal inspection of the suspected wealthy households.[58]

In addition to slowing the flow of taxes up to the state, power brokers could also block relief measures aimed down at the people— measures that in this period of economic disruption were extremely important. In 977, it was reported that "powerful individuals and criminous clerks" (*haomin xiali*) were profiteering in government relief salt, buying it up at 70 cash per catty and selling it to the people at several hundred cash.[59] Similarly in the 990s, "local potentates" (*haoyou*) quickly gained control of government vouchers issued to the poor for relief salt and rice.[60]

In the eyes of Song officials, however, the most dangerous aspect of magnate power was the ability of influential families to direct their large retinues of dependents against imperial rule. In 996, while Sichuan was still reeling from the impact of the Wang Xiaobo– Li Shun rebellion, officials offered the following analysis of the relationship between powerful families and their "collateral" *(panghu)* dependents:

> In the past the inhabitants of Ba and Shu arrived at a mutual accommoda-
> tion based on the wealth of some and the labor of others. Every wealthy
> family possesses dependents numbering several thousand households. The
> small folk pay rents and labor service each year, and both sides consider
> the arrangement appropriate. Those reporting to the throne argued that
> the Shu masses rebelled simply because the powerful people whistled and
> summoned together these collateral households.[61]

It was this bond between master and dependent that Song officials felt compelled to break, in order to open Sichuan up to centralized control. The solution proposed in the 996 report entailed
inserting "village magnates" *(xianghao)* between the most powerful
barons and their *panghu* dependents, by appointing designated village magnates to leadership positions as community elders *(qizhang)*; after three years, all those who had successfully pacified their
jurisdictions would be rewarded with public office.[62] But the officials sent in to implement this policy of social control argued against
it, memorializing that "[t]he *panghu* have long been dependent on
the powerful families, and their relationship mutually acknowledged for many generations. If this is suddenly changed and they
are put under the control of other leaders, it is to be feared that
their hearts will be made anxious, and that this will provoke further
crises."[63]

This attempt to coopt intermediate, or nascent, elites into driving a wedge between the local magnates and their dependents in
order to prevent future unrest was consequently shelved. But the
same goals were achieved by the rebellion itself. As Karl Deutsch
speculated at an abstract level, and Chalmers Johnson demonstrated
in the special case of Japan's invasion of China, the violence and
chaos of wars and revolutions can suddenly destroy old social bonds
and habits of thought and action, thereby opening previously resis-
tant social groups to political mobilization and national integration.[64] The social upheaval of the mid 990s erupted with sufficient
fury to shake the locally entrenched elites out of their circumscribed
spheres of influence and make them available to recruitment by the

centralized Song bureaucracy, as the poor turned against the rich and the rich turned for protection to the state. These rebellions stand as the dividing line between a regional elite that was integrated into the national policy and one that was not, and they mark as well the point at which the regional economy became subject to effective centralized exploitation. Ironically the major cause of the rebellion was not the obdurate resistance of anti-imperial elites, but the general economic chaos brought on by imperial plunder of the wealth of Shu.

REBELLION AND POLITICAL MOBILIZATION DURING THE SONG

Impartial contemporaries and modern historians agree that it was the confiscatory polices of the Song conquerors of Sichuan that kindled the greatest rebellion the dynasty would face until 1120 and the uprising of Fang La. By expropriating the wealth accumulated by Later Shu, destroying the region's currency system, and imposing immoderate taxes on an already troubled economy, official Song policy drove the people of Sichuan into the rebellion that was to open the region to centralized control.

Sichuan's wealth and the "Daily Offering Convoys" that were organized to remove it, are described in a contemporary account of the Wang Xiaobo–Li Shun rebellion:

> The land of Shu was wealthy and filled with abundance. With its raw silk thread and silk products such as moire, silk twill, and embroidered silks, it was known as "the crown of all under heaven" (*guan tianxia*). The storehouses of the Mengs were filled to overflowing, but the [Song] imperial armies took it all: The heavy goods, coppers, and cloths were carried through the [Yangzi] gorges and sent for storage in Jiangling, where they were transferred onto boats and transported to the capital [at Kaifeng]. For the light goods, figured silks, and grains a series of courier posts were set up from the capital to [eastern and western] Sichuan, and troops despatched to do the carrying. Every forty soldiers were organized into one convoy (*gang*), called the "Daily Offering," and in a few years all that the Mengs had stored was returned to the "Interior Storehouse."[65]

These land and water convoys must have begun immediately: Later Shu submitted in the first month of 965; by the third month there was an order for all prefectures to send any precious metals and silks that were not needed to meet expenses to the capital without delay; and at about the same time the court announced the establishment of the Reserve Treasury to handle the overflow of goods pouring into the Left Treasury.[66]

The convoys continued for over a decade. One of their most valuable cargoes must have been the copper coins circulating in Sichuan, which the court coveted for use in North China.[67] In 955 Later Shu, threatened by invasion from the north, began the emergency minting of iron coins, which from then on circulated concurrently with copper. But Song conquering officials almost immediately prohibited the use of copper coins, which were siphoned out of circulation and shipped up to the capital. At the same time, they began minting exorbitant quantities of iron coins. Prices in Sichuan soared, and the value of iron coins plummetted 400 percent in relation to copper, from 10:4 to 10:1.[68] Government policy on the use of copper vacillated unpredictably over the next two decades, to the benefit of private and official speculators alone. In 982 the fiscal vice- and co-intendants and their associates throughout the provincial government were found guilty of manipulating currency directives to maximize the speculative returns on their salaries, which were paid in copper.[69] From this point to the end of the dynasty, no further attempts were made to reintroduce copper currency into Sichuan. But efforts to reform the iron cash also met with little success. As a result, one of the empire's economic centers was left with no reliable currency until the end of the century, when Chengdu mercantile houses invented the paper "exchange media" (*jiaozi*) that eventually became the region's basic stock of money.[70]

The consequences of the currency crisis were compounded by extra levies in cash or its equivalent, and the monopolization of such important handicraft commodities as silk, hemp, and linen cloth that were most people's main source of cash. Thus when rebellion did break out, it originated in the highly commercialized districts of the Chengdu plain, where market-oriented cultivation and manufacture of consumers' goods and the implements necessary to their production had long played a critical role in the regional and household economies. The size of the irregular commercial exactions is impossible to assess, but they affected consumers and producers in all sectors of the economy. In 973, for example, the people of Sichuan were ordered to pay a surtax on all cash, silk cloth, silk floss and wadding, tea, and straw used to pay the twice-yearly taxes in summer and autumn, thus initiating the later ubiquitous "supplementary trade tax" *(touziqian).*[71] The government earned further profits on the twice-yearly tax by fixing the commutation rate of silk to cash at old, outdated rates, while the market price soared as a result of currency debasement. Local government officials were periodically warned against engaging in speculation, the manipulation of commodity prices, and illegal imposts and exactions; but these prohibitions were largely ignored.[72]

Government intervention in the fragile and troubled economy continued without interruption, fomenting unrest that in 993 exploded in uncontrollable violence. To continue with the account begun above:

> Policy advisors competed to raise the promise of gain in order to delude the emperor. In Chengdu, in addition to the regular taxes, monopoly purchase bureaus were set up, with every prefecture levying the people's weaving and manufacturers. Merchant travelers were prohibited from privately buying and selling hemp and silk cloth, and the "Daily Offerings" continued to increase. The regular government profits were taken out of the extra autumn levy, but the [arable] lands of Shu are narrow and the people crowded in, and the [harvest] from plowing and sowing was not enough to meet their needs. Thus the small folk were impoverished and embittered, while the greedy monopolists bought cheaply and sold dear to grasp at profits. A man of Qingcheng County, Wang Xiaobo, gathered his followers and arose to lead them in mass rebellion. Wang addressed the crowd, proclaiming: "I hate the inequality between the poor and the rich; today I will level it for you."[73]

Wang's rebellion broke out in early 993. Su Che claimed, a century after the event, that Wang and his brother-in-law Li Shun were tea merchants, thrown out of work by the government's repressive controls.[74] Although Su Che is the only source to link the rebellion and the tea trade, the charge is certainly credible, since Qingcheng (a part of modern Guanxian) and the hilly lands around it were major areas of tea production.[75] Temples and scattered plot-lands characterized the entire area surrounding Qingcheng, which is likely to have made the local population dependent on commercial crops and handicraft production to pay taxes and rents and to meet household needs, and hence extremely sensitive to currency debasement and disruption in the commercial economy in all its forms.

The rebels directed their initial violence against government officials in the commercial centers of the Chengdu Plain, such as the notoriously rapacious county magistrate of Pengshan (in Meizhou); the military inspector, clerks, and officials of Shuzhou; and the Prefect and Vice-Prefect of Qiongzhou.[76] The total size of the rebel contingent can only be estimated from specific instances: In 994 the rebels sent 50,000 men against the salt capital of Lingzhou, and that same year Li Shun led 200,000 followers in an eighty-day siege of Chengdu.[77] Geographically, the rebellion spread to virtually every area of the Sichuan basin. Following Wang's death in the final month of 993 the new leader, Li Shun, led his troops through the cities of the Chengdu plain and then north to Jianguan and the passes into the Hanzhong Basin. The government was able to reverse this assault on "the throat of Shu," but the rebel forces then headed east and south, where they attacked every major riverine city between the Min River and the Yangzi Gorges.[78] After losing Chengdu in mid 994, the rebels moved their headquarters to Jiazhou, from which city they were not expelled until 995. At this point the government declared the rebellion in western Sichuan to be over, but in fact there was general unrest throughout the region through 996 and 997.[79] Then in 999, when Sichuan was still tense in the aftermath of the rebellion, one of Chengdu's two provost marshals, Wang Jun, took advantage of the resentment caused by the government's tardiness in paying for brocades it had requisitioned to lead an uprising of his own.[80] Wang himself was defeated in the tenth month of 1000, but the aftershocks of his rebellion were still being felt in 1002 and 1003, and it is very difficult to say when calm finally returned to Sichuan.[81]

Although the rebels' first acts of violence were directed almost exclusively against the government, they soon turned their attention to the wealthy citizenry as well. The historian Tan Kyoji, building on Shen Gua's observation that the rebels initially sought only to confiscate "surplus wealth" from the rich and great lineages of the countryside, has claimed to find in the rebellion a pattern of progressive radicalization, culminating in outright polarization between rich patrons and poor dependents.[82] Although the chronological progression from a relatively cooperative relationship between elites and rebels to one of outright class hatred would be hard to demonstrate, there is certainly evidence of both poles of behavior.

Deng Chen of Zizhou, for example, a sixth-generation descendant of the Deng Yuanming who had opened his coffers to Wang Jian, in turn offered his own riches to the rebels under Li Shun and even exhorted his wealthy cohorts not to be stingy with the townspeople. Deng was able to save his family, but he lost all his possessions and later migrated to Shuangliu (Chengdu), where he became a well-known scholar.[83] Further along the radical continuum, Huang Tingjian described retrospectively how the local elites of Shu were made to suffer at the hands of the rebels, citing as evidence the case of Shi Duanchen, whose family scattered the contents of their granaries and fled into hiding.[84] At the extreme pole of unrestrained hatred is the case of one Wang Sheng, a villager in Jiangyuan County, Shuzhou. Wang joined the rebels in 994, and on their occupation of Chengdu was made a "hay-replenishment commissioner." Wang roamed the city with a band of a hundred "assistants," forcing poor residents to guide them to the homes of the rich, after which both rich and poor were robbed and murdered.[85] Temples too became the objects of rebel plunder, as was the case with the Shouning Monastery in Chengdu and the Fahua Monastery in Ziizhou.[86]

Families of wealth and position were soon compelled to organize against the rebels. Again, our information is richest for the *shidafu* class. Guo Renwo, whose family came to Sichuan during Emperor Xizong's exile, organized a village defense force against Li Shun that was able to save the family's country villa, although Guo was later killed in Wang Jun's revolt.[87] Similarly the Changs of Qiongzhou, another late-ninth-century lineage, set up a formidable village defense unit that was subsequently linked to the government forces.[88]

Yet another family to establish defense units were the Yangs of Mianzhu County, Hanzhou. The Yangs, whose most famous member was the financial expert Yang Yungong, had wielded wealth and power in Mianzhu for many generations. When the rebels entered the Mianzhu region, Yungong's two brothers Yunsheng and Yunyuan led brigades composed of village and ward residents against them, and later served as village guides to the government troops. Subsequently, Yunsheng was appointed magistrate of Mianzhu, and Yunyuan magistrate of Shifang County, also in Hanzhou.[89] There is also evidence of militia formation at more popular levels. In early 1000, for instance, during the renewed rebel outbreak under Wang Jun, propertied residents of Shuzhou formed mutual defense groups that they called "Pure Altar Vigilantes" (*qingtanzhong*). Later some seventy chiefs of these popular guards were selected as militia heads by the prefect of Shuzhou, as part of his attempt to assemble an inter-prefectural militia network to contain the rebellion emanating from Chengdu.[90]

Despite certain similarities to the situation at the end of the Tang, when local elites and the government cooperated for defense, the relationship between the Song government and the Sichuan elites at the end of the tenth century was different in two important respects. The first and most obvious was the status of the central government itself: Although it faced a difficult challenge in Sichuan, the Song government was otherwise firmly in control of the Chinese interior, and equally in control of the military commanders it sent into the region to quell the revolt.[91] The second departure from the Tang case follows as a corollary of the first: Because it possessed firm control over the military, early Song policy-makers enjoyed relative flexibility in building up a centralized bureaucratic apparatus. Unlike the mid- and late-Tang courts, the Song court was in a position to recruit local elites into its bureaucracy rather than farm the bureaucracy out to local elites. In 965, the Song wiped the official slate clean in Sichuan and from that point on maintained strict control over officialdom in the province, as it did in all the newly conquered regions of the south.[92] For example, inhabitants of western Sichuan, as well as natives of Lingnan and the Middle and Lower

Yangzi circuits, were barred from holding posts in their home circuits, while sojourning officials posted to these regions were prohibited from bringing along members of their family.[93] Only under the extreme provocation of a major social upheaval did the Song court begin to reward militia leaders with bureaucratic posts, and then, as in the case of Yang Yungong's two brothers, the men were already members of bureaucratically oriented families. But the rebellion reshaped the mutual perceptions of both Song policy-makers and the Sichuanese elites: After the shock of regionwide upheaval the Song began courting those influential members of Sichuanese society to whom rebellion had provided an opening wedge, and gradually these same elites began to respond.

One of the earliest architects of the movement to recruit Sichuanese into the bureaucracy was the post-rebellion Prefect of Chengdu, Zhang Yong. Zhang relished his role as social engineer, and boasted that, "Li Shun intimidated subjects into becoming thieves; now I have transformed thieves into subjects." In praising Zhang's transformative influence in Sichuan, Zhang's biography observes,

> At first the literati of Shu attained the highest reaches of scholarship, but took no pleasure in serving as officials. Zhang Yong learned that the scholarship and probity of the [Chengdu] men Zhang Ji, Li Tian, and Zhang Kui were proclaimed in their native villages, and he proceeded to sponsor them with the greatest enthusiasm. All three men passed the {jinshi} examinations, and from this point onwards the scholars [of Shu] were greatly encouraged.[94]

Li Tian went on to a career that included a lectureship in the Directorate of Education, magistrate of Huai'an county in Fujian, and back to Sichuan as prefect of the salt-rich prefecture of Rongzhou. In Rongzhou he is said to have won the remission of 200,000 catties of salt a year and the reduction of miscellaneous labor services for 315 households. Zhang Ji served as Linqiong County magistrate, where he gained distinction for blocking the attempts of prefectural officials to cut off irrigation in the area in order to raise the water level of a main stream they wanted to use for boat traffic. During Emperor Renzong's reign (1023–1063), Zhang held office in the Finance Commission and served as Fiscal Intendant of Huainan.

Zhang's career, like Li's, illustrates that Sichuanese were not merely being put into local positions to fill in the gap between the central government and local society, but rather that they were being consciously brought into the bureaucracy and circulated throughout the empire, returning to office in their home regions, when they did so, not so much as local power-holders but as representatives of the central government. And by protecting their fellow Sichuanese from the short-term abuses of centralized power in this post-rebellion return to gradual calm, men such as Li Tian and Zhang Ji helped lay the political foundation for long-term, systematic taxation.[95]

To be sure, the anti-imperial habits of generations and the anti-Song resentments of decades could not be changed immediately; and at least in some quarters of Sichuanese society, the response to Song overtures remained cautious. Li Fan, Zizhou man and student in the late 1060s, has described how long it took for the people of his county (Shehong) to embrace imperial political ideals. First Li provides the background:

> After Shu went through the usurpations of the Five Dynasties, people were rid of troubles and vexations, took pleasure in resting, and were not anxious to hold office or advance; with no one seeking renown, the scholars [of Sichuan] were less numerous than in the interior prefectures.

He then describes the local economic conditions:

> The land of our village is barren and the people poor, and families in the middle level must work hard until year's end. Even then they must worry about not having enough. That they do not have the leisure or energy for arts and literary culture cannot be thought odd. When I was a child, I saw the elders of the villages and alleys, while in the midst of their everyday lives, command their sons and younger brothers: "Do no go beyond energetically plowing and harvesting, and respecting the laws and regulations. Do this and no more."

Li then relates the local attitude towards literati, and his own personal situation:

> If those in Confucian gowns and caps [should happen to appear, the townspeople] would hurriedly gather and jeer, regarding them as having set aside the constant occupation, discarded their first duty, and lost themselves in

what is improper, and as being no better than gadabouts and indolent folk. At the beginning of the Xining period [1068–1077], I began to follow a village teacher and sought to enter office through examination. In the previous period, those who traveled as *jinshi* and were advanced to the county chambers numbered but four or five men. If at this time, when there had already been peace for a hundred years, those who rushed forward were still so few, then the perpetuation of these [anti-official] customs can [well] be understood.[96]

Thus it can be seen that even after the rebellion Sichuanese aloofness towards the state persisted. But gradually this distance began to erode, as Sichuanese became increasingly involved in the two most representative activities of imperial political culture, taking *jinshi* examinations and holding office. Whether one interprets the examination system as a channel of mobility for new families into the elite or as a mechanism by which families that already enjoyed elite status extended their power even further, there is no doubt that the vastly expanded Song examination system dramatically altered mobility strategies, adding examination success to marriage politics as a springboard to power and prestige.[97] John Chaffee's careful study of the role of the examinations in civil-service recruitment, social and regional mobility, and changing cultural trends during the Song affords us an important indicator of the political integration of Sichuan. As Li Fan and his contemporaries asserted, Sichuanese took very little part in the examination culture of the early Song, producing only one or two degree-holders annually for the first sixty years of the dynasty.[98] After 1021, however, Sichuanese participation in the examination system jumped dramatically, as the region produced escalating averages of 7.9 (1021–1063), 10.5 (1064–1085), 14 (1086–1100), and 19.8 (1101–1126) new *jinshi* holders per year. Sichuan's representation in the total pool of *jinshi* holders showed a similar pattern: Claiming just 2.8 or 2.9 percent of the new degree holders during the first sixty years of the dynasty, Sichuan's representation jumped to a fairly constant 7.8 percent from 1021 through the end of the Northern Song. Half of Sichuan's degree-holders during the Northern Song came from the prefectures of the Chengdu Plain.[99] The Upper Yangzi as a whole came nowhere close to the scholarly density of Fujian, which won between 11.3 and 17.5 percent of all degrees conferred from 998 on; nor did it approach the cumulative scholarly success of the Lower Yangzi circuits of Liangzhe and Jiangnan, which claimed 13.6 percent of all the *jinshi* graduates for the first two decades of the eleventh century, then jumped to between 23 and 30.4 percent for the remainder of the Northern Song. But Sichuan's pockets of success were impressive: Chengdu ranked fifth among all South China prefectures for the first century of the Song (all four leaders were Fujian), and Meizhou ranked tenth.[100] In short, within two or three decades of the Wang-Li rebellions, Sichuan's academic profile had completely changed, as Sichuanese became assimilated into the dominant political culture.

The increase in *jinshi* graduates was paralleled by the growing number of Sichuanese office-holders. Still wary of Sichuan's recalcitrance, the post-rebellion court maintained a variety of specific controls over Sichuanese civil servants and sojourner officials in Sichuan on the books; but gradually these restrictions were reversed.[101] In very general terms, the eleventh-century career pattern for Sichuanese appears to have included posts in Sichuan and in the neighboring regions of Northwest China and the Middle Yangzi, with movement up the administrative hierarchy from county to prefectural to circuit-level positions. Similarly the pattern of office-holding in Sichuan gradually moved towards native incumbency in the posts of county magistrate *(xianling)*, vice-prefect, prefect, and finally such circuit positions as fiscal intendant *(zhuanyunshi)* and judicial intendant *(tidian xingyu)*. Several examples will serve to illustrate the cumulative movement of Sichuanese into bureaucratic posts in the generations following the rebellions.

One member of the early post-rebellion generation of *jinshi* graduates was Guo Fu (degree ca. 1025), a son of the Guo Renwo killed in the rebellion of Wang Jun.[102] With recommendations by Fan Zhongyan, Han Qi, and other high officials, Guo was transferred from Prefect of Fengzhou to the same post in the more important Xingyuanfu, where he put down rebellions in Jin and Fang prefectures. Promoted then to Fiscal Intendant of Zizhou Circuit, Guo was subsequently killed suppressing a tribal revolt in Luzhou, which earned entry into the civil service for his three sons. The most illustrious of these was Guo Zigao (1033–1087), who was given the post of registrar of Xinfan County (Chengdu), followed by magistrate of Dayi County (Qiongzhou), where he gained a reputation for his water-control works. Zigao's later career in Sichuan included a position in the Chengdu Bureau of Exchange Notes, and Prefect of Changzhou and then Lizhou.[103] A relative of Ziguo's generation, Guo Yuyi, was also a county magistrate, in Wanzhou in eastern Sichuan, acquiring his post as a 1040s *jinshi* holder.[104]

Another early *jinshi* graduate (1027) who was to have an illustrious career was Chen Xiliang, whose family had migrated to Meizhou in the 880s. In a career that reached as high as Fiscal Intendant of Jingdong Circuit, Chen passed through county magistrates' posts in Sichuan and out, as well as four prefectural administratorships, one of which, Luzhou, was in Sichuan.[105]

Chen Xiliang's biographer, the eminent Sichuanese Fan Zhen, observed that initially natives of Sichuan were barred from the important post of vice-prefect in their home circuits. Promulgated in 982 and reaffirmed in 1033, by mid century the ruling appears to have lapsed. Xianyu Shen, a twelfth-generation descendant of Zhongtong whose own father, grandfather, and great-grandfather all declined official service, was Vice-Prefect of Mianzhou, en route to a career capped by circuit intendancies in Sichuan and Shandong.[106] Chang Gong, of the Chengdu branch of his lineage, served as vice-prefect in two Sichuanese prefectures as well as one in Shaanxi. Chang's career took him to Hubei and Fujian as well, and included a term as Prefect of Qiongzhou, home territory of the more illustrious branch of the lineage.[107]

Chang Gong got his jinshi in 1046, an examination that produced eighteen graduates from Chengdufu alone.[108] The mid eleventh century marked a watershed in Sichuanese examination success, and of Sichuan's integration into the imperial political arena as well. Zhou Biaoquan and Zhou Yin, uncle and nephew whose terms as prefects of Hanzhou and Zizhou overlapped, earned their degrees in this period, as did Wu Shimeng and Wen Tong, whose family claimed to have been in Sichuan since the Han.[109] But the transformation of Sichuanese from cloistered provincials to cosmopolitan citizens of the empire is best symbolized by the explosion into the literati cultural world of Su Xun and his brilliant sons Shi and Che. Residents of Meizhou since perhaps the seventh century, at the founding of the Song the Sus were still modest landowners and local silk traders who "could not bear to forsake their ancestors and emerge to take office in the world."[110] Su Xun himself showed no scholarly aspirations until relatively late in life; but a trip to the capital in 1047, where he failed his second major examination, nonetheless fired him with creative energy and a driving ambition to join ranks with the empire's greatest intellects. In 1056 Su returned to Kaifeng in search of patrons, bringing with him his two sons. When Shi and Che earned honors in the 1056–1057 *jinshi* exam personally supervised by Ouyang Xiu, all three Sus were dramatically thrust into the political and intellectual limelight. Along with Fan Zhen, Zhen's nephew Bailu, Bailu's nephew Zuyu, and Lü Tao, whose family had been long-time natives of Meizhou before moving to Chengdu, Su Shi and Su Che formed the nucleus of Sichuan's most prominent generation of officials. The importance of this "Shu" circle is reflected in the relatively high percentage of central offices held by Sichuanese under Emperors Shenzong (r. 1068–1085) and Zhezong (r. 1086–1100), at 11 and 12 percent the highest percentages over an extended period between the founding of the dynasty and 1162.[111] And while as individuals these men rose to prominence on the basis of quite formidable talents, from a demographic perspective their coming to power in the central government as a group can be seen as part of the long process of political integration of Sichuan into the larger state system.

By 1068 and the onset of the New Policies, the court was ready to gamble that this long-term political integration would sustain intensified taxation in Sichuan. Since its suppression of the Wang-Li rebellion the government had taxed Sichuan relatively lightly. Sichuan provided a substantial portion of the textiles purchased by the state for the military, which in turn imposed a heavy burden on individuals conscripted into transport service.[112] But as the thir-

teenth-century Sichuanese historian Li Xinchuan observed, until the
New Policies Sichuan's tea, salt, and wine industries went unregulated.[113] And Sichuan's share of total direct *(liangshui)* taxes over
the century—5 percent (as recorded in 1077)—was comparatively
low, measuring only half the region's share of total population.[114]
With the mounting fiscal crisis of the 1060s, however, fiscal administrators began looking to Sichuan for greater contributions; and,
as we saw in Chapter One, by the middle of the decade a link
between the Sichuanese economy and the horse trade had been forged.
Unlike the early Song, however, when the government had sought
to impound Sichuan's wealth with an army of conquering officials,
the New Policies leadership proposed to intensify its exploitation of
Sichuan's economy by mobilizing the growing corps of native
degree-holders and incumbent and expectant officials into taxing
their home region for the state.

The key to transforming Sichuanese into the fiscal agents of the
state was the new "law for the appointment and transfer of officials
from distant places" *(yuanguan jiuyi zhi fa)*, promulgated in 1070.
Commonly referred to as the "new law for eight circuits" *(balu xinfa)*,
the directive was nominally aimed at a set of problems that hampered personnel administration not only in Sichuan, but in Guangnan, Fujian, and Jinghu South as well. First, because travel times
from the capital to these regions was so long, the standard requirement of alternate appointments close to and far from the capital,
with an appearance in the capital between each new posting, resulted in long delays and even complete neglect in the filling of
vacancies. And second, precisely because the distant regions were
so far from the centers of power and cosmopolitan culture, officials
from the interior were reluctant to serve in them.[115]

The new 1070 regulations suspended the rule of alternative near
and distant service and the obligatory trip to the capital for the
designated regions, and allowed officials whose terms were drawing
to an end to apply personally *(zishe)* for appropriate vacancies, including other offices in the same location. In particular, the ruling
specified that "officials in a given prefecture who wish to be appointed to another assignment in that prefecture, and natives of one

of the four circuits of [Sichuan] who wish to be appointed to another assignment in that circuit will all be permitted to do so."[116] The only restriction was on serving in one's own or neighboring prefecture or district; but, in fact, even the avoidance of neighboring prefectures seems to have been disregarded.[117]

It was quite clear to opponents of the new measure that Sichuan was its chief target. Feng Jing, Wang Anshi's perennial critic, complained to the emperor that the appointment of native Sichuanese to successive posts as administrator in their own region would inevitably foster the pursuit of family interests (*jiabian*) in office.[118] A second opponent of the law predicted that because the number of Sichuanese on the official rolls was especially great, "[with this new ruling] because all officials from prefect on down can apply for appointment [to a home] assignment, the greater half of the officials in any prefecture will be local men, and the minor officials, clerks, and general populace below them will all be their relatives and confidantes. These administrators will encounter great difficulty in prosecuting the public interest and will naturally form into cliques."[119] But Wang Anshi responded that the new regulation benefitted everyone:

> The reason for alternating near and distant posts is to ensure an equal distribution of the hardships and benefits of service. At present, residents of the interior do not wish to go to the four circuits [of Sichuan] but [Sichuanese] do wish to enjoy the benefits of home service. If we enact this new law, both sides will obtain what they desire. So why must everyone complain about it, and seek to deprive both sides of this great convenience? Moreover, this ruling is not only of benefit to members of the official class. It will also save clerks and soldiers the trouble and expense of accompanying [incoming and outgoing officials to and from distant places]. This is a particularly good law.[120]

Promulgated just as the government was intensifying its claims on Sichuan's silks, tea, and paper currency for the horse and state commerce trades in Shaanxi, the new rule offered the quid pro quo of home service (and all of the licit and illicit opportunities for individual and family enrichment that home service provided) to the 333 *jinshi* degree-holders graduated between 1021 and 1063, another 222 men who had or would receive their degrees between 1064 and 1085, and the increasing number of men eligible for office because of their fathers' service through the mechanism of "protection" *(yinbu)*.[121] The trade of successive positions in Sichuan in return for serving as fiscal agent of the central government was attractive to a wide range of Sichuanese. In 1075 even Wen Tong, then coming to the end of his term as Prefect of Xingyuanfu, cited family financial problems as an excuse against traveling to the capital and requested direct assignment to neighboring Yangzhou. One argument Wen gave in support of his request was that "formerly [as Prefect of] Lingzhou, I carried out the New Policies."[122] And indeed in 1072 it was Wen Tong, later a critic of the New Policies, who had called the court's attention to the revenues being lost by the proliferation of untaxed "lofty-pipe" salt wells.[123]

By the start of the New Policies, that restructuring of goals, priorities, and commitments that must precede the construction of an effective bureaucracy had been completed in Sichuan: Successful fulfillment of state-defined policy objectives was transformed into the fastest and surest path to bureaucratic authority, and bureaucratic authority was made the dominant form of power in society at large. Wang Anshi was prepared to merge the fiscal goals of the state and the career goals of Sichuanese bureaucrats in the intensive exploitation of the region's economy.

Wang demonstrated his confidence to the emperor in late 1073, as plans were underway to establish a State Trade Bureau in Chengdu. Feng Jing attempted to dissuade the emperor from the project, saying that "it was precisely the government control of commercial goods that led to Wang Xiaobo's rebellion. Yet now almost everyone is talking about State Trade . . ." But Wang Anshi countered that

> Wang Xiaobo gathered people together in banditry because the government made no attempt to relieve the starving masses. And the reason for all this was that the clerks and officials loaded the goods of Sichuan onto boats and shipped them out as tribute; they did not know what effect

shipping the wealth of the Meng family treasuries would have on the starving people. I would beg Your Majesty to put aside doubt. This minister guarantees that the state trade policy will not cause the people of Shu to rebel. [124]

Emperor Shenzong "wished to plumb the matter in depth" and ordered investigator Pu Zongmin to proceed to Sichuan. The consequences of Pu Zongmin's investigation forms the second part of our story.

Part Two

Introduction to Part Two: Wang Anshi's Theory of Bureaucratic Entrepreneurship

The fiscal and geopolitical problems that hindered Song horse supply, the potential solution latent in the Sichuan tea industry, and the political means of linking the Sichuan tea industry to the Qinghai horse trade were pieces in a puzzle ready to be fitted together when Emperor Shenzong assumed the throne in 1067. The puzzle was finally completed by Shenzong's Chief Councilor, Wang Anshi, who mobilized Sichuanese into creating a vast enterprise devoted to supplying Qinghai horse traders with Sichuanese tea, and frontier defense agencies with surplus revenues. That enterprise was the *duda tiju chamasi,* the Superintendancy for Tea and Horses or Tea and Horse Agency (THA). The new agency was a crucible in which were mixed all the components most typical of New Policies economic activism; and as an epitome of the New Policies, it affords a window on Song economic activism in its most concentrated form.

That activism arose out of long-term political and economic trends, but the New Policies movement itself was deeply imprinted with Wang Anshi's personal vision of radical reform. To be sure, many of the specific policies enacted during the sixteen-year reform campaign drew directly on classical, and particularly Han, precedents, or originated with Wang Anshi's associates or from the field. And in some cases the most radical extensions of state power took place after Wang's retirement in 1076, under the impetus of Wang's colleagues, field officials, and the emperor himself.[1] But it was Wang Anshi who turned vague calls for political reform into a widespread political movement, Wang Anshi who elicited and maintained imperial support for change in the face of extraordinary opposition, and Wang Anshi who provided the action blueprint that translated separate policy proposals into an integrated and coherent reform campaign. Wang's theories of the activist state and bureaucratic entrepreneurship animated the enactment of the New Policies, and fueled the ascent to power of the Sichuan Tea and Horse Agency.

From a contemporary perspective, we might say that Wang attempted to superimpose an idealized model of a relatively simple and undifferentiated feudal society onto the complex, commercialized, bureaucratic society of the eleventh century. As Peter Bol has shown in a study of the political visions and ambitions of Sima Guang and Wang Anshi, from very early on Wang dedicated his career to recreating in the present an idealized unity of the past that would eradicate the barriers between public *(gong)* and private *(si)* spheres, and collapse the distinctions between the state and society.[2] This commitment to reunifying state and society defined the ideological thrust of the New Policies and informed many of its most characteristic measures. In his reforms of the subbureaucracy and the *baojia* system of local security, for example, Wang gave concrete form to his conviction that "the first obligation of imperial governance is to unite clerks and officials and farmers and soldiers as one."[3] But it was in his theory of public finance that Wang's goal of relinking the public and private sectors was most sharply enunciated. Wang Anshi saw the state as the necessary and sufficient intermediary between the natural and household economies; if any one sector was to be enriched, they all must be enriched together.[4] Because of this interpenetration of public fisc and household economy, Wang invested public finance with a sense of moral mission and placed it at the very center of public affairs: "[The art of] governing," Wang instructed a colleague, "is to manage resources, and managing resources is what is meant by moral duty."[5] And as Wang proclaimed in his "Myriad Word Memorial" of 1058, the appropriate goal of public finance (*zhicai,* governing resources) had always been "to utilize the energy of all under heaven to produce wealth for all under heaven, and to use the wealth of all under heaven to meet the needs of all under heaven."[6]

Wang's model of an activist state under moral obligation to govern the economy generated an unconventional diagnosis of the contemporary fiscal crisis. Ever since the Tangut Wars of 1040–1042, high officials had indicted irresponsible spending for impoverishing the state and over-burdening the people; and by the end of Emperor Yingzong's reign, denunciations of "superfluous clerks, superfluous officials, superfluous soldiers" had assumed the status of a political cliché.[7] Sima Guang continued the tradition at the start of Shenzong's reign, admonishing the new emperor that "the current deficits in the national treasury have been caused by wasteful administrative expenditures, unrestrained bestowal of emoluments and rewards (attendant on the deaths of two emperors in four years), an overly lavish imperial household, a bloated bureaucracy, and an inefficient army."[8] Shenzong dutifully instituted a campaign to trim expenses in the imperial household; and for the second time in ten years, an Office of Economizing was established.[9] But calls for fiscal responsibility, however apposite they may have been in fact, no longer seemed an adequate solution to economic crisis; and in 1069 the emperor turned instead to Wang Anshi.

Wang rejected excessive expenditures as the cause of the financial crisis. Instead, he fixed the blame on a sluggish state manned by incompetent administrators, who allowed private monopolists and engrossers (*jianbing*) to slip between the state and society. During the idealized Zhou period that served as Wang's model society, public economic authority was secured against private encroachment by the Treasury Officer (*quanfu*), master wielder of the basic techniques of economic regulation. As Wang informed Shenzong, "The Treasury Officer was the instrument by which the Former Kings controlled and regulated would-be engrossers, measured and equalized the differences between rich and poor, transformed and circulated the wealth of all under heaven, and caused all benefits to flow from a single source."[10]

But now, as Wang and the emperor agreed, there were too few

officials trained in the techniques of economic management *(licai)*. Officials had "lost the Way of creating wealth,"—that is, they had lost control over the institutions and techniques by which the state could enrich itself and stimulate the economy, by suppressing private monopolies, redistributing wealth, and ensuring the smooth flow of resources throughout the empire.[11] Consequently, the state had forfeited its fiscal prerogatives to private economic actors. As Wang argued in his plea for the establishment of a Finance Planning Commission, "Most of the commodities used by the court are levied from places where they are not produced, or demanded before their season. Wealthy merchants and great traders have taken advantage of the crisis this causes both public and private interests to usurp control over the ratios of exchange *(qingzhong)* and the collection and disbursement of money and goods."[12]

In order to supply its needs, the Song court relied on an inadequate and inflexible command structure to siphon off goods and services from a complex and bustling market economy. This provided well-capitalized merchants enormous opportunities to profit from the gap between "plan"—typically represented by outmoded quotas—and reality. Wang's solution was to enhance centralized state control by augmenting the capacity of the state's financial administration to participate in the market economy. The Finance Planning Commission was to spearhead this intensified penetration of the economy. On the one hand, the Finance Planning Commission was intended to "promote the arts of economic management," by functioning as a clearing-house to which "individuals of all sorts"— probably meaning merchants as well as officials—in the capital and in the provinces could send their views on economic affairs.[13] On the other hand, Wang Anshi intended to use the new commission as the command center through which the state would "recapture its authority over the ratios of exchange and collection and disbursement [of money and goods] and return it to the public domain."[14] Wang and Chen Shengzhi established the Finance Planning Commission in the second month of 1069, thereby (according to the authors of the *Song History*) formally inaugurating the New Policies.[15]

The new campaign to enlarge the state's economic presence was advertised as an attack on the long-term targets of Wang Anshi's resentment—the *jianbing* engrossers. In 1053 Wang had written a poem denouncing the "wicked engrossers" who had shattered the ancient unity between public and private property; and in 1059 he had inveighed against engrosser tea-guild merchants, as he would again in 1072.[16] During the New Policies the term was used to categorize classes of economic actors, such as large landlords or great guild merchants, whose wealth and power the state viewed as destabilizing or coveted for itself, and to identify potential or actual targets of state campaigns. In the ninth month of 1069, for example, the Finance Planning Commission launched its new rural credit program (the "Green Sprouts" policy) with an attack on the "engrossing households who take advantage of [seasonal credit] crises to demand interest rates of 100 percent."[17] Similarly when the State Trade Act was enacted in the capital in 1072, the state used as its rationale the fact that "traveling merchants from all over the empire who bring goods to the capital are put in great distress by the 'engrossing houses,' and must sell at a loss and [often] go out of business."[18] Under the direction of Wang Anshi and his reform cadre, the state forged direct links with producers, small merchants, or consumers, in order to oust large-scale economic actors from dominant market positions. In the case of the "Green Sprouts" policy, the state sought to displace large landlords as the primary suppliers of rural credit by providing cheap loans to farmers at 20 percent interest for the state; in the case of the State Trade Act, the state trade bureaus assumed the function of primary wholesale distributor, inserting themselves between the smaller merchants and the great metropolitan trading houses in order to neutralize the powers of the largest guild merchants and gain the wholesalers' mark-up for the state.

Wang Anshi's commitment to pitting state agents against private "engrossers" had two important consequences for New Policies statecraft. First, in direct contradiction of conventional fiscal wisdom, widening the scope of government activities required expanding rather than reducing the size of government and its expenditures. But Wang Anshi openly encouraged bureaucratic expansion, and the increased expenditures this entailed, as a means of stimulating economic activity and generating greater revenues. In response to calls for the abolition of a water-works post, for example, Wang wrote that "only with many officials can [essential] tasks be accomplished. So long as these tasks are accomplished, there is nothing wrong with great [official] activity. And large expenditures will stimulate increasing prosperity. So long as they stimulate prosperity, then what is the harm in great expenditures?"[19] Although Shenzong was never as sanguine as his Chief Councilor about the wisdom of bureaucratic expansion, under Wang Anshi's direction the number of qualified officials registered the greatest increase of the entire dynasty, jumping 41 percent from 24,000 in 1067 to over 34,000 men in 1080.[20]

Many of these new officials staffed the multitude of circuit agencies that were created to fulfill reform tasks at the regional level. As Winston Lo showed in an analysis of circuit intendencies and Song territorial administration, instead of working through existing machinery and entrenched personnel, Wang Anshi preferred to create new institutions to carry out reform tasks.[21] Rather quickly the reform leadership created a parallel administrative apparatus that concentrated bureaucratic power in those classes of participants and administrative echelons that were most strategically placed to meet the reform goals of military security and enrichment of the state. At the political center, the reformers breached the traditional boundaries between financial, military, and executive authority (in the Finance Commission, Bureau of Military Affairs, and Secretariat-Chancellery) by placing the new Finance Planning Commission under the direct supervision of the executive branch, and by routing orders around such elite opponents of the reforms as Wen Yanbo, the Director of Military Affairs. These moves centralized general policy-making and command functions in the executive branch of government, dominated by Wang Anshi and his followers, and placed both financial control and operational funds at their disposal.[22] Specific reform initiatives were then delegated to such new single and multi-circuit intendancies as the intendancies for state trade in the capital and throughout the provinces; the *baojia* and militia intendancies and the offices for the management of frontier finances, established primarily in the north; the Ever-Normal Granary intendancies set up in virtually every circuit of the empire; and, of course, the Superintendancy for Tea and Horses.[23] In addition, the reformers increasingly empowered circuit intendants to by-pass conservative prefectural administrators in exercising administrative control over the counties, by giving them greater powers over the appointment and promotion of county magistrates.[24] These many new functionally specific circuit intendancies, retrospectively denounced by Sima Guang in 1086, came to serve as the central link in a chain of command that circumvented prefectural centers of opposition to the forceful implementation of New Policies initiatives, and allowed the reform leadership to penetrate directly into the local society.[25]

But if the state were to compete successfully with powerful private interests in the expanding market place, then it was not enough simply to make government larger: the agents of the state had to think and act not like rule-bound bureaucrats, but like innovative entrepreneurs.[26] It was precisely this vision of a society transformed by bureaucratic entrepreneurs that Wang Anshi put forth in his "Myriad Word Memorial" of 1058. There Wang blamed the economic, military, and moral ills of society on the deficiencies of the state, which was overwhelmingly staffed by men selected by the examination system for their strong memories and literary skills rather than for the practical experience essential for good government. Wang proposed a four-stage process of instruction, nurture, selection, and employment that could produce the appropriate moral and political leadership over the long term. But there was urgent need for immediate change as well, and in his last two stages Wang provided a theory of mobilizing existing talent for immediate reform.

In brief, Wang argued that men with the skills and abilities to meet the needs of the time had to be mustered from all levels of society, tested in actual government affairs, and the truly able ones "appointed for long terms of office to posts that suit their qualifications. In this way, intelligent, able, and energetic officials will be able to put all their intelligence into the pursuit of achievement, without having to worry that their projects will go unfinished and their accomplishments be incomplete . . . Once appointed, they must be given exclusive authority, and not be hampered or bound by this or that regulation, but be permitted to carry out their ideas."[27] Once a man has been appointed to office, Wang continued, he should be trusted to "select men of like character and put them to the test for a period of time, then appraise their abilities and make recommendations to the ruler, at which point they will be granted salaries and ranks." Above all, Wang stressed the need for full discretionary authority, writing that "there has never been a single case in history that has shown it possible to obtain good government even with the right man in power if he is bound by one regulation or another so that he cannot carry out his ideas."[28]

To summarize Wang's argument, the mobilization of bureaucratic entrepreneurship incorporated five key elements: First, men with the requisite practical and managerial skills were to be recruited from all levels of society. Second, the most able of them were to be assigned strategic posts or tasks on the basis of their proven skills, and not their formal credentials. Third, these action-oriented cadres were to remain in their respective positions for as long as it took to accomplish their assigned goals. Fourth, they were to be permitted to choose their own subordinates. And, fifth, they were to be given exclusive authority to experiment in the achievement of their tasks.[29]

Wang Anshi's action strategy allowed a reform-minded leadership to define critical political and economic tasks, delegate these tasks to aggressive and innovative officials in the field, and decentralize extraordinary power to the men who were most successful in meeting reform goals. This emphasis on inducing entrepreneurial officials to devise their own solutions to centrally defined problems provided the critical link between Wang's activist economic vision and the enactment of practical policies. In the realm of reform economic policy, economic vision and action strategy converged in the creation of new public agencies empowered to participate directly in the market economy, administered by officials chosen for their entrepreneurial characteristics. To varying degrees, activism and entrepreneurship pervaded the New Policies as a whole, but nowhere more strikingly than in the exchange of tea for horses.

FOUR

The Entrepreneurial Leap

In the fourth month of 1074, investigators Li Qi and Pu Zongmin were ordered to buy tea in Sichuan for Wang Shao's new horse markets in the northwest.[1] Less than a decade later, the enterprise they and their successors created, the Sichuan Tea and Horse Agency, had become the most powerful state agency in all of Northwest China and the Upper Yangzi.* In the course of a decade the Agency's chiefs commandeered control over all the tea produced in western Sichuan and the Hanzhong Basin, and all the tea sold in North-

---

*The tea and horse enterprise that constitutes the focus of Part Two is designated in a variety of ways in the sources. At its broadest it is entitled the Superintendancy for Tea and Horses *(duda tiju chamasi)*. But for most of the New Policies era (1074–1085) the regulation and sale of tea for cash was administered separately from, and overshadowed, the exchange of tea for horses. The horse trade itself was managed by the Shaanxi Intendant for Horse Purchases and Pastures *(tiju maima jianmusi)*, who competed with the Tea Intendants until the two sides of the enterprise were formally merged in 1086. Through 1085 the tea administration is referred to as the Tea Monopoly Agency *(quechasi)* or Tea Market Agency *(chachangsi)* of all or some of the relevant circuits of Sichuan and Shaanxi. Because these changes of title reflect important stages in the evolution of the tea and horse enterprise, I have retained the distinctions in the following way: In discussions of the enterprise during the New Policies era I use the label Tea Market Agency (TMA); for all subsequent periods I use the label Tea and Horse Agency (THA). Where a general reference to the organization is called for, I refer simply to the Agency, or less often to the Intendancy.

west China and along the northwestern frontier. In addition they wrested control over a significant portion of Sichuan's commerce in salt, textiles, handicrafts, and credit. By the end of the reform era, moreover, the Tea and Horse Agency had gained a degree of autonomy in its dealings with the court, with other agencies, and with its own personnel that was unrivaled by any other Song field agency.

Was the Agency's rise to dominance a bureaucratic fluke? Had distance provided a shield behind which cunning bureaucrats could wheel and deal free from the scrutiny of the court? Did the Agency represent bureaucracy run out of control? To all of these questions the answer is, no. The dynamism of the Agency, the ambitious empire-building of its chiefs, was exactly what Wang Anshi had anticipated in his "Myriad Word Memorial," and what he expected from his bureaucratic entrepreneurs.

Throughout his written works, and especially in the records of his audiences with the emperor, it is clear that Wang Anshi understood and delighted in the use of power, particularly the techniques of motivating individuals and groups to act in desired ways. Wang's perception of both bureaucratic dynamics and the interaction between bureaucracy and society anticipated many of the conclusions of modern social scientists. This is especially true of Wang's theory of bureaucratic entrepreneurship and economic activism. Here, for example, is how Joseph LaPalombara characterizes the type of bureaucrat needed for state-sponsored economic development: "The economic development of a society, particularly if it is to be implemented by a massive intervention of the public sector, requires a breed of bureaucrats different (e.g., more free-wheeling, less adhering to administrative forms, less attached to the importance of hierarchy and seniority) from the type of man who is useful when the primary concern of the bureaucracy is the maintenance of law and order."[2]

LaPalombara is just one of many social scientists who now recognize, with Wang Anshi, that effective state economic intervention requires bureaucrats who can act like entrepreneurs. The most technically precise definition of entrepreneurs was offered by Joseph Schumpeter, in his *Theory of Economic Development*. Operating within the framework of an equilibrium model of the economy, Schumpeter defined economic development as "a spontaneous and discontinuous change in the channels of the [economic] flow, a disturbance of equilibrium, which forever alters and displaces the equilibrium state previously existing."[3] The sole source of economic development for Schumpeter is the carrying out of new combinations. These include the introduction of a new good or of a new method of production; the opening of a new market, or conquest of a new source of raw materials or half-manufactured goods; and the "carrying out of the new organization of any industry, like the creation of a monopoly position . . . or the breaking up of a monopoly position."[4] Entrepreneurs are any individuals whose function it is to carry out these new combinations.[5] Schumpeter's definition is analytically useful because it excludes the whole array of actors—owners, heads of firms, managers, and so forth—who merely operate an established enterprise, while including under the rubric of entrepreneur anyone who in fact carries out a new combination, whatever the individual's position in or relationship to the firm.

Schumpeter's model incorporated the wide range of participants in the complex capitalist economy of the early twentieth century, but it was nonetheless limited to firms in the private sector. In the years since Schumpeter's theory was published in 1911, social scientists have come to recognize not only that public bureaucracies play a large role in even the most competitive market economies, but also that the neoclassical model of a competitive economy can help us understand the competitive behavior of public bureaucracies.[6] As a result, various scholars have found it appropriate to apply the notion of entrepreneurship to agents of the state.[7] One of the most interesting syntheses of entrepreneurship and public bureaucracy, and one that retains Schumpeter's critical distinction between entrepreneurs and managers, is Eugene Lewis' *Public Entrepreneurship,* which analyzes the organizational lives of Hyman Rickover, J. Edgar Hoover, and Robert Moses.[8] Where Schumpeter sees entrepreneurs as individuals who change the economy, Lewis sees public entrepreneurs as individuals who transform public organizations. Because Lewis' formulation of public bureaucracies as competitive, autonomy-seeking entities highlights many of the key features of the Tea and Horse Agency, it is worth quoting at length:

> No large formal organization is simply a tool for carrying out [its formal mandate]; it consists of persons who are structured into hierarchies, bounded by highly refined expert knowledge, and who have interests which always and everywhere diverge to a greater or lesser extent from the formal needs of the organization . . .
>
> Public organizations are neither neutral nor neutered creatures of the state. Rather, they are from time to time unusually potent political forces, led by people who reject normal system maintenance norms and attempt to expand the goals, functions, and power of their organizations in ways unprecedented or unforeseen by their putative masters. Such people we shall call public entrepreneurs . . . A public entrepreneur may be defined as a person who creates or profoundly elaborates a public organization so as to alter greatly the existing pattern of allocation of scarce public resources.[9]

The THA intendants we will be dealing with were entrepreneurs in Schumpeter's sense, in that they promoted new economic combinations that induced economic development; but they did so as creators and promoters of a public agency who conformed in all important ways to Lewis's description above.

Lewis's overall model assumes a state of relative equilibrium in which routine dominates organizational activities but in which entrepreneurs (individuals who have not been perfectly molded to the company line) build empires by exploiting contradictions within the organizational and political climate.[10] During the New Policies, however, entrepreneurship was explicitly courted. The New Policies leadership was prepared, in theory, to sacrifice bureaucratic routine and organizational restraint in order to expand the overall capacity of the state. They sought, in effect, to routinize entrepreneurship.

How did the mobilization of bureaucratic entrepreneurs operate in practice? As we just saw, Wang Anshi's reform blueprint first entailed seeking out precisely those men who were most likely to act in an entrepreneurial manner, regardless of their formal credentials, and putting them in critical New Policies posts for long terms of office. Once in office these innovators were to be allowed to staff their own organizations, and encouraged to experiment in the fulfillment of their tasks unfettered by bureaucratic red tape. The first set of characteristics describes the selection of entrepreneurial types, the second set the exercise of entrepreneurial power. By examining the attributes of the THA Intendants, I hope to show that they were selected precisely for their entrepreneurial traits.

ATTRIBUTES OF THE INTENDANTS

The executive tier of the Northern Song Tea and Horse Agency was composed of at first two, and from 1079 on three, positions: the Intendant or Superintendant, the Co-Intendant, and the Assistant Intendant *(tong zhuguan* or *guangou).* [11] After 1079 the Superintendant served in Qinzhou and the Co-Intendant in Chengdu, with the venue of the Assistant Intendant varying according to the actual relationship between the tea and horse sides of the enterprise at a given time. [12] We can measure how fully the executive leadership of the enterprise (the Tea Market Agency up to 1085, the Tea and Horse Agency thereafter) conformed to the first two components of Wang Anshi's entrepreneurial strategy—selecting action-oriented and innovative men and disregarding formal credentials—by examining how the incumbents entered the agency and their formal civil service rank at the time of appointment.

MODE OF ENTRY AND CIVIL SERVICE RANK. All seven men appointed to one of the executive positions in the Agency between 1074 and 1085 fit the classic profile of the eleventh-century fiscal specialist outlined by Hartwell in 1971. [13] It is a particular indicator of entrepreneurship, however, that six of the seven men were appointed to office not just as fiscal experts, but as fiscal experts who had already displayed their aggressiveness, ingenuity, and loyalty to the reform cause in previous New Policies posts or tasks. [14]

The first Intendant, Li Qi (served 1074/11–1075/12), had been specially commended for his management of the currency and commodities that were used to buy military provisions in Shaanxi just prior to his assignment to Sichuan. [15] His colleague and Co-Intendant, Pu Zongmin (1074/11–1086/2), was an inspector for the reform movement in eastern Sichuan when he was ordered to Cheng-du in 1073/12, where he remained for the next twelve years.[16] Li Qi's successor, Liu Zuo (1076/4–1077/7), had been a division chief in the Capital State Trade Bureau, where he helped produce a sur-plus of over 100,000 strings of cash for his section before being sent by Wang Anshi to Hanzhou (against vehement resistance of the reform apostate Han Jiang) to investigate a tea-transport bottle-neck.[17] In the midst of this assignment Liu was appointed to replace the ailing Li Qi as chief Intendant of the TMA, at which time he initiated a campaign to wrest the vigorous Sichuan tea and Jiezhou salt trade away from private Shaanxi merchants and add it to the Agency's domain. Liu became a political liability after his entrepre-neurial zeal occasioned a temporary collapse of the salt-voucher mar-ket in Shaanxi and a tea-cultivator's riot in Pengkou; and to appease Sichuanese opponents of the New Policies and make way for a more effective Intendant, Liu was summarily cashiered.[18]

Wang Anshi was forced from office in 1076, more a victim of factionalism within the reform ranks than of opposition from the conservatives. But Emperor Shenzong himself commanded the re-forms for the next nine years, and under his leadership the mobili-zation of entrepreneurship actually intensified.[19] Consequently Liu's replacement, Li Ji (1077/7–1082/10), was able to further Liu Zuo's expansionist designs while neutralizing the Sichuanese opposition. Himself a native of Sichuan, from the manufacturing center of Qiongzhou, Li Ji served in 1074 in the Directorate of Military Sup-plies directly under Wang Anshi's lieutenant, Lü Huiqing.[20] That same year Li was named Fiscal Supervisor of Hebei West Circuit, where he was accused by Cheng Fang of "exceeding the limits of his office," and by the Sichuanese censor Zhou Yin of pitiless and relentless efforts to suborn and humiliate other officials—especially the anti-reform elder statesman and Xiangzhou Prefect, Han Qi.[21] By the time Li Ji was appointed Intendant in mid 1077, Zhou Yin had sent up two additional denunciations of Li's "inexperience" and lack of moral character—as manifested by his insufficient reverence for his dead father's bones.[22] But the TMA had already begun to assume that charismatic shield that protected it as a money-making enterprise; and within two months of his appointment as Intendant, Li Ji got Zhou Yin transferred out of the censorate and his uncle Biaoquan cashiered as Prefect of Hanzhou.[23] Lü Tao, Su Shi, and Su Che were also dismissed or banished to minor provincial posts around this time, effectively silencing prominent Sichuanese opposition to the tea monopoly and the New Policies until Shenzong's death in 1085 ushered in the Restoration.[24]

In recognition of his continuing prowess in generating revenues, in 1079 Li Ji was named Superintendant of Tea Markets, Concurrent Provisional Fiscal Intendant for Shaanxi, and Regulator of Jiezhou Salt.[25] Li's successor as Superintendant, Lu Shimin (1080/12–1086/6), first appears in the records in 1077 as one of Li Ji's managing supervisors. We must assume that Lu made his mark in the Agency in the next three years, for in 1080 he was promoted to Co-Intendant.[26] In 1083 Lu Shimin exploded into prominence, expanding the functional and territorial prerogatives of the Agency with such deftness that "his power caused trembling and dismay, not one of his requests was denied [by the Court], and no other officials could guess what he would do next."[27] Lu's rise through consecutive levels of the Agency, a career course followed by two other Northern Song Intendants, highlights the willingness of the New Policies leadership to permit specialization within specific organizations as a means of maximizing the effectiveness of the individual enterprise.[28]

Not surprisingly, bureaucratic entrepreneurs were no more likely to have attractive personalities than their modern business or public counterparts. The ruthlessness and arrogance that was probably typical of the potential bureaucratic entrepreneur was captured in a street ditty that made the rounds of Chang'an when Li Ji, as concurrent TMA chieftain and Shaanxi Fiscal Intendant, ran the region with his crony Li Cha:

> Better to run into the black death (*heisha*)
> Than to encounter Ji or Cha.[29]

But it was also this very willingness to flaunt social, professional, and even moral conventions that marked an individual as a potential entrepreneur, one who could be trusted to translate broad policy goals into action.

A second "entrepreneurial" attribute of the men appointed to head the TMA was their low rank in the civil service. In his "Myriad Word Memorial," Wang Anshi had prescribed choosing men for office on the basis of their practical knowledge and qualifications, regardless of their formal credentials; and under his stewardship the reform administration courted ideas and innovators from the fringes of official circles and beyond.[30] Wang Shao, as we have seen in Chapter One, had abandoned an official career for frontier adventurism before sending up the irredentist call to arms in Qinghai that came to serve as the cornerstone of reform foreign policy. Similarly the commoner Xu Xi earned a variety of trouble-shooting posts in the New Policies administration as a result of his twenty-four-part response to Wang Anshi's reform decrees.[31] In 1072 Wei Jizong, a self-described "man of weeds and marshes" *(caozeren)*—a popular epithet for an individual outside the official class—sent up a memorial on trade in Kaifeng that led to establishment of the Metropolitan State Trade Bureau, an agency that routinely employed merchants as managing supervisors *(goudang guan)* because of the complexity of the commercial transactions involved.[32] The reform leadership was committed in the most practical ways to mobilizing talent and ideas from every quarter.

In the case of the TMA executive body, this commitment translated into a strategy of granting power to men near the bottom of the official hierarchy, who had everything to gain by allying themselves with the activist goals and programs of the reforms. Collectively, the TMA Intendants represented men with good connections in official service who were themselves on the lowest rungs of the administrative ladder. The Sichuanese Pu Zongmin, for example, was a brother or cousin of Pu Zongmeng, whose career was sponsored by the elder statesmen of Emperor Yingzong's reign;[33] Li Ji entered the civil service through the *yin* protection privilege of his father, an Auxiliary Academician in the Longtu Academy;[34] Fan Chuncui (1079/5–ca. 1081/11), who was transferred to the Agency after a term as Ever-Normal Granary Intendant in Eastern Shaanxi, was the son of the famous Qingli reformer Fan Zhongyan (and brother of the New Policies opponent Fan Chunren);[35] and Lu Shimin had entered Sichuan with his father Lu Shen, a highly respected expert on border affairs who served as Prefect of Chengdu just before his death in 1070.[36]

Raised as the sons and nephews of officials, these men would have been intimately familiar with the politics and culture of official life, and would have absorbed its values and aspirations. But by the 1060s the pool of potential office-holders had become extremely crowded, and even well-connected men could expect to languish four to six years between positions.[37] As a group the TMA Intendants had to wait for Wang Anshi to open up the scope and size of government before their careers took off, and they entered the Intendancy towards the bottom of the graduated hierarchy of nine full and twenty half grades, or stipendiary offices (*jiluguan*), that identified an official's titular status and basic salary.[38]

To take the example of Pu Zongmin once again: Although Pu obtained his *jinshi* degree in 1053, he was still only at Grade 8B at the time of his appointment as Co-Intendant in 1074, though his success in the Agency earned him successive promotions to Grade 6B.[39] Other than one exceptional 6B (Liu Zuo), none of the Intendants held a rank higher than 7B at the time of appointment.[40] Moreover, the court acknowledged that the Intendants stood at the bottom of the official hierarchy and took steps to offset their low status. In 1080, for example, the court granted Co-Intendant Fan Chuncui a titular commission in the Finance Commission at the request of Superintendant Li Ji, who had complained that "since Chuncui is only a 'Critic Advisor to the Heir Apparent,' his rank is low (8B), and I fear he will not be able to awe (*tanya*) the [prefects] and [county magistrates]."[41] And in 1083, in approval of Lu Shimin's expansion of the TMA's geographic and functional domain, Emperor Shenzong himself ordered that the post of Superintendant be regarded as equivalent in status to the Fiscal Intendant of Shaanxi, since "although the ranks of the [Intendants] are low, they must be permitted to use authority as they see fit."[42]

As a professional cohort, the seven men appointed to the TMA

The Entrepreneurial Leap

executive during the New Policies were not at all unique; men like Pu Zongmin, Li Ji, and Lu Shimin gained key administrative posts throughout the New Policies administration. As I showed in an earlier study, for example, the seventy-one men appointed Intendant or Co-Intendant of the empire's twenty-three circuit-level Ever-Normal Granary systems exhibited precisely the same pattern of technical skills, New Policies affiliation, good official connections, and low civil service rank.[43] But the widespread employment of men fitting this entrepreneurial profile was unique to the New Policies, and in the eyes of reform opponents set the New Policies era apart. Contemporaries and later generations excoriated Wang Anshi for his "exclusive use of mean and petty men";[44] and in his brief tenure as Restoration Chief Councilor, just prior to his death in 1086, Sima Guang specifically lambasted Wang's appointment of such men to positions as intendants:

> When Wang Anshi got hold of the reins of government he wanted to press forward vigorously with his New Policies. In every circuit he set up an Intendant of Ever-Normal and Universal Charitable Granaries and Farming Lands and Irrigation. Afterwards he added new intendants' positions for every type of matter . . . while also increasing the number of fiscal vice-intendants and fiscal supervisors. Moreover, for each post he selected young, low-ranked, and frivolous officials, with seniority status no higher than vice-prefect, county magistrate, or market supervisor . . . Officials such as these showed no concern for the affairs of state nor sympathy for the plight of the common people, but just devoted themselves to banding together to scheme for advancement and profit.[45]

In the aftermath of the New Policies, the court recentralized control over its field administration and shifted away from entrepreneurship as an explicit objective of personnel policy. But during the four decades of the Restoration (1086–1094) and the Post-Reform eras (1095–1127), the Tea and Horse Agency still had no fixed routine; and there were no alternatives to its output of horses and funds. Because the court required men who could keep the far-flung and essential enterprise running smoothly, it tended to appoint to Intendants' posts men already familiar with the Agency. Consequently Lu Shimin was reappointed for a second term, from 1094/6 to 1099/11; and a man who had served as managing supervisor in 1075, Sun Aobian, was rotated through all three posts in the executive triad between 1104 and 1107.[46] One other managing supervisor (in 1113), He Jian, was later made Intendant (ca. 1121–1123), in He's own opinion because of his earlier experience.[47] And two additional Post-Reform Intendants (Cheng Zhishao, 1091–1094 and 1099–1105; and Zhang Hui, ca. 1111–1114 and ca. 1120–1122) were reappointed in times of crisis. It was not until Emperor Gaozong successfully consolidated his Southern Song government in the early 1140s that the court could afford to abandon the internal recruitment of THA specialists and begin to move men into and out of the Agency in a routine manner.

LENGTH OF TENURE AND SICHUANESE REPRESENTATION. Two further aspects of the appointments to the TMA were related to entrepreneurial effectiveness. The first was length of tenure in office. The second had to do with bringing into play the newly won willingness of Sichuanese officials to tax their region for the state.

Wang Anshi, who envisioned office-holding as a mandate for experimentation, specifically called for long terms in office in order to give incumbents full opportunity to see their projects through to completion.[48] The TMA Intendants exemplified Wang's theory fully: No statutory limit was placed on the length of time a TMA Intendant served; and the early chiefs were kept in office as long as they kept innovating and increasing revenues, their ambitions sated with imperial awards, greater authority, and promotions in rank. Consequently the average term of office for the New Policies TMA Intendants was a remarkable 49 months, nearly twice that of other intendancies. This figure is only slightly skewed by Pu Zongmin's service in Chengdu for the entire eleven years.[49] Moreover, the TMA Intendants rarely went on to other posts. Fan Chuncui was transferred out in an unexceptional manner, and Liu Zuo was cashiered.[50] But the remaining Intendants served until death, illness, or the Restorationist policy reversal intervened.[51]

Long tenures promoted the development of local and intra-agency networks that were indispensable to decentralized bureaucratic entrepreneurship, but they also posed the risk that power might be abused or that long-time specialists might monopolize the performance of critical tasks. As one aspect of their plan to recentralize authority that had been delegated to the circuit intendants, Restoration policy-makers set a term of 30 months for five circuit offices, including the tea-monopoly intendant.[52] But in the case of the Agency the ruling was not enforced: Yan Ling (1087/4–1092/8 +) served over 64 months, while Lu Shimin added 65 months to his original 66 during his second term as Superintendant in the 1090s.[53] The average term for the Restoration and Post-Reform periods together was 40.7 months by term (out of 692 accountable man-months for 17 terms), and 43 months by individual (16 men).[54] The Southern Song, however, kept its intendants more firmly under control: an average of 26.6 months (480 man-months and 18 terms) by term or 28.2 months by individual. In order to thwart the development of just those local power bases that were essential to entrepreneurial experimentation, the Southern Song court, like the Ming and Qing, placed close limits on how long a man stayed in a single post.

Long tenures also helped ensure a continual Sichuanese presence at the executive level of the Agency. For although, as Table 1 shows, only two of the seven men appointed during the New Policies (Pu Zongmin and Li Ji) were actually Sichuanese themselves, Pu Zongmin remained in his post in Chengdu for the entire period. It was Pu Zongmin's ability to neutralize conservative Sichuanese opposition to the monopsony, especially after the Pengshan tea riot of early 1077, and to steer the Agency through changes at the Superintendant's level that allowed successive Agency chiefs to focus on the cumulative expansion of the monopoly market in Shaanxi.[55] There was a strong Sichuanese presence in the Restoration and Post-Reform periods as well, with four natives out of twenty incumbents serving during half of the remaining forty-two years.[56] During the first decade and a half of the Southern Song, the THA was run almost entirely by three Sichuanese (Zhao Kai, Zhang Shen, and Feng Kangguo), largely as a consequence of Governor-General Zhang Jun's sponsorship of his fellow Sichuanese for key financial posts throughout the province.[57] After 1143, for reasons connected more

Table 1 Sichuanese in Intendants' Positions

Period	Sichuanese Intendants	Non-Sichuanese Intendants	Intendants of Unknown Origin	Total Number of Intendants	Sichuanese Intendants as Percentage of Total
1074–1085	2	3	2	7	28.6
1086–1093	1	1	2	4	25.0
1094–1127	4[a]	4[b]	10	18	22.0
1128–1204	3	13	16	32	9.4
Total	10[a]	21[b]	30	61	16.4

Sources: Appendices A and B.

Notes: [a]Counts Cheng Zhishao twice. [b]Counts Lu Shimin twice.

with court factionalism and the rise to power of Emperor Gaozong's chief minister Qin Gui than with the internal dynamics of the tea and horse trade, not a single identifiable Sichuanese was appointed to the post.[58] But at this point it no longer mattered, since (as we will see in Chapter Five) by the mid twelfth century almost all the positions below Intendant would have been staffed by Sichuanese.

THE TEA MARKET ENTERPRISE

In Eugene Lewis's model of the natural history of the public entrepreneur, a promising individual is first recruited within the organization and guided by a mentor in such a way that his failure to adopt perfectly the customary routine is transformed into creative energy in the organization's service; then the innovator begins to make his mark on the world through an *entrepreneurial leap*, "an act that either creates or elaborates an organization in unforeseen ways such that major existing allocation patterns of scarce public resources are ultimately altered."[59] In the case of our bureaucratic entrepreneurs, that initial entrepreneurial leap was manifested in the creation of a tea monopsony (exclusive purchaser) in Sichuan and a tea monopoly (exclusive seller) in Shaanxi. But entrepreneurial activity did not stop with the first team if Intendants: Because Sichuan had been (from the perspective of the state) underregulated prior to the New Policies, and the New Policies in any event significantly widened the scope of state regulation, the Upper Yangzi and Northwestern macroregions constituted an open organizational field, with abundant opportunities for establishing new regulatory domains. With room to maneuver, and a mandate to experiment, successive New Policies TMA Intendants were free to alter and expand their original enterprise. These men created the markets, operational domain, organizational apparatus, and bureaucratic perquisites that propelled the tea and horse enterprise to power. The precedents they established, moreover, were invoked and manipulated by their successors. The foundation of the enterprise was the monopsony in Sichuan and monopoly in Shaanxi (see Map 6), which together generated the enormous profits that the Intendants could trade to the central government for autonomy and support in their expansionist endeavors.

THE TEA MONOPSONY IN SICHUAN. On their appointment as chief tea purchasers in Sichuan, Li Qi and Pu Zongmin were charged with one implicit and two explicit tasks. Explicitly, they were to set up a reliable supply network for tea and to arrange a system for transporting the tea to Shaanxi. Implicitly, they were expected to make the procurement and transport operations self-financing. In the New Policies atmosphere of state activism and direct competition with merchants for the profits of commerce, creating a self-financing tea-and-horse exchange inevitably meant monopolizing the tea trade.[60] The two men moved first to earmark choice tea regions for the horse exchange and then to monopolize the entire industry.

As will be recalled from Chapter Two, for the first century of the Song the state played no role in the Sichuan tea industry, although up to suspension of the southeastern tea monopoly in 1059, Sichuanese tea was barred from export outside the region. Consequently when Li Qi and Pu Zongmin began to buy tea for the horse trade, there were very few state markets to fall back on. The Intendants inherited one pre-Song government market at Pengkouzhen

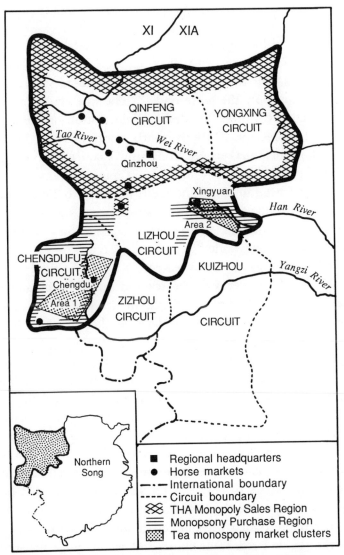

Map 6 Geographic Domain of the Northern Song THA

Notes: North to south, government monopsony markets in Area 1 north of Chengdu include Zhangming, Long'an, Mianzhu, Pengkou, Shifang, Jiulong, Yongkang, Daojiang, Yongchang, and Qingcheng. South of Chengdu: Dayi, Huojing, Qiongzhou, Lushan, Mingshan, Danleng, Yazhou, Hongya, and Rongjing. In Area 2, west to east lay the government monopsony markets of Xingyuan, Chenggu, Yangzhou, Xixiang, and Jinzhou. Other markets scattered between Qinzhou in the north and the Yangzi river include Wenzhou, Sanquan, Bazhou, Dongxiang, Quzhou, Guangan, and Hezhou. For a more detailed map, see Smith, "Taxing Heaven's Storehouse" (Ph.D. diss.), Map 15.

in Pengzhou and four markets in Qiongzhou, established between 1005 and 1072.[61] These two prefectures were long noted for their fancy cake teas, but they would not have produced sufficient volumes of tea to supply the horse trade.[62] The Intendants cast about for additional tea sources, guided by information on commercial activity and tax receipts.[63] By the tenth month of 1083, Li Qi had opened additional markets in Yongkang County, Shuzhou, and Mingshan County, Yazhou.[64] Mingshan County, seventy-five miles southwest of Chengdu along the main highway to Tibet, was Sichuan's most prolific producer, with a capacity of 4,000,000 jin of tea. It was soon designated the major supplier of "convoy tea" (*gangcha*) for the horse trade.[65]

The following month the investigators turned to the Hanzhong Basin. Under the impetus of the tea and salt trade organized by Shaanxi merchants, "every household in the prefectural, county, market town, village, and hamlet-level markets [of Hanzhong]," according to Wen Tong, "engaged in the tea trade."[66] The Hanzhong Basin tea-export trade was only fifteen years old, a product of the 1059 southeastern monopoly rescission; but in that relatively short period, it had radiated south to Bazhou and Dazhou, east to Jinzhou, and north to Tibetan and Han consumers throughout Northwest China.[67] By 1074 the tea trade was so robust that the capital of the Basin, Xingyuanfu, generated 47,000 strings in point-of-purchase taxes—half the prefecture's total commercial tax quota—on 7,400,000 catties of tea.[68] Li Qi was quite impressed by the quantity of tea produced in Xingyuanfu and neighboring Yangzhou, "heretofore traded without restriction." In 1074/11 Li challenged the region's free-trade status and set up three government markets in each prefecture.[69] Four of the Hanzhong teas, designated the "four-varieties convoy-tea" (*sise gangcha*), joined that of Mingshan as the staple of the Sino-Tibetan trade.[70] By the time of the monopsony decree of late 1076, the TMA had opened twenty-seven markets in eleven prefectures of Chengdu and Lizhou Circuits. All but two of the markets shared sites that also had commercial tax stations and had probably been centers for the local and regional tea trade all along. In 1076 the entire complex was designated the "Chuan-Shu tea-production region."[71]

During the first two transitional years, the TMA primarily bought just the tea it required for the horse exchange and the government grain trade in Shaanxi.[72] Moreover, it had to buy tea at market prices, in competition with traveling merchants, resident shop households, and wealthy private warehousers *(tingta zhijia)*. But it was clear early on that Li Qi and Pu Zongmin intended to push for exclusive control, first of the tea they needed for the horse trade and then of the entire industry. With an industry-wide monopsony, the TMA could buy all the cultivators' tea cheaply, earmark what was needed for the non-profit-earning horse and grain trades, and sell the rest at high prices to shops and merchants in Sichuan or directly to consumers and foreign merchants in Shaanxi. With the profits it earned on this unreserved tea, the TMA could not only finance the purchase and transport of tea for the horse trade without requiring inputs of capital, it could also produce surplus revenues.

The push for monopsony began with Mingshan. In the fourth month of 1075 the new Intendants requested exclusive rights to the entire Mingshan crop, which had already become the staple of the horse trade. Thereafter merchants who wanted Mingshan tea had to buy it from the government.[73]

At this time the tea market administration was still in flux, which may have retarded the widespread imposition of monopsony controls. But from 1074 to 1076 the Intendants focused on acquiring key enterprise personnel, and by the end of 1076 they were ready to impose deeper control: the "new law," as the monopsony was called, was extended to the entire Chuan-Shu tea-production region of western Sichuan and the Hanzhong Basin.[74]

After three years of selective and competitive tea purchases by the government, the promulgation of monopsony controls caught many participants in the tea industry off guard. Lü Tao, who was Prefect of Pengzhou when the "new law" was enacted there in 1077, described the stunning swiftness with which the TMA flushed out all old stocks of tea and imposed the new monopsony regime:

On the twenty-fourth day of the second month this prefecture received a
directive from the Tea Market Agency ordering that within half a month
garden households must completely sell out all their old tea. This tea must
not be mixed in with tea sold to the government. Once the time limit has
been reached [the order permitting private sales] will no longer be in effect.
All violators will be dealt with according to the laws [against smuggling].
Although I immediately sent notice down to each district, the liquidation
order will expire on the tenth day of the third month. Over the years many
people have stored tea in preparation for high prices, at which point they
planned to sell. Now all of a sudden because the government plans to buy
new tea, of which [the people] were not previously notified, they must
frantically sell all their old tea under the time limit. Should they exceed
the limit without having liquidated their stocks, they face denunciation
and seizure by private individuals . . . and cudgeling on the spine with
the heavy rod. But how is it possible to sell off all their tea in a few days?
The price of old tea will plummet, and shiftless men will be incited to
[acts of] denunciation and seizure.[75]

Lü sent his memorial to the court on the eighth day of the third
month, two days before the liquidation order was scheduled to expire. Twice before he had directly solicited the TMA, probably Pu
Zongmin in Chengdu, requesting that garden households and private warehousers be given until the end of the eighth month to sell
out their stocks; but his messages had been ignored.[76] Lü fared little
better with the court, however: Four months later he was "dismissed from office in mid term (*chongti*)"; a year after that the Intendancy was given the right to select new Prefects and Vice-Prefects for Pengzhou and Hanzhou or to reappoint officials whom it
judged cooperative.[77]

With the onset of monopsony the twenty-seven tea markets were
taken over by Agency-hired brokers, scale operators, warehouse-
men, and other local-service personnel, placed in at least seven locations under the charge of a market inspector.[78] Nor was the TMA
bound to its own markets in buying tea. The "new law" of 1076/
11 also authorized the agency to depute officials of the seventy-one
tax stations of Chengdu Circuit to buy tea on its behalf;[79] and by
mid 1083, tax and other officials were authorized to represent the
TMA where there was no regular supervisory official in all the tea
purchase or sales markets, border stations, walled towns, market

towns, districts, and prefectures in Chengdu and Lizhou Circuits, and the six sub-circuits of Shaanxi.[80] Where the TMA needed to penetrate beyond the limits of formal government to reach deep into the rural tea economy, as in Yangzhou's Xixiang County, the Intendants hired or franchised local-service supply masters (*yajiao*) and tax farmers (*maipuren*) to purchase, inspect, register, and control the smuggling of tea.[81]

The monopsony imposed very fundamental restrictions on cultivators who had previously been free to choose which teas to harvest, where to market, and whom to sell to. Production choices, for example, were limited by the Agency's desire to buy only certain seasonal crops and to keep all others off the market. Sichuan's cultivators typically harvested four crops, or "flushes": "bud tea" (*yacha*) around March, "early tea" (*zaocha*) from April through June, "late tea" (*wancha*) in July and August, and the "old yellow-leaf tea of autumn" (*qiu huanglao yecha*).[82] Of these only "early tea" fit the Agency's commercial needs. Consequently, cultivators were prohibited from processing or selling the two latest harvests, which deprived them of a small but useful cash income at the time of autumn taxes and the preparations for winter.[83]

Restrictions on where to sell and whom to sell to were the defining features of the monopsony. Whereas cultivators had previously been free to sell to traveling merchants, shop households, and directly to consumers, or to barter with tribesmen at the southwestern frontier markets, under the monopsony they could sell only to the government and only in official markets.[84] As recodified by Lu Shimin in 1083, the restrictions specified that "[A]ny cultivator who bears tea to places where there is no market, or who illicitly sells 1) tea for which licenses have been filled out, 2) contraband tea with licenses that have been left blank, or 3) any tea that has not been sold [through official markets], to any category of individual, [or who] attempts to evade paying commercial taxes, can be informed on and seized by commoners."[85]

On the distribution side, shop households and tea merchants had to buy their tea from the official markets, and resell where and in a manner specified by the TMA. By inserting itself between producer and distributor, the TMA could drive down prices paid the cultivators, raise prices charged the intraregional distributors and all consumers, and collect the difference between the two as profit. In Chapter Six I will describe the methods used by inspectors, brokers, and service personnel to create a profit margin of 10 to 30 percent.

From 1078 to the termination of the New Policies in 1085 the TMA established twenty additional markets. The new markets, all run on the monopsony principle, allowed the Agency to increase its exports of "convoy tea" for the horse and provisioning trades in the northwestern frontier from 3,300,000 catties in 1077 to around 5,000,000 catties by 1085.[86] They also provided another 24,500,000 catties of tea to be sold as "consumer tea" (*shicha*—"drinking tea") in Sichuan or as "government tea" (*guancha*) in the steadily expanding restricted monopoly zones of Western and Eastern Shaanxi.[87]

Fourteen of the new markets were opened in Chengdu and Lizhou Circuits, and merely filled in the gaps around key production centers—for example, the Lushan and Rongjing markets of Yazhou— or reclaimed sites that had been rejected during the early days of selective procurement, such as in Bazhou.[88] The six markets opened in the constituent counties of Jinzhou, down the Han River valley from Xingyuan and Yangzhou, were an exception. Until 1130 and its incorporation into Lizhou Circuit, Jinzhou was not even part of the Upper Yangzi administrative structure. Part of Jingxi South Circuit, its ultimate economic orientation was the downriver trade between the Hanzhong Basin and Wuhan, at the confluence of the Han and Yangzi Rivers. But with the tea of Hubei currently unrestricted, there were no other agencies close enough to have a proprietary interest in the Jinzhou crop, which thus offered an easy and inviting target for the expansionist Intendants of the TMA.

Lu Shimin, the most ambitious of the Intendants, devised a plan to monopolize Jinzhou's tea. Some he planned to sell to itinerant merchants, who could peddle it in the prefecture's border regions. The rest he would ship up to Yongxing Circuit—the eastern half of Shaanxi—for direct government sale to consumers. Lu's plan began to take shape in early 1083, when Eastern Shaanxi was made a restricted monopoly zone for TMA tea. In rapid order Jinzhou was monopsonized, its tea all cornered by six new Agency markets, while a new spur in the TMA's cart-transport relay system (*chezi dipu*) was opened to ship the tea up to Eastern Shaanxi.[89] The number of TMA purchase markets now stood at forty-seven, and its power to commandeer all the tea of southwestern China was essentially complete.

THE TEA MONOPOLY IN SHAANXI. The Sichuan tea monopsony imposed restrictions over the cultivator that on their own might have led to a decline in production. Under similar circumstances the first southeastern tea monopoly had caused registered tea production to fall by over half, from 23,000,000 catties at the end of the tenth century to 10,700,000 catties in 1055.[90] But the TMA monopsony was coupled to a policy of monopoly expansion in the northwest that made Sichuan the sole supplier of tea to the Tibetan and Central Asian merchants that traded in the frontier markets of Qinfeng and Xihe Circuits and to the roughly 7,000,000 resident Chinese who bought tea for household consumption in both the eastern and western circuits of Shaanxi. In response to the entrepreneurial creation of a new marketing region, Sichuanese tea production surged and TMA revenues grew five-fold in little over a decade.

The Agency earned revenues from the tea it bought in two ways. In the twenty-seven to forty-seven government markets of western Sichuan and the Hanzhong Basin, the TMA sold "consumer tea" to shop households and traveling merchants. In Shaanxi, the Agency sold Mingshan and Hanzhong Basin tea left over from the horse trade to foreign merchants and Tibetan and Chinese residents. As the eastern terminus of the Central Asian trade routes and the region of Song China that was farthest from all sources of tea, Shaanxi was traditionally the most lucrative of all China's markets.[91] It was the goal of the TMA Intendants to exploit this market as intensively as possible, by driving out competing southeastern merchants and excluding competing southeastern tea. By 1083 Li Qi, Pu Zongmin, Li Ji, and Lu Shimin had created a "Sichuan-tea restricted zone" (*Chuancha jindi*) that encompassed all of Northwest China and its frontier markets, in which tea was sold solely by the TMA and its agents.

Government takeover of the Shaanxi marketing region began in the west, in the prefectures central to the horse trade. It took several years to develop a reliable tea-transport system, and initially the Intendants were forced to employ merchants to transport tea for them from Mingshan and Hanzhong to the markets of Qinfeng and Xihe Circuits. But merchants were allowed to earn only the transport cost of shipping tea; the lucrative price difference from selling tea in distant markets was claimed wholly by the Agency. As of the seventh month of 1074, merchants could buy tea in Yazhou, Yangzhou, and Xingyuan, and transport it over the Qinling Shan passes. But once in Western Shaanxi, they could sell it back only to the TMA. To prevent merchants from selling tea illicitly a "long license" control system was employed. As clarified in an order of 1074/9, the long license ensured that all the tea leaving a market in Sichuan reached its appointed designation in Shaanxi:

> The appropriate tea-producing prefectures and counties are ordered to supply a license to all guest merchants intending to sell Yazhou's Mingshan tea, Yangzhou tea, and Xingyuan's "Great Bamboo" tea in Qinfeng Circuit. This license permits merchants to sell tea only in the government's tea markets in Xizhou, Qinzhou, [Minzhou], Tongyuan Commandery, and Yongning Stockade. Following the precedent [of 1074/7/16], on each license the presiding official must write the guest merchant's family and surname, the quality and amount of tea, and the month and day of departure. At each customs-reporting station this will be entered in the register. When the guest arrives [to the specified market], the tea will be bought without delay. If the merchant greatly exceeds the estimated travel time, an investigation and pursuit will be undertaken. [This assumes that a copy of the license was sent ahead.] If the guest merchant sells tea privately to any category of [unauthorized] person, passes off Qinfeng-bound tea as tea intended for Eastern Shaanxi [as yet unrestricted], or evades customs-reporting sites, then all of these cases are to be judged and rewards [to informers] paid according to the Xining period Camphorated Tea Restriction and Monopoly Act.[92]

The license, for which the merchant was charged an ad valorem tax of 10 percent, also served as the primary tax and regulatory mechanism for controlling intraregional tea merchants.[93]

Between 1075 and 1076 the TMA intensified its sales capacity in this core marketing region, blanketing the border territory with fifty-two government tea-sales markets in the twelve westernmost prefectures and commanderies of Qinfeng and Xihe circuits.[94] At the same time tea merchants were prohibited from all activities in the lucrative western prefectures, including transport services.[95] One aspect of the siting of the new monopoly markets is especially revealing. Although the twelve prefectures and commanderies contained a greater number of commercial tax stations at this time (ninety-one as of 1077), it was the tea markets that advanced the economic presence of the government westward.[96] In contrast to the structure of tea-purchase markets in western Sichuan and Hanzhong, which followed existing commercial flows, the tea-sales markets of the Longxi Basin served as the vanguard of Song expansion into the former Tibetan domains, dispensing the economic salve to colonial expansion that Wang Anshi recommended to Wang Shao in Xizhou in 1072.

This convergence of revenue-gathering and defensive interests in the government sale of tea provides a counter example to William Skinner's hypothesis about late imperial China that "revenue and defense were inversely related in regional space such that in the central areas of regional cores local government was preoccupied with taxation to the virtual exclusion of defense, whereas along regional frontiers local government was preoccupied with defense and security to the virtual exclusion of fiscal affairs."[97] In the northwestern—and southwestern—frontier of the Song Empire, trade and defense were inseparable.[98] Making trade available to favored foreign polities was one of the key strategems of defense and a primary source of government revenues. The congruence of revenue and defense is illustrated by the distribution of the fifty-two markets in the administrative hierarchy: twelve were in prefectural or commandery cities, eleven were in county centers, seven were in market towns, two were in walled towns, while seventeen were located in stockades and three in military enclaves protected by low earthen walls (*bao*). The last two, explicitly defense-related categories, not only made up 38 percent of the total number, they were also situated in the most westerly locations of Qinzhou (six stockades), Xizhou (one stockade and two *bao*), Minzhou (four stockades and one *bao*), and Tongyuan (two stockades). The tea trade was not only a center-piece of financial policy during the New Policies, it was also a basic component of defense.

The chief contribution of the TMA to the horse trade during the New Policies was to supply the horse markets with tea; the horse trade itself was administered by the Shaanxi Intendant for Horse Purchases and Pastures. As a result, the major concern of the TMA Intendants was to increase their sales of tea. As of 1077, the TMA shipped a quota of 40,000 one-hundred-catty *tuo* (literally "saddle-bags," or bales) of convoy tea, the equivalent of about 2,600 tons, to the fifty-two northwestern markets for the horse and provisioning trades and for cash sales.[99] During this early period of the tea and horse trade, the exchange value of tea was at a peak of one bale of tea per horse and horse procurement used only about 15,000 to 16,000 bales of the allotted convoy tea.[100] Subventions to the grain trade at this time took an unspecified amount (in 1083 an extra 10,000 bales were added to the convoy quota expressly for provisioning),[101] but the bulk of the non-horse surplus was diverted by Agency design to sales for revenue production.

Most of the Agency's cash flow came from a favorable balance of trade and taxes on the sale and transit of tea. Tibetans and other Central Asian traders bought tea with their own native products, or with the goods they themselves acquired further inland in return for Chinese tea and manufactures. Commonly mentioned Central Asian commodities included gold, mercury, musk, camel's hair, soft and coarse woolens, oxen and sheep, and pearls, ivory and jade.[102] Pearls, ivory and jade were probably obtained from the merchants of Khotan (Yutian) who traded in the Xihe and Qinzhou markets, and were exempted in 1078 from paying tea taxes to the Agency, which was recompensed for the loss.[103] Because most of these commodities were of little use to the TMA, which required liquid assets for recapitalizing tea and transferring to client agencies, government markets were instructed to convert the goods they obtained for tea into cash within six months.[104] It is probable that in Shaanxi the conversions were accomplished by reselling the foreign valuables to Chinese merchants.

Central Asian merchants would also have purchased tea with

Chinese commodities they obtained in exchanges with other government agencies. The horse markets run by the Intendant for Horse Purchases and Pastures paid out silk, silver, and cash (up to 10 percent of the value of a horse) as the horse merchants desired, or to equalize the exchange value between horses and units of tea.[105] In addition, the various frontier agencies involved in grain and fodder procurement paid Tibetan provisioners with a wide array of media, including cash, tea, and salt vouchers.[106] In the first decade of the tea and horse exchange, when of all Chinese goods tea was said to hold the greatest attraction for Tibetan merchants, many foreigners apparently converted all other commodities into tea at the Agency's markets.[107] The tea would then be exported through Amdo and as far west as Khotan.

Possessing as it did the most valuable current item of foreign trade, the Agency was in a position to realize substantial profits for presentation to the court; and in order to keep these revenues flowing, the court allowed the Intendants to expand their geographic domain. The process was a further component in the court's trade-off of bureaucratic power for revenues. The next stage in the creation of a supraregional tea monopoly came in 1078, with an order excluding "southern"—that is southeastern—tea from Xihe, Qin-feng, and Jingyuan Circuits of Western Shaanxi.[108] The order created two clear marketing zones in Northwest China: To the west, the twelve frontier prefectures with their fifty-two markets, serving about 300,000 registered households and the entire Tibetan and Central Asian trade, made up a "restricted [monopoly] zone" (*jindi*) reserved for 4,000,000 catties of Sichuanese tea shipped and sold by the Tea Market Agency. To the east, the nineteen prefectures of Eastern Shaanxi with Fengxiangfu and Fengzhou, housing roughly a million households, constituted a "free-trade zone" (*tongshang di-fen*), open to merchant sales of both Sichuanese tea bought in the monopsony markets and "southern tea" bought in the southeastern circuits.[109]

The court's sponsorship of the Agency's monopoly in Western Shaanxi was well rewarded. From the end of 1077 to the autumn of 1078, the TMA accumulated or transferred to other agencies 767,066 strings of cash, prompting an imperial accolade and promotion for

Li Ji to Superintendant of the Tea Market Agency and concurrent Provisional Fiscal Intendant of Shaanxi and Regulator of Jiezhou Salt.[110] In the fourth month of 1079 the TMA received permission to retain 1,000,000 strings of copper coins a year to meet operating expenses, indicating a substantial cash turnover from its Shaanxi concerns.[111] And four months later Li Ji reported that capital funds and surpluses of cash and silks in the Shaanxi markets were too great to transport, whereupon he obtained permission to invest 200,000 strings of cash in the local grain trade on the stipulation that this not interfere with the grain purchases of other agencies.[112] At the same time the administrative center of the TMA was transferred from Chengdu to Qinzhou, the traditional base of the Shaanxi Fiscal Intendant.[113] As Agency efforts shifted from buying tea for the horse trade to selling tea for profits, the surpluses continued to increase. Late in 1080 it was reported that the markets in Qinzhou, Xizhou, Tongyuan Commandery, and Yongning Stockade amassed gross returns from tea sales of over 700,000 strings annually, more than twice the amount of the tax quota for Qinfeng and Xihe Circuits.[114]

Eastern Shaanxi remained open to merchant sales of both Sichuanese and southeastern tea until 1083, but that year Lu Shimin successfully claimed the twenty prefectures and one million households of Eastern Shaanxi for the Agency's export monopoly.[115] Lu aimed to blanket the entire region with Sichuanese and Jinzhou tea, though he couched his objective in expressions of concern for the consumer:

> The only tea available in [Eastern Shaanxi] is from Jinzhou, or is non-government tea smuggled out from [the Hanzhong basin] or scrapings and imitations of southern milled tea. The prices are high, which embitters the people of Shaanxi. I request permission to estimate the volume of surplus tea produced in the circuits of Sichuan and to transport it for sale in all the prefectures and commanderies of Shaanxi. [The sales] should all be implemented according to the articles of the [Western Shaanxi] Restricted Tea Zone.[116]

The full impact of the restrictions was made clear in the second of Lu's thirty-eight amendments to the Revised Orders of the Tea Market

Agency of 1083/6, which delimited the government's marketing region:

> [Eastern and Western Shaanxi] along with Xihe and Lanhui Circuits constitute a Government Tea Restricted Region *(guancha difen)*. Commoners are permitted to inform on and seize any merchant from any circuit selling Sichuanese tea, southern tea, camphorated tea, or any variety of unlicensed tea within the borders of the restricted region. All violaters will be dealt with according to the regulations on violation of the Camphorated Tea Act. [117]

Five months later, in special recognition of this expansion of the TMA monopoly-sales domain, the court promoted the entire Agency to the status of a Superintendancy and made the Superintendant's post equal in rank to the Fiscal Intendant (the paramount Northern Song circuit official), explicitly in spite of Lu Shimin's low civil service grade. [118]

In order to saturate its new marketing domain, the Intendancy increased its number of markets in Shaanxi from the 52 of 1076 to a total of 332 by 1085. [119] The distribution of the added markets has not been recorded, but the density of the enlarged system is suggested by the fact that the number of tea markets exceeded the total number of commercial tax stations by 69. In other words, we can conclude that the Tea Market Agency sold tea to consumers and small retail shops at every level of the administrative and economic hierarchy. Although the TMA would not itself have staffed all of these 332 markets, the same rule authorizing the Agency to depute tax-station and other officials to buy tea for it in Chengdu and Lizhou circuits also applied to the sale of tea in the counties, market towns, walled cities, and stockades of Shaanxi. [120] All markets set up quotas based on the returns in 1078 or the first full year of operation after that, and these quotas provided the basic guidelines for an incentive system that turned the TMA functionaries into extremely aggressive sellers of tea. [121]

Lu Shimin's creation of a "Government Tea Restricted Zone" extending from the Sino-Tibetan horse markets of Xihe in the west to the cities of Chang'an, Hezhongfu, and Tongzhou in the old Chinese heartland of the Wei and Yellow River valleys in the east, almost doubled over its 1059 limits the marketing region for Sichuanese tea. Moreover, the 1083 regulations made 1,300,000 Chinese households as well as all the foreign traders of the northwest directly dependent on the TMA for their tea. And once again the court was recompensed for its sponsorship of Intendancy expansion. In late 1083 the TMA set a quota of 1,000,000 strings on net receipts to its tea and salt business; in 1084 it showed net returns on tea sales and taxes of 1,600,000 strings; and in 1085 the Intendancy "presented" *(xian)* revenues of 2,000,000 strings to be used at the discretion of the court.[122] Excluding its subsidy of the horse trade, the value of the multiregional tea monopoly had increased five-fold since 1074, and provided between 1.5 and 3 percent of the government's cash receipts of 60,000,000 strings annually during the New Policies era.[123]

The Shaanxi markets, reserved entirely for the government, were by far the most profitable component of the monopsony-monopoly enterprise, delivering the highest returns to investments. In 1085, for example, Lü Tao reported that the TMA could buy and transport a hundred-catty bale of Mingshan tea to Qinzhou for less than 10 strings of cash, and sell it for between 30 and 40 strings, for a net profit of between 200 and 300 percent.[124] By 1105 the Agency sold Pengkou tea to consumers outside the horse trade in Western Shaanxi at 130 strings 453 cash per bale. Even if we allow for a doubling of the price of Pengkou's costliest tea after the 1080s (to 120 cash per catty), the TMA would have made a gross profit of over 400 percent on the export.[125]

Only the least profitable intraregional domestic markets were left to the merchants under the 1083 regulations. In fact after the fifteen years from 1059 to 1075 in which merchants could freely sell Sichuanese tea, followed by seven years in which they could at least sell in Eastern Shaanxi, the private marketing region was possibly more restricted than it had been under the rules of the southeastern monopoly. For in 1083 Wen and Long prefectures in Sichuan's northwest mountain fringe were closed to private merchants because of their proximity to the Jiezhou horse market.[126]

Nonetheless, the sale of tea to merchants for distribution throughout the four circuits of Sichuan played a significant (although incalculable) role in the total income of the Tea Market Agency. Lü Tao indicated that the value of the interregional trade to the government if it had been simply taxed rather than run as a monopoly would have been around 500,000 strings.[127] Tea markets operated with a target profit margin of 10 to 30 percent, and consequently it was necessary to make the local trade as lucrative as possible for the regional traders.[128] Merchants were given extra measures of tea, called "wastage tea" *(haocha)* or "indulgence tea" *(raocha)*, and eventually (in 1110) even the prime markets of Zizhou Circuit were set aside for merchants selling tea from the Chengdu government markets, all in an effort to encourage sales of Agency-owned tea.[129] But the distance over which merchants could carry tea before entering a restricted zone, and hence their profits, were limited. We have no figures on returns to merchants for the Northern Song, but information supplied by Wang Zhiwang for the Southern Song demonstrates the point: After paying 40 strings of cash for the basic purchase price *(benqian)*, transit taxes, and license fees for 100 catties of second class "guest-trade Sichuan tea" *(kefan chuancha)*, the traveling merchant could expect to earn a net profit of 10 strings, or 25 percent.[130] This was a far cry from the 200 to 400 percent earned by the TMA in Shaanxi.

Other than the approximately 5,000,000 catties of tea shipped to Western Shaanxi annually in the late eleventh century, we have no data on the total proportion of Sichuan's 29,000,000 catties of tea transported by the TMA to its 332 northwestern markets. As Intendant Cheng Zhishao pointed out in 1103, the Chinese households of Eastern Shaanxi were by custom and (to 1059) by government mandate drinkers of "southern tea";[131] and there may have been consumer resistance against the legislated switch to Sichuanese tea. But as a government organization with the powers to both tax and intimidate, the TMA could market its product much more aggressively than could private merchants; and there is evidence that the TMA oversupplied Shaanxi with tea that it then forced on consumers and local retail outlets. According to Lü Tao and Su Che,

There are limits to the amount of tea the people of Shaanxi can consume. But the Tea [Market] Agency, in its greed for increased profits, transports more tea than can be sold. Every prefecture has places that are below quota. Moreover, in order to produce surpluses over the yearly [profit] quotas, [the TMA] raises the sale price per catty, and everywhere forces it *(peimai)* on the people . . . ([Original note:] This year Fengzhou increased the price 100 cash per catty, following a TMA directive to all prefectures.) . . . Thus the harms of monopoly reside not only in [Sichuan], but flow also to [Shaanxi].[132]

Yet despite elements of compulsion in the way the TMA distributed tea in its new market domain, from the perspective of the Sichuanese tea industry the result was that its monopsonistic purchaser—the TMA—was buying and exporting unprecedented amounts of tea.

The impact of the TMA monopoly enterprise on the Sichuanese tea industry is taken up in Chapter Six. Here I would like to draw attention to the question of why, in view of the administrative segregation that had characterized imperial policy towards Sichuanese tea since the late eighth century, the TMA was permitted to claim ever more territory for its tea.

The first and most obvious factor was the Agency's profitability. Following full establishment of the monopoly enterprise in 1077, the only regular outside subvention to the TMA consisted of 30,000 to 100,000 strings of iron cash provided by local mints. Indeed the TMA went well beyond financing the purchase of 15,000 horses annually and regularly brought in surplus revenues, which eventually exceeded 1,000,000 strings a year. From 1074 to 1078, for instance, profits of at least 400,000 strings a year were recorded; for 1079, a surplus of 1,000,000 can be estimated from various records; and in 1085 a profit of 2,000,000 strings was recorded along with evidence that 1,000,000 strings were presented to the court. By 1115 claims of 3,711,111 strings of "tea profits" were made. (See Appendix D for a compilation of figures on revenues and subventions paid to other agencies during the years 1074–1115). All along the TMA Intendants argued, and the court agreed, that monopolistic exploitation of an expanding market was the key to surplus revenues.

But the court's support for TMA expansionism also hinged on a very rare set of circumstances in the Song fiscal environment—unregulated markets in the tea lands of the southeast. On dismantling the monopoly apparatus in 1059, the state's interest in the southeastern tea economy was reduced to local tax collections. With no over-arching regional-level agencies holding a direct stake in the movement of southeastern tea, the expansion of the TMA into Eastern Shaanxi was not perceived as threatening; no other agencies stood to lose by TMA control of the lucrative northwestern market.

By around 1070 even Fujian's camphorated *la* tea had been deregulated, in an attempt to dispose of the inevitable backlog that plagued state monopolies. Control of the industry was given back to the merchants, who between 1070 and 1084 were allowed to sell the tea freely south of the Yangzi River, but not in the TMA's Shaanxi markets or in a large tract of North China that was reserved for the State Trade Agency.[133] In fact, the first official to show an interest in re-intensifying the marketing of Fujianese tea was Lu Shimin. In the last month of 1083 Lu, eager to exploit to the fullest the marketing potential of his domain, recommended that merchants be allowed to transport camphorated tea from Kaifeng to Shaanxi, where the TMA would either market it directly or collect taxes on its sale. In return for the privilege, Lu offered to pay what amounts to a franchising fee (*jingliqian*) of 14,100 strings of cash to the Ministry of Finance.[134] Since total production of the expensive camphorated tea was only about 355,000 catties annually, probably only small amounts were handled by the TMA in such metropolitan centers as Chang'an, without affecting the saturation of Shaanxi with Sichuanese tea.[135]

The court took a direct interest in the consumer tea markets of the capital and North China during the reform era, but this, too, was neither a threat to nor threatened by TMA hegemony in the northwest. The State Trade Agency bought 3,000,000 catties of tea annually from southeastern merchants, which it resold on credit to small peddlers—"vagrant avaricious debtors," according to Lü Tao—who hawked the tea throughout the northeast, in Hebei and Shandong.[136] And in the capital region itself the Intendancy for Bian River Embankments regulated the grinding and distribution of water-milled powder tea, but its operation was confined largely to the river systems of the capital and North China.[137]

The success of the Sichuan tea monopoly did prompt a succession of calls for the re-monopolization of southeastern tea; and had this movement not been aborted by the death of Emperor Shenzong, it would have eventually challenged the TMA hegemony in Shaanxi. During the last third of 1084, for example, the tea lands of Guangxi were monopolized for the first time in their history;[138] a request that the tea of eastern Sichuan be monopolized was seriously considered;[139] and Lu Shimin was given permission to investigate replicating his Upper Yangzi–Northwest China enterprise in the Middle Yangzi–North China marketing system, to "return the profits of the tea trade to the commonwealth."[140] Only a recommendation that all six of the original southeastern circuits be re-monopolized in their entirety was rejected out of hand.[141] Evidence of the direct link between monopoly status and market protectionism was provided in the tenth month, when the Fiscal Vice-Intendant for Fujian succeeded in again monopsonizing the circuit's camphorated tea: Within four months a government marketing region for camphorated tea had been created south of the Yangzi, and Kaifeng and Shaanxi opened to merchant sale of the tea to extend its markets.[142] Although Lu Shimin had earlier offered to sell limited quantities of camphorated tea in Shaanxi, this new policy might well have threatened his hegemony over the region. But it, too, fell prey to the Restoration in 1085. The TMA did not lose its hold over Eastern Shaanxi until 1103, when the central government under Cai Jing claimed that marketing region for the re-monopolized southeastern tea industry.[143] The impact of this and subsequent stages in the long-term cycle of market expansion and decline on the Sichuanese tea industry and the tea cultivators is taken up in Chapter Six. But first we will examine what entrepreneurs do after they have made their leap.

FIVE

Autonomy, Risk Reduction, and Entrepreneurial Expansion

No organizations operate in a vacuum. Like their sub-set, the business firm, organizations interact with one another and compete for power and resources. In the analytical scheme synthesized by James Thompson, organizations function within a "task environment"— "those parts of the environment which 'are relevant or potentially relevant to goal setting and goal attainment,' " such as suppliers of inputs, recipients of outputs, and regulatory authorities.[1] Every organization must establish a viable "domain," consisting of its range of products, the population it serves, and the services it renders, that defines the organization in relation to its task environment. But as Thompson stresses,

> The attainment of a viable domain is, in essence, a political problem. It requires finding and holding a position which can be recognized by all of the necessary "sovereign" organizations as more worthwhile than available alternatives. It requires establishing a position in which diverse organizations in diverse situations find overlapping interests. The management of interorganizational relations is just as political as the management of a political party or of international relationships. It can also be just as dynamic, as environments change and propel some elements out of and new elements into a task environment.[2]

Precisely because a viable domain must be created and held in a competitive organizational world, the process is disruptive and costly.

Therefore "organizations subject to norms of rationality seek to design themselves so as to minimize the necessity of maneuvering and compromise."[3] In short, they strive for power. In a bureaucratic context, power may be defined as the independence an organization has to determine its supply of inputs (whom to tax, where and whom to buy from); the disposition of its output (for example, whether an agency can distribute its goods and services in ways that best serve its own needs or must allocate them according to some externally imposed criteria); and its own internal structure (most critically, the appointment of personnel).

The organizational imperatives that Thompson describes for all organizations apply with particular force to those led by public entrepreneurs. In Eugene Lewis's terms, public entrepreneurs "engage in characteristic strategies of organizational design that simultaneously grant them high degrees of autonomy and flexibility, minimize the external interference with core technologies, and which appear to be isomorphic with the most inclusive needs, wants, values and goals of crucial aspects of the task environment."[4] The first stage in that characteristic strategy consists of the entrepreneurial leap, in our case creation of the monopoly enterprise. But bureaucratic entrepreneurs must protect and expand their enterprises with the same unique intensity that they use to create them. In Lewis's model, the entrepreneurial leap is followed by three further steps that are relevant to the rise of the TMA. First is the "struggle for autonomy," in which the entrepreneur "must bargain, threaten and seduce others into allowing him the autonomy over his mission and over the organization(s) which he must command to achieve that mission."[5] The entrepreneur must then turn to the "reduction of uncertainty in the task environment," by making as secure as possible those "organizations and groups upon which [his] organization is highly dependent for sources of input and for absorption of output . . ." And finally (for our purposes), once the entrepreneur has established and consolidated his original domain, he will, if his ambition to dominate is still unsatisfied, transcend the boundaries of his organization and his mandate to expand his entrepreneurial domain.

Lewis's model elucidates what makes public entrepreneurs special, and I will use his categories to analyse the political power of the TMA. But first it is necessary to highlight the fact that unlike private firms, public organizations (excluding the military) rise or fall at the sufferance of the state. The state is the central element of their task environment; and though public organizations may jockey for power and independent authority, it is the prerogative of the state to decide if they keep it. Insofar as autonomy and independence can be granted or withheld by a political center, as opposed to flowing from opportunities and constraints imposed by, for example, the market or external features of the environment, an organization derives power to the extent that it can satisfy those needs viewed as most critical by the center, and to the degree also that it can monopolize that capacity.[6]

In the case of the New Policies regime, it is clear that the reformers, including the emperor, came to perceive the creation of new and expandable sources of revenue as the state's most pressing need. We have seen that the tea-monopoly enterprise—the Intendants' entrepreneurial leap—enabled the TMA easily to fulfill its original assignment as suppliers of tea to the horse trade, and to produce in addition substantial revenues that could be allocated to defense agencies in Shaanxi or deposited in court-controlled discretionary funds in Shaanxi and Sichuan. As an indication of the role played by TMA funds in the always thorny problem of financing Shaanxi defense, of the two million strings allocated to the Xihe-Lanhui Regional Frontier Defense Financing Office in 1084, the largest single sum—600,000 strings—came from the TMA. (Another 550,000 strings were provided by two other Sichuanese sources, 648,000 strings came out of three Shaanxi accounts, and a relatively minor 200,000 strings were supplied by the court.)[7] Moreover, the TMA still had over 1,000,000 strings left, and it paid for the horse trade. Therefore, although it did not monopolize the role of defense financier in Shaanxi, it was by far the greatest contributor. In exchange for their capacity to satisfy critical revenue needs, the court gave the TMA Intendants extraordinary support in their drive for autonomy, the reduction of risk, and continued entrepreneurial expansion. This exchange of revenues for power is highlighted by the TMA's success in neutralizing rivals, selecting personnel, controlling subsidiary markets, and establishing a unique incentive system for maximizing profits.

AUTONOMY AND THE NEUTRALIZATION OF RIVALS

In return for a steady flow of funds, the court granted the TMA Intendants a degree of freedom from supervision and extra-agency scrutiny that contradicted basic Chinese precepts of organizational checks and balances, and that was rare even in the activist atmosphere of the New Policies.[8] The TMA Intendants successfully sheltered their operation from interference by parent and allied agencies, neutralized opponents and critics within and outside the New Policies administration, and established the principle of inviolability for TMA tea and funds.

As we saw in Chapter One, the tea-purchase operation grew out of parallel investigations by the State Trade Agency and the Finance Commission; and both agencies sought a continuing foothold in the potentially lucrative enterprise. The court itself quickly severed all ties between the TMA, its Intendants, and the Finance Commission, thwarting Commissioner Zhang Dun's effort to involve himself in personnel selection and the control of surplus revenues.[9] Links to the State Trade Agency took longer to break, however, since the two organizations shared common functions, marketing regions, and customers. In the fourth month of 1075 the Xihe Circuit branch of the State Trade Agency solicited the Secretariat-Chancellery for a decision on whether it had jurisdiction over the TMA; the Secretariat ruled that the TMA and Xihe State Trade bureau shared equal status and joint responsibility for both the tea and state-trade markets, and made the TMA subordinate to the Superintendant for State Trade in Kaifeng.[10] But tea was the most valuable commodity in Sichuan and Shaanxi, and tea was controlled by the TMA. Consequently the TMA soon outgrew its State Trade affiliation, which came to be seen as burdensome. In late 1077, just as the Agency's surplus revenues had begun to surpass 500,000 strings annually, Li

Ji complained that outside agencies were meddling in the internal affairs of the tea monopoly; in response the court relieved the TMA of all connections with either the State Trade Agency or its Xihe branch, and prohibited all other agencies from interfering in TMA affairs.[11] By the fourth month of 1079, when Li Ji was made concurrent Superintendant of Tea and Fiscal Intendant of Shaanxi, the TMA had become the paramount fiscal agency in the Upper Yangzi and Northwest China.

The most persistent jurisdictional challenge to the TMA was issued by the Intendant for Horse Purchases and Pastures, Guo Maoxun. In 1081 Guo accused the TMA of diverting the preferred Mingshan tea away from the horse trade in order to maximize revenues and was appointed Co-Intendant of the tea agency to protect the horse-procurement operation. But two years later Lu Shimin protested that "[e]ver since the horse purchasing office obtained concurrent control over the tea markets, the tea policy has been deprived of its independence. Moreover, all the [horse purchase officials] devote themselves to is getting more horses. [To do so] they take what they need from the tea enterprise and use their influence to take from [tea] to augment [horses]."[12] The court swiftly abolished Guo's concurrent position in the TMA and reaffirmed that all TMA affairs, including questions of resource distribution and internal discipline, were the exclusive concern of the Agency, in which "other agencies may not interfere." This blanket protection against outside interference was reiterated in an Imperial Rescript of 1085, and not reversed until well into the Restoration, in the tenth month of 1086.[13]

The TMA enjoyed equal protection against critics who sought not to coopt the tea monopoly, but to alter or dismantle it; the list of individuals transferred, demoted, cashiered, fined, or censured for tangling with the TMA Intendants is impressive. The chief Sichuanese opponents of the tea monopoly, in particular Lü Tao, Zhou Yin, Zhou Biaoquan, and Wu Shimeng, were all neutralized through transfers or dismissals in 1077, not least of all owing to the machinations of their fellow Sichuanese, TMA chief Li Ji.[14] These four men had opposed the very principle of monopolization, but even more pragmatically oriented critics of the TMA were censured as well. In 1077, after eighteen months of charging that the TMA employed too many officials in Shaanxi and was inefficient, the Fiscal Supervisor of Qinfeng Circuit, Sun Jiang, was informed that because the emperor had given his support to the Agency, such criticisms had become disruptive.[15] The following year, when the first ban on outside interference with the Agency was issued, the Fiscal Intendant and Fiscal Supervisor of Lizhou Circuit were each demoted at Li Ji's insistence for recommending that the tea monopoly be abolished and tea taxation handed over to their office. At the same time the Sichuanese Fan Bailu was fined for contending with the TMA over the choice of a road through the Qinling Mountains.[16] And to take one final instance, in 1083 four officials in the central government were fined 6 to 8 catties of copper each for criticizing Lu Shimin's net-profit-based incentive system.[17]

Perhaps the most impressive display of autonomy was the TMA's power over the distribution and pricing of Agency tea. In the case of the southeastern tea monopoly, cash revenues from the sale of tea had been sacrificed in favor of using heavily discounted tea vouchers as an inducement to northern grain merchants to provision the frontier armies—the so-called *ruzhong* policy—causing paper claims on tea to soar well beyond capacity and bringing the trade to a halt.[18] But during the New Policies, it was revenues that were most wanted by the court, which consequently supported the TMA's quest to seek out the most profitable uses for tea. In 1078 Li Ji was asked his opinion about replicating the *ruzhong* provisioning policy with Sichuanese tea, and he promptly convinced the court that allowing other agencies to trade Sichuanese tea for grain would destabilize tea prices and undercut the profitability of the monopoly.[19] When exceptions to this understanding were made during the Lanzhou campaigns of 1082–1083, they were either at the initiative of the TMA, which could bolster its influence further by allowing beleaguered frontier outposts to sell its tea to meet emergency expenses, or with the proviso that the agency involved would pay the TMA for the tea it obtained.[20] It was the Intendancy for Horse Purchases and Pastures that had the most routine need for extra tea, and in 1083 the TMA established a fixed procedure that required the horse purchase office to pay for extra-quota allotments of tea with an equivalent amount in cash or silk *(duishu jiaoyi)*.[21] The greatest challenge to Agency control over its tea came from the horse purchasing intendant, Guo Maoxun, who in 1081 pressed the court to prohibit TMA sales of Mingshan tea until the annual horse quota was met. But the TMA countered that shackling Mingshan tea to the horse trade would create backlogs of its most lucrative product and cut into TMA profits, and the court agreed that everything beyond the fixed horse-purchase allotment of Mingshan tea could be sold by the TMA as it saw fit.[22] It took longer to resolve the issue of prices, but again the TMA position prevailed. As Li Ji noted in 1078, horse-procurement officials sought a low price for tea as an inducement to foreign horse sellers, whereas tea-market officials wanted a high price for tea to maximize their profits.[23] Once again Guo Maoxun was the chief TMA adversary, in a debate that is discussed in detail in Chapter Seven. Here I will note only that when the War Ministry interceded in mid 1083, it showed unusual deference to a field agency in recognizing the TMA's rights over the price of tea: Each bale of tea used to buy horses was discounted 2 strings in value, yielding foreign merchants more tea for their horses, but the TMA was allowed to register the transfer at the full market price, so that total Agency profits—the basis for individual and collective incentive awards—would not appear to have declined. In addition the same order mandated that for any extra-quota subvention of tea that the horse purchase office required, it had to pay the TMA in full by the end of the year.[24] Ultimately the various ministries of the central government also came to acknowledge that the TMA owned discretionary control not only over its tea but also its funds; in 1085 even the Finance Ministry declared that "the funds of [the TMA] are its own to manage."[25]

RISK REDUCTION THROUGH PERSONNEL CONTROL

One of the most critical levers of power for the bureaucratic entrepreneur is control over his own personnel. The leader intent on smashing routine and building new empires must have followers whose abilities and loyalty he can trust. Like their leader, the subordinates must also thrive on change. Hide-bound bureaucrats, appointed by seniority and devoted to routine, can undermine even the most modest initiatives; and they represent one of the entrepreneur's greatest risks. Many contemporaries thought that the source of TMA power was the control it wielded over its own men.

When Li Qi and Pu Zongmin were first ordered to buy tea and ship it to the Xihe horse markets in 1074, they possessed neither executive assistants nor on-site staff. Because the reform leaders were intent on expanding the power of the state in society, however, they encouraged the creation of new bureaucratic posts; and as a result, the new Intendants encountered little difficulty gaining authorization for the positions they required. Between 1074 and 1085 the Intendants created approximately thirty-five new supervisory positions, including managing supervisors *(gandang gongshi)*, managing secretaries *(guan'gan wenzi)*, tea-transport relay-station inspectors *(xunxia banchapu shichen)*, and tea-purchase and tea-convoy-market inspectors in Sichuan *(chachang jianguan, gangchang jianguan)*, and tea-sales-market inspectors *(maichachang jianguan)* in Shaanxi.[26] Subordinate to these management positions were office, market, and transport functionaries that added an estimated 100 to 200 subbureaucrats and military servitors *(shichen)*,[27] 200 local service personnel and an equal number of government brokers,[28] and 5,000 hired or conscripted porters to the Intendancy's roster.[29] Only during the Southern Song did the Intendants face serious challenges over the size of their staff and court-ordered reductions.[30]

But it was more difficult for the Intendants to get the right to make their own appointments. The early phase of the New Policies capped a long process in which rights of personnel selection, and of recommendation for promotion from executory, junior level *(xuanren)* to administrative, senior level *(jingchaoguan)* status came to be vested not in the central government, but in the circuit offices, especially the fiscal intendant.[31] In Sichuan and the other "distant circuits" the fiscal intendant became primary administrator of the entire personnel procedure, and this authority had to be wrested from the fiscal intendants when the TMA was established in 1074. The key to its success, as usual, was the Agency's extraordinary profitability. In 1077 Emperor Shenzong gave special recognition to the relationship between productivity and personnel control by vesting in Intendant Li Ji the unlimited authority to recommend and impeach (*juhe*) officials—the bureaucratic equivalent of hiring and firing.[32] The impeachment provision was aimed at the anti-reform faction of Sichuanese that opposed the tea monopoly on principle and at the officials of other circuit agencies (especially the Lizhou and Qinfeng Circuit Fiscal Intendancies and the Xihe bureau of the State Trade Agency) that opposed the TMA as a threat to their spheres of interest. It was soon expanded into the general prohibition against interference in the official routine of the TMA by any other agencies that shielded the Agency until the Restoration.[33]

The right of unlimited appointment was a generous gesture by a grateful emperor and could not be sustained. By 1078 the court had begun to impose quotas on the numbers of officials of various categories the combined intendants might select or sponsor for office, with the numbers intended to decrease as the administrative apparatus took shape.[34] But the second half of Shenzong's reign, the years between 1078 and 1085 known as the Yuanfeng era, proved to be a period of tremendous growth for the Agency, creating a continual need for more officials. Since every expansion brought in greater revenues, the cash-hungry court granted the TMA Intendants almost every request to make new appointments. Moreover, even after the court rescinded all rights of appointment by capital and provincial officials in 1081, as part of a recentralization of personnel procedures in the Ministry of Personnel (*libu*), the TMA recovered its right of autonomous selection.[35] The rights acquired by the Yuanfeng Intendants in turn served as the precedents for succeeding chief administrators, earning for the Agency unique status, according to the *Song History*, as an organization "that was permitted to appoint its own personnel (*guanshu xu zi bizhi*)."[36] Two aspects of the TMA's selection privileges, the right of irregular appointment for managing supervisors and market inspectors, and the right to recommend key county magistrates and prefectural vice-administrators, will highlight this special status of the TMA.

The managing supervisors (*gandang gongshi, ganban gongshi,* or *goudang gongshi*) were part of a class of middle-level administrators attached to many of the circuit intendancies and central financial and production agencies.[37] They formed the administrative backbone of both the TMA and its post-1085 expansion into the THA, with responsibility for coordinating the purchase and transport of tea and its exchange for horses or resale for cash. Between five and nine managing supervisors were appointed at a time up to 1127, and between three and four in the Southern Song.[38] Each was responsible for the overall performance of a regional cluster of tea-purchase markets in Sichuan or tea-sales markets in Shaanxi. Li Ji, in an attempt to get imperial recognition for the good work of the managing supervisors, described them as being "on the road day and night."[39] To allow them to wield independent authority, each supervisor was equipped with a "vermilion Seal of the Managing Supervisor of the Tea Market Agency," a perquisite of power that in the fiscal intendancy was reserved for the functionally higher circuit supervisor (*panguan*).[40]

The managing supervisors could be selected from executory and administrative-class civil officials, or from servitors major or minor (*daxiao shichen*) in the military bureaucracy.[41] Despite the substantial authority vested in these officials, three of whom (Lu Shimin, Sun Aobian, and He Jian) went on to become Agency Intendants, the majority appear to have been junior, that is, executory class officials.[42]

The market inspectors (*jianguan, jiandangguan*) occupied the next echelon down in the Agency's administrative hierarchy, and provided the critical link between bureaucracy and the economy. The inspectors formed part of a class of functionaries (termed *service agents* by Kracke) responsible for collections and payments in the government's monopoly markets, commercial tax stations, and at least some of its warehouses and manufactures.[43] The TMA regularly assigned inspectors to its key convoy-tea purchase (*qigangchang*) and retail-tea purchase and sales *(shichachang)* markets in Sichuan and the Hanzhong Basin, and to its principal tea sales markets in Shaanxi. Ten inspectors were assigned to the convoy-tea markets of Yazhou and the Hanzhong Basin in 1083 in order to supervise the purchase of tea in bulk and its packing and transport to the 332 markets in Shaanxi where it was exchanged for horses or grain and fodder or sold directly for cash.[44] It is not clear how many of the retail-tea markets (that is, markets that bought tea primarily for the domestic trade) were assigned inspectors, but the officials would probably have been clustered in the markets of Pengzhou, Qiongzhou, and Yongkangjun that supplied Chengdu.[45] The specific responsibility of the retail-market inspectors, and the one to which their incentive schedules were indexed, was to generate revenues. This meant buying tea as cheaply as possible from the cultivator and selling it high to traveling merchants and to local tea shops *(chapu)*.[46] Both categories of markets might have vice-inspectors *(tong jianguan)* as well,[47] and those TMA markets to which no inspectors were assigned were managed by the local tax-bureau supervisor, or in some cases franchised out to wealthy individuals *(maipu)*.[48] Inspectors also manned the monopoly sales markets in Shaanxi, where the vast bulk of the TMA's cash surplus was generated. Although by 1085 the Agency operated 332 state markets in the region, inspectors were appointed only for the seven major sales centers of Qin, Xi, Min, He, and Jie prefectures, Tongyuan Commandery, and Yongning Stockade. The four most profitable of these—Qin, Xi, Tongyuan, and Yongning—each got two inspectors.[49]

All of the TMA purchase and retail-tea markets were staffed by a variety of commoner service personnel *(gongren)*. These most commonly included the stock controller and his assistant *(zhuandian)*, warehouse men *(kuzi)*, scale operators *(chengzi)*, and bookkeepers *(dianli)*.[50] The actual business transactions of the markets were handled by brokers *(yaren)*, hired from among local men of substance and connections to serve as salaried agents of the TMA.[51] Brokers, service personnel, and tea-market inspectors were linked by a system of shared incentives, discussed below, that bridged the gap between formal government and local society and supplied a powerful impetus to government control of the economy.[52] These three classes were not only most directly responsible for executing government policy, they were also the most visible agents of government exploitation. As a result they became the specific targets of the only recorded mass demonstration against the tea monopoly, the Pengkou riot of 1077.

The managing supervisors and market inspectors were the first posts the new TMA Intendants sought to fill. The earliest recommendations all followed the long-established procedure for guaranteed sponsorship, with Li Qi and Pu Zongmin guaranteeing that their principals had committed and would commit no crimes of rapacity, and assuming equal liability for themselves if such crimes did occur. The recommendations then had to be approved by the appropriate personnel agencies in the capital, or in some cases by the fiscal intendant, before the appointment could take effect.[53]

In late 1077, just after Emperor Shenzong granted Li Ji an unlimited mandate to hire and fire, the TMA Intendants were given their first authorization to select three managing supervisors "in contravention of regular procedure" (*buyi changzhi jubi*).[54] In general, the right of irregular appointment permitted an administering official (most often it seems to have been a circuit intendant or prefectural administrator) to fill critical vacancies or shuffle personnel immediately, without awaiting approval from above. It might be granted on an ad hoc basis in military emergencies or in the aftermath of natural disasters, such as flooding. Or certain categories of positions could be placed under irregular authorization to protect the continuity of essential operations, such as the movement of tea to the horse markets.[55]

Irregular authorization also allowed administrators to place men with special skills into appropriate positions. Generally, neither irregular authorization nor the Eight-Circuit Laws sanctioned appointing to office a man without the requisite formal status, unlike the acting officials from outside the civil service often used in Guangxi.[56] But able and experienced men could be drawn from the large pool of officials whose previous commissions had been terminated (*baren*), whose replacements had arrived (*deti*), who were

awaiting vacancies *(daique)*, or who were currently serving elsewhere in the agency in question.[57] Because of the surplus of officials
at the lower levels, this pool could be quite large. And since any
single official might otherwise have to wait four to six years before
gaining a second post, the right of irregular authorization not only
allowed an agency to keep critical posts filled, it probably also fostered great loyalty on the part of the men whose careers were has-
tened by being chosen in this manner.[58]

Cognizant of the danger of irregular authorization as an avenue
for favoritism, the court abolished routine use of the privilege in
late 1077, the same month that it was first granted to the TMA.
The reason given was the fear that "in isolated and rustic places
. . . criminally involved and questionable individuals will use entreaties to obtain positions."[59] Thereafter most agencies throughout
the empire had access to the right on a very limited basis only.[60]
But in the TMA, where the experiment in bureaucratic entrepreneurship was beginning to show unexpected financial returns, irregular authorization became standard. In late 1080, for example, Li
Ji memorialized that the seven tea-market inspectors in Qinfeng
Circuit earned net profits from tea sales of over 700,000 strings of
cash—twice the commercial tax quota for the entire circuit. Li noted
that the seven officials had been selected through irregular authorization all along; and he requested, and received, the right to add
four more inspectors to the roster on the same terms.[61]

Similarly, when the rights of all capital and provincial officials to
make appointments were rescinded in 1081, it took Lu Shimin only
two years to regain not only selection rights but the irregular authorization for all his managing supervisors and inspectors. In mid
1083, when the Agency was showing a net profit of 1,000,000
strings yearly, the Minister of Personnel himself recommended that
the TMA get back its rights to the Shaanxi market inspectors despite the rescission.[62] Towards the end of the year, the Ministry
relinquished its possession of five of seven managing supervisors to
Lu Shimin and gave him two new managing secretaries as well.[63]
Then in the final month of the year, the Agency was granted irregular authorization for the ten tea-purchase and convoy-despatch market

inspectors in Sichuan.[64] The TMA thus gained almost full autonomy in the selection of its key personnel at a time when other organizations throughout the empire had lost most of their independence. Because of the court's hunger for revenues, entrepreneurial autonomy was granted to the TMA well after it had ceased to characterize the New Policies in general.

Succeeding regimes were stingier about the delegation of power, and the Restoration, Post-Reform, and Southern Song eras witnessed a steady deterioration of the Agency's independence. Nonetheless, the appointment rights acquired between 1078 and 1085, referred to as the "Yuanfeng precedents" (*Yuanfeng jiufa*), served as the basis of personnel selection into the Southern Song. The "Yuanfeng precedents" were reapplied in full at least twice during the twelfth century, in 1106 and during the 1120s.[65] But after the New Policies era, irregular authorization was enjoyed on a much more limited basis. Even Lu Shimin, who always appears to have sensed just how much he could ask for from the central government, made very few requests for the prerogative; in one case he asked only that his market inspectors be protected from the irregular appointment rights of other agencies.[66] Early in the second decade of the twelfth century, irregular selection was repeatedly denied the joint Tea and Horse Agency, and was not regained until the 1120s, when the Jurchen threat gave renewed urgency to requests by the THA Intendants.[67] During the Southern Song, the only post that appears to have routinely come under irregular authorization was the combined registrar and sheriff's office of the twenty-three to thirty-four contract markets (*hetongchang*) that taxed and regulated the Sichuan tea trade during the twelfth century.[68] But there is evidence that at this time even the Governor-General could be denied the right.[69]

We cannot tell from biographical data the extent to which the Tea Market Agency used its appointment prerogatives to fill key posts with Sichuanese, since in most cases even where we have the names of staff members their native places have not been preserved.[70] But both the "law for the appointment and transfer of officials from distant places" and the statutory evidence from the

Post-Reform period, when the Agency came under closer scrutiny, suggest that at least below the level of the managing supervisors the men staffing the Agency were largely natives of Sichuan. In 1099, for example, relatives of all tea-market inspectors, co-inspectors, stock controllers, weighers, and warehouse men under the Tea Market Agency, as well as the equivalent officials in the region's official salt markets, were prohibited from opening tea (or salt) stores, from accepting a tax or sales franchise, or from doing business with the official markets—tacit evidence that these staff members were Sichuanese.[71] In 1113 tea-transport relay-station inspectors *(xunxia bancha shichen)* were allowed, at the completion of their terms, to "indicate their preference for an appointment close to home," a provision of the "distant offices" law specifically applicable to Sichuan.[72] An imperial edict of 1115 accused the Agency of appointing only Sichuanese to its offices, and prohibited any further selection of natives.[73] This reversal appears to have been only momentary, however. Otherwise the only restraint seems to have been that in the case of dual appointments—for example, one market with two inspectors, or with a chief and an assistant inspector—only one of the appointees could be a native.[74] Moreover, even after 1142, when the Intendants were all non-Sichuanese, we can expect the Agency staff to have remained primarily native. For during the Southern Song the tea and horse enterprise was superimposed over select prefectural and county governments, and all evidence indicates that Sichuanese local government during the Southern Song was native-run.[75]

AGENCY INFLUENCE OVER COUNTY MAGISTRATES

Organizations face the most unpredictable contingencies not from their own members, whose goals and values will at least minimally accord with those of their organizational patron, but from the functionaries of other organizations on whom they must rely for critical goods or services. These outside functionaries, motivated by a separate set of tasks and goals, represent a crucial element of the task environment; and to the degree that a given organization can obtain power over these elements of the task environment, either through competitive or cooperative strategies, it can reduce the uncertainties it must confront.[76] The most crucial outside participants in the Agency's domain were the magistrates of those counties that produced tea or through which tea was transported north. (During the Southern Song, by which time the Agency in its later guise as the THA was directly responsible for horse procurement, the vice-prefects of prefectures containing horse markets also became objects of Agency concern.) The founding Intendants gained significant influence over these extra-Agency participants through a combination of selection, impeachment, and incentive rights that forced local government officials to take heed of Agency power and concerns. Although it was the post–New Policies Intendancy that enjoyed rights to the greatest number of county magistrates, the precedents were established by the New Policies Intendants.

Appointment rights were requested for a total of fifteen counties from the Yuanfeng period on. The targeted counties were all either major producers of convoy tea (Mingshan, Yongkang, and Qingcheng in Sichuan and Xixiang in the Hanzhong Basin) or centers for its distribution. Early in the tea and horse exchange, district magistrates in all tea-purchase and resale counties were given nominal supervisory authority over the tea markets, but probably only in the case of the markets for the bulk purchase of convoy tea did this entail concrete responsibility for such operations as grading, smuggling control, and labor recruitment.[77] Similarly it was the responsibility of the magistrates in each of the districts traversed by the convoys to register and recruit porters (*jiaohu*) and their guarantors (*jiatou*); and of the district militia inspector (*xunjian*), sheriff (*wei*), and military servitors (*shichen*) to expedite some 4,000–5,000 catties of tea through their borders each year.[78]

In the case both of counties that produced convoy tea and counties through which it was transported, therefore, the Intendants could legitimately argue that the success of the tea and horse enterprise depended on placing the right men as magistrates. The argument took on special force in the case of the tea-transport counties along the upper reaches of the Jialing. For the main public task performed in these districts was the transport of tea; yet because they were small and out of the way, talented men were unwilling to serve in them. Therefore, in order to attract and motivate capable individuals, successive Intendants requested that even where they did not appoint these officials, they at least be allowed to provide a liberal incentive schedule tied to the volume of tea transported.[79]

Li Ji was the first Intendant to request selection rights for the producing and transporting districts. Again capitalizing on his extraordinary mandate to hire and fire, Li was given shared rights to select (*xuanchai*) the magistrates of Mingshan and Yongkang production counties and the Miengu and Shunqing transport counties in conjunction with the fiscal intendant.[80] But following the personnel recentralization of 1081, only the prerogative of impeachment was retained.[81] The Mingshan County magistrate continued to receive career incentives for the purchase of 1,000,000 catties of tea—a feature later adopted by the twelfth-century southeastern tea monopoly—but the Yuanfeng Intendants had no further control over the appointment of district magistrates.[82]

Ultimately, however, the purchase and transport of tea came to be viewed as one of the routine functions of local government in Sichuan, and the Tea and Horse Agency as an integral component of regional administration. In 1089, in the midst of the Restoration era, THA Intendant Yan Ling requested permanent appointment rights (*zouju*) for three key counties (Mingshan, Yizheng, and Zhaohua) and one-time rights for three others. Despite the hostility of Restoration leaders to THA empire-building and their suspension of the Eight-Circuit appointment laws, Yan was granted the three permanent counties.[83] Mingshan at least was retained throughout the Northern Song, and in 1112 Zhang Hui added the Hanzhong Basin county of Xixiang.[84] The following year, with 5,900,000 catties of Agency tea backlogged in the Zhaohua and Changju warehouses, Zhang requested that seven transport-county magistrates be covered by promotional incentives keyed to the successful movement of 4,000,000 catties of tea. Although the rewards were less generous than he asked for, they expressed the court's recognition that transporting tea had become a central task of local government.[85] In 1121 the court went even further, granting THA Intendant He Jian the right to select the appropriate magistrates of three production and seven transport counties in conjunction with the fiscal intendants in accordance with "the Yuanfeng precedent."[86]

In the decade between the fall of the Northern Song and the reestablishment of the THA in 1137, all the Agency's selection privileges reverted to the regional fiscal intendants. But in 1143 THA Intendant Jia Sicheng charged that the fiscal intendants based their appointments solely on a man's rank and hiring priority (*mingci gaoxia*); their disregard for functional competence, he argued, had jeopardized the tea and horse operation. Jia merely requested that the fiscal intendant be ordered to choose men for the THA staff positions, market inspectors, and magistrates of Xixiang, Changju, and Shuncheng counties more judiciously. Surprisingly the Personnel Ministry transferred all these appointments to the THA.[87] Then in 1168 two Jiezhou districts not previously covered by tea-transport incentives were brought into the system on the same basis negotiated by Zhang Hui in 1113. This gave the Southern Song THA, in other ways considerably less powerful than its Northern Song predecessor, appointment rights to three districts and incentive powers over another three, including Mingshan.[88]

To opponents of the tea monopoly and of statist experiments in general, Agency influence over county and prefectural officials seemed like nothing more than a pernicious method of undercutting local government's role as the guardian of the people, by turning local government officials into agents of state profiteering.[89] But from the perspective of the central government, as Sichuan and the tea and horse trade became inextricably associated in the decades following the creation of the THA, Agency tasks became an increasingly legitimate responsibility of the local government, and Agency control an increasingly legitimate exercise of organizational power.

BOUNDARY SPANNING AND AGENCY CONTROL OF SUBSIDIARY MARKETS

The Agency's right to select its own men and offer incentives to them and to officials in other organizations meant that the Intendants had secure control over all the functionaries needed to carry out the Agency's mandate of supplying tea and generating revenues. Beyond control, they gained the men's loyalty and enthusiasm by directly tying promotions and bonuses to good service, which caused subordinates and outsiders to identify their own interests with those of the Agency. The Agency's entrepreneurial experiment was not limited to its original mandate, moreover, but expanded across economic sectors into key subsidiary markets. During the New Policies years especially, the TMA Intendants encountered a rich opportunity for this economic boundary spanning through the Intendancy's early displacement of the State Trade Agency from a position of influence in Sichuan, which left an administrative vacuum surrounding the accepted reform objective of intervening in local commodity markets. The two most striking examples of the TMA's entrepreneurial expansion into subsidiary industries were its involvement in the Jiezhou salt trade and the establishment of the Chengdu Metropolitan Tea Bureau. Both activities illustrate the ways in which the tea monopoly drove an opening wedge for the state beyond the traditional limits of the Sichuan textile industry into the wider commercial economy, including salt and wine.

THE JIEZHOU SALT TRADE. Prior to the reform era, regulations on the Sichuan salt trade approximated those for tea. In general, the region's salt could be traded freely across the four circuit boundaries but could not be exported.[90] Production was divided between the large state-managed salt pits located in six or seven industrial centers (*jian*) in Chengdu, Zizhou, and Kuizhou Circuits, and the small but increasingly numerous "lofty-pipe wells" (*zhuotongjing*) scattered throughout all four circuits. These lofty-pipe wells constituted an eleventh-century technological advance that enabled wealthy households to bore and reap the returns from as many as ten to twenty wells.[91] Well-owners paid a tax based on assessed value; but the wells were extremely difficult to regulate, and smuggling was endemic.

Each of the four circuits produced salt, and early in the dynasty each was expected to be self-sufficient. But salt and population were unequally distributed throughout the region: Chengdu Circuit, with 41 percent of the population but only about 27 percent of the salt (out of a late-tenth century total of 15,500,000 catties), and Lizhou Circuit, with 22 percent of the population and only 3.9 percent of the salt, had chronic shortages; while Zizhou Circuit (24 percent of the population and 46 percent of the salt) and Kuizhou Circuit (12 percent and 23 percent respectively) enjoyed continual surpluses.[92] When salt shortages became apparent in the late tenth century, the state used tax exemptions to encourage merchants to transport the mineral in from elsewhere; and gradually Daningjian in eastern Sichuan and Jiezhou in modern Shanxi became the most prominent suppliers. In addition, an increasing part of the deficit was filled by the new lofty-pipe wells from the 1040s on.[93]

During the Qingli reform of the 1040s, policy makers began to perceive western Sichuan's salt shortage as an opportunity to generate state revenues. At that time it was decreed that merchants bringing in Daning salt had first to make deposits of money or goods in Chengdu, but this import-licensing policy brought the trade to a standstill and had to be revoked. Nonetheless financial experts continued to be attracted to the flow of salt into western Sichuan; and in the next wave of reform, New Policies administrators zealously sought to generate more income for the state by plugging up the lofty-pipe wells, damming the flow of salt from the east, and appropriating the Jiezhou import trade.

In 1074 the State Trade Agency, not yet ousted from influence in Sichuan, made the first attempt to suppress private salt trade in the west by requesting that the lofty-pipe wells be banned and filled in order to make room for the state's sale of Jiezhou salt. Shen Gua dissuaded Emperor Shenzong from the measure by arguing that despite its hypothetical advantages, the cost of enforcement would be unacceptably high. But officials hungry for revenues still longed to replace local private well-salt with state-owned shipments from Jiezhou.[94] In 1076 Liu Zuo was captivated by the great profits merchants made trading Jiezhou salt for Sichuanese tea. He proposed that the government commandeer the trade by exchanging about 7,600 tons of Jiezhou salt for what amounted to 3,900 tons of tea, that is, about one-seventh of Jiezhou's salt production for one-quarter of Sichuan's tea.[95] Liu recommended that private commercial trade be completely prohibited and predicted that revenues from the exchange would save the government 2,000,000 strings in capital expenditures, at least part of which would have gone to purchase tea. In approval of his plan, the court named Liu to replace the retiring Li Qi as TMA Intendant. That same year (1076) the Fiscal Supervisor for Chengdu Circuit obtained the long-sought order to fill in the lofty-pipe wells, in order to facilitate the sale at inflated prices of government salt from the Pujiang, Lingjing, and Daning works.[96] At the same time, salt from eastern Sichuan was barred from private import into the west. The degree of cooperation between the TMA and the Chengdu financial administration is unclear, but the effect of their joint assault on the private salt trade was to substitute high-priced government and imported salt for all the cheap local sources.

The salt restrictions joined tea as the two issues that most catalyzed the Sichuanese anti-reform faction against the TMA. Just three months after Liu Zuo's proposal was approved, Wen Tong, who in 1072 had supported government regulation of the Lingjing salt wells, now argued that in Yangzhou the government salt monopoly was unable to meet consumer demand.[97] Then towards the end of 1076 Zhou Yin charged that the joint ban on lofty-pipe wells and private salt from eastern Sichuan had forced a thousand salt households out of work and driven the price of salt in Chengdu from 70 to 250 cash per catty.[98] Opponents of the salt restrictions were aided by a periodic collapse of the Jiezhou salt-voucher system in Shaanxi, which obliged the court to suspend TMA salt sales and cashier Intendant Liu.[99] Shortly thereafter, however, Li Ji neutralized the Sichuanese opposition; and by 1078 he and Pu Zongmin had regained the right to import 760 tons of salt from Jiezhou to serve as "tea capital" (*chaben*), without, however, prohibiting private trade.[100] TMA salt continued to compete with private salt in western Sichuan, sold at putatively market prices by TMA officials or by tax-bureau officials on the TMA's behalf. By 1083, when the import volume was up to 988 tons, salt came under all the same regulations for smuggling, profit quotas, bonuses, transportation, and local responsibility as tea.[101] Although no figures on the actual contribution of Jiezhou salt to the Intendancy's total income have been preserved, we know that Lu Shimin expected the Agency to make a net profit of 25 percent on its salt sales.[102] The Jiezhou trade not only swelled Agency profits, it also enabled the TMA to make more efficient use of its tea relay-station network, since the salt could be carried back over the Qinling Shan roads in the same carts that were used to transport tea northward (see Chapter Seven).[103]

LOCAL COMMODITIES AND THE CHENGDU METROPOLITAN TEA MARKET. From very early on the TMA Intendants showed an almost obsessive concern (shared by their masters) for generating revenues. This obsession was most dramatically expressed in notices sent to market officials exhorting them to

> Expedite Rapid Purchases and Sales,
> Prevent the Stagnation of Capital.[104]

In a policy-making environment that encouraged official involvement in local commerce, it was natural for the TMA to reinvest its enormous reserves of cash and countertrade goods in local handicrafts and commodities, replicating in Sichuan the functions of the State Trade Agency in other commercial centers of the empire.

The TMA slipped into the local commodities trade in 1075, when the court granted the Agency permission to buy for resale an annual quota of 100,000 strings' worth of cloth to help meet tea-transport expenses.[105] Lü Tao charged that the Agency sold the cloth to swell its profit statements; but even if true, the court was unlikely to have been concerned. Soon the TMA had added salt from the government works in Daning and earthenware implements to its sales of tea and Jiezhou salt.[106]

Lu Shimin provided a separate administrative apparatus for the commodities trade in mid 1083, as part of his multifaceted campaign of territorial and jurisdictional expansion In his memorial of the fourth month of 1083 Lu requested permission to set up a Metropolitan Tea Barter and Sales Market (*bomaicha duchang*), giving the same rationale that had been used to justify opening the Metropolitan State Trade Bureau in Kaifeng eleven years earlier: the eradication of private monopolistic speculation. Lu argued that

> [b]ecause Chengdu is at the conjunction of riverine and dry-land routes there are numerous tea merchants. They are often troubled by the stagnation of commercial goods, which are inevitably bought up cheaply by lodge-cum-storehouse owners (*juting zhijia*). I request that a metropolitan tea trade and sales market be established in Chengdu, with permission to increase the price [of tea] as appropriate and sell it, and to barter and trade for a wide variety of commodities that will all be liquidated for cash (*bianzhuan*). The additional profits will all be dealt with in the same manner as [the profits from] consumer-tea sales in Sichuan and the barter-exchange trade in Shaanxi.[107]

It was in fact the generation of a steady cash flow that was the most important function of the Metropolitan Market and its prefectural and county offshoots, as was made clear in the seventeenth of Lu's thirty-eight articles:

> All government markets that have traded tea and salt for silver, textiles, grains, and assorted goods must liquidate them into cash within half a year. Ten percent of the net profits will be given to the chief official and clerks as a bonus . . . But if after half a year the goods have not been turned into cash, no bonus will be given.[108]

The motivational effect of tying the incentive schedules directly to net profits was electric. Local tea-market officials were given license to go out into the countryside and corner the local markets. According to Lü Tao and Su Che, market inspectors were permitted to go outside the market area to "summon and entice" buyers and sellers, and to send brokers into the hinterland districts to "tie up and obstruct" commercial goods. The list of commodities dealt in by the Metropolitan and prefectural markets catalogues the most important commercial goods of western Sichuan: Among the textiles were raw silk thread, silk wadding, pongee, plain tabby, gauze, open tabby, and figured damask, as well as quilting and hempen cloth. There was also another of western Sichuan's famous products, fine paper, and gold and silver, skins and medicinals, and aromatics, probably from as close as the western mountains and as distant as Khotan in the case of frankincense, as well as rice and legumes from the local markets. The silks in particular angered Lü and Su, for they charged that market inspectors and brokers conspired to use government funds to buy and export fancy and plain silks up to Shaanxi, thereby cutting into one of the few long-distance trades still allowed to Sichuanese merchants in Western Shaanxi.[109]

The Tea Market Agency used the funds and goods that it obtained from these local trades to expand into the credit market, paralleling another activity of the Kaifeng State Trade Bureau. The Agency's debtors were by no means limited to the garden households. Lü and Su, for example, describe the dunning of a Chengdu franchise manager of a wine-making and selling establishment *(maipu jiufangren)* for a pledge on 10,000 strings' worth of glutinous rice.[110] But manipulation of the terms of credit and repayment gave the tea markets a systematic lever for obtaining more tea cheaply. The mechanism for the bonded loans was laid out by Lu Shimin in his thirty-eight articles:

> All tea-producing prefectures and counties will make available cash and measures of grain each year in advance of the time of dearth [i.e., autumn], and will summon those tea-garden households who so desire to enter into a bond and borrow *(jiebao jieqing)*. Interest on each string of cash will be 20 percent. When the tea is harvested, [they] must give notice, and be ordered to take the tea to the government [markets] and repay the loan equivalent. If after summer they have not paid, a tax expeditor will be sent. If by fall the loan is still not fully repaid, then the [interest] will be adjusted accordingly.[111]

We do not know whether or how much interest had been required on the deposits merchants left for the following year's harvest in Pengzhou (see Chapter Two); the 20 percent required by the Tea Market Agency was standard for the State Trade Agency as well. Evidently brokers provided the bond, or guarantee, which was also a typical State Trade Agency practice. According to New Policies opponent Liu Zhi, the brokers oversaw repayment of the loan, no doubt at extra cost to the cultivator.[112]

Critics of the monopoly were unanimous in asserting that the Intendancy forced loans on the cultivator as a means of claiming extra tea. The almost indentical charges made by Lü and Su are combined below, with Su's comments given in italics:

> Every autumn when the rice crop has matured, the Tea Agency buys granary rice and, setting it at a high price, allots it to the tea households. This is called "tea capital" *(chaben)*. The Agency even makes advance allotments of rice to those who do not want it. If the rice costs [the government] 800 cash per *dan*, then the Agency allocates it at one string and still adds interest of 20 percent, making it a total of 1,200 cash. *Then in spring when the tea is out, the garden households pay with tea that has been pushed down to half price, with the total value further deflated by "heavy weighing."* This is called "Green Sprouts tea" *(qingmiaocha)*.[113]

There is little reason to doubt the charges made by Lü, Su, and Liu Zhi. Overall, the financial contribution of the Metropolitan Tea Barter and Sales Market and its associated businesses must have been substantial and may have constituted much of the "presentation" *(xian)* of 1,000,000 strings beyond the quota that Lu Shimin made to the throne in 1085.[114] The Metropolitan Market (but not the provision of credit) was abolished by Huang Lian in the eighth month of 1086, when he ordered that the Agency's involvement in local goods be cut back to its original scope in the tea-producing districts—a somewhat ambiguous decision.[115]

Because the tea trade with the non-Chinese tribes was inevitably based on barter and brought in a wide array of goods other than horses, barter and exchange markets *(boyisi)* were periodically set up and abolished in such frontier districts as Liizhou and the hinterland districts of Yazhou.[116] But these markets constituted a limited and necessary mechanism for controlling tea sales to the border tribes and did not represent an unusual projection of state power into the commercial economy as had the Yuanfeng Metropolitan Market. Similarly the Intendancy always retained great power over sources of credit to the tea cultivator, but the New Policies era was probably the only time that it systematically manipulated local credit as a major source of revenues.

The Southern Song Tea and Horse Agency did control one collateral industry that had been untouched by the Yuanfeng Intendancy: the manufacture and sale of brocades. But this did not so much reflect profit-oriented activism as it did the imperatives of a horse-market system pushed south into the tea-producing regions. The Man and Tibetan tribes who sold horses in southern Sichuan had a limited interest in tea, and the government was unwilling to part with excessive amounts of silver. But brocade and other silks were acceptable to both sides. As the Yuan scholar Fei Zhu wrote in his "Treatise on Shu Brocades," "In 1129 the Tea and Horse Agency began to weave and manufacture brocade, damask, and bedding to pay for horses in Liizhou and other places . . . From this point on, prohibitions against private trade arose . . . and the weaving and ornamental art of the Middle Kingdom clothed and covered the people with mallet-braided hair and the tongues of shrikes."[117]

Originally the Intendancy ran three factories in the vicinity of Chengdu; but in order to increase surveillance over private weaving and trade, these were supplanted by a new Brocade Factory in 1168. The silk-loom households were compelled to live on the premises of this state-operated factory and to produce specified qualities of goods, although the overall volume of production varied from year to year according to the number of horses brought to market.[118] The Intendancy prohibited its weavers not only from trading privately, but also from weaving for other government agencies.[119]

Unlike the Tea Market Agency, its predecessor, the Southern Song Tea and Horse Agency was prohibited from trading its stocks of silk to produce revenues. As the value of tea declined in relation to horses, silk became increasingly central to the horse exchange. Any diversion of silk away from the trade affected the government's ability to attract horses to market, and was regarded by the court as reckless speculation.[120] At the same time, the Southern Song government imposed a strict functional division of authority over most circuit agencies in order to foster a recentralization of power, which confined the Agency to activities directly concerned with tea and horse procurement. As we will see in Chapter Six, the combination of bureaucratic recentralization, the devaluation of tea, and a much more limited supply of horses provided the Southern Song

THA Intendants with little opportunity for expanding their regulatory authority into wider economic spheres.

The Tea Market Agency's empire-building did not end with geographic expansion, personnel autonomy, or acquisition of new markets and commodities. Agency chiefs still had to breathe life into the system by motivating their subordinates towards the same entrepreneurial goals as their own. The incentive system devised by the TMA Intendants served to animate the organization they controlled by turning general policy goals originating from the top into specific and quantifiable objectives linked to predictable and desirable rewards for every participant in the system. Rewards brought the apparatus to life and translated the public interest of the state in taxing Sichuan into the private interests of the natives who were the agents of that taxation.

In the literature on personnel control during the late imperial era, the emphasis is placed on the use of negative sanctions to restrain bureaucratic offenses. C. K. Yang suggests that administrative law itself stressed the inhibition of official wrongdoing over the positive inducement of desired action, and Thomas Metzger devoted an entire monograph to delineating how the administrative punishment of civil officials served as a cornerstone of Qing personnel management.[121] The Song state also employed negative sanctions, and *shangfa*—rewards and punishments—were the opposite poles of every control system. But in its financial agencies, and above all in the TMA, the overriding emphasis was on the positive inducement of dynamic performance. This choice of the carrot over the stick probably does not reflect any great change in views of the nature of man between Song and Qing times, but rather a different notion of the role of the state and hence a different set of expectations for the state's functionaries. As Metzger points out, Qing policy-makers generally sought to establish and reaffirm a fixed order that limited the executive process and that favored "realistic" adjustment over "radical reform" in solving major problems. In this relatively quietist view of the state, the restraint of official misdeeds would naturally outweigh the encouragement of adventurous decision-making.[122] But during the Song, and particularly during the New Policies, the state was seen as an active agent of large-scale change; and this role required that the agents of the state themselves be mobilized into action.

Song administrators and philosophers viewed bureaucratic man as an actor motivated by self-interest. Therefore, successful mobilization of personnel entailed allying that self-interest with the interest of the state. Wang Anshi, in calling for higher salaries for officials and clerks, wrote that the vast majority of people will act in a petty (and thus selfish) manner when poor and in a noble (and thus public-spirited) manner when prosperous. This was recognized by the Former Kings, who guided the desires and abilities of the mediocre majority into serving posterity and the social good. Wang conceded that men wish to do good, but no less do they want to possess a good reputation, honorable rank, and handsome material benefits; it was these desires that the Former Kings manipulated in order to spur on their *shi* officials.[123]

The basic method used by the Song to exploit the desires and ambitions of its officials and employees, especially at the lower level, was a predictable system of career and material incentives. The establishment of an appropriate reward schedule was seen as the key to eliciting official cooperation. In 1078, for example, Li Ji called for the creation of a schedule linking rewards (*choushang gefa*) to yearly returns, "in order to cause one and all to pursue achievement, so that the affairs of office can be managed effortlessly."[124] In 1113 Intendant Zhang Hui asserted that the main cause of a 5,900,000-catty backlog of tea was that the ten key county magistrates and warehouse inspectors involved in tea transport "have exclusive responsibility [for the affairs of the THA], but not the rewards."[125] And in 1168 THA Intendant Zhang Song, the Minister of War, and the Minister of Personnel all agreed that without an effective system of rewards the Min and Jiezhou Vice-Prefects could not be expected to attend to horse administration; nor could regular civil officials be induced to serve as inspectors in the Minzhou tea market.[126] The formula, "no incentives, no work," was fully accepted in the financial bureaucracies of the Song.

Administrators also had concrete evidence that when faced with choices, officials structured their performance to maximize their rewards. In their condemnation of the tea monopoly in 1086, Lü Tao and Su Che claimed that the tax returns on tea sales and transit, which should have gone to the circuit fiscal intendants, were instead registered as profits to the tea monopoly because of an incentive system that distributed 5 percent of net profits above quota back to the administering officials and service personnel.[127] In 1101 the incentive system placed different operating units of the tea and horse enterprise in contention. THA Intendant Cheng Zhishao reported that the market inspectors, service personnel, and administering superiors from local governments (probably the county magistrates) of Mingshan and two other counties in Yazhou were specifically rewarded for buying and shipping tea to the Shaanxi markets, with the reward schedule activated when 80 percent of the convoy tea had been dispatched. Since there were no bonuses for sending tea south to the Liizhou horse market, the Yazhou tea-market officials first filled the statutory and then the supplemental orders for Shaanxi before sending any tea to Liizhou. In an effort to force market compliance, Cheng barred allocation of any of the Yazhou bonuses until 80 percent of the Liizhou convoy-tea quota was met.[128]

Because of the obvious power of the incentive system to channel the efforts of Agency personnel, it was essential that performance-minded Intendants, whose own power depended on their ability to deliver essential outputs, index the reward schedules to an appropriate measure. The Intendant of 1111, for example, found it necessary to rule that even when the tea-monopoly markets in Sichuan showed increases over the quota *in terms of cash profits,* no rewards would be given unless *the volume of tea bought and sold* also reached its quota. It is probable that inflation had devalued the monetary returns to tea, putting functionaries in higher reward brackets than their actual performance warranted.[129] And Zhao Kai, when he took over management of the tea and horse trade in 1128, changed the basis of horse-purchase rewards from the number of animals purchased—an index that encouraged market officials to buy large quantities of useless nags that died on the road—to the number of animals to reach the capital. [130]

But the most telling example of the attention devoted to designing a productive incentive system is provided by Lu Shimin, the master of bureaucratic politics. In late 1083 various agencies in the southeastern circuits began to re-impose tea monopolies on a selective basis, borrowing for their incentive index the system of "gross-profit quotas" (the "market-and-bureau tax-levy system," *keli changwufa*) used by the salt monopolies. In this system an official could be penalized even if he showed a profit, if the total of net profit and investment came to less than the quota. The officials responsible for promoting this method tried to have it imposed on the Sichuan tea monopoly as well. But Lu Shimin responded that the Tea Market Agency used a "net-profit quota" (*yi jingli wei e*) to determine its incentives, which encouraged maximizing the returns on a small investment (not least by squeezing cultivators and consumers). Lu's charge that foisting the gross-profit quota on the Agency would undermine its productivity was sufficiently compelling for the court to fine the presumptuous officials 6 to 8 catties of copper each. [131]

Rewards could be manipulated to serve a variety of purposes beyond the obvious one of motivating individual effort. One of the most important of these was to link clusters of performers into collective action units. Vertical integration within the Agency was achieved, for example, by grouping Intendants, middle-level managers (managing supervisors and secretaries), and clerical staff together for periodic rewards based on the performance of the Agency as a whole. [132] Vertical linkage between the Agency and its non-official employees was fostered by common schedules and shared rewards for market inspectors and service personnel, and shared penalties for these two groups and the managing supervisors. [133]

Horizontal integration between Agency and non-Agency personnel was promoted by authorizing local government officials to serve as co-supervisors of the TMA's purchase and sales markets. One official, most often the county magistrate, vice-prefect, or director of surveillance, was responsible for tallying the returns to ensure that the quota was met, a legitimizing function for which he received a reward half as great as the market inspector's.[134] Critics charged that this subverted the functions of inter-bureaucratic surveillance and popular advocacy that were central to the jobs of the vice-administrator and county magistrate, which was no doubt in part its intent.[135]

The incentive system could also be used to extend the reach of the Intendancy beyond the range of its own personnel by rewarding other bureaucrats or civilians to act on its behalf. The most important example of the first case is the extension of promotional rewards to the magistrates and warehouse inspectors involved in tea transport. The most prominent extension of rewards to the civilian populace was the use of cash bounties to incite popular denunciation and seizure of smugglers. (See Chapter Six.)

Three categories of incentives were employed by or for the Tea and Horse Agency itself: normative, career, and material. Kracke has written that because of the liberality with which such normative rewards as dignities, prestige titles, decorations, and the right to wear certain restricted colors were handed out, by the second half of the eleventh century they had ceased to confer real prestige.[136] Normative awards did not play a prominent role in the Tea and Horse Agency, although one author has left an image of an Agency official and a tea broker in the 1090s swaggering through the streets of Chengdu in finery above their station, obtained by augmenting the tea returns.[137] Posthumous awards may also be regarded as normative, although they were manifested in concrete ways: In 1080 Li Qi's son was given office in commemoration of his father's achievements, and in 1083 Li Ji was posthumously granted about 139 acres (10 *qing*) of government land.[138]

The largest category of incentives involved different ways of hastening or retarding a man's career. Of these the most prominent were promotions in stipendiary office (*zhuanguan*), promotion from the executory to administrative division (*gaiguan*), reductions or

extensions in the number of years before the promotional case review *(mokan)*, and the conferral of degrees of seniority within the
executory division *(xunzi)*. [139]

Promotion in stipendiary office *(jiluguan)* was reserved for the
administrative class, and propelled them up the hierarchy of twenty-
nine grades *(guanpin)* that determined their basic salary scale. [140]
Each grade promotion (for example, from *chengwulang* 9B to *chengfenglang* 9A) conferred an average raise of 4 strings monthly over a
salary range of 7 to 120 strings per month in the 1080s, and 3.3
strings over a range of 7 to 100 strings per month in the Southern
Song. [141] (Promotions in stipendiary office did not necessarily imply
a change in functional office, or commission—*chaiqian*.) Because
the Agency was staffed primarily by executory-level officials, the
main recipients of office promotions were the Intendants themselves, prefects and vice-prefects for horse purchasing, and the minority of managing supervisors and secretaries in the administrative
division. The court generally granted promotions in three categories: First, persons like Pu Zongmin, who rose successively from 8B
to 6B, could be recognized for individual merit. [142] Second, the
Intendants and all eligible subordinates might be promoted for the
achievement of the Agency as a whole. [143] Third, at the request of
the Intendant, a class of officials like the managing supervisors could
be singled out for promotion. [144]

The relatively higher status and greater task complexity of the
administrative-class positions appears to have militated against the
widespread use of simple quantified formulas for dispensing grade
promotions. But there were some exceptions, including horse-market officials who bought 3,000 head during the Post-Reform period;[145] horse-convoy masters *(guanya shichen)* who safely delivered
to the Southern Song capital a specified percentage of the fifty-head
convoy;[146] and Mingshan tea-market inspectors whose purchases of
convoy tea, probably 1,000,000 catties, put them into the highest
reward category. In this last case, a Yuanfeng incentive that remained in effect through the twelfth century with only little mod-
ification, the Mingshan County magistrate would also have his promotional case review pushed forward three years. [147]

This same Yuanfeng incentive schedule for the Mingshan market also specified that if the first-class inspector were in the upper four of the seven executory grades, collectively designated as the prefectural and district civil aides' offices *(muzhiguan),* then he would be promoted directly into the administrative division.[148] This is an example of the *gaiguan* promotion from junior to senior status, the most important promotion in an official's career.[149] As with many formal organizations, this critical passage presented policy-makers with some difficult dilemmas. Between the mid eleventh and early thirteenth centuries the ratio of executory to administrative officials varied between above 2:1 and 5:1, representing an average range of about 12,000 executory-class to 3,600 administrative-class functionaries.[150] As was typical of the late imperial era, the Song bureaucracy contained far fewer posts than it did qualified officials. Therefore in every era, the desire to promote especially talented or otherwise useful individuals faster by providing alternatives to the long climb up and out of the executory class had to be balanced against the need to restrict passage into the administrative division, where the number of appropriate positions was especially limited.[151]

A variety of ways existed for hastening a man's promotion to the administrative class, but none was more direct than automatic promotion for satisfying quantified performance criteria. As far as I have seen, the Agency employed the automatic mechanism only in the case of the Mingshan tea-market inspector. But the Intendants could also recommend a varying number of men for promotion to the administrative division. In 1083 Lu Shimin got the Agency's quota for the number of such recommendations it could make annually raised from nine to twelve.[152] Although this was less direct than automatic promotion, it could still leap-frog a man over most of the executory grades. In 1105, for example, Supervisor Zhang Cha was promoted from the seventh and bottom grade of the executory division *(jiangshilang)* to grade 8B in the administrative division *(xuandelang)* for his "first class" contribution to tea transport.[153] Similarly long jumps were apparently standard in the case of the Mingshan market inspector as well, although they were not legally sanctioned.[154]

A second way of translating satisfactory performance into career progress was to reduce the amount of time required before a man's promotional, or *mokan*, review. The *mokan* review applied to both progress within the administrative class and the *gaiguan* promotion into it, but it was especially important in the latter case.[155]

In the absence of such expediting factors as sponsorship (*ju, zoujian*) or "reward and commendation" (*choujiang*), a formally qualified, degree-holding official (*you chushen*) at the seventh grade of the executory division (defined by the posts of local-government supervisor, inspector, registrar, and sheriff) would have to serve for seven annual merit ratings (*kao*) before coming up for his *gaiguan* promotional review. Since the merit ratings did not begin until a man had been in office a year, and also because consecutive office-holding at the lower levels was fairly rare, at the mandated rate it would take at least eight years before the *mokan* review.[156] But the waiting time could be reduced or extended in recognition of a man's performance, providing a valuable way of motivating individuals whose major hope for mobility lay in the civil service.

Both in the Tea and Horse Agency and in other financial bureaucracies, manipulation of the *mokan* waiting period was typically indexed to quantifiable performance criteria. In 1078 Li Ji established a five-class bonus schedule for convoy-tea market inspectors, keyed to purchases of 500,000 to 4,000,000 catties of tea, that provided *mokan* reductions.[157] A similar schedule based on net profits was set up for consumer-tea (*shicha*) markets in Sichuan and Shaanxi, with a return of 20,000 strings earning a one-year reduction for the market inspector.[158] So liberally were *mokan* reductions given out under the Yuanfeng Intendants that the staunch Restorationist Liu Zhi complained, no doubt with some exaggeration, that in one term a man could amass reductions of thirty years.[159]

The specific schedules for tea-market inspectors in subsequent periods have not been preserved, but the principle remained the same.[160] Managing supervisors and secretaries could also have their review pushed up. In the five notices of promotions and rewards preserved for 1105 to 1123, for instance, four levels of achievement worth *mokan* reductions of three to one years were specified: "premier," first, second, and third class.[161] And horse-purchase officials were similarly rewarded and penalized: A horse-purchase managing supervisor would have his review advanced two years for reaching the quota at the end of his term and extended two years for falling below 80 percent of quota.[162] At the same time the convoy masters could have *mokan* reductions added to their grade promotions (e.g., a promotion of one grade plus *mokan* reduction of four years for the arrival of forty-nine out of fifty horses), allowing the government to set a precise marginal value for each horse.[163]

A third career incentive often used to mobilize the efforts of executory-level personnel was the conferral of ranks of seniority that could otherwise be acquired only by completing terms of office in successive lower offices. To take the seventh executory grade again as an example, a formally qualified entrant without sponsors would have to serve through two terms *(ren)* of three years each, passing four merit ratings, before he could be promoted to the first of two positions in the fifth executory grade as a prefectural or county "executive inspector" *(lushi canjun)*. Other types of entrants, for example "formally qualified transfers from the clerical services" *(liuwai chushen)* and men "lacking formal qualifications" *(wu chushen)*, would have to serve even longer.[164] Each completed term constituted one seniority grade; and by accumulating seniority, an official could skip various rungs in the otherwise tedious climb up the executory ladder.[165] But seniority grades could also be conferred (or retracted) in recognition of an official's performance, making him eligible for promotions beyond his actual number of years in office.

The THA conferred seniority grades on both its regular and clerical personnel. In 1105, for example, three men in the first-class bonus category were given two seniority grades *(xun liangzi)*, while one in the second class was given one seniority grade and allowed to indicate his preference for a new commission *(zhanshe chaiqian yici)*.[166] And in 1116 all supervisory personnel in the "premier" bonus category were promoted in office if in the administrative class and given two seniority grades if in the executory class; those in the "first" bonus category were given a three-year *mokan* reduction or one seniority grade and a new commission respectively.[167]

Clerical staff in the superlative category were promoted one se-

niority grade in the 1105 rewards. But because clerical transfers to
the regular civil service had to serve through four terms and ten
merit ratings before becoming eligible for the next executory level,
even with an additional seniority grade worth three years they still
had to serve at least nine years before being promoted.[168] Therefore,
clerks who wished to do so could exchange their seniority promotion for twenty lengths of plain silk, the usual medium for rewarding clerical staff.[169] A similar choice was offered to the military
attachés and other functionaries that made up the official component of each horse-convoy crew: Each was promoted two seniority
grades for delivering the entire convoy, and one grade for one to
five losses; seniority-grade demotion began at fifteen deaths for each
fifty-horse convoy. Each grade promotion, however, could be commuted to 30 strings of cash.[170] As with the clerks, a realistic assessment of one's limited future in the civil service could make a
cash bonus more attractive than a minor career boost.

As the sociologist Amitai Etzioni has argued, the methods employed by an organization to control and motivate participants resemble the methods used to acquire those participants in the first
place.[171] Not surprisingly, then, material incentives in general and
cash rewards in particular were typically limited to those lower-level
subofficial and commoner participants whose relationship to the
Agency was purely utilitarian and who had little hope or interest in
pursuing an official career. In addition to the silks given to the
THA clerks and the cash made available to the hired convoy crews,
for example, wealthy commoners authorized to buy tea for the Agency
in its outlying markets were given cash bonuses for purchases beyond the quota,[172] and smuggling informants were given cash rewards based on the amount of tea recovered.

The major exception to this policy of rewarding lower participants with material bonuses and regular civil servants with career
incentives occurred in the New Policies' Yuanfeng Intendancy, when
profit-sharing plans were used to animate the entire hierarchy of
Agency personnel involved in buying and selling goods for the TMA.
By profit-sharing, I mean the setting aside of a specified percentage
of the net returns as a bonus for the functionaries responsible. Pu

Zongmin first suggested such a plan for market inspectors in 1082, as an alternative to the *mokan* reduction. Inspectors making less than the 20,000 strings' net profit needed for a one-year reduction or those who did not want the reduction would receive a cash bonus of 2 percent of their net earnings instead.[173] As executory or lower administrative-division officials, the market inspectors would have received base salaries of between 7 and 25 strings monthly, or 84 to 300 strings annually.[174] An inspector earning 20,000 strings net for the Agency would be eligible for a 400-string bonus; and thus by forgoing the one-year *mokan* reduction he could multiply his base salary for that year 1.3 to 4.7 times. Even lesser net profits could substantially increase his pay.

Pu Zongmin's plan was systematically expanded by Lu Shimin in his amendments to the Revised Regulations of the TMA of mid 1083. Lu set in motion a system of shared earnings that drove Agency and local government officials into fulfilling the major objective of the Yuanfeng Intendancy: making money.

In Shaanxi, where the Intendancy earned the bulk of its profits from the direct resale of tea to foreign traders and domestic consumers, Lu retained Pu Zongmin's schedule of one year's *mokan* reduction or 2 percent of the net profits for the market inspectors. No other functionaries were tied into the cash incentive system.[175]

In Sichuan and the Hanzhong Basin, political control of the region being taxed required a greater reinvestment of profits. Therefore, 5 percent of the net profits earned on the resale of tea to merchants and tea shops was distributed back to the market inspector and the service personnel: 2 percent went to the inspector, as in Shaanxi, and 3 percent was shared by the stock controller and assistant, the bookkeeper, and the scale and warehouse men.[176] The TMA's sales of Jiezhou salt came under the same provisions. In addition, the local government agent deputized to act as tea-market auditor, that is, the vice-prefect or the county magistrate, received a bonus one half that of the market inspector's, which would have been 1 percent of the net profit.[177] Furthermore the TMA used its profit from tea and salt to trade in a wide variety of local commodities, including grains, textiles, precious metals, and the herbal medicines for which Sichuan was famous. In order to ensure a fast cash turnover, market officials (not necessarily TMA subordinates) and service personnel were given six months to liquidate these goods for cash *(bianzhuan xianqian);* to ensure that no opportunity to realize a profit was lost, if (and only if) the half-year time limit was met, the supervisory official and service personnel were allowed to keep 4 percent and 6 percent of the net resale profit respectively.[178]

This incentive plan of sharing net profits is one of the most striking manifestations of bureaucratic entrepreneurship and resembled, in intent at least, the incentive systems employed in modern business firms. Consider, for example, these comments from a former head of the Bechtel Corporation:

> When I was part of a good well-administered bonus system the idea was that if you've got somebody who's really performing well, you load 'em up with money. You give it out. That's the way to make the system work. I think reward is more important than punishment.[179]

From their actions it would seem that Pu Zongmin and Lu Shimin shared the Bechtel Corporation's desire to make money and the belief that to do so, it was necessary to spend money; indeed that belief was adumbrated in Wang Anshi's claim, quoted in the Introduction to Part Two above, that "large expenditures will bring about increasing prosperity." Large the expenditures may have been. In his denunciation of the Sichuan tea monopoly Liu Zhi charged that in the course of a term officials might make thousands of strings of cash in bonuses. Similarly Lü Tao and Su Che portrayed the districts occupied by the TMA as transformed by the lure of bonus money into the bureaucratic equivalent of company towns.[180] How exaggerated Liu's claim might be is impossible to say. The Intendancy's net profit in 1084 was 1,600,000 strings of cash.[181] If we guess that 1,000,000 strings of this was earned in Shaanxi, then the Agency could have distributed around 56,000 strings of cash to its subordinates and associates that year.[182] In addition to the countless illegal opportunities for enrichment provided by the monopoly trade, the profit-sharing system clearly made the interests of the TMA and of its participants one and the same.

But profit-sharing also aggravated all the worst abuses of a government monopoly, including confiscatory purchases from the tea cultivators in Sichuan and forced sales to consumers in Shaanxi. The post-entrepreneurial phases of the tea and horse enterprise abandoned the cash-sharing plan. Indeed, in 1097 Lu Shimin himself explicitly prohibited the practice, writing that "tea-market [inspectors and] service personnel are all well paid: It is impermissible to divide up the net profits proportionally to be used as bonuses for officials and clerks."[183] Local officials, THA subordinates, and service personnel continued to be linked through reward systems based on a common set of criteria, but ranked categories replaced proportional division, and career incentives replaced cash bonuses for the regular civil servants. For the profit-sharing plan encouraged an unrestrained exploitation of producers and consumers that threatened political stability and channeled a flow of cash from the TMA to its network of Agency, commoner, and local-government functionaries that threatened to suborn the allegiance of officials and undermine the due process of government in Sichuan. No post–New Policies court was prepared to trade political power for revenues, nor to risk the potential for political disruption posed by the profit-sharing incentive policy.

In these last two chapters I have portrayed the structure of bureaucratic power in the context of bureaucratic entrepreneurship. The Intendancy for Tea and Horses arose out of a New Policies blueprint for military, political, and economic reform that delegated authority to bureaucratic entrepreneurs, who were given a mandate to experiment in the fulfillment of New Policies objectives. Building on the profits and political capital generated by their entrepreneurial leap—the creation of a tea monopsony in Sichuan and a tea monopoly in Shaanxi—the New Policies Intendants gained extraordinary authority to protect and expand their organization, and to staff it with men of their own choosing. The New Law for Eight Circuits provided a precedent for filling the Agency with Sichuanese, who served as representatives of the state in return for the right to hold office near their homes and the opportunity of using bureaucratic posts to augment family power. The first Intendants, in large part Sichuanese themselves, joined native incumbency to a broad set of appointment rights and an action-oriented incentive system to create an organization that projected state power deep into Sichuanese society, and that transformed the fiscal objectives of the state in taxing Sichuan into the material and career goals of a growing cadre of Sichuanese. Chapter Six will trace the evolution of the THA in the Post-Reform era, and assess the impact of bureaucratic entrepreneurship on the Sichuan tea industry.

SIX

The Impact of Bureaucratic Power on the Sichuan Tea Economy

In its entrepreneurial heyday the Tea Market Agency and its Intendants enjoyed extraordinary powers. Throughout the New Policies the TMA chiefs were granted a level of personnel autonomy, immunity from outside supervision, and freedom of entrepreneurial expansion that was quite possibly unique. Many cases can be adduced in which the court, besieged by crisis, granted extraordinary powers to key individuals on the spot. But in the case of the TMA these powers were conferred not in crisis but routinely, and not to an individual but to an organization. As the TMA generated ever greater revenues in the course of the New Policies, it acquired as an enterprise the charismatic powers that are normally associated with individuals.[1]

But if the power of the TMA was unique, it also flowed from a unique—and unpredictable—set of circumstances. The Agency could enjoy its prerogatives and sustain high productivity only as long as the court was willing to let it go its own way in fulfilling centrally defined goals and only as long as the geopolitical environment favored the expansion of state-sponsored markets to supply what the central government wanted most: new sources of revenues. But neither condition could be counted on to last forever, and both were

beyond the control of the Agency's chiefs: To reinvoke James
Thompson's model, they came from outside the immediate "task
environment." In the century and a quarter that we can trace the
history of the tea and horse trade following the New Policies, the
combined Tea and Horse Agency succumbed to changes in policy
and geopolitics that undermined its productivity and transformed
the Intendant from the charismatic and free-wheeling chief of a
growing enterprise to the tightly restricted manager of a deteriorating concern. On the tea side of the enterprise, quotas for tea volume
and sales revenues that were pushed higher and higher during the
New Policies era, when opportunities for expanding the market for
Sichuanese tea seemed limitless, hit a plateau in 1103, when the
southeastern tea monopoly began to compete with the Post-Reform
Intendancy for the consumers of Shaanxi, and then became absolutely unattainable after the Jurchen conquest of North China in
1127. The dwindling ability of the Agency to satisfy critical tasks
naturally eroded its claims to extraordinary powers; and in the second part of this chapter we will see how, as the Intendancy's entrepreneurial authority was trimmed, it came to resemble a typical
circuit agency. But dwindling output also shaped the impact of the
tea monopoly on the Sichuanese tea industry. In an effort to shore
up their power and perquisites, Intendants and functionaries were
forced to extract the revenues lost with the destruction of the Shaanxi
market out of the incomes of the tea cultivators. Entrepreneurship
gave way to expropriation; and as we will see in the third part of
this chapter, by the beginning of the thirteenth century the once-
prosperous tea industry was characterized by destitute tea households, abandoned or confiscated tea gardens, and mountains of rot-
ting, worthless tea. The power and profitability of the Agency's
empire began to unravel when it lost its tea markets first to bureaucratic competition, and then to the ravages of war.

REVERSING THE ENTREPRENEURIAL LEAP

Emperor Shenzong's death in March of 1085 brought back to power
a broad spectrum of officials momentarily united by their opposition
to the New Policies under the titular leadership of the regent, Em-

press Dowager Xuanren, and the elder statesman Sima Guang. The leaders of this conservative Restoration moved quickly to reverse and dismantle key facets of the reform policies, including the campaigns of military expansion, the *baojia* militia registration, and such interventionist economic policies as the "Green Sprouts" farming loans, Tribute and Distribution (*junshu*), and the State Trade Act.[2] As we saw in Chapter Four, the last year of the reform era had also seen increasingly vigorous attempts to re-monopolize the tea industries of the southeast, including for the first time Guangxi. Su Che and Liu Zhi, both members of the central government during the Restoration, made the reversal of this burgeoning state control over all of tea their special goal.[3]

But distance and self-containment isolated Sichuan from trends in the "interior," and the power of the Intendancy continued unabated even as the New Policies were being dismantled in the east.[4] As a result, Su Che lamented early in 1086, "the people of Shu weep blood":

> The court recently abolished State Trade and will no longer compete for profits with the merchants, allowing the four classes to obtain their livelihoods . . . But in the Circuits of Chengdu, Lizhou, Qinfeng, and Xihe the Tea Market Agency still oppresses the people. It uses the tea regulations like a shadowy and concealed State Trade Law to buy and sell the hundred goods, and prefectural and county investigating officials do not dare look and ask what is going on. The damage is not inconsiderable, yet up to now the Court has done nothing to prohibit it.[5]

The TMA Intendants, however, had dominated western Sichuan for close to a decade, long enough to weave a net of complicity and fear around the region's officials. Su Che charged that while investigating TMA salt and tea sales, the Chengdu Fiscal Intendant (Guo Kai) had disregarded abuses that were "as clear as black and white, and that all who have eyes and ears have known about."[6] After repeated importuning by Su and Liu, an outside investigator, Huang Lian, was sent to Chengdu by the Ministry of Finance;[7] at about the same time Pu Zongmin was prohibited from responding to charges made during the investigation, to encourage officials to testify without fear of recrimination.[8] But Superintendent Lu Shimin proved more difficult to dislodge: he was not demoted in rank and functional office until mid 1086, after Liu Zhi memorialized that he had blocked prefectural and district officials from giving evidence, and had engineered the removal of tea-monopoly records from the public files.[9]

But even with Pu Zongmin muzzled and Lu Shimin cashiered the Agency remained largely intact. Not even Su Che nor Lü Tao recommended that the court abandon horse procurement, and the lure of Sichuanese tea had brought the Song court its greatest bounty of horses yet.[10] The most conservative critics hoped for a return to free commerce (*tongshang*) in tea, and to the old "traders' caravan" (*quanma*) for the purchase of horses.[11] But the court instead redefined horse procurement and the tea monopoly as the appropriate task of a truly unified Tea and Horse Agency and in mid 1086 named Huang Lian to replace Lu Shimin as Superintendant.[12]

Huang was expected to root out a wide spectrum of fiscal abuses in Sichuan without sacrificing the self-financing nature of the tea and horse trade, and he consequently made very few changes in the structure of the operation. In Shaanxi, Huang offered a compromise to the free-traders, without, however, acknowledging that free trade was more efficient than state management: "If the monopoly system is abandoned, then the hundred goods will not flow freely; porterage and transportation will not be provided for; and not only will the products of the garden households become backlogged, but the very route by which wealth is born will be severed. If [as a consequence] trade in the Tibetan markets should also cease, this would damage our long-lasting policies."[13]

In order to establish a judicious balance between state and mercantile interests, Huang divided the Shaanxi market in half, reserving Western Shaanxi with its rich foreign trade for the THA and offering Eastern Shaanxi back to commercial sellers of Sichuanese tea. But he insisted that all of Shaanxi, east and west, remain a protected Sichuanese market, closed to southeastern tea. Huang founded his argument on the imperatives of national defense:

[The Sichuan tea-marketing region] occupies all the prefectures and counties of Shaanxi . . . as well as Jinzhou in Jingxi Circuit. Viewing the matter from the southeast, this may look suspiciously like an attempt to monopolize profits for Sichuan. But surveying it from the perspective of all under heaven, it is a question of vigorously promoting profits in Sichuan and Shaanxi for the sake of frontier preparedness, and not an attempt to cause injury to the southeast . . . [It is true that] the marketing of tea has been oppressive and extortionate, and there are still irregularities in the system of government sales. Now these old abuses must be eradicated. But at the same time we must prohibit southeastern tea from entering Shaanxi, so that Sichuanese tea does not go below a median price. In this way [not only will frontier defense be assured but] the people of Sichuan will not know the drawbacks of monopolization.[14]

Huang Lian's recommendations were adopted in full, leaving the Restoration Intendancy still holding proprietary rights to the entire northwest marketing region claimed in the New Policies' entrepreneurial leap. Consequently when Emperor Zhezong's majority brought many of the old reformers back to power in 1094, it was relatively simple for Lu Shimin, reappointed that year as Superintendant, to retract merchant privileges in Eastern Shaanxi and restore the THA sales operation.[15]

Nonetheless the THA's rights to the tea consumers of Shaanxi was built on an unstable foundation: free trade in southeastern tea. Though the Sichuan tea monopoly could finance frontier defense, a southeastern tea monopoly was potentially even more valuable to the court. For by selling licenses for the resale of southeastern tea in its Monopoly Bureau in Kaifeng, the court could generate revenues for its expenses in the capital as well as along the frontier. This had been the utility of the first monopoly, and efforts to re-monopolize southeastern tea in the mid 1080s had been arrested only by Emperor Shenzong's death. By the turn of the century pressure had again mounted for state control of southeastern tea; and in late 1102 Cai Jing, just beginning his quarter-century domination of Emperor Huizong's government, was finally able to act. In a memorial reviewing the history of eleventh-century tea policy, Cai Jing complained that after the monopoly was abolished in 1059, government tea revenues plummetted from over 5,000,000 strings of cash a year to just over 800,000 strings. He concluded that since its suspension "neither public nor private interests have been served, and the source of profit has lain dormant and withered."[16] The following year Cai established new Intendancies to administer the official purchase and resale of tea in the seven circuits of the southeastern tea region (modern Jiangsu, Zhejiang, Fujian, Anhui, Hubei, and Hunan provinces). Tea merchants could buy licenses to trade not only in the tea-producing prefectures but also in the capital, providing the central government with an immediate source of cash. The new monopoly returned about 2,500,000 strings annually to the government, split among the Ministry of Finance, the privy purse, and, according to the *Song History,* Cai Jing himself.[17]

The two state tea monopolies were now in competition; and because the southeastern monopoly was worth so much to the central government, Sichuan was soon forced to relinquish part of its lucrative northwestern market. In early 1103 all of North China was set aside for southeastern tea, including the circuits of Hedong and Jingxi that bordered the THA's Shaanxi domain.[18] Within half a year so much relatively cheaper (and probably better) southeastern tea had been smuggled into Eastern Shaanxi that even THA Intendant Cheng Zhishao, unable to suppress the illicit trade, recommended that all of Shaanxi east of the Liupan Mountains be transferred to the southeastern tea monopoly.[19] In 1104 Cheng's disinterested recommendation, unimaginable in the years of entrepreneurial expansion, was adopted in an edict proclaiming that henceforth "Sichuanese tea must not be transported for sale in the Shaanxi Southeastern Tea Zone."[20]

The THA lost twenty-two prefectures and commanderies to the southeastern monopoly, making Sichuan's marketing region smaller than it had been in 1076.[21] The reduction, which represented a loss of about 34 percent of Sichuan's total domestic consumers and 81 percent of its Shaanxi buyers, quickly spawned troublesome tea surpluses.[22] By 1111, according to Intendant Zhang Hui, the THA was holding over 7,500,000 catties of "consumer tea," tying up an investment of over 4,000,000 strings of cash.[23] Zhang blamed the problem on the loss of Eastern Shaanxi, and offered to buy back rights to the region with a yearly payment equal to the value of the central government's profits and taxes from the sale of "southern tea" and "water-milled saddle-bag tea" in the four eastern subcircuits. The Ministry of Finance initially agreed to this leasing of market rights and arranged that the THA should pay 167,000 strings yearly to the Shaanxi Fiscal Intendant, in lieu of the court's own annual subvention, in return for access to Eastern Shaanxi.[24] But the plan was aborted by a comprehensive reform in 1112 that, among other things, replaced government purchases with a regulated contract-market *(hetongchang)* system in the southeast and fixed the boundaries of imperial tea markets for the remaining years of the Northern Song. Southeastern tea was allotted two zones: the capital city of Kaifeng, in which the government retailed water-milled tea; and (to switch to macroregions) all of Southeast China, the Lower and Middle Yangzi, North China, and the four eastern subcircuits of Northwest China, or Shaanxi, in which itinerant merchants sold tea bought in the southeastern contract markets. Sichuanese tea, on the other hand, was sold by merchants in four circuits of Sichuan excluding the western borderlands, and by the THA in the western borderlands and the two western subcircuits of Shaanxi.[25]

With its marketing region thus restricted, the THA faced surpluses for the remainder of the Northern Song. In 1113 Zhang Hui again reported accumulations of about 5,900,000 catties of tea (5,000,000 of it from Mingshan) in transshipment warehouses in the Qinling Mountain counties of Zhaohua, Shuncheng, and Changju.[26] Transport difficulties and government restrictions on the use of tea compounded the difficulties, but it is clear that there was simply too much tea. No further memorials call attention to the problem during the last fifteen years of the dynasty, in part because the concern of officials was focused on buying extra horses for the continuing wars against the Xi Xia, the Khitan, and the Jurchen. These increased purchases may have consumed part of the tea surpluses, but a shift in the terms of trade in favor of horses highlights the excess tea supplies: the price of a horse doubled from a single hundred-catty bale of tea in the 1080s to two bales by the last decade of the Northern Song.

Despite the loss of a third of its total tea markets to bureaucratic competition, horse supply remained unaffected; and during the last two decades of the Northern Song the THA could still deliver 15,000 to 20,000 horses and 1,000,000 to 2,000,000 strings of cash to the court each year. But war exacted a graver toll. In 1119 the Jurchen subjects of the Khitan suddenly swarmed out of their Manchurian homeland to overwhelm the Liao Supreme Capital of Linhuang (in modern Inner Mongolia), sending the first waves of apprehension through the Song court. Seven years later Jurchen cavalry routed the Song capital of Kaifeng and pursued the imperial retinue south of the Yangzi and out into the sea. When the international borders were redrawn in 1127, the Song had lost all of North and Northwest China, from the north slope of the Qinling Mountains east along the Huai River to the sea. The impact on the tea and horse trade was especially severe, for the THA lost not only its remaining tea markets in Western Shaanxi, but also its major horse suppliers and foreign buyers of tea (see Map 7). Of the original fifty-two foreign-trade tea markets of 1076, only two—Danchang and Fengtie—remained as long-distance outlets for Sichuanese tea. The remaining markets were all either under the control of the Jin, who prohibited the squandering of national resources on tea wherever possible, or closed down by the Song to stem the flow of tea to potential horse dealers.[27] At the same time the Agency was now cut off from its principal Tibetan horse suppliers in Koko Nor, Xining, and the Longxi Basin. Only the local tribes of Taozhou, Minzhou, and Leizhou, clustered in the southernmost part of Longxi and the northern part of the Songpan grasslands, remained able to provide the Song with its coveted war horses. The consequences of this drastic cut in horse supply are taken up in Chapter Seven. From the perspective of the tea trade it meant that the THA could buy only about 4,500 horses with its tea.

Because there was so much tea in relation to horses, Intendancy officials were forced to close off all possible alternatives to the horse trade as a source of tea; and therefore rather than promoting foreign sales of Sichuanese tea, they sold as little as possible. Licit foreign trade was limited to about 2,000,000 catties of tea traded for horses in Danchang and Fengtie, and 200,000 to 500,000 catties sold to the hinterland Tibetan tribes of Weizhou to discourage periodic raids[28]—in sum only about half the volume of tea shipped by the New Policies Intendancy to Xizhou and Qinzhou markets alone.

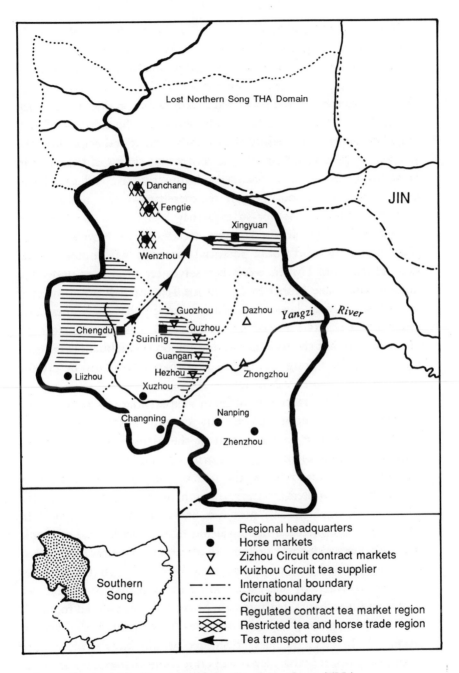

Map 7 Geographic Domain of the Southern Song THA

Nor could the contraction of the foreign trade be balanced by expanding extraregional domestic sales, since the Jurchen conquest barred all of China's tea producers from profitable northern markets. Because sixty prefectures in ten circuits of South China and about sixteen prefectures in the four circuits of Sichuan produced tea, much of Southern Song China had ready access to the beverage.[29] All available markets, including the carefully controlled trade with the Jin, had to be divided among the competing claims of the court in Hangzhou, the regional financial administrations, and to a lesser degree the unruly southeastern tea-merchants. The allocation of market territories was not so explicitly laid out in the Southern Song as it had been in the last two decades of the Northern Song. But because Sichuan's only potential extraregional domestic markets, Hunan and Hubei, were themselves tea producers under the jurisdiction of the Hubei Intendant for Tea and Salt and protected by anti-smuggling laws, it is almost certain that Sichuanese and Hanzhong tea was confined to the Upper Yangzi.[30] Therefore we can conclude that the total marketing region for Sichuanese tea during the Southern Song was little larger than it had been before the lifting of the export prohibition in 1059.

The drastic contraction of Sichuan's export markets removed the government's incentive for directly owning vast stocks of tea, prompting the first major reform of the Sichuan tea monopsony since its establishment.[31] The reform was undertaken by the Sichuanese Zhao Kai, who, as the first of what was to become four General Supply Masters *(zongling)* throughout the empire, was charged with rebuilding Sichuan's post-war financial administration.[32] In 1128 Zhao submitted a denunciation of the THA's use of credit manipulation and forced purchases to obtain tea at confiscatory prices; he recommended that the monopsony be lifted, that tea procurement be managed by the fiscal intendants and that producers' tea quotas and merchants' tea-purchase prices both be lowered to match the precipitous drop in demand that accompanied the loss of Shaanxi.[33] In fact, the loss of Shaanxi would have made a state monopsony unprofitable, for it was on its long-distance trade in the northwestern markets that the government realized its greatest profits from tea. And profits on the tea trade within Sichuan itself would not have justified the costs of buying all the tea and reselling it to merchants.

As a result of his memorial, Zhao was ordered to reform the tea monopoly system. Zhao replaced direct tea purchases by the THA with the same contract-market system first introduced by Cai Jing in the southeast: in place of the direct purchase of tea by the state, the contract markets regulated and taxed the trade between cultivators, shop households, and merchants. Zhao's biographer, Li Tao, has provided the clearest description of the contract-market reform:

> The direct government purchase and sale of tea were both abolished, and the articles and regulations of 1112 on the Eastern Capital Metropolitan Tea Bureau consulted. Tea licenses were printed and merchants permitted to bear these licenses with them to trade face-to-face with the tea households. The old tea-purchase and sales market of Chengdu was renamed the Contract Market License Bureau *(hetongchang maiyinsuo);* and in all the [prefectural and district] contract markets, tea markets were set up. Trade could take place only in these markets, and the licenses and [volume and type] of tea actually exchanged had to correspond.
>
> Ten or fifteen tea households formed one guarantee-unit *(bao);* and the surnames and personal names of the tea [households and tea] shops were registered and fixed; and they were charged with mutual responsibility for investigating illicit trade. Licenses cost 70 cash per catty in the spring and 50 cash per catty in the summer. Payment of such earlier taxes as the *shili* [market maintenance] and *touzi* [supplementary trade] was unchanged, and a transit tax of 1 cash per catty and a point-of-purchase tax of 1.5 cash per catty were charged. Recklessly increasing these fees was prohibited. Other than inspecting licenses, weighing the tea, and wrapping and marking it for release, the contract-market inspectors were prohibited from interfering in the transaction between the tea merchants and the tea cultivators.[34]

Following the reform, the Tea and Horse Agency (formally reestablished in 1137) bought only the 2,000,000 catties of tea it needed for the horse trade, principally in Mingshan county.[35] The revenues that it had once earned from direct sales in extraregional markets now had to be obtained by taxing the intraregional commerce in tea. The largest single source of income came from the sale of licenses to merchants, who could buy them either in Chengdu or in the twenty-three to thirty-four local contract markets opened in the course of the century.[36] As we see from the following description by Li Xinchuan, although license sales provided the Intendancy with ample revenues through the mid 1140s, officials were inevitably tempted into pushing this revenue source beyond its limits:

> During the Jianyan era [1127–1130] the monopoly system deteriorated and Intendant Zhao Kai . . . put the tea license system into practice. The cultivator and the merchant were permitted to trade in the [contract] market, and the government just collected the license and market usage fees *(shiliqian)*. A long license covered 100 catties of tea, and the guest merchant paid no more than 6 strings 500 cash in license fees and 300 cash in market usage fees for each license. Based on *the tea quota then current,* yearly receipts would not have exceeded 1,059,000 strings of cash, which is not very far from the Xining [1068–1077] quota. In addition, early in the Shaoxing era [1130–1162], the viceroy appropriated not more than 400,000 strings annually to meet military expenses.
>
> But after this the price of commodities soared, and the profits reaped by merchants [still paying low license fee] were substantial. [In order to capture a portion of these profits] successive Intendants raised the long-license and other fees, until by 1144 each license had doubled over Zhao Kai's [original price] to 12 strings 300 cash.[37] Tea was then sold dear, and every contract market greatly exceeded its revenue quota. Although the number of horses purchased did not increase by much, in this early period the wealth of the Tea and Horse Agency armored all under heaven; and yearly surpluses sent to the court as tribute amounted in good years to 2,000,000–3,000,000 strings.[38]

If we take Li Xinchuan's comment about tea quotas literally, then Zhao Kai trimmed the yearly output of Sichuanese tea from its peak of 29,000,000 catties at the end of the New Policies to a more appropriate 16,000,000 to 18,000,000 catties.[39] But because the THA Intendants could no longer expand outward, in order to increase their incomes—or to hold their income steady against inflation and the declining value of tea—they chose to exploit their fixed regional market more intensively. The tactics employed by successive Intendants to generate short-term gains all tended to undermine the long-term solvency of the Sichuan tea industry. The most notorious representative of short-sighted "fiscalism" (*julian,* "exploitative revenue-gathering") was Han Qiu, who in his short term as Intendant (1147–1149) both widened the geographic range of the THA monopsony and forced more tea out of Sichuan's cultivators and onto already saturated markets.

In 1148 Han Qiu extended THA control to Sichuan's central and eastern circuits of Zizhou and Kuizhou Lu. Northern Song Intendants had periodically attempted to hegemonize Sichuan's eastern tea industry but had each time been fended off by administrators of these largely independent circuits.[40] But the Jurchen occupation of Northwest China transformed the Qinling Mountains into a militarized defense zone against the Jin, financed and provisioned almost wholly by Sichuan. The intensified mobilization of Sichuanese resources this required fostered the emergence of new or expanded supraregional agencies, superimposed over the old circuits, that could command the resources of the entire macroregion. This resulted in the first set of agencies whose jurisdiction was designated by the term "Sichuan" rather than by specific circuit, including the General Supply Master of Sichuan, Viceroy of Sichuan, and, by 1146, the Sichuan Tea and Horse Intendant.[41] As as result of this administrative integration, the THA was finally able to breach the old circuit barriers to monopolize tea production in Zhong and Da prefectures of Kuizhou Circuit, and erect contract markets for the sale of eastern tea in the adjoining prefectures of Hezhou, Guozhou, Quzhou, and Guang'anjun in Zizhou Circuit.[42]

Han Qiu expected to earn 8,000 strings of cash on transactions of 80,000 catties of tea annually from the new monopoly—sums so negligible that they can only mean that the mid-century THA was desperate for expandable resources. But in fact the Agency made the trade in Kuizhou tea so unprofitable that the actual returns were even less. In 1160 Provisional Intendant Wang Zhiwang described for the court the stifling impact of the new monopoly:

According to a notification from the [Dazhou authorities]: Dongxiang County produces both loose tea and packed-cake tea. Heretofore merchants have only dealt commercially in the cake-pack tea. Each pack contains 25 catties, which with the tea priced at 120 cash per catty comes to 3 strings. If it is sold in Quzhou [about 60 miles downriver], the transit taxes along the way come to 3 strings 50 cash, and the "customs license" (*guanyin*) is another 2 strings 500 cash. Thus the merchant pays a total of 8 strings 550 cash. But on arriving in Quzhou the tea can only be sold on average for 6 strings 500 cash. As a result, guest travelers no longer come to trade.[43]

On the Dongxiang-Quzhou transaction, then, a merchant stood to lose 2 strings 50 cash, or 8 strings 200 cash for a standard hundred-catty license. (In western Sichuan, by contrast, a merchant paid 40 strings for tea that he could then sell for 50 strings.) Not all of the designated exchanges could have been this costly to the trader, since Wang informs us that 5,000 strings were collected in 1158 on licenses for 50,000 catties, but even this was 3,000 strings below quota. The depressing effect of the Kuizhou Circuit monopsony and Zizhou Circuit monopoly had been publicly deplored since at least 1157, but Wang was able to get no more than a temporary suspension of the license sales.[44] Despite the very low returns involved, the contract-market apparatus in Zizhou and Kuizhou Circuits was never dismantled; and a branch office of the Intendancy was opened in Suining in 1166 to administer the eastern circuits.[45]

Han Qiu's eastward expansion of the Sichuan tea monopoly illustrates how easily state intervention could, in the absence of accompanying expansion of commercial opportunities, raise the price of doing business so high that trade itself was smothered. But merchants had an economic advantage with respect to the Southern Song THA not shared by the tea producers. For when the cost of business soared too high, merchants could invest their capital in other ways or withdraw from the market altogether. As we shall see in the next section, even during the Northern Song, when the original Tea Market Agency had earned its greatest profits by retailing tea in its own state markets in Shaanxi, Agency officials had courted merchant involvement for the trade within Sichuan itself. In the reduced marketing environment of the Southern Song, when the THA could not afford to operate its own retail markets, merchant participation was absolutely indispensable. Consequently when taxation threatened to drive merchants out of the tea trade, THA officials were forced to devise ways to re-ignite mercantile interest. The solution employed by Han Qui in 1147 transferred a growing share of the fiscal burden to the tea producer, while forcing more tea on an increasingly glutted market.

Government tea markets traditionally provided extra measures of tea on each transaction to lubricate the trade. This premium was usually called "wastage tea" *(haocha),* in reference to its justification as a guarantee against spoilage, and generally amounted to 10 percent by weight, although 50 percent was not unknown.[46] In Sichuan in the early 1130s the same practice was referred to as *raocha,* or bonus tea, and the cost was absorbed by the Tea and Horse Agency.[47] But in 1147 Han Qiu, probably already faced with declining revenues and shortfalls in his profit quotas, transferred the bonus-tea responsibility to the cultivators. In addition he used this opportunity to increase total tea-production quotas by an alleged 4,600,000 catties, with local increases of as much as 200,000 to 300,000 catties in some markets.[48] All of this extra tea was thrown at the merchant in an effort to preserve the price of a hundred-catty tea license at 12 strings 300 cash, and to reach financial targets that had become pegged to it.

Han Qiu's tea-quota increase, which forced more tea on a market that was already oversupplied, was characteristic of short-term efforts by producers to preserve incomes in the midst of declining demand by raising output still higher. The imposition of an additional bonus-tea quota on cultivators was part of a cluster of revenue-gathering policies linked to militarization of Sichuan's northern frontier that by mid century had taken a dangerous toll on the region's economy. In 1157 a major investigative committee on the Sichuanese economy was convened, consisting of the senior financial officials of the region: Pacification Commissioner Xiao Zhen, Supply-Master General Tang Yungong, Chengdu Circuit Fiscal Intendant Xu Yin, Zizhou Circuit Fiscal Supervisor Wang Zhiwang, and THA Intendant Li Run.[49]

Overall the investigation led to immediate reductions in such wartime levies as the "matching rice purchases," the "exhortation silks," and the plain-silk commutation tax. In the tea industry the 4,600,000-catty quota increase attributed to Han Qiu was rescinded, tea-merchant license fees were reduced 3 strings to about 9 strings 300 cash, and the Agency's overall profit quota was cut by 950,000 strings.[50]

These 1157 reductions signaled an acceptance in principle, by regional and court officials both, that tea production and revenues had to be adjusted to the circumscribed market. But quotas resist change, and significant reforms were extremely slow. Twenty years later, for example, the Sichuanese official Yan Cangshu complained that in Danchang and the surrounding pasture lands Yongkang's "fine tea" had become "as cheap as mud." Yan called for strict restraints on production and sales, and shrewdly noted that, "because tea is plentiful, northern folk disdain tea and esteem silver, tabby, and pongee. As a result the power of the Tea and Horse Agency has flowed to other offices."[51]

Yan's charge prompted separate investigations by the Supply-Master General, Military Regulator, and THA Intendant that yielded quota rescissions of 1,000,000 catties, worth 152,994 strings of cash in fees to the government.[52] In 1185, 76,729 catties were cut from Mingshan's quota, followed five years later by a deduction of 160,000 strings of cash from the Agency's tea-license quota.[53] By the turn of the century, however, western Sichuan and the Hanzhong Basin were still producing 20,900,000 catties of tea. Although output had been cut back 30 percent from the 1085 peak, the THA was still forcing about 4,000,000 catties more on the market than had Zhao Kai at the beginning of the contract-market reform.[54]

Inevitably, contraction of the tea industry induced a drastic decline in the profitability of the tea and horse enterprise. As is shown in Table 2, not only did THA surpluses diminish during the twelfth century, by the last third of the century the Agency even had difficulty meeting its own operating expenses.[55] Gross receipts appear close to those for the Northern Song (Appendix D), but they must be placed in perspective. First, although the tea markets returned between 1,000,000 and 3,000,000 strings during the first fifteen years of the Southern Song, Sichuan alone spent an average of 35,000,000 strings annually at this time, largely for defense.[56]

Whereas net profits to the New Policies TMA provided between 1.5 and 3 percent of the imperial government's cash income of 60,000,000 strings, even at the height of its productivity gross receipts to the Southern Song THA equaled no more than 6 percent of provincial income, far less than the taxes on Sichuanese salt, wine, or textiles.[57] And secondly, the Southern Song figures reflect a price inflation of about 400 percent since the New Policies era.[58] Moreover, because they were tied to a declining trade, THA revenues inexorably dwindled. The Agency found it impossible to meet the new 1,130,000-string cash quota that it was given in 1155;[59] and from 1149 to 1162 the Intendants steadily fell behind in their cash payments, forcing the court to reduce the Agency's surplus-revenue quota to 200,000 strings in 1165 and to cancel accumulated debts of 664,900 strings in 1167. Two years later the THA was in the red, with an operating deficit of 200,000 strings. And in 1184, despite gross receipts of 2,400,000 strings, the Intendant reported a net cash surplus of only 20,000 strings. By the end of the century revenue production had essentially dropped out of the THA's task agenda.

TRIMMING THE AGENCY'S SAILS: FROM ENTREPRENEUR TO MANAGER

The diminishing productivity of the THA had a baleful effect on the bureaucratic power of the Agency itself; for as THA revenues declined, the court withdrew the mantle of immunity and autonomy that had made the New Policies TMA very nearly unique. The Agency was transformed into but one strand in a web of regional organizations. As early as the first years of the Post-Reform era, the court began to pare down the THA's privileges and recentralize decision-making, though the basic structure built up during the New Policies era was retained through the fall of the Northern Song. The chief indication that THA dominance had been reversed was a drop in the formal rating of its top post in relation to other circuit offices (its *xuquan* ranking). Initially, the TMA Intendant had been ranked the equivalent of a circuit judicial intendant; then in 1083, four years after being raised to the status of Superintendant, the

Table 2 Revenues, Disbursements, and Deficits of the Southern Song THA

Year	Gross Revenues (strings of cash)	Source of Revenue	Subvention or Net Surplus (strings of cash)	Recipient	Deficit
1129–1130[a]	1,700,000	Sales of tea licenses at 6.5 strings per 100-catty license			
1130s[b]	1,059,000/year	Sales of tea licenses			
1144[c]	2,000,000–3,000,000/year	Sales of tea licenses at 12.3 strings per 100-catty license			
1145[d]			400,000/year	General Supply Master	
1150[e]	2,493,000	Total value of all commodities used in the horse trade			
1155[f]			1,130,000/year quota	General Supply Master	Agency unable to meet the quota

Date			
1149–1162[g]			664,900 strings in accumulated debts to other agencies, canceled in 1167
1165[h]	100,000–200,000/year quota	All other agencies	
1169[i]			200,000 strings operating deficit
1184[j]	2,460,000	20,000 net surplus	Gross receipts from all operations
1204[k]	1,230,000	700,000 quota	Current balance — The horse trade

Sources: [a] *SHY* shihuo 32/25b–26a; [b] *XNYL* 167/5327; [c] *XNYL* 148/4688; [d] *XNYL* 154/4883; [e] *XNYL* 154/4883; *CYZJ* jia 14/440; [f] *XNYL* 169/5389–91, *CYZJ* jia 14/440; [g] *SHY* shihuo 31/18a–b; [h] *CYZJ* jia 14/440; [i] *CYZJ* jia/14/440; [j] *SHY* bing 23/5a–b; [k] *SHY* bing 26/16b–17a.

chief post was made the peer of a fiscal intendant, the highest circuit position. In 1107, however, the THA Superintendant was demoted in rank to the equivalent of an assistant fiscal intendant of Shaanxi. In 1121, he fell still lower when the Tea and Horse Agency was deprived of its standing as a super agency *(duda)*.[60]

The Southern Song court went well beyond questions of relative prestige to restructure the nature of the Tea and Horse Agency radically. First, because of the reduced geographic range of the enterprise, the executive triad was judged superfluous and the posts of Co- and Assistant Intendant abolished.[61] More fundamentally, the Intendancy was embedded in a cluster of covalent regional offices that transformed it from a decentralized entrepreneurial agency, with high autonomy and an open mandate, to a managerial agency, subject to tight centralized control in the performance of a fixed task agenda. The principal indicator of this transformation involves the way incumbents moved into and out of the THA.

In Chapter Four I emphasized three indicators of an entrepreneurial appointment: mode of entry, rank at the time of appointment, and length of tenure in office. To recapitulate my argument, entrepreneurial mobilization, as epitomized by the New Policies Intendancy, was characterized by the willingness of the court to grant extraordinary functional power to proven innovators regardless of their formal rank, and to encourage career specialization within the Tea Market Agency in order to maximize the effectiveness of the enterprise. The reform court appointed to the Intendancy executive men who had proven themselves in other New Policies' posts or who, like Lu Shimin, had come up through the Agency itself. Moreover, it kept Intendants in position for an average of 49 months, long enough to develop the local and intra-agency networks of power that were indispensable to decentralized bureaucratic entrepreneurship. During the Post-Reform era the Agency had still not acquired a fixed routine, and the court tended to appoint as Intendant men who had served in the enterprise before and to keep them in position only 6 months less than the New Policies tenure, an average of 43 months.

One important corollary of Agency specialization and internal

Table 3 Service prior to and following the Northern Song THA
Intendancy

Category of Post (or Other Status)	Number Entering from Post	Percentage Entering from Post	Number Exiting to Post	Percentage Exiting to Post
Central Gov't, Special New Policies Assignment	3[a]	11.1		
Sichuan, Special New Policies Assignment	2[b]	7.4		
THA	3[c]	11.1		
Central Gov't, Regular Assignment	1[d]	3.7	1[k]	3.7
Sichuan Circuit Post	3[e]	11.1		
Shaanxi Circuit Post	5[f]	18.5	6[l]	22.2
Other Circuit Post	1[g]	3.7	2[m]	7.4
Sichuan Prefectural Post	1[h]	3.7	1[n]	3.7
Shaanxi Prefectural Post			2[o]	7.4
Other Prefectural Post	1[i]	3.7	3[p]	11.1
Retired			1[q]	3.7
Cashiered, Demoted, or Denied Reappointment			4[r]	14.8
Died in Office			1[s]	3.7
Unknown	7[j]	25.9	6[t]	22.2
Total	27	99.9	27	99.9

Source: Appendix C.

Notes: (Individuals holding post in category): [a]Li Ji, Li Qi, Liu Zuo; [b]Pu Zongmin, Yan Ling; [c]He Jian, Lu Shimin, Sun Aobian; [d]Huang Lian; [e]Cheng Zhishao, Song Gou, Wang Fan; [f]Fan Chuncui, Guo Maoxun, Pang Yinsun, Sun Zhen, Wu Zeren; [g]Zhang Hui; [h]Yuwen Chang; [i]Han Zhao; [j]Cheng Tang, Chou Boyu, Guo Si, Huang Minyong, Li Jii, Wang Wan, Zhang Youji; [k]Huang Lian; [l]Chou Boyu, Fan Chuncui, Guo Maoxun, Huang Minyong, Yan Ling; [m]Pang Yinsun, Wu Zeren; [n]Yuwen Chang; [o]Cheng Tang, Cheng Zhishao; [p]Han Zhao, He Jian, Zhang Youji; [q]Li Qi; [r]Liu Zuo, Lu Shimin, Pu Zongmin, Zhang Hui; [s]Li Ji; [t]Li Jii, Song Gou, Sun Aobian, Sun Zhen, Wang Fan, Wang Wan.

recruitment was a fairly high degree of unpredictability in the careers of the men who served. As is illustrated in Table 3, there was no regular rotation of posts that led into the Intendancy, other than an association with the reforms or the Agency itself (29.6 percent), or service in a Shaanxi circuit post (five men for 18.5 percent).

Similarly there was little predictability about what an incumbent could expect down the line, although a circuit post in Shaanxi (22.2 percent) or demotion (18.5 percent) were the likeliest possibilities. The trade-offs for this uncertainty were power and career rewards.

During the first decade of the Southern Song, when the survival of the dynasty still hung in the balance, the Tea and Horse Intendants shared some of the open-ended features of their Northern Song predecessors. Responsibility for defense of the Sichuan-Shaanxi perimeter was vested in the Sichuanese leader of the irredentist party, Zhang Jun, who was appointed Governor-General of the two macroregions and given the right to "dismiss and appoint men to office as he sees fit."[62] Zhang sponsored a number of his fellow provincials for key fiscal posts in Sichuan, including Tea and Horse Intendant. Three of Zhang's candidates headed the Agency for thirteen of the first fourteen years of the Southern Song, including Zhao Kai, who held the post twice (for a total of 107 months) in conjunction with his umbrella responsibility for Sichuanese finances.[63] In 1138 Zhang Jun and the war party was ousted by Qin Gui, the much-vilified chief of the appeasement faction who served as Emperor Gaozong's Chief Councilor for the next seventeen years.[64] Emperor and Chief Councilor capitalized on the relaxation of border tensions with the Jin to recentralize political and military power wherever possible at home. In order to strengthen central control over its field administration, including the THA, the Southern Song court employed a system of checks and balances that Winston Lo has described as functional interchangeability and overlapping jurisdiction.[65]

In order to decrease the court's dependence on any single revenue agency in Sichuan, revenue production and collection were distributed among a wide array of overlapping regional agencies, including the Tea and Horse Intendant, the trans-regional General Supply Commissioner, and the sub-regional circuit fiscal intendants and vice-intendants. All of these agencies could be made jointly responsible for the solution of specific problems, and almost all the funds collected by them were subject to appropriation for specific needs by the viceroy, a prototypical provincial governor-general who coordinated military and fiscal affairs intraregionally and linked up with the center.[66]

Table 4 Service prior to and following the Southern Song THA
Intendancy

Category of Post	Number Entering from Post	Percentage Entering from Post	Number Exiting to Post	Percentage Exiting to Post
Central Gov't Post	2[a]	6.2	6[j]	18.8
Sichuan Circuit Post	11[b]	34.4	7[k]	21.8
Jinghu Circuit Post	1[c]	3.1		
Other Circuit Post	5[d]	15.6	2[l]	6.2
Sichuan Prefectural Post	3[e]	9.4	1[m]	3.1
Contiguous Prefectural Post	2[f]	6.2	1[n]	3.1
Other Prefectural Post	1[g]	3.1	1[o]	3.1
Military	2[h]	6.2	1[p]	3.1
Retired			2[q]	6.2
Cashiered, Demoted, or Denied Reappointment			4[r]	12.5
Died in office			1[s]	3.1
Unknown	5[i]	15.6	6[t]	18.8
Total	32	99.8	32	99.8

Source: Appendix C.

Notes: (Individuals in each category): [a]Tang Yungong, Tao Kai; [b]Feng Kangguo, Jia Sicheng, Li Dazheng, Wang Fei, Wang Zhiwang, Xu Yin, Yang Jing, Zhang Deyuan, Zhang Song, Zhao Kai, Zheng Ai; [c]Ding Feng; [d]Chen Mizuo, Han Qiu, Li Dai, Wang Ning, Wang Wo; [e]Fu Xingzhong, Wang Daguo, Zhang Shen; [f]Wang Zhen, Xu Bi; [g]Chao Gongwu; [h]Peng Ge, Wu Zong; [i]Hu Dacheng, Li Run, Qian Wu, Zhao Yanbo, Zhu Quan; [j]Chen Mizuo, Ding Feng, Hu Dacheng, Li Run, Wang Wo, Zhu Quan; [k]Chao Gongwu, Fu Xingzhong, Tang Yungong, Wang Ning, Wang Zhiwang, Xu Yin, Zhang Shen; [l]Li Dai, Zhang Song; [m]Han Qiu; [n]Tao Kai; [o]Zhao Yanbo; [p]Peng Ge; [q]Wang Fei, Zhao Kai; [r]Wu Zong, Xu Bi, Yang Jing, Zheng Ai; [s]Feng Kangguo; [t]Jia Sicheng, Li Dazheng, Qian Wu, Wang Daguo, Wang Zhen, Zhang Deyuan.

The interdependence of Southern Song circuit offices is perfectly reflected in the career patterns of the THA Intendants. Because the court sought men who could manage the Agency as an integrated component in a well-defined cluster of offices, the THA Intendancy became fixed as part of a regular rotation of Sichuanese circuit positions. As is shown in Table 4, by far the largest proportion of THA chiefs—eleven of thirty-two identifiable men, for 34.4 percent—was appointed directly from other Sichuanese circuit posts. These included a circuit judicial intendancy (four cases), fiscal vice intendant (two cases) or fiscal supervisor (two cases), general supply commissioner (two cases), and pacification commissioner for Kuizhou Circuit.[67] Similarly the largest proportion of Intendants—seven men, for 21.8 percent—succeeded directly to another Sichuan circuit post, in five cases that of general supply master.[68] In addition, a total of eleven men held three or more circuit positions in Sichuan during their careers, with thirteen men all told holding the majority of their career positions in the region.[69] In this respect, too, the THA was completely typical; for, as Robert Hartwell has argued, during the twelfth century intraregional careers in diverse fields replaced interregional careers in specific branches of the bureaucracy as the typical career pattern throughout the Southern Song field administration.[70] This pattern of regional as opposed to enterprise specialization, which was presaged during the New Policies by the intendants for Ever-Normal Granaries, allowed the court to benefit from a man's knowledge of a region yet retain centralized control over his performance, by preventing officials from exploiting a particular office for personal ends without sacrificing his close familiarity with the problems and resources of his assigned region.[71]

As Winston Lo has observed, when men moved from one kind of job to another and agencies had overlapping authority, the court exercised greater control because officials in a given region had the opportunity to keep an eye on each other, the means for assessing each other's performance, and a measure of collective responsibility for what happened.[72] Functional interchangeability and overlapping jurisdiction also ensured that experience in a specific enterprise was not monopolized by a single person or group. Both strategies can be illustrated by the 1157 committee discussed earlier in this chapter, which was convened to provide emergency relief for tea, salt, textile, and rice producers.[73] To review its members, the committee included General Supply Master of Sichuan Tang Yungong, the fiscal supervisors of Chengdu and Zizhou Circuits, Xu Yin and Wang Zhiwang, Tea and Horse Intendant Li Run, and Pacification Commissioner and Administrator of Chengdu Xiao Zhen. Tang Yungong had been Tea and Horse Intendant in 1153. The year after the committee was convened Tang and Li Run went to posts in the central government, Xu Yin took Li's post as THA Intendant, and Wang Zhiwang replaced Xu as Chengdu Fiscal Vice-Intendant. Subsequently Xu Yin was made General Supply Master and then sent to the central government, followed directly by Wang Zhiwang as Tea and Horse Intendant and then General Supply Master.[74]

The rotation of posts fed a variety of opinions into the decision-making process and provided a mechanism of checks and balances. For example, when Wang Zhiwang was Intendant in 1160, he was able to reverse what he judged to be a premature decision by Xu Yin to continue the Kuizhou Circuit tea monopoly.[75] But more importantly, the rotation of posts prevented essential bureaucratic output from becoming tied to the skills and personal connections of particular individuals. Because it was forced to depend on military entrepreneurs like Wu Jie to defend northern Sichuan, the Southern Song court installed a succession of interchangeable managers to operate the region's financial administration. In sharp contrast with the internal recruitment that characterized the Northern Song Intendancy, only one man, Zhang Song, held an Agency-related post prior to his appointment as Intendant (1167–1170), and that twenty years before when he was Vice-Administrator of Liizhou in 1145.[76] And only Zhao Kai was recalled to the Intendancy.[77] Otherwise Intendants were rotated in and out, after an average of 26 months of service, in an absolutely predictable manner. However much it might have enhanced the effectiveness of the tea and horse enterprise, specialization in the Agency was viewed by the Southern Song court as politically undesirable.

In addition to its reconfiguration as one link in a cluster of inter-connected agencies, the THA also forfeited immunity to outside scrutiny and supervision as its output of funds and horses declined. The only prerogative retained by the Southern Song THA out of the array of privileges built up by the New Policies Intendancy was the right to select certain local government personnel. We saw in Chapter Five that because tea purchase and transport became an intrinsic duty of local government in counties producing or expediting tea for the horse trade, the Southern Song THA kept selection or incentive rights for a total of five county magistrates. The same logic applied to the selection of vice-prefect *(tongpan)*, who since the early Northern Song had been most directly in charge of horse management.[78] Indeed in the frontier prefectures that housed horse markets, horse procurement was probably the most important local government function. Southern Song THA Intendants played on this fact to argue that when vice-prefects were appointed, rewarded, and fined by the central government rather than the Agency, they paid little attention to buying horses, protecting native traders, managing hostelry and fodder supplies, or suppressing the contraband trade in tea and silks.[79] In almost all cases the court agreed, and consequently as late as 1168 the THA appointed vice administrators in seven prefectures, at a time when all other vice-prefects were selected "in camera," that is, by the court.[80]

In all other respects, however, the Southern Song THA was kept on a much tighter leash than its Northern Song progenitor. Whereas the New Policies TMA had enjoyed virtual immunity from outside interference, during the Southern Song central and regional officials routinely intervened in Agency operations by sending out surveillance agents, taking over the selection of key operational staff, and restructuring the Agency's incentive system to maximize the delivery of usable mounts.[81] Finally, during the last quarter of the twelfth century, the THA was balkanized by powerful client agencies that could no longer tolerate its inadequate performance. Because of the Agency's financial debts the Military Regulator *(zhizhishi)* was ordered to take over joint control of its accounts in 1186.[82] Six years later the Agency owed horses as well, and the court transferred its capital funds for the year to the Supply Master of Huguang to buy horses locally.[83] By the end of the century revenue production had essentially dropped out of the THA's task agenda, and its ability to buy and convoy horses had become extremely erratic. As final testimony to the Agency's loss of independence and power, in 1203 the THA was split into two enterprises, one in Xingyuan under a military official and the other in Chengdu under a civil official; and both were put under the control of the Bureau of Military Affairs.[84] Although the split was only temporary, horse procurement became even more precarious in the course of the thirteenth century, making it impossible for the Intendancy to achieve the level of organizational effectiveness necessary for holding and wielding independent bureaucratic power.

THE THA AND THE SICHUAN TEA INDUSTRY

The same boom-and-bust cycle that shaped the power of the Tea and Horse Agency determined the capacity of Sichuan's tea producers to absorb the costs of state monopolization. The founders' entrepreneurial leap—the creation of a tea monopsony in Sichuan and a tea monopoly in Shaanxi—forced a rapid and fundamental transformation of the Sichuan tea industry into a bulk producer of tea for the long-distance trade. From the very beginning of the enterprise the Agency paid the cultivators less for their tea than had private merchants; but because the horse trade and the Shaanxi monopoly increased demand, cultivators could sell much more tea than they had before, and production consequently soared. Although the state drove merchants out of the interregional trade and reaped enormous returns from the cultivators' tea, these profits were by and large entrepreneurial returns to the expanded long-distance commerce. By adapting to the bulk requirements of the state-run trade, participants in the Sichuan tea industry could absorb the sudden onset of state intervention with acceptable declines in household income.

But the loss of the Sichuan tea-marketing region to bureaucratic competition and war sapped the resiliency of Sichuan's tea cultivators. Although the central government continued to expect that the Intendancy would produce surplus revenues, its opportunities to sell tea steadily declined. Shrinking markets and tea surpluses left no room for entrepreneurial expansion, forcing Agency officials to extract their revenue quotas out of the incomes of tea cultivators. In the absence of opportunities for growth bureaucratic entrepreneurship—the creation by public agencies of new avenues of economic expansion—degenerated into confiscatory exploitation, gradually exhausting the capacity of the cultivators to absorb the costs of state control.

THE THA AND TEA PRODUCTION. Statistics on Sichuanese tea output during and after the monopoly era (there are none from before) demonstrate how dramatically market expansion after 1059 propelled tea production. By 1074 suspension of the barriers isolating Sichuanese tea had stimulated the production of 7,400,000 catties in Hanzhong alone, as families throughout the basin harvested leaves for the eager Shaanxi tea-and-salt merchants. But growth was by no means aborted by state control: By linking Sichuanese tea to the Qinghai horse trade and carving out richer and more extensive markets than the region had ever enjoyed before, the TMA's founding Intendants pushed Sichuanese tea output to unprecedented levels. According to Lü Tao, whose fervid opposition to the tea monopoly would have disinclined him to exaggerate production under the TMA, aggregate output for the two circuits of Chengdu and Lizhou soared to 29,147,000 catties (ca. 37,800,000 pounds) in 1084, and reached 29,548,000 catties (38,400,000 pounds) by 1085.[85]

The significance of these figures can be highlighted by three simple comparisons. First, as shown in Table 5, tea production in the Upper Yangzi during the New Policies era far surpassed regional tea output for any subsequent period up to the 1930s. Second, tea production under the New Policies Intendancy exceeded the aggregate output of the entire southeastern tea region at any time during the Song: 23,000,000 catties in the late tenth century, 10,700,000

Table 5 Tea Production in the Upper Yangzi, 1085–1930
        (in catties)

	Sichuan	*Hanzhong*	*Total*
1085[a]	29,548,000	—	29,548,000
ca. 1200[b]	16,100,000	4,800,000	20,900,000
ca. 1500[c]	6,000,000	1,000,000	7,000,000
ca. 1800[d]	13,900,000	2,200,000	16,100,000
ca. 1930[e]	30,000,000	1,000,000	31,000,000

Sources: [a]Lü Tao, *Jingde ji* 3/9b; [b]*XNYL* 17/704, *CYZJ* jia 14/440; [c]*Ming shi* 80/1951–1953; [d]*Shaanxi tongzhi* (1735) 42/1a; *Sichuan tongzhi* (1816) 69; [e]Zhang Xiaomei, *Sichuan jingji cankao ziliao*, vol. N, p. 42; Perkins, *Agricultural Developments in China*, p. 285.

Table 6 Tea Production per Upper-Yangzi Household, 1085

	Chengdu and Lizhou Circuits	Upper Yangzi	Upper Yangzi plus Western Shaanxi	Upper Yangzi plus Western and Eastern Shaanxi
Number of households	1,184,570	1,917,102	2,217,176	3,263,658
Tea Production (in catties)	29,548,000	same	same	same
Tea Production per household (in catties)	24.9	15.4	13.3	9.0

Sources: Lü Tao, *Jingde ji* 3/9b; *Yuanfeng jiuyuzhi*, zhuan 3, 7, 8.

catties in 1055, 17,800,000 catties in 1162, and 19,600,000 catties around 1165.[86] And finally, as shown in Table 6, throughout the era of Agency control western Sichuan and the Hanzhong Basin produced far more tea per producing-circuit household than southeastern China—an astonishing 25 catties per household in 1085. Even when the two non-producing circuits of Zizhou and Kuizhou Lu are included, the Upper Yangzi macroregion still produced over 15 catties of tea per household—five to ten times greater than household tea production in the southeast at the time.[87] Such enormous output per household can only be explained as a response to the new export opportunities opened up by the horse trade and the protected Shaanxi monopoly. The southeastern tea industry probably did not attain similar production density until its linkage to the burgeoning world economy in the eighteenth and nineteenth centuries, by which time the Sichuanese industry had deteriorated into a localized Yazhou speciality sending almost 90 percent of its low-quality brick tea to Tibet. By World War I the southeast was producing an estimated 12 catties per household, led by the 38.5 catties per household in Hunan, where export-oriented tea production was helping to restructure the province's economy.[88]

Judging from both total tea production and production per household, then, there can be little question that the opening of the extraregional market to Upper Yangzi tea in 1059, followed by the bureaucratic expansion of the exclusive marketing zone for Sichuanese tea between 1074 and 1085, made the tea industry more central than ever before to the local economies of (to use Su Che's list) Qiong, Shu, Peng, Han, Mian, and especially Ya prefectures in western Sichuan, and Yangzhou and Xingyuanfu in the Hanzhong Basin.[89]

THE THA AND THE TEA PRODUCERS. At the same time that total output increased under the Intendancy, the monopsony system imposed on each tea household increasingly stringent controls that, in comparison with the earlier competitive market, increased the costs of cultivating and selling tea. The monopsony system introduced at least six serious disincentives to production, by first, decreasing the price paid the cultivator; second, restricting production choices; third, increasing the tax burden; fourth, monopolizing credit; fifth, criminalizing previously legal dispositions of the crop; and sixth, preventing withdrawal from the market through registered quotas. Nonetheless output soared.

Drawing on Lü Tao's observation of the interaction between Intendancy officials and tea cultivators in Pengkouzhen, Pengzhou, we can construct a model for the New Policies phase that both accounts for an increase in production under the monopsony despite the demonstrable disincentives imposed on the tea households, and highlights the ways these disincentives threatened the cultivator's solvency only during the subsequent market decline.

Let us return to the tea cultivators introduced in Chapter Two: Mou Yuanji, Dang Yuanji, and Shi Guangyi, from the mountainous western border of Pengzhou. Lü portrays a household economy in the Han-dominated mountain hamlets that is centered on producing tea for the market to obtain rice and other staples, manufactured goods, and cash for the payment of taxes. Because of the location of their holdings the Pengzhou cultivators have no alternative uses for their land. Although Lü does not say so, for the sake

of our model we will assume that their demand for staples, manufactured goods, and cash is fairly constant. A small Pengzhou cultivator, according to Lü, produced about 200 catties of tea a year
before the monopoly and, on tea of the medium grade worth 90
cash, earned a net profit of 20 cash per catty, or 4,000 cash annually.[90] Again, we must assume that his net income is just equal
to his fixed expenses.

When the monopsony was first imposed in Pengzhou, in the
second month of 1077, its twin goals were a large volume of tea
and a 30 percent profit on each resale transaction. The 30 percent
was a literal profit target. For example, between the twelfth and
fifteenth days of the third month of 1077 Pengkou market officials
bought 886 catties of early, high-priced tea for 106 strings 320
cash (120 cash per catty). A few days later this was sold for a net
profit of 31 strings 896 cash, a mark-up of exactly 30 percent.[91] As
we saw in Chapter Five, officials were exhorted to turn their tea
over quickly in notices urging them to "expedite the rapid purchase
and sale of tea and prevent the stagnation of capital."

State economic intervention during the New Policies was based
on the theory that by breaking up private economic concentra-
tions—the *jianbing* elements, or engrossers—economic activity could
be increased and the state enriched without sacrificing the interests
of producers or consumers. The state's enhanced revenues were to
come at the expense of merchants and large landlords, not producers
and poor peasants. In the case of the new tea monopoly, this meant
that *in theory* the 30 percent profit margin was to be generated on
the resale of tea to merchants. But *in practice,* it was recognized that
merchant demand for tea was far more elastic than producer supply:
that is, merchants would cease to buy tea at high prices before
cultivators stopped selling at low prices. Therefore, in the key government markets the inspector, brokers and service personnel conspired together to transfer the burden of the government's profit
margin to the cultivators.

In his memorial of 1077/3/18, Lü Tao documents a variety of
schemes used by the Pengkou market officials to drive down the
price paid the cultivators. One stratagem involved a simple con-

spiracy by the government, brokers, and merchants to intimidate the cultivator into discounting his tea by 30 percent. As Lü describes it, a broker and a merchant would intercept a cultivator outside the market and frighten him with stories of fixed government scales or rejected tea crops. Because the monopsony had been instituted in Pengkou only the month before, the cultivators were extremely apprehensive; and some agreed to sell their tea to the government at 70 percent of market price, guaranteed by the broker and merchant, rather than take their chances with the officials on their own. Lü gives the following illustration: "A cultivator has 100 catties of tea, with an average value of 130 cash per catty. The total value is thus 13 strings. Now if the cultivator, paralysed by fear, agrees to go along with the scheme, he sells his tea to the government for only 10 strings. Thereupon the merchant shows up and buys the tea for 13 strings [rather than the 16 strings 900 cash he would have to pay if the cultivator got full value]. The records are thus correct [since the government has made 30 percent profit], but the evil is great."[92] Through this conspiracy of intimidation, then, a merchant could buy his tea from the government at no more than he would have previously paid the cultivator, yet the state would still earn its mandated 30 percent. Moreover a cultivator might find that it was indeed wise to accept the 30 percent protection fee. In a memorial written the following month, Lü describes how Shi Guangyi took a loss of 48 percent when he tried to sell his tea independently: "On the fifth day of this month [April 29] Shi put his tea up for sale. Each sack *(dai)* weighed an even 18 catties. Because he did not consign his tea to a tea broker to manage, it was weighed at just 14 catties per sack. Shi's tea was of the second class, worth a standard price of 90 cash per catty. But that day prices were reduced, and each catty just brought in 47 cash in large iron coins. On the thirteenth day [May 7] Shi returned with third-class tea, worth 70 cash per catty. This time the price was reduced to 37 cash in large iron coins."[93] Indeed, Shi Guangyi would have been fortunate to get even his 37 cash per catty in hard currency, for it was standard practice for the Tea Market Agency to pay only fractional amounts with iron coins; all full string amounts (1,000 cash) would be paid with *jiaozi* notes. In this way the Agency could value the notes at prices above the market rate for each issue (*jie*), adding still another 20 to 40 cash on its profits for each 1,000-cash transaction.[94]

The market strategies described by Lü Tao would have netted huge one-time profits for the TMA, but would also have quickly driven producers out of the industry. We know, for example, that on the eve of the monopsony it cost a Pengzhou cultivator 70 cash to grow, harvest, process, and transport to market a catty of medium-grade tea worth 90 cash.[95] The mandated 30 percent profit margin would have reduced the price paid to the cultivator to 63 cash, or 7 cash below the cost of production. If all markets employed the same confiscatory practices as did Pengkou, cultivators would have soon been driven out of the industry. In fact, Lü Tao was able to point to a three-year decline in tea output in neighboring Yongkang Commandery, site of the famous Qingchengshan tea industry, as evidence that "out of fear of punishments and the loss of their businesses tea households have [already] begun to produce less tea."[96]

But on May 13th of 1077, just when market activity was reaching its peak in Pengkou, 5,000 frustrated tea cultivators broke out into a spontaneous riot that forced the Agency to lower its profit margin.[97] Here is Lü's description:

According to the two petitionary reports of the Pengkou Market Inspector, Executive Assistant of the Imperial Library Yin Gu, and the Registrar of Mengyang County and Assistant Tea Purchaser, Xue Yi, on the seventeenth day of this month 60,000 catties of tea were purchased at 3,600 strings of cash (60 cash per catty). The payments exhausted all the [allotted] tea-purchase capital and the profits [from previous sales]. Thereupon, on the eighteenth day, they petitioned the prefectural [Tea Market Agency] requesting that it transfer 6,000 strings in *jiaozi* notes to finance the tea purchase [scheduled for] the nineteenth and twenty-first days. On the nineteenth day, just at dawn, the garden households brought their tea to sell at the market. But because by 11:00 A.M. the requested notes still had not arrived, and moreover it was raining, [Yin] Gu addressed the cultivators, saying:

"We have requested *jiaozi* notes, and they will arrive soon. If you wait until the weather clears, we will weigh your tea for you."

But the cultivators, suiting themselves, took their tea and proceeded directly to the [tea-market] yamen, where they piled it all up. Surrounding Yin Gu and the others, they demanded that their tea be weighed. Then they addressed the brokers:

"You all have put goods up as collateral in the government yamen. Now the government has no money to buy tea. You brokers had better come up with some money to buy a market [session's] worth of tea."

Yin Gu and the others retreated into the yamen and other places of safety. Registrar Xue Yi walked towards the gate of the Hall of the Pure Multitude, but the tea cultivators began to beat the tea-market service personnel and ripped open the sleeves of Xue Yi's gown. Then the cultivators went looking for the [twelve] brokers, intent on fighting with them. But the brokers, on seeing that this was the case, all scattered.[98]

The frustration of the cultivators was directed at the same three classes of functionaries that were linked together in pursuit of profits and low-cost tea by a common incentive system: the inspectors, the service personnel (stock controllers, scalemen, warehouse men, and scribes), and the brokers. As Prefect of Pengzhou, Lü Tao organized his own inquiry. Rather than punishing the rioters, Lü despatched an official to re-weigh and re-price the cultivators' tea and demanded that the TMA provide adequate capital.[99] Although Lü was charged with negligence in the affair and dismissed, the direct link he had demonstrated between the tea riot and the 30-percent profit margin was irrefutable: Pu Zongmin, temporarily in charge of the Agency during its only anxious moment of the New Policies, was forced to reduce the profit margin to 10 percent.[100]

Garden households could absorb a 10 percent loss to the government. At 10 percent the cultivator could still earn a net profit of 11 cash on a catty of tea. But in order to meet his hypothetically fixed marketing and tax needs of 4,000 cash a year, he would have to produce and sell 364 catties of tea, rather than his earlier 200 catties. Moreover, he had to do this in only two (albeit the most productive two) of four harvests, since under the Yuanfeng monopsony (but not the Southern Song contract markets) cultivators were not permitted to sell the "late tea" of summer or the "old yellow-leaf tea of autumn" (*qiu huanglao yecha*). Although these last two crops did not add much volume to the total output, they provided a small but useful cash margin to the cultivator in the late seasons.[101]

My argument, therefore, is that one strategy for cultivators who had fixed cash needs was to increase production when the price paid them was lowered to a figure close to but not below their costs. Some would do so because, first, having more tea to sell could earn them the same income from a smaller profit margin and, second, they could achieve the increase in production largely through labor. Unlike the land, fertilizer, or other inputs of production for a farmer in a peasant economy, his own and his family's labor are, up to a point, under his control: within human limits, how much to expend is a matter of choice. In fact, labor's supply curve is sometimes described as "backward bending": an "increase in price may result in smaller amounts of the input being supplied."[102] In other words, like any other laborer, the peasant farmer may work less if he can make ends meet while selling a smaller amount. But the inverse is also true: given the desire for a certain level of well-being (which in marginal cases may merely be subsistence), leisure will be sacrificed to increase production when prices for his commodity go down and he has no other way to make up the difference. From the Tea Market Agency's point of view, paying less for tea elicited more of it.

But could a marginal tea household almost double its crop, from, for example, 200 catties to 364 catties with increased inputs of labor alone? I think it could. Most importantly, the cultivator could harvest for volume rather than quality, by taking all but enough leaf to keep the plant healthy, rather than just the fine leaves of each stalk, and by plucking each flush early to increase the number of harvests. Similarly he could increase the bulk of his harvest by including stems and even twigs, a common response to government tea purchases.[103] The tea household could also increase the number of trees under cultivation. Even in the case of small householders with limited land, it is possible that there was unused capacity, since limited demand up to 1059 and new demand for primarily export-quality tea from 1060 to the beginning of monopoly, in combination with the absence of alternative uses for the most marginal hill land, would have left room for more intensive tea cultivation even on small tracts. With uncultivated tea bushes probably available in abundance throughout the hills, the cultivator could transplant shrubs to his own land, or propagate new trees from seed, which produces useful leaf within three years, or from cuttings, which requires only two.[104]

The cultivator could also have reduced costs and labor needs by processing his tea less intensively, in particular by firing the tea in his eighteen-catty sacks only long enough to get them by the market inspectors, without reducing all the watery bulk that more careful processing would call for. Finally those householders who, like Mou Yuanji and Shi Guangyi, hired seasonal laborers at 60 cash per day plus food, could either forgo this outside help and exploit family labor more intensively, or, where the absence of alternative employment permitted, pay less to their helpers.[105] Although it is impossible to say how much a cultivator could increase output without increasing costs by these methods, and thus still satisfy his basic market needs at the reduced price paid by the monopoly system, I believe the increase was both theoretically and actually substantial.

But the adjustments I have described would all lead to a decline in tea quality. This is in fact what occurred. At the beginning of the monopoly, for example, the incentive system promulgated by Li Ji in 1078 not only rewarded market inspectors and co-inspectors for buying given volumes of tea, it also punished them for buying tea that was "mixed, ersatz, coarse, or rotten" or for allowing the "old autumn-leaf tea" to get through.[106] Because of the monopoly's pricing policy, however, the two goals were mutually exclusive; and in later references to market-inspector reward schedules, particularly Lu Shimin's comprehensive regulations of 1083, the question of tea quality is not raised at all. In his indictment of 1128 Zhao Kai specifically charged that by underpaying cultivators the Agency openly sacrificed quality for quantity, as tea-market functionaries cynically referred to half-rotten stacks of tea as "current government funds."[107]

Until 1103, however, the THA enjoyed a seller's monopoly in Shaanxi and the western frontier markets, sheltering it from the consequences of a decline in tea quality. The advantage of a protected market is reflected in the stability of the price ratio between tea and horses: Although 1085 marks the end of the expansionist period, up to 1104 the price of a 13¼-hand pony in Qinzhou oscillated only slightly between 100 and 112 catties of tea.[108] I think it is also probable that despite the eternal battle between market officials and tea cultivators over price, fairly steady commodity prices during this period allowed the Agency to pay the cultivator a price that forced him to produce more without ruining him. And once quality controls were relaxed, the possibility of selling unlimited amounts of tea to the government would have brought a flood of inferior tea to market regardless of price. Harsh and unpredictable application of the anti-smuggling laws and fiscal exploitation unquestionably made the lot of the small, unprotected cultivator difficult, as was expressed in the popular Sichuanese lament that because of the monopsony "the land does not produce tea; in truth it produces trouble."[109] Nonetheless, for households on marginal land with cash needs tea was still probably an asset rather than a liability during the first thirty years of the monopsony. Our evidence, to be sure, is mostly negative. Yet it is significant that after the Pengkou riot of 1077 the tea industry gave rise to no further instances of collective violence. Nor do any of the indictments of the tea monopoly up to the early twelfth century—by Lü Tao, Su Che, and Liu Zhi in 1086, and Yang Tianhui and Li Xin around 1100— seriously claim that cultivators were being driven into insolvency and flight.[110]

THE TIGHTENING NOOSE. The price of tea in relation to horses deteriorated as soon as Eastern Shaanxi was transferred to the southeastern tea monopoly. In mid 1105 the Tea and Horse Agency was forced to pay 174 catties of tea for the standard 13¼-hand pony, and horse prices rose steadily after that.[111] And as the value of tea in horse and then consumer markets fell, the monopsony began to weigh more heavily on tea cultivators. In 1128 Zhao Kai lodged the first accusation that THA credit manipulation and confiscatory prices had driven garden households into insolvency (*pochan*), although he does not indicate how long this had been going on.

In his attempt to reform state control of the industry, Zhao adjusted tea quotas to the severely reduced Southern Song markets, as we saw earlier in this chapter. As a result of Zhao's adjustment the 1130s were prosperous for both tea merchants and the THA alike, and it is likely that pressure on the tea cultivators was somewhat relieved. But this short interlude of stability peaked in the mid 1140s, when Agency officials had jacked up the price of each hundred-catty tea-license to 12 strings of 300 cash, the maximum that tea merchants would pay. As they had up to 1077, THA officials used a variety of tactics to squeeze more tea out of cultivators for the sake of tea merchants, most notoriously Han Qiu's tea premium. But the political and economic circumstances were different in 1150 from what they had been 1077, and there as no rapid rebound: Native opposition to the monopoly was muzzled by chief minister Qin Gui's boycott of Sichuanese at court, so that the policy went unchallenged for almost a decade; and the generally robust upward cycle of the 1060s and 1070s had been definitively reversed with the loss of the Shaanxi horse and consumer markets.

The mid twelfth century stands as a turning-point in the fortunes of the Sichuanese tea cultivators. By the time Qin Gui's death in 1154 released a storm of protest against state fiscal policies in Sichuan, the industry was irreparably damaged. The following year the Sichuanese official Zhang Zhen charged that by driving the people into misery in order to reward the merchants, Han Qiu's tea premium had "dredged the flow but exhausted the source." The signs of that exhaustion were unmistakable: since state and merchant collaborated to pay less for tea than it cost to produce, tea cultivators were either forced into smuggling in an effort to remain solvent, or were impoverished and forced to flee their homes.[112] The actual fall in prices to the producer is unknown, since not a single tea-purchase price for western Sichuan during the Southern Song has been preserved. But on the basis of Wang Zhiwang's assertion that a merchant paid 40 strings of cash in taxes, license fees, and purchase price for second-class tea in 1160, we can estimate a price to the cultivator of about 250 cash per catty.[113] If we reckon that between 1077 and 1160 tea prices rose 2.7 times (from 90 to 250 cash per catty) while rice prices rose 5 times (from 1,200 cash per *dan* to 6,000 cash per *dan*), it is clear that the small cultivator who depended on tea sales to obtain staple grains would find that the value of his crop had deteriorated badly. And when drought drove rice prices in the west up to 12 to 13 strings of cash, as happened in 1167, the small cultivator had no cushion at all against disaster.[114]

Han Qiu's quota increase deprived large numbers of garden households of the marginal profits that had kept them solvent. But withdrawal from the market did not absolve a cultivator of his tea and tax quotas, and consequently tea households were forced to go into debt to meet their assessments and then to risk selling good tea privately for cash to pay of these debts. The cycle of debt and insolvency that ensued transformed the problem of the cultivator from a rallying point for native opponents of the tea monopoly to a central concern of Sichuan's financial administrators, including the Tea and Horse Intendants. The three issues that converged with the most destructive impact on the cultivators, and that became the focus of relief legislation, were the smuggling laws, tax assessments, and of course the tea quotas themselves.

SMUGGLING LAWS. The laws against tea smuggling aroused particular opposition because they suddenly transformed what had been a basic livelihood—the cultivation and sale of tea—into a potentially criminal act. Lü Tao described with great passion his anger and feeling of helplessness when as Administrator of Pengzhou in early 1077 he was directed by the Tea Market Agency to order all tea cultivators and shop households to dispose of their stocks of old tea within half a month in order to clear the market for the new, monopolized harvest. Anyone in possession of as little as one catty of pre-monopoly tea after the time limit could be informed on or seized and punished for smuggling.[115] The specter of a previously law-abiding population turned into criminals by the tea laws was raised again twenty-three years later by the Sichuanese official Li Xin, then serving as a local official in Xingyuanfu. In a memorial to the emperor, Li described the collared necks and shackled feet of alleged tea smugglers whose interrogation led to an ever-widening circle of arrests, until there were "no empty places in the prisons . . . and the sounds of injustice and pain had become unbearable to hear." Li charged that tea-related cases were over ten times more numerous than any other category of crime reported by the Lizhou Circuit Judicial Intendant to the throne.[116]

This criminalization of a previously legal trade must have been one of the most traumatic aspects of the New Policies' projection of state power into the region. But the smuggling laws during the Northern Song were neither so severe nor so endemically destructive as they were to be in the Southern Song. As codified in 1083, smuggling entailed "bearing tea to places without government markets, or forging or abusing tea licenses in order to sell tea to unauthorized persons or to evade commercial taxes."[117] The situation was not much changed under the contract markets, except that instead of selling to the government directly the cultivator sold to merchants and registered tea shops under the supervision of the government.[118]

There were two ways in which the punishments for smuggling became more severe between 1080 and the mid twelfth century, as oversupply and the greater proximity of the horse markets jeopardized the Intendancy's purchasing power. First, the degree of punishment typically meted out rose over time up the graduated scale known as the five punishments (*wuxing*), comprising the light rod, the heavy rod, forced labor, deportation, and execution. And second, two sets of special codes that increased the gravity of the punishments, the "heavy penalties" (*zhongduan zui*) and martial law (*junfa*), were gradually applied in an increasingly routine manner.[119]

Under the Yuanfeng Intendancy, for example, although penalties for smuggling were initiated from as little as a single catty, the punishments remained within the fourth and the third categories, the heavy rod and forced labor. The punishments for smuggling were inordinately severe. For example, illicit sale of 40 catties of tea, worth only 800 cash, would earn the unfortunate cultivator a sentence of one year's forced labor. A common thief, by contrast, had to steal property worth 2,000 cash before being punished in the same degree.[120] But despite the very real hardship imposed on the cultivator by the Yuanfeng laws, it does not appear that the "heavy laws" were invoked. The heavy-law regulations made punishments more severe, extended liability on the part of accomplices and kin further, and offered rewards that were greater than ordinary penalties for certain types of crimes and in periodically redesignated regions.[121] They were first applied by the Intendancy to the single case of a commoner caught smuggling tea in Xizhou in 1092 and were made the categorical punishment for any horse-market official or merchant who sold Mingshan tea to Tibetan traders for commodities other than horses in 1101.[122] In both cases it took a threat to the tea and horse trade in Shaanxi to elicit the heavy-law provisions.

During the Southern Song, however, any smuggling automatically affected the terms of trade between tea and horses, since the western tea lands communicated directly with the two principal horse markets at Dancheng and Fengtie. A parallel situation existed in the southeast, where merchants illegally supplied by cultivators could reach the Jin frontier from every tea-producing circuit. Consequently officials in both tea regions sought to make swift use of the heavy-law provisions but were restrained by fears that the draconian penalties might agitate local populations before the newly restored dynasty had consolidated its power. The court traditionally offset the awesome majesty of imperial rule with the benevolent mercy of imperial amnesties, including "amnesty reductions of original penalties" (*sheyin yuanmian*). But in the case of the tea and salt monopolies, "the sole source of funds for nurturing the nation's troops," liberality was sacrificed to prudence. Early in 1133, after two years of prompting by regional tea and salt officials, the court specifically excluded tea and salt smugglers from "all amnesties granted however many times."[123] Later that year the court denied the protection of amnesties to Sichuanese smugglers as well, after Zhao Kai complained that without a clear mandate "officials would take a wait-and-see attitude and hold back on the prohibition of illicit trade." Henceforth, "the sub-celestial tea and salt administrations all employed the heavy laws."[124]

It was also Zhao Kai who introduced martial law into the Sichuanese tea monopoly. Zhao made anyone caught smuggling Sichuanese tea west to the tribal capitals of the "submissive Tibetans" or north to within ten *li* of the Sino-Jurchen border automatically subject to martial law, which under the circumstances almost certainly meant execution. Punishment was decreased one degree for violators who crossed the Tibetan border but had not reached the tribal capitals, making them liable to deportation at a distance of 3,000 *li*.[125]

Deportation also served as the fulcrum of Intendancy efforts to prevent tea cultivation from spreading to the Tibetan borderlands and in 1142 was made the mandatory penalty for smuggling tea seeds to the Tibetans:

> If garden householders gathering tea seeds dare to sell to unauthorized people, thereby causing the seeds to be traded or sold to the Tibetans, then both the cultivators and the intermediary buyers will be deported 3,000 *li*. Storehousers *(tingzang)* and carriers *(fuzai)* will be separated one from the other and sent 500 *li* for three years of forced labor. There will be no amnesty reductions of original penalties. All categories of persons are permitted to inform on and seize [suspected smugglers] and will be rewarded with a bounty of 500 strings of cash for each violator. The tea gardens of the cultivators involved will be confiscated by the state. Prefectural and county officials who are lax in investigating the problems will be put in penal servitude for two years and fined.[126]

Twenty-five years later the identical regulations were applied to the sale of tea shoots. The efforts to keep Tibetans from producing their own tea met with little success, however; and around this time reports filtered back that the Tibetan tribes on the Yazhou border had acquired the art of tea cultivation, increasing their contempt for Sichuan's common "convoy-tea."[127]

The 1142 ruling also introduced confiscation of a cultivator's tea garden at the very time that cultivators were becoming most deeply pressed by quota shortfalls and cash debts into smuggling tea to meet past obligations. At an unspecified date, confiscation was made the mandatory penalty for cultivators in Long'anxian (Mianzhou) who were caught illegally selling ten catties of tea or more. The value of the cultivator's garden was assessed, and individuals found to contract for its purchase *(chengmai)*. Half of the purchase price went to the state, and half was returned to the convicted smuggler as partial compensation. In 1163 the Long'an precedent was applied by Intendant Xü Bi to all of Chengdu and Lizhou Circuits, becoming in effect the standard penalty for smuggling in western Sichuan.[128]

The Long'an precedent was applied at the same time that officials had begun to frame quota and tax-relief measures for the beleaguered tea cultivators. Because it threatened both producers and the public peace in the most fundamental way, by enlarging the population of homeless and destitute, six years later the law was rescinded at the request of the Tea and Horse Agency itself. The drought of 1167 had more than doubled the price of rice in at least three tea-producing districts (Mianzhou, Hanzhou, and Shiquanjun), which must have produced a wave of smuggling cases.[129] In 1169 the Intendant acknowledged that frustrated officials had extended the antismuggling law to at least seven milder transgressions: first, exceeding the contracted delivery time; second, mismatching the contracted and actual varieties of tea; third, employing the contracted amount as a ruse for wholesaling; fourth, mismatching the actual and contracted amounts; fifth, not taking the processed tea to the government markets; sixth, cultivating tea shrubs without registering in a mutual-surveillance unit; and seventh, taking tea to the market when no government official was available to complete the transaction. It is clear that administering officials, themselves intimidated by severe penalties for negligence in the suppression of smuggling, indiscriminately applied the confiscation clause to any violation that might be construed as smuggling. The Intendant himself was forced to admit that official overreaction had forced "the impoverished peoples of the mountains and valleys to break up their families and lose their occupations." As a result the ruling was revoked, and the adjudication of smuggling offenses "returned to the status quo ante."[130]

Because some officials continued to blame declining prices for government tea on smuggling rather than oversupply, periodic attempts were still made to tighten smuggling regulations.[131] Moreover, captured tea, if not the gardens it came from, continued to be confiscated; but the market was so saturated that the Intendancy could no longer find buyers for the contraband, yet refused to burn it. It became customary to force the unwanted tea on shop households and local tax farmers *(lantou)* at a fee paid in advance, with the recipients instructed to dispose of the tea however they could. This practice was not officially prohibited until 1185.[132]

The steady increase in smuggling penalties was accompanied by increasingly generous rewards for commoners who informed on or apprehended alleged smugglers. In 1083 Lu Shimin offered a bounty of 3 strings of cash for every 10 catties of tea recovered in smuggling or tax evasion, starting at 1 catty and with a maximum bounty of 30 strings of cash.[133] At that rate the reward equaled an average of 300 cash per catty over the range, or about six times the worth of the tea itself. By 1085 the bounty had swelled to 30 strings for only 40 catties of tea worth 800 cash, or 37.5 times the value of the tea.[134] Zhao Kai again increased informants' rewards around 1128, as his sponsor Zhang Jun was reluctantly forced to admit.[135] We have no information on the proportional relationship between tea and bounty values for small amounts, but the total sums were much greater. As of 1135, a commoner who reported cultivators or merchants selling tea to Tibetans in the west or to Jurchens in the north earned an unspecified sum of money per catty up to 1,000 strings' worth of tea and the tea itself beyond that. At the wholesale price of 500 cash per catty current in 1160, a bounty-hunter could gain over 2,000 catties of tea.[136] The last bounty price we have is for 1142, repeated in 1167, when 500 strings of cash per head were provided for denouncing or seizing cultivators and others who allowed tea seeds and sprouts to pass to the Tibetans.[137] So substantial a sum would clearly have been generous enough to "incite mean-spirited people to inform on and seize their fellows," as Lü Tao had earlier feared.

Of course the Tea and Horse Agency also charged its own and collateral officials with suppressing tea smuggling; a partial list of responsible functionaries includes the managing supervisors, military intendants (*junbei chaishi*), contraband-tea inspectors (*xunzhuo sicha shichen*), sheriffs, constables, and prefectural and county civil aides.[138] But the twelfth-century Chinese police capacity was not dense enough to contain tea or salt smuggling in the mountainous lands of Sichuan, or indeed of Hunan, Hubei, Jiangnan and elsewhere, without buying the services of the local inhabitants.[139] Thus a practice that had been used with great reluctance in early Tang, when the arena of state power was still circumscribed, had become a basic feature of government in the Song, when the state and its monopolies reached out to every corner of the society.[140]

TAXATION. Monopoly taxation added a second burden that became insupportable once oversupply and declining prices turned tea production into a liability. Prior to the monopoly Sichuanese tea was not subject to crop-specific levies of any industry-wide significance. There were only four government markets in the entire region, and local tribute was probably limited to token amounts of the best teas.[141] The government earned revenues from the industry by taxing local and regional trade: 6 cash per catty paid by the merchant at the time of purchase in a fixed market (*zhushui*), 6 cash per catty paid at the time of sale (*fanshui*), and 2 cash per catty for each tax station traversed (*guoshui*), with a typical range of two to ten tax stations.[142] The cultivator on the other hand simply paid the twice-yearly tax on his plantation and other holdings and the surtaxes this entailed, but no special tax as a tea producer.[143]

Under the monopsony and contract-market systems the twice-yearly tax duties remained, but in addition the cultivator was charged with a wide assortment of taxes either levied on his individual transactions or distributed by quota to the garden-household community to which he belonged. In the first category the most significant were the supplementary trade tax (*touziqian*), the market-usage fee (*shiliqian*), the broker's fee (*yaqian*), and the local products tax (*tuchan*).

The supplementary trade tax originated in 973 as a surcharge on the payment by Sichuanese of their twice-yearly tax, including a payment of 1 cash per catty on payments made in tea, and was not made universal until 1040.[144] Lu Shimin's thirty-eight articles specify a rate of 5 cash per 1,000 that, following a New Policies precedent of 1069, was assessed twice: once on payments by the tea market to the cultivator and again on payments by the merchant to the tea market.[145] As with virtually all Song taxes the rates rose steadily, reaching 43 cash per 1,000 by 1140 and peaking at 56 cash per 1,000, or 5.6 percent, by 1165.[146]

A second tax paid by both cultivator and merchant was the market-usage fee, a general surtax of 10 percent on the payment of commercial taxes and other fees that in the case of the monopoly was used to pay the tea-market service personnel.[147] The cultivator also paid the "broker's fee," a cash sum deducted from the state's payment to the cultivator and put into a common fund for the payment of market brokers. Originally the rate was supposed to vary with local custom, which in Pengzhou amounted to 6 percent.[148] The local products tax, which was also imposed on salt-well households, appears to have been unique to the contract markets. Along with the broker's and market-usage fees, it formed a fixed package of levies, totaling 2.3 strings per hundred-catty license transaction, that the cultivator had to pay on selling his tea.[149] If my estimate of a price to the Southern Song cultivator of an average of 250 cash per catty is correct (see above), then these three taxes alone would have consumed almost 10 percent of his return; moreover, because the rate was fixed, they absorbed an increasing proportion of the cultivator's profit as the price of tea declined.

A second category of taxes consisted of levies that were distributed by quota to specific locales to be shared by the cultivators, most likely in inverse proportion to their power and status. The most prominent of these was the "tea-tax commutation fee" (*chake zhegu*), a monetary assessment either in lieu of, or in addition to, deliveries in kind to the monopoly markets. Most of the cash-crop and handicraft industries, such as salt, wine, and silk and hempen textiles, were responsible for such fees; quotas were set at the circuit level and distributed down to the industry, or possibly the general populace.[150] The garden households of the eight tea-producing townships of Long'anxian were assigned a commutation tax of 927 strings 114 cash (6 cash per catty on 154,519 catties) around 1078.[151] Tea cultivators were also made collectively responsible for the "monopoly-goods and government rents" surtax *(chengtiqian)*. This was a surtax of 3 percent on the payment of tea, salt, and wine taxes and taxes and rents to the government, created in 1144 to help subsidize minting and military expenses. The total assessment for Chengdu, Zizhou, and Lizhou circuits was fixed at 431,690 strings 291 cash, of which Sichuan's cultivators shared 3,148 strings 290 cash.[152]

REGISTERED QUOTAS. What made the plethora of taxes and the risks of smuggling so damaging to the cultivator in a declining market was the impossibility of withdrawing from the industry. The garden households were assigned fixed quotas that bore no intrinsic relation to current capacity or market demand and that persisted even if they were forced to suspend production. As a result, they were unable to allocate their land and labor to more productive uses, yet could no longer subsist on what they were paid for their tea. Consequently the cultivators were forced to borrow cash or smuggle tea in order to meet their tax and consumption needs, risking debt and foreclosure in the first instance, and denunciation, arrest, and severe penalties in the second.

But even after regional officials and the court had perceived the problems caused by tea quotas in excess of capacity and demand, no easy solution was at hand. For just as the individual cultivator faced a given tea or tax assignment, so, too, the Intendancy as a whole had to meet revenue quotas that had been set in more prosperous days, when the value of tea was greater. These quotas had long been allocated to the thirty or forty markets in the system, run by officials whose careers rose or fell with their ability to meet them and whose instinctive response to falling prices or declining revenues was to demand still more tea or cash from the cultivator. In order to relieve the pressure on the tea households, financial expectations had to be brought into closer alignment with economic reality all through the system; but this in turn meant sacrificing political in-

fluence. Thus the process of winding down the monopolized industry was slow and extremely wrenching.

Under the Yuanfeng Intendancy each retail-tea market had a profit
quota, and each convoy-tea market a tea delivery quota. Although
no text specifies that cultivators were registered and made responsible for specific amounts of tea, when Lu Shimin reestablished the
full monopsony in 1097 he specifically forbade the registration of
fixed quotas for individual garden households, which suggests that
the practice had existed.[153] Registration of cultivator households
was a hallmark of the contract-market system, although its original
intent was to limit entry into rather than exit out of the market.[154]
Household registration did not necessarily entail responsibility for
a fixed quota; but when Han Qiu increased the government's total
demand for tea in 1148, it was through household quotas that he
wrung more tea out of the underpaid cultivators. As the Sichuanese
official Sun Daofu lamented in 1156, "Officials have no sympathy
for the cultivators and endeavor only to increase tea quotas in search
of greater surpluses. . . . The contract-market estimates have no
basis in fact."[155] Moreover, in many cases the increases were so
precipitous that cultivators were forced into stripping and damaging their trees to meet the new target, making it impossible to
satisfy their quotas the following year. For them the cycle of debt
began immediately, since the new quotas remained.[156]

The history of the tea monopoly from 1155 to the end of the
century is largely one of attempts to reduce the household tea and
tax assessments in the face of resistance by line administrators. The
first battle in this war of wills was fought in 1157, when Han Qiu's
quota increase of 4,600,000 catties was rescinded at the request of
the region's chief financial officials. Four years later an imperial
amnesty *(she)* charged that individual tea markets had taken advantage of the remission to cover their own quota shortfalls without
actually reducing the so-called "empty quotas" *(xu'e)* of the middle-
and lower-level garden households. This obstructionism was later
blamed on Intendant Zheng Ai (1154–1155), who was said to have
ordered his subordinates to press cultivators for the higher quotas
despite the remission. But at the time of the 1161 amnesty, the

Intendant was Wang Zhiwang, a member of the investigating committee that had originally recommended the reduction and a staunch advocate of tax relief.[157] Clearly reform was no easy matter.

At the heart of the matter lay the political reality of the Song bureaucracy. As Sima Guang had deplored in 1086, officials gained political influence and career rewards by meeting output targets rather than by securing the well-being of the population.[158] However forcefully the court enunciated platitudes about the livelihood of its imperial subjects, officials knew that they would be judged on the basis of their bureaucratic output. As Agency productivity began its inexorable decline at mid century, many Agency chiefs chose to disregard imperial bromides in order to hit their all-important financial quotas. Consequently, minor adjustments ordered from above could not keep pace with the industry's deterioration.

In the late 1160s, for example, Intendant Zhang Song began to force extra tea licenses on individual contract markets, in a ruthless effort to prop up his revenues and prestige. Zhang sent out agents at the end of each month to collect the additional fees, regardless of whether the licenses had been sold. In Xingyuanfu and Yangzhou the market officials in turn forced the tea licenses directly onto the cultivators, leaving it up to them to meet the required sums however they could.[159] These practices ruined many cultivators, but they were not thereby relieved of their tea quotas. In 1177 Pacification Commissioner Hu Yuanzhi called attention to the swelling number of families "burdened with quotas long after they have lost the means of producing tea, or forced by officials to accept ineradicable tea quotas simply because they once sold a little loose tea."[160]

As a result of Hu Yuanzhi's charge, another 1,040,300 catties of tea were trimmed from the Agency's tea production quota, and investigators were ordered to adjust household quotas to actual capacity wherever the two were out of line.[161] But some officials rejected accusations that the Agency was squeezing its cultivators with unrealistic quotas. In 1185, for example, Intendant Wang Wo insisted that other than Mingshan, whose quota was an insignificant 76,729 catties over actual capacity, the THA's targets were accurate. Moreover, Wang Wo blamed the Mingshan imbalance not on exploitative officials but rather on avaricious cultivators, greedy for advance loans:

> Every year the Agency sends capitalization money (*benqian*) down to the Mingshan market to be distributed as deposits on 2,000,000 catties of tea for the horse trade. These funds are divided equitably, based on each household's production of retail tea. But the cultivators are greedy for these advance deposits, and many of them put in a claim for unrealistic amounts of tea. Tea-market officials record the cultivator's base quota and the additional amount of tea contracted for; but when it comes time to sell the tea, many of the cultivators cannot even reach their original quota. Afterwards a market official is sent out to investigate, and he can only use the amounts acknowledged by the cultivator in the "Register of Convoy-Tea Purchases" (*mai gangcha buji*) as his guide. As a result, it is said that the tea quota is excessive and that cultivators are being dunned for amounts of tea beyond their quotas.[162]

Wang Wo was probably quite correct in his assertion that cultivators took larger advances in cash than they could repay in tea; the same phenomenon had occurred under the "Green Sprouts" rural loan measure during the New Policies. But as with the "Green Sprouts" loans, cultivators were driven into oversubscription not by greed, but by a financial system that manipulated all taxable households into paying a constantly escalating proportion of their tax burden in cash, as a means of furtively increasing tax revenues.[163] As tea prices continued to fall (as contemporaries noted), cultivators had no choice but to oversubscribe on the next crop to pay past debts; and oversubscription of course got them more deeply in debt.

Court and high regional officials understood the situation, and they rejected Wang Wo's disclaimer of responsibility. But the court limited its response to admonitions that included no mechanisms for enforcing compliance. Two months after Wang Wo's memorial an "Amnesty on the Occasion of the Suburban Sacrifices" again condemned prefectural and county officials who ignored quota reductions to squeeze Sichuanese tea, salt, and wine producers. The amnesty specifically prohibited the use of forced donations and faked registers, as well as the practice of dumping confiscated tea on shop households and tax farmers. But no specific penalties were promulgated, and enforcement was predictably toothless: Victimized producers were allowed to file complaints; and the provincial Regulator, Commissioner of Supply, and THA Intendant—the very offices most dependent on monopoly revenues—were instructed to investigate the claims and impeach culpable officials.[164]

The 1185 Amnesty revealed how deeply the problems of debt, foreclosure, and property confiscation had cut into the Sichuanese tea industry, threatening not only the cultivator but his kin as well: "In the case of tea, salt, money, and goods not fully repaid according to law *(weiqian)* the value can only be judged against the fixed and moveable property of the debtor *(guqianren)* and the broker-guarantor *(yabaoren)*. No precedent authorizes either the imprisonment of relatives to force them to pay back the debt or the continued dunning of widows who have remarried."[165]

This first amnesty made no distinction between debts to the state and debts to the merchants, but it was repromulgated in 1191 under circumstances that suggest the possibility of multiple debts public and private, with collection of the public debt taking precedence over the private. After repeating the 1185 amnesty, the later text continues as follows: "People owe money to traveling merchants and stores because, having fallen behind in their delivery of goods to the monopolies, their household property has already been confiscated without sufficient compensation. If the broker-guarantors and others continue to be imprisoned, the cyle of bankruptcies will go on without end. Let the debts of all be canceled, so that there will be no mistakes."[166]

The document evidences an ever-widening circle of debt, insolvency, and importuning, in which garden households and salters lose their property to the state before they can repay their debts to private lenders, who in turn seek compensation from the broker-guarantors. The debt cancellation seems to have had no lasting consequence. The 1191 directive affords the first evidence that the economic tide could turn against the brokers, generally the most flexible and least risk-prone class of actors in a monopolistic environment. But in a final amnesty on the question, issued in 1203, the previously exempt second husband was given part of the broker's responsibility: Broker-guarantors remained jointly liable for collection *(jianna)* in the case of tea or salt debtors (to the state it

seems) who had died long before, leaving only a single wife or or-
phans; but if the wife had remarried, the debt now came under the
supervision (*jianli*) of her new husband, subject to an official's estimate of his ability to pay.[167] The text suggests that a shift had
already taken place over the decade on the transfer of debt to a new
household through the wife, with the government simply stepping
in to ensure that the second husband was not also ruined.

Only a change in the system, from tea quotas to market-deter-
mined supply, could have ended the distortions introduced by fixed
assignments. But the Southern Song state was even more starved
for funds than its Northern predecessor, and was never solvent enough
to initiate real reform. As of 1203, when information on the tea
side of the THA enterprise ends, no such changes had occurred; and
the 79,000 catties of Mingshan tea remitted by Wang Wo in 1185
mark the last tea-quota reduction on record. As we have seen, by
the turn of the century the court was forced to acknowledge that
the THA could no longer produce revenues beyond what was needed
for the horse trade. This acknowledgment brought several reductions in the cash burden on Sichuan's tea cultivators during the final
decade of the century, worth a total of about 270,000 strings by
the year 1200.[168]

We have very little information on the Sichuanese tea industry
after 1203. But as I will show in the next chapter, horse procurement became increasingly precarious and foreign markets remained
saturated with tea, making it unlikely that deterioration of the industry was reversed. Moreover the cultivators' lives would certainly
have become harsher still after the 1230s, when the Mongols launched
repeated assaults against western Sichuan in preparation for their
final invasions of Southern Song China.[169] The last reference to the
Sichuanese tea industry during the Song comes from the Mongols
themselves, who symbolically suspended tea and salt taxes upon
invading Sichuan in 1271, to ameliorate "the exhaustion of the
people."[170]

To review the argument of this chapter, there can be little question that by the early thirteenth century the state-induced cycle of

growth in the Sichuanese tea industry had come full circle. Through the first half of the eleventh century, interregional trade had been prohibited; but the regional population was growing steadily, adding an average of 2,667 households annually since 742. At the same time, taxes were low and cultivators who produced high quality tea were probably fairly prosperous. From 1060 to 1074, the suspension of the southeastern monopoly opened up the northwest to Sichuanese tea; and merchants from Shaanxi created a triangular trade linking salt from Jiezhou, tea from the Hanzhong Basin and western Sichuan, and the animal and mineral products imported by traders from Qinghai and Inner Asia to Qinzhou and Tongyuan. On the evidence of Wen Tong in Yangzhou and Lü Tao in Pengzhou, this was a period of prosperity and rapid growth, the beginning of a boom.

Beginning in 1074 bureaucratic innovators replaced private merchants as the prime exporters of Sichuanese tea. Operating under authorization of the New Policies to experiment in obtaining tea and generating revenues for the defense and enrichment of the state, the first Intendants for Tea and Horses created extensive and protected markets for Sichuanese tea by monopolizing the foreign and domestic trade of the northwest. Although cultivators were paid less per unit of tea, because of the entrepreneurial creation of new markets they could sell much more of it. Therefore, despite the introduction of new taxes and harsh restrictions on the cultivator's disposition of his crop, the boom continued. New growth ended by 1085; but the price ratio between tea and horses suggests that there was no drastic decline before 1103.

But the major factor in the growth of the tea industry, the availability of extraregional markets, was reversed once in 1103 by the transfer of eastern Shaanxi to the new southeastern tea monopolies and again in 1127 by the loss of Northwest China to the Jin. Regional population continued to grow, adding another 6,939 households a year for a total increase of 645,388 households from 1080 to 1173; but this was not enough to offset the loss of 1,300,000 domestic buyers in Shaanxi and the native traders of Amdo and points west. Moreover, after 1173 even the modest contribution to demand provided by population growth was halted; for from 1173 to the last census of 1223, the population registered a net loss of 131,819 households, or 2,636 households annually.[171] In addition, although more tea had been produced for the monopoly, quality had declined, so that by the middle of the twelfth century there was not only too much tea, too much of it was of poor quality. With few exceptions, Sichuan was never again known as a producer of fine teas.[172]

Lacking room for territorial expansion, the Tea Market Agency was forced to maintain its previous revenue levels by exploiting the region's merchants and cultivators more intensively. But merchants could not be compelled to trade, whereas cultivators could be compelled to produce more tea or to pay a tax in lieu of production. Hence the burden of the Agency's attempts to maintain high revenues and political influence in a declining market fell on the garden households. By the 1150s a change in the central political leadership allowed information about the deteriorating economic condition of the cultivators, as well as Sichuan's salt, wine, and loom households, to surface, prompting a half-century of tax relief. But even the minimal adjustments called for at the top were obstructed by official resistance at the agency, market, and local government levels, and each decade up to the end of the century uncovered yet another layer of deterioration.

By the thirteenth century, phases of growth that in many industries can be traced back to the early eleventh century and earlier had succumbed to the militarization of northern Sichuan in the 1130s and the overextension of taxation to pay for it. By way of illustrating the consequences (if not demonstrating the causality) for centers of cash-crop and handicraft industries, I will conclude with a lament by a resident of Qiongzhou, one Zhang Shangxing, preserved in Zhu Mu's thirteenth-century "Surpassing Sights all over the World" (*Fangyu shenglan*):

> In former times [Qiongzhou] had four [sources of] profit; now it has four [sources] of suffering. They are tea, salt, wine, and iron. To have four [such sources] of benefit! Other places just had one, or perhaps two, but only our Qiong had them all. In former times when they were profitable, the people

strove for great wealth; now that they have become injurious, the people are all impoverished.[173]

In the absence of new opportunities for growth, bureaucratic entrepreneurship had been transformed into confiscatory taxation and had systematically destroyed the capacity of Heaven's Storehouse to produce new wealth.

SEVEN

The Limits of Bureaucratic Power in the Tea and Horse Trade

The early relationship between Sichuan's tea cultivators and the tea monopoly's procurement officials was intended to mimic a market transaction, with the state paying fair value for goods voluntarily supplied. Over time, however, the fiction of a market relationship gave way to the reality of compulsion, as THA agents squeezed cultivators into supplying tea and its attendant cash fees regardless of price or the logic of supply and demand. Voluntary sales of tea were supplanted by inescapable obligations, and the once-free garden households were transformed into indentured servants of the state.

Reliance on authority to mobilize and distribute resources is the hallmark of a command economy; but though a country can bully its own people, generally speaking it has to rely on trade to get needed supplies from beyond its borders.[1] Trade is cheaper and more reliable than raiding your neighbors. But trade can also be precarious, especially if it subjects critical needs of the state to the vagaries of the marketplace—as the oil embargo of the 1970s demonstrated dramatically during modern times. Nevertheless, in a study of historical command economies, market forces, and the technology of war, William H. McNeill contends that in most cases, "the commodities really important for the maintenance of armies and administrative bureaucracies . . . were available from within the bound-

aries of the state, and could be effectively mobilized by command."
Where this was not the case, however, dependence "on distant suppliers who were not firmly subject to imperial words of command
constituted a limit upon the management of ancient empires."[2]

During the Song, reliance on imported cavalry horses constituted
the most severe constraint on the management of the Chinese empire. As we saw in Chapter One, after almost a century of abortive
efforts to create a national herd, New Policies administrators dismantled the state pasturage system, conceding that all war horses
would have to be purchased abroad. Many factors entered into the
relationship between the Song state and its foreign horse suppliers,
including considerations of prestige, power, and social control. But
the relationship was fundamentally an exchange transaction, dominated by the Song's utter reliance on Tibetan, Man and Yi breeders
for its cavalry horses.

Because they lived safely outside the pale of Song military power
and administrative authority, these tribal herdsmen would trade
horses only if they obtained something sufficiently desirable in return. Consequently, Song horse purchasers were thrust into the
awkward role of buyers in a seller's market, a position that affected
even the nature of the face-to-face relationship between agents of
the Tea and Horse Agency and the tribal horse merchants. Whereas
the tea-purchase officials, for example, could browbeat and abuse
the hapless tea suppliers, their counterparts in the frontier horse
markets were obliged to coddle coarse and bizarrely garbed herdsmen who probably excited their repugnance.[3] Even in the 1080s,
when the Song was buying more horses than it ever had before,
officials were reproved for "haughtily reviling [the Tibetan traders]
with foul language" and were ordered to provide frequent feasts of
food and wine for all the Tibetan horse sellers[4]

Distinctions in the relationship between THA officials and their
tea and horse suppliers went well beyond questions of propriety.
Because they were backed by the coercive power of the state, tea-
purchase officials could force cultivators to sell more tea for less
money; they could transform tea procurement into a form of confis-

cation. Under the market conditions that defined the horse trade, however, the number, quality, and price of the horses that THA agents could buy depended on two factors beyond their control: the overall supply of horses and the foreign demand for China's trade goods. When the government's demand for horses exceeded supply, while its stock of trade commodities exceeded foreign demand, control over the terms of trade shifted conclusively to the horse suppliers. By the twelfth and thirteenth centuries, as we shall see below, tribal horse traders could manipulate the Song state into paying higher prices for fewer horses, and for horses of poorer quality.

EXCHANGING TEA FOR HORSES

With the creation of the tea and horse trade, horse procurement acquired a much higher level of integration than it had previously enjoyed. As will be remembered from Chapter One, until 1060 the principal horse-purchasing mechanism was the "traders' caravan." Under the traders-caravan procedure, Tibetan and Han horse merchants first assembled their herds in the frontier markets, then drove them directly to Kaifeng, where at least three separate bureaus took part in evaluating the horses and paying and entertaining their owners. This expensive operation was supplemented by a variety of routine and ad hoc procurement measures that located the transaction closer to the frontier, a trend followed by Xue Xiang in his reforms of the early 1060s. In a variety of experiments undertaken while he was chief financial officer of the Shaanxi region, Xue attempted to decentralize both the financing and actual management of the horse trade to Shaanxi, or at most Shaanxi and Sichuan.

Because Xue served as concurrent Intendant for Horse Purchases and Pastures, Assistant Fiscal Intendant of Shaanxi, and Regulator of Jiezhou Salt, he was personally able to coordinate horse-procurement policy. But horse procurement and financing were not integrated into a single, specialized operation until the onset of the tea and horse trade in 1074; and they were not unified into a single enterprise—the Superintendancy for Tea and Horses—until 1086.[5]

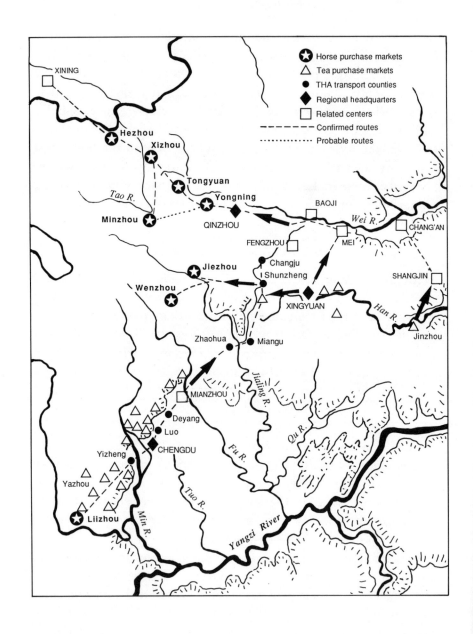

Legend:
- ★ Horse purchase markets
- △ Tea purchase markets
- ● THA transport counties
- ◆ Regional headquarters
- □ Related centers
- – – – Confirmed routes
- ·········· Probable routes

XINING

Hezhou

Xizhou

Tongyuan

Tao R.

Yongning

BAOJI

Minzhou

QINZHOU

Wei R.

CHANG'AN

FENGZHOU

MEI

Jiezhou

Changju

Shunzheng

SHANGJIN

Wenzhou

XINGYUAN

Han R.

Jinzhou

Zhaohua

Miangu

Jialing R.

MIANZHOU

Deyang

Fu R.

Qu R.

Luo

CHENGDU

Yizheng

Yazhou

Tuo R.

Liizhou

Min R.

Yangzi River

Map 8 Tea Supply Routes to Horse Markets under the Northern
Song THA

The tea and horse trade made horse procurement a decentralized, regionally based operation, and relieved the central government of the need to manage or subsidize the purchase of horses.

SHIPPING TEA. The rhythms of the tea and horse trade were geared to the Inner Asian cycles of pasturage and transhumance. In 1083 one official reported that because "by nature horses thrive in the cold and suffer in the heat," the supply of marketable horses was plentiful in winter, scarce during the summer, and unpredictable in the spring.[6] During the hot months of late spring and summer, Tibetan horse breeders grazed their horses in the cool pastures of Qinghai, at an elevation of 10,000 feet; as the cold season approached, they drove their herds to the lower and warmer markets of the Tao and Wei River valleys.

The marketing season began in the eighth month of the year.[7] Between the first tea-picking in the third and fourth months and the opening of the horse markets, 4,000,000–5,000,000 catties (ca. 2,600–3,000 tons) of tea had to be hauled 900 miles from Yazhou and 400 miles from the Hanzhong Basin to the government's foreign trade markets in Western Shaanxi. In order to supply these markets, some 150 tea convoys were issued annually; and the work gangs struggling with their loads of tea must have been a ubiquitous sight along the paths and trestle roads that spanned the 9,000-foot Qinling mountains.[8]

The Intendants employed the same combination of organizational sophistication and political command to ship tea that they used to obtain it in the first place. In this they were aided by the value of the tea and horse trade to the court, which allowed them to make tea transport a primary obligation of local government and subjected local officials to the scrutiny and evaluation of the Tea and Horse Agency.

Local government officials were directly enlisted in the mobilization of transport labor. Along less troublesome stretches of roadway, the THA relied on hiring porters for the short term as needed. Every prefecture and county along the tea (and up to 1086 salt) convoy routes was required to maintain registers of people liable for porterage service, and to conscript them (*hegu,* literally "harmoni-ously hire") at the appropriate time at seasonal rates. Local govern-ment officials were also required to levy "persons of means and good judgment" to serve as "heads of tithing" (*jiatou*), who were charged with providing surety against the porters absconding with govern-ment property. These same officials were also expected to set up sheds to serve as "convoy pavillions" (*gangyuan*) at strategic points where the convoy crews were exchanged and to open the temples, sheds, pavillions, postal stations, and empty yamen offices under their jurisdiction to tea and THA-salt convoys that encountered inclement weather.[9]

The system of short-term hiring was supplemented by a network of permanently manned tea-transport relay depots (*chezi dipu*) set up along the most critical and heavily traveled segments of the distri-bution system, where a reliable and constantly available labor force was essential. By the end of the New Policies era, the system in-cluded over a hundred depots, each manned by fifty "tea-transport depot soldiers" (*banchapu junren* or *banchapu bingshi*).[10] According to Su Che, the Agency employed roughly 5,000 transport soldiers, at a cost to the government of about 20 strings of cash per head in food and clothing annually.[11] The Agency also paid wages based on the amount of tea carried and the distances traversed.[12] Tea-depot soldiers served one-year terms, and were mustered from among those households normally liable for labor service. If civilian manpower proved insufficient, replacements could be made first from among runaway militiamen that had been recaptured and then from the roster of active prefectural and county troops.[13] In emergencies the Agency could even draw the provincial army (*xiangjun*) into trans-port duty: Around 1080, according to Lü Tao, several hundred members of the Chengdu Circuit provincial army were impressed into service, and "in no more than one or two years they had all died or run off."[14]

Each depot and its soldiers was managed by a "convoy foreman" (*gangguan*), selected from among military men with previous expe-rience convoying tea in Sichuan. Overall coordination was provided by five or six military men appointed by the THA as tea-depot inspectors *(xunxia chapu shichen)*; they were aided by a convoy expeditor *(cuifa gangyunguan)*, whose responsibilities included making payments and collections.[15] But perhaps the most critical aspect of the system was that responsibility for actually supervising both the relay depots and local conscription was extended from the THA-appointed officials to the functionaries of local government. County magistrates were given general responsibility for moving tea through their jurisdictions, and military inspectors *(xunjian)*, sheriffs *(wei)*, postal inspectors *(xunxia madipu)*, and military attachés *(shichen)* were specifically charged with speeding the convoys on to the next border.[16]

The tea-convoy operation imposed an enormous burden on its porters. Unlike the nineteenth- and twentieth-century tea porters described by von Richthofen and Baber, carrying as much as 400 pounds on their backs in wooden frames equipped with support crutches, Song porters made use of a cart.[17] No details about the vehicle itself have remained, but it was most likely a variant of the traditional Sichuanese single-wheeled barrow attributed to Zhuge Liang.[18] These tea carts were loaded with four bales *(tuo)*, or over 520 pounds, of tea; and both opponents and administrators of the tea and horse trade admitted that convoying tea could cost a man his life. In 1086, for example, Su Che wrote:

> The roads of Shu, crossing mountains and rivers, are reputed to be the most dangerous and terrible. As a result, shipping tea to Shaanxi exacts the most awful burdens on a man's strength. In the tea relay one man transports four bales, or about 400 and some catties of tea, each day. Moreover, in the return cart he carries Jiezhou salt, traveling sixty *li* [20 miles] back and forth in the mountains. If mud or slippery stretches are encountered, a man's strength is exhausted; and the porters run off and seek [relief in] death. Alas, anger fills the roads. Last year, in the eighth and ninth months, all the men of the Jianyang Depot in Jianzhou fled. The tea depots along the way are called "death traps" *(namingchang)*.[19]

Twenty-seven years later, Intendant Zhang Hui portrayed the burden in the same region in similar terms: "Because of poor harvests and famine up to [1110] the strength of the local people is still [in 1113] depleted, and those among the former heads of tithing (*jiatou*) and porter households who have not yet become 'floating corpses' have run off to escape their service obligation. As a result hiring and levying of porters has come to a standstill."[20]

Hirees and conscripts did attempt to challenge the convoy system. Around 1080, for example, a man from Yangzhou issued a formal complaint about his transport burden to the Administrator of Yongxingjun, the anti-reformer Liu Xiang, who in turn ordered compulsory hiring in his prefecture stopped.[21] But convoyers could also profit from their transport duty. In 1100 the monopoly opponent Li Xin charged that "depot soldiers are among the most criminal elements. As a result they turn around and rob the 'good citizens' (*liang min*) in order to fill their mouths and bellies."[22] And around 1170 Yuan Xingzong complained that porters adulterated the tea they carried with tree leaves plucked along the way, so that they could sell off the best tea for private profit. "When it comes time to trade for horses," Yuan reported, "the Tibetans recoil in horror."[23]

Transport bottlenecks occasionally disrupted the horse trade. Over 59,000 bales of tea stood backed up in three Qinling warehouses as of mid 1113, for example, in part because of the shortage of transport workers revealed by Zhang Hui.[24] And in 1156 horse merchants became so irritated at having to wait up to a month for their tea to be delivered to Wenzhou that trade at the local market stalled.[25] Moreover, the system produced enormous waste. In 1077 Zhou Yin charged that backlogged tea, "spoiled by the wind and the rain, lies abandoned by the side of the road like piles of shit."[26]

But because the THA possessed so much more tea than it needed, the transport system could absorb enormous losses; and there is no evidence that tea-transport problems ever placed more than temporary obstacles in the way of the horse trade. Transport bottlenecks could generally be solved through administrative adjustments that tightened the Agency's control over the local populace. By embedding the organization of transport labor into the structure of local government, the Intendancy could draw on a labor pool of almost three-quarters of a million households between the tea lands of Sichuan and the horse markets of Shaanxi to move its tea, while delegating the on-site surveillance and control of that labor pool to the county magistrates and other local officials. The capacity of the state to exploit local laborers at low cost, in conjunction with a growing tea surplus that made enormous waste tolerable, absolved the transport system from the need for economic efficiency. This transformation of political inputs into labor was simply an extension of the same system that compelled tea cultivators to part with their tea for non-economic returns. But transporting tea was the last phase of the tea and horse trade that could be successfully manipulated through administrative techniques.

BUYING HORSES: THE QIN BRANCH. The Tea and Horse Agency operated a primary marketing system in Shaanxi that purchased horses with tea and a secondary system in southern Sichuan that relied increasingly on silk.[27] During the Southern Song the two components were differentiated as the Qin and Chuan branches (*si*).[28]

The cornerstone of the Shaanxi system were the six markets in or adjoining the territories captured by Wang Shao between 1068 and 1074: He, Xi, and Min prefectures in the Tao River valley, and Tongyuan Commandery, Yongning Garrison, and Qin Prefecture along the upper reaches of the Wei River. This cluster of markets skirting the southwestern corner of the great Longxi Basin projected Song purchasing activity out towards the rich pasturelands of Qinghai, in northeastern Tibet. By the late eleventh century these Qinghai grasslands were China's sole source of war horses.[29]

The Jurchen conquest deprived Song China of its principal Shaanxi markets. The Southern Song THA was forced to fall back on the two more southerly markets of Danchang and Fengtie Gorge Garrisons, tucked among the jagged 10,000-foot peaks separating Min and Jie prefectures and much less accessible to the Qinghai breeders.[30] A third market, Wenzhou, occupied an intermediate position in the THA marketing network. Memorialists differed on the quality of the Wenzhou horses, which probably originated in the Tibeto-Sichuanese borderlands of Songpan; but in the end they were grudgingly given "war-horse" status.[31]

Who were the Tibetan participants in the tea and horse trade? In contrast to the precise identification of tribal suppliers in the early eleventh century, our information for the Shaanxi tea and horse exchange is frustratingly incomplete.[32] But even through our very imperfect sources it is possible to discern the outline of a tea and horse trade suspended in a web of relationships linking herder/merchants, Tibetan political elites, assimilated "cooked" tribes, and the purchasing agents of the Song state.

The most obscure actors in the trade are the suppliers themselves. Song sources variously refer to Tibetan horse sellers as *maima Fanbu* (horse-selling Tibetan tribesmen), *Fanshang* (Tibetan merchants), *Fanke* (guests), or *yuan Fan* (distant Tibetans). These and other generic terms provide no clue to whether herdsmen and merchants were differentiated. But it is clear that the herders and merchants were distinct from the Tibetan political elites with whom the Song state dealt directly. The rulers of northeastern Tibet, such as the scions of Juesiluo's Qingtang federation, occupied the towns in and around Xining and the Tao River valley; and they controlled the roads to China's frontier markets.[33] The herdsmen occupied the higher pasturelands to the west of the principal Tibetan polities, through whose lands they had to drive their herds en route to the Song markets. Although they were probably subordinate to the Tibetan political elites in more than just economic exchanges, what we know for certain is that they paid substantial premiums in tea, horses, and other goods in return for use of roads controlled by the political chieftains.[34]

Song procurement officials depended on their Tibetan political allies to help promote the horse trade. In 1082 Intendant for Horse Purchases Guo Maoxun, who held a concurrent post in the TMA, recommended that *Fanguan*—prominent Tibetans who had been given frontier posts—be routinely enlisted to help buy horses:

> Every prefecture and commandery in Xihe Circuit contains tribal officers (*Fanguan*), such as Bao Xun, Bao Cheng, and Zhao Cunzhong. All of these officers are close to the top Tibetan chieftains and have the trust of the Tibetan tribesmen; they are influential enough to summon the Tibetan horse merchants to market. I beg that an Imperial Rescript be granted ordering each tribal officer to entice the Tibetan tribes into selling their horses in the frontier markets.[35]

Tibetan political leaders were no less important to the Southern Song horse trade. In 1133, for example, Tibetan officer Zhao Jizhi was awarded an official Song military rank for helping General Wu Lin buy horses from the "thirty-eight small Tibetan tribes."[36] We know more about Madame Bao of Taozhou:

> At first Madame Bao's husband Alingjie served the military commander of bandit-slave controlled Taozhou. When the imperial troops reached Taozhou in 1162, Alingjie went out to meet them. At this point the Jin armies had not yet submitted. But Madame Bao led the officials, soldiers, and commoners to open the gates and submit to Song. Madame Bao was honored with the title Meritorious Woman. Thereafter the Minzhou resident Zhao Yanbo went to Danchang to buy horses for the government, and he urged Madame Bao to summon the Tibetan merchants of the Tao-Die-Xi-Gong region. As a result the number of horses purchased swelled way beyond the yearly quota.[37]

In 1171 Madame Bao was further ennobled as First Lady of the Prefecture at about the same time that Zhao Yanbo was named Intendant of Tea and Horses.

Song horse purchasers employed a variety of additional mechanisms to summon herdsmen to market and to keep them coming back. Han as well as native agents were sent out into the hinterlands to "promote the horse trade" (*zhaoyou boma*); feasts were laid on to "make distant folk happy to sell horses in the frontier markets"; premiums were advertised for sales of unusual volume or quality; and market officials were under standing orders not to cheat or revile the horse sellers.[38] But once they got the horse traders to market, Song officials had to rely on "gate households" (*menhu*)—native retainers in the employ of the Song state—to help them bridge the cultural and linguistic gap between the herdsmen and themselves. *Menhu* were selected from the pool of assimilated non-Han known generically as "cooked households" (*shuhu*). Most of the "cooked households" employed in the horse trade were probably Tibetan. But one observer indicates that some of these *shuhu* may have been Uighurs, and states unequivocally that "whenever Tibetans and Chinese trade, if there is no [Uighur merchant] serving as middleman (*kuai*) they cannot complete the transaction."[39]

Native brokers performed essential services for the horse purchasers, including advertising the horse trade, negotiating the tea and horse exchange rates, and probably also interpreting. But their brokerage services were costly and, in contrast to the tea-monopoly side of the operation, were paid for by the THA. Native brokers were eligible for premiums of silver and silk for bringing in specified numbers of horses, and they were permitted to buy units of teas that were otherwise earmarked exclusively for the horse exchange.[40] Most importantly, they also earned a percentage on each transaction. According to Yuan Xingzong, during the latter half of the twelfth century native brokers and other market functionaries earned one-third of the cost of each horse: "When buying horses, it is essential to employ 'gate householders,' who are similar to China's brokers *(yakuai)*. In the case of a fine horse valued at over 150 [strings of cash worth of tea], the actual purchase price [to the government] will be over 200 strings. [This is because] the gate households and the market laborers *(benwu lixu zhi tu)* will take one quarter [sic] of the value. In this way the state forfeits its goods, and private parties gain the profits."[41] Eventually the native brokers acquired the same stereotyped reputation for cunning and deceit as their Chinese sub-bureaucratic counterparts. Zhang Hui's complaint of 1113 was typical: He charged that the native horse brokers "conspire with the market clerks and functionaries to commit evil. They engross the government's earnings, and block the profits of tea from reaching the 'raw Tibetans' *(sheng Fan)*."[42]

The structure of horse procurement in Shaanxi, then, reveals an operation aimed at reaching out to Tibetan pastoralists whose only direct contact with the Song state took place at the horse markets. Nor did either side seem eager to prolong that contact. Horse merchants appear to have favored a speedy settlement of their business, and market officials were instructed to price the Tibetan's horses and pay them their tea with all due haste. Guo Maoxun described the essential elements of the tea and horse transaction in 1081:

> The Tibetan tribesmen drive their herd to the market and wait for the market officials to make a selection. That day they are issued a receipt indicating the amount of tea they are to receive. They then go to the tea market and request their tea, which must be paid out at the appointed

time. Those who wish to make additional requests for silver, silk, or cash [in return for livestock, medicinal, and mineral products] may do so at the horse markets, which must pay them out that same day. If there are delays or backlogs, the implicated officials will be judged severely.[43]

This two-fold procedure—pricing horses and paying out tea—was not much changed by the de facto consolidation of the tea and horse agencies in 1086.[44] Moreover, it was at this very point that the same hippological incompetence that undercut the early Song pasturage program compromised the tea and horse operation as well. For even with the help of their native brokers, Han market officials were too inexperienced to judge horseflesh accurately. Yuan Xing-zong, a former horse-market official himself, condemned the market functionaries as "unprofessional" (*buzhi*), and charged that "they mistake sick horses for strong ones, small ones for large, and old ones for young."[45] In 1170 one official concerned about the high mortality rates of horses in convoy down to the capital traced the problem back to the selection procedure, which was as likely to imperil the animals as to reveal their flaws:

> At the beginning of the transaction, the horses are all tied together in a corral and given absolutely nothing to eat. As a result they are ravenous. The next day they are inspected for purchase. First, they are fed hay, gruel, and beans and given water. Because they are so hungry, they eat twice as much as normal. Although this gives them a moment's color and bright-ness, in fact they are bloated. Then the horses are run at a gallop back and forth, exhausting them, in order to "test" their strength. In this way hun-ger and satiety lose their proper balance, and work and idleness are both excessive. It is hoped that [the court] will command [Sichuan Tea and Horse Agency officials] to investigate personally. We must not be swindled by traders and brokers.[46]

I will have more to say about the futility of asking commanding officials to perform tasks beyond their competence below. Here I would like to conclude this overview of the tea and horse transaction in Shaanxi with a brief look at the distribution of tea among the Tibetans. As usual, the sources are least informative about questions that arouse the greatest interest. Consequently it is impossible to trace the progress of tea into Inner Asian trade networks with any precision, or to define the exact role of Tibetan horse merchants in that Inner Asian trade. But Song administrators assumed that much of the tea acquired in exchange for horses was intended for resale to other tribes, and they emphasized the utility of tea's resale value as a lure to bring in horse merchants.[47]

Evidence of the commercial nature of the Inner Asian tea trade is provided by the existence of preferences among the non-Han groups for different kinds of Upper Yangzi tea. At the very broadest level, Han consumers were said to prefer "tender" teas, such as the fine "drinking teas" of Hanzhou, Pengzhou, and Yongkangjun, while Tibetan consumers were thought to prefer "aged" teas.[48] These Tibetan-oriented teas were further differentiated by production region. The premier export tea, Yazhou's Mingshanxian tea, was the staple of the horse trade and the favorite of the "distant Tibetans".[49] According to Huang Lian's investigative report of 1086, Mingshan tea was traded through Lanzhou to the Qingtang capital of Miaochuan; it was even carried to Khotan (Yutian), though the agents in this case were not horse merchants but rather Khotanese "emissaries" engaged in the frankincense trade.[50]

Mingshan tea was supplemented in the export trade by the "four varieties of convoy tea" *(sise gangcha)* from the Hanzhong Basin. "Convoy tea" was the staple of the Agency's cash retail trade in Western Shaanxi, and the tea of choice of the local "light Tibetan cooked households" *(qian Fan shuhu)*.[51] But even these convoy teas were traded west to Qinghai and as far north as Saiyinlonghe, probably in Outer Mongolia.[52]

Because profits were as important as horses to the Northern Song Intendants, the THA traded tea for a wide range of native products with the expectation that tribal merchants could profitably resell their tea throughout Tibet.[53] During the Southern Song, however, the constant threat of a tea glut in the Tibetan pasturelands compelled the THA Intendants to dampen the inter-tribal trade. The anti-smuggling laws reviewed in Chapter Six served as the centerpiece of this effort to stifle all but the most essential tea exports. In addition, the THA refused to regularize trade with local tribes who might resell their tea to the "war-horse" suppliers. For example, in 1135 Zhao Kai vetoed the establishment of horse markets in Yongkangjun, Maozhou, and Weizhou, out of fear that the sale of tea to the Weizhou Tibetans, linked by back roads to the northwestern tribes, would compromise the all-important war-horse trade.[54] Nonetheless it was imprudent to deny the Weizhou Tibetans completely, since if they were not sold tea they would steal it. As a result they were allowed to purchase 200,000 catties of tea annually for the first half of the twelfth century, and 500,000 catties yearly after 1168.[55] We do not know whether the Weizhou Tibetans did in fact sell their tea to the Qinghai tribes, but Zhao's fear that tea sold to Tibetans in Yongkang, just east of Chengdu, could contaminate a horse trade on the far side of the Qinlings over 500 miles away was well founded. For when THA Intendant Zhang Song loosened restrictions on the delicate Yongkang tea around 1170, Tibetan interest in the tea traded at Danchang completely collapsed, and natives from Tao, Min, Die, and the Songpan region of Yanzhou staged a run on "heartland" markets in quest of "this wellspring of profit" in Yongkang.[56]

BUYING HORSES: THE SICHUAN BRANCH. The THA also operated between one and five horse markets along the southern rim of the Sichuan basin, from Liizhou in the southwest to Zhenzhou in the southeast. The highlands of southern Sichuan produced horses in abundance, but they were typically too small and weak to be used as cavalry mounts.[57] Historically these animals were bought simply as a means of manipulating and pacifying Man and Yi tribes, who were being increasingly goaded into violence by Han expansion into southwestern tribal domains.[58] In 1136, after angry tribesmen had provocatively slaughtered and eaten unfit horses rejected by hard-nosed market officials, the prefect of Luzhou reminded the government of the real function of the southwestern horse trade: "In the autumn of each year the southwestern tribes request a 'mutual trade' (*hushi*) for their horses. The markets are opened for 'broad exchanges.' Trade is enhanced with gifts of gold and silk, in order to bait [the tribes] with profit. It is profit that expresses the real art of the 'halter and bridle' technique of controlling the non-Han tribes. The significance of this trade is far-reaching indeed."[59]

Debates over the wisdom of buying Sichuan's "halter and bridle" horses recurred throughout the Song. At one end of the spectrum, officials whose sole concern was to supply the cavalry with horses deplored the waste of tea, gold, silver and silk on Sichuan's broken, stunted creatures, most of whom (it was charged) never survived the convoys out of the region.[60] These administrators—who almost never included the THA chiefs—were convinced that the nation would fare just as well without the Sichuan horse trade, and they periodically tried to pare down the procurement quotas at Sichuan's principal horse market in Liizhou.[61] But for those local and regional officials whose responsibilities included securing the stability of the southwestern frontier, the "halter and bridle" horse trade was absolutely essential. Some administrators adopted a conciliatory position, recommending that the Liizhou horse sellers be gradually weaned from entitlement purchases to a "genuine mutual trade" as they became "docile and submissive."[62] But the Liizhou tribes could not be tamed. As the "Affair of the Five Tribes" reveals, the natives of southwestern Sichuan were easily able to make the cost of marketing efficiency in Liizhou unacceptably high.

The Five Tribes *(wu buluo)*, so named for the five Chinese surnames into which they were divided, occupied Flying and Leaping Peak, 30 miles west of Liizhou. Although their herds were limited to small numbers of "broken nags," men of the Five Tribes "can all speak the language of China, and are much craftier than the other tribes."[63] They first demonstrated their cunning in 1176. That year Nuerjie, chieftain of the Blue Qiang, staged a series of raids that earned him a preferential "enrichment" price for his horses in Liizhou.[64] The Five Tribes jealously eyed Nuerjie's preferential rates, but their own horses continued to fall under the old regulations. Moreover, market officials routinely rejected the worst of their animals. But Song marketers fell victim to tribal cooperation: Nuerjie slipped the Five Tribes' rejects into his own herds and sold them for the Five Tribes at his "enriched" rates.

The Five Tribes–Blue Qiang deception might have developed into yet another entitlement had it not been superseded by the perfidy of one Tao Dun, a corrupt official in the Liizhou tea market. For years Tao Dun had embezzled money, tea, and other commodities from both the government and its tribal trading partners, including the Five Tribes. In 1179 the vice-prefect exposed Tao Dun and confiscated his ill-gotten gains, but the government was unable to fully compensate the Five Tribes for the money and goods they were owed. In a fury the Five Tribes chieftain Zhao Alie denounced the government: "For generations we have been loyal and submissive, but now we would be better off rebeling than selling horses. The Qiang and the Han both owe us money; moreover, the government permits the market brokers to slander us, causing us to lose face."[65] In March of 1180 Zhao Alie hung the carcass of a dead dog from a tree atop Flying and Leaping Peak in the traditional tribal call to arms, then led his comrades in raids against Liizhou's frontier villages. For six months Zhao Alie's fighters baffled and embarrassed Sichuan's frontier armies: In two raids alone the Five Tribesmen penetrated deep inside Liizhou's borders, killing 12 officers and 568 regular troops, pillaging 29 villages, and taking 211 "local conscripts" (*tuding*) prisoner.[66] THA Intendant Wu Zong was made responsible for quelling the uprising, but only after he called in over 2,000 troops from as far away as the Qinling defense forces did the Five Tribes decide they had made their point and request a covenant (*qingmeng*) of peace. The court immediately reestablished their "mutual marketing" privileges, and blamed the fiasco on the greed of the horse-purchase officials. In mid 1181, Wu Zong was demoted and fired from his position as THA Intendant.[67]

Buying horses in Sichuan, in short, confronted the THA with a very different task from the one it faced in Shaanxi. In the frontier markets of the northwest, officials were instructed to buy as many horses as they could, and to continually attract new sellers to market. In Sichuan, on the other hand, officials had to prevent those tribes whose horses were too feeble even for pack or courier work from establishing entitlement quotas that could provide a permanent excuse for violence. At the same time, they had to force those tribes whose horses they did buy into filling their quotas with an acceptable proportion of usable, healthy animals. Ultimately the THA was defeated in both of its marketing regions, as we will see below.

LOSING CONTROL OF THE TRADE

How successful was the tea and horse trade? As shown in Table 7, the first half century of the trade brought the Song its most reliable supply of horses. The basic criterion of a successful horse procurement policy is the capacity to purchase and deliver enough animals

Table 7 Horses Purchased in Shaanxi Markets, 998–1195

Year	Actual Purchases, Shaanxi Market	Quota, Shaanxi Market	Quota, All Southern Song Markets
998[a]	—	5,000	—
1006[b]	—	27,585	—
1027[c]	34,900+	—	—
1044–1052[d]	3,333*	—	—
1060[e]	—	8,000	—
1068–1070[f]	5,700*	—	—
1075[g]	—	15,000	—
1081[h]	—	20,000	—
1082[i]	14,700+	—	—
1083[i]	16,100+	—	—
1084[i]	ca. 12,000	—	—
1086[j]	—	18,000	—
1105[k]	20,000	—	—
1113–1114[l]	22,510*	—	—
1116–1118[m]**	17,356*	—	—
1120[n]	22,834	—	—
1122[o]	21,940	—	—
1145[p]	—	3,800	8,800
1165[q]	—	4,150	9,846
1170[r]	—	5,900	11,900
1195[r]	—	4,620	10,966

Sources: [a]*XCB* 43/14a; [b]*SHY* bing 24/2a; [c]*XCB* 104/21a; [d]*WXTK* 160/1390; [e]*SHY* bing 22/5a; [f]*XCB* 218/18a; [g]*SHY* zhiguan 43/50a; [h]*SHY* zhiguan 43/55a; [i]*SHY* zhiguan 43/68a; [j]*XCB* 381/22a; [k]*SHY* bing 24/28a; [l]*SHY* zhiguan 43/99b; [m]*SHY* bing 24/30b; [n]*SHY* zhiguan 43/101b; [o]*SHY* zhiguan 43/102b; [p]*XNYL* 154/4883; [q]*SHY* zhiguan 43/110b–111b; [r]*CYZJ* jia 18/596–597.

Notes: The horse marketing season opened in the eighth month of the year and extended into the following winter. Where exact dates are given in the sources, I have supplied the first year of the market season.

* Annual average.

** Entry covers two marketing seasons.

to meet replacement needs. One early Song official estimated that the Northern Song state required about 22,000 horses annually to meet the replacement needs of its metropolitan and frontier cavalries.[68] Pre-THA horse procurements met this target so rarely that over three-quarters of the empire's 60,000 cavalrymen were stranded without horses as of 1060.[69] But Sichuanese tea enticed Tibetan breeders to drive great herds of horses to market. THA procurement quotas during the Northern Song ranged between 15,000 and 20,000 horses annually, with actual purchases amounting to between 12,000 and 23,000 head. For the first time in its history, Song horse supply approached demand.

This delicate equilibrium between supply and demand was snapped by the loss of North China. Although naval installations along the Yangzi River supplanted massive standing armies as the front line of Southern Song defenses, cavalrymen were still needed to patrol the Huai and Yangzi River marches and to provide mobility in the Upper Jialing and Huai River valleys.[70]

Statutory horse quotas for the capital Guards *(Sanya)*, the Six Armies of the Yangzi *(Jiangshang zhujun)*, and the Three Outer Armies *(Guanwai jun)* of the Qinling Mountains are shown in Table 8. All told, Southern Song troops required about 11,000 head annually to meet their replacement needs. How were these horses supplied? From figures given in Tables 9 and 10, we can calculate the following horse-purchase quotas:

Year	Total
1145	8,800
1165	9,846
1170	11,900
1195	10,966
1204	12,994

In other words, the Southern Song expected to purchase quotas totaling about 10,000 head annually. Danchang and Fengtie, principal suppliers for the Capital Guards, bought an average of 5,061 horses;[71] Wenzhou purchased between 1,000 and 1,500 head; and Sichuanese markets bought about 4,500 "halter and bridle" horses

Table 8 Distribution of Demand for Cavalry Horses during the Southern Song

Army Division	Total Horse Quota	Actual Annual Replacements
Three Palace Commands	"Several myriad"	4,500
Palace Command	10,700	2,500
Cavalry Command	—	1,000
Infantry Command	—	1,000
Six Yangzi River Commands	50,000	4,000
Zhenjiang	—	750
Jiankang	—	750
Chizhou	—	500
Jiangzhou	—	500
Ezhou	—	750
Jingzhou	—	750
Three Outer Armies	13,142	1,400+
Xingzhou	—	605
Xingyuanfu	—	400?
Jinzhou	—	400?
Sichuan Governor-General	—	720–1,000
Total	73,000+	ca. 11,000

Sources: *CYZJ* jia 18/566, 603–604; Hua Yue, *Cuiwei xiansheng beizheng lu* 1/7b; *SHY* zhiguan 43/108a–b.

for the Riverine Commands. A third marketing system was opened in Guangxi's Hengshan Stockade in 1131, with a working quota of 1,500 head.[72] At an average height of 12½ hands the Guangxi horses were smaller than those bought in Danchang, and when possible the armies that were assigned quotas of horses from Guangxi might try to exchange them for the larger Shaanxi warhorses.[73]

Military planners expected the Shaanxi, Sichuan, and Guangxi systems to buy about 11,700 horses annually, roughly equal to the minimal demand. The real test of a centralized supply system, however, is not its procurement quotas but its actual deliveries. In the case of the Southern Song horse-supply system, reality fell short of plan by about 30 percent. At the marketplace, purchase quotas

Table 9 Horse-Purchase Quotas for the Southern Song THA, Qin Branch

	Danchang	Fengtie	Branch Total
1145[a]	—	—	3,800
1157[b]	3,600	500	4,100
1165[c]	—	—	4,150
1170[d]	5,100	800	5,900
1195[d]	3,920	700	4,620
1204[d]	—	—	7,798
Branch Annual Average			5,061

Sources: [a]XNYL 154/4883; [b]SHY zhiguan 43/109a–b; [c]SHY zhiguan 43/110–111b; [d]CYZJ jia 18/596–597.

Table 10 Horse-Purchase Quotas for the Southern Song THA, Sichuan Branch

	Wenzhou*	Liizhou	Xuzhou	Nanping-jun	Changning-jun	Zhenzhou	Branch Total
1144[a]	1,000	3,000	850	—	395	—	5,245
1145[b]	—	—	—	300+	—	—	5,000
1165[c]	—	—	—	—	—	—	5,696
1170[d]	—	—	—	—	—	—	6,000
1195[d]	1,500	3,000	800	400	396	250	6,346
1204[d]	—	—	—	—	—	—	5,196
Branch Annual Average							5,580

Sources: [a]SHY zhiguan 43/105b–106a; [b]XNYL 154/4883; [c]SHY zhiguan 43/110–111b; [d]CYZJ jia 18/596–597.

Note: *Wenzhou was officially transferred to the Qin Branch between 1170 and 1195; CYZJ jia 18/596.

often went unfilled or were met by buying horses so small and weak that even the most intrepid officials hesitated to slip them into the standard fifty-head delivery convoys. As a result, Southern Song horse markets issued an annual average of only 200 convoys empire-wide, 9 percent short of the 220 convoys needed to meet minimal demand.[74] Moreover, even this estimate is based primarily on quotas and is probably too generous.[75] Nor did the shortfalls end at the point of issue. As I will show in greater detail below, at least 20 percent of the horses shipped out from Shaanxi, Sichuan, and Guangxi were expected to die in transit. Thus in any given year the actual number of horses delivered to waiting cavalrymen could be expected to fall about 30 percent below immediate need. This disparity between plan and reality was built into the system.

Endless efforts were made to fill this deficit. The court issued emergency procurement orders; it tried to reform the convoy system; and by the end of the twelfth century it even began to buy the indigenous—and heretofore scorned—ponies of Hunan, Hubei, and Anhui.[76] But none of these policies filled the gap, suffusing Song strategists with a growing sense of apprehension. We turn now to how Tibetan, Man, and Yi horse merchants played on Song fears of an irremediable horse gap to manipulate the terms of trade.

BARGAINING OVER THE TERMS OF TRADE. The Song demand for war horses was almost always less elastic than the Tibetan demand for China's manufactured and agricultural goods: That is, the Tibetans were seldom likely to part with a horse for less silver, silk, tea, or salt, whereas the Chinese were almost always inclined to pay more if need be to get one. Thus, all else being equal, the price of horses would tend to rise in relation to all Chinese goods. This is in fact what happened, as Table 11 illustrates.

The only exception to this rising trend occurred at the beginning of the tea and horse trade. Two factors explain the temporary drop in the price of horses. First, having created the Sichuan tea monopoly to pay for horses, the court's demand for cash generated by that monopoly came to exceed its demand for the animals themselves. And second, novelty, a still inefficient tea-transport network, and a production system that had not yet shifted to the bulk processing of low-quality tea sufficed to keep the price of tea high in relation to horses. Therefore throughout the decade of the 1070s the price of a horse held steady at around a hundred-catty bale of tea.[77]

Table 11 Price of Horses in Shaanxi Markets, 979–1178

Prices are given for a 13¼-hand horse where available. The unit of value is a string of copper cash (*guan, min*).

Year	Value in Cash	Commodities Offered
979[a]	20.000	Currency
1016[b]	20.618	Implements and currency
1040[c]	35.000	Currency
1064[d]	35.000	Currency
1081[e]	<25.000	Less than 1 *tuo* (100 catties) of Mingshan tea, at ca. 25 strings per *tuo* or 250 cash per catty
1104[f]	86.128	112 catties of Mingshan tea at 769 cash per catty
1105[g]	136.590	174 catties of Mingshan tea at 785 cash per catty
1111[h]	104.183	Tea
1120[i]	125.098	—
1164[j]	300.000	700 catties of tea, 70 rolls of silk, gifts
1170[k]	200.000	—
1177[l]	—	1,000 catties of tea for an inferior horse; silver and silk for good horses
1178[m]	300.000	—

Sources: [a]*WXTK* 160/1389b; [b]*SHY* fanyi 6/2b; [c]*SS* 198/4934; [d]ibid., p. 4936; [e]*SHY* zhiguan 43/58b–59b; [f]ibid., p. 80b; [g]ibid, pp. 84a–b, 85b–86a; [h]*SHY* zhiguan 43/92b–93a; [i]ibid., pp. 101b–102b; [j]*SHY* bing 25/7b; [k]Yuan Xingzong, *Jiuhua ji* 7/5a; [l]*Songdai Shuwen jicun* 61/1a; [m]*SHY* shihuo 31/25a–b.

Once the novelty of the new trade wore off, merchants began to demand more tea for their animals; but because of the separation between the tea and horse enterprises through the end of the New Policies era, tea resisted devaluation. The Tea Market Agency and the Shaanxi Horse Purchase Bureau responded to a contrary set of expectations and imperatives, as TMA Intendant Li Qi acknowledged in 1078:

> The TMA benefits from high tea prices, from which great profits can be made . . . But the Horse Purchase Bureau gains from low tea prices. For

in that case the Tibetan tribes will profit handsomely, and there will be plenty of horses from which to choose.[78]

This disparity in goals set the scene for a three-year battle between the Tea Market Agency and Horse Purchasing Intendant Guo Maoxun over the pricing and allocation of tea to the horse trade.

Guo's sole objective was to buy as many horses as possible; and in order to do so, he was prepared to give Tibetan merchants whatever they wanted in return. In 1081 Guo charged that the TMA's myopic obsession with profits threatened to sabotage the horse trade. Of all the commodities employed in the Shaanxi trade, including silver, silk, cash, and salt vouchers, Guo claimed that only tea excited the interest of Tibetan horse merchants. Lately, however, the TMA had tried to jack up the price of tea and even sought to withhold tea from the horse markets entirely to seek a better price elsewhere. Tibetan merchants, in response, had begun to keep their horses off the market.[79] Guo proposed three steps to save the horse trade: first, tie Mingshan tea, the favorite of Tibetan horse merchants, exclusively to the horse trade until each year's horse quota was reached; second, offer Mingshan tea to the horse merchants at a subsidized price one string per unit lower than the market rate; and third, make Guo himself concurrent TMA Intendant, to ensure that "the Tibetans will obtain the tea they desire, and the Middle Kingdom will get the many horses it needs for mounted battle."[80]

In its rejoinder the TMA stressed the opportunity cost of earmarking Mingshan tea for the horse trade. According to the TMA petitioners, the horse trade used only 15,000 bales of Mingshan tea, at a rate of 1 bale or less per horse. The remaining 20,000 to 25,000 bales shipped annually to Western Shaanxi were traded for Central Asian products that the TMA then liquidated domestically for cash:

> The Tibetan tribes that come to China to engage in trade do not deal only in horses. They also bring gold, silver, measures of grain, mercury, musk, soft and coarse woolens, and oxen and sheep. They exchange these products for tea, which they in turn sell to the other Tibetan tribes. If the Tea Market Agency is not permitted to sell Mingshan tea, then because the Tibetan guest merchants will not buy anything else, not only will the wealth and profits of this Agency be severely diminished, there will also be a backlog of Mingshan tea.[81]

The Intendancy retained the right to the unrestricted sale of all Mingshan tea beyond the yearly quota to the Horse Purchase Bureau.

In a second petition, the TMA contested Guo's request for a preferential tea price to Tibetan horse merchants. From the Agency's perspective, decreases in the price of tea to horse sellers were identical to an increase in the amount of tea allocated to the horse markets. Since otherwise this tea would be sold in its most profitable markets, free disbursement of tea to the Horse Purchase Bureau constituted yet another threat to the TMA's profits. In order to protect its capacity to meet profit quotas, the Intendants insisted that the Horse Purchase Bureau buy any extra-quota tea it required with funds or goods of equal value.[82] Eventually a system of accounts was partially substituted for the actual remittance, authorizing the TMA to credit all extra-quota disbursement to horse markets in Shaanxi and Sichuan to its yearly profit statement at the price the tea would have earned on the market.[83] On the basis of this system the price of Mingshan tea to horse merchants was lowered 2 strings per bale in 1083.[84]

The court's operational preference for TMA cash over Horse Purchase Bureau horses was demonstrated repeatedly at this time. In 1083, for example, Guo Maoxun complained that although the Tibetan horse merchants selling horses in Jiezhou had been accustomed to receiving payment in "Great Bamboo" tea priced at 14 strings 640 cash per unit, recently the value had been raised to 20 strings to match the price in neighboring markets. Guo charged that at this higher tea price the Tibetans would refuse to sell horses. The court, however, ordered that the increased price should stand and instructed Guo that "if the Tibetans do not want tea [at this price], buy [their horses] with cash, [miscellaneous] commodities, or silk."[85]

Guo's insistence that the escalating price of tea was depressing the horse trade eventually proved correct, but at the time he received no support from the court. Late in 1084 the War Ministry charged Guo with consistently missing his quota of 20,000 head despite "clandestinely increasing the price of horses" in relation to tea; and in the ninth month of 1085 the horse-purchasing operation was transferred to the control of Lu Shimin in his capacity as Super-intendant of the TMA. The tea monopoly and horse-purchase operations were formally unified into a single Tea and Horse Agency the following year under Lu Shimin's successor, Huang Lian.[86]

In retrospect it is clear that the court's obsession with revenues, in conjunction with an administrative and incentive structure that completely isolated the TMA from responsibility for horse purchases, depressed horse prices in relation to tea during the New Policies era. The functional unification of the two operations into a single enterprise in 1086, along with a concommitant shift in what was expected of the organization by the court, forced the ratios of tea to horses to respond to actual market conditions. Gradually these conditions came to favor the horse sellers.[87]

Intendant Cheng Zhishao demonstrated the practical impact of this change in attitude and organizational structure when he reversed the position of his Yuanfeng predecessors and proposed linking Mingshan tea exclusively to horses. As Cheng argued in 1101, profit-oriented sales had forced too much Mingshan tea on the market, depreciating its value in the horse trade:

> It is the nature of the Tibetan tribes to delight in Mingshan tea. Indeed they cannot do without it for even a day. For the past number of years, there has been a substantial decrease in the number of horses we have been able to purchase. This is surely because government officials and Chinese guest travelers buy Mingshan tea and trade it to Tibetan merchants for a variety of goods. By custom they take fat profits. But the Tibetan lands are already saturated with tea. For this reason the Tibetans do not bring horses to sell to us.[88]

Thereafter the THA remained legally prohibited from selling Mingshan tea outside the horse trade, despite the entreaties of later Intendants.[89] In practice, unauthorized trade in Mingshan tea by market officials was irrepressible, and periodically swelled to crisis levels. Still, the 1101 ruling did momentarily staunch the flow of tea into Qinghai; even in early 1104 a standard 13¼-hand war horse cost just 112 catties (1.12 bales) of tea in Qinzhou.[90]

Two factors suddenly shook this relative price stability, and unleashed a horse-price spiral that the Intendancy was helpless to stop. The first was the initiation around 1103 of the "universal horse-purchase" measure *(fanpao maima)*, which called for unlimited horse purchases, with no restrictions on size, in Shaanxi and Liizhou to obtain mounts for the final phase of the expansionist campaign in Qinghai.[91] In order to pay for these horses and for the provisions needed to feed the men and animals converging on Xining and other Qinghai towns, the THA was forced to flood markets with 30,000 to 50,000 extra bales of tea.[92] Even as this so-called "doubling the amount of tea" *(liangbeicha)* policy put enormous amounts of extra tea into Tibetan hands, the central government enacted its transfer of Eastern Shaanxi to the southeastern tea monopoly, depriving the THA of a third of its domestic consumers. Either one of these factors would have been sufficient to devalue tea in relation to horses, but in combination they were irresistible.

In Liizhou, for example, horse market officials were suddenly ordered to pay extra premiums of 120 catties for each pony of 12¾ hands or more in stature, after an attempt to reduce the amount of tea had provoked a slowdown.[93] In Minzhou the price of a 13¼-hand horse had already risen 42 catties of tea by mid 1105, as shown in Table 12. Even so, the Prefect of Minzhou, under orders to buy 10,000 extra horses, complained that "recently the Tibetan guests

Table 12 Tea-Horse Exchange Rates in
Minzhou, 1105

Class and Size of Horse (in hands)	*Price in Mingshan Tea (to the nearest catty)*
"Fine Horses"	
14¼ and up (superior)	250
14¼ and up (inferior)	220
"Convoy Horses"	
14¼	176
14	169
13½	164
13¼	154
13	149
12¾	132

Source: SHY zhiguan 43/84a–b.

have come in fewer number, and the markets cannot buy any horses. If we do not give the traders more tea, I am afraid that ultimately it will be difficult to make any purchases."[94] The THA added a premium of 30 catties per head for each "fine horse" *(liangma)*, and 20 catties for each "convoy horse" *(gangma)*. The new price of 174 catties for a standard 13¼-hand pony represented a 55 percent increase over the 1104 price of 112 catties.

Still more tea was made available to horse merchants as an "added sale" *(tiemai)* allowance. Although the specifications of the allowance changed periodically, in general, for each horse he traded for Mingshan tea, a merchant could buy an additional hundred-catty bale of "convoy tea." At first the "added-sale" tea was priced about 70 percent higher than when it was exchanged directly for horses (the *duimai* category), but later it was set at "current prices" in the state-run retail markets.[95] Differential pricing and the subsidized tea-for-horses price are illustrated in the 1105 schedule for Xihe Circuit shown in Table 13, the only such schedule preserved. As of

Table 13 Differential Tea Prices in Xihe Circuit, 1105
(Strings of cash per 100-catty bale of tea)

Tea Variety	Producing Prefecture	Horse-Trade Price	Added Sale Price	Retail Tea Price
Mingshan	Yazhou	78.523	81.651	—
Ruijin	Xingyuanfu	129.413	173.348	—
Wanqun	Xingyuanfu	87.036	173.348	—
Yangzhou	Yangzhou	70.542	173.348	86.230
Youmaba	Xingyuanfu	—	—	93.230
Chongning	Pengzhou	—	—	81.866
Yangcun	Hanzhou	—	—	101.973
Xingyuanfu	Xingyuanfu	—	—	122.571
Yongkangjun	Yongkangjun	—	—	98.724
Weijiang	Shuzhou	—	—	93.414
Pengkou	Pengzhou	—	—	130.453

Source: SHY zhiguan 43/85b–86a.

1106 or 1107 Mingshan was removed from the "added-sale" category; and by 1111 all "added-sale" tea was offered at retail-tea prices.

In 1110 the government attempted to abolish the "universal horse purchase" and "doubling the tea" policies. But tribal merchants, having become accustomed to an average of 2 bales of tea per horse (according to the Intendant of 1111), staged an almost immediate slowdown. To bring the merchants back to market, the THA chief was not only forced to augment the "added purchase" privileges, but to extend them as well to the "gate household" horse-market brokers.[96]

Tea-horse ratios for the remainder of the Northern Song are difficult to reconstruct. In an effort to emphasize its putatively more stringent pricing policy, it became customary for the THA to refer to its "horse-purchases-at-reduced-tea-volume" (*jiancha maima*) and their commutation into so-called "reduced payments" (*jiansheng qian*). These yield average prices of 104.182 strings per head in 1111, 125.098 strings per head in 1121–1122, and 137.947 strings per head in 1122–1123.[97] The soundest guess is that beneath the self-congratulatory labels actual tea-horse ratios fluctuated around 2 bales of tea per head. But perhaps of greater significance, the final decade and a half of the Northern Song represents the last period in which tea was sufficiently attractive to elicit horses on its own. Before destruction and demoralization brought procurement to a halt sometime after the 1123 market season, the THA Intendants successfully bartered tea for 45,021 horses (ca. 1113–1114), 34,713 horses (1116–1118), 22,834 horses (1120/8–1121/10), 10,000 horses (to 1121/12), and a final 21,940 horses (1122/9–1123/9).[98]

Under the supply curves for tea and horses that obtained during the Southern Song, with its truncated markets, tea alone was no longer valuable enough to attract good horses. Not only did the unit ratio of tea to horses spiral to 10:1; by mid century it had become necessary to add silk, cash, and silver as well, in return for smaller and weaker horses that had less chance of surviving the caravans out of Sichuan, and were less able to carry mounted soldiers if they did.

The deteriorating value of tea became obvious in 1155, when

horse merchants at Danchang began to trade their tea to private agents for silk before leaving Chinese domains. The THA was ordered to honor "the convenience of the Tibetan guests" by offering silk as well as tea, but at least 100,000 bolts of that silk had to be supplied by the provincial fiscal intendant.[99] As tea lost its value, the horse trade could no longer finance itself.

Thereafter, the purchasing power of tea plummeted. In 1164 an anonymous official complained that horses in the Danchang and Fengtie markets cost a base price of at least 7 bales of tea, the equivalent of 70 bolts of silk. Moreover, both the Shaanxi and Sichuan markets had to offer promotional inducements of brocade, silk ribbon, and wine and viands to attract traders, all of which helped to drive the price of a delivered horse up to 300 strings of copper cash.[100]

By 1172 the situation that Guo Maoxun had complained of a century earlier had come full circle. As one official put it, "now the THA ignores tea and brocade and uses only silver and specie to purchase horses . . . Silver and valuables are flowing out of our borders, to the great disadvantage of the Middle Kingdom."[101] But whereas in 1082 the Tea Market Agency withheld tea from the horse markets because it could be sold more profitably elsewhere, in 1172 the problem was that because of oversupply and debasement, tea was of little value at all. Five years later Yan Cangshu charged that because of the glut of tea, "now an inferior horse of 13¼ hands costs an average of 10 bales of tea in Danchang, and a superior animal cannot be gotten at all without silver or silk."[102]

But the surfeit of tea was only one reason for the rising price of horses. Even in Guangxi horse vendors from the southwestern tribes, generically referred to as the Man, could demand their choice of payment. In 1164 it was reported that "each year horse-purchase administrators in Yongzhou buy horses with gold and silver, commuting the price into whichever commodity is agreeable to the Man tribesmen. But since Yongzhou Prefect Guang Sheng took office, he has not followed the old regulations and has caused losses to the traders. Therefore, this year they have not wanted to bring in horses for sale."[103] And several years earlier Hong Cun had described the

Yongzhou suppliers as indifferent to any but the most lucrative transactions: "The government has been buying horses in Yongzhou . . . for many years. The sellers are paid with gold and silver; otherwise they will not bring horses. But the Man peoples are insatiable: If the slightest thing is not to their liking, they hold up their horses in order to force the government to meet their price; and many use the inferiority of the exchange goods as an excuse not to trade."[104]

Thus in markets as far apart as Danchang and Hengshan, tribal horse-sellers could use their control over a much needed but scarce resource to pry loose ever greater quantities of Chinese goods, confident that by slowing down the flow of horses they could force the Southern Song government to pay a better price.

BIG TEETH AND SMALL FRAMES. Given its enormous wealth, Song China could probably have absorbed even greater increases in the cost of its horses, if cost alone were the problem. But it was not. Because Southern Song horse suppliers enjoyed a seller's market, they not only raised the price of their horses, they also lowered the quality. By the latter half of the twelfth century, Song markets were forced to buy so many sub-standard animals—horses "so long of tooth [the sign of advanced age] that they cannot pass inspection, and frames so weak and small they cannot be ridden"—that the quality as well as the quantity of Southern Song cavalry horses was fundamentally undermined.[105]

Horse market administrators were barraged with orders to enforce regulations on size, age, and quality, and to enjoin their subordinates from squandering the nation's wealth on useless nags. But many these same commands also warned that quotas must not go unfilled. Since the number of horses an official bought was immediately obvious, whereas the quality of the horses was not, a beleaguered market official would be more inclined to slip a nag or jade into the convoy than to reject it and risk not meeting his quota.[106] Moreover, officials in Sichuan faced the additional problem of tribal violence if they actually did reject sub-standard animals. There is no evidence that the many statutes governing horse procurement had much effect on the performance of market officials. But officials were routinely punished for inciting border incidents, as we saw in the case of Liizhou, and this would have influenced the market decisions of even the most diligent buyers.

The two most objective measures of a horse's quality were age and size. In a horse-supply system without expandable pasturage and feed, the ideal age to buy horses is in their early maturity, when immediate use and a long and healthy life can be anticipated.[107] Qualitative evidence indicates that Southern Song market officials were forced to buy both adolescent animals, which were less likely to survive the cross-mountain caravans, and old horses near the end of their working lives. In 1159, for instance, the Bureau of Military Affairs complained that most of the horses driven to the capital were already nine or ten years in age (by Chinese count, which would be eight or nine years by Western count), and too old to ride. The memorialist requested that horses be bought only up to eight years of age, but the recommendation could not be enacted.[108] In fact, it often became necessary to disregard age restrictions entirely in order to meet size qualifications, by buying under-age horses with the expectation that they would reach a useful height, or over-age animals that were, at 13½ hands or more, unusually large.[109]

We can be more precise about size. Horse suppliers forced the minimum acceptable size for "western war horses" at Danchang from 13¼ hands down to 12¾ hands; 12¾ hands became the average size in Liizhou and Wenzhou; and all size restrictions were abandoned in Guangxi.

A stature of 13¼ hands served as the de facto standard for Qinghai horses through the mid twelfth century. But in 1171 the Bureau of Military Affairs complained that the average size of the horses dispatched from Danchang and Fengtie had fallen three inches, to 12½ hands. Orders were issued to the Sichuan Governor-General and the THA that made the purchase of undersized horses an administrative offense, but the regulations proved impossible to enforce.[110] Seven years later a compromise was effected that set 13¼ hands as the minimum for horses of five years of age, but permitted buyers to purchase down to 13 hands for four-year-olds and 12¾ hands for two-year-olds.[111] This compromise was soon transformed by suppliers and buyers alike into a general license to trade in smaller animals. In 1190 the Palace Command tried to reinforce size discipline by demanding that horses of 12¾ hands be rejected, but the THA dissented: "This Agency has been buying horses of 12¾ hands and specially rotating them into the caravans as stipulated in the directive of 1178 . . . Now the Tibetan tribes hew to these regulations as long-established precedent. If we suddenly reject the 12¾ hand horses completely, I fear that this will throw up barriers against the good will of the Tibetans and may give rise to trouble."[112] Thus the 1178 compromise had to be readmitted, making 12¾-hand ponies a permanent and growing part of the Southern Song's stock of cavalry mounts.

Similar concessions had to be made in southern Sichuan and Guangxi. In Liizhou and Wenzhou, which between them provided about 3,600 of Sichuan's 5,500 horses, the THA was authorized in 1180 to fill the caravans with ponies of 12¾ hands until the southwestern tribes became "awestruck and submissive."[113] In Guangxi, efforts to enforce size limitations provoked a slowdown of all horses, forcing the court to temporarily suspend all restrictions.[114] Eventually a minimum size of 12¾ hands became the norm in Guangxi as well.[115]

Minimal standards for riding horses vary with time and place: In the United States today horses of less than 14½ hands are called ponies and used as children's mounts and pets.[116] By contrast, the famous Khotanese war horse "Fine-Head Red" painted by Li Gonglin in 1087 was only 13¾ hands. But even by the standards in force in China during the Song, it is clear that many if not most of the horses being sent to the Riverine and Capital Armies approached the minimum size for riding, as opposed to pack work. In order to prevent a complete deterioration in the quality of the herds, it was imperative to buy at least some mounts of large stature. To get them, however, the THA was forced to establish two special purchasing categories: "good and fine" horses (*liangxi ma*) in Sichuan, and "broad and strong" horses (*kuozhuang ma*) in Shaanxi.

The *liangxi* measure represented an effort to salvage some utility out of Sichuan's "halter and bridle" trade. In 1168 former THA Intendant Chen Mizuo reported just how badly the Sichuanese trade had deteriorated:

> The Founders established the policy of mutual trade in order to "halter and bridle" distant peoples. At first, obtaining horses was not the aim of the policy. Therefore when useless wrecks were put on the market, they were all accepted. Tibetan and southwestern Man tribesmen long depended on the liberality of the court; and whenever their wills were opposed, they became disorderly. Officials were afraid to provoke incidents, and so none dared to question [the policy]. As a result, out of every fifty head of ordinary convoy horses purchased in Liizhou, Xuzhou, or Nanpingjun, no more than three or four are "fine horses," while not over twenty are mediocre. The remainder are well below par and cannot even be ridden. If they are slipped in to meet the convoy quotas, then they drop dead en route.[117]

Chen recommended that by selling off the inferior horses locally, officials could use the returns to offer extra premiums of tea and brocade for more "good and fine" horses. In this way, Chen insisted, horse markets could raise their percentage of "good and fine" horses to 20 percent, without antagonizing the horse merchants.

In 1182, however, the THA chief reported that the policy had backfired. During the 1179 market season Liizhou officials had purchased 540 out of 1,129 head, or 48 percent, at *liangxi* premium prices; in 1181 1,988 undersized and inferior animals, or 59 percent of the total, were slipped in as *liangxi* mounts; and in some years entire shipments from the Tibetans were passed off as "good and fine." The *liangxi* measure had doubled the average price of all horses at Liizhou, from 10.8 bolts of silk to 22.5 bolts of silk per head, while making a sham of the horse procurement policy. Liizhou's Prefect and Vice-Prefect were dismissed from their posts and demoted in rank for the fiasco, and the Intendant recommended that the *liangxi* "entitlement" be reduced to 30 percent of all purchases. But so precipitous a cut in profits to the suppliers was deemed to be provocative, and the 1179 figure of 540 head was set up as the new *liangxi* quota.[118] Yet even this could not be protected: Between 1190 and 1194 Liizhou paid the premium on a mean of 1,014 head, which was increased to 1,504 head in 1195.[119] By skillfully combining monopoly and intimidation, the southwestern tribes had turned the *liangxi* policy from a purchasers' quota for good horses into a suppliers' entitlement for premium payments, without at all altering the quality of their stock.

The *kuozhuang* policy at Danchang reveals the dilemma of the Song state caught between its need for large horses and its reluctance to use silver in its foreign trade. As Robert Hartwell has demonstrated, once *huizi* paper notes became a central component of the Southern Song currency supply in 1160, gold and silver became directly linked to the monetary system. Consequently, for the first time in the Song dynasty, legislation was passed restricting or prohibiting entirely the use of these precious metals in foreign trade.[120]

Silver had been traded freely for horses up to the establishment of the tea monopoly, and as an auxiliary counter-trade good thereafter. But as Hartwell argues, until the empire-wide establishment of a paper currency backed by silver, the greatest monetary fear had been the hemorrhage of copper currency, not precious metals.[121] Therefore, it was only after 1160 that the use of silver to buy horses became controversial. Yet it was at this very time that tea, and even silk, became insufficient to elicit large horses from the Tibetans. In order to obtain large horses, the government had to pay what the suppliers desired.

At first the *kuozhuang* measure by-passed the THA completely. In 1165 Wu Ting, then Frontier Military Commissioner, was authorized to spend 20,000 *liang* of silver and 10,000 bolts of silk from a discretionary fund controlled by the Sichuan General Supply Commissioner on 1,500 "broad and strong horses."[122] Two decades later the THA had become the major buyer, but it was able to purchase only 700 head with the 20,000 *liang* of silver. And not only had the *kuozhuang* horses become more costly; according to Emperor Xiaozong they had also become indistinguishable from the ordinary convoy horses.[123] Therefore, in an effort to phase out the use of silver, the special *kuozhuang* purchases were periodically suspended from 1183 on, and markets as a whole exhorted to "attempt to reduce the use of silver in buying horses."[124]

In the heavily militarized Danchang market region there was little fear that suspending the *kuozhuang* trade would provoke violence, but it did lead to a Tibetan embargo on the sale of large horses. In 1191 the new Emperor Guangzong expressed fears that without the special trade Tibetan merchants would sell only their smallest animals. The policy was restored for the year and at least periodically thereafter.[125]

Song efforts to reduce its silver payments were further thwarted by Jurchen competition for the horses of Tibet. Around 1170 it was reported that the Jin had spent 200,000 *liang* of silver on Tibetan horses; by the early thirteenth century the trade was regularized, with the Jurchen paying between 30 and 50 *liang* of silver per horse.[126] In circa 1210 the Southern Song strategist Hua Yue observed that at Danchang and Fengtie the government continued to use silver because it was easier to transport than tea.[127] It is more probable, however, that Song horse purchasers were forced to use silver simply to compete with the Jin. In either case the result was the same: the Southern Song government was perpetually frustrated in its attempts to exclude silver from the horse trade. But in view of the long-term decrease in the size of the horses bought at Danchang, and skepticism about the quality of the *kuozhuang* horses, we can conclude that by the end of the twelfth century, rather than bringing forth horses of unusual size, silver simply succeeded in attracting animals that a few decades earlier had been regarded as standard.

Rising prices, deteriorating quality, and horses withheld from markets throughout Song China indicate that the pastoralists of Qinghai, Sichuan, and Guangxi could use their oligopolistic control of a scarce resource to prevent government markets from buying up to capacity. Because there were more Chinese tea and other commodities in relation to demand than there were horses, foreign horse merchants held a bargaining advantage over the Chinese. By selling fewer horses, they could extract a better price. Thus the grasslands surrounding the Southern Song held a clear if immeasurable surplus of horses to which the government was denied access by the devaluation of its trade goods.[128]

Could Song administrators have reversed the terms of trade? Certainly a short-term improvement might have been possible. For example, around 1220 the Jin, already under siege by the forces of Chinghiz Khan, took advantage of bad harvests in Qinghai to drive the price of Tibetan horses down to between 5 and 10 *liang* of silver per head.[129] Faced with a scarcity of essential commodities, the Tibetans could have been forced to part with their horses cheaply. This suggests that if the THA had succeeded in stemming the flow of tea across Song borders and had improved the quality of its stocks, then it could have bought more and better animals despite the very real limitations of total supply.

As we saw in Chapter Six, however, the Southern Song THA sought to prop up its sagging revenues by pumping more tea into already saturated markets. Moreover, by wringing tea out of the industry with confiscatory prices, the THA drove cultivators into challenging the smuggling laws by meeting government quotas with inferior tea while selling their good tea illegally. This stream of contraband tea flowing to its best markets north and west was swelled by illegal speculation engaged in by the market officials themselves. It was always tempting for market functionaries to trade tea for jade, ivory, and Inner Asian valuables, both to help meet THA revenue quotas and to line their own sleeves.[130] But following Han Qiu's notorious mid-century tenure as Intendant, official irresponsibility and malfeasance became epidemic. The inevitable result, according to Hong Cun, was to "devalue the price of [tea] in the purchase of horses, so that [we] cannot choose between good horses and nags."[131] By abandoning economic discipline, in short, the THA employed a strategy exactly the opposite of the one used by its Tibetan suppliers and forfeited all the advantages that it might have enjoyed as a monopolist in the tea and horse trade.

Ultimately even the THA monopoly over the tea and horse trade was lost. In a final assault on Song horse procurement measures, Jin officials set up a rival tea and horse trade in the prime marketing region of the northwest. In order to prevent just such a possibility, the THA had reserved its severest penalties for the contraband sale of tea to the Jin. But the THA had no control over the sale of tea from the southeast, which poured into Jurchen territories in enormous quantities through official markets along the Huai River and illegal smuggling routes along the coast and inland.[132] The teas entering North China included the finest products of Fujian and Jiangnan, which by all accounts far surpassed those sold by the THA.[133] Around the turn of the century, Jin horse purchasers added these teas to the silver with which they bought Tibetan horses, thus completely outmaneuvering Song horse buyers. The Sichuanese scholar Wu Yong lamented this final loss of control over the trade in the 1220s:

> These days, because the Jin cavalry and army are strong, they routinely make light of our intentions; whereas because we treasure the profits from tea, we are unable to manipulate the foreigners' desires. It has even gotten to the point that at the customs stations and markets there are no inspections against smuggling, and in the mountains and woodlands there are no prohibitions against private cultivation and sale. The roads over which the private merchants ply their trade are as broad as an open thoroughfare, and across the northern battlements everyone in the land of kumiss-drinkers imbibes fine tea. The Jin see that they can easily obtain our finest products, while we face great difficulty getting the horses bred in the west. Thus everywhere they sweeten their prices in order to entice our merchants to sell them tea and use the tea they do not consume to trade for horses from the Tibetans. The Jin used this technique to set up a market in Taozhou. Thus it is that the handle of trade that ought to be in the hands of the Middle Kingdom is instead in the firm grasp of the Jurchen.[134]

FLYING DRAGONS IN ROCKS AND MUD

When domestic markets failed to meet the demands of the Chinese state, government bureaucrats could employ authority and coercion to extract most of the goods and services they needed at a cost they were willing to pay. Coercion and authority were sufficient to assure the THA a constant supply of tea and to guarantee that their tea would be transported to Shaanxi. But we have seen that foreign suppliers were impervious to the authority of the Chinese state; indeed they often held Chinese authority in justifiable contempt. Unable to draw on the mechanisms of command to obtain its horses, the THA was forced to buy them in an increasingly competitive market. When the total supply of horses and the total demand for tea both plummeted after the fall of North China, the THA was reduced to playing a passive role in the tea and horse trade; it was consistently outmaneuvered by foreign horse suppliers who could play on the Song state's dependence on their herds to sell fewer horses, and horses of poorer quality, for more Chinese goods.

Unfortunately for Southern Song cavalrymen, the inadequacies of bureaucratic power did not end at the market place. After buying horses in Shaanxi and Sichuan, officials had to assemble them in convoys and drive them to the armies of the Yangzi River and the capital.[135] The convoy operation confronted the state with two problems that resisted bureaucratic solution. The first was physical terrain: there were no tractable routes between the markets of the west and the armies of the east. The second was the alienation between man and beast: there was no administrative system that could bridge the distance between Chinese convoyers and Tibetan horses. Southern Song policy-makers employed every available organizational strategy to move horses from market to front, but no strategy could wholly overcome the challenges of space and personnel.

ADMINISTERING PHYSICAL SPACE. Southern Song policy makers learned to welcome a horse mortality rate of 20 percent per convoy; in fact, many caravans killed more than half their horses. Many of the horses simply succumbed to high mountain passes, treacherous plank bridges, rocky ravines, and dessicated valleys through which they were led from market to the front.

Natural geography and the long Sino-Jurchen border placed severe limits on the possible convoy routes (see Map 9). The trestled pathway out of Danchang, where the best horses were purchased, was especially perilous. Already footsore and emaciated from the drive out of their native pasturelands, Danchang horses had to be driven twenty travel days or stages (*yicheng*) to Xingyuanfu before they could be rested.[136] But as Hua Yue tells us, many of them never made it: "The cocks crow and the horses whinny. The track from Dancheng to Xingyuan traverses twenty-eight towering peaks.

Map 9 Southern Song Horse Markets and Convoy Routes from Sichuan

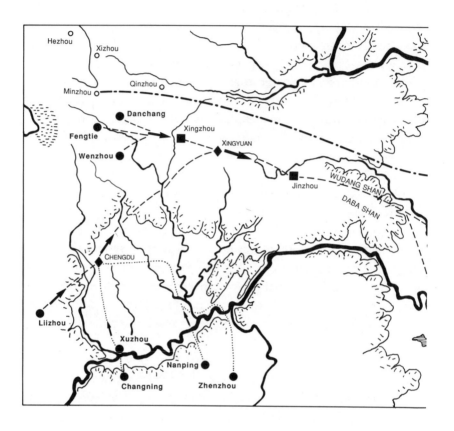

Countless numbers of horses plummet from the cliffs to be smashed to bits below."[137]

The survivors still faced a trip of approximately 1,600 miles, or eighty stages, to the capital at Hangzhou. This spur included a treacherous passage over the Wudangshan range east of Jinzhou, whose tight passes were festooned with jutting rock that split the horses' unshod hooves and in some cases even killed them.[138] The

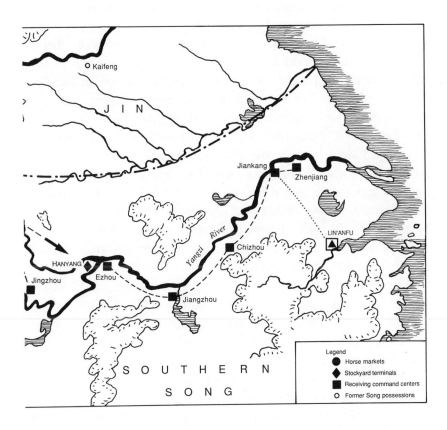

route followed by the sixty caravans issued out of Sichuan was almost as bad, especially the month-long caravan from Chengdu to Xingyuan; from Xingyuan east the routes were identical. Depending on the lay-up times in Chengdu, Xingyuan, and Hanyang, any given horse might be in transit for half a year. [139]

Were there no easier passages to the east? To military planners desperate for horses, the riverine route out of Sichuan through the

Yangzi Gorges presented a tempting possibility; but the problems proved insurmountable. Significant commercial traffic between Sichuan and its downriver neighbors was a relatively recent phenomenon, and even in the twelfth century the Gorges presented formidable obstacles. Because of the sheerness of the cliff walls, horses could not be walked through the Gorges.[140] Nor, as it turned out, could they be floated through on boats. In 1165 Governor-General Wu Lin, with the strong backing of the court, ordered Sichuan's riverine prefectures to build two hundred river boats of 125-ton (500 *liao*) and 175-ton (700 *liao*) capacity to ferry Danchang horses down the Jialing River to the Yangzi and out through the Gorges. At Xiazhou (mod. Yichang) the horses were off-loaded for the overland drive to the capital. After two years the experiment succumbed to the excessive cost of building, manning, and provisioning the boats and to the great number of horses lost to drowning in the perilous rapids. Wu Lin had pushed the experiment forward against strong opposition from prefectural and regional administrators in eastern Sichuan, who bore much of the cost; and when Wu died in late 1167, the policy was abruptly halted.[141] As Yuan Xingzong gloated, Ouyang Xiu's dictum that shipping objects of value through the Yangzi gorges was equivalent to throwing them away had once again been proved true.[142]

Thus, military planners had no choice but to send their horses overland, around the perimeter of the empire. In order to neutralize the harsh and stingy frontier terrain, Song administrators laid down careful rules for provisioning the caravans; and they experimented to find the best way of deploying their convoy crews. Most importantly, they punctuated the convoy routes with three major stockyard terminals, linked one to the other by a belt of relay depots.

Stockyard terminals *(majian)* were set up at Chengdu, Xingyuan, and Hanyang. At Chengdu, horses from the five markets of southern Sichuan were assembled in fifty-head convoys, branded with the insignia of their intended riverine command, and sent out on the twenty-four day journey to Xingyuan.[143] The Xingyuan terminal processed not only all the horses issued from Sichuan, Danchang-Fengtie, and Wenzhou, but also their convoy crews. Here advance teams from the Capital Guards, sent to pick up war horses for the capital, converged with THA crews working the first leg of the trail drive out of Danchang and Sichuan. Over the course of the year at least eighty crews from the capital billeted for up to a month at a time, while another seventy crews passed through the city, supposedly on strict schedule, as they made their way to Hanyang.[144] Hanyang terminal, at the confluence of the Han and Yangzi Rivers, was the hub of the horse convoy system. Spaced forty travel-days from Xingyuanfu, the Hanyang terminal was opened in 1163 to equalize the convoy burden between Sichuanese and eastern crews by moving the transfer point downriver, and to provide a veterinary-care facility where the animals could be rested and tended to after the ravages of the Wudang Mountain stretch. Between 1163 and 1173 about 80 percent of the THA's 160 convoys were driven directly by Sichuanese crews to Hanyang, where after recuperating for five days to a month they were picked up by Yangzi River and Palace Command teams and driven the rest of the way.[145] As at Xingyuan, strict schedules were meant to govern the movement of men and horses, lest "men be held up awaiting horses or horses be held up awaiting men." To facilitate coordination, the THA was required to post estimated arrival dates at Hanyang to the court, which would then act as despatcher for the recipient commands.[146] This concern with scheduling was by no means trivial, for the threat of equine epidemics caused or aggravated by overcrowding made the orderly arrival and departure of herds at Hanyang especially crucial. THA Intendant Zhang Song stressed this problem in 1169: "As soon as the horses bought in the markets of Sichuan and Danchang enter the Middle Kingdom, nothing suits their basic nature. As a result, they commonly develop all varieties of diseases that can then become contagious. Because so many horses arrive at the Hanyang stockyards at the same time, even if there is only a single sick horse among them, within a month the entire herd will be diseased."[147]

In order to care for the herds, Hanyang administrators shipped out healthy horses as soon as they were rested and well fed, and kept back the diseased animals for more intensive treatment. But the level of veterinary training at Hanyang was apparently inadequate, and diseased horses tended to linger at the stockyards without improving. [148] The government treated this as a problem of personnel management rather than medical knowledge, and in 1173 ordered the Hubei Fiscal Intendant to inspect the Hanyang stockyards every ten days and to report to the THA and the capital. [149] But as we learn from the raconteur Hong Mai, no amount of administrative surveillance could provide reliable insurance against disaster at Hanyang:

> The horses bought in Sichuan and Danchang are sent east in convoys of fifty head. At first Sichuanese soldiers were assigned to drive them, but large numbers of animals kept dying in transit. Thereupon a terminal was opened at Hanyang, where the convoys rested for five days and waited to be picked up by crews from the Capital Guards and the Yangzi River Armies.
>
> First the convoys are driven to the yamen of the Huguang Supply Master General (in Ezhou, just across the river from Hanyang), to check that the markings and age match the advance roster sent by the Sichuan Horse Agency. Thereafter they are sent on the road.
>
> In 1173 the Palace Command sent Cheng Fu to perform this task. On arriving in Hanyang, Cheng used divination to choose the right day to cross the river to Ezhou.
>
> The battallion leader said, "By old custom you must offer sacrificial wine, go to the Temple of the City God, pay obeisance, and proceed. Then there will be nothing else to worry about on the long journey."
>
> Cheng did not answer, and the chief repeated his advice. Suddenly Cheng became angry, and berated the chief:
>
> "I am picking up government horses. Of what concern is that to gods?"
>
> Reviling the chief, Cheng sent him away.
>
> Late that day the convoy crossed the river and encamped at the relay depot below Ezhou. Precisely at 4:00 A.M. the horses were led towards the yamen of the Supply Master General. While waiting for the gate to be opened to enter, the crew suddenly heard the sound of horses coming from the west. The drivers assumed that another convoy was arriving and got up to rouse one another. Each grabbed hold of the horses' reins to prevent them from colliding into each other. But suddenly the horses were upon them, and in the darkness it was impossible to tell how many there were. Then the two groups collided, and their kicking and biting were beyond restraint. It was like this for thirty minutes. But then, when the sun arose,

the men could see that it had not been another convoy at all, but all part of the same one. Half the horses lay dead, their flanks ripped open and their intestines flowing as though they had run into spears and lances. Everyone said that it was revenge for General Cheng's rude treatment of the God of Walls and Moats.[150]

The same year as the Hanyang tragedy it was decided that the crews mustered by the THA could not get the horses down to Hanyang without unacceptably high losses, and so the transfer point was moved back to Xingyuan.[151] Although the first objective of the Hanyang facility, to provide a central point for the equal distribution of the convoy burden, was thus abandoned, the stockyard continued to serve as a recuperation and veterinary center.[152]

Horse markets, regional stockyards, and the Riverine and Capital armies were further linked by a belt of relay depots *(mayi)* that girdled the perimeter of the empire, from Danchang and Liizhou to the capital at Lin'anfu. The depot system represented the best administrative solution to the hardships of a long convoy route through harsh terrain, by providing food and shelter for men and beasts at predictable intervals. The depots were intended to be placed a day's journey apart—generally between 50 *li* (17 miles) in the mountains and up to 70 *li* (24 miles) on level ground—though Hua Yue did complain that "one can be on the road for many days without seeing a single depot-shed."[153] Excluding Guangxi, the system operated about 145 depots: twenty or so from Liizhou to Chengdu, 24 from Chengdu to Xingyuan, and 100 from Danchang to Lin'anfu.[154] Most of the sheds were no doubt "small and decrepit," like those between Danchang and Hanyang, though the depot outside Yukang Gate at the capital was a relatively spacious structure of twenty-four rooms.[155]

All the superordinate organizations concerned with horses—the emperor and his military advisors in the capital, the THA, the Governor-General of Sichuan, and heads of the Yangzi River commands-general *(dutongsi)* in their respective regions—participated in the collective effort to maintain and provision depot facilities on the edge of the empire. Their most intractable problem was supplying depots located along grassless mountain tracks with provender for the horses and rice for their drivers. Provisioning rations were substantial. Each convoy of fifty horses was allotted 345 quarts of barley and 847 pounds of millet-grass a day.[156] Food rations for the drivers ranged between 1.5 and 2.5 *sheng* (2.6 to 4.4 pints) of uncooked rice per man, for an average daily allotment of 120 *sheng* or 105 pints of rice (1.6 bushels) per thirty-man convoy.[157] Depots along the main trunk line connecting Xingyuan and Hanyang had to feed 160 convoys in the course of the year. In theory each depot was responsible for only a single day's feeding per convoy. But when bad weather knocked out bridges and flooded the roads, caravans were forced to lay up well beyond their time limit. In such cases, "enough food for one day of satiety is stretched to meet nine days of hunger."[158] When food rations could not be stretched, some animals starved to death.[159]

The costs of provisioning were shared, however unequally, by local governments and superordinate civil and military agencies.[160] But the actual tasks of procuring grain, cutting hay, and stocking each depot had to be performed locally. Yet local functionaries could not be charged with the provisioning task without careful surveillance, since they would inevitably be tempted to embezzle the supplies for their own private use.[161]

Thus this seemingly straightforward task—stocking 145 depots with enough food for between 60 and 160 convoys—prompted an endless search for the appropriate supervisory structure: the problem of hay became an exercise in bureaucracy. Nor was the problem ever adequately solved. At first the vice-prefects were made the chief supervisory officers and were even equipped with a seal pronouncing them "Administrator of Horse Convoy Relay Depots."[162] But vice-prefects held extremely broad and complex obligations. Consequently, actual responsibility for depot provisioning slipped further down the administrative hierarchy, to the county magistrates, sheriffs, and registrars. Yet even under these men, according to Yu Yunwen, "fodder procurement is taken lightly, and provisioning goes unattended." As a result, many horses starved to death.[163] In subsequent experiments the military was given responsibility for the depots, but they, too, failed to devise an optimum solution to the hay problem.[164]

Why did surveillance and control of the horse-convoy depots prove more intractable than the administratively analogous tea-transport relays? Three possible reasons stand out. First, the horse-convoy route was almost four times longer than even the longest Northern Song tea convoys. Second, where the tea-transport corridor between Sichuan and Shaanxi was administered by a single superagency to which the most critical counties could be appended, the horse caravans traversed over twenty-five prefectures, spread out over seven administrative circuits encompassing three physiographic macroregions. Because of the political, geographic, and communications barriers presented by so widely dispersed a network, no single agency existed, nor could be effectively designed, to which all key counties could be subordinated. And third, although the transport of tea could be designated as the primary function of local government in the strategic but sparsely settled counties of the Upper Jialing River, convoying horses could hold only a limited place among the multiple tasks for which administrators in counties along the Han and Yangzi Rivers had to be held responsible. And since incentives— the key to compliance in the tea-transport counties—inevitably channeled official energy to the activity most highly rewarded (to the detriment of other functions), it would have been imprudent to design incentive rewards that focused the efforts of multi-task county administrators too single-mindedly on provisioning and maintaining the stage depots: exhortation had to substitute for rewards and fines.[165]

Further experiments can be documented into the thirteenth century, but none of the reforms could guarantee that the depots would be perpetually well supplied or maintained.[166] Under the circumstances, the stage depots represented perhaps the most effective strategy for dividing up physical space; but scarce food resources and widespread administrative dispersion made a high level of maintenance and preparation for contingencies impossible.

TIBETAN HORSES AND CHINESE MEN. The problems of physical space that thwarted Chinese convoyers were compounded by the difficulty of assembling trail crews in a culture where the horse was an alien intruder. Experienced wranglers, attuned and sympathetic to the skittish and willful personality of their charges, might have overcome the mountain barriers that stood between the markets of Danchang and Sichuan and the armies of the Yangzi and the capital. But in a culture dominated by intensive hoe agriculture and literati values, experienced horse handlers were exceedingly rare. The THA and the recipient armies had little choice but to entrust their valuable cargo to men whose basic attitude to horse and state alike ranged from indifference to hostility and fear.

As usual, Song administrators fell back on the tactics of bureaucratic organization to solve a thorny problem of labor mobilization. Song convoy crews were large in relation to the number of horses they drove, and they were elaborately staffed. A comparison with American cattle drives (no figures are available for horse roundups) indicates how Song planners employed numbers and organization to offset the lack of skill and commitment. In the American cattle drives of the 1870s and 1880s, fourteen men on horseback were sufficient to drive 3,000 "half-wild, nervous longhorns" and a riding stock of sixty-five to a hundred spare horses over prairie and desert from Texas to Dodge City.[167] In the Song horse convoys of the twelfth century, by contrast, thirty or more men on foot were needed to lead fifty horses over the mountains, across the trestle bridges, and down the river valleys from Sichuan to the Lower Yangzi. Moreover, the Chinese support staff was considerably more elaborate. On the American range, eleven cowboys were led, fed, and kept in gear by a trail boss, a cook, and a wrangler. In the mountains and valleys of China, on the other hand, twenty-five drivers (*qianma bingshi*) required a foreman (*yama shichen*), assistant foreman (*xiao guanya* or *jiangjiao*—military attaché), one or two cooks (*huotou*), a stockman (*jundian*), a veterinarian (*yishou*), and a signaler (*xianpai*) to provide adequate maintenance and supervision.[168]

In terms of numbers, the horse-convoy crews made an insignificant claim on total Southern Song labor power: approximately 10,000 to 11,000 individuals annually out of a population that approached 100,000,000 people.[169] Yet every one of the key positions in the convoy teams required skills that native Chinese did not normally possess.

The foreman's post should have been the easiest to fill. Only one foreman was required per convoy, and his tasks—overseeing the convoy and managing its travel allowances of silver and travel certificates—were primarily managerial.[170] But some familiarity with horses was essential, a job requirement that eluded both the civil and military incumbents of the position. The THA appointed both civil and military men to head its caravans, but neither group registered great success.[171] An imperial edict of 1152, for example, charged that "the trail foremen assigned by the THA know nothing about the nature of horses. They neither water nor feed them on time, and hence many of the horses have been injured or killed."[172] By 1189 most of the THA foremen were drawn from among the prefectural armies and militias; yet according to an official in the Anterior Palace Command, they still "do not understand the nature of the horse. This is the reason so many convoy horses die [in transit]."[173]

The government attempted to compensate for the incompetence of its foremen by assigning a veterinarian to each convoy, but in practice the veterinary position did little more than highlight the impotence of the bureaucratic state. For in a horse-poor economy the collective experience of its veterinary staff was abysmally low. Indeed their ministrations could prove deadly: "When horses sicken on the road, by long-established precedent they cannot be left behind, but must follow with the caravan. The practitioners of curing do not understand that the horses are frail, exhausted, and starved. They tie them all together and drag them step by step over a thousand *li*. Thus horses that start out only one-percent sick wind up competely diseased. How is it that officials do nothing about this?"[174]

But the weakest link in the convoy system were the trail drivers, the men who actually handled the horses. Each convoy employed twenty-five drivers, assigning two horses to each man. Excluding Guangxi, the convoy operation required between four and eight thousand drivers annually, depending on the deployment system in force.[175]

Soldiers, whether regular or auxiliary, were the preferred source for trail drivers; but they were not always available for transport duty. In Danchang the THA periodically drafted drivers, some of them probably minority tribesmen, from among the local populace:

> Roughly a hundred families live in the Danchang horse market. About twenty-five men, half of whom are usually boys around fourteen years old, are pressed into service for each convoy. Their job is to drive the horses. They are given hay, half of which they feed to the horses and half of which they use to make their beds.[176]

In Sichuan, drivers were mustered from among the imperial, provincial, or local troops, or conscripted from the population liable for labor service.[177] The Capital Guards and the Yangzi River Commands might send members of the new "Martial Vanguard Army" (*wufengjun*) to pick up their horses at Hanyang, Xingyuan, or Chengdu; but they usually despatched the lowest ranks of regular soldiers (*bingji*) or service auxiliaries (*baizhi renbing*).[178]

As a group the trail drivers would have had the least familiarity with horses and been the most resentful of the convoy burden. Moreover, since the men impressed into convoy service were generally of low military or socio-economic rank, they were minimally committed to the state and its authority and inclined to abscond if pressed too hard. As far as can be determined from the sources, no interpersonal bond, or *guanxi,* linked the drivers to their foremen; and certainly no absorption in an equestrian culture linked the drivers to their horses. As a result it was especially difficult to enforce discipline among the convoy crews during the half year they might be on the road.

Military and civilian convoyers were equally unreliable. In 1194, for example, THA Intendant Yang Jing reported that the trail drivers sent to Xingyuan by the Three Palace Commands sold off the specially purchased "broad and strong" (*kuozhuang*) mounts and replaced them with smaller animals bought locally; on arriving at inspection stations down the line, they asserted that the dimunitive substitutes had been issued by the THA itself.[179] This was only the most brazen of the misdeeds with which the military crews from downriver were charged. Hua Yue asserted that they also "use the funds for hay and provisions to gamble" and exchanged the convoy-depot vouchers (which should have been under the control of the foremen) for wine and roasted meats. Some demanded bribes; others used convoy funds to "buy up commodities and sell them at the distant markets passed on route." "And the horses? At night they are not stabled; by noon they have not been fed. Only if they encounter a mountain pasture can they graze; only if they hit a mountain spring do they get to drink."[180] As an anonymous memorialist of 1216 lamented, "no wonder half the horses are starved to death."[181]

By overwhelming consensus, however, the crews assembled in Sichuan and Danchang by the THA presented special problems of discipline and incompetence. No rotation that included Sichuanese drivers could be counted on to move horses safely.[182] Sichuanese civilians conscripted into convoy duty were dumbfounded by the responsibility and terrified of the consequences should their charges die. As one sympathetic official observed in 1146, "the convoy routes are long and remote, and the months and days on the road exhaust a man's strength. On top of this, while on the road hay and fodder are frequently not delivered on time, causing up to 40 or 50 percent of the horses to die. Because these convoy soldiers fear being charged with the responsibility, many of them flee."[183] Nonetheless, for many of the men hired by the THA, horse convoying represented a ready opportunity for graft and embezzlement. In a catalogue of corruption and hooliganism among all the crews, a complainant of 1216 singled out the Sichuanese: "The horse-convoy soldiers despatched from Sichuan are the most unrestrained. On arriving at a county seat, they cause trouble in a hundred ways. If the slightest thing is not to their liking, they agitate the entire herd and let the horses collide or tie some to the yamen buildings and let others roam loose through the porticoes. They will not leave without a fat bribe."[184]

Whatever combination of temperament and custom accounts for the unique unwillingness and inability of the Sichuanese to drive horse caravans safely and with discipline, the phenomenon itself dominated the evolution of the convoy deployment system. The various deployment strategies were differentiated primarily by whether single crews drove the horses all the way from market region to recipient army, or whether crews from both ends exchanged somewhere in between. At one extreme, crews despatched by the THA drove the horses all the way from the horse markets to the armies of the Yangzi River and the capital; at the other extreme, these same armies sent their own crews to Chengdu and Xingyuan to pick up the herds and drive them back. In an intermediate strategy, crews from the THA and the recipient armies exchanged the herds at Hanyang.

In general, the military commands preferred to accept delivery of their horses from the THA in their home prefectures—the deployment system that was first employed. The most equitable and effective system in terms of shared costs and labor burdens was the intermediate transfer at Hanyang.[185] By far the most cumbersome system was for a crew from one of the armies to pick up their horses at Chengdu or Xingyuan. For unlike the Sichuanese crews sent downriver, who could deliver their horses and immediately head back, the army-despatched crews had to wait in Chengdu and Xingyuan for unpredictable lengths of time while the convoys were assembled. And according to one observer, their time on the road was doubly costly: First, because they were regular soldiers drawing salary in addition to their convoy wages, the wage bill for sending them to Sichuan was high; and second, since they were on the road for over half a year (this informant, in fact, claims two years for the roundtrip journey), they would "abandon the practice of the martial arts"—that is, the time spent training them would be lost.[186]

Despatching crews from the Jiangnan to pick up horses in Sichuan was therefore the least attractive strategy to military policymakers. But the disadvantages had to be weighed against the need to save the horses from the Sichuanese, and in the end it was the client-crew system that prevailed. In 1154 a two-decade policy of market-to-army convoying by the THA was suspended after equine mortality rates had soared to half the herd.[187] At first, crews from the Three Palace Commands were sent directly to Danchang and Fengtie; but the two garrisons proved unable to feed and house the extra 2,400 men that came through each year. Therefore in 1158 the crews were rerouted to Xingyuan instead, to await the horses brought in by the "short-haul" *(duansong)* gangs.[188] But even this system was costly, and in 1163 the court established the Hanyang-terminal transfer-system in an effort to at least keep the soldiers of the Yangzi River and Palace Armies east of the great mountainous divide.[189] Yet this intermediate system left it to the Sichuanese crews to negotiate the perilous Wudang Mountain stretch from Jinzhou to the Xiangyang flatlands, and once again their incompetence intervened. After a decade that saw also the two-year experiment in riverine transport, the deaths en route to Hanyang forced an abandonment of the compromise policy and acknowledgment that the Sichuanese could not be safely trusted to drive horses beyond their home regions. In 1173 Palace Army crews were redirected to pick up their horses at Xingyuan, with an advance team sent to Danchang and Fengtie to supervise the short haul to the terminal; at around the same time, the Yangzi River armies were charged with escorting their herds from Chengdu.[190] From this point on, the client-convoy system was standard.

The 1173 deployment system was the best the state could do; all later recommendations merely reiterated rotations that had already been tried and abandoned.[191] Yet an incentive schedule promulgated that year by the War Ministry reveals how low were the state's own expectations for success. The comprehensive incentive schedule specifies the rewards and punishments for each class of participant in each type of convoy, as differentiated by despatching command (e.g., Palace or Riverine Armies) or agency (e.g., the THA).[192]

Each class of participants was governed by a separate schedule, calculated according to the number of horses out of each fifty-head convoy that arrived safely at the designated terminus. The size of the reward or punishment for men in a given category varied according to the distance they had to travel between their despatching unit and the market: A foreman from the Three Palace Commands in the capital, for example, was rewarded or punished more heavily

than a foreman from the Ezhou Command halfway up the Yangzi
River. But the neutral point—that is, the point at which neither
rewards nor fines were called for *(buli shangfa)*—was identical for
each category of participant. These neutral points provide an operational measure of the state's most realistic goals.

The foreman most clearly represented the bureaucratic presence
of the state in each convoy, and consequently only career incentives
were used to motivate his performance. If nine or fewer horses died
in transit, he received some combination of promotion in rank and
a hastening of his promotional review. If eleven or more horses died,
he was demoted and the time until his promotional review was
lengthened. If he delivered exactly forty horses, he was neither rewarded not penalized. In the case of the convoy foreman neither
cash bonuses nor fines were employed—only rank and the timing of
promotional reviews.[193]

The foreman's schedule represents the best-case scenario and implies that the state aimed for a minimal loss of ten horses per convoy, or 20 percent. In practice, however, military planners knew
that a mortality rate of 20 percent was unrealistic. Therefore they
were compelled to hold lesser functionaries, whose commitment to
the state was correspondingly weak, to a lower standard of achievement. Unlike their foremen, drawn from the regular civil and military bureaucracies, members of the support staff were less likely to
possess official rank. As a result, they could commute their grade
promotions into cash; conversely, their grade demotions could be
commuted for them into corporal punishment. Under the 1173
rulings, the support staff—the military attaché, cooks, veterinari-
ans, signalmen, and stockmen—received no rewards, as measured
in grade promotions and as much as 60 strings of cash, for anything
over nine deaths.[194] But their punishments, measured by demotions or up to one hundred floggings with the light rod, did not
begin until fifteen deaths. In other words the support staff was allowed a combined mortality of 28 percent of the herd.

Yet even this compromise target of 28 percent was undermined
by the incompetence and unruliness of the trail drivers, by far the
weakest link in the convoy system. Because they were the most
likely to flee the convoy and abandon the horses, the government

could make only the most modest of demands on the trail drivers in terms of delivery rates: If a trail driver delivered two healthy animals, he was promoted a seniority grade (for the officially attached) or given 30 strings of cash. If one of the animals had scabies lesions or was gaunt and emaciated—the two most commonly encountered health afflictions—the driver would still receive half a grade promotion or fifteen strings of cash. And the neutral point on the scale of incentives for trail drivers, emblematic of the state's most realistic assessment of what it could expect, was two sick animals or one dead in transit. Only if both horses died would the driver be demoted or flogged.[195] Thus at the lowest and most critical level of the convoy crew, the state was forced to accept a projected attrition rate of 50 percent. Policy makers could only hope that the convoy foreman, who had the most at stake, could devise ways to elicit a better overall arrival rate.

In addition to their incentive bonuses, support crew and trail drivers received cash wages and a rice ration for every day of convoy service.[196] As of 1165 trail drivers attached to the military earned 100 copper cash daily, worth an estimated 8 strings of cash for the Xingyuan to Hangzhou convoy, a trip of about eighty stages. Thus a trail driver who delivered two healthy animals to the capital stood to gain 38 strings of cash for his troubles, if the incentive schedule was strictly followed.[197] But even this combination of wages and incentives failed to improve the survival rates for horses in convoy. The administrative record documents a continued deterioration in horse transport through the twelfth and thirteenth centuries, as stagnation and demoralization overtook Southern Song fiscal and military agencies. Towards the end of the reign of Emperor Ningzong (r. 1195–1224), whose horse-administration records are the last to have been preserved, an official submitted what may serve as a final testament to the failure of the horse-convoy system: "I have inquired into the reasons that our herds do not increase. It is because the horses are born in the northwest and are driven to the southeast, where they are deprived of what is natural to them. Moreover, they are driven swiftly for 10,000 *li*, allowed to stay just one night in the relay depots along the way, unable to rest. And further, most of the provisions for the horses supplied by the government are sold off for cash, or embezzled and stolen by the clerks and soldiers."[198]

In retrospect it may appear that the Southern Song squandered enormous effort on a relatively simple logistical problem. Why couldn't a powerful bureaucratic state transport ten thousand horses a year? Again a comparison with the tea transports will put the problem into sharper perspective and help to highlight the limits of command mobilization.

Tea-transport "soldiers" were no more committed to pushing tea barrows over the mountains than were trail drivers to leading horses. The labor pool for tea transporters was similar to that for trail drivers, and the attitudes of the two groups to their assignment—hostility or opportunism—were identical. But two features distinguished the tea-transport task from the convoying of horses. First, carrying tea required nothing more than submitting passively to brute, physical labor, however back-breaking and at times dangerous; but driving horses required, in addition, skill and judgment of a kind the men usually lacked and active dealings with unhappy, demanding animals. Second, because of the great surplus of tea, the transport system could absorb considerable waste. But in the case of horses the Song state started out undersupplied by an average of 9 percent each year. Any loss in transit exacted an enormous marginal cost. In an operation such as tea transportation, defined by passive compliance and low efficiency, the command system of the Song state could surmount the hostility and indifference of its conscript work force sufficiently to elicit a minimal level of satisfaction. But when the task required active commitment and high efficiency, as did the horse convoy operation, then the usual means of control available to the state—coercion and material incentives—proved unable to exact an acceptable level of satisfaction.[199]

Over the long run it is possible that the market might have produced a solution that evaded the bureaucratic state, by stimulating the development of a specialized horse-transport industry that brought skill and commitment to the convoy task. But Southern Song administrators never turned to private contractors, native or Chinese, to transport their horses, and in any event the dynasty was not to be granted very much time.[200] For by the late twelfth century the entire Southern Song defensive system had begun to unravel. The extent of the deterioration was revealed by Chief Councilor Han Tuozhou's revanchist campaign against the Jurchen in 1206. In the course of a humiliating defeat that cost Han Tuozhou his head, the Southern Song's regular standing armies—the Three Armies of the Capital and the Riverine Commands—proved to be completely ineffective. In the end it was only the success of newly emergent regional armies under the ad hoc control of civil officials, as well as such popular militia as the Righteous and Brave Tea Merchant Army of De'anfu and the Daring and Brave Tea Merchant Army of Xiangyang, that temporarily saved the dynasty.[201]

Regional and local armies and popular militia played an increasingly important role in Song defenses through the fall of the dynasty in 1279. This was especially true in Sichuan, which was left by the court to defend itself against waves of Mongol shock troops who repeatedly laid waste to the province from 1234 on.[202] At the same time, horses and cavalry became increasingly insignificant. Hua Yue deplored the ineffectiveness of Song horse power in the aftermath of the 1206 war with the Jin:

Earlier generations have said that China is unable to defend itself against the mounted soldiers of [the Jin]. The enemy's strength derives from its cavalry; their ability lies in riding and archery. . . Their lands in Henan and the northern marches are broad in expanse, and there are numerous pastures. In our country there is not four- or five-tenths of the number of pastures. The Danchang and Hengshan horse markets are extremely far from the front, and the convoy-relay depots are spaced irregularly. Therefore our nation does not even have two- or three-tenths as many horses as our enemy, the Jin. Although the horses for the Cavalry Guards and Three Armies of the Capital are said to number many ten thousands, in fact the emaciated, weak, old and sick among them number over half. The horses of the Yangzi River Armies do not exceed fifty thousand, yet most of this quota is still outstanding, and less than one-third have actually been rotated into their brigade. This is why China cannot resist the horses of the Jin. Moreover, our horses traverse rocks and are injured; they traverse mud and sink in. But the horses of the enemy—it can rain and snow for months on end and they still seem to be leaping; they go over a thousand *li* of sand and rock as fast as if they were flying. Our horses cannot defend against these animals. As for our horses, when it comes to noon they must be watered; when it gets to late afternoon, they must be fed. But the horses

of the enemy—they get to drink without cease during months of pasturing, and then they can go hungry for days on end yet still be ridden without tiring. This is something our horses cannot achieve. How then are we
to prevail over them?[203]

By the early thirteenth century, then, Song horse supply had
dwindled to insignificance. Outmaneuvered at the marketplace by
tribal merchants and Jin competitors, THA purchasers were forced
to squander valuable resources on the worst products of Tibetan and
southwestern pastures. Moreover, very few of the stunted ponies
bought in the THA markets, already frail, old, and sickly, stood a
chance of surviving the trip to the front: The court was even more
fortunate now than it had been fifty years earlier if half the year's
herd made it to their destinations alive. Under these circumstances
the Song state could not rely on horses to defend itself.

Yet it was not simply the collapse of the horse-supply system
that caused the fall of the Southern Song. Mounted soldiers were
only one part of a multi-faceted defensive network. Even without
horses the Song state still possessed its walled cities, its navy, and
its military technology. From a purely strategic point of view the
really crucial problem for the dynasty was that even as the horse gap
widened beyond repair, "[Song] rulers faced a narrowing technical
gap between themselves and their principal rivals."[204] At the same
time that Song forces lost all capacity to engage nomad horsemen
on the nomad's terms, the mounted warriors of the Jin and then the
Mongols acquired mastery of every one of China's defensive arts.
One after another, Song defenses were neutralized, as the techniques
of iron working, siege warfare, and even gunpowder seeped out to
the steppe. The Mongols inherited all of these when they conquered
the Jin in 1234, though they were still barricaded from the southern Chinese heartland by the formidable navy of the Southern Song.[205]
But in 1270 Qubilai built a navy of his own and proceeded to
besiege the towns of the Yangzi River and the coast. In 1279 the
Mongol fleet destroyed the Chinese navy, and "the Devil's Horsemen" floated to victory over the Southern Song.

Conclusion

The leaders of the New Policies sought the same two goals that have traditionally motivated Chinese reformers: to "enrich the state and strengthen its defenses" (*fuguo qiangbing*). Recent Chinese commentators, reacting against the encomiums to Wang Anshi that were standard during the Cultural Revolution, have uniformly agreed that in the second of its aims, strengthening the nation's defense, the New Policies almost completely failed. In an article in 1980 that launched the critical reappraisal of the reforms, the historian Wang Zengyu argued that of all the New Policies military reforms and strategic initiatives only one, Wang Shao's preemptive invasion of the three easternmost prefectures of Xihe, was successful. [1]

Wang Shao's Xihe campaign was intended to spearhead the conquest of all of the Gansu-Qinghai frontier, the initial stage in a plan to neutralize the Tangut Xi Xia. Follow-up campaigns in the 1080s and the first two decades of the 1100s, however, led to either outright disaster or costly stalemates, without ever unseating the Tanguts from their commanding position in the Ordos. From the perspective of the horse trade Wang Shao's accomplishments in Xihe were critical, for they opened up supply lines to the major Qinghai pastures and provided a safe haven for the horse markets, enabling the Tea and Horse Agency to wield its bureaucratic authority to supply Song armies with their greatest bounty of horses. But the inability of Song generals and their massive but ineffective armies to capitalize on the first reliable supply of horses to stabilize the frontier eventually doomed the tea and horse trade. Once the Jin conquered North China in 1126 and severed the dynasty's access to the last good Asian pastures, there was little a bureaucratic procurement agency could do to keep the cavalry supplied with mounts. Within the Southern Song geopolitical context, it seems fair to conclude, there was nothing that the Song state could offer that would have attracted an adequate supply of good foreign horses to its markets. The government compensated for its irreversible shortage of horses by creating a powerful navy, tolerating the existence in the Qinlingshan frontier of a strong but autonomous and hereditary army, and strengthening its fortified city walls; and these systems of passive defense kept the Song dynasty alive for a century and a half beyond the fall of North China. But without cavalry horses there was no way to project power outward beyond the barrier of rivers, mountains, and city walls that protected South China from the north, and hence no way to recreate a new environment for the successful mix of bureaucratic power and marketing capacity. Though the tea and horse trade issued from the New Policies' only strategic success, its eventual failure a half century later reflected the inadequacy of New Policies achievements in the field of military reform.

The New Policies, then, failed to strengthen the nation's defenses in any fundamental way. But it did enrich the state, and quite dramatically. Here the chief questions are at whose cost, and with what long-term effect. The history of the Sichuan Tea and Horse Agency provides some useful answers.

As enacted in Sichuan, New Policies economic activism followed two basic premises. The first of these, enunciated by Wang Anshi in the debate over the "law for appointments and transfers to distant posts," was that political integration served as the bedrock for centralized economic control. The experience of the Sichuan tea monopoly demonstrates that by interweaving the private and career interests of a region's native population into the fiscal interests of the state it is possible to mobilize native elites into taxing their own region for the state. By building on the gradual integration of Sichuanese into the larger political culture, the New Policies merger of bureaucratic entrepreneurship and native office-holding embedded bureaucratic power deeply into Sichuanese society and facilitated government exploitation of the region's economic resources on an unprecedented scale, without requiring a significant expansion of the state's police presence. Political mobilization of native elites proved to be a cheap and efficient way of maximizing the taxing power of the state, and it was enduring. Even after the Southern Song court discontinued the practice of appointing Sichuanese to the THA Intendant's post, employment of natives elsewhere throughout the Agency and its related institutions enabled the state to keep a firm grip on the tea economy. On a regionwide scale, the New Policies and its attendant "laws for distant offices" initiated a dynasty-long trend that put Sichuanese in the majority of posts at most echelons of local and regional government, yet kept them dependent on the state for their professional and material advancement. Thus, instead of promoting separatism and autonomy, the combination of elite bureaucratization and native service in Sichuan allowed the state to apply the lessons of the tea monopoly to the entire region. This enhanced taxing power of the state was put to the test during the Southern Song, when the tea, salt, wine, textile, and mining industries and regional grain supply were all forced to support the militarization of the Qinlingshan frontier and horse procurement in southwestern and northwestern Sichuan. Despite the obvious and crushing burden that defense taxation placed on the regional economy, Sichuanese elites embraced centrally defined goals and stayed loyal to the center. The proof of their loyalty came in 1206, when Sichuanese were quick to suppress the separatist rebellion led by a scion of the militarist Wu clan, Wu Xi. Thus, by turning the successful fulfillment of state-defined fiscal goals into the fastest and surest path to bureaucratic authority and by transforming bureaucratic authority into the dominant form of power in Sichuan, New Policies mobilization strategies opened the door to systematic control of the Sichuanese economy.

Political mobilization facilitated the taxation of a region that had previously repulsed efforts at centralized economic control: by capitalizing on the eleventh-century metamorphosis of magnates into bureaucrats, the New Policies regime opened the door to Heaven's Storehouse. But New Policies economic activism also entailed a second metamorphosis—of bureaucrats into entrepreneurs. Wang Anshi sent bureaucratic agents out into the countryside to take over key economic functions—transport, rural credit, wholesale and even retail distribution—from the so-called "engrosser" elements of the commercial economy in order to generate new revenues for the state. By using financial experts (*shan licaizhe*—what I have called bureaucratic entrepreneurs) to break the power of these private monopolists, Wang Anshi promised his emperor that he could "multiply the state's revenues without adding to the people's taxes (*min bujia fu er guoyong rao*)."[2]

Was Wang Anshi's promise fulfilled? The history of the Sichuan tea monopoly shows that under ideal circumstances Wang's strategy of bureaucratic entrepreneurship could succeed. By promoting an expanded foreign trade, opening new markets, and restructuring the Sichuan tea industry, the New Policies TMA Intendants fostered an enormous expansion in Sichuanese tea output and created a new source of entrepreneurial profits for the state without critically diminishing the income of the tea producers. The Sichuan tea monopoly demonstrates that, given an opportunity to innovate and to expand the arena of economic activity, even a state agency could stimulate rapid short-term economic growth.

Over the long run, however, the results were much less benign. The history of the Sichuan tea monopoly in the periods following the New Policies illustrates how when opportunities for economic expansion level off or are reversed, bureaucratic entrepreneurship can degenerate inexorably into confiscatory taxation. As government fiat and then military disaster carved away its marketing region, the Agency was as helpless to create new buyers for tea as it was to find new suppliers of horses. And without extraregional markets the THA was unable to generate surplus revenues from the sale of tea. Still, producing revenues was the Agency's most immediate source of bureaucratic influence, was expected of it by its central government masters, and was built into the system of incentives that determined the prosperity and career progress of its personnel. With each decrease in the Intendancy's ability to deliver surplus funds, the autonomy and influence of the organization and the material and career expectations of its participants withered apace. The entire system was thus put under enormous pressure to replace the entrepreneurial and monopoly profits that had been generated by the sale of tea in extraregional and foreign markets with increased and inescapable imposts levied directly on the producers of tea.

The chief allies of the THA's efforts to squeeze more money out of Sichuan's dying tea economy were the very targets of the original monopoly: the tea merchants. In the truncated markets of the Southern Song a state retail operation would have been too costly and inefficient. In order to generate any revenues at all, the THA was forced to share its profits with merchant distributors of Sichuanese tea. And in order to entice merchants into distributing tea in a glutted and overtaxed market, the THA chose to squeeze more tea at less money out of the most vulnerable participants in the industry: resident tea cultivators who had no alternatives but to meet impossible quotas or abscond. A policy born out of the impulse to "capture the profits of merchants and traders and return them to the commonweal *(gongjia)*, without increasing the burden on the people," had in the end "rewarded the merchants and impoverished the people."[3]

This degeneration of bureaucratic entrepreneurship into a collaboration between state and merchant against the producer mirrored a more general failing of the New Policies activist strategy. Because of the hunger for revenues that drove the New Policies regime, the redistributive rationale that animated the "anti-engrosser" campaign was subverted by a need to court the owners of capital in order to keep revenues flowing. The most prominent example of this transposition of allegiance was the "Green Sprouts" rural credit measure. In 1069 Wang Anshi enacted a plan to provide poor peasant households with seasonal loans at an interest fee (20 percent) well below the putative "market" rate. By supplanting private landlords and usurious moneylenders as the principal source of rural credit, the theory went, the state could "enable the peasants to hasten to their affairs, without monopolist households taking advantage of their [seasonal credit] crisis."[4] But the intent of this plan to "suppress engrossers and relieve the poor and weak" was undermined first by the enormous revenue potential of the "Green Sprouts" loan fund (capitalized by selling off Ever-Normal Granary stocks), and second by the inability of the neediest peasants to repay their loans on time. Very shortly after announcing the measure, the state imposed a variety of restrictions to prevent defaults by poor peasant borrowers at the same time that it offered relatively generous loans to middle and wealthy landlords—the very elements previously condemned as "engrossers." The "Green Sprouts" loan fund soon became one of the most profitable of the New Policies revenue sources: In 1082 its administrators deposited 8,000,000 strings in surplus revenues into Shenzong's Yuanfeng Treasury, while rich landowners invested their loans and stood by to snatch up the property of peasant defaulters. Though many poor peasants may have benefitted from the "Green Sprouts" loans, the impression preserved in the historical record is of a policy that shifted from a social welfare measure for poor peasants to a revenue-gathering scheme that aided the rich and the state.

Other interventionist, anti-engrosser measures, such as the state trade *(shiyi)* and labor exemption *(mianyi)* acts and expanded monopolies on salt, wine, and later southeastern tea, were similarly subverted by revenue-gathering imperatives into allying the state with the most powerful private actors in the economy. The historian Wang Shengduo has elaborated on an insight by the eleventh-century statesman Ouyang Xiu to argue that economic intervention by the Song state promoted throughout the economy the type of predatory collaboration exhibited by the THA and the tea merchants of Sichuan. Three decades before the New Policies, Ouyang Xiu resisted an earlier wave of anti-engrosser sentiment by arguing that if the state attempted to "commandeer the profits from commerce and return them exclusively to the commonweal," those profits would surely disappear. As Ouyang Xiu explained, profit *(li)* derives from the rapid and widespread distribution of goods throughout the economy. Any attempt to monopolize profit will dry up the flow of goods, and hence the source of profit itself. Great merchants—the hated "engrossers whose drive for profits gets more ingenious by the day"—understand that in order to distribute their commodities, they must share their profits with the peddlers and petty merchants who will sell them in local markets. "Although the returns [on each transaction] are small, commodities circulate rapidly, and therefore small profits mount up and become large." In this model of an unimpeded market Ouyang Xiu found a lesson for the activist state: "Great merchants who are expert in the arts of trade do not begrudge profits to entice peddlers: Great nations well versed in the arts of fiscal management should not begrudge profits to entice great merchants. This is the art of sharing profits with merchants and traders, and by collecting small amounts acquiring a great deal."[5]

For Wang Shengduo, Ouyang's analysis helps illuminate the collaboration between the state and mercantile interests that grew out of Song efforts to commercialize the economy and divert mercantile profits to the public treasury. Because the Song did constantly expand its monopoly controls over such commodities as salt, wine, tea, and the foreign trade in spices and incense, Wang points out, the state was obliged to fashion a panoply of schemes to divide commercial profits between government tax collectors and what Susan Mann has recently referred to as "merchant liturgies."[6] Moreover, as Song fiscal agents penetrated ever more deeply into the commercial economy, they turned private commercial interests into retail agents for a state that had become the nation's largest merchant, albeit a merchant that stayed resolutely outside the production process. Reflecting an historical perspective that has flourished in the midst of China's post-Mao market-oriented reforms, Wang Shengduo concludes that Song experiments in centralized economic control "contracted the scope of activity essential to the survival and development of private commerce. [State intervention] destroyed the normal relations between merchants and producers, restricted merchants' freedom of management, seized the merchant community's rightful profits, and most devastatingly, so squeezed out the surplus labor of producers that future productivity was undermined, thereby impeding the normal development of the commercial economy."[7]

Based on the lesson of bureaucratic entrepreneurship and the Sichuan tea economy, what conclusions can we draw about the impact of economic activism on the Sichuanese economy as a whole? In the long run, it seems inescapable that the centralized economic control spearheaded in Sichuan by the THA went beyond merely "impeding normal development" to cripple key sectors of the economy. During the ninth, tenth, and eleventh centuries, although Sichuan was no longer a major exporter of goods to interior cosmopolitan China, our sources project the image of a commercial economy shielded from the taxing power of the state and growing steadily in response to regional population growth and the stimulus of trade with immediate neighbors: an autonomous and self-sufficient region, in short, of great productive capacity and commercial prosperity. When we move up to the twelfth and thirteenth centuries, yet still short of the devastating Mongol invasions that began in 1236, the documentary image changes to one of a region whose productive resources have been exhausted and whose people impoverished, with population leveling off in the core regions and sharply depressed in the periphery. The transition from prosperity to decline coincides precisely with the era of bureaucratic mobilization and the integration of Sichuan into the imperial polity. There seems little question that bureaucratic penetration of the Sichuanese economy helped reverse a centuries-long cycle of economic development, by substituting unpredictable government decisions about resource allocation in the tea, salt, wine, textile, and metallurgical industries for predictable and long-standing patterns of regional and extraregional trade; exposing the regional economy immediately and directly to changes in the wider and more precarious political system; and imposing the potentially destructive power of command mobilization over the economy's cash crops, handicrafts, staple grains, and labor force. For Sichuanese in the late-Northern and Southern Song, political integration exacted an exorbitant price.

To the extent that Sichuan's experience mirrored trends in the

Song political economy as a whole, it is worth asking whether Song intervention in the commercial economy ultimately sapped the vitality of the medieval economic revolution. It is well known that by the fourteenth century, following the violent rise and fall of the Yuan, the medieval economic revolution had been reversed: population, productivity, and commercial activity were all depressed, not again to reach Song levels until the second commercial revolution that began in the sixteenth century.[8] But as Hartwell and others have proposed, the economic downturn may have begun much earlier.[9] There is no question that in many geographic regions and economic sectors of Song China people were worse off in the twelfth and thirteenth centuries than they had been in the eleventh: peasants were more vulnerable to subsistence crisis, merchants were more exposed to commercial recessions, and even relatively privileged individuals were more likely to slide down than to climb up the ladder of mobility.[10] Some scholars have seen connections between the economic inertia of the twelfth and thirteenth centuries and the economic policies of the Southern Song, although we are still very far from a synthetic interpretation of economic policy and the end of the medieval economic revolution. Nevertheless, it seems fair to generalize that by the twelfth century the Song state was draining far more out of the economy than it was contributing to society as a whole—by the Southern Song the state had become parasitic. As the constantly escalating costs of defense following the Jin conquest of North China intersected with an ossifying and increasingly ineffective bureaucracy, Southern Song fiscal administrators wielded Northern Song techniques of taxation, monopoly, and currency expansion with an increasingly heavy hand. The entrepreneurial state of the eleventh century, which aided a buoyant economy through its investments in agriculture, transportation, mining, and industry, gave way to the rentier state of the twelfth and thirteen centuries, which vitiated an economy already exhibiting Malthusian symptoms by inflating its currency, erecting widespread trade barriers, and imposing taxes and surcharges on every possible commodity and transaction.[11] As it had in Sichuan, economic activism degenerated into confiscatory taxation.

The fall of the Song in 1279 marked the end of an era of direct bureaucratic participation in the commercial economy. The political economy of the Ming and Qing was characterized by a withdrawal of the state from direct intervention in commerce, and a transition from command to market-oriented strategies of resource mobilization.

For some scholars, the transition from a command to a market orientation represents the most significant trend in fiscal administration during the Ming and Qing, and a major contributor to the second commercial revolution of the sixteenth to nineteenth centuries.[12] But other scholars differentiate between premodern commercial expansion, such as that experienced in late-imperial China, and the type of modern economic growth chararcterized by increases in capital formation and productivity. For them, modern economic growth is closely associated with the rise of strong, aggressive states that can help restructure the economy and society to foster capital formation and entrepreneurship.[13] From this perspective the growing distance between the Chinese state and the late-imperial economy resulted in a financial system that was too weak to support essential government functions or to push China into the transition from premodern commercial expansion to modern economic growth.

The strongest proponent of this weak-state view has been Ray Huang. In his pioneering study of Ming taxation, Huang characterized the Ming financial administration as "remarkably self-denying, in that it reduced its own operational capacity to the minimum, neglected to develop revenues from industrial and commercial sources, and refused to consider the possibility of seeking assistance from private quarters. The whole tone of the administration was regression rather than progress."[14] In contrast to historians who extol the laissez-faire policies of the Ming, Huang argues that the underfinanced government was unable to provide basic public services, which in turn retarded the progress of technology as a whole and forced administrators to shift the costs of government to those portions of the population that were least able to resist ad-hoc taxes. Marianne Bastid concurs in her assessment of the Qing financial administration, writing that "the principle of personal direct responsibility to the emperor of all officials, together with a rapid turnover except in the highest and lowest grades, limited the possibility of developing a body of regulations and conventions specific to financial institutions which would allow such institutions to protect themselves and expand while still assuring their own internal policing."[15] Similarly the sociologist Frances Moulder, one of an expanding group of comparative sociologists to incorporate recent Sinological research into broader theoretical studies of the state, society, and economic development, has chararcterized the very weak interaction between the late-imperial state and the Chinese economy as "provisioning" in nature. For Moulder, a political economy oriented to provisioning seeks

> above all to acquire revenues and supplies for a static or relatively slowly expanding state civil and military apparatus to ensure an adequate supply of food and other necessities to the rural and urban populations in order to forestall riots and rebellions against the upper classes. The state that has a provisioning policy plays a relatively passive role in the economy. Provisioning policies generally neither suppress commerce, industry, and private capital accumulation nor especially encourage their development.[16]

Moulder, following Eli Heckscher, contrasts provisioning policies with the political economy of mercantilism. "The key element of mercantilism," in Moulder's formulation, "is the conception of the economy as a national economy whose wealth and strength can be increased in part through government action"—including the promotion of capital accumulation, territorial expansion, technical diffusion, and the promotion of a national marketing infrastructure through, for example, currency unification and the improvement of internal transportation.[17]

For Moulder, as well as such mentors and colleagues as Barrington Moore and Theda Skocpol, the provisioning policies of late-imperial China stand in sharp contrast to the mercantilist orientation of the state-building regimes of Europe from the eighteenth century on, and the industrial capitalist states of the present day. They stand in equally sharp contrast to the activist, interventionist political economy of the Song. I would like to return to the theme of fiscal sociology that began this book to speculate on the social basis for the transition from a "mercantilist" to a "provisioning" political economy in the post-Song era.

No simple explanation can account for shifts in the Chinese political economy over the last millienum, and any complete assessment would have to consider changing international contexts and the limited administrative capacity of a premodern agrarian state.[18] But here I would like to emphasize changes in the relationship between the state and the dominant elite as an underlying factor in the transformation of the Chinese political economy. Following Twitchett and Hartwell, I argued in the Introduction that economic activism from the late Tang through the Northern Song was promoted by the rise of a professional bureaucratic elite that depended on government service for its power and income and that therefore benefitted from the expansion of government activities. As Hartwell has demonstrated, long-term social, economic, and demographic changes in the structure of elite power from the eighth century on were exacerbated by the intense factional power struggles of the New Policies and its aftermath, which nullified the formal organizational tactics used by professional elite lineages to guarantee government careers for their offspring. With the intensification of factionalism and political purges, separate lineages of the national hereditary elite increasingly abandoned the endogamous marriage practices and career specialization on which their power had rested, gradually becoming indistinguishable from the local gentry.[19]

Recently Robert Hymes, following up on Hartwell's model of the medieval social transformation, has shown how elite mobility strategies in Fuzhou, the political and economic center of Jiangxi, shifted dramatically between the Northern and Southern Song. In the eleventh century, elite lineages kept their eyes on the state, and aimed at placing as many sons as possible in high office. During the twelfth century, however, and especially after the fall of the Northern Song, elites shifted to a diversified strategy that included occasional office-holding for the sake of social prestige and legal privilege, but that was founded on "a solid property base and firm involvement in local elite social networks." As both the predictability of office-holding and the power and prestige of the state declined during the course of the Southern Song, Hymes argues, a separation opened between state and elite: The gap between elite and state interests at the local level widened, and elite status and social position became independent of the state.[20]

Thanks to the work of many historians working on the social and intellectual history of the Song, we can now associate the rise of the local gentry with a paradigmatic shift from the centralized bureaucratic state to the local voluntaristic community as the focus of elite concern during the Southern Song. Though Southern Song intellectuals might still look to the emperor for solutions to pressing social and economic problems, they rarely looked to the bureaucracy.[21] What I would like to argue is that the rise of the local gentry in the twelfth century, a watershed in the evolution of the Chinese elite, ultimately transformed the foundation of state power and the political economy of the late-imperial era. As Elvin, Beattie, and Wiens have shown for the Ming and Qing, social, institutional, and demographic factors all continued from the twelfth century on to diminish the role of government service in the lives of the dominant gentry elite.[22] Even the examination system drove a wedge between the elite and the state, for the increasing ratio of degree-holders to government positions made entry into the civil service progressively remote and turned the examination system into as much a mechanism for acquiring status and connections as a ladder to official success.[23] Thus, although official position probably remained the quickest route to power and fortune throughout the late-imperial era, for any given lineage the downward slide out of the civil service was far more predictable than entry into it.[24] Under the circumstances, elite mobility strategies gradually clustered around the control of land, commerce, and credit, supplemented by the widespread pursuit of the social and cultural rather than the official rewards of education. As elites came to focus on mobility strategies that were independent of the state, the autonomous state of the eleventh century gave way to the autonomous elite of the late-imperial era.

This transformation in the basis of elite power from the twelfth century on—the differentiation of state and elite—helped foster the shift from a mercantilist to a provisioning political economy in at least two ways. First, the growing localism and independence from government service of the gentry as a class fostered a preference for minimalist, non-interventionist, provisioning economic policies on the part of individual gentrymen when they did serve as members of the government. And second, when under the impetus of dynastic crisis the late-Ming and late-Qing states did attempt to expand their power in the economy, these efforts were easily repelled by a powerful and independent elite.[25]

In the end, then, China's medieval social transformation—the rise to political prominence of an independent local gentry—had a much more profound impact on the political economy of the late-imperial era than the glorious but abortive medieval economic revolution. A gentry whose power was based on property and trade could successfully counter economic intervention by the state and force the state to concede revenues in return for political stability. Faced with a relatively autonomous elite, the activist economic policies of the Northern Song—whatever their ultimate efficacy—would have been impossible during the Ming and Qing. The social foundation of the late-imperial political economy was not definitively broken until the Chinese Communist Revolution destroyed the foundation of elite autonomy and fostered the rise of a new elite of bureaucratic cadre that was utterly dependent on the state. This rebureaucratization of the Chinese elite has promoted a new, modern phase of economic activism and reintensified the debate over the proper scope of state control of the economy.

Appendices
Notes
Bibliography
Glossary
Index

Northern Song Tea and Horse Agency Chiefs, Co-Intendants, and Assistant Intendants by Year

In the following table, incumbent Agency Chiefs, Co-Intendants, and Assistant Intendants are listed in order of their rank in the THA. The first entry for each name is given in all capital letters. A man's cumulative record of service in all three ranks between 1074 and 1125 is given in months at the first appearance of his name for each period of incumbency. Where exact dates of appointment and transfer are unavailable, terms of office and number of months served are based on the first and last references in the sources to a man's holding a post, his appearance in a new post, and evidence from context for continuity. The final column lists whether a man is known to have been born in Sichuan. For sources, see Appendix C. For exact offices held by each man, see Paul J. Smith, "Taxing Heaven's Storehouse" (Ph.D. diss).

Incumbents	Term of Office	Total Months of Service	Native Place
1074 LI QI	1074/11–1075/12	13	Unknown
PU ZONGMIN	1074/11–1086/2	135	Sichuan
1075 Li Qi			
Pu Zongmin			
1076 LIU ZUO	1076/4–1077/7	15	Unknown
Pu Zongmin			
1077 Liu Zuo			
LI JI	1077/7–1082/10	63	Sichuan
Pu Zongmin			
1078 Li Ji			
Pu Zongmin			
1079 Li Ji			
Pu Zongmin			
FAN CHUNCUI	1079/5–1081/11	28	Other
1080 Li Ji			
Pu Zongmin			
Fan Chuncui			
LU SHIMIN	1080/12–1086/6	66	Other
1081 Li Ji			
Pu Zongmin			
Fan Chuncui			
Lu Shimin			
GUO MAOXUN	1081/7–1083/6	23	Other
1082 Li Ji			
Pu Zongmin			
Lu Shimin			
Guo Maoxun			
1083 Lu Shimin			
Pu Zongmin			
Guo Maoxun			
1084 Lu Shimin			
Pu Zongmin			
1085 Lu Shimin			
Pu Zongmin			
1086 Lu Shimin			
Pu Zongmin			
HUANG LIAN	1086/6–1087/12	18	Other
1087 Huang Lian			
YAN LING	1087/4–1092/8+	64+	Unknown
CHOU BOYU	1087/12–?	?	Unknown

Incumbents	Term of Office	Total Months of Service	Native Place
1088 Yan Ling			
Chou Boyu			
1089 Yan Ling [?]			
1090 Yan Ling [?]			
1091 CHENG ZHISHAO	1091/12–1094/4+	28+	Sichuan
Yan Ling			
1092 Cheng Zhishao			
Yan Ling			
1093 Cheng Zhishao			
1094 Cheng Zhishao			
LU SHIMIN	1094/6–1099/11	65	
1095 Lu Shimin			
1096 Lu Shimin			
SONG GOU	1096–?	?	Sichuan
1097 Lu Shimin			
HUANG MINYONG	1097/8–1098/6	10	Unknown
1098 Lu Shimin			
Huang Minyong			
1099 Lu Shimin			
CHENG ZHISHAO	1099/2–1105/6	76	
SUN ZHEN	1099/2–1103/10	56	Unknown
1100 Cheng Zhishao			
Sun Zhen			
1101 Cheng Zhishao			
Sun Zhen			
1102 Cheng Zhishao			
Sun Zhen			
1103 Cheng Zhishao			
Sun Zhen			
1104 Cheng Zhishao			
Sun Zhen			
SUN AOBIAN	1104/2–1107/11	45	Unknown
1105 Cheng Zhishao			
Sun Aobian			
WU ZEREN	1105/2–1107/1	22	Other
1106 Sun Aobian			
Wu Zeren			
1107 Sun Aobian			
PANG YINSUN	1107/2–1109/5+	?	Other
1108 Pang Yinsun			

Incumbents	Term of Office	Total Months of Service	Native Place
1109 Pang Yinsun [?]			
WANG WAN	1109–?	?	Unknown
1110 ?			
1111 ZHANG HUI	1111/1–1114/11+	46+	Unknown
LI JII	1111–?	?	Unknown
1112 Zhang Hui			
1113 Zhang Hui			
GUO SI	1113/1–1121/12	108	Other
1114 Zhang Hui			
Guo Si			
1115 Guo Si or CHENG TANG			
1116 Guo Si			
CHENG TANG	1116/2–1118/8	32	Sichuan
1117 Guo Si			
Cheng Tang			
1118 Guo Si			
Cheng Tang			
1119 Guo Si			
YUWEN CHANG	1119/8–1122/4+	32+	Sichuan
1120 Guo Si			
Yuwen Chang			
1121 Guo Si			
Yuwen Chang			
ZHANG YOUJI	1121/4–1121/12	8+	Unknown
HE JIAN	1121/4–1123/6+	26+	Unknown
1122 Guo Si			
ZHANG HUI	1120/8–22/4+	20	
He Jian			
Yuwen Chang			
1123 He Jian			
HAN ZHAO	1123/12–1125/10+	24	Other
1124 WANG FAN	1124/8–?	?	Other
Han Zhao			
1125 Han Zhao			

Southern Song Tea and Horse Agency Intendants

Incumbent	Term of Office	Total Months of Service	Native Place
Zhao Kai	1128/11–1136/8	93	Sichuan
Li Dai	1136/8–1138/2	18	Other
Zhang Shen	1137/11–1139/2	15	Sichuan
Zhao Kai	1139/2–1140/4	14	Sichuan
Tao Kai	1140/2–1140/3	2	Unknown
Feng Kangguo	1140/4–1142/3	24	Sichuan
Jia Sicheng	1142/6–1143/10+	?	Unknown
Han Qiu	1147/12–1149/5	17	Other
Fu Xingzhong	1149/5–?	?	Other
Tang Yungong	?–1154/12	?	Other
Zheng Ai	1154/12–1155/12	?	Unknown
Li Run	pre-1156/10–1157/3	12+	Unknown
Xu Yin	1157/11–1159	?	Other
Wang Zhiwang	1160/2–1160/8	6	Other
Wang Fei	1160/6–1162/6	24	Unknown
Xu Bi	1162/6–1165/1	31	Unknown
Chen Mizuo	1165/1–1167/2	24	Other
Chao Gongwu	?–1167/6	?	Other
Zhang Song	1167/8–1170/4	32	Unknown
Zhang Deyuan	1169/6–?	?	Unknown
Zhao Yanbo	pre-1171/5–1172/7	ca.24	Other
Zhu Quan	1176/1–1178/2	24+	Unknown
Wu Zong	pre.1178/6–1181/6	36+	Other

Incumbent	Term of Office	Total Months of Service	Native Place
Wang Wo	1181/7–1185/9+	50+	Other
Li Dazheng	1187–?	?	Unknown
Yang Jing	pre-1194/3–1196/3	24+	Unknown
Ding Feng	1197	?	Other
Qian Wu	1198	?	Unknown
Wang Ning	1199	?	Unknown
Wang Zhen	1201	?	Unknown
Hu Dacheng	1202	?	Unknown
Wang Daguo	1203	?	Unknown
Peng Ge	1203/8–1204/2+	?	Unknown

Sources on Careers of the Northern and Southern Song Tea and Horse Agency Intendants

The following list of sources to Appendices A and B cites only those entries directly pertinent to the reconstruction of each Intendant's career. For fuller references, see Wang Deyi, *Song huiyao jigao suoyin*; Zhang Bide et al., *Song ren chuanji ziliao suoyin*; and Umehara Kaoru, *Zoku shiji tsugan chōhen jinmei sakuin* (Name index to *XCB*) and *Ken'en irai keinen yōroku jinmei sakuin* (Name index to *XNYL*).

THE NORTHERN SONG INTENDANTS (1074–1127)

Cheng Tang 程唐: *SHY* zhiguan 6/14a–b; *SHY* zhiguan 43/99b, 100a; *SHY* zhiguan 70/13b; *SHY* fangyu 8/24a, 19/21b–22a; *XNYL* 30/1156.

Cheng Zhishao 程之邵: *XCB* 320/6b, 366/21b, 468/15a, 506/3a–b; *SHY* zhiguan 43/74a–b, 77a–b, 77b–78a, 79a; *SHY* shihuo 30/26b, 33b–34a, 34b; *SHY* bing 24/28a–b; *SS* 351/11150.

Chou Boyu 仇伯玉: *XCB* 407/16a, 499/5b; *SHY* shihuo 24/30b.

Fan Chuncui 范純粹: *XCB* 266/8b–9a, 298/6b, 303/15a–b, 319/1b; *SS* 184/4500, 314/10279–10280.

Guo Maoxun 郭茂恂: *XCB* 298/17b, 314/1b–2a, 315/2b, 335/20a, 340/9b, 347/16a, 372/14a, 395/13b; *SHY* zhiguan 43/53b–56b, 56b–58a, 59a–61a, 62b–63a, 63b.

Guo Si 郭思: *SHY* zhiguan 43/100a, 101b, 101b–102a; *SHY* shihuo 32/3a–b; *SHY* xuanju 33/33a; *SHY* bing 22/14b; *SHY* fangyu 10/36a; *SHY* xingfa 2/88b–89a; Lu Xinyuan, *Songshi yi* 38/4b.

Han Zhao 韓昭: *SHY* zhiguan 3/49a; *SHY* zhiguan 43/102b, 103b; *SHY* xuanju 31/6a; *SHY* fangyu 15/30a–b.

He Jian 何漸: *SHY* zhiguan 43/94a, 98b, 100b–101a, 101b–102a, 102b, 103a; *SHY* zhiguan 69/16b; *SHY* xuanju 33/36b, 37b.

Huang Lian 黃廉: *XCB* 277/5a, 364/16b, 366/2a, 381/22a–23b, 390/1b, 399/10b, 401/15b–16a, 448/7a, 473/5b.

Huang Minyong 黃敏用: *XCB* 490/7a, 499/3b, 510/2a.

Li Ji 李稷: *XCB* 253/7a, 255/2a, 277/6a–b, 278/2b–3a, 280/9a–b, 283/10b, 297/13a, 297/16b, 299/12b, 312/3b, 312/15b, 318/1b, 327/10b, 330/9a–b.

Li Jii 李稷: *SHY* zhiguan 43/93a, 93a–b; *SHY* shihuo 30/39b.

Li Qi 李杞: *XCB* 247/20a, 252/4b, 258/5a, 267/12b, 269/17b, 271/2b, 303/14b–15a.

Liu Zuo 劉佐: *XCB* 245/12b, 256/9b, 263/22b, 264/9b, 264/17b, 265/7a, 266/8b, 270/3a, 274/10b, 274/11a, 278/13b, 283/9b, 298/11a.

Lu Shimin 陸師閔: *XCB* 495/9b, 17a, 501/15a, 504/6a, 507/12a, 516/3b; *SHY* shihuo 30/18a–b, 18b–22a, 23a, 23a–b, 23b–24a, 26b–27a, 27a–b, 28b–29a, 29a–30a; *SHY* zhiguan 43/55a, 70a, 71b–72a; *SS* 332/10682–10683.

Pang Yinsun 龐寅孫: *SHY* zhiguan 41/126b; *SHY* zhiguan 42/27a; *SHY* zhiguan 43/89b; *SHY* shihuo 30/36a.

Pu Zongmin 蒲宗閔: *XCB* 248/23a–b, 249/6a, 258/17b, 282/12b, 290/3b, 292/1a, 303/14b, 326/15a–16b, 334/13b, 341/4b, 368/12a–b, 391/10a–b; *SHY* zhiguan 43/47a, 52a, 53a, 61a–b; Su Che, *Luancheng ji* 30/5a.

Song Gou 宋構: *XCB* 350/10a, 377/11b–12a.

Sun Aobian 孫鼇林: *XCB* 269/3b, 280/22a; *SHY* zhiguan 43/49a, 81a, 86b, 90b–91a; *SHY* shihuo 30/36a; *SHY* xuanju 19/16b.

Sun Zhen 孫軫: *XCB* 506/1a, 516/5b, 517/3a; *SHY* zhiguan 43/79a.

Wang Fan 王蕃: *SHY* zhiguan 43/103a; *SHY* zhiguan 57/6b; *SHY* fanyi 4/41b; *SHY* xuanju 29/14b.

Wang Wan 王完: *XCB* 275/7b; *SHY* shihuo 30/37a.

Wu Zeren 吳擇仁: *SHY* shihuo 30/35b–36a; *SHY* bing 24/28b; *SHY* zhiguan 42/32b, 36a.

Yan Ling 閻令: *XCB* 309/12b, 399/10b, 476/2a; *SHY* zhiguan 43/71a–b; *SHY* shihuo 30/26a–b.

Yuwen Chang 宇文常: *SHY* zhiguan 43/101a, 101b–102a; *SHY* bing 22/14a; *SHY* xuanju 33/37b; *SS* 353/11149.

Zhang Hui 張翬: *SHY* zhiguan 43/93a, 93b, 94b, 101b–102a; *SHY* zhiguan 48/33b; *SHY* xuanju 33/25a, 27a.

Zhang Youji 張有極: *SHY* zhiguan 43/101a–b; *SHY* bing 22/14b; *SHY* xuanju 33/37b.

THE SOUTHERN SONG INTENDANTS *(1128–1204)*

Chao Gongwu 晁公武: *XNYL* 178/5784–5785; *SHY* xuanju 34/15b, 20a, 23a; *SHY* zhiguan 6/61b; *SHY* zhiguan 17/21b; *SHY* zhiguan 37/7a; *SHY* zhiguan 59/26a; *Quan Shu yiwen zhi* 26/12b.

Chen Mizuo 陳彌作: *XNYL* 199/6605; *SHY* bing 23/1b–2a, 3b–4a; *SHY* zhiguan 11/50b, 52a; *SHY* zhiguan 20/60b; *SHY* zhiguan 24/30a; *SHY* zhiguan 43/110a, 110b, 114a: *SHY* zhiguan 47/69b; *SHY* zhiguan 54/38b; *SHY* xuanju 25/29a; *SHY* xuanju 34/15b.

Ding Feng 丁逢: *SHY* bing 23/27b; *SHY* bing 26/17a; *SHY* zhiguan 72/24b, 38a; *SHY* zhiguan 73/26a; *SHY* zhiguan 74/13a; *SHY* xuanju 21/7b; *SHY* shihuo 31/30a; *SHY* shihuo 44/15a; *SHY* shihuo 62/72b.

Feng Kangguo 馮康國: *XNYL* 90/2933, 97/3140, 135/4234, 141/4433, 144/4541; *SHY* zhiguan 40/7b; *SHY* zhiguan 77/19a; *SHY* shihuo 2/20b; *SHY* fangyu 12/8a; *SS* 375/11619–11621.

Fu Xingzhong 符行中: *XNYL* 159/5059–5060, 167/5329.

Han Qiu 韓球: *XNYL* 156/4985–4986, 159/5059; *SHY* zhiguan 43/106b, 149a, 157b–158a; *SHY* zhiguan 57/99b; *SHY* shihuo 31/11a; *SHY* xuanju 31/6b; *SHY* xuanju 34/5a; *SHY* shihuo 64/48a, 76a.

Hu Dacheng 胡大成: *SHY* bing 26/17a; *SHY* zhiguan 73/43b; *CYZJ* yi 14/1064; Yu Chou, *Cunbaitang ji* 5/2b–3a.

Jia Sicheng 賈思誠: *XNYL* 133/4184–4185, 145/4563; *SHY* zhiguan 43/105a–b; *SHY* shihuo 31/3b–4b; *SHY* bing 21/10b.

Li Dai 李迨: *XNYL* 90/3042, 104/3314, 108/3453, 118/3737, 128/4066; *SHY* shihuo 49/43b; *SS* 374/11592–11596.

Li Dazheng 李大正: *SHY* bing 23/19a, 19b; *SHY* zhiguan 43/167a, 174a; *SHY* zhiguan 72/44a; *SHY* shihuo 14/43a; *SHY* shihuo 34/21a–b.

Li Run 李潤: *XNYL* 111/3510, 183/5993, 184/6053; *SHY* bing 24/37b–38a; *SHY* shihuo 63/13a–b.

Peng Ge 彭輅: *SHY* 20/8b; *SHY* bing 26/16a, 16b; *SHY* zhiguan 62/14b; *SHY* zhiguan 79/21a–b; *CYZJ* yi 14/1064–1065.

Qian Wu 錢鍪: *SHY* bing 26/17a.

Tang Yungong 湯允恭: *XNYL* 167/5351, 169/5389–5391, 176/5704–5705; *SHY* zhiguan 40/12a–b; Zhou Linzhi, *Hailing ji* 13/10b–11a; *Songdai Shuwen jicun* 51/17b.

Tao Kai 陶愷: *XNYL* 92/2999, 129/4085–4086, 134/4218, 4244; *SHY* shihuo 26/10b; *SHY* zhiguan 70/17a, 32a.

Wang Daguo 王大過: *SHY* shihuo 62/72a; *SHY* zhiguan 73/26a; *CYZJ* yi 14/1065.

Wang Fei 王弗: *XNYL* 185/6090; *SHY* zhiguan 41/52a; *SHY* zhiguan 71/13a; *SHY* shihuo 2/18a; *SHY* shihuo 3/13a; *SHY* shihuo 63/52a.

Wang Ning 王寧: *SHY* bing 26/17a; *SHY* xuanju 21/6b; *SHY* xuanju 22/12b; *SHY* zhiguan 73/31b; *SHY* zhiguan 74/2a, 11a.

Wang Wo 王渥: *SHY* zhiguan 24/37b; *SHY* zhiguan 62/23b, 25b; *SHY* zhiguan 75/4a; *SHY* bing 23/16b–17a; *SHY* shihuo 31/27b–28a; *SS* 396/12074.

Wang Zhen 王珍: *SHY* bing 26/17a; *SHY* bing 29/44b.

Wang Zhiwang 王之望: *XNYL* 165/5275–5276, 168/5373, 174/5628, 175/5650, 176/5684, 177/5720, 179/5812, 184/6032, 185/6096–6097, 189/6212, 198/6566; *SHY* zhiguan 43/109b.

Wu Zong 吳揔: *SHY* bing 23/15a, 15b–16a; *SHY* shihuo 31/25a–b; *SHY* zhiguan 47/40a–b; *SHY* zhiguan 74/14a–b; *CYZJ* yi 14/1063–1064.

Xu Bi 續觜: *XNYL* 178/5785, 200/6639; *SHY* zhiguan 43/110b–111b; *SHY* zhiguan 47/26a; *SHY* zhiguan 71/10a; *SHY* xuanju 34/10a, 14b; *SHY* shihuo 31/15b.

Xu Yin 許尹: *XNYL* 181/5899, 183/5973, 184/6032, 191/6277; *SHY* zhiguan 41/48a; *SHY* zhiguan 77/74b–75a; *SHY* shihuo 1/40a–b; *SHY* shihuo 3/7a; *SHY* shihuo 8/6a; *SHY* shihuo 31/13a; *SHY* shihuo 63/13a–14a.

Yang Jing 揚経: *SHY* bing 23/24b; *SHY* bing 26/2a, 6a, 9a; *SHY* zhiguan 73/65a; Lou Yue, *Gongwei ji* 37/10a.

Zhang Deyuan 張德遠: *SHY* shihuo 8/9b; *SHY* shihuo 14/38a; *SHY* shihuo 65/93b; *SHY* xuanju 34/11b, 18a–b.

Zhang Shen 張深: *XNYL* 48/1676, 66/2164, 116/3675, 130/4117; *SHY* zhiguan 41/27b; *SHY* zhiguan 63/10b, 11b; *SHY* zhiguan 68/27b; *SHY* bing 24/35b; *Quan Shu yiwen zhi* 55/6b.

Zhang Song 張松: *SHY* zhiguan 41/113a; *SHY* zhiguan 43/114b; *SHY* bing 22/25a; *SHY* bing 23/2b, 4a, 13b–14a; *SHY* bing 25/16b–17a, 23a, 33a; *SHY* xuanju 34/15b, 22a, 23b.

Zhao Kai 趙開: *Songdai Shuwen jicun* 54/1a–8a; *XNYL* 18/742, 28/1121, 32/1251, 48/1689, 75/2391–2392, 95/3070, 99/3175, 104/3314, 125/4234.

Zhao Yanbo 趙彥博: *SHY* bing 17/30b; *SHY* bing 23/16b; *SHY* bing 25/38b; *SHY* xuanju 34/25b; *SHY* li 62/69a; *SHY* zhiguan 72/20b.

Zheng Ai 鄭靄: *XNYL* 157/5008, 167/5329, 167/5351, 170/5475, 172/5546; *SHY* zhiguan 70/43a; *Huang Song zhongxing liangchao shengzheng* 55/1177.

Zhu Quan 朱佺: *SHY* bing 23/14a–b; *SHY* shihuo 31/24b–25a; *SHY* zhiguan 10/35a; *SHY* zhiguan 61/57a; *SHY* zhiguan 62/21a; *SHY* zhiguan 72/50b; *Huang Song zhongxing liangchao shengzheng* 55/2087.

Tea and Horse Agency Revenues and Subventions Paid to Other Agencies, 1074–1115.

The following table includes both individual figures and those for a range of dates. Quota figures are given in boldface. Where a mean average is useful as an estimate of an annual figure, it is given in parentheses following the actual recorded number and is italicized. The unit of measure is the guan, or one string of 1,000 cash. No adjustment has been made for fluctuations in the number of cash per actual string.

Year(s)	Net Revenues	Subventions to Other Agencies
1074	**400,000 strings net profit quota** from sales and taxes on tea.[a]	—
1074–1077	1,229,000+ strings net profits and taxes (*=409,666 strings per year average*).[b]	—
1077	600,000 strings, including sales of salt and cloth.[c]	—
1077–1078	767,066 strings, including new monopoly returns, previous tax receipts, and funds disbursed to other agencies.[d]	—
1078–1082	4,280,000+ strings earned under Li Ji (*=856,000 strings per year average*).[e]	—
1079	1,000,000 strings (probably from Shaanxi tea sales) retained as capitalization.[f]	50,000 strings to Fiscal Intendant; 100,000 strings to await court dispensation.[g]
1080	700,000+ strings earned on tea sales in West Shaanxi.[h]	300,000 strings' worth of gold and silk put in discretionary fund (*fengzhuang*).[i] 200,000 strings to Jinguanlu Pacification Commissioner for grain and fodder procurement.[j]
1081		200,000 strings annual grant-in-aid to Xihe Circuit.[k]
1082		400,000 strings to Qinfeng Military Affairs Commission for grain and fodder procurement.[l]

Year(s)	Net Revenues	Subventions to Other Agencies
1083	**1,000,000 strings annual net profit quota.**[m]	—
1084	1,600,000 strings in net profits and taxes.[n]	600,000 strings to Director of Frontier Finances, Xihe and Lanhui Circuits for provisioning.[o]
1085	2,000,000 strings net profit.[p]	1,000,000 strings "presented" *(xian)* to court.[q]
1092	3,000,000 strings generated for capitalization *(eben)*.[r]	—
1098	**2,000,000 strings net profit quota.**[s]	—
1101	600,843.867 short strings' surplus over quota from sales of Mingshan tea in Shaanxi horse markets.[t]	—
1102	1,872,153.136 short strings' surplus over quota.[t]	—
1103	—	2,532,997.103 short strings deposited with a Judicial Intendant (probably of Shaanxi).[t]
1114–1115	4,835,000 strings profits and taxes.[u]	—
1115	3,711,111 strings of "tea profits."[u]	111,098.750 strings to various prefectures.[u]

Sources: [a]*SHY* zhiguan 43/48b. [b]*SHY* shihuo 30/16b. [c]Lü Tao, *Jingde ji* 3/7a. [d]*SHY* shihuo 30/15b–16a. [e]*XCB* 334/12b. [f]*SHY* shihuo 30/16a. [g]*XCB* 297/16b. [h]*SHY* shihuo 30/17b. [i]*SHY* shihuo 30/17a. [j]*XCB* 308/3b. [k]*SHY* zhiguan 43/58b. [l]*XCB* 323/3b. [m]*XCB* 340/12b. [n]*XCB* 334/13b. [o]*XCB* 348/12b. [p]Lü Tao, *Jingde ji* 3/7a. [q]Lü Tao, *Jingde ji* 3/7a. [r]*Song shi* 184/4501. [s]*XCB* 501/4a; *Songdai Shuwen jicun* 26/10b. [t]*SHY* zhiguan 43/77b–78a. [u]*SHY* zhiguan 43/99b–100a.

Abbreviations Used in the Notes

CBBM   Yang Zhongliang, *Zizhi tongjian changbian jishi benmo.*
CYZJ   Li Xinchuan, *Jianyan yilai chaoye zaji.*
SHY   *Song huiyao jiben.*
SS   *Song shi.*
WXTK   Ma Duanlin, *Wenxian tongkao.*
XCB   Li Tao, *Xu zizhi tongjian changbian.*
XNYL   Li Xinchuan, *Jianyan yilai xinian yaolu.*

Notes

INTRODUCTION

1. Joseph Schumpeter, "The Crisis of the Tax State," in Alan T. Peacock, Ralph Turvey, Wolfgang F. Stoper and Elizabeth Henderson, eds., *International Economic Papers: Translations Prepared for the International Economic Association,* vol. 4, pp. 6–7.
2. The Naitō thesis is summarized in Hisayuki Miyakawa, "An Outline of the Naitō Hypothesis and its Effects on Japanese Studies of China," *Far Eastern Quarterly* 14:533–552. The best surveys of this transformation in English are Mark Elvin, *The Pattern of the Chinese Past,* and Robert M. Hartwell, "Demographic, Political, and Social Transformations of China, 750–1550," *Harvard Journal of Asiatic Studies* 42.2:365–442. For a recent study of the impact of the medieval transformation at the local level, see Robert Hymes, *Statesmen and Gentlemen: The Elite of Fu-chou, Chiang-hsi, in Northern and Southern Sung.* Richard von Glahn traces its effect on both Chinese and native peoples in the Sichuanese border region of Luzhou in *The Country of Streams and Grottoes: Expansion, Settlement, and the Civilizing of the Sichuan Frontier in Song Times.*
3. Regional population proportions are based on Hartwell, "Transformations of China," Table 1, p. 369. See also ibid., pp. 383–394; Hans Bielenstein, "The Census of China during the Period 2–742 A.D.," *Bulletin of the Museum of Far Eastern Antiquities* 19:125–263; and Elvin, *Pattern,* pp. 113–130 and 203–215.
4. Francesca Bray, *Agriculture,* pp. 597–615. Note that several of the government policies that Bray identifies as central to this "Green Revolution," such as the "Green Sprouts" farming loans, have since been reinterpreted in a less favorable light. For other works in English on the Song agrarian revolution

see Elvin, *Pattern*, pp. 113–130, and Peter Golas, "Rural China in the Song," *Journal of Asian Studies* 39.2:291–325, both of which provide bibliographical entrée to the crucial Japanese literature.

5. See Shiba Yoshinobu, "Urbanization and the Development of Markets in the Lower Yangtze Valley," in John Winthrop Haeger, ed., *Crisis and Prosperity in Sung China*, pp. 13–15, an article which synthesizes the work of a generation of scholars. On market expansion and the growth of trade during the Tang-Song transition, see Denis Twitchett, "Merchant, Trade, and Government in Late T'ang," *Asia Major* (n.s.) 14.1:63–95; Shiba Yoshinobu, *Sōdai shōgyoshi kenkyū,* and the synopsis of this work by Mark Elvin under the title *Commerce and Society in Sung China.*

6. The social background of "the newly risen bureaucrats of the Song" is another field in which the Japanese have done pioneering work. For a descriptive bibliography in English of representative Japanese studies, see Hasegawa Yoshio, "Trends in Postwar Japanese Studies on Sung History: A Bibliographical Introduction," *Acta Asiatica* 50:115–120.

7. See Denis Twitchett, "The Composition of the T'ang Ruling Class: New Perspectives from Tunhuang," in Arthur F. Wright and Denis Twitchett, eds., *Perspectives on the T'ang*, pp. 47–85; David Johnson, *The Medieval Chinese Oligarchy*, and "The Last Years of a Great Clan: The Li Family of Chao Chün in Late T'ang and Early Sung," *Harvard Journal of Asiatic Studies* 37.1:5–102; and Patricia Buckley Ebrey, *The Aristocratic Families of Early China: A Case Study of the Pō-ling Ts'ui Family.*

8. Hartwell, "Transformations of China," p.406. Hartwell identifies only thirty-five of these professional lineages as truly important, but notes that while they constituted less than 5 percent of the families supplying holders of policy-making offices, they filled 23 percent of these positions between 998 and 1085; see p. 413.

9. On the transformation of landlords and magnates into a new bureaucratic elite, see Sudō Yoshiyuki *Sōdai kanryōsei to daitochi shoyū*, pp. 5–102. Winston Lo argues that the Song founders explicitly utilized the examination system to create a new, compliant elite to replace the defunct aristocracy and the unsuitable militarists, an elite that "owed their status wholly to the grace of the emperor." See Lo, *An Introduction to the Civil Service of Sung China*, p. 82.

10. See Zhu Jiayuan and Wang Zengyu, "Songdai de guanhu," in Deng Guangming and Cheng Yingliu, eds., *Songshi yanjiu lunwen ji*, pp. 8–14. As Brian McKnight points out, however, the fiscal privileges enjoyed by Song officials were far less substantial than those held by their peers in either the Tang or the Yuan and Ming; on the other hand, any given individual probably had a greater chance of entering officialdom during the Song. See

McKnight "Fiscal Privileges and the Social Order in Sung China," in John Winthrop Haeger, ed., *Crisis and Prosperity in Sung China*. pp. 79–100.

11. See John Chaffee, *The Thorny Gates of Learning in Sung China*. pp. 28–30; and Lo, *Introduction to the Civil Service*. pp. 102–109.

12. For statistics on the size of the civil service, see Chaffee, Table 4, p. 27. The registered population of the empire in 997 was 4,100,000 households; by 1083 the registered population had quadrupled to 17,200,000 households: *WXTK* 11/113–114.

13. Hartwell, "Transformation of China," p. 422. Hartwell's propositions about the collapse of a national elite orientation and the rise of localist strategies during the twelfth century have been richly substantiated by Hymes in *Statesmen and Gentlemen*. Patricia Ebrey surveys the recent literature on the Song elite in "The Dynamics of Elite Domination in Sung China," *Harvard Journal of Asiatic Studies* 48.2:493–519.

14. As Hartwell demonstrates for the empire as a whole and Hymes for the elite of Fuzhou, Northern Song officials tended to seek marriage partners for themselves and their relatives from among the national membership of the civil service, and to migrate out of their native places to the political and economic centers of the empire. During the Southern Song, however, political elites reverted to a much more localist focus in their marriage and residence patterns. At the same time the local community, a cornerstone of Neo-Confucian concern, displaced the state as the ideological center of attention for socially concerned intellectuals. See Hymes, chs. 3 and 4. Current work by Peter Bol sheds light on the place of the state in the intellectual and professional concerns of successive generations of Northern Song intellectuals. Part of his findings appear in his "Principles of Unity: On the Political Visions of Ssu-ma Kuang (1019–1086) and Wang An-shih (1021–1086)."

15. For a discussion of "state autonomy," see Theda Skocpol, "Bringing the State Back In: Strategies of Analysis and Current Research," in Peter B. Evans, Dietrich Rueschemeyer, and Theda Skocpol, eds., *Bringing the State Back In*, pp. 9–11.

16. I rehearse much of the present argument in "State Power and Economic Activism during the New Policies, 1068–1085: The Tea and Horse Trade and the 'Green Sprouts' Loan Policy." For useful discussions, see Albert Feuerwerker, "The State and the Economy in Late Imperial China," unpublished manuscript, 1983; William Rowe, "Approaches to Modern Chinese Social History," in Olivier Zunz, ed., *Reliving the Past: The Worlds of Social History*, pp. 236–296; and an important new study by Susan Mann, *Local Merchants and the Chinese Bureaucracy, 1750–1950*.

17. Denis Twitchett, *Financial Administration under the T'ang Dynasty*, pp. 97–123; Denis Twitchett, "The Salt Commissioners after the Rebellion of An

Lu-shan," *Asia Major* (n.s.) 4.1:60–89; Robert M. Hartwell, "Financial Expertise, Examinations, and the Formulation of Economic Policy in Northern Sung China," *Journal of Asian Studies,* 30:281–314; and Hartwell, "Transformations," pp. 394–425.

18. By Yingzong's reign (1064–1067) the career advantages enjoyed by technically oriented officials had produced serious morale problems. As Ouyang Xiu explained to the emperor, it was generally felt that only specialists in finance and law were rising in the government rapidly, and that such specialist commissions *(chaiqian)* had preempted the *jinshi* exams and recommendations as a way to get ahead, leaving scholars and generalists out of the competition: *XCB* 208/15b–17a. By way of confirmation, Robert Hartwell shows that thirty-eight out of eighty-five Finance Commissioners between 960 and 1083 made it to the Council of State, twelve as Chief Councillor; moreover there was at least one former Finance Commissioner on the Council 75 percent of the time; see "Financial Expertise," pp. 292–293.

19. The Song state monopolized the staples of foreign trade and the products of "the mountains and the marshes" *(shanze):* gold, silver, copper, iron, lead, and tin among the metals; incense and alum; and most importantly from the perspective of revenues, salt, wine, and tea. In combination these last three monopolies contributed 51 percent of the state's cash income in 997–998; 80 percent of the cash and 25 percent of the total income around 1050; and an estimated 69 percent of the cash and 34 percent of the total income around 1077. See Quan Hansheng, "Tang-Song zhengfu suiru yu huobi jingji de guanxi," in his *Zhongguo jingjishi yanjiu,* vol. 1, pp. 209–263, for a full discussion and valuable statistical tables. Commercial transit and sales taxes were levied through a network of 1,850 to 2,011 tax bureaus and stations during the eleventh century, located in most of the 1,235 county seats and in favorably situated garrison towns, markets, stockades, passes, and ferry crossings. Total sums collected ranged from 4,000,000 in 997–998 to a peak of 19,700,000 strings around 1045, and back down to 7,000,000 strings in 1077, representing an average of about 26 percent of the cash receipts and 7 percent of the total receipts to the government during the eleventh century. In addition to Quan Hansheng, see Katō Shigeshi "Songdai shangshui kao," in the Chinese translation of his *Shina keizaishi kōshō* as *Zhongguo jingjishi kaozheng,* pp. 626–627; Song Xi, "Songdai de shangshui gang," in *Songshi yanjiu ji,* vol. 3, p. 332, and his "BeiSong shangshui zai guojizhong de diwei yu jianshui guan," in *Songshi yanjiu ji,* vol. 5, pp. 229–236. All three articles are based primarily on the prefectural and subprefectural tax quotas for 1077 and "of old" listed in *SHY* shihuo 15–17. According to the financial councillor Zhang Fangping, combined receipts from the commercial sector amounted to 15,000,000 strings around the turn of the eleventh century, for 23 percent of the government's total income of 65,600,000 units. By the

late 1040s commercial receipts had tripled, to constitute about 36 percent
of the total income of 126,000,000 strings. Although total income for 1077
has not been preserved, we do not know that the quota for direct *(liangshui)*
taxes in 1077 was 52,000,000 units, each unit theoretically worth a string
of cash. Assuming that there were no other significant sources of government
income, we can conclude that by the 1070s 49 percent of the state's financial
resources were derived from the commercial sector. See Zhang Fangping,
Lequan ji 25/25b—26a.

20. During the Ming the land tax, calculated in grain (26,700,000 *dan* in 1502),
constituted 75 percent of government revenues; and total revenues and financial capacity were well below that of the Song: Ray Huang, *Taxation and
Government Finance in Sixteenth-Century Ming China,* p. 46. The situation was
quite similar during the early and mid Qing. According to Wang Yeh-chien,
74 percent of the government's total receipts in 1753 (worth a silver value of
73,800,000 taels) was contributed by the land tax; another 12 percent was
provided by the salt monopoly, 7.3 percent by native customs, and the rest
from miscellaneous sources. But by 1908, as Wang estimates, the proportions had changed radically: out of a total income of 292,000,000 taels, the
land tax provided 25 percent while the salt monopoly and likin, maritime
customs, and native customs levies contributed 42 percent, with 22 percent
derived from miscellaneous sources: Wang Yeh-chien, *Land Taxation in Imperial China, 1750—1911,* Tables 4.2 and 4.4, pp. 72 and 80. These changes
are put into perspective in Mann, ch. 3.

21. For summaries of the rise of the steppes empires, see J. J. Saunders, *The
History of the Mongol Conquests,* pp. 17—43; and Luc Kwanten, *Imperial Nomads,* pp. 49—104.

22. See Wang Gungwu, "The Rhetoric of a Lesser Empire: Early Sung Relations
with its Neighbors," in Morris Rossabi, ed., *China Among Equals: The Middle
Kingdom and its Neighbors, 10th—14th Centuries,* pp. 47—65; and Benjamin I.
Schwartz, "The Chinese Perception of the World Order, Past and Present", in John K. Fairbank, ed., *The Chinese World Order,*
pp. 280—281.

23. See Zhou Bodi, *Zhongguo caizheng shi,* pp. 259—260. William H. McNeill,
The Pursuit of Power: Technology, Armed Force, and Society since A.D. *1000,* Ch.
2, deftly synthesizes Western scholarship on the interrelationship between
war, markets, and technology in Song China.

24. A long literature has emerged on the relationship between the state and the
medieval revolution in science and industry. Robert M. Hartwell has produced two classics in 'Markets, Technology, and the Structure of Enterprise
in the Development of the Eleventh-Century Chinese Iron and Steel Industry," *Journal of Economic History* 26.9:29—58 and "A Cycle of Economic Change
in Imperial China: Coal and Iron in Northeast China," *Journal of the Economic*

and Social History of the Orient 10:103–159; Elvin, *Pattern,* chs. 7 and 9–13, is also extremely important. An extraordinarily rich vein of material is to be found in the many volumes of *Science and Civilisation in China,* produced under the authorship or direction of Joseph Needham, all of which emphasize the positive contributions of the Song state to the medieval economic revolution.

25. Sogabe Shizuo *Sōdai zaiseishi,* p. 3; Shiba Yoshinobu, "Sōdai shiteki seido no enkaku," in *Aoyama Hakushi koki kinen Sōdaishi ronsō,* p. 128; Huang, *Taxation,* p. 46.

26. On salt, see Dai Yixuan, *Songdai chaoyan zhidu yanjiu.* I discuss the issues surrounding the collapse of the southeastern tea industry in "Interest Groups, Ideology, and Economic-Policy-making: The Northern Sung Debates over the Southeastern Tea Monopoly."

27. Skocpol, "Bringing the State Back In," p. 9.

28. The costs of imperial funerals and associated ceremonies and gifts were considerable; and according to officials such as Zhang Fangping, Han Jiang, Han Qi, and others, the imperial treasuries still stood empty as a result of Renzong's death in 1063. See their requests for ceremonial restraint, *XCB* 209/1b–3a.

1. LINKING TEA AND HORSES: GEOPOLITICS AND HORSE SUPPLY DURING THE NORTHERN SONG

1. The nature of the Inner Asian threat to China is discussed by Owen Lattimore, *Inner Asian Frontiers of China,* pp. 6–7 and 60–61; Herlee C. Creel, "The Role of the Horse in Chinese History," in his *What is Taoism,* pp. 162–165; and John King Fairbank, "Varieties of the Chinese Military Experience," in Frank Kierman and John Fairbank, eds., *Chinese Ways in Warfare,* pp. 11–14. Jagchid Sechin provides a useful and interesting interpretation of the relationship between Chinese agriculturalists and the steppes nomads in his *Beiya youmu minzu yu zhongyuan nongye minzu jian de heping zhanzheng yu maoyi guanxi.*

2. See, for example, Yang Lien-sheng, "Historical Notes on the Chinese World Order," and Susuki Chusei, "China's Relations with Inner Asia: The Hsiungnu, Tibet," both in John K. Fairbank, ed., *The Chinese World Order;* Jagchid Sechin, *Beiya youmu minzu,* pp. 25–182; and Luc Kwanten, *Imperial Nomads,* pp. 9–26. For Chinese foreign relations during the Song period in particular, see the essays collected in Morris Rossabi, ed., *China Among Equals.*

3. On Chinese walls, see Joseph Needham, Wang Ling, and Lu Gwei-djen, *Civil Engineering and Nautics,* pp. 38–57.

For an extremely useful overview of the Song military system, see Wang Zengyu, *Songchao bingzhi chutan.* See also Lin Ruihan, "Songdai bingzhi chutan," *Songshi yanjiu ji,* vol. 12, pp. 113–145; and his "Bei Song zhi bian-fang," *Songshi yanjiu ji,* vol. 13, pp. 199–229. Military provisioning is dis-cussed by Aoyama Sadao *Tō Sō jidai no kōtsū to chishi chizu no kenkyū,* pp. 327–398; and Shiba Yoshinobu, "Sōdai shiteki," pp. 123–159. For Ming provi-sioning needs and the role of the Shanxi merchants, see Terada Takanobu, *Sansei shōnin no kenkyū,* chs. 1–4.

For good summaries of Chinese military technology in the context of the medieval economic revolution, see Elvin, *Pattern* pp. 84–90; and McNeill, pp. 24–62. The classic basic study of military technology during the Song-Yuan era is Yoshida Mitsukuni, "Sō Gen no gunji gijutsu," in Yabuuchi Kiyoshi, ed., *Sō Gen jidai no kagaku gijutsu shi,* pp. 211–234. On siege warfare, see Herbert Franke, "Siege and Defense of Towns," in Frank Kier-man and John K. Fairbank, eds., *Chinese Ways in Warfare.*

Basic works on Song naval history include Lo Jung-pang, "The Emer-gence of China as a Sea Power," *Far Eastern Quarterly* 14:489–503; his "Mar-itime Commerce and its Relationship to the Song Navy," *Journal of the Eco-nomic and Social History of the Orient* 12:57–107; and Sogabe Shizuo, "Nan Sō no suigun," in his *Sōdai seikeishi no kenkyū,* pp. 249–271. For an overview of the history of Chinese nautical history, see Needham, Wang, and Lu, pp. 379–699.

On mobility, see Creel, p. 163.

4. Lü Yihao, "Lun qi yu Yongzhou zhi maimasi zhuang," *Zhongmu* ji 5/11a. The same memorial is included in *Lidai mingchen zouyi* 242/10a–b. Lü's bold-ness and skill at horses and arms are noted in his biography, *SS* 362/11324.

5. Xu Mengxin, *Sanchao beimeng huibian* 36/8a–b, translated by Tao Jing-shen in *The Jurchen in Twelfth-Century China,* pp. 22–23.

6. For a very useful collection of articles on the role of the horse in all facets of Central Asian culture, see the special issue of *Central Asiatic Journal* 10 (De-cember 1965) devoted to the subject.

7. Creel, p. 173, quoting the *Hou Hanshu.*

8. Edward Schafer, *The Golden Peaches of Samarkand,* p. 58, quoting the *Xin Tangshu.*

9. *Yuan shi* 100/2553.

10. *Lidai mingchen zouyi* 242/9a–b: *XNYL* 6/354–6.

11. Tao, p. 91. The Mongols began to cut off the Jurchen from their native pasture lands around 1198, forcing the Jurchen to compete with Song for Tibetan horses. See *CYZJ* jia 14/599 and Chapter Seven below.

12. For Han figures, see Michael Loewe, "The Campaigns of Han Wu-ti," in Frank Kierman and John K. Fairbank, eds., *Chinese Ways in Warfare,* p. 98; and *WXTK* 159/1384c. For the Tang, see *WXTK* 159/1386c. For the Ming, see Xie Chengxia, *Zhongguo yangma shi,* pp. 191–192. Xie Chengxia, pp. 185–186 and 231–242, also provides partial enumerations of the Yuan and

Qing herds. On the problems early Yuan rulers faced in acquiring horses during the first four decades of the dynasty, when they were cut off from native pasture lands by a revolt of the Mongol princes, see Jagchid Sechin and C. R. Bowden, "Some Notes on the Horse Policy of the Mongol Dynasty," *Central Asiatic Journal* 10:246–268. Northern Wei and Liao figures are from *WXTK* 159/1386b, *Liao shi* 34/397, and Xie Chengxia, p. 176. For the Jin, see *Jin shi* 44/1005. To put these national herd figures in perspective, the People's Republic of China registered 7,100,000 horses in the late 1950s, pastured primarily in Manchuria, Inner Mongolia, Sinkiang, and the Yunnan-Kueizhou plateau; the total world population of horses at that time was about 61,000,000 head. See Xie Chengxia, pp. 267–88; and *Encyclopedia Americana,* vol. 14, p. 389.

13. *SS* 198/4929; *WXTK* 160/1391a; *SHY* bing 24/24a–b.
14. Because the best horse were always bred outside its perimeters, sedentary China never had horses as good as those of the steppes nomads. See, for example, Chao Cuo's assessment of the superior quality of the steppes horses during Han in *Han shu* 49/2281, cited by Loewe, p. 98. The issue of horse quality during the Song is taken up in Chapter Seven.
15. See Elvin, *Pattern,* p. 88.
16. Song Qi, "Lun fu Hebei-Guangping liang jian Chan-Yun liang jian," *Jingwen ji* 29/6a, 11a. The figure of 60,000 horses, for a complete roster of 120 commands, is from 1047, supplied by Zhang Fangping: *XCB* 161/13a.
17. *Lidai mingchen zouyi* 242/12b.
18. On the sixteen prefectures of Shanxi and Hebei that remained under Liao control, see Zhao Tiehan, "Yan-Yun shiliu zhou de dili fenxi," *Songshi yanjiu ji,* vol. 3, pp. 385–411. For a comparison of the geographic extent of the Song in relation to other dynasties, see the maps in Albert Hermann, *An Historical Atlas of China.*
19. See Lin Ruihan, "Bei Song zhi bianfang," pp. 220–226.
20. On the horses of Fujian, see *WXTK* 160/1390b. Song Qi and Fan Zhongyan both recommended policies to prevent the horses of Huainan and Jiangnan from being slipped among the animals bought up in government requisitions. Song Qi also included the horses of Sichuan: Song Qi, "You lun Jingdongxi Huaibei zhoujun minjian yangma fa," *Jingwen ji* 29/7b–8a; *XCB* 112/20a. For the horses of Lingnan, see *CYZJ* jia 18/601–602.
21. Li Gang, in *Lidai mingchen zouyi* 249/9a. From mid Tang on, the horse became increasingly marginal to elite Chinese, as is indicated by the dwindling popularity of polo during the Song. See James T. C. Liu, "Polo and Cultural Change: From Tang to Song China," *Harvard Journal of Asiatic Studies* 45.1:203–224. On Chinese farms the ox was the fundamental beast of burden, according to the great thirteenth-century agronomist Wang Zhen; see his *Nong shu* 6/5a. According to D. B. Grigg, even in northern Europe horses

replaced oxen in the fields only very slowly and were still outnumbered by oxen by the eighteenth century; see *The Agricultural Systems of the World,* pp. 52, 172. See also Alexander Sowerby, "The Horse and Other Beasts of Burden in China," *China Journal of Science and the Arts* 26:282–287. On the history and use of donkeys and mules in China, see H. Epstein, *Domestic Animals of China,* p. 113. For illustrations of the farm use of donkeys and mules, see Wang Zhen, *Nong shu* 15/6a–b seq., 19/14a–b. Donkeys and mules were used by private merchants to carry tea over the Qinling Shan roads: *SHY* shihuo 30/13a–b. The entry of what appears to be a traveling merchant's mule team into the capital city of Kaifeng opens Zhang Zeyuan's painting, the "Qingming shanghe tu." See the reproduction of the original Song scroll in *Zhongguo wenwu,* No. 3. The scroll portrays donkeys and mules used as pack animals, ridden by apparently wealthy women, harnessed to light carts; oxen harnessed to large carts; camels bearing loads; and horses ridden by officials.

22. The figure of 22,000 head was offered by the military observer Ding Du as an estimate of the number of horses the state needed to purchase after suspending its pasturage system in 1028; see *WXTK* 160/1390b. His figure can serve as an estimate of total replacement needs.

23. *Xin Tang shu* 50/15b–18b; *WXTK* 159/1386–1387; Ouyang Xiu, "Lun jianmu zhazi," *Ouyang wenzhonggong ji* 13/33. For a survey of Tang horse policy, see Xie Chengxia, pp. 113–139.

24. On the pasturage inspectorate system, see *SHY* bing 21/4a–5b; *WXTK* 160/1389–1392; *SS* 198/4928–4932; Xie Chengxia, pp. 142–154; and Sogabe Shizuo, "Sōdai no basei," in his *Sōdai seikeishi no kenkyū,* pp. 67–74.

25. See the memorial by Li Jue in *WXTK* 160/1389a–b. Li offers an interesting comparison of the semi-feral horses of the steppes and the stabled animals of China. He implies that because rearing practices were so different, imported foreign horses inevitably suffered under Chinese management, while native-raised horses did not.

26. Song Qi complained that mismatched mares and stallions produced foals that were too small and weak for battle use: "Lun yangma zhazi," *Jingwen ji* 29/8a. But note that when in 1072 Wang Anshi initiated a policy of using Tibetan tribesmen to raise horses for the government in Deshun Commandery (modern Gansu), "the foals were inferior, fines were imposed for losses, and the Tibetan tribes were embittered": *SS* 198/4949. Birth rates over the first century of the Northern Song fell steadily from Li Jue's target of 500 foals per 1,000 mares to an actual figure of 200 foals per 1,000 mares in 1063. See *WXTK* 160/1389a–b; *XCB* 36/17b–18a; *SS* 198/4932. On the 1075 investigation of the pasturage system, see *SS* 198/4941; *WXTK* 160/1391a; *CBBM* 75/2287.

27. See Aoyama Sadao, pp. 352–353; and Shiba Yoshinobu, "Sōdai shiteki," p.

129. In 1033 Fan Zhongyan sent up an important memorial on the necessity of reducing the burden on the six grain-tribute circuits of the southeast by reducing military, including pasturage, costs: *XCB* 112/18a–20b. The chief public monopolies used to pay for provisioning were tea and salt. See Saeki Tomi, "Sōsho ni okeru cha no sembai seido," in his *Chūgokushi kenkyū*, vol. 1, pp. 377–408, for tea; and Dai Yixuan, *Songdai chaoyan zhidu yanjiu* on salt and the voucher system in general; see also Edmund H. Worthy, "Regional Control in the Southern Sung Salt Administration," in John Winthrop Heager, ed., *Crisis and Prosperity in Sung China*.

28. *XCB* 104/20a–b. For amounts of feed used in the stables of the capital, see *WXTK* 160/1390a; *SS* 198/4930.

29. Peter Golas, p. 300n29, citing Yanagida Setsuko. Dwight Perkins calculates a plot of 15 modern *mou* (2.3 acres, or about the same as the Song figure) as standard for tenant farmers in the early twentieth century. See his *Agricultural Development in China, 1368–1968* p. 96n12.

30. The government reported losses of 18,000 *qing* in the 990s, and another 5,000 *qing* in 1069: *SS* 198/4936, 4941; *WXTK* 160/1391a.

31. On disestablishment of the pasturage system, see *CBBM* 75/2380–2383; *SS* 198/4939–4942; *WXTK* 160/1390–1392.

32. On the *baoma* and *huma* policies, see *SS* 198/4946–4950; *WXTK* 160/1391b–1392b; *CBBM* 75/2381–2393, 109/3443–3454; and Sogabe Shizuo's clear discussion in "Sōdai no basei," pp. 77–91. On *jidi muma* see *WXTK* 110/1393a–c and *CBBM* 138/4165–4174.

33. *CYZJ* jia 18/609/10.

34. Jagchid Sechin, *Beiya youmu minzu*, pp. 385–406, gathers and analyzes the sources on this trade.

35. For the Ming pastures, see maps in Tani Mitsutaka, *Mindai basei no kenkyū*, pp. 290, 309, and 345; and Xie Chengxia, pp. 191–228.

36. Jagchid and Bowden, p. 264.

37. The most famous of the Transoxanian animals were the "blood-sweating horses of Ferghana" that are said to have inspired Han Wudi's western expeditions. On Han Wudi's efforts to obtain these animals and their impact on Chinese breeding stock, see Sima Qian, *Shi ji* 123/3177; Loewe, pp. 98–100; and W. Perceval Yetts, "The Horse: A Factor in Early Chinese History," *Eurasia Septentrionalis Antiqua* 9:231–255. On the horses of Tianshan, see Yetts, p. 232; *Jiu Tang shu* 194B/3b; and Xie Chengxia, pp. 240–242.

38. Li Gonglin's paintings of five Khotanese tribute horses are discussed and reproduced in Zhang Anzhi's slim but useful volume entitled *Li Gonglin*.

39. *SHY* bing 22/9b–10a; Xu Mengxin *Sanchao beimeng huibian* 3/8a. In 1002 Zhang Qixian estimated the earlier Jurchen trade at "not less than 10,000 head a year." Since the Khitan blockade, however, yearly horse purchases had fallen below mortalities, for a net annual deficit. See *XCB* 51/14a.

40. *Liao shi* 91/389. Xi Xia did occasionally sell horses to Song, as will be seen below; but the periods were irregular. See also Liao Longsheng, "Bei Song dui Tubo de zhengce," *Songshi yanjiu ji,* vol. 10, p. 109. Cao Wei, sent as emissary to the Xi Xia, was reported to have said early in the eleventh century that although the Xi Xia ruler Li Deming traded horses for Chinese goods, if the goods did not meet his expectations he had the traders killed. Deming's son Li Yuanhao (r. 1031–1048), at the young age of ten, protested that there was no advantage in trading Xi Xia's foundation for China's useless luxuries, and thus the trade was stopped: *SS* 291/9750.

41. On the Tangut campaigns in Liangzhou and the Gansu corridor, see Maeda Masana, *Kasei no rekishi chirigaku teki kenkyū,* pp. 551–572. Details on the horse trade are taken up below. The entries in *SHY* fanyi 4/1b and following indicate that from the mid 970s on, the Uighurs of Hexi sent small numbers of fine horses to Song, rather than large herds.

42. On Sichuanese horses, see Song Qi, *Jingwen ji* 29/7b; *SHY* bing 22/2a; *CYZJ* jia 18/597; and Chapter Seven.

43. The Guangxi marketing system is outlined in *CYZJ* jia 18/599–602. See also Sogabe Shizuo, "Sōdai no basei," pp. 128–133.

44. Norton Sydney Ginsburg, ed., *The Pattern of Asia,* p. 203.

45. Basic sources on Liangzhou and the Liugu Tibetans include *SHY* fangyu 21/14a–23b and *SS* 492/14151–14169. The most important secondary studies are Maeda Masana, pp. 362–407, and Iwasaki Tsutomu, "Seiryōfu Hanrashi seiken shimatsu kō," *Tōhōgaku* 47:25–41.

46. Qingtang refers to the town, modern Xining, that served as Juesiluo's capital from about 1030 on. Because his first capital was Zongge (Tib. Tsong kha) just east of Xining, Juesiluo's federation is often designated in the sources as the Zongge Tibetans, but for the sake of clarity I will use the term Qingtang throughout. The basic sources on Juesiluo are *SHY* fanyi 6/1a–5b; *SS* 492/14160–14164; and the short biography by Zhang Fangping, "Qinzhou zou Juesiluo shi," in his *Lequan ji* 22/20a–22b. The most useful secondary sources include Iwasaki Tsutomu, "Sōkajō Kakushira seiken no seikaku to kōhai," *Ajiashi kenkyū* 2:1–28; Liao Longsheng, "Bei Song dui Tubo"; and Wu Tianchi, "Juesiluo yu Hehuang Tubo," in Deng Guangming and Li Jiaju, eds., *Songshi yanjiu lunwen ji,* pp. 470–501. See also Luciano Petech, "Tibetan Relations with Sung China and with the Mongols," in Morris Rossabi, ed., *China Among Equals,* pp. 173–203; and Luc Kwanten, "Chio-ssu-lo (997–1065): A Tibetan Ally of the Northern Song," *Rocznik Orientalistyczny* 39:92–106.

47. On these tribes, see *SS* 492, *passim.* In 1001 Zhang Qixian placed them at the most Sinicized end of a gradient that included also "shallow Fan" *(qian Fan)* and "distant Fan" *(yuan Fan): XCB* 49/12b. In his chapter on the Tibetans, Tubo, Ma Duanlin contrasts the "cooked" *(shu)* and "raw" *(sheng)*

Fan as follows: "Those who belong to the Chinese polity *(nei shu)* are called cooked households; the remainder are called raw households." See *WXTK* 334/2628c.

48. Juesiluo himself had between 60 and 70 thousand troops: *SS* 492/14160. In 1015 he sent the one-time chief of Liangzhou, Panluozhi's brother Siduodu, to launch a surprise attack against the Buluo tribes with a reported 100,000 troops: *SHY* fanyi 6/1b.

49. The relationship between road networks, political alliances, and the rise and fall of states and principalities in Hexi is one of the major themes of Maeda's study. The impact of the rise of the Xi Xia state on the communications map of Hexi and the political and economic fortunes of the Liangzhou and Tsong kha federations is dealt with in parts five and six of *Kasei no rekishi*, especially pp. 479–677.

50. *SS* 492/14161–14162.

51. *SHY* zhiguan 43/58b–59a, 74a–b.

52. Qinghai is still recognized as a distinct region of horse production, with at least three identifiable breeds: the Xining horse, bred primarily in the Huangshui valley east of Kokonor; the Datong pony, from the river valley just north of Xining; and the Khetsui pony of southern Qinghai, western Gansu, and northwestern Sichuan. Though these strains have been altered by modern breeding programs, at an average height of about 13 hands (52 inches) these modern Qinghai ponies are comparable in size to the horses sold by the Qingtang Tibetans to the Song, and come from the same regions. See Epstein, pp. 109–110.

53. See *XCB* 50/6a for Wu Shu's policy recommendation of 1001, where he makes the characteristic claim that the way to set barbarian against barbarian is to play on their greed.

54. On the strategic significance of Lingzhou, see *XCB* 44/16a–20a; *XCB* 49/11b–12b; and Maeda Masana, pp. 434–492.

55. *XCB* 51/14b.

56. *XCB* 44/16b–17a; see 16a–20a for the entire memorial.

57. In 1002 Li Jiqian sent two emissaries to persuade Panluozhi to join him in an alliance against Song, but Panluozhi reported the attempt to the Song court, which commended him. One month later Panluozhi sent Song a "tribute" of 5,000 horses, for which he was paid generously, given gifts of silk and tea, and his tribesmen feasted and entertained: *XCB* 53/7a; *SS* 492/14156; *SHY* fangyu 21/17a, which records 1,000 head. In 1003 Panluozhi ambushed and killed Li Jiqian in a feigned submission; he was in turn assassinated by a pro-Tangut party in 1004: *SHY* *fangyu* 21/19a–20a. In 1004 the Weizhou, Kangu, and Laijiazu tribes of the Longxi Basin, through which Liangzhou horses had to pass once Lingzhou was lost, sent a presentation of fine horses to Song with the boast that "the road over which Liang-

zhou sells its horses passes through our tribal lands. We guarantee that henceforth there will be no cause for worry": *SS* 492/14157.

58. See, for example, Jagchid Sechin, *Beiya youmu minzu,* p. 361; Liao Longsheng, p. 99.

59. Song tribute included the yearly payment of 200,000 lengths of plain tabby (*juan*) silk and 100,000 *liang* of silver that constituted the Shanyuan settlement with Liao in 1004; the settlement of 255,000 units of silk, tea, and silver annually that Song settled on Xi Xia in 1044; and the many extravagant gifts with which these were supplemented. See Li Zhi, *Huang Song shichao gangyao* 3/102; *SS* 485/13999.

60. For the consequences of the quantity theory of money on Chinese attitudes towards foreign trade during Tang and Song, see Robert M. Hartwell, "Classical Chinese Monetary Analysis and Economic Policy in T'ang-Northern Sung China," *Transactions of the International Conference of Orientalists in Japan* 13:6–7. Bronze coins were prohibited from the horse trade as early as 981, after reports that Tibetans melted the coins down to make implements. Purchase agents were instructed to use silk, tea, and other commodities instead: *SS* 198/4933; *SHY* bing 24/2a. The most prominent exception to this currency exclusion was during the New Policies, when one-tenth of the value of a horse could be paid in currency to equalize the monetary value of the horse and Chinese commodities—that is, to make change: *SHY* zhiguan 43/54a–b.

61. On the responsibility of local officials to buy horses and aid tribal convoyers en route to the capital, see *SHY* bing 22/1a. Buying horses was defined as an integral part of a frontier prefectural administrator's task. For the case of Lingzhou Administrator Zhang Quancao, cudgeled and banished for cheating and then murdering fourteen Tibetan horse dealers in 976, see *XCB* 18/5a–b. On the use of emissaries in Taizu's reign (960–976), see *SS* 198/4933.

62. *SHY* fangyu 21/15a–b; *SS* 492/14154. Ding was still in Liangzhou in 1003: *XCB* 54/13b. Another man sent to protect the Fan horse caravans around the same time was Zhou Renmei. Zhou's biography states that "every tribute of horses by the various Fan was intercepted by Li Jiqian on the way to the capital. Renmei led cavalry troops to act as escort, and the bandits did not dare clash with them." *SS* 279/9492, cited by Liao Longsheng, p. 97.

63. SHY *fangyu* 21/15b; *SS* 492/14154–14155; *XCB* 43/12b–13a.

64. Details of the marketing system can be found in *XCB* 43/13b–14a. See also Sogabe Shizuo's discussion in "Sōdai no basei," p. 68.

65. *SS* 198/14928; Sogabe Shizuo, "Sōdai no basei," pp. 69–70. For Chen Yaosou's strengthening of the Directorate against a flurry of calls for disestablishment of the pasturage system, see *XCB* 66/9b–10a.

66. *SS* 198/4932.

67. *SHY* bing 22/4b–5b.
68. *SHY* bing 24/2a. I have interpreted the date Jingyou 3 (1036) as Jingde 3 (1006), since the list of prefectures is almost identical to the markets identified for this period in *XCB* 104/20b–21a, most of which had been closed down by the later year. In addition though the text does not label the larger set of figures for each prefecture, it does designate the smaller set as *shengma*, making it almost certain that the *shengma-quanma* dyad is intended.
69. *XCB* 51/10b; Maeda Masana, pp. 434–479; Wu Tianchi, *Xi Xia shigao*, pp. 20–22.
70. *SS* 485/13989–13990. Minor players eager to pursue a blood feud with the Tanguts, particularly the Liugu and Uighur tribes, were restrained and quieted by the Song: *SHY* fangyu 21/19a–20a. The geopolitical significance of the treaty is discussed by Wang Gungwu; see esp. pp. 54–59.
71. *SHY* bing 24/2a; *SS* 198/4929; *XCB* 66/9b–10a.
72. Details of the dispersal of the Liugu (Six Valleys) tribes are sketchy. The basic sources are *SHY* fangyu 21/23a–b, *SS* 492/14160–14161, and *XCB* 85/15a–b. For discussions, see Liao Longsheng, p. 104; Maeda Masana, pp. 551–555; and Iwasaki Tsutomu, "Seirōfu." On the recapture of Liangzhou by the Ganzhou Uighurs, see *SHY* fangyu 4/6a–8a; Iwasaki Tsutomu "Sōkajō," pp. 16–23; and Maeda Masana, pp. 555–558. Iwasaki argues that Uighur control of Liangzhou preserved the Liang-Lan highway for Sino-Central Asian trade through the 1020s. But if the number of tribute animals offers a valid indication, as a satellite of Ganzhou the former Liugu territories ceased to be a major supplier of horses: in 1024 a total of five horses were presented by the Uighurs, and in 1025 something over thirty. Thus although from 1016 to 1028 the Liangzhou region kept a precarious position in the barrier of foreign states protecting Song from the Tanguts, it was no longer an active supplier of horses. See Iwasaki, "Sōkajō," pp. 20–23; and *SHY* fanyi 4/8b–9a.
73. *SS* 492/14160–14162; *SHY* fanyi 6/1a–b.
74. This is based on a comparison of the lists in *XCB* 43/14a and *XCB* 104/21a, which reviews horse policy and the Tangut impact on market distribution to 1026.
75. *XCB* 104/20a–21a.
76. The following discussion is based on *SS* 485/13992–13995; *SS* 492/14161–14162; Wu Tianchi, *Xi Xia shigao*, pp. 30–33 and 49–68; Liao Longsheng, pp. 105–109; and Enoki Kazuo, "Ō Sei no Kasei keiryaku ni tsuite," *Mōko gakuhō* 1:90–94.
77. *SS* 492/141562; Liao Longsheng, pp. 106–108.
78. On the course of the war, see *SS* 485/13994–14000; Wu Tianchi, *Xi Xia shigao*, pp. 59–71; and E. I. Kychanov, "Les guerres entre le Song du nord et le Hsi Hsia," in Françoise Aubin, ed., *Etudes Song in Memoriam Etienne*

Balazs, Sér. I, no. 2, pp. 102–118. The annual settlement cost Song 255,000 units of silver, silk, and tea; in addition the Song court had to enter into an oath agreement *(shibiao)*—a diplomatic instrument that indicated equal international status between Song and Xi Xia—and reopen border trade with the Tanguts: *SS* 485/13999; Wu Tianchi, *Xi Xia shigao,* pp. 68–69.

79. The circuits included Jingdong and Jingxi, Huainan, Shaanxi, and Hebei, excluding only the seven prefectures along the Liao border. See *XCB* 133/2a.

80. *CBBM* 44/1398–1399. Han Qi, then general of the Shaanxi armies, argued that donkeys were in any event more versatile. In an appendix to a requisition order for 50,000 donkeys from the capital region and Shansi, Han Qi commented that "I have already requisitioned all the donkeys of Guanzhong (Shaanxi) in order to transport provisions. The donkey moves quickly and can keep pace with the troops. And if perchance we should penetrate deep into Tangut territory, we can slaughter the donkeys and eat them."

81. See *SS* 198/4932; and *SHY* bing 22/1b–2a, 3a, and 6b.

82. *SHY* bing 22/3a–b; *SS* 485/13999. Trade at the two markets, Baoan and Zhenrong Commanderies, was suspended in 1057; *XCB* 185/9a–10b; 186/7a.

83. *SHY* bing 22/3a; *SHY* fanyi 6/3b–4a.

84. *SHY* bing 22/4a; *SS* 198/4935.

85. On the Qingli reforms, see James T.C. Liu, "An Early Sung Reformer: Fan Chung-yen," in John K. Fairbank, ed., *Chinese Thought and Institutions.* Army sizes are recorded in *SS* 187/4576.

86. Total receipts for 1065 amounted to 116,138,405 units, of which 60,000,000 strings were cash. Ten million strings of this cash income went to general expenditures, while 50,000,000 strings were consumed by the military: see Shiba Yoshinobu, "Sōdai shiteki," p. 128. Total expenditures, on the other hand, were 131,864,452 units, for a deficit of 15,726,047 units. This was the first *recorded* shortfall for the dynasty. (Ca. 1021 had seen receipts of 150,850,000 units over expenditures of 126,775,200 units; and 1049 had a balanced budget at 126,215,964 units: *SS* 179/4349, 4352, and 4353. Cheng Minsheng argues that the deficit, which is traditionally put at 4,200,000 units (excluding an emergency expenditure of 11,500,000 units), was a statistical fiction that resulted from the inability of Song financial officials by 1065 to keep track of the nation's accounts. See his "Lun Bei Song caizheng de tedian yu chengpin jiaxiang," *Zhongguoshi yanjiu* 3:27–40. Wang Shengduo, on the other hand, argues on the basis of contemporary memorials that fiscal deficits began even earlier in the Song: "Songdai caizheng yu shangpin jingji fajan," in Deng Guangming and Li Jiaju, eds., *Songshi yanjiu lunwen ji,* pp. 32–57.

87. For the information and deliberations of the committee, see *XCB* 192/4a–b,

7a–9b. For Ouyang Xiu's statement, see also his "Lun jianmu zhazi," *Ouyang wenzhonggong ji* 13/32–34. On the high-level ad hoc committee as a specific type of policy mechanism see Hartwell, "Financial Expertise," p. 298.

88. For Wang Anshi's proposal, attributed to committee chair Wu Kui in *XCB* 192/7a, see "Xiangdu mumasuo ju Xue Xiang zhazi," *Wang Linchuan quanji* 42/243–244. His "Myriad Word Memorial" and the concept of bureaucratic entrepreneurship are taken up in Introduction to Part Two. On Xue Xiang's appointment and career, see *SHY* bing 22/4a–b and *SS* 328/10585–10588.

89. When Xue took office in 1060 only Qinzhou was open. He revived the Yuan and Wei markets, and opened three new ones in Deshunjun, Guweizhai, and Yongningzhai, placing markets west of the Liupan Shan for the first time: *SS* 198/4935; *XCB* 192/9a–b.

90. *SS* 198/4935. Xue Xiang's own descriptions of the *quanma* system illustrates the mechanism of direct payments: *SHY* bing 22/4b–5b. For examples of subventions from the center, see *SHY* bing 22/3a, 41a.

91. *Wang Linchuan quanji* 42/244.

92. *SHY* bing 22/4b–5b. On the inventory of financial instruments of which the salt certificates were a part, see Dai Yixuan, pp. 85–110, and Lien-shang Yang, *Money and Credit in China,* pp. 56–58.

93. *XCB* 192/9b; *SS* 198/4935. This time the government allocated 40,000 *liang* of silver and 75,000 lengths of silk.

94. *SS* 198/4936.

95. In contrast to the bronze coins used elsewhere in the Song empire, Sichuan's currency was iron. Because these iron coins did not circulate outside the region, Sichuanese merchants and government officials used Sichuan's unique paper exchange notes (*jiaozi*) and silver to remit taxes to the capital and do business with the outside world. The Sichuanese mercantile community was the chief conduit by which silver and exchange notes were transferred back into the province. Katō Shigeshi's classic articles on the *jiaozi* paper notes are collected in his *Shina keizaishi kōshō,* translated into Chinese as *Zhongguo jingjishi kaozheng.* The standard source on early Song currency in general is Miyazaki Ichisada, *Godai Sōsho no tsūka mondai.* On Sichuanese silk merchants in the provisioning trade in the 1920s, see *SHY* shihuo 36/19a–b; on the role of Sichuanese silk merchants in bringing silver back into the region, see *SHY* shihuo 37/10a–11a. For both, see Miyazaki, pp. 301–348.

96. *SS* 198/4936. In 1066 the central government's annual subvention was changed from 40,000 *liang* of silver and 75,000 *pi* of silk to 100,000 *pi* of silk alone, disbursed by the Finance Commission: *SHY* bing 22/6a–b.

97. *SHY* bing 22/7a–b.

98. Kawahara Yoshirō discusses the impact of government taxation and requisitions on the Sichuan silk industry in *Hoku Sōki tochi shoyū no mondai to shōgyō*

shihon, pp. 275–284. Li Xinchuan records that up to the New Policies the state bought 300,000 bolts of plain tabby *(juan)* silk and 700,000 bolts of hempen cloth annually for the armies, paying at 300 cash per bolt a price that was out of date by 1004. See *CYZJ* jia 16/1123.

99. Wang Shao's role in shaping the New Policies agenda is highlighted by Enoki Kazuo, who analyses Wang's "Three-Part Proposal for Pacifying the Western Barbarians" in "Ō Sei no kasei," pp. 96–99. For Wang Shao's biography, see *SS* 328/10579–10582. Shenzong's summons is in *SHY* zhi-guan 60/3a–4a. On the emperor's sensitivity to the military weakness of the Song, see James T.C. Liu, *Reform in Sung China,* p. 57.

100. *SS* 492/14163, 14167–14168; *SHY* fanyi 6/4b–5b; Enoki Kazuo, p. 90.

101. *SS* 492/14162; Wu Tianchi notes Muzheng's defection in his useful chronology, *Xi Xia shigao,* p. 318, but I have not located his source.

102. *XCB* 204/1a; *SS* 485/14002; *SS* 492/14162.

103. *XCB* 218/18a–b; *SHY* bing 22/6b–7a.

104. *SS* 328/10579.

105. The Qingtang campaigns, directed by Wang Shao's son Wang Hui and Cai Jing's eunuch confidant Tong Guan, are detailed in *CBBM,* zhuan 139 and 140. On Dongzhan's loyalty, see *SS* 492/14164; *SHY* fanyi 6/6a.

106. For the campaign against Muzheng, see Enoki Kazuo, pp. 113–140. Xihe Circuit and its constituent prefectures were designated in 1072, before the region had been pacified. See *SS* 87/2143. Xihe was a subdivision of Shaanxi. Shaanxi's administrative history is as follows: In 1041 the Shaanxi border-lands were divided into the four circuits of Qinfeng, Jingyuan, Huanqing, and Fuyan, without altering the civil administration of Shaanxi as a whole. In 1072, with the westward expansion towards Hezhou underway but not yet complete, the civil administration of Shaanxi was divided between Yongxingjun Circuit in the east and Qinfeng Circuit in the west. A Fiscal Intendant and Judicial Intendant were appointed for each of the two cir-cuits, although in each case one man could hold the post for both east and west concurrently. At the same time the military administration of Shaanxi was divided into six subcircuits: Yongxing, Fuyan, and Huanqing under Yongxing Circuit, and Qinfeng, Jingyuan, and Xihe under Qinfeng Cir-cuit. For each of the six subdivisions a military affairs commissioner *(jing-luesi)* and a pacification commissioner *(anfusi)* were designated. See *XCB* 240/37b–38a.

107. Sima Guang was the principal critic of frontier expansionism. See his "Ying zhao yan chaozheng queshi zhuang," *Sima wenzhenggong chuanjia ji* 45/571–578.

108. On the reopening of Sichuan's horse markets, see *SHY* bing 22/8a–9a and *XCB* 267/1a, which notes that building roads into the Tibetan territories

to facilitate the passage of horses disturbed and provoked the southwestern tribes. One private trade mission, by the Emei *jinshi* Yang Zuo, is recorded in Song Ruyu's "Yunnan maima ji," preserved in *XCB* 267/1a–2a.

109. *XCB* 259/7a and 272/14a; *SHY* bing 22/7a.

110. *SHY* zhiguan 27/38a; *SHY* shihuo 37/14a–17b. The specialized literature on the State Trade Agency, especially in Japanese, is quite substantial. For an annotated list of twelve items, see Higashi Ichio, *Ō Anseki jiten,* pp. 269–270, and his discussion pp. 50–60. For general discussions of State Trade in the context of the reforms as a whole, see Higashi's *Ō Anseki shimpō no kenkyū,* pp. 610–690; and Qi Xia, *Wang Anshi bianfa,* pp. 157–163.

The state trade act achieved its goals of price stability and revenue generation in three ways: first, the government lent money at 20 percent to officially connected guild merchants and brokers who put up local goods as collateral (the *didang fa,* or collateral policy); second, the government lent money and goods (eventually only goods) to associations of five guild merchants or brokers (forming a *bao*) who gave their own or borrowed property, gold, and silver as collateral, charging interest of 10 percent per half year (the *jiebao sheqing* credit-purchase by guarantee-association); and third, the government bought up goods that itinerant merchants from outside the capital were unable to sell, paying a price determined by negotiation between the guest merchant and resident guild merchants and brokers, based on the demand and capacity of the guild merchants to resell the commodities. These were lent to the guild merchants, at the usual rate, according to the size of their collateral. The guest merchant could take goods as well as money, and non-guild merchants could also participate (the *maoqian wuhuo,* trade and transfer policy.) See *SHY* shihuo 37/15a–b, 29a.

111. *SHY* shihuo 37/14a. Wang Shao did not exaggerate the volume of trade. In 1070 Wen Yanbo, Feng Jing and others criticized moving the State Trade bureau to Guwei, out of fear that the 300,000+ strings' worth of commodities and cash collected there would "arouse the barbarian hearts to greed." Wang Anshi dismissed the sums involved as insignificant. "Nowadays," he rejoined, "all the rich Tibetan households are worth 200,000 or 300,000 strings": *XCB* 213/10b–11b. Wang Shao may have had in mind the guild shops of Qinzhou, which engaged in substantial credit transactions with foreign merchants. See *SHY* shihuo 37/14a–b and *XCB* 213/10b–11a.

112. *XCB* 213/11b.

113. Wang Anshi, "Yu Wang Zichun shu," *Wang Linchuan quanji* 73/464–465. The Xizhou bureau was established immediately with a capitalization of 500,000 units of cash and silk: *SHY* shihuo 37/15b.

114. In 1070, for example, the Fiscal Intendant for Chengdu Circuit was ordered to ship all the regional tax commodities (silks, silver, specie, etc.) not needed

for his administrative expenses to the Fiscal Intendant of Shaanxi, who would in turn use the goods to buy back Jiezhou salt certificates that the government had over-issued. Wang Anshi endorsed the plan to the emperor personally, observing that "transferring the goods of Ba and Shu [the classical toponymns for eastern and western Sichuan, respectively] to Shaanxi will not only reduce the transport burden of the people of Shu [who would otherwise have to accompany the tax goods to the capital], but will obviate the expense of making disbursements from the capital." The policy was successively halted then revived. See *XCB* 217/9b–10a and 219/8b.

115. *SHY* zhiguan 27/38a. The contemporary observer Shao Bowen wrote that the notes had accumulated over the years, like uncashed cheeks, and so were now used to buy Sichuanese goods for the Tongyuan market, where they were in turn sold to "help open Hehuang and recover the old lands." Quoted by Katō Shigeshi in his "Sansei koshi ko," *Zhongguo jingjishi Kaozheng*, p. 514. Chen Jun, *Huangchao biannian gangmu beiyao* 19/848, observes that the main Tibetan commodity purchased with these goods was horses. This is the first sign that the Tibetan horse trade was reviving.

116. *XCB* 245/14a.

117. In 1073/10 the Kaifeng State Trade Bureau was transformed into the Superintendancy for State Trade and given jurisdiction over all provincial bureaus: *SHY* zhiguan 37/14a. By 1075 there were at least ten provincial bureaus scattered throughout North and Northwest China and the Lower Yangzi, with a Canton bureau added somewhat later. See *SS* 186/4551 and the map in Higashi Ichio, *Ō Anseki jiten*, p. 58.

118. According to a report by Wang Shao in 1074, the Tongyuan bureau had amassed gross profits of over 500,000 strings of cash since its inception, for an annual favorable balance of trade of about 190,000 strings: *SHY* shihuo 37/18b.

119. Wang Anshi sent Pu Zongmin from eastern Sichuan in 1073/12, and the Finance Commission sent one of its managing supervisors (*goudang gongshi*), Li Qi, in 1074/1. At the same time, the Superintendent of State Trade sent one of its registrars, Liu Mo: *SHY* zhiguan 43/47a; *SHY* shihuo 37/17b–18b.

120. *XCB* 251/2a; *SHY* shihuo 37/20a; *SHY* zhiguan 43/47a.

121. *SS* 167/3969; *SHY* zhiguan 43/47b.

122. *SHY* shihuo 37/20a; *SHY* zhiguan 43/47a; *SS* 167/3969. Cancellation of the market and exchange planning investigation and the order to Li Qi to concentrate on buying tea for the horse markets are dated earlier than Wang Shao's memorial on tea and horses, but the sources make it fairly clear that the order of events is as I have portrayed it here.

123. *SHY* zhiguan 43/47a; *SHY* shihuo 30/11b.

2. MARKET SEGREGATION AND THE STRUCTURE OF THE SICHUANESE TEA
INDUSTRY ON THE EVE OF THE TEA AND HORSE TRADE

1. *XCB* 22/16a.
2. For the Upper Yangzi macroregion as defined by Skinner, see "Cities and the Hierarchy of Local Systems," in G. William Skinner, ed., *The City in Late Imperial China*, Map 1, p. 289. I explore the spatial development of the macroregion in Smith, "Commerce, Agriculture, and Core Formation in the Upper Yangzi, 2 A.D. to 1948," *Late Imperial China* 9.1:1–78.
3. *WXTK* 4/59.
4. Ginsburg, ed. *Pattern of Asia*, p.215.
5. The literature on the history of tea in China is substantial and growing steadily, and the more technical studies are referred to in the course of this chapter. The most interesting historical overview is still Yano Jinnichi, "Cha no rekishi ni tsuite," in his *Kindai Shina no seiji oyobi bunka*, pp. 218–319. Two other useful reviews are Cheng Guangyu, "Cha yu Tang-Song sixiangjie de guanxi," in *Songshi yanjiu ji*, vol. 3, pp. 489–534; and Saeki Tomi, "Cha to rekishi," in his *Chūgokushi kenkyū*, vol. 3, pp. 21–36. The most helpful work in English remains William Ukers, *All About Tea*, 2 vols. Three modern collections of primary sources on tea deserve immediate mention. Chen Zugui and Zhu Zizhen, eds., *Zhongguo chaye lishiziliao xuanji*, contains punctuated and dated transcriptions of all the major treatises on tea, as well as a rich selection of government and literary sources from the Han to the Qing. Saeki Tomi, *Sōdai chahō kenkyū shiryō*, is an encyclopedic anthology of public and private prose sources on tea during the Song, chronologically arranged. And Nunome Chōfū and Nakamura Takashi, eds., *Chūgoku no chasho*, provides fully annotated translations into Japanese of the ten major treatises on tea from Tang through Ming. In addition Zhu Zhongsheng has compiled much useful information in his *Bei Song cha zhi shengchan yu jingying*.
6. See Yano Jinnichi, p. 234; Saeki Tomi, "Cha," p. 22; Nunome Chōfū's introduction to *Chūgoku no chasho*, pp. 5–6; and Cheng Guangyu, "Cha yu Tang-Song,"pp. 492–94.
7. Wang Bao, "Tongyue," *Guwen yuan* 17/3b. C. Martin Wilbur's translation is quoted by Yü Ying-shih "Han," in K. C. Chang, ed., *Food in Chinese Culture*, p. 70.
8. Two of the five Han sources Lu cites are by Sichuanese—Yang Xiong and Sima Xiangru—while a third, the *Erya*, employs the idiomatic Sichuanese term for tea, *tu*. The two remaining sources identify tea in Chalingxian, Hunan, and in Lingnan. See Lu Yu, *Chajing*, xia, 4a, 8b.
9. Lu Yu, *Chajing*, xia, 5a. In my translation I have largely followed the annotations of Nunome Chōfū, *Chūgoku no chasho*, pp. 107–108.

10. Major evidence for the spread of tea to the southeast is found in the fifth-century "Record [of Picking Herbals]" by Tong Jun *(Tong Jun caiyao lu):*

> The good tea of Xiyang [Hubei], Wuchang [Hubei], Lujiang [Anhui], and Xiling [Jiangsu] is made by all easterners into a "clear *ming*-tea." [This] *ming* has a froth, and drinking it is beneficial to people . . . Batong [Sichuan, Fengjie County] also has "genuine *ming*-tea," which if decocted and drunk causes people not to sleep . . .

The fragment is cited in *Chajing,* xia, 8a; and Wu Shu (947–1002), "Cha fu," in his *Shilei fu* 17/1a–4b. Yano Jinnichi pp. 248–249, dated the text to between 420 and 502.

11. See Edward Schafer, "T'ang," in K. C. Chang, ed., *Food in Chinese Culture,* pp. 106, 109. The most notorious instance of the northern preference for kumiss was provided by the minister Wang Su, who fled to the Northern Wei court after Qi overthrew Southern Song in 479. When Wang first arrived north, he brought with him his preference for fish stew and tea. But years later, though he still thought fish stew as good as mutton, he declared that "tea is not fit to be a slave to kumiss": *Luoyang jialan ji,* quoted in Lu Tingcan, *Xu chajing,* xia 3/1a–2a.

12. The point is made by Yano Jinnichi, who quotes Lu Deming on p. 252.

13. *Xinxiu bencao* 13/305, 18/417. See also Yano Jinnichi, p. 251, and Nunome Chōfū, and Nakamura Takashi, p. 10.

14. For an illustration of the settlement of the Xiang and Gan river valleys of Hunan and Jiangxi, the middle and lower reaches of the Yangzi, and of Anhui, see Bielenstein, Plate VI. Fujian at this point was still relatively unpopulated. This is reflected in Lu Yu's statement that although he knows of Fujian's tea, he has no detailed information on it: *Chajing,* xia, 9b–10a. Settlement and economic development of the south constitute major features of the Tang-Song transition. For an overview of this medieval transformation, see Elvin, *Pattern,* chs. 5 and 9–13; and Hartwell, "Social Transformations." On the relationship between development of the south and state finances, see Denis Twitchett, *Financial Administration,* esp. pp. 182–89 on the Sui-Tang canals. For an extended discussion of the impact of the canals on the middle-period empire, see Quan Hansheng, "Tang-Song diguo yu yunhe," in his *Zhongguo jingjishi yanjiu* vol. 1, pp. 265–396. On the specific effects of the canals on the spread of tea, see Nunome Chōfū and Nakamura Takashi, pp. 9–10; and Cheng Guangyu, "Cha yu Tang-Song," p. 494.

15. On the Sichuanese lacquer industry, see Yü Ying-shih, *Trade and Expansion in Han China,* p. 24; and Shiba Yoshinobu, *Sōdai shōgyoshi kenkyū,* pp. 295–299. On Sichuan's paper industry see Shiba, pp. 241–265, and the short treatise by the Yuan Sichuanese literatus Fei Zhu, "Qianzhi pu," in *Quan Shu yiwen zhi* 56 shang, 8b–11a.

16. Feng Yan, *Fengshi wenjian ji* 6/1a–2a.

17. Feng Yan, *Fengshi wenjian ji* 6/2a. It was also discovered around this same time that tea drinking had spread to the Tibetans. The *Tang guoshibu* records the tale of Master Chang Lu, who during an embassy to the Tibetans was brewing tea in his tent. "The Tibetan chief asked, 'What is this thing?' Master Lu said, 'Able to overcome ennui and slake thirst, it is called tea.' The chief said, 'I too have [tea],' and thereupon ordered that it be brought out. He pointed and said, 'This is from Shouzhou [Anhui], this is from Shuzhou [Anhui], this from Guzhu [Huzhou, Zhejiang], this from Qimen [Hubei], this from Changming [Sichuan], and this from Yonghu [Hunan].'" *Tang guoshibu deng bazhong*, part 3, p. 66. Yano Jinnichi (p. 263) speculates that tea drinking was probably introduced to the Tibetans in the first half of the fourth century through Sichuan, when Tibetan tribes occupied the western part of the region for some forty years.

18. See Twitchett, *Financial Administration,* Maps 5 and 6, pp.84–85.

19. *Jiu Tang shu* 105/6b. The construction of the canals, the use of "light commodities" to replace the tremendous surplus of grain thus made available, and their display in a great exhibition are described by Twitchett, *Financial Administration,* p.90.

20. See Lu Yu's biography in the *Tang shu* 196/16b–17b. For other sources, see Nunome Chōfū and Nakamura Takashi, pp. 11–14; and Cheng Guangyu, "Cha yu Tang-Song sixiang," pp. 499–503.

21. Lu Tingcan, *Xu chajing,* xia, zhuan 5, gives a bibliography of works of various genres. Yano Jinnichi (p. 261) lists ten Tang authors of tea treatises.

22. Fragments of the *Chapu* have been preserved in Wu Shu's *Shilei fu,* zhuan 17; and in Yue Shi, *Taiping huanyu ji;* they are now collected in Chen Zugui and Zhu Zizhen, *Zhongguo chaye,* pp. 24–27. For Mao's role in the Former Shu court, see Peng Yuanrui, *Wudai shi jizhu,* 63 shang, 39–40a.

23. On the "thank you" genre, see Cheng Guangyu, "Cha yu Tang-Song sixiang," p. 507. A selection of such poems written on the receipt of Sichuanese tea can be found in Cao Xuequan, *Shuzhong guangji* 65/6b–7b.

24. Bo Juyi, "Pipa xing," *Bo Juyi xuanji,* pp. 175–81. On Fuliang's importance as a tea producer during the Tang, see Li Jifu, *Yuanhe junxian tuzhi* 28/375.

25. Both government and merchant benefitted from the use of "flying money." As Denis Twitchett notes, the chanceleries used the merchant deposit to pay provincial tax quotas, the merchants could travel safely, and the considerable trouble and expense of transporting large sums of money were avoided by both sides. See Twitchett, *Financial Administration,* p. 72, and the sources he cites.

26. *Tang guoshibu deng bazhong,* part 2, p. 34. For Ouyang Xiu's statement, see Cheng Guangyu, "Cha yu Tang-Song sixiang, p. 503.

27. On Tang increases in commercial taxation, see Twitchett, *Financial Administration,* p. 49ff.

28. See Quan Hansheng, "Tang-Song zhengfu suiru yu huobi jingji de guanxi," in *Zhongguo jingjishi yanjiu,* vol. 1, pp. 230, 240, 246–248.

29. A convenient source on tea taxation in the Tang is *WXTK* 18/173a–c. See also *Jiu Tang shu* 49/6a–b and 13a–b. The standard secondary sources are Kanei Yukitada, "Tō no chahō," *Bunka* 5.8:35–53; and Twitchett, *Financial Administration,* pp. 62–65 and accompanying notes.

30. For examples of direct participation by the Tang state in the southeastern tea economy, see Kanei Yukitada, "Tō no chahō," pp. 41–43. In 838 the government appointed a commissioner for tea production to administer preparation of the tribute tea of Huzhou, especially the "russet shoot" tea of Guzhushan. To produce Guzhushan's tribute tea, it was said to be customary to impress into service 30,000 local residents for several months every year. See Li Jifu, *Yuanhe junxian tuzhi* 25/338; Twitchett, *Financial Administration,* p. 64; Kanei, "Tō no chahō," p. 43. Sichuan also sent tribute teas to the Tang court. But only Yazhou's Mengdingshan tea commanded any real notice, and that was mostly ceremonial. Every May the Mingshan County magistrate picked an auspicious day to ascend the mountain, leading the priests and officials of the district to pick tribute leaves (including 360 leaves for the emperor and the imperial sacrifices), and to process tea cakes for tribute. This practice continued from Tang through Qing: *Mingshanxian xinzhi* 4/9b. Altogether seventeen prefectures sent tribute teas to the Tang court; the sources from the geographical chapters of the *Tang shu* are collected in Chen Zugui and Zhu Zizhen, *Zhongguo chaye,* pp. 463–464.

31. For short synopses of the early Song monopoly system, see *WXTK* 18/173a–c; *SS* 183 and 184; *XCB* 100/3a–4b. Among the basic secondary discussions are Katō Shigeshi, "Sō no cha sembei to kanjukuhō," in his *Shina keizaishi kōshō,* vol. 2, pp. 165–175; Saeki Tomi, "Sōsho ni okeru cha no sembaiseido", in *Chūgoku shi kenkyū,* vol. 1; Umehara Kaoru, "Sōdai chahō no ichi kōsatsu," *Shirin* 55.1; Hua Shan, "Cong chaye jingji kan Songdai shehui," in *Song-Liao-Jin shehui jingji luncong.*

32. In 1005 Emperor Zhenzong personally refused a request to open a tea monopoly bureau in Xingyuanfu, out of fear that the move would provoke the populace: *SHY* shihuo 30/3a.

33. The prohibition of extraregional sales of Sichuanese tea were suspended when the southeastern monopolies were abolished in 1059. See *WXTK* 18/175b and *XCB* 189/3a–4b. Yue Shi, *Taiping huanyu ji,* cites evidence of a tea trade between Sichuanese and the border tribes for late Tang and early Song that almost certainly was unaffected by monopoly restrictions. The first case, from a lost fragment of the *Chajing,* concerns Qiongzhou: "[Linqiong] also produces tea cakes, called *huofanbing.* Each cake weighs forty *liang.* It enters the lands of the Tibetans and the Tanguts, who esteem it as much as tea from China's more famous tea mountains": Yue Shi, *Taiping huanyu ji* 75/81. We

know from Lü Tao's memorials (see below) that the Sino-Tibetan tea trade
was still important in the eleventh century. Tribal groups also traded for
Sichuanese tea in Liizhou: "In the borderlands of mixed Tibetan and Manyi
occupance there were originally no official market places. When Chinese and
[tribals] engaged in trade, they did not use cash. The Chinese offered *chou*
and *juan* silks, tea, and homespun, while the Tibetan tribals offered red
peppers, salt, and horses": Yue Shi, *Taiping huanyu ji* 77/596.

34. By far the greatest number of treatises, including one by Emperor Huizong
(r. 1101–1125), concerned the teas of Fujian, as a glance at the bibliography
in Lu Tingcan, *Xu chajing,* xia 5/1b–3a, will show. For a bibliographic review of the major Song treatises, see Cheng Guangyu, "Songdai chashu kaolue,"
in *Songshi yanjiu ji* vol. 8, pp.415–444.

35. Teas can also be compared along the continuum from unfermented (green) to
fermented ("black" to the Westerner, "red" to the Chinese). Unfortunately
the early evidence for the second set of criteria, consisting mostly of poetic
reference to the colors of the leaf or brew, is too ambiguous to permit more
than the simple conclusion that Tang and Song teas were available in both
fermented and unfermented form and that the latter probably predominated.

36. *WXTK* 18/173–4.

37. Government-purchase prices for Gaozong's reign (1127–1162) are given in
SHY shihuo 29/8b–10a; sales prices in 10a–14a. Both are by weight. *WXTK*
18/174a gives price ranges, but for solid teas quotes only the unit and not
the weight. *WXTK* includes "wax tea" *(lacha,* tea treated with an aromatic,
usually Baroos camphor *{longnao}),* as a separate category, but *SHY* shihuo
29 does not. The quoted price range assumes that the price for Muzhou,
given as 342 cash per catty, is a mistake for 242 (see Saeki Tomi, *Sōdai chahō,*
p. 123), and excludes several exceptionally low *pian* prices. Unfortunately
tea prices for Sichuan are not included, nor are there comparable lists. The
SHY lists are given in much more legible form in Saeki, pp. 113–126 and
128–161.

38. *SHY* shihuo 29/9b. For examples of regions specializing in the manufacture
of loose tea only, e.g., Huainan West Circuit, see *SHY* shihuo 29/8b.

39. On the evolution from "ground-paste" tea *(yangaocha)* to "cake-pack" *(bingtuancha)* tea, see Lu Tingcan, *Xu chajing,* xia 3/21a–b. Illustrations of the
molds are included in *Zhongguo chaye* pp. 55–81. Two of the basic sources on
the government-operated plantations in Fujian are Xiong Fan, *Xuanhe
beiyuan gongcha lu* (1158), in *Shuofu* 60/20a–23b; and Zhao Ruli, *Beiyuan bielu*
(1186), in *Shuofu* 60/23b–33a. Both works are also anthologized in Chen
Zugui and Zhu Zizhen, *Zhongguo chaye,* pp. 48–94. The production of molded
powdered tea, both with and without the addition of aromatics, began in the
late Tang, and by the late eleventh or early twelfth centuries had assumed
the status of a fad among the court-connected elite. But labor requirements

and cost were extravagant (a single mold of tribute tea was said to be worth 30,000 cash), and by the middle of the twelfth century the molded teas (although not Fujian tea in general) had lost much of their allure. The production process, as described in the *Beiyuan bielu,* 60/24a–26a, may be summarized as follows: 1) grade the tea; 2) wash and steam the buds; 3) press them under a high-pressure press overnight to express the oils; 4) grind them in a mortar and pestle, adding water to make a paste; 5) put the paste into a mold; 6) alternatively roast the mold and immerse it in water three times, then dry it over a fire overnight; 7) smoke the mold for 7 to 15 days, depending on the thickness of the mold, and afterwards pass it over boiling water, put it into a closed room, and fan it vigorously to bring out the color and luster. The packaging is separate. A nineteenth-century approximation of the powdered molds, but without the over-refinement, was the brick tea made of milled tea-dust by the Russians in their own factories in Hankou (Hubei), Fuzhou (Fujian), and Jiujiang (Jiangxi). See Ukers, vol. 1, pp. 96–97.

40. See *SS* 184/4507–4508; *CBBM* 137/4139–4145. Water-milled teas are discussed further in Chapter Six.

41. *SHY* shihuo 32/30b–31a. An entry for 1134 (ibid., p. 31a) states that Fujian powder tea did not travel well, and there was a (presumably temporary) order to halt government purchases.

42. Requests for Jiangxi *mocha* permits by government officials looking to sell them to merchants to generate revenues abound after 1160. See, for example, *XNYL* 185/6100.

43. *SHY* shihuo 30/43a has the following statement: "The weights of the basketed leaves are divided into two categories, with a limit of 130 catties."

44. Ouyang Xiu, *Guitian lu* 1/8, mentions the rise of Hongzhou (Jiangxi, Nanchang xian) as a producer of *caocha*—leaf tea—from the early eleventh century on. Since *SHY* shihuo 29/9a lists only *san* tea for Hongzhou, the identification of *san* with *caocha* seems secure.

45. The evidence is scattered through the tea records for the 1160s to the 1240s, i.e., *SHY* shihuo 31/16b *seq.*

46. For a standard account of southeastern tea manufacture during the Ming, see Xu Cishu, *Chashu.* On the demise of compressed tea in the southeast, see Lu Tingcan, *Xu chajing,* shang 3/12a–b.

47. Lu Yu, *Chajing,* xia 4a; Li Fang, *Taiping yulan* 867/2b–3a has the same text and attribution. The *Guangya* is a third-century text, but Yano Jinnichi (p. 242) argues that the present text is inconsistent with the original *Guangya,* extant versions of which do not contain the fragment. See also Chen Zugui and Zhu Zizhen, *Zhongguo chaye,* p. 203.

48. The method employed by the aboriginal tribesmen of Luzhou, as recorded in Yue Shi, *Taiping huanyu ji* 88/663, is as follows:

"The Yi-Liao of Luzhou who pick tea often carry a gourd, in the side of which is put a hole. Each [person] climbs the tree and picks the tea [leaf] buds, holds them in his mouth until the leaves have spread out, then puts them into the gourd and stoppers the opening. On returning it is put into a warm place. The flavor is extremely fine."

For rich study of the tribal economy of Luzhou during the Song, and the interaction between southwestern tribes and Chinese colonists, see Richard von Glahn, *Country of Streams and Grottoes.*

49. Lu Yu, *Chajing,* zhong 3a–b. In appending the implements, I follow Nunome Chōfū and Nakamura Takashi, p. 52. They are described in *Chajing,* zhong 1b–3b.

50. Lu Yu, *Chajing,* shang 2b–3a states that although in Jiangdong the weight of a stringer, or tie, of cakes ranged from 4 or 5 *liang* to 1 *jin,* in Xia—the territory on either side of the Yangzi gorges—the weight ranged between 50 and 120 jin. Nunome Chōfū and Nakamura Takashi (p. 51 note 8) are suspicious of the figures, which may indeed be a mistake. On the other hand, since the range approximates the tea-bale or saddlebag *(tuo)* weight of 100 *jin,* the large weights may reflect a method of packaging the tea for overland transport. The *chuan* was a standard unit of tea in Tang. Cheng Guangyu, "Cha yu Tang-Song sixiang," has a number of examples on pp. 500, 507, and 508.

51. For descriptions of Sichuan's tea cakes wrapped in paper, see Bo Juyi's short poem "Xie Li liu langzhong qi Shu xincha," in *Mingshanxian xinzhi* 15/27b; and Kong Pingzhong *(jinshi* 1065), "Meng xi hui mo da yi Shu cha," in his *Chaosan ji* 2/5b–6a.

52. Lu Yu, *Chajing,* xia 1a–2b. For alternative methods of consumption, see ibid., p. 3a.

53. For a poetic and formalistic description, apparently from the Song, of manufacturing tea cakes in Mingshan for the Tea and Horse Agency, see Min Qun's short poem "Cha," in *Mingshanxian xinzhi* 15/31b–32b. Min (who cannot be further traced) describes the eight stages of production as 1) cultivation, 2) plucking, 3) grading, 4) roasting, 5) making the cake, 6) storing, 7) presenting as tribute (i.e., selling to the government), and 8) trading the tea for horses.

54. Yue Shi *Taiping huanyu ji* 74/513; *Tang guoshibu deng bazhong,* part 3, p. 60; *SHY* shihuo 31/12b–14a.

55. Yue Shi, *Taiping huanyu ji* 75/583; Lu Yu, *Chajing,* xia 9b.

56. Yue Shi, *Taiping huanyu ji* 75/581; Wu Shu, *Shilei fu* 17/a; *Tang guoshibu deng bazhong,* part 3, p. 60; Cao Xuequan, *Shuzhong guangji* 65/5a; and *SHY* shihuo 29/15.

57. *SHY* shihuo 31/12b–14a.

58. *Ming shi* 80/1951; *Sichuan chaye,* p. 195. The *Ming huidian* 37/1063, in an entry for 1371, gives the basic unit for Hanzhong tea as the *bao,* a package

of 50 *jin*. *Bao* later referred to solid tea in Sichuan, but whether it does so here is not clear.

59. For a description of the Sichuan-Tibetan tea trade in the late nineteenth century, see Colborne Baber, *Travels and Researches in Western China,* pp. 192–201.

60. Baber, pp. 194–197; Alexander Hosie, *Three Years in Western China,* pp. 94–95.

61. In 1596 Xu Cishu (p. 66) wrote, "When the ancients spoke of tea, they naturally placed Mengding tea [of Yazhou] first . . . But now [the tea] is no longer manufactured; or if it is, all is cornered by the surrounding Yi [tribes] and does not leave the [western] mountains. If even the people of [Sichuan] cannot obtain [Mengding tea], then how is it to get to North China or Jiangnan?"

The Qing figure is based on the distribution of permits given in *Sichuan tongzhi* 69/19b–37b.

62. Ukers, vol. 1, pp. 305–306; and vol. 2, pp. 96–97. The impact of the Sino-Russian tea trade on the economy of Hubei and Shaanxi is dealt with in Liu Ts'ui-jung, *Trade on the Han River and its Impact in Economic Development, c. 1800–1911,* pp. 47–58. See also Moriya Takeshi, *Ocha no kita michi,* pp. 71–74, and Table 6, p. 72.

63. It should be emphasized, however, that in terms of organization and technology there were no major changes in Chinese tea production until the late nineteenth and early twentieth centuries, when government commissions were established to study the organization and factory technology of the Indian and Ceylon industries. See Ukers, vol. 1, p. 308.

64. See, especially, Xiong Fan, *Xuanhe beiyuan gongcha lu;* and Zhao Ruli, *Beiyuan bielu.*

65. See Lü Tao's biography in *SS* 346/10977–10980. The three memorials of 1077 are in his *Jingde ji,* zhuan 1: "Zouju zhi chang maicha lüxing chumai yuanfang bubian shizhuang" (4a–11b); "Zou wei cha yuanhu anzhe sanfen jiaqian ling kelü naguan chongxi qi jianhui qianzou zaoxi gaigeng, shizhuang" (11b–14a); "Zou wei guanchang maicha kuisun yuanhu zhi you sisu xunnao shizhuang" (14b–23b). The two memorials of 1086, "Zou wei jiaolian xian zhi Pengzhou ri sanci lunzou quemai Chuancha bubian bing tiaoshu jinlai lihai shizhuang" and "Zou qi ba que Mingshan deng sanchu cha yi guang deze yi bu que beibian zhi fei zhuang," are at *Jingde ji* 3/1a–10b. See also 11/1a–3b for Lü's summary of the arguments in his first set of memorials.

66. Total population of the four circuits grew from 1,174,598 to 2,027,702 households *(hu).* I discuss Sichuan's demographic development in "Commerce, Agriculture, and Core Formation" pp. 6–18.

67. On the throngs of people wandering around the tea braziers and herbal med-

icine displays of the Dazhengzi Temple market in Chengdu, see Zhang Pu, "Shouningyuan ji," in *Quan Shu yiwen zhi* 38 xia 2b–4a. During the mid eleventh century, a fad was begun by Linqiong man Zhou Zhichun, who taught "tea toast lyrics" (*chaci*) to prostitutes for the entertainment of their literati clients. Song Qi, during his tenure as Prefect of Chengdu in the 1050s, banned the diversion during official banquets. See Fei Zhu, "Suihua jili pu," in *Quan Shu yiwen zhi* 58/2a. Lü Tao refers to tea as an item of daily consumption in Sichuan, as was standard for China as a whole during the Song: *Jingde ji* 1/7a.

68. *Chajing,* xia 9b.
69. Lü Tao, *Jingde ji* 1/6b.
70. The story of Zhang Shougui's plantation is reproduced in the *Chongxiu Pengxian zhi* 11/9a–b. The tale is partly apocryphal, but its mention of Zhang's hiring of more than a hundred pickers at least indicates that plantations of that size existed. The Later Shu official Wu Shousu presented a tea garden to Emperor Taizong after the Song conquest that must have been substantial, but no details have been preserved: *SS* 479/13893. Monasteries may also have operated tea gardens, but again the evidence is scanty. From the scattered notices on monastic plantations in, for example, Mengding (*Mingshanxian xinzhi* 13/23a–24b), Qingchengxian (*Sichuan tongzhi* 38/54a), Dayixian (*Dayi xianzhi,* wenhui 4b and 26a–29b), and Emei Shan (Cao Xuequan, *Shuzong guangji* 65/3a), it appears that tea production would have been more important to individual monasteries than would total monastic production have been to aggregate regional output. But the monastic economy of Song Sichuan still remains to be charted.
71. Lü Tao, *Jingde ji* 1/19a–21b; 11/2b–3b.
72. Lü Tao, *Jingde ji* 1/146–18a.
73. Mao Wenxi, "Chapu," quoted in Yue Shi, *Taiping huanyu ji* 73/2b.
74. Lü Tao, *Jingde ji* 1/14b, 15b. Baber (p. 193) describes the uncultivated state of Yazhou's tea trees; and in a caption to a photograph of tea cultivation down river from Sichuan, Ukers (vol. 1, p. 300) writes, "It is amazing what good quality tea comes from China, considering the haphazard way in which it is grown."
75. *Sichuan chaye* pp. 178–179, gives the basic schedule by subregion. The northwest subregion, including Pengxian, has an average first-harvest time of ca. April 20. Picking might continue until autumn, but the later flushes in most areas were probably kept for household consumption.
76. See, e.g., *Chajing,* xia 9b.
77. Lü Tao, *Jingde ji* 1/17a; *Sichuan chaye,* p. 179.
78. Lü Tao, *Jingde ji* 1/18a.
79. Lü Tao, *Jingde ji* 1/17b.

80. Lü Tao, *Jingde ji* 1/15b–16a, describes how unprotected cultivators would have their sacks under-weighed by government-connected brokers under the monopsony system. Government perfidy is detailed in Chapter Six.

81. Lü Tao, *Jingde ji* 1/7a.

82. Bernard Read, *Chinese Materia Medica,* p. 34.

83. The term *maocha* refers to tea that has passed through the initial stage of processing that fixes the degree of fermentation, and thus determines the color, aroma, and flavor of the tea: *Sichuan chaye,* p. 197. The term appears to be applicable here.

84. Ukers (vol. 1, p. 306) describes how after a rudimentary firing and sun-drying by the cultivators, the leaves "are placed in large bags or loose bales and sold to agents of the brick-tea hongs in the towns where the [brick-tea] factories are located." See also Baber, p. 194; and Hosie, p. 94.

85. Lü Tao, *Jingde ji* 1/6b–7a. For prices, see 15b–16b. On p. 18a Lü reports that a laborer earned 60 cash per diem plus food, and that it took four laborers one day to fill an 18-catty sack. Thus a single laborer manufactured 4.5 catties daily, and earned 13.3 cash per catty in wages.

86. Lü Tao, *Jingde ji* 1/6a–b.

87. Yue Shi, *Taiping huanyu ji* 77/596.

88. Lü Tao, *Jingde ji* 1/6b.

89. Lü Tao, *Jingde ji* 1/8a–9b.

90. On the tea license, see *WXTK* 18/176c.

91. See, for example, *SHY* shihuo 32/5a–b.

92. *SHY* shihuo 31/29a–30a.

93. *SHY* shihuo 32/2b.

94. *SHY* shihuo 32/29b–30a.

95. *XCB* 334/13a.

96. Wen Tong, *Danyuan ji* 23/190a–191b.

97. I have encountered only a single reference to tea "guild merchants" *(hang-shang)* in connection with Song Sichuan, in Li Xinchuan's description of Zhao Kai's "contract market" reform of 1128: *XNYL* 18/743. But this is an abridged and variant version of Li Tao's original description in his funerary inscription for Zhao Kai, "Zhao daizhi Kai muzhiming," *Songdai Shuwen jicun* 54/1a–8a, and neither Li Tao nor any of the other sources that quote him employ the term.

98. Su Che's observations on Wang Xiaobo's rebellion are taken up in Chapter Three; on the raids of 1126–1127, see *Songdai Shuwen jicun* 54/2b–3a.

99. *XCB* 236/13a–b. The passage is translated in Katō Shigeshi, "On the Hang or Associations of Merchants in China," *Memoirs of the Research Department of the Toyo Bunko* 8:68.

100. On the relationship between the government and the great merchants, see

Wang Anshi, "Chashang shier shuo," *Wang Linchuan quanji* 70/444. On the solicitation of tea-merchant opinion in policy debates, see *SS* 183/4479 and *WXTK* 174.

101. *SS* 184/4492.

102. Shiba Yoshinobu, *Sōdai shōgyoshi,* p. 456; Shiba/Elvin, *Commerce and Society,* p. 198.

103. Shiba Yoshinobu, *Sōdai shōgyoshi,* p. 120; Shiba/Elvin, *Commerce and Society,* pp. 33–34; *SHY* xingfa 2/107a–b.

104. *SHY* shihuo 31/51–6b.

105. *XNYL* 166/5315 and 185/6064.

106. *XNYL* 181/5908–5909. The government subsequently attempted to place the merchants in farming or military service.

107. *SHY* bing 5/29a.

108. *SS* 34/659; Saeki Tomi, "Sōdai chagun ni tsuite," in his *Chūgoku shi kenkyū,* vol. 1, p. 411.

109. On De'an, see Saeki Tomi, *Chūgoku shi kenkyū,* vol. 1, p. 413; on Xiang-yang, see Zhao Wannian, *Xiangyang shoucheng lu* (1207), pp. 2b and 3a. Franke suggests that the Xiangyang merchants were connected with the Sichuanese tea trade ("Siege and Defense," p. 181). But the text does not say so; and it is, in fact, more likely that the merchants were from Hubei and Hunan, whose traders would have passed regularly through Xiangyang as they smuggled tea up to the Jin. See *XNYL* 177/5730–5731.

110. Zhou Qufei, *Lingwai daida* 5/10b.

111. Max Weber, *General Economic History,* p. 165.

112. *XCB* 189/3a–4b; *WXTK* 18/175b.

113. *SHY* shihuo 24/9a–b. See also Lü Tao, *Jingde ji* 3/5a; Su Che, *Luancheng ji* 36/8a.

114. *SHY* shihuo 24/10a–11a.

115. See Terada Takanobu, *Sansei shōnin no kenkyū.*

3. BUREAUCRACY, SOCIAL MOBILIZATION, AND THE POLITICAL INTEGRATION OF SICHUAN

1. Dietrich Rueschemeyer and Peter B. Evans, "The State and Economic Trans-formation: Toward an Analysis of the Conditions Underlying Effective Inter-vention," in Peter B. Evans, Dietrich Rueschemeyer, and Theda Skocpol, eds., *Bringing the State Back In,* p. 50. For Weber's own formulation see his *Economy and Society,* pp. 956–1005.

2. Rueschemeyer and Evans, p. 51.

3. Bibliographical notices of several important Japanese works on government as the focus of mobility strategies in general and by region during the Song are provided in Hasegawa Yoshio, pp. 115–120. For general statements on the social role of government service in Song in English, see Hartwell,

"Transformations"; Chaffee, *Thorny Gates;* and Lo, *Introduction to the Civil Service.*

4. There are a number of technical studies of Sichuan between the Tang and Song to which I shall refer to in the course of the discussion. The most useful general works on the socio-political history of Sichuan during this era include Matsui Shuichi, "Tōdai zenhanki no Shisen—ritsuryōsei shihai to gōzokusō kankei o chūshin to shite," *Shigaku zasshi* 71.9:1–37, and "Tōdai kōhanki no Shisen—kanryō shihai to dogōsō no shutsugen o chūshin to shite," *Shigaku zasshi* 73.10:46–88; Satake Yasuhiko, "Tōdai Shisen chiiki shakai no henbō to sono tokushitsu," *Tōyōshi kenkyū* 44.2:1–39; Klaus-Peter Tietze, *Ssuch'uan vom 7. bis 10. Jahrhundert: Untersuchungen zur frühen Geschichte einer chinesischen Provinz.* Richard von Glahn traces many of the same processes of development and state-building in southern Sichuan (especially Luzhou) that I am concerned with for the Chengdu Plain in *The Country of Streams and Grottoes.* I have many disagreements with Winston Lo's book, *Szechwan in Sung China: A Case Study in the Political Integration of the Chinese Empire,* whose main points are much more clearly developed in his *Introduction to the Civil Service.*

5. *Sui shu* 29/829–830. The last five sentences are taken, with a few amendments, from the translation by von Glahn, *Country of Streams and Grottoes,* p. 40.

6. See Matsui Shuichi, "Tōdai zenhanki no Shisen," p. 11.

7. Ibid., p. 2.

8. Chen Zi'ang, *Xinjiao Chen Zi'ang ji* 4/111–112. Much of the available biographical material on Chen is gathered at the end of this collection, p. 241ff.

9. In 627 the Governor-General of Sichuan, Gao Shilian, was repeatedly rebuffed in his efforts to recruit the hermit-scholar Zhu Taozhui into the government. First Confucian students, sent out to lecture on the classics and search out local talent, tried to press Zhu into service as village head. Offered a new suit of clothes as an inducement to serve, Zhu flung them to the ground and ran off babbling into the mountains. Gao later sought Zhu out personally, but Zhu spurned him. *Jiu Tang shu* 65/2b–3a. The same contempt for office was expressed on a more sophisticated level by the famous scholar and seer Yuan Tiangang of Chengdu, whose life spanned Sui and early Tang. Yuan repeatedly (and with uncanny accuracy) foretold the unhappy destinies that would accompany high office for others and was utterly uninterested in it for himself: *Jiu Tang shu* 191/5a–8a. In "Tōdai zenhanki no Shisen," Matsui Shuichi concludes (p. 3) that office-holders were mostly non-Sichuanese. This is supported in a random way by the funerary inscriptions in Chen Zi'ang, *Xinjiao Chen Zi'ang ji,* zhuan 5, which include only one native out of a total of four local officials given epitaphs.

10. Sima Guang, *Zizhi tongjian,* 199/6261–6262; *Jiu Tang shu* 3/19a–b.

11. Chen Zi'ang, *Chen Zi'ang ji* 8/176. Chen claimed that grain prices jumped 400 cash per *dou*.

12. Matsui Shuichi argues that the Tang control structure began to crumble in Sichuan from Emperor Gaozong's reign (650–683) on. He points to Sichuan's low ratios of households to individuals (as low as 1:2 or 1:3 in many prefectures of eastern Sichuan), and to the very low rate of increase of individuals in relation to households as evidence of magnates' enhanced ability to shelter dependents and the state's dwindling capacity to count them. See his "Tōdai zenhanki no Shisen," pp. 19–20. On the enslavement of non-Han tribes by the magnates, see ibid., p. 18.

13. Chen Zi'ang, *Chen Zi'ang ji*, p. 251.

14. For an analysis of elite stratification and channels of mobility during the Tang, see Twitchett, "Composition of the T'ang Ruling Class," pp. 78–83.

15. Matsui Shuichi, "Tōdai zenhanki no Shisen," p. 11; Denis Twitchett, "Hsuan-tsung," in Denis Twitchett, ed., *The Cambridge History of China*, vol. 3, pp. 366–370.

16. Wu Tingxie, "Tang fangzhen nianbiao," in *Ershiwushi bubian*, vol. 6, p. 7456. The third incumbent, Huo Tingyu, was a Sichuanese.

17. For the Xianyus, see *Jiu Tang shu* 122/10a–11a; and the material cited by Matsui Shuichi, "Tōdai zenhanki no Shisen," pp. 5–6. On the Yans, see *Jiu Tang shu* 117/1b–2a, 10b–14b.

18. Matsui Shuichi, "Tōdai zenhanki no Shisen," pp. 21–23. See also Kurihara Masuo, "Tōmatsu no dōgoteki zaichi seiryoku ni tsuite—Shisen no I Kunsei no baai," *Rekishigaku kenkyū* 243:1.

19. Sima Guang, *Zizhi tongjian* 222/7113.

20. Du Fu, "Dongxi liangchuan shuo," *Du Gongbu shiji* 19/19b. Around 698 Chen Zi'ang had memorialized that the widespread conscription of commoners into transport duty had forced thousands of families to seek the protection of local magnates and great families, who thereby gained control of "the taxes and labor services that rightfully belong to the state": *Chen Zi'ang ji* 8/174.

21. Charles Peterson, "Corruption Unmasked: Yuan Chen's Investigations in Szechwan," *Asia Major* (n.s.) 18:34–78.

22. Matsui Shuichi "Tōdai kōhanki no Shisen," pp. 49–53.

23. The Nanzhao invasion lasted only a short time, but the invading armies captured and enslaved thousands of Chengdu's craftsmen and youth. For a colorful discussion of the invasion and the military incompetence that made it possible, see Charles Backus, *The Nan-chao Kingdom and T'ang China's Southwestern Frontier*, pp. 105–126.

24. For a table of foreign attacks on Sichuan during the ninth century, see Matsui Shuichi, "Tōdai kōhanki no Shisen," pp. 57–64.

25. Sources and background on Tian Lingzi are provided by Robert Somers, "The End of the T'ang," in Denis Twitchett, ed., *The Cambridge History of China*,

vol. 3, pp. 715–717 and 748–751. On the power struggle in Sichuan at this time, see Guo Yundao, *Shujian* 7/88–98.

26. Somers, pp. 748–750; Matsu Shuichi "Tōdai kōhanki no Shisen," pp. 73–79. For both revolts, see Guo Yundao, *Shujian* 7/88–90.

27. The basic source on Wei Junqing is the commemorative stele erected on the completion of his fortress in Changzhou, "Wei Junqing jian Yongchangzhai ji," in Lu Yaoyu, *Jinshi xubian* 12/7b–22a. The basic study is Kurihara Masuo, "Tōmatsu no dōgoteki." On militia formation in late-Tang Sichuan in general, see Satake Yasuhiko, "Tōdai Shisen," pp. 13–36.

28. Lu Yaoyu, *Jinshi xubian* 12/7b–8a. Somers (p. 751) gives a total of 34 militia units; Kurihara Masuo (pp. 4–5) lists 32 of them.

29. Kurihara Masuo, p. 4, Table 1.

30. Ibid., p. 5. See also von Glahn, *Country of Streams and Grottoes*, pp. 42–44. Magnate society persisted in eastern Sichuan long after it had given way to "bureaucratization" of the elite in the west, as von Glahn demonstrates in the course of his study.

31. See Satake Yasuhiko, "Tō Sō henkakuki ni okeru Shisen Seitofuro chiiki shakai no henbō ni tsuite," *Tōyōshi kenkyū* 35.2:115.

32. Kurihara Masuo, p. 1.

33. The *locus classicus* for the analysis of patrimonial authority and its place in the range of authority types, from charismatic to bureaucratic, is Max Weber, *Economy and Society*. See esp. chap. 3, pp. 226–240; and chap. 12, pp. 1006–1069.

34. Denis Twitchett, "Provincial Autonomy and Central Finance in Late T'ang," *Asia Major* (n.s.) 11.11:216. Twitchett lists the complete set of figures, taken from the *Tongdian*, in *Financial Administration*, p. 193, Table C.

35. *Jiu Tang shu* 117/6b–7a; Matsui Shuichi "Tōdai zenhanki no Shisen," p. 25.

36. Charles Peterson, "Court and Province in Mid- and Late-T'ang," in Denis Twitchett, ed., *The Cambridge History of China*, vol. 3, p. 524. See Wei Gao's biography, *Jiu Tang shu* 140/1a–6b.

37. Sources on tea are listed in Chapter Two. On the taxation of salt under the Tang, see Kanei Yukitada, "Tō no empō," *Bunka* 5.5:9–45.

38. For a characterization of these new rulers of China, see Somers, pp. 762–789.

39. For the basic chronology of the two Shu states, see Guo Yundao, *Shujian*, zhuan 7 and 8; and Zhang Tangying, *Shu taowu*. For greater detail, see Peng Yuanrui, *Wudai shi jizhu*, zhuan 63–64, shang and xia.

40. Ouyang Xiu, who authored the *Xin wudai shi*, had only contempt for the Tang aristocrats who flocked to Sichuan because of its wealth and safety and served Wang Jian despite his bandit origins. See Peng Yuanrui, *Wudai shi jizhu*, 63 shang 1051–1052, which includes a list of Wang's ministers, as does Zhang Tangying, *Shu taowu*, pp. 3a–b. For Later Shu and the large

number of ministers from Henan and Shandong, see Zhang Tangying, pp. 17b–20a. The fullest biographical material for the two regimes is to be found in Lu Zhen, *Jiuguo zhi* (early Song); and Wu Renchen, *Shiguo chunqiu* (early Qing).

41. Fei Zhu's "Shizu pu" is anthologized in *Quan Shu yiwen zhi,* zhuan 53–55. Individuals who served the Wang or Meng regimes include (in alphabetical order by patronym) DENG Hong and Long (55/5b–6a), FANG E (53/10b–11b), FEI Zongdao and Shuneng (55/7b–8b), LIU Mengwen and Changyu (54/3a–b), WEN Gu (55/9a); and WU Gun (53/3b–4a). Individuals who rejected service include three generations of the FAN lineage (53/4a–5a), GOU Hui (53/9a–10a), and GUO Zhen (53/5a–6a). Fan Zhen of the very obdurate FANs wrote in his funerary inscription for Chen Xiliang that "Chen's family fled to the hills of Meizhou to escape the bandits that filled the cities under the Wangs and Mengs, emerging only when Song rose and Shu was peaceful": *Songdai Shuwen jicun* 10/18b–21a. Yet despite claims by the Fan and Gou clans to have refused service, it is evident from biographies in Wu Renchen, *Shiguo chunqiu* 56/3b–4b, that members of both lineages cooperated with the Shu states. Su Xun, whose lineage resided in Sichuan since about the seventh century, summed up the situation (with a certain amount of preening) as of the early Song: "At this time the Wangs and Mengs had controlled Shu in succession. None of the great talents and honorable men of Shu had wanted to serve in office. The shortage of officials increased daily. The only scholars who served in Shu were the youthful and recklessly clever." See his "Zupu houlu xiabian," *Jiayou ji* 13/6a.

  For a useful study of Fei Zhu's "Shizu pu" see Morita Kenji, "Seito shizokufu shōko," *Tōyōshi kenkyū* 36.3:101–127.

42. Peng Yuanrui, *Wudai shi jizhu* 63 xia 1066; Zhang Tangying, *Shu taowu,* pp. 9a, 13a–b.

43. Lu Zhen, *Jiuguo zhi* 7/82–3.

44. *XCB* 6/6b.

45. Wang Jian's relative and Prefect of Pengzhou seized an estate from the wealthy Shi family: Kawahara Yoshirō, p. 261. The Later Shu ministers Zhang Ye and Shen Gui used bribes, extortion, and imprisonment and terror to obtain lands and possessions: Peng Yuanrui, *Wudai shi ji zhu* 64 xia 1101; Wu Renchen, *Shiguo chunqiu* 51/5b–6b. Li Tinggui, Han Baozhen, Wang Zhaoyuan, and Wu Shousu all presented lands, buildings, and in Wu's case a tea garden to Song Taizu, for which they were each compensated 3,000,000 cash: Wu Renchen, *Shiguo chunqiu* 53/5b, 55/1b–4a; *SS* 479/13893.

46. The basic source on the events surrounding the Correct Dharma Monastery is Yang Tianhui's "Zhengfayuan changzhutian ji," written in 1117. The text was originally preserved in *Chengdu wenlei* 39/6a–10a, and is reprinted in *Songdai Shuwen jicun* 26/7b–9b. Tian Qinquan cannot be positively traced,

but it may be more than coincidental that an official from Henan with the same surname and generational name—Tian Qinzuo—was involved in administering post-surrender Sichuan: *XCB* 6/2b, 3b.

Because it sheds unique light on the problems of land and class stratification in Sichuan during the first century and a half of Song rule, Yang Tianhui's "Record" has attracted a great deal of scholarly attention, particularly in Japan. The basic studies include two articles by Sudo Yoshiyuki: "Sōdai Shisen no tenko sei: saikin no kenkyū o yonde," in his *Tō Sō shakai keizaishi kenkyū*, pp. 321–387, and "Hokū-Sō Shisen no tenko sei sairon," in his *Sōdaishi kenkyū*, pp. 449–468. Sudo's arguments are debated in two articles by Tan Kyoji:"Sōsho no shōen ni tsuite—Seitofu Goshoku koku setsudoshi Ten Kinsen no shoryō o chūshin to shite," *Shicho* 87:1–25; and "Sōsho Shisen no Ō Shōha—Ri Jun no ran ni tsuite—Tō Sō henkaku no ichi mondai," *Tōyōgaku* 61:67–102.

47. The Feis of Shuangliuxian (Chengdu), who claimed to have resided in Sichuan since the Han, set up lineage segments in Guangduxian (Chengdu) and Shazhuzhen (Qiongzhou) just after the branch founders held office under Wang Jian. Wen Gu, originally of Mianzhou and a third-generation resident of Sichuan who held the office of general censor under the Mengs, dug a salt well and built houses and a family compound in Wenjiangxian (Chengdu). In the same generation the family also set up branches in Hanzhou, Qiongzhou, and Zizhou, while still retaining the Mianzhou branch. On the Feis, see *Quan Shu yiwen zhi* 55/7b–8b. On Wen Gu, his well, traces of his house, and the family compound, see *Quan Shu yiwen zhi* 55/9a, and *Wenjiang xianzhi* (1921), 1/12b, 2/33a. In these and the following examples I am making the assumption that segmentation is a sign of prosperity or entrepreneurial activity. See Maurice Freedman, "The Politics of an Old State: A View from the Chinese Lineage," in his collection, *The Study of Chinese Society,* p. 336.

48. Lu Zhen, *Jiuguo zhi* 7/82–3, quoted by Tan Kyoji, "Ō Shōha Ri Jun no ran," p. 85.

49. See Su Xun, "Sushi zupu," "Zupu houlu shangbian," and "Zupu houlu xiabian," in his *Jiayou ji* 13/1b–7b.

50. On subregional economic development in Sichuan during the Song, see Smith, "Commerce, Agriculture, and Core Formation."

51. The two Shu states amassed great fortunes, apparently without gouging their subjects. The mid-eleventh-century Sichuanese Zhang Tangying, whose regional history "The Fearsome Beasts of Shu" *(Shu taowu)* is a major source for the regimes, concluded that following a long period of peace Shu had become quite wealthy: Taxes and labor service were modest, the price of rice was low, the coffers were filled with treasure, and brocades and embroideries were everywhere to be seen. The reason for this great prosperity, Zhang maintained (pp. 206–21a), was that of all the valuables accumulated in the

treasuries and storehouses not one silk thread nor one grain of rice had to be sent to the imperial heartland.

As was typical of peer regimes elsewhere in the commercially buoyant south, the two Shu states imposed a wide range of indirect taxes and monopoly controls. Both regimes regulated the wine, salt, and tea industries; and Former Shu occasionally engaged in the official interstate trade of tea and cloth. Wang Jian threatened to tax mulberry trees, though whether he actually did so is unclear. And from 955 on Later Shu was compelled to monopolize iron, in response to an emergency need for currency brought on by Later Zhou's threatened invasion of the region. For tea, salt and wine controls in Former Shu, see Peng Yuanrui *Wudai shi jizhu* 63 shang 1053; on the official sale of tea and cloth, see He Guangyuan, *Jianjie lu* 4/6b–7a. On tea regulations in Later Shu, see Su Che, *Luancheng ji* 36/6b; and *SS* 479/13886. On salt, see Guo Yundao, *Shujian* 8/110–111.

52. On the Tang and Song periodic markets in general, see Katō Shigeshi, *Shina keizaishi kōshō*, vol. 1, pp. 380–421. For the Song, see Shiba Yoshinobu *Sōdai shōgyō*, pp. 337–390; and Sogabe Shizuo, *Sōdai seikeishi no kenkyū*, pp. 495–509. For Sichuan in particular the basic article is Ju Qingyuan, "Tang Song shidai Sichuan de canshi," *Shihuo* 3.6:28–34.

53. Su Shi, "Meishan Yuanjinglou ji," *Su Dongbo ji* ci 6 zhuan 32/29–30. Satake Yasuhiko "Shisen Seitofuro," p. 110, cites Su's observation as part of his evidence for the long-term collapse of magnate domination in Western Sichuan.

54. The process of encroachment went on for over a century and was periodically contested by the abbots of the Correct Dharma Monastery. In 1105 4,775 *mou* were returned to the temple at the intercession of Cai Jing. See Sudō Yoshiyuki, "Sōdai Shisen no tenko sei," in his *Tō Sō shakai keizaishi kenkyū*, pp. 328–330.

55. *XCB* 9/4a–b. Satake Yasuhiko interprets the prohibition as an early effort by the Song court to coopt local magnates, whose power would be diminished by early property divisions: "Shisen Seitofuro," p. 118.

56. By 1050 crowding in Sichuan, particularly the Chengdu Plain, was so bad that the court was obliged to permit voluntary out-migration. The policy applied to Fujian as well: *XCB* 168/15b–16a.

57. Von Glahn, *Country of Streams and Grottoes*, pp. 54–58. By 1080 guest households accounted for 27.7 percent of the population in the west and 68.3 percent of the population in the east.

58. *SHY* shihuo 7/3b; *XCB* 21/1a–b. The court subsequently ordered *xingshi banbu* to be kept in all prefectures and made collecting taxes from the influential families the exclusive responsibility of the vice prefect.

59. *XCB* 18/9b–10a.

60. *SS* 315/10302–10303.
61. *SHY* xingfa 2/5b–6a. There are two additional versions of this report: a parallel version in the *Taizong huangdi shilu,* zhuan 78, and a somewhat different version in Liu Shidao's biography, *SS* 304. Sudō Yoshiyuki, "Shisen no tenko sei," pp. 345–353, and Tan Kyōji, "Ō Shōha Ri Jun no ran," p. 71, explicate the parallel versions. Von Glahn (pp. 54–55) takes *panghu* as roughly equivalent to the European *villein.*
62. The *SS* 304 text has *panghu* in place of *xianghao;* i.e., putting *panghu* over *panghu.* For attempts to resolve the textual discrepancy, see Sudō and Tan, cited above in note 72. Sudō (p. 349) identifies the *xianghao* as rich peasant landowners of household grades 1 or 2.
63. *SHY* xingfa 2/6a; *SS* 304/10064.
64. Karl Deutsch, *Nationalism and Social Communication,* chs. 5–6; Chalmers A. Johnson, *Peasant Nationalism and Communist Power: The Emergence of Revolutionary China, 1937–1945.* Although I reject Johnson's overall interpretation of the nature and causes of the Chinese Revolution, as well as his notion of revolution as "social pathology," his use of Deutsch's theory of social mobilization as an explanatory link between the Japanese invasion and the success of the Chinese Communist Pary in North China is deft and convincing.
65. *CBBM* 13/325–326. Tan Kyoji, "Ō Shōha Ri Jun no ran," pp. 77–78, has arrayed the primary sources chronologically, starting with Zeng Gong's *Longping ji,* published posthumously in 1142. The same material can also be found in *Wang Xiaobo Li Shun qiyi ziliao huibian.* Shimasue Kazuyasu, "Ōshōha Ri Jun no ran no seikaku—Sōdai Shisen no jinushi tenosei tono kanren ni oite," *Tōyōshi kenkyū,* 29.1:1–30, has a useful summary of the Japanese literature on the significance of the rebellion, although he himself misreads the history and exaggerates the role of the tea industry in the rebellion.
66. *XCB* 6/2b.8b. See also Miyazaki Ichisada *Godai Sōsho no tsūka mondai,* pp. 153–154, who argues, along with the original notes appended to the *XCB* entry, that the timing of the order to divert surpluses to the capital is prima facie evidence that it was directed at Sichuan.
67. Miyazaki Ichisada, *Godai Sōsho no tsūka mondai,* p. 154; Tan Kyōji, "Ōshōha," p. 77.
68. *CBBM* 11/279; *XCB* 23/12a; *SS* 180/4376. The issue of early Song monetary policy in Sichuan is taken up in Miyazaki Ichisada, *Godai Sōsho no tsūka mondai,* pp. 152–168.
69. *XCB* 23/12a–13a; Miyazaki Ichisada, *Godai Sōsho no tsūka mondai,* pp. 167–168.
70. On the iron cash, see *CBBM* 11/279–283. The basic source on the *jiaozi* exchange notes is Li You, *Songchao shishi* 15/5a–7b. For an analysis, see Katō Shigeshi, *Shina Keizaishi Kōshō,* vol. 2, pp. 1–26. See also Lien-sheng Yang,

Money and Credit in China; and Robert M. Hartwell, "The Evolution of the Northern Sung Monetary System, A.D. 960–1025," *Journal of the American Oriental Society* 87:280–289.

71. *WXTK* 4/555a. The *touziqian* is taken up in greater detail in Chapter Six.

72. *XCB* [*Yongle dadian* 12,306] 18a (vol. 1, p. 135); *XCB* 23/12b, 13a. In 982 the government suspended requisitions of fancy silks that required high levels of skill and labor and began demanding only basic textiles used in clothing the troops. See *SHY* shihuo 64/22b–23a. Kawahara Yoshirō, pp. 272–284, interprets such reductions as an effort to preserve productivity for essential items.

73. *CBBM* 13/325–326. One specific example of the rich buying cheap and selling dear is preserved for the year 977, when *hao* magnates were accused of buying salt from the government cheaply and selling it at inflated prices to the people: *SHY* shihuo 23/21a.

74. Su Che, *Luancheng ji* 36/7a.

75. Qingcheng County was already well known for its loose-leaf and powder teas by the mid Tang, but government purchases of it would not have been systematic. Only one governmental tea market was in operation in Sichuan prior to the rebellion, in Pengzhou's Pengkouzhen, although three more (all in Qiongzhou) were added soon after the rebellion, in 1005: *SHY* shihuo 29/7b. Shimasue Kazuyasu stresses the role of tea in the rebellion, as does Zhang Yinlin, "Songchu Sichuan Wang Xiaobo–Li Shun zhi luan," in *Songshi yanjiu ji*, vol. 1, pp. 251–271. The most interesting discussion of the problem I have seen is in *Wang Xiaobo Li Shun*, pp. 133–139, which includes field surveys (of an admittedly non-systematic nature) of temple occupance and tea cultivation in the Qingcheng region that gave birth to the rebellion. The authors place more emphasis on temple than on government control of tea at the time.

76. This and the following information is taken from *CBBM* 13/326 *seq.*, which includes much material left out of the *Changbian*. Another useful account is Li You's *Songchao shishi*, 17/20b–24b.

77. *CBBM* 13/332, 335.

78. A list of cities held or attacked by the rebels after they had lost Chengdu in mid 994 reads like a catalog of all the riverine cities of the region, and includes the occupation of Liangshan, Guang'an, Quzhou, Guozhou, and major assaults on Jia, Rong, Lu, Yu, Zhong, Wan, Kai, and Kui Prefectures, followed by a siege of Shizhou: *CBBM* 13/328, 334–335.

79. See *XCB* 39/3b–4b; Li You, *Songchao shishi* 17/23a–24b.

80. *CBBM* 25/739–52.

81. See, for example, *XCB* 51/17a and 54/4a.

82. Tan Kyōji, "Ō Shōha," pp. 87–88; Shen Gua, *Mengqi bitan* 25/815–818

83. Fei Zhu, "Shizu pu," *Quan Shu yiwen zhi* 55/5b–6a.

84. Huang Tingjian, quoted in Tan Kyōji, "Ō Shōha," p. 88.
85. Huang Xiufu, *Maoting kehua,* 6/2b–3a.
86. See, for example, Zhang Pu's "Shouningyuan ji," in *Quan Shu yiwen zhi* 38 xia 4a; and Xie Yong's "Chongxiu Ziizhou Fahuayuan ji," in *Songdai Shuwen jicun* 4/15b–17a.
87. Fei Zhu, "Shizu pu," *Quan Shu yiwen zhi* 53/5a–6a.
88. One of their members, Chang Yanyou, followed the Song general Lei Youzhong in his pacification drive and later established a branch lineage in Chengdu: Lü Tao, *Jingde ji* 24/4a.
89. *SS* 309/10159–10160. See Tan Kyōji "Ō Shōha," p. 89.
90. *XCB* 46/6b. Satake Yasuhiko hypothesizes that the 70 "chiefs" were rich peasants, part of what he sees as the growing stratum of "village magnates" *(xianghao):* "Shisen Seitofuro," p. 119.
91. One of Song Taizu's earliest concerns was to centralize—some commentators would say eviscerate—the military apparatus under his command. On these centralization policies, see Edmund H. Worthy, "The Founding of Sung China, 950–1000: Integrative Changes in Military and Political Institutions."
92. *XCB* 6/6b.
93. *XCB* 22/16a (981); *XCB* 23/17a (982). In 981 the prohibition on accompanying relatives was relaxed to permit one family member. Winston Lo understates the extent to which these rulings applied to all of southern China (which he refers to as the periphery of the empire), thereby implying that Sichuan was treated by the court as a special case. See his "Circuits and Circuit Intendants in the Territorial Administration of Sung China," *Monumenta Serica* 31:78; and his *Szechwan in Sung China,* pp. 24–25. My interpretation of Song personnel policies towards post-rebellion Sichuan is almost the exact opposite of Professor Lo's.
94. See Zhang Yong's biography in *SS* 293/9800–9804. Zhang's efforts at restoring civil order were much appreciated by Sichuanese. Huang Xiufu, for example, applauds Zhang's understanding of the roots of the rebellion and quotes in full his "Lament for Shu" in *Maoting kehua* 6/1a–b.
95. For Li Tian and Zhang Ji, see the biographies of 453 Sichuanese prefaced to *Songdai Shuwen jicun,* p. 27.
96. See Li Fan's "Shehong xian xiuxue ji," in *Songdai Shuwen jicun* 59/15b–16b. The appended biography lists (p. 31) Li as a *jinshi* of 1148, but this is implausible in view of his own account.
97. In "Transformations" Hartwell argues (pp. 416–420) that examination success joined endogamous marriage alliances and protection *(yin)* as part of a tripartite set of tactics used by the professional elite to perpetuate its domination of the civil service during the eleventh century. At the same time, the civil service examination system "provided the institutional means through

which newly risen local gentry families could perpetuate their enhanced social and political positions" (p. 420). But for Hartwell, examination success was predicated on prior attainment of a foothold in the local political and economic elite, a foothold typically acquired through marriage. While not denying the importance of marriage alliances, Chaffee argues (pp. 10–12) that examination success could also initiate mobility and identifies cases where marriage into the elite was predicated on acquiring a degree.

98. I have disregarded the actual number of examinations. These and the following calculations are based on Chaffee, Table 21, pp. 132–133. Following Chaffee (Table 20, p. 126), I have based the percentages on the number of *jinshi* graduates found in local histories—comprising one- to two-thirds of the total number of degree-holders—divided by the total number of degrees conferred. Since according to Chaffee the greatest lacunae apply to North and Northwest China, particularly the capital of Kaifeng, these percentages are likely to be fairly representative for southern China.

99. For the regional distribution of *jinshi* degrees in Sichuan from 670 to 1814, see Smith, "Commerce, Agriculture, and Core Formation," Table 3.

100. Chaffee, p. 149.

101. In 1020 the government allowed Sichuanese members of the civil service who had appropriate recommendations and had not been accused of crimes of rapaciousness to spend one term out of three in a post 300 *li* or more from their native place; at the same time elderly officials ready for retirement would be allowed to return to their villages: *XCB* 95/6b–7a. In 1033 inhabitants of western and eastern Sichuan were prohibited from holding the posts of prefect or vice-prefect in their native circuits: *XCB* 112/14a. In 1034 it was ordered that incumbents of the posts of fiscal intendant, fiscal vice-intendant, and judicial intendant in any of the circuits of Sichuan could house their families in the neighboring circuit, but could not visit them for more than ten days annually: *XCB* 114/9b.

102. Fei Zhu, "Shizu pu," *Quan Shu yiwen zhi* 53/5a–6a.

103. See *Songren chuanji ziliao suoyin,* vol. 3, pp. 3129–3130.

104. Fei Zhu, "Shizu pu," *Quan Shu yiwen zhi* 53/6a.

105. *Songdai Shuwen jicun* 10/18b–21a.

106. The rulings, previously noted, are in *XCB* 23/17a and *XCB* 112/14a. For Xianyu Shen's biography, see *Songdai Shuwen jicun* 10/10a–11b and *SS* 344/10936–10939.

107. Fei Zhu, "Shizu pu," *Quan Shu yiwen zhi* 53/10a–b; Lü Tao, *Jingde ji* 24/3b–6b.

108. In 1049 Chengdufu produced 24 *jinshi.* Tan Kyōji, "Ō Shōha," p. 96, citing Tian Guang.

109. Wu Shimeng was appointed Intendant of Ever-Normal Granaries in Zizhou Circuit, but he quit in disagreement over the New Policies and was then

appointed prefect of Shuzhou. His son Wu Zhen was prefect variously of Qiong, Qu, Yang and Wan prefectures, all in the Upper Yangzi, having earned his entry by examination: Fei Zhu, "Shizu pu," *Quan Shu yiwen zhi* 53/3b–4a. Wen Tong held the post of vice prefect in both Qiongzhou and Hanzhou, and prefect in Puzhou and Lingzhou in Sichuan, Yangzhou in Hanzhong Basin, and Huzhou in Liangzhe: *SS* 443/13101–13102, and Wen Tong's chronology, appended to his collected works, *Danyuan ji*.

110. This and the following information is from George Hatch's biography of Su Xun in Herbert Franke, ed., *Sung Biographies*, pp. 885–900. See also Su's geneological studies in his *Jiayou ji* 13, esp. pp. 5b–7b.

111. See Hartwell, "Transformations," Table 10, pp. 414–415. The single year of 1126 had a higher percentage of policy officials, at 13 percent.

112. On a national scale Sichuan provided 17 percent of the plain tabby requisitioned by the state, 20 percent of the pongee, and 36 percent of the hempen cloth. Yearly production quotas for the empire, by circuit, are recorded in *SHY* shihuo 64/1a–16a and compiled by Shiba Yoshinobu, *Sōdai shōgyoshi*, pp. 275–276. The Sichuan textile industry during the Song is discussed by Jia Daquan, *Songdai Sichuan jingji shulun*, pp. 65–84. On the silk transport burden, see *SS* 304/10071; *SHY* shihuo 64/19b–20a; *XCB* 96/26a–b; *XCB* 106/8a; and *XCB* 217/10a.

113. *CYZJ* yi 16/1123.

114. Bi Zhongyan's compilation of tax figures for the empire contained in *WXTK* 4/59–60 lists Sichuan's twice-yearly tax burden, as of 1077, at 2,575,407 units (strings of cash, bolts of cloth, etc.). The circuit breakdown is as follows: for Chengdufu Circuit 926,732 units; for Zizhou Circuit 832,187 units; for Lizhou Circuit 665,306 units; for Kuizhou Circuit 141,182 units (p. 60b). Total tax quota for the empire was 52,011,029 units. Sichuan's population at this time was 1,933,162 households, and the total population 16,471,830 households: figures from Wang Cun, *Yuanfeng jiuyu zhi*, as compiled by Katō Shigeshi, in *Shina keizaishi kōshō*, vol. 2, pp. 371–403.

115. Early in the dynasty, punishments were set for men who attempted to evade their distant rotation. Exceptions were made for men such as executory class officials of over 60 *sui*. It was especially difficult to fill posts in the periphery of these "frontier" regions. To fill the magistrates' posts in outlying counties, the government often had to increase the bonus schedules in those districts traversed by tea convoys (*SHY* zhiguan 43/97a–b), use local men as "acting officials" *(sheguan)*, or appoint military men to civilian posts (*Libu tiaofa*, in *Yongle dadian* 14625/8b).

116. *XCB* 214/21b. Winston Lo discusses the "eight-circuit measure" in "Circuits and Circuit Intendants," pp. 77–80, and *Introduction to the Civil Service*, pp. 200–216.

117. For example, three Chengdu luminaries all served as administrators of

neighboring prefectures: Lü Tao in Pengzhou (*SS* 346/10978); Wu Shi-meng in Shuzhou (*Quan Shu yiwen zhi* 53/3b–4a); and Zhou Biaoquan in Hanzhou (*Quan Shu yiwen zhi* 55/4a–b).

118. *XCB* 214/22a.
119. *SS* 159/3723.
120. *SS* 159/3723; *XCB* 214/22b. Although temporarily suspended during the Restoration, the "distant offices" rule was revived in 1094 and remained in effect in Sichuan through the Northern and Southern Song. Fujian and Guangnan, no longer far from the center of government, were dropped from its provisions around 1127. See *SS* 159/3723–3724.
121. *Jinshi* figures from Chaffee, Table 21, pp. 132–133. The new laws were extended to entrants coming in through *yin* protection at the beginning of the Post-Reform: *SS* 159/3723.
122. Wen Tong, "Zou wei qi zhi Yangzhou yici zhuang," *Danyuan ji* 4/354.
123. Ibid., pp. 356–357. Wen Tong had requested that a capital-class official be assigned to Jingyan County to protect government interests.
124. *SHY* shihuo 37/18a.

INTRODUCTION TO PART TWO: WANG ANSHI'S THEORY OF BUREAUCRATIC ENTREPRENEURSHIP

1. On Emperor Shenzong's role in the reforms, especially after Wang's depar-ture, see Wu Tai, "Xining-Yuanfeng xinfa sanlun," *Song-Liao-Jin shi luncong,* pp. 19–24.
2. Bol, "Principles of Unity."
3. *XCB* 237/8a. Clerical venality was a chief target of the reforms, but as usual Wang took an institutional rather than a moralistic view of the problem. According to Wang, clerical venality and corruption stemmed from their financial need and could be solved by providing clerks with adequate salaries financed by Farming Loan and Service Exemption funds: see, for example, *XCB* 248/21a. Moreover by making clerical offices financially rewarding, "upstanding literati"—*shanshi*—might then be attracted to the posts, so that "clerical and official [classes] can again be combined into one as of old." For more on this eradication of barriers between clerks and officials, see Miyazaki Ichisada, "Ō Anseki no ri-shi gōitsu saku—sōhō o chūshin to shite," in his *Ajiashi kenkyū,* vol. 1, pp. 311–364.
4. Wang Anshi, "Yu Ma Yunpan shu," *Wang Linchuan quanji* 75/479.
5. Wang Anshi, "Da Zeng Gongli shu," *Wang Linchuan quanji* 73/464.
6. Wang Anshi, "Shang Renzong huangdi yanshi shu," *Wang Linchuan quanji* 39/222–223.
7. This particular phrasing is in fact by Su Che early in Emperor Shenzong's reign, on the occasion of his official break with the economic policies of

Wang Anshi and Lü Huiqing: *XCB* shibu 4/8b. Calls for expenditure reductions rose to a crescendo from the mid 1060s on. In 1066 Li Duanyuan used the appearance of a comet, *hui,* to pun on the need for a clean sweep, *hui* (same character) of "superfluous officials, false scholars, unrestrained expenses, and cocksure (but incompetent) troops": *XCB* 207/23a.

8. *XCB* shibu 3A/14b–15a; *WXTK* 24/232c.
9. The prototypical economizing bureau, the *shengjianju,* was set up in 1058. See Edward A. Kracke, Jr., *Civil Service in Early Sung China,* p. 17n24.
10. *XCB* shibu 4/5a–b.
11. Wang Anshi, *Wang Linchuan quanji* 39/222 and 75/479.
12. Wang Anshi, "Qi zhizhi sansi tiaoli," *Wang Linchuan quanji* 70/445.
13. *CBBM* 66/2097. There was ample precedent for bringing merchants into the economic deliberations of the eleventh-century state, particularly in monopolized industries such as tea and salt. See Smith, "Interest Groups, Ideology and Economic Policy-making." For a recent discussion of the close relationship between merchants and the state during the Song, see Zhu Ruixi, "Songdai shangren de shehui diwei jiqi lishi zuoyong," *Lishi yanjiu* 2:127–143.
14. Wang Anshi, *Wang Linchuan quanji* 70/445.
15. *SS* 14/270.
16. For the poem "Jianbing" see Wang Anshi, *Wang Linchuan quanji* 5/22. On tea-guild merchants, see "Yi chafa" and "Chashang shier shuo," *Wang Linchuan quanji* 70/443–444; and *XCB* 236/13a. The term *jianbing* was used at least as early as Xunzi (fl. 298–238 B.C.) to denote individuals who used extraordinary wealth and power to expropriate the property of others. Ch'ü T'ung-tsu writes that the "term {*bingjian*} or {*jianbing*} suggests a person whose extraordinary wealth and power enabled him to encroach upon the people. Literally, it means to swallow up, to encroach, and thus to grab the property of others." See his *Han Social Structure,* p. 394n7. Wu Tai (pp. 26–27) analyses the inherent tension between suppressing "engrossers" and increasing state revenues.
17. *SHY* shihuo 4/16a.
18. *SHY* shihuo 37/14a. That same year Wang Anshi described to the emperor the practices of "engrosser" comb wholesalers who tried to depress the price of raw materials brought to the capital by traveling merchants, and the "engrosser" tea-guild magnates who tried to raise the price of tea sold wholesale to less powerful guild members. Intervention by the state trade bureaus should have equalized prices to the advantage of the smaller commercial interests. In the case of the comb market, the traveling merchants had themselves taken their case to the *shiyiwu,* which bought up their goods. According to Wang Anshi's report, "the 'engrossers' then wanted to utilize the new [state trade] laws to buy the entire lot, but the [state trade administrator] instead distributed it to the local comb shops": *XCB* 236/11b. In the case of the tea

industry, Wang reported that "since we have now established a State Trade [Bureau], these ten or so [greatest guild] houses—the 'engrossing houses'— will have to buy and sell at the same price as the poor merchant houses, which is why these ten houses dislike the new policy and slander it. [I] recently obtained this information from a report by a member of the tea guild, but the same situation is to be found in all other guilds": *XCB* 236/11b–13a, discussed at length in Katō Shigeshi, "On the Hang," pp. 68–69.

19. Wang Anshi, "Kanxiang zayi," *Wang Linchuan quanji* 62/391; see also James T. C. Liu, *Reform,* p. 48.

20. See Chaffee, Table 4, p. 27. The *Changbian* records an attempt by Wang to instruct Shenzong in the economic benefits of appointing additional officials to administer the local Farming Loan and Service Exemption funds. "The number of [county-level] officials in charge of distribution and collection of the Service Exemption and Ever-Normal funds does not exceed 500, and salaries for these 500 is not more than 100,000 strings [annually]. This year profits [from the two accounts] reached 3 million strings, at a [total administrative] cost of but 300,000 strings. Establishing new offices does not lead to unnecessary expenses": *XCB* 250/14a–b.

21. Lo, "Circuits and Circuit Intendants," p. 89.

22. For a detailed analysis of the structure, authority, and personnel of the Finance Planning Commission as the command center of the reforms, see Higashi Ichio, *Ō Anseki shimpō no kenkyū,* pp. 264–393. See also Sogabe Shizuo, *Sōdai zaiseishi,* pp. 3–36; and James T. C. Liu, *Reform,* pp. 86–7.

23. On the Ever-Normal Granary intendancies, see Smith, "State Power." On the *baojia,* "bowman" militia, and frontier finance intendancies, see *SHY* zhiguan 44/51a–52b, 53a–55b; and *SS* 167/3927.

24. For Lo's model of the Song system of dual control over county magistrates, see "Circuits and Circuit Intendants," pp. 94–95. On the increasing importance of the county rather than the prefecture as the basic unit of government by the Song, see Hartwell, "Transformations," pp. 394–397.

25. Sima Guang was particularly incensed by Wang Anshi's practice of creating new intendants, assistant intendants, and staff supervisors for each reform policy, and staffing them with young, low-ranked, and frivolous men with seniority status no greater than prefectural vice-administrator, county magistrate, or market inspector: *XCB* 368/23b–24a.

26. This transformation of officials into entrepreneurs was recognized, and condemned, by traditional Chinese historians. Ma Duanlin, writing in the early fourteenth century, complained that in order to break the power of monopolist merchants who hoarded goods in anticipation of a high price, New Policies "officials copied the practices of merchants and traders, and then

held them up as the 'art of enriching the nation' ": *WXTK,* zixu (preface), p. 5a.

27. Wang Anshi, *Wang Linchuan quanji* 39/220; see also p. 224.

28. Wang Anshi, *Wang Linchuan quanji* 39/224.

29. My interpretation of Wang's "Myriad Word Memorial" as a theory of bureaucratic entrepreneurship is informed by Joseph Schumpeter, *The Theory of Economic Development,* esp. ch. 2; James D. Thompson, *Organizations in Action: Social Science Bases of Administrative Theory;* and Eugene Lewis, *Public Entrepreneurship: Toward a Theory of Bureaucratic Power.*

4. THE ENTREPRENEURIAL LEAP

1. The history of the tea and horse enterprise is recorded in *SHY* zhiguan 43/47a–118b, which, however, goes up to only 1173. The tea side of the enterprise is documented in *SHY* shihuo, zhuan 29–32, which contains usefully detailed records of the Sichuan tea industry up to 1204. Note that zhuan 31 and 32 have been misnumbered, so that the records in 31 pick up where 32 leaves off. Horse policy, including the horse side of the enterprise, is recorded in *SHY* bing, zhuan 22–26, which covers events in Sichuan up to 1219. Most articles on the Agency as an integrated operation focus on the New Policies era. Of these the most useful are still Umehara Kaoru, "Seitō no uma to Shisen no cha," *Tōhō gakuhō* 45:195–244; Kawakami Koichi, "Sōdai Shisen ni okeru kakuchahō no kaishi," *Tōhōgaku* 23:65–78, and the same author's "Sōdai Shisen no kakuchahō, *Shigaku zasshi* 71.11:1–25.

2. Joseph LaPalombara, "An Overview of Bureaucracy and Political Development," in Joseph Lapalombara, ed., *Bureaucracy and Political Development,* p. 12.

3. Schumpeter, *Theory,* pp. 64–65.

4. Schumpeter, *Theory,* p. 66.

5. Schumpeter discusses the institutional barriers against entrepreneurial activity, and the psychological profile of entrepreneurial types, in *Theory,* pp. 74–94. Successful entrepreneurial activity, for Schumpeter, is one of only two sources of economic profit. If a new combination is successful, the entrepreneur earns a temporary surplus of receipts over costs "to which no liability corresponds, [and which] is an entrepreneurial profit." This surplus will persist until the allure of profit attracts new competitors into the industry, shifting the supply curve to the right and driving the price of the good or service in question down to total production costs. If the new combination is also a monopoly, economic profits will continue until the monopoly is broken. See esp. p. 152.

6. See, for example, Thompson's *Organizations in Action.* For a recent survey of

the many fields to which economic theory is now being applied, see the essays in Gerard Radnitzky and Peter Bernholz, eds., *Economic Imperialism: The Economic Approach Applied Outside the Field of Economics.*

7. See, for example, Stuart Holland, *The State as Entrepreneur.*

8. I arrived at my own notion of bureaucratic entrepreneurship independently of Lewis' work, on the basis of my reading of Wang Anshi and James Thompson (who also provides the theoretical foundation for Lewis' book). But I am pleased to defer to the sophistication of Professor Lewis' synthesis.

9. Lewis, pp. 8–9.

10. Lewis, pp. 9, 15–17.

11. *SHY* zhiguan 43/47a and 52a–b. From mid 1081 to mid 1083, the Intendant for Horse Purchases, Guo Maoxun, served concurrently as a second co-intendant: *XCB* 314/1b–2a and 335/20a; *SHY* zhiguan 43/62b–63a.

12. The Superintendant's office was moved from Chengdu to Qinzhou in 1079 to accommodate Li Ji's concurrent leadership of the TMA and the Shaanxi financial administration: *XCB* 299/12b. It apparently remained there throughout the Northern Song. Yu Yunwen wrote in 1168 that the Superintendant spent half a year in Chengdu and half a year in Xingyuan, according to the tea-harvest and horse-market cycles: *SHY* zhiguan 43/114a–b.

13. Hartwell, "Financial Expertise," p. 285; see also his "Transformations," p. 399. Names, dates of tenure, and sources on the Northern and Southern Song Intendants are given above in Appendices A–C.

14. The exception is Guo Maoxun, whose position in the Agency was purely nominal. The records of Guo's quite typical financial career start with him as a managing supervisor in the Finance Commission, from which post he moved to Supervisor of Herds and Pastures and then to Intendant of Horse Purchases in Shaanxi: *XCB* 298/17b and 314/1b–2a.

15. Like Guo Maoxun, Li Qi also served as managing supervisor of the Finance Commission, in which capacity he was sent to Shaanxi, and then to investigate the establishment of a State Trade Bureau in Chengdu: *XCB* 247/20a and 249/6a.

16. *XCB* 248/23a–b. Pu Zongmin had once been approved for the post of Prefect of Xingyuan by his later opponent, Su Che: Su Che, *Luancheng ji* 30/5a.

17. *XCB* 256/9b and 265/7a. Han Jiang's hatred of Liu Zuo, for reasons not clearly reported, forced Wang Anshi to send a second investigator as well. Han Jiang took the issue directly to the emperor, who agreed not to use Liu Zuo (Liu's dismissal never materialized); but Han Jiang nonetheless insisted on retiring over what the emperor, greatly puzzled, called "this little affair." Ultimately Han Jiang accepted the post of Prefect of Xuzhou. The event, as recorded in *SS* 315/10304, is reported by H. R. Williamson, *Wang Anshi,* vol. 1, pp. 355–356.

18. On disruption of the salt trade, see *SS* 181/4420–4421 and *SS* 184/4498.

The Pengkou tea riot is discussed in Chapter Six. Liu was dismissed in mid term in 1077/7, as was his chief accuser Lü Tao: *XCB* 283/9b.

19. For a discussion of the factional battles that undermined Wang Anshi's position, see Qi Xia, pp. 199–217. Wu Tai (pp. 24–28) discusses the direction of the reforms under Emperor Shenzong's stewardship.

20. *XCB* 253/7a.

21. *XCB* 277/6a–b.

22. *XCB* 278/2b–3a and 280/2b–3b; *SS* 334/10724–10725. Zhou Yin charged that twenty years after his father's death, Li Ji had still not properly interred his father's bones. Zhou may have obtained this information as a native of a neighboring prefecture: Zhou was from Chengdu, Li Ji from Qiongzhou.

23. *XCB* 284/15a–16a.

24. *XCB* 283/9b; *SS* 339/10823.

25. *XCB* 297/16b.

26. *SHY* zhiguan 43/55a; *SS* 332/10682–10683. Lu entered Sichuan with his father, the expert on frontier matters, Lu Shen, when Shen served as Prefect of Chengdu towards the end of his life in 1070. The only information on Lu Shimin before he joined Li Ji is by Chao Yuezhi, who writes that Lu married a Ms. Fan of Wen'an County (Hebei) around 1060, while holding the rank of *hubu shilang: Songshan wenji* 19/41b.

27. *SS* 332/10682.

28. Internal recruitment remained a relatively prominent feature of the Agency for the remainder of the Northern Song. Two men in addition to Lu Shimin, Sun Aobian (1104–1107) and He Jian (pre-1121–1123), were made Intendant sometime after holding the position of managing supervisor. Sun Aobian, who held all three posts in the triad, was a managing supervisor in 1075 (*SHY* zhiguan 43/49a, 81a, 86b, 90b–91a). And He Jian held the post in 1113 (*SHY* zhiguan 43/94a, 98b, 101b–102b; *SS* 167/3969–3970). In addition Lu Shimin, He Jian, Cheng Zhishao, and Zhang Hui were reappointed to the Intendant's office in times of later crisis.

29. *XCB* 297/16a–b.

30. Wang Anshi, *Wang Linchuan quanji* 39/220.

31. *SS* 334/10721–10722.

32. For Wei Jizong's memorial, see *SHY* shihuo 37/14b–15a. The prototype for the state trade agency, it will be recalled, was crafted in Shaanxi by Wang Shao. On the use of merchants in the various state trade bureaus, see Wang Anshi's remarks to Emperor Shenzong, *XCB* 240/3b.

33. *XCB* 208/17b.

34. *SS* 334/10724.

35. *SS* 314/10279.

36. *SS* 332/10682–10683. On Lu Shen's prowess as a border expert, see *XCB* 208/6b.

37. *SS* 159/3723. Winston Lo discusses the problem of over-recruitment and the need for job rationing in *Introduction to the Civil Service,* pp. 29–33 and ch. 4.

38. The *jiluguan* system is described in *SS* 169/4049. For guides in English, see Lo, *Introduction to the Civil Service,* ch. 5 (but note that he does not refer to the term). In Japanese, see Miyazaki Ichisada's "Sōdai kansei josetsu," which serves as the introduction to Saeki Tomi, *Sōshi shokkanshi sakuin;* and Umehara Kaoru, "Sōsho no kirokuhan to sono shūhen," *Tōhō gakuhō* 48:135–182. Umehara's article has been enlarged in his *Sōdai kanryō seido kenkyū,* pp. 3–98, and is summarized in English as "Civil and Military Officials in the Sung: the *Chi-lu-kuan* System," *Acta Asiatica* 50:1–30.

39. *SHY* zhiguan 43/47a; *XCB* 258/17b–18a, 274/10b–11a, 341/4b.

40. For sources, see Appendix C.

41. *XCB* 303/15a–b.

42. *XCB* 341/2a; *SHY* zhiguan 43/65a.

43. See Smith, "State Power."

44. Many of these complaints are anthologized in *CBBM* 64/2053–2071. Fan Zuyu's diatribe on the subject includes Wang Shao, Li Ji, Lu Shimin, and one of the most brilliant scientific minds of his age, Shen Gua: *SS* 337/10798–10799.

45. *XCB* 368/23b–24a.

46. On Lu Shimin, see *SHY* zhiguan 43/71b–72a; *XCB* 516/3b. On Sun Aobian, see *SHY* zhiguan 43/49a, 81a, 86b, 90b–91a.

47. *SHY* zhiguan 43/94a, 98b, 100b–101a, 101b–102b; *SS* 167/3969–3970.

48. Lewis (p. 11) also assumes as a precondition for entrepreneurial experimentation that "sufficient time is available for the development of the specific issue or area upon which the budding entrepreneur wishes to work."

49. For the dates of terms in office, see Appendix A. It is with the criterion of length of time in office that the TMA and Ever-Normal Granary Intendants begin to diverge. Although appointed for their entrepreneurial qualities, once in office the Ever-Normal Granary Intendants were relatively tightly restrained and, in most identifiable cases, held office an unremarkable 15 to 25 months. See Smith, "State Power."

50. Fan was transferred back to Shaanxi as a Fiscal Supervisor: *XCB* 319/1b.

51. Modes of entry and exit for the Northern and Southern Song Intendants are compared in Tables 3 and 4, Chapter Six.

52. *XCB* 393/22b.

53. *XCB* 399/10b; *XCB* 476/2a.

54. For individual terms, see Appendix A. Lu Shumin's second term falls in the Post-Reform era; and the two terms of Cheng Zhihui and Zhang Hui are each counted separately. Total average for the entire Northern Song period was 43 months.

55. As a 1053 *jinshi* Pu Zongmin was probably the oldest of the men in the New

Policies Intendancy. He had, as noted earlier, received Su Che's endorsement
for the important post of Xingyuan Prefect. On his mediation after the Pengkou tea riot and Liu Zuo's monopolization of the Shaanxi salt trade, see *XCB*
282/12b–13a. Pu was also the mediator (although not neutral) in Guo Maoxun's attempt to exert control over TMA resources and was praised for his
efforts in an imperial rescript that went, "Pu Zongmin is able to work in
harmony in affairs of office, does not agitate with his objections, and can
avoid [being the object of] accusations." As a result Pu was promoted in
rank from 7A to 6B. See *XCB* 341/4b. But Pu was never made Chief Intendant, the post always going to men who were either younger (we do not
know their ages) or more aggressive. Pu Zongmeng—either Zongmin's brother
or cousin, also from Langzhou—was an important member of the reform
administration, regarded as one of Wang Anshi's "mean and petty" under-
lings: *SS* 328/10571–10572.

56. The four Post-Reform Sichuanese Intendants were Song Gou (Int. 1096);
Cheng Zhishao (Int. 1091/12–1094/4; 1099/2–1105/6); his son Cheng Tang
(Int. ca. 1115–1118/8); and Yuwen Chang, from one of the oldest Si-
chuanese elite lineages. For sources, see Appendix C.

57. See *SS* 361/11297–11311. Zhang enjoyed the right to "dismiss and promote
men in office as he saw fit" (*bianyi chuzhi*). For the background of Zhao Kai,
Zhang Shen, Li Tai (the only non-Sichuanese in this period), and Feng Kangguo as Intendants during the rise of Wu Jie, see *SS* 174/4223–4225.

58. Qin Gui was the leading advocate of peace with the Jin. After coming to
power as Chief Councilor, he waged a campaign against the most prominent
representatives of the "war party," particularly Yue Fei (whom he caused to
be executed in 1142) and Zhang Jun. Zhang Jun was impeached from his
position in the Bureau of Military Affairs in 1137, and many of his followers
were demoted. Contemporaries believed that Qin Gui waged a vendetta against
Sichuanese, so many of whom were sponsored by Zhang Jun. For example,
Yu Yunwen's biographer comments that "Qin Gui took over the nation and
many [men of] Shu were discarded. When Gui died [in 1155], Gaozong
wished to employ Sichuanese again": *SS* 383/11791. For Qin Gui's biography, see *SS* 473/13747–13765.

59. Lewis, p. 17. Although not all phases of Lewis's model apply or can be tested
in the case of TMA Intendants, Lewis has added an extremely useful evolu-
tionary dimension to Thompson's propositions on bureaucratic power.

60. *SHY* zhiguan 43/47a; *SHY* shihuo 30/11b.

61. *SHY* shihuo 29/7b.

62. Lu Yu, *Chajing* xia 9b; Yue Shi, *Taiping huanyi ji* 73/565–566 and 75/581.

63. In 1074/7/8, the Secretariat ordered Li and Pu to investigate reports that tax
returns on exported tea (lit. "guest," or "merchant" tea) in Da and Fu Prefectures in eastern Sichuan were high. Nothing came of the matter, however,

and the tea industry of eastern Sichuan was not monopolized until the Southern Song: *SHY* zhiguan 43/47b.

64. *SHY* zhiguan 43/48b. The tea was earmarked for shipment to Qinfeng and Xihe Circuits for sale and barter for horses.

65. In 1101 Mingshan had a standing supply-quota of 120 convoys *(gang)*, each with a standard capacity of 30,000 catties (or a combined total of 3,600,000 catties) for the markets supplied out of Qinzhou; to this were added orders for 15 additional convoys for a total of 4,500,000 catties (2,976.75 tons): *SHY* shihuo 30/28a.

66. *SHY* shihuo 24/10a–11a.

67. *SHY* shihuo 30/16a–b; *SHY* shihuo 24/10a–11a.

68. Lü Tao, *Jingde ji* 3/5a.

69. *SHY* zhiguan 43/48a; *SHY* shihuo 29/7b. A third site, Jizhou, on the Sichuan basin side of the mountains, was rejected because of insufficient production.

70. *SHY* zhiguan 43/88a, 96a. See also Chapter Seven.

71. *SHY* shihuo 30/13b. For commercial tax stations, see *SHY* shihuo 16/15a–17a (Chengdufu Circuit), 18a–19b (Lizhou Circuit). The two exceptions were Yumachang in Xingyuan and Siduodian in Yangzhou. Opening a market in Siduodian turned out to be an error in judgment, for the tea was of poor quality and small quantity. And because of low returns and hence little expectations of bonuses, no official would consent to serve as inspector. In 1080 the market was absorbed into the prefectural market: *SHY* shihuo 30/17a–b.

72. *SHY* zhiguan 43/50a.

73. *SHY* shihuo 30/12b.

74. The TMA obtained five middle-level managing supervisors *(gandang gongshi)* by 1075: *SHY* zhiguan 43/49a. In early 1077 the Pengkou market was still managed by one special inspector with the assistance of a registrar reassigned from neighboring Mengyang County: Lü Tao, *Jingde ji* 1/19a. The first recorded TMA recommendations for market inspectors *(jianguan)* are not until 1078: *SHY* shihuo 30/17a–b.

For the extension of the monopsony to the entire Chuan-Shu region, see *SHY* shihuo 30/13b.

75. Lü Tao, *Jingde ji* 1/8a–b.

76. Lü Tao, *Jingde ji* 1/9a.

77. *SHY* shihuo 30/15a. The rights lapsed in 1081, but the TMA retained the authority to impeach uncooperative officials in Ya, Han, Qiong, Peng, and Li prefectures: *SHY* zhiguan 43/53a. Lü Tao was made to take the blame for the Pengkou tea riot (described in Chapter Six), with the charge that he "had not immediately investigated the complaints of the Pengkou cultivators": *XCB* 283/9b.

78. *SHY* shihuo 30/17a–b notes seven inspectors for 29 markets as of the ninth month of 1080, when the Siduodian market was closed.

79. *SHY* shihuo 30/13b.

80. *SHY* shihuo 30/20a.

81. From about 1074 to 1077, the TMA employed *yajiao* (also referred to as *yaqian*)—local-service supply masters, drawn from wealthy families—to inspect, register, and tax tea in five sites on the perimeter of Xixiang County. When the posts were allowed to lapse in 1077, smuggling rose dramatically, forcing Li Ji to re-employ one *yajiao* and add four *maipu* tax farmers to buy and tax tea for the TMA in Xixiang. In addition to whatever basic fees the men received, they were also rewarded with 1,000 cash for every 10,000 catties of tea over the quota that they purchased: *SHY* shihuo 30/16a–b; *XCB* 247/18a.

82. Su Che, *Luancheng ji* 39/5b.

83. Lü Tao, *Jingde ji* 1/23b, 11/3a–b; *SHY* shihuo 30/15b. Su Che, *Luancheng ji* 39/5b, claims that cultivators were also prohibited from selling their bud tea (*yacha*), but a 1086 entry calling attention to the TMA practice of milling and forcing the sale of bud tea in Hezhou indicates that the government bought the cultivators' earliest flush: *XCB* 376/11b–12a.

84. See Chapter Two. Zhang Pu, in his "Shouningyuan ji," describes merchants lined up and tea braziers and herbal medicines displayed at the great Dazhenzi Temple market in Chengdu: *Quan Shu yiwen zhi* 38 xia 2b–4a. It appears, or at least is possible, that the tea braziers were manned by cultivators who brewed and sold their own product. According to Lü Tao, after imposition of the monopoly the cultivators of Zhide Mountain, also in the western mountains of Jiulong county, first sold their tea to the government, then bought it back (at a 30 percent markup) in order to peddle it themselves. Whether they had been in the habit of peddling their own tea prior to the monopoly is unclear. See Lü Tao, *Jingde ji* 1/17a.

85. *SHY* shihuo 30/19a.

86. The export increase was necessitated by the joint Song-Tsongkha war against Xi Xia waged around Lanzhou. The TMA exported 33,737 bales in 1077 and 36,500 bales in 1078: *SHY* zhiguan 43/51b. In 1082 Pu Zongmin recommended shipping tea to Lanzhou for sale to the local Tibetan tribes in order to finance grain and fodder procurement, in lieu of disbursing 100,000 strings of cash to the Military Regulator: *SHY* zhiguan 43/61a–b. The plan was put into action in late 1083 when 10,000 bales were added to the Agency's quota. The value of the tea was deducted from the TMA's cash subvention to the Regulator's office: *SHY* shihuo 30/23a. This additional sum is reflected in Lü Tao's estimate that 50,000 bales were shipped to Xihe annually by the TMA: *Jingde ji* 3/9a–b.

87. Huang Lian defined *shicha* as "that [tea] which is monopolized in the four

circuits of [Sichuan]," and *gangcha* as "that which is disbursed up to the six circuits of Shaanxi" (*XCB* 381/22b), but an alternate usage for *shicha* appears to have been tea sold to domestic consumers rather than in the horse and provisioning markets. The term *guancha* simply denotes any tea sold by the government. See, for example, *SHY* shihuo 30/19b.

88. Bazhou tea had been rejected as unfit for export in 1074, but reconsidered and monopolized in 1082 as government tea needs grew: *SHY* zhiguan 43/48a, 61b.

89. *XCB* 334/12b–13b; *SHY* shihuo 30/18b, 24b–25b.

90. *SS* 183/447; *SS* 184/4494. The decline in output stimulated a debate that finally led to the suspension of the monopoly in 1059.

91. *WXTK* 18/175a includes the observation, in reference to the eleventh-century southeastern monopoly system, that "merchant-traders transport [the tea] to the northwest in order to spread it among the Yi and Di [peoples], where the profits are especially great."

92. *SHY* shihuo 30/12a–b.

93. *XCB* 282/12b.

94. The 52 sales markets are listed in *SHY* shihuo 29/14b–15a.

95. *SHY* shihuo 30/13b.

96. Commercial tax stations for the twelve tea-marketing centers are listed in *SHY* shihuo 15/17b–20a.

97. Skinner, "Cities," p. 308.

98. For the intermingling of commercial and defensive interests in southern Sichuan, see von Glahn, *Country of Streams and Grottoes,* Parts II and III.

99. *XCB* 282/12b. By far the greatest proportion of this convoy tea, about 35,000 bales, went to the 28 or 29 submarkets of Qin, Xi, He, and Min prefectures, Tongyuan Commandery, and Yongning Stockade: *SHY* zhiguan 43/51b; and Paul J. Smith, "Taxing Heaven's Storehouse: The Szechwan Tea Monopoly and the Tsinghai Horse Trade, 1074–1223," Table 13, p. 464.

100. *SHY* zhiguan 43/58b–59a.

101. *SHY* shihuo 30/23a.

102. See, for example, *SHY* zhiguan 43/59b (1081), 74a–b (1100), 108b–109a (1156); *XNYL* 116/3664 (1137). The intra-Asian tea trade is discussed more fully in Chapter Seven.

103. *SHY* fanyi 4/16a.

104. *SHY* shihuo 30/20a.

105. *SHY* zhiguan 43/54a–b.

106. *SHY* zhiguan 43/54a.

107. In 1081 Gua Maoxun wrote that "of all the things the Tibetan tribes desire, it is tea they are most anxious for": *SHY* zhiguan 43/53b.

108. *SHY* shihuo 30/15a. The order was enforced with a set of anti-smuggling regulations.

109. *XCB* 282/12b–13a. The household populations for Qinfeng and Yongxing Circuits are based on Wang Cun, *Yuanfeng jiuyu zhi,* zhuan 3.

The exceptions made for Fengxiangfu and Fengzhou illustrate some of the problems associated with enforcing monopoly restrictions. Although administratively part of Qinfeng Circuit (in fact Fengxiang was the circuit capital), the two prefectures could only be successfully restricted when all of Eastern Shaanxi, or Yongxing Circuit, also came under Agency control. In the case of Fengxiangfu, its southwestern county of Baoji served as the northern terminus of the Baoye Road, and the transshipment point for points west: *SHY* fangyu 10/3b–4a; *SHY* shihuo 32 1a–b. But the prefectural center and its eight eastern counties were oriented economically downriver towards Yongxing Commandery (modern Xi'an), and an administrative barrier separating Fengxiang and Yongxing was apparently impossible to enforce. Consequently when Eastern Shaanxi was open to southeastern or private Sichuanese tea, either all of Fengxiangfu (e.g., 1075–1083) or the prefectural seat and the eight eastern counties (e.g., from 1104 on, with a short interruption in 1111) were linked to it: *XCB* 282/12b–13a; *SHY* shihuo 30/38a–39b; *SHY* shihuo 32/1a–b. In the case of Fengzhou, we can only assume that since all the roads from Sichuan to Yongxing Commandery traversed the prefecture, any time that Yongxing Circuit was designated for free trade, the trade in Fengzhou had to be unrestricted as well.

110. *SHY* shihuo 30/15b–16a; *XCB* 297/16a–b.
111. *SHY* shihuo 30/16a.
112. *XCB* 299/19b.
113. *XCB* 299/12b. On the location of the Fiscal Intendant, see *XCB* 299/37b–38a.
114. *SHY* shihuo 30/17b. The total tax quota was 343,095 strings of cash: *SHY* shihuo 15/17b–20a.
115. For Lu Shimin's expansionist memorial, see *XCB* 334/12b–13b. The twenty prefectures and population increment included Fengxiangfu and Fengzhou.
116. *XCB* 334/13a.
117. *SHY* shihuo 30/18b. The original text reads "Shanfu West," i.e. the entire Shaanxi region. Three months later the two Sichuanese border prefectures of Wenzhou and Longzhou were added: *SHY* shihuo 30/23a.
118. *SHY* zhiguan 43/65a; *XCB* 341/2a.
119. *XCB* 334/13b.
120. *SHY* shihuo 30/20a.
121. See *SHY* shihuo 30/19b–20a.
122. *XCB* 334/13b, 340/12b; Lü Tao, *Jingde ji* 3/7a–b.
123. For cash incomes to the government during the Northern Song, see Quan Hansheng, *Zhongguo jingjishi yanjiu,* vol. 1, pp. 226–227. Of the 60,000,000 strings about 22,000,000 strings came from salt (p. 242), about 12,000,000

12,000,000 strings from wine (p. 244), and 8,000,000–11,000,000 strings from commercial taxes (p. 251).

124. Lü Tao, *Jingde ji* 3/9a.

125. *SHY* zhiguan 43/85b–86a. The horse trade provides a second indication of the greater relative profitability of the Shaanxi market. In 1104, for example, a horse of 13¼ hands could be bought in Qinzhou for 112 catties of Mingshan tea, worth 769 cash per catty. In the southern Sichuanese market of Liizhou, on the other hand, only about 50 miles from Mingshan, the same size horse cost a total of 350 catties of tea (worth only 30 cash per catty), 6 *liang* of silver (at 1 string 200 cash per length), 6 mats of coarse silk wadding (at 50 cash per mat), and 1 length of grey hempen cloth (at 500 cash per length): *SHY* zhiguan 43/80a–b. On the evidence of the horse trade, Mingshan tea was worth 25 times more in Qinzhou than it was in southeastern Sichuan.

126. *XCB* 334/12b–13a; *SHY* shihuo 30/18a–b, 23a. In 1090 the restrictions were extended to the entire arc formed by the western counties of Yazhou, all of Wei, Mao, and Longzhou, and the westernmost county of Mianzhou; *SHY* shihuo 30/26a–b. They were lifted one year later at the urging of the Military Director, who argued that a free trade in tea was essential to pacifying the Tibetan and Man tribes, but were reimposed by Lu Shimin in 1096. Lu set up government markets from Liizhou in the southwest to Wenzhou in the north in order to regulate the amount of tea flowing into tribal networks near or linked up to the Wen and Jiezhou horse-marketing region: *SHY* shihuo 30/26b, 28b–30a.

127. Lü Tao, *Jingde ji* 3/9b–10a. The estimate is based on a sales volume of 25,000,000 catties and include merchant sales of tea to eastern Shaanxi.

128. The original profit margin of 30 percent was lowered to 10 percent following the Pengkou disturbance: *XCB* 282/12b–13a.

129. *SHY* shihuo 30/37b.

130. *SHY* shihuo 31/12b–14a.

131. *SHY* shihuo 30/34b.

132. Lü Tao, *Jingde ji* 3/5b; Su Che, *Luancheng ji* 36/9a.

133. *XCB* 349/5a–b; *WXTK* 18/176b; *SS* 184/4505.

134. *XCB* 341/16b; *SHY* shihuo 30/23b.

135. *SHY* shihuo 29/15a.

136. *SHY* shihuo 37/23b–24a; *SS* 184/4501. For Lü Tao's comment, see his memorial against the credit sales of tea to itinerant peddlers for resale in Shandong and Hebei: "Zou qi ba Jingdong-Hebei Lu shefang cha zhuang," *Jingde ji* 3/10b.

137. The watermill tea operation required merchants to take their tea directly to government mills, where shopowners from outlying counties would convene to buy the milled tea. At its peak the system included over 260 mills

in Jingxi, Hebei, and after 1103 Yongxingjun Circuits, with requisitions of as much as 8,000,000 catties of leaf tea *(caocha)* annually. But the extended system fell prey to high costs, low profits, uncontrollable smuggling, and finally an embargo by southern leaf-tea merchants, and in 1112 was reduced to the confines of the capital city. See *XCB* 343/3b; 346/2b–3b; 370/4a–5b, 20a; *SHY* shihuo 30/34b–35b, 39b–44a; *CBBM* 134/4140–4144; *SS* 184/4507.

138. *SHY* shihuo 30/24a–b. The Guangnan monopoly was reversed in 1082/2.
139. *XCB* 350/10a.
140. *XCB* 348/11a. Lu Shimin encouraged the government to "harmoniously purchase" the tea of Hunan, Hubei, and Anhui for sale in Hebei and Hedong as a way of financing defense expenditures in these two circuits. Eventually, however, the proposal was "put to sleep" *(qin)*.
141. *XCB* 348/11a, with a probable transcription error of *da* for *liu*.
142. *XCB* 349/5a–b; 351/4b; *SHY* shihuo 30/25b. Marketing of the Fujianese camphorated tea was divided by circuit, with sale entrusted to the Fiscal Intendants of Fujian, Liangzhe, Jiangdong, and Guangdong; and all private sale of Jianzhou's powder tea was prohibited.
143. See *SS* 184/4502–4505, and Chapter Six below.

5. AUTONOMY, RISK REDUCTION, AND ENTREPRENEURIAL EXPANSION

1. Thompson, p. 28.
2. Thompson, p. 36.
3. Thompson, p. 38.
4. Lewis, p. 9.
5. Lewis, pp. 18–21.
6. Thompson, pp. 30–31.
7. *XCB* 334/12b, 365/23b–24a.
8. See Smith, "State Power," for a comparison of the levels of autonomy granted the TMA and the more tightly centralized Ever-Normal Granaries.
9. *SHY* zhiguan 43/48a–b.
10. *SHY* zhiguan 43/49a–b.
11. *SHY* zhiguan 43/50b; *XCB* 284/12b.
12. *SHY* zhiguan 43/62a.
13. *SHY* zhiguan 43/62b–63a, 70b–71a; *SHY* shihuo 30/22a; *XCB* 334/12b–13b.
14. *XCB* 282/16a; *Quan Shu yiwen zhi* 53/4a–b; 55/4a–b. In 1078 Li Ji obtained the right to co-select the prefect and vice-prefect of Pengzhou and Hanzhou, where Lü Tao and Zhou Biaoquan had served: *SHY* shihuo 30/15a.
15. *SHY* shihuo 30/13a, 13b–14a; *XCB* 285/9b–10a.
16. *SHY* zhiguan 43/50b; *SHY* shihuo 30/15a; *XCB* 294/6a–b.

17. *XCB* 341/7a–b.
18. See Hua Shan, pp. 51–54; and Smith, "Interest Groups."
19. *SHY* shihuo 30/14a–b.
20. *SHY* zhiguan 43/61a; *XCB* 334/23a.
21. *SHY* zhiguan 43/61b–62a.
22. *SHY* zhiguan 43/53b–56b, 59a.
23. *SHY* zhiguan 43/50b–51b. Li Ji suggested what he termed a median price (*zhongjia*).
24. *SHY* zhiguan 43/63a–b.
25. *SHY* zhiguan 43/69a.
26. I can account for the following supervisory offices created by the New Policies Intendancy:

Office	Number Created
Managing supervisors[a]	7
Managing secretaries[a]	2
Tea-transport relay-station inspectors[b]	6
Tea-purchase and convoy market inspectors[c]	10
Tea-sales market inspectors[d]	11

Sources: [a]*SHY* zhiguan 43/65–66a; [b]*SHY* shihuo 30/25b and, by analogy, 26b–27a for the year 1094; [c]*SHY* xuanju 28/14a; [d]*SHY* shihuo 30/17a–b.

27. Subordinate functionaries include an indeterminate number of clerks (*li*) and scribes and/or bookkeepers (*tiesi jundian*): *SHY* shihuo 30/21a. In addition the TMA employed a large number of servitors major and minor (*daxiao shichen*)—lower-division members of the military bureaucracy whose job assignments took them back and forth between the civil service (often as service agents, *jiandang*) and the army. One hundred servitors were deployed in 36 markets of Western Shaanxi as of 1078: *SHY* zhiguan 43/52a. There is no information on how many of these officials were added during the Yuanfeng growth phase, when 332 markets were opened in Shaanxi.

    Servitors also played a central role in the transport of tea and the convoying of horses. For good descriptions of their role in the Song civil service, see Lo, *Introduction to the Civil Service*, pp. 62–67, 137–140; and Umehara Kaoru, *Sōdai kanryō seido kenkyū*, pp. 105–120.

28. Each purchase market had, in general, a stock controller (*zhuandian*), warehouse man (*kuzi*), scale man (*chengzi*—or warehouse-cum-scale man—*kucheng*), and scribe (*dianli*): *SHY* shihuo 30/19b–22b. At 47 markets by around mid 1083 (*XCB* 334/31b) the full roster would come to 188 men. Each market would also have hired an average of five brokers.

29. Su Che, *Luancheng ji* 36/8b.

30. For example, the Southern Song THA had to fight to keep its managing supervisors, and indeed only retained three to four: *SHY* zhiguan 43/110a. In 1107 Pang Yinsun had to fight to save two out of six supervisory posts that the court wanted to abolish; but by arguing that they were paid for out of THA receipts and not central government funds, he won his point: *SHY* zhiguan 43/89b–90a.

31. For the gradual decentralization of recommendation and sponsorship procedures during the course of the eleventh century, see Kracke, *Civil Service,* pp. 137–185.

32. *XCB* 284/5b–6a.

33. *SHY* zhiguan 43/50a; *XCB* 284/12a.

34. In 1078 the Intendants were given the right to sponsor for appointment (*ju*) ten Servitors of the Three Echelons (*sanban shichen*) yearly for three years, after which the number was to decline: *SHY* zhiguan 43/52a; *SHY* xuanju 28/12a. In 1080 the three active Intendants (Li Ji, Pu Zongmin, and Lu Shimin) were given combined selection rights to four administrative-class officials, two county magistrates, and promotion rights for two military officials; but the quotas were to decrease by one-third each year: *SHY* zhiguan 43/53a. On the phenomenon of sponsorship during the Song, see Kracke, *Civil Service,* esp. ch. 6; and Lo, *Introduction to the Civil Service,* pp. 191–199.

35. See *WXTK* 38/361b–c. Ma Duanlin's summary says that "abolishing the right of the various agencies to make recommendations and transfer of selection procedures to the Ministry of Personnel was implemented during the Xining era (1068–1077)." The *WXTK* entry is copied in its entirety into the *SHY* xuanju 28/9b–10a, suggesting a gap in the original material. Under the Yuanfeng reforms of the administrative structure (i.e., the return to the Tang system of the Six Boards and the Three Ministries), the Ministry of Personnel (*libu*) absorbed all the personnel functions that had previously been distributed to the Bureau of Executory Personnel (*liuneiquan*) and the Bureau of Evaluations (*shenguanyuan*) See Miyazaki Ichisada, "Sōdai kansei josetsu," pp. 16–22; and Lo, *Introduction to the Civil Service,* pp. 70–78.

36. *SS* 167/3969. No other circuit office described in this chapter of *SS* is so characterized.

37. The three terms are variants for the same office. On the managing supervisors of the Finance Commission, see Sudō Yoshiyuki, "Hoku Sō ni ikeru sanshi no kohai," in his *Sōdaishi kenkyū,* pp. 63–65.

38. The fullest lists of Northern Song managing supervisors are found in the bonus and promotion edicts of 1111 (*SHY* zhiguan 43/92b–93a), 1122 (ibid., 101b–102a), and 1123 (ibid., 102a–b). For Southern Song, see *SHY* zhiguan 43/107b, 110a, 113b; *SHY* bing 23/9a–b. The Southern Song supervisors were located in Chengdufu, Xingyuanfu, and Suiningfu, with a special supervisor for the Danchang horse market.

39. *SHY* shihuo 30/17b. In order to facilitate their travel, the supervisors could

ride post-horses *(dima)* and pay for their needs with relay-system travel vouchers *(yiquan)*: *SHY* zhiguan 43/49a.

40. In 1080 the Office of Buildings and Works was ordered to strike five copper seals with the designated inscription: *SHY* zhiguan 43/56b. On the fiscal supervisor, see Lo, "Circuits and Circuit Intendants," p. 82.

41. *XCB* 258/5a.

42. Two of the first three managing supervisors appointed, Sun Aobian and Zhang Chang, had been executory-class civil aides and the third, Duan Xian, a lower-division military official: *SHY* zhiguan 43/48b, 49a. Six out of eight managing supervisors and secretaries given promotions in 1105 were of the executory class: *SHY* zhiguan 43/83a–b.

43. Kracke, *Civil Service,* pp. 50, 88; *SS* 167/3983; *SHY* zhiguan 48/138a–147a for the late twelfth century. Yuki Tōru estimates that at least 2,500 inspectors were employed at the height of the Northern Song: "Hoku Sō jidai no seiji ni okeru kantōkan no haichi jōtai ni tsuite," *Tōyōshi kenkyū* 23.2:167. As a low-level position in the regular civil service, the post was generally given towards the end of a man's career in the executory class. See *SS* 169/4041.

44. *SHY* shihuo 30/23b; *XCB* 341/14a. The market sites are not named, but were probably concentrated in Yazhou, Xingyuan, Yangzhou, with at least one or two in Jinzhou, and Yongkangjun and Pengzhou.

45. These were the major tea-producing prefectures outside of Yazhou and Xingyuanfu. Yongkangjun produced 1,580,000 *jin* in 1074; 1,410,000 *jin* in 1075; and 1,360,000 *jin* in 1076: Lü Tao, *Jingde ji* 1/7b. On the role of the market inspectors in the Pengkou tea riot of 1077, see *Jingde ji* 1/19a–22b; 11/1a–3b.

46. *SHY* shihuo 30/15b, 19a–b. The interaction between the market inspector and the cultivator is taken up further in Chapter Six.

47. *SHY* shihuo 30/15b, 31a–b.

48. *SHY* shihuo 30/17a–b, 20a.

49. *SHY* shihuo 30/17b, 19b; *SHY* zhiguan 43/63b–64a. An additional two were added in Huangzhou (Qinghai, Leduxian) in 1103 to capitalize on the invasion of the core Qingtang cities. Intendant Cheng Zhishao observed that Huangzhou was right on the herding route for the Qingtang breeders and that foreign traders moved through the city freely. He added that "the Tibetan tribes rely on the tea and horse [trade] for their existence" and called for the selection of two market inspectors, one of whom would concurrently manage the horse market: *SHY* zhiguan 43/78b–79a. The TMA also provided incentives to, but did not necessarily appoint, three to five inspectors of government warehouses in Lizhou, Fengzhou, Xingzhou's Changjuxian, and Yangzhou's Xixiang on the routes linking the tea production and sales regions: *SHY* zhiguan 43/97a–b, 98a–b, 98b–99a; *SHY* bing 22/25a–b.

50. Lu Shimin's 38-article amendments to the revised regulations of the tea market agency of mid 1083 (*SHY* shihuo 30/18b–22b) discuss service personnel at pp. 19b, 20a, 20b, 21a, and 22a.

51. Lu Shimin addressed the hiring of brokers in his 38 amendments of 1083: "Each tea-purchase market will estimate the complexity of its affairs and summon and hire [an appropriate number of] men possessing material assets and guarantors [to serve] as brokers. These will take in, buy, and arrange to despatch convoy tea, for which they will be paid a broker's fee according to local custom and also take in and buy retail tea [for which they will be paid at the same rate]. The broker's fee will be withheld from the tea-price [paid to the cultivator] . . . and the fees paid out equally to all the brokers": *SHY* shihuo 30/21a. The reference to "local custom" *(xiangli)* implies that brokers' fees could vary.

    From Lü Tao we know also that the brokers put up part of their assets as collateral, which was kept in the offices of the local government; that in Pengkou the broker's fee amounted to 6 percent of the tea-purchase price, deducted from the cultivators' profit; and that at the height of the season the Pengkou market employed twelve agents. Brokers also guaranteed and collected the off-season loans made to cultivators by the TMA, and acted as its agents in the local commodity trade. See *Jingde ji* 1/16b, 19b; 3/2a; 11/2b. Miyazawa Tomoyuki interprets the use of collateral as similar to the *hangyi* payments made by guild merchants to the government: "Sōdai no gajin," *Tōyōshi kenkyū* 39.1:3–6.

52. Brokers are not included among the beneficiaries of the incentive system in the formal regulations, but Liu Zhi (*XCB* 366/3a), Lü Tao (*Jingde ji* 3/2a, 5b), and Su Che (*Luancheng ji* 36/6b) charge plausibly that they were. Service personnel and brokers were also involved in the Shaanxi sales markets, although their statutory role is unclear. The use of brokers in the horse trade is taken up in Chapter Seven.

53. *XCB* 258a; *SHY* zhiguan 43/48b–49a. See Kracke, *Civil Service*, pp. 174–175; *SS* 159/3722. Central government approval of recommendations made in the field was standard even under the "new law for distant offices," which would simply have allowed officers already in Sichuan to apply for and go directly to their new posts.

54. *SHY* zhiguan 43/40b.

55. For various examples, see *SHY* xuanju 28/10b–12a.

56. In 1077, for example, a ruling from the Secretariat-Chancellery stated that despite irregular authorization, executory class officials could not be appointed beyond their seniority ranks to such posts as county magistrate: *SHY* xuanju. In 1125 the THA was refused a request to appoint an administrative-class man (8B) to the post of vice-prefect of Xingyuanfu, on the grounds that the designate's seniority entitled him to a first post as county magistrate but

not to a vice-prefect's post, despite the irregular authorization: *SHY* zhiguan 43/103a–b. Zhang Hui also waged and lost a battle to have seniority specifications for county magistrates waived in 1113, even though eight-circuit and Ministry of Personnel regulations stated that "if no properly ranked man is available, it is permitted to contravene regulations *(poge)* in making appointments": *SHY* zhiguan 43/98a. On *poge* (irregular) appointments, see Lo, *Introduction to the Civil Service,* pp. 126–130.

57. See examples at *SHY* xuanju; *SHY* shihuo 30/20b, 27a.
58. The estimate is by Shangguan Jun, who complained that, in circumventing this waiting period, the eight-circuit provisions gave men coming under its jurisdiction an unequal advantage: *SS* 159/3723.
59. *SHY* xuanju 28/11b; *XCB* 285/1a.
60. A review of the entries in *SHY* xuanju 28 covering the New Policies era shows just one instance after 1077 of an agency other than the TMA enjoying the right: in 1078/6/7 Huang Lian, as Investigatory Pacification Commissioner in Jingdong Circuit (Shandong) was given the privilege in order to make emergency appointments in counties suffering from severe flooding.
61. *SHY* shihuo 30/17b. The circuit tax quota of 337,448 strings comes from *SHY* shihuo 15/17b–20a, as compiled by Katō Shigeshi, *Zhongguo jingjishi kaozheng,* p. 644.
62. *SHY* zhiguan 43/63b–64a; *XCB* 340/12b; *XCB* 334/13b.
63. *SHY* zhiguan 43/65a–66a; *XCB* 341/2a–b.
64. *SHY* shihuo 30/23b; *XCB* 341/14a; *SHY* xuanju 28/28a.
65. *SHY* zhiguan 43/88b–89a, 102b–103a.
66. *SHY* shihuo 30/30a–b.
67. In 1124 Intendant Wang Fan was given the right to irregular appointment once for each vacancy as it came up: *SHY* zhiguan 43/102b–103a.
68. *Libu tiaofa,* in *Yongle dadian* 14625/3a.
69. Ibid., 6b. In 1181 the Governor-General was ordered to follow regulations in the appointment of administrators for stockades and walled towns.
70. For example, I have identified 37 managing supervisors and managing secretaries from the Northern Song TMA. Of these, two are Sichuanese: Cheng Dunlin (*SHY* zhiguan 43/102a; *XNYL* 166/5315; *Songren chuanji ziliao suoyin* (4/3046–3047); and He Lun (*SHY* zhiguan 43/103b). Three men, although not natives, had long association with the region: Lu Shimin, Chao Gongyu (*SHY* zhiguan 43/102b; *Songren chuanji* 3/1949); and Duan Xian (*SHY* zhiguan 43/49a). But nothing is known about the native places of the remaining 32 men.
71. *SHY* shihuo 30/31a–b.
72. *SHY* zhiguan 43/98b–99a, specifically reinvoked in 1168; *SHY* bing 23/2b–3a.
73. *SHY* zhiguan 43/99a–b.

74. *SHY* zhiguan 43/102b–103a. A similar rule prohibited Sichuanese from filling both the administrator's and vice-administrator's post of a prefecture at the same time: *Libu tiaofa*, in *Yongle dadian* 14620/4a–b.

75. Ihara Hiroshi presents abundant evidence of the many Sichuanese who served as local officials in Sichuan in "Nan Sō Shisen ni okeru teikyo shihin—Seitofuro Shishuro o chūshin to shite," *Tōhōgaku* 54:47–62. Further support is provided by the material in Fei Zhu's "Shizu pu." In addition a broad but non-systematic perusal of extant Ming prefectural gazetteers for Sichuan suggests that during the Southern Song Sichuanese routinely served as county magistrates in the province and often as prefects.

76. See Thompson, pp. 33–34; Lewis, p. 20.

77. *SHY* shihuo 30/20a; *SHY* zhiguan 43/93b.

78. *SHY* shihuo 30/21a–b. Tea transport is taken up in Chapter Seven.

79. See Intendant Zhang Hui's argument of 1113 at *SHY* zhiguan 43/97a–b.

80. *SHY* shihuo 30/15a; counties interpolated from *SHY* zhiguan 43/53a.

81. *SHY* zhiguan 43/53a.

82. Incentives for the Mingshan county magistrate are discussed below.

83. *SHY* zhiguan 43/71a–b. For Restoration antipathy to the eight-circuit laws, see *SS* 159/3723.

84. *SHY* zhiguan 43/93b.

85. The court allowed one year off the waiting period before the promotional case review rather than Zhang's two, and the right to petition for a next assignment close to home: *SHY* zhiguan 43/97a–b, 98b–99a.

86. *SHY* zhiguan 43/100b–101a. The producing counties were Mingshan, Yongkang, and Qingcheng; the transport counties were Miangu, Shenzheng, Yizheng, Zhaohua, Deyang, Luo, and Changju. See Map 8 in Chapter Seven.

87. *SHY* zhiguan 43/105a–b.

88. *SHY* bing 23/2b–3b. The two new counties were Jiangli and Fujin, on the road to the Danchang and Fengtie markets. The Finance Ministry quoted in its own memorial excerpts from the ruling of 1113 granting Zhang Hui incentive rights to the seven transport counties; but this appears to have been for reference only and did not, apparently, grant the 1168 THA the same rights. Mingshan is included by association: the chief supervisor of the administrative unit containing a THA market received half the bonus of the market inspector (*SHY* shihuo 31/15b), and Mingshan was the THA's chief market. See *SHY* zhiguan 59/21a–b; *SHY* shihuo 31/27b. There is no evidence that the THA lost its rights to the three counties of Xixiang, Changju, and Shunzheng, although in a fluid political environment such negative evidence is by no means conclusive.

89. See, for example, Lü Tao, *Jingde ji* 3/2a–b, 5b; and Su Che, *Luancheng ji* 36/6b.

90. Sichuanese salt laws are reviewed in *SS* 183/4471–4476 and *WXTK* 15/155a–

b. See also Jia Daquan, pp. 128–157. For a study of the impact of New Policies state activism on the salt industry of Luzhou, see von Glahn, *Country of Streams and Grottoes*, ch. 3. I trace the relationship between salt and demographic redistribution in Sichuan in "Commerce, Agriculture, and Core Formation," pp. 52–57.

91. Wen Tong, "Zou wei qi chai jingchaoguan zhi Jingyan xianshi," *Danyuan ji* 34/256–257. For a translation, see von Glahn, *Country of Streams and Grottoes*, pp. 75–76.

92. Statistics compiled from *WXTK* 15/155a.

93. *SS* 183/4472–4473.

94. *XCB* 255/8b–9b; *SS* 183/4474.

95. *XCB* 263/22b, 274/10b–11a; *SHY* shihuo 24/9a–b; *SHY* shihuo 30/13a. The original units were 100,000 mats *(xi)* of salt for 60,000 bales *(tuo)* of tea. Production figures for Jiezhou salt are conveniently tabulated in Guo Zhengzhong, "Songdai Jiechi yanchan kaoxi," in Deng Guangming and Li Jiaju, eds., *Songshi yanjiu lunwen ji*, p. 83.

96. Lü Tao, *Jingde ji* 4/15a–16b; *XCB* 279/7b–8a. Fiscal Supervisor Duan Jie had wanted to include Zizhou Circuit in the order; but the circuit Fiscal Intendant fended off this move, arguing that it would disrupt revenues for circuit administration.

97. Wen estimated demand at about 3,000 catties of salt daily for 240,000 individuals (or 4.56 catties per person annually), and complained that not a single shipment of salt had arrived since the monopoly began: *SHY* shihuo 24/10a–11a.

98. *SHY* shihuo 24/11a–12a; *XCB* 279/7b–8a.

99. *XCB* 281/8b; *XCB* 283/9b; *SS* 181/4420–4423.

100. *SHY* shihuo 24/16b–17a; *XCB* 290/6a.

101. *XCB* 334/13a–b; *SHY* shihuo 30/18b–22b passim.

102. *XCB* 340/12b. At the 1076 prices of 250 cash per catty in Chengdu, the 13,000 mats would have yielded a gross return of 378,625 strings, worth about 95,000 strings of cash net at a 25 percent return. But there is no way of confirming whether this was the range Lu Shimin had in mind.

103. Ultimately the TMA's involvement in the Jiezhou salt trade was severed because of competing government interests rather than principle. By 1086 and the onset of the Restoration, western Sichuan had become saturated with salt, since in addition to the TMA's Jiezhou salt, small-well salt from Zizhou and Kuizhou Circuits had begun to flow westward again, although Chengdu's lofty-pipe wells were still banned. Both sources jeopardized the ability of the regional financial administration to dispose of the salt produced for it at its well in Pujiang, County, Qiongzhou. Because Pujiang salt could be sold for 120 cash per catty, compared to 70 to 80 cash for salt from the east, officials had begun forcing it on consumers. Huang Lian, the

Restoration investigator who became the first TMA Intendant after the New Policies, decided to preserve the Pujiang monopoly against all competitors, by cutting the price of its salt on the one hand, but prohibiting both small-well and government-imposed salt from entering the region on the other. Although there was no general pronouncement, this appears to have severed the TMA's involvement in the Jiezhou salt trade. The lofty-pipe well proscription was lifted in 1089 as a result of Lü Tao's prodding; and by 1105 all of Sichuan's salt could circulate freely in the west, although it could not be exported to regions designated for Jiezhou salt. See *XCB* 369/13a–b; *XCB* 381/23a; *XCB* 421/11a–b; *WHTK* 16/162c.

104. The placards read *Wuling maimai tongkuai; wuzhi fangzhi qianben,* as reported in 1077 by Lü Tao, *Jingde ji* 1/12a.
105. *SS* 184/4498
106. Lü Tao, *Jingde ji* 3/4a.
107. *XCB* 334/13a.
108. *SHY* shihuo 30/21a.
109. Lü Tao, *Jingde ji* 3/4a; Su Che, *Luancheng ji* 36/7b–8a.
110. Lü Tao, *Jingde ji* 3/4b; Su Che, *Luancheng ji* 36/7b–8a.
111. *SHY* shihuo 30/19a.
112. Liu Zhi, *Zhongsu ji* 5/13a.
113. Lü Tao, *Jingde ji* 3/3b; Su Che, *Luancheng ji* 36/7a–b.
114. Lü Tao, *Jingde ji* 3/7a–b.
115. *XCB* 384/18b. Huang Lian is not mentioned by name in the entry.
116. *SHY* zhiguan 43/92a–b: both Liizhou and Yazhou had barter and exchange markets from 1102 to 1106 and then again in 1111. See *XNYL* 167/5326 for their reestablishment in 1154.
117. Fei Zhu, "Shujin pu," *Quan Shu yiwen zhi* 56 xia 1b.
118. Ibid., p. 2b, which lists the varieties of silk cloths produced for each horse market.
119. In 1171 the THA accused the Chengdu fiscal intendant of attempting to suborn the Agency's loom households into weaving 1,000 bolts of silk for it while the THA chief was at the Qin Branch horse markets. The THA got the court to agree that other agencies requiring its silk must send in an order and the appropriate funds, and then wait for the goods to be woven and sent to them: *SHY* zhiguan 43/113a–b. Around this same time Yuan Xingzong observed that because of peculation by the clerks and brocade-weaving households, although the Agency paid for top quality brocade, most of what it received was of medium grade, with the difference going to the clerks and producers: *Jiuhua ji* 7/5a.
120. See, for example, *SHY* zhiguan 43/108b–109a.
121. C. K. Yang, "Some Characteristics of Chinese Bureaucratic Behavior," in David Nivison and Arthur Wright, eds., *Confucianism in Action,* p. 157;

Thomas A. Metzger, *The Internal Organization of the Ch'ing Bureaucracy,* esp. pp. 235–417.

122. Metzger, pp. 34–35, 74–80.
123. Wang Anshi, *Wang Lichuan quanji* 39/222, 226.
124. *SHY* zhiguan 43/51b.
125. *SHY* zhiguan 43/97a–b.
126. *SHY* zhiguan 43/115a–116a.
127. Lü Tao, *Jingde ji* 3/5a–b; Su Che, *Luancheng ji* 36/8a.
128. *SHY* zhiguan 43/76b–77a. The incentive system followed the profitability of the trade. A catty of Mingshan tea could be priced for the horse trade at 769 cash in Qinzhou, but only 30 cash in Liizhou: *SHY* zhiguan 43/80a–b. A similar problem cost the THA its selection rights to the two inspectors of the Xingyuanfu commercial tax and concurrent tea-contract market in 1182. The prefect complained that the two officials "regard tea as important and casually disregard tax-bureau affairs. Moreover those who are [selected] by the tea agency must stick with it in order to climb. [As a result] Xingyuan has become a dependent appendage *(shubu)* [of the THA]. And who dares question this?" *SHY* zhiguan 48/138a–b. Implicit in the problem is the role of incentives in channeling official activity.
129. *SHY* shihuo 30/39b. The price of tea in relation to horses roughly doubled in the three decades from 1080 to 1111, from 100 catties per head to 200 catties per head (see Chapter Seven). We have no information on the retail price of tea in Sichuan at this time, however. But government over-printing of Sichuan's paper money between 1102 and 1107 had devalued the region's money supply (and created a crisis of confidence in the paper notes), and this would have raised prices generally. On the paper inflation, see *CYZJ* jia 16/519–521; *SS* 181/4404.
130. *Songdai Shuwen jicun* 54/3b.
131. *XCB* 341/7a–b.
132. For example, in 1080 (*SHY* shihuo 30/16b); 1105 (*SHY* zhiguan 43/83a–b); 1111 (ibid., 92b–93a); 1116 (ibid., 99b–100a); 1122 (ibid., 101b–102a); and 1123, but without the intendants (ibid., 102a–b).
133. The shared rewards for inspectors and service personnel gave 2 percent of the extra-quota profits to the inspector, and 3 percent to the assorted service personnel: *SHY* shihuo 30/19b. Shared penalties began at deficits of 5 percent, as follows: At 5 percent the inspector would be fined half a month's salary (i.e., between 6 and 12.5 strings of cash, assuming the inspector is an official of the executory class) and the service personnel given 40 strokes with the light rod. At a deficit of 10 percent the inspector was liable for 20 strokes of the light rod and the service personnel 60 strokes of the heavy rod. The penalties increased by two degrees for each subsequent deficit of 10 percent (i.e., 2 x 10 strikes for beatings, 2 x 6 months for incarcerations,

and 2 x 500 *li* for deportations), up to a maximum deficit of 30 percent. The managing supervisor, who was in charge of a cluster of markets, was fined one degree less severely than the rate for inspectors, according to the total average deficit for all the markets in his jurisdiction. Therefore it was up to the managing supervisor to spur the inspectors under him into at least meeting their net profit quotas and up to the inspectors to drive their service personnel into generating profits beyond the quota.

134. *SHY* shihuo 30/20a. Late in 1083 Lu Shimin claimed that the practice had been stopped, but it was in effect again from at least 1101 and remained standard through the twelfth century: *XCB* 341/7a; *SHY* zhiguan 43/76b–77a; *SHY* shihuo 31/15b. On the role of the local officials Lu's 1083 amendments specify that "in all prefectures and commanderies that buy and sell tea, the prefect and vice-prefect will act as co-supervisors. In prefectures that are the site of the yamen of a military affairs commissioner, the vice-prefect will co-supervise. In prefectures with a tea market the surveillance director *(dujian)* will supervise. And in counties with a tea market the magistrate will co-supervise": *SHY* shihuo 30/20a. Thus local government officials had umbrella authority over, and responsibility for, all tea markets; and direct responsibility over those tea markets that were placed in a seat of local government.

135. Lü Tao, *Jingde ji* 3/5b; Su Che, *Luancheng ji* 36/6b.

136. Kracke, *Civil Service,* pp. 81–82.

137. Zhu Yu, *Pingzhou ketan,* zhuan 3, quoted in Saeki Tomi, 65ōdai chahō, p. 545.

138. *XCB* 303/14b–15a; 334/13b.

139. For clear technical discussions of these terms, see Lo, *Introduction to the Civil Service,* and Umehara, *Sōdai kanryō seido.*

140. See *SS* 169/4023–4038. See also Umehara Kaoru, *Sōdai kanryō seido,* pp. 37–80; Miyazaki Ichisada, "Sōdai kansei josetsu," pp. 40–53, esp. the table on p. 44.

141. Computed from Kinugawa Tsuyoshi, *Songdai wenguan fengji zhidu,* Table 5, pp. 34–37. Lo notes that the salary schedule varied not by grade but by groups of grades, which he analyses in *Introduction to the Civil Service,* pp. 159–162.

142. Pu Zongmin was a *zhuzuo zuolang* (8B) when appointed Co-Intendant in 1074 (a very low rank for a man who had been *jinshi* in 1053 and considered for Prefect of Xingyuanfu); sometime before 1083/11 he was promoted to *chaoqinglang* (7A), and was then promoted again to *duguan langzhong,* one of a category of offices that denoted rank 6B. See *SS* 168/3993; *XCB* 341/4b. With each promotion Pu's functional office remained the same.

143. See the class promotions of 1111, 1116, and 1122, listed in n. 132 above. Note that in 1122 two of the four Intendants, Guo Si and He Jian, were

denied promotions on the grounds that "the succession of months and days is not great, and thus we do not again offer recognition": *SHY* zhiguan 43/101b. Because He had been in office since before 1021/4, and Guo (as far as I can determine) since before 1113, I interpret the denial to refer to the men's stipendiary, and not functional, office. For career sources, see Appendix C.

144. For instance, in 1080 Li Ji memorialized that his managing supervisors "are on the road day and night accomplishing things of great merit but have not as yet received imperial recognition"—even though promotions had been ordered for them in 1079 and earlier in 1080. See *SHY* shihuo 30/16b, 17b. On receiving Li's complaint the TMA was authorized to establish quota guidelines for evaluating the supervisors' performance.

145. *Songdai Shuwen jicun* 54/3b.

146. *SHY* bing 24/39a; *SHY* bing 25/41b.

147. Lü Tao, *Jingde ji* 3/6a; *SHY* zhiguan 59/21a–b; *SHY* shihuo 31/15b (1163), which repeats the 1083 provision that the managing official of an administrative unit with a tea market (in the case of Mingshan the county magistrate) would get half the promotion of the inspectors.

148. *SHY* zhiguan 59/21a–b. This 1162 entry documents an attempt to curtail the indiscriminate use of the automatic *gaiguan* promotion. In 1148 the Mingshan tea-and-tax market inspector Jia Zun, at the very bottom of the executory-class ladder of seven steps (a *digonglang*) and only in office four seasons, had achieved first-class status and was promoted into the administrative class. In 1162 the Executive of the Ministry of Personnel compared Jia's case with that of Wang Xiang, a man at the top of the executory ladder (*chengzhilang*) with six years seniority. Wang also achieved first-class purchases and issuance of convoy tea, and was properly promoted into the administrative class. But the Executive insisted that according to the Yuanfeng regulations Jia Zun's promotion had been improper, for he should only have been raised two seniority steps within the executory class. The Executive requested that henceforth only men with the appropriate standing be given the automatic *gaiguan* promotion.

149. On the procedure and its implications for a man's career, see Umehara Kaoru, *Sōdai kanryō seido*, pp. 250–258; Lo, *Introduction to the Civil Service*, pp. 165–170.

150. *WXTK* 38/441a; Lo, *Introduction to the Civil Service*, Table 2, p. 28.

151. *WXTK* 38/363b–c; Kracke, *Civil Service*, pp. 89, 118–125.

152. *SHY* zhiguan 43/65a–66a.

153. *SHY* zhiguan 43/83b.

154. *SHY* zhiguan 49/21a–b.

155. On the *mokan* review, see Lo, *Introduction to the Civil Service*, pp. 151–158.

156. For the *mokan* schedules, see *SS* 169/4042. Kracke estimates the range of

time required from first entry to promotion into the administrative class as between six and ten years: *Civil Service,* p. 89. In 1105, the only year for which information is supplied, four out of eight of the managing supervisors and secretaries rewarded for meritorious tea-transport service were at the bottom, entry level (*jiangshilang,* changed ca. 1111 to *digonglang*) of the civil service. One of these men had his *mokan* review pushed up three years: *SHY* zhiguan 43/83a–b.

157. *SHY* shihuo 30/15b; *XCB* 290/6b; *SS* 184/4499. The number of years is unspecified. The top class was revised downward to 1,000,000 jin by 1085, according to Lü Tao, *Jingde ji* 3/6a.

158. *SHY* shihuo 30/18a, 19b.

159. Liu Zhi, *Zhongsu ji* 5/14a; *XCB* 366/3a.

160. In 1097, for example, it was decided that in a market district served by two inspectors, the net monetary returns would be split down the middle to determine the bonuses for each man, with a limit to the *mokan* reduction of three years: *XCB* 493/10b.

161. *SHY* zhiguan 43/83a–b, 92b–93a, 99b–100a, 101b–102a, 102a–b; *SHY* shihuo 30/16b.

162. *SHY* zhiguan 43/105b–106a (1144); *SHY* bing 23/15a (1179).

163. *SHY* bing 25/41b (1173). Pp. 41b–48b contain a variety of reward schedules for different participants in the horse convoys. These are analysed further in Chapter Seven.

164. *SS* 169/4040–4041.

165. For example, a man in the lowest grade, grade 7 (*bansibuwei*), who had completed one term and had one seniority grade, could be promoted up to grade 6 (*zhilinglu*); a man with two terms to his credit could skip grade 6 and go directly to grade 5 (*linglu*): *SS* 169/4040. Conferral of seniority grades would give a man who had served, say, for one term, the seniority of a man who had served two.

166. *SHY* zhiguan 43/83a–b.

167. *SHY* zhiguan 43/99b–100a.

168. See *SS* 169/4041 (*xunzi*).

169. *SHY* zhiguan 43/83a–b. The option was obligatory in the case of "clerks who have no seniority [beyond which] they can be promoted"—i.e., hired commoners. Silk bonuses for the four schedules from 1105 to 1122 ranged from a low of 5 lengths for third class achievement to a high of 20 lengths for first class (in 1105) or premier class (1116) achievement. In 1122 the range was only 5 to 8 lengths: *SHY* zhiguan 43/83b, 93a, 100a, 102a.

170. *SHY* bing 25/42a–b. See also Chapter Seven

171. Amitai Etzioni, *A Comparative Analysis of Complex Organizations,* p. 256.

172. *SHY* shihuo 30/16a–b.

173. *SHY* shihuo 30/18a; *XCB* 330/12b.

174. See Kinugawa Tsuyoshi, *Songdai wenguan,* Table 5, pp. 34–38.
175. *SHY* shihuo 30/19b.
176. *SHY* shihuo 30/19b, 22a. By these figures, the stock controller, his assistant, and the bookeeper, warehouseman, and scale man each earned 600 cash for every 100 strings in net profits generated by their market, a sum surely large enough to inspire profit gouging.
177. *SHY* shihuo 30/20a. I am assuming that in the New Policies era, when market inspectors were rewarded with cash, the local government agent also received cash, although this is partly supposition. That money flowed to the county magistrates and vice-administrators as a result of TMA profit-seeking is irrefutable, however. Lü Tao, for example, charged that "these days [the vice-prefect and the county magistrate] both reckon on the amount of tea sales, and divide the profits equally with the brokers": *Jingde ji* 3/5b–6a. But whether this was embezzlement or part of the TMA strategy is not clear.
178. *SHY* shihuo 30/20a. In the event of a net deficit the supervising official and stock controller were equally responsible for making up the losses. Moreover, the official was not permitted to leave his post, even if his term had ended and his replacement arrived, until the shortage had been made up. I have taken *zhuandian,* stock controller, to refer to all the service personnel.
179. Comment by George Schultz to James Reston, *New York Times,* May 25, 1983.
180. Liu Zhi claimed that "the least [bonus] was not [under] a few thousand strings of cash": *Zhongsu ji* 5/14a. See also Lü Tao, *Jingde ji* 3/4a–b, on brokers and officials cornering the trade in local commodities; 5a, on TMA officials "terrorizing" tax officials into complicity in counting taxes paid on tea (which would go to the Fiscal Intendant's office) as profits of the sale on tea (which went into TMA accounts); and 5b–6a on brokers, prefectural vice-administrators, and county magistrates splitting profits. The charges are all seconded by Su Che, *Luancheng ji* 36/5a–10b.
181. *XCB* 334/13b.
182. Lü Tao estimated that if the monopsony in Sichuan were replaced with the taxation of free trade, the government could earn 600,000 strings yearly from Sichuan alone: *Jingde ji* 3/9b–10a. In connection with other reports showing the profits from the Shaanxi enterprise to be between 750,000 and 1,000,000 strings, Lü's figures can serve as an estimate of the value of the Sichuan monopsony as well. See also *SHY* shihuo 30/15b–16a, 17b; *XCB* 334/12b. Five percent of 600,000 would have gone to the market inspectors and service personnel, for 30,000 strings; 1 percent would have gone to the supervisory local officials, for 6,000 strings; and 2 percent of 1,000,000 strings would have gone to market inspectors in Shaanxi, for 20,000 strings,

for a total of 56,000 strings as the estimated upper limit for total yearly bonus costs to the TMA.

183. *SHY* shihuo 30/30a.

6. THE IMPACT OF BUREAUCRATIC POWER ON THE SICHUAN TEA ECONOMY

1. For a reinterpretation of charisma as "the ability of an actor to exercise diffuse and intense influence on the normative orientation of other actors" that "can be achieved in an office," see Etzioni, pp. 305–312.

2. For useful summaries of the Restoration and its participants, see Chen Bang-zhan, *Songshi jishi benmo* zhuan 43–45, pp. 411–442; and Higashi Ichio, *Ō Anseki jiten,* pp. 149–211.

3. Liu got the re-monopolization of Fujianese tea reversed in 1085/11:*XCB* 361/9b–10a. Liu and Su together got the state monopoly over water-milled tea in the capital abolished: *XCB* 370/3a–4a, 4a–5a, 5a–b, 20a. And Liu, Su, and Lü Tao forced the court's attention on the Sichuan monopoly.

4. For example, as late as the ninth month of 1085 Lu Shimin was granted concurrent control of Shaanxi Horse Purchases and Pastures and Sichuan Horse Purchases; he also retained power over the Sichuan-Shaanxi tea monopolies: *SHY* zhiguan 43/70a.

5. Su Che, *Luancheng ji* 36/5a, 9a; *XCB* 366/23b–29a.

6. *XCB* 369/13a–14b.

7. *XCB* 366/2a.

8. *XCB* 368/12a–b. Pu was demoted to Fiscal Vice-Intendant of Lizhou Circuit before being cashiered at Lü Tao's request in 1086/11:*XCB* 391/10a–b.

9. *XCB* 381/21a–b.

10. Lü Tao, *Jingde ji* 3/5b–7a, 8b–9a; Su Che, *Luancheng ji* 36/9a–b. The horse procurement side of the enterprise is taken up in Chapter Seven.

11. *XCB* 381/22a. Su and Lu, occupying an intermediate position, recommended that the government tax the free market in tea and use the proceeds to buy what tea it needed for the horse trade on the open market. Lü Tao *Jingde ji* 3/9b–10; Su Che, *Luancheng ji* 36/9a–b.

12. *XCB* 381/22a. Su Che requested in vain that another man be sent in immediately to continue the investigation, since Huang Lian could no longer be regarded as impartial: *Luancheng ji,* 37/14b–15a; *XCB* 378/16b.

13. *XCB* 381/22b.

14. *XCB* 381/22b–23a.

15. *SHY* zhiguan 43/71b–72a; *SHY* shihuo 30/26b–27a, 28a. By 1097 Lu had reestablished the entire "Yuanfeng system": *SHY* shihuo 30/29a–30a.

16. *SHY* shihuo 30/31b–32b; *SS* 184/4502; *XCB* shibu 20/22a–b. On Cai Jing's political career, see Xu Ziming, *Song zaifu biannianlu jiaobu,* zhuan 11–12.

17. *SS* 184/4503, 4505; *SHY* shihuo 30/38b. Sales and transit taxes were remitted to the Ministry of Finance, and profits from the sale of southern tea to guest merchants and sales of "saddlebag tea" *(tuocha)* were remitted to the use of the emperor. *SS* 184/4503 claims that 1,000,000 strings a year from the emperor's portion were lavished as "private emoluments" on Cai Jing's friends and followers.

18. *XCB* shibu 21/3a–b.

19. *SHY* shihuo 30/34b. Cheng admitted that prior to establishment of the Sichuan tea monopoly people in Eastern Shaanxi had consumed tea from the southeast, which should be considered their natural supplier.

20. *SHY* shihuo 32/1a–b (1113) cites the 1104 ruling.

21. In addition to greater Yongxing Circuit the THA also lost the eight eastern counties of Fengxiangfu, the capital of greater Qinfeng Circuit, retaining only the southwestern county of Baoji that served as the northern terminus for the Baoye Road and transshipment point for points west: *SHY* shihuo 32/1a–b; *SHY* fangyu 10/3b–4a.

22. That is a loss of 1,094,315 households (1080 census, Wang Cun, *Yuanfeng jiuyu zhi*), including Yongxingjun's three subcircuits, Fengxiangfu, Jingzhou, Weizhou, and Yuanzhou.

23. *SHY* shihuo 30/38a–39b.

24. Ibid. Some Sichuanese tea must have been brought up to Eastern Shaanxi, however, since article 37 of the 40 reform articles of 1112 permitted Sichuanese tea currently in the region to be sold out (ibid., 43b).

25. *SHY* shihuo 30/39b; *SS* 184/4504–4505.

26. *SHY* zhiguan 43/96a–b.

27. See for example *Jin shi* 49/1108–1109. An exception was made in 1164, when the Sichuan Zongling was ordered to use 1,000,000 strings of cash to buy dried ginger, plain silk, silk thread, hempen cloth, and manufactured tea for (Sichuanese) merchants for use in a government-run trade with the Jin. One reason for the policy was to circumvent smuggling: *SHY* shihuo 38/38b–39a, cited by Quan Hansheng, "Song-Jin jian de zouzi maoyi," in his *Zhongguo jingjishi luncong*, vol. 1, p. 217.

28. *SHY* shihuo 31/24b–25a. See also Chapter Seven.

29. Circuits, prefectures, and production quotas for the southeast are given in *SHY* shihuo 29/2a–5a.

30. For Hunanese smuggling laws, see *SHY* shihuo 31/3b–4b and the inquiry by Tea and Salt Intendant Jia Sicheng (made THA Intendant in 1143), dated 1142, on how to divide up bounties for informants; *XNYL* 177/4730–4731 on Hunanese smuggling to the Jin in 1157; and *SHY* zhiguan 48/134b–135a on improving smuggling control in Sichuan's Shizhou that was probably oriented towards Hunan.

31. Huang Lian had made minor adjustments in 1086, limiting government

purchases to the two prefectures of Yazhou and Xingyuanfu that supplied the horse trade. But even these changes were reversed by Lu Shimin after 1094, as he gradually reimposed the Yuanfeng monopoly-monopsony system. See *XCB* 381/22b–23a; *SHY* zhiguan 43/71b–72a; *SHY* shihuo 30/ 29a–30a.

32. Zhao Kai wove together a financing apparatus that included tea, salt, and wine monopolies; copper-cash currency notes; direct taxes on all textile production; and a "matching rice purchase" *(duidimi)* that doubled the amount of grain claimed by the government. To these were later added substantial surtaxes on all commercial transactions (the *jingzongzhi qian,* worth 5,400,000 strings) and on the payment of monopoly taxes and government rents (the *chengtiqian*). On these taxes, see *SS* 174/4222–4228 and *XNYL* 111/3516–3525. The fullest source on Zhao Kai is Li Tao's funerary inscription, "Zhao Daizhi Kai muzhiming," in *Songdai Shuwen jicun* 54/1a–8a. See also *XNYL* 18/742–743 and *SS* 374/11596–11597. On the office of General Supply Master, see Uchigawa Kyūhei, "Nan Sō sōryō kō," *Shichō* 78–79:1–26; and Guo Zongzheng, "Nan Song zhongyang caizheng huobi suishou kaoban," in Zhongguo shehuikexueyuan lishi yanjiusuo, comp., *Song-Liao-Jin shi luncong,* pp. 168–191.

33. The five drawbacks of the monopoly system in its own right and as a mechanism for buying horses were 1) the purchase of too many useless animals in Liizhou at a quota of 4,000 head per annum; 2) the exchange of tea for luxury goods by tea-market officials, who also tried to cheat the foreign horse merchants out of a fair price; 3) the high cost to the fiscal intendancy and Ever-Normal Granary system of capitalizing the monopoly; 4) the use of credit manipulation and forced "harmonious purchases" to obtain tea from cultivators at confiscatory prices, forcing producers to strip their trees for unpotable leaves that "accumulated like mountains along the side of the road"; and 5) the maintenance of high production quotas despite the loss of Shaanxi, making surpluses, forced sales, and the wasteful expenditure of funds for clothing and feeding the transport soldiers inevitable. See *Songdai Shuwen jicun* 54/2a–b.

34. *Songdai Shuwen jicun* 54/3a–b.

35. *XNYL* 108/3453. On Mingshan procurement, see *SHY* zhiguan 59/21a–b; *SHY* shihuo 31/27b–28a.

36. *CYZJ* jia 14/440 and *XNYL* 154/4883 note 20 markets for 9 prefectures of Chengdu Circuit, with an output of about 16,170,000 catties; and 3 markets for 2 prefectures of Lizhou Circuit with an output of 4,840,000 catties. Jin and Ba prefectures had apparently been dropped. Although the *XNYL* 154 notice is appended to an entry for 1145 as a point of information, the *CYZJ* entry begins with the heading "Now" *(jin)*—i.e., around 1202 when the book was presented. On this basis I date the 21,000,000 catties total to the

late rather than the mid twelfth century. *SHY* shihuo 31/32a–b (1195) notes 34 markets (none identified), which probably includes eastern Sichuan.

37. In 1137 Li Dai raised the price to 8 strings; in 1138 Zhang Shen raised it to 12.5 strings, lowered the next year by Zhao Kai in his second term to 9.5 strings. Feng Kangguo jacked the price up again to 11 strings in 1140, followed in 1144 by Jia Sicheng who increased the price to 12.3 strings. See *XNYL* 148/4667–4668.

38. *XNYL* 167/5326–5327.

39. At a total license and market-usage fee of 6.8 strings, 1,059,000 strings in revenues would be worth 15,573,529 catties (1,059,000 ÷ 6.8 × 100). Another 2,000,000 catties went to the horse markets.

40. At the very beginning of the enterprise, in 1074, Li Qi had been ordered by the Secretariat-Chancellery to investigate tea stocks in Dazhou and Fuzhou, Kuizhou Circuit, but nothing had come of the matter: *SHY* zhiguan 43/47b. In 1084 the fiscal staff supervisor of Kuizhou Circuit, Sung Gou (later THA Intendant), tried to monopolize the tea of Dazhou for licensed sales in Zizhou Circuit, but no decision was ever made: *XCB* 350/10a. In 1110 the THA attempted to monopolize a newly emergent tea industry in Zizhou Circuit, but the circuit fiscal intendant fended off the attempt with a request that the new industry be given several years to develop: *SHY* shihuo 30/37b. Then in 1122 the THA tried to duplicate Sung Gou's 1084 plan, but under its own auspices. It was instead permitted to claim Zizhou Circuit's consumers for the "Chuan tea-marketing zone," i.e., as part of its protected market; at the same time, the teas of Qu, He, and Lu prefectures and Changning Commandery in central and southern Sichuan were confined to purely local circulation: *SHY* shihuo 32/15a.

41. *SHY* zhiguan 43/106a–b. For a list of some of these offices, see Saeki Tomi, *Sōshi shokkanshi sakuin,* p. 141. Although the term *Sichuan* was used as early as 981 (see *XCB* 22/16a), I know of no office that was designated by the name until the Southern Song.

42. *CYZJ* jia 14/441–442; *SHY* shihuo 31/12b–14a (memorial by Wang Zhi-wang), which adds Guozhou and gives a date of 1154 for the contract markets.

43. *SHY* shihuo 31/13b–14a.

44. *XNYL* 184/6032. Tea in Zizhou Circuit was apparently also monopsony purchased. The practice was halted in 1157 (*XNYL* 176/5704–5705), although the TMA continued to *monopolize* the sale of Kuizhou tea in Zizhou Circuit until 1161, and to regulate the trade with licenses after that. Li Xinchuan lists the *shuinan* tea of Hezhou, in Zizhou Circuit, as one of Sichuan's few good teas by the end of the twelfth century, but notes that there was very little of it: *CYZJ* jia 14/441.

45. *SHY* zhiguan 43/111b–112 (1166). This was actually a reopening of a man-

aging supervisor's office first noted in 1150 (ibid., 107b). At some later point the tea licenses were revived, although this time market officials lubricated the trade with an extra 50 catties of free tea for every 100-catty license.

46. The practice had been in effect since the early Song (see *SS* 183/4484). In 1109 it was reported that in the southeastern markets merchants would only buy tea where there was a *haocha* bonus of 10 percent: *SHY* shihuo 30/36b.

47. This follows the explanation given by Zhang Zhen in 1156, which appears to be standard: *SHY* shihuo 31/11a–b. But in *XNYL* 156/4985–4986, Li Xinchuan refers to *haocha* as an exemption of 10 percent on the cultivator's quota.

48. *XNYL* 176/5704–5705; *SHY* shihuo 31/11a–b.

49. The committee was convened in response to a chorus of Sichuanese complaints unleashed by the death of Prime Minister Qin Gui, whose anti-Sichuanese stance had silenced opposition from the region's political elites. The critics were led by Zhang Zhen and Sun Daofu (see *SHY* shihuo 31/11a–b and *XNYL* 175/5665 respectively). Zhang has a short biography in *Sichuan tongzhi* 144/38b–39b. Both Zhang and Sun are represented in *Songdai Shuwen jicun,* zhuan 60 and 64 respectively. On the background, formation, and reports of the committee, see *SHY* shihuo 63/12a–14a.

50. *XNYL* 175/5664–5665; *SHY* shihuo 31/12b–14a. Much of the available information on taxation in Sichuan during the 1150s was provided by Wang Zhiwang during the roughly seven years (1156–1162) he served in the region. Many of his memorials on Sichuan are collected in his *Hanbin ji,* in particular zhuan 5 and 8–10.

51. *Huang Song zhongxing liangchao shengzheng* 55/3087.

52. *CYZJ* jia 14/440; *SHY* shihuo 31/251–b; *Huang Song zhongxing liangchao shengzheng* 55/2161–2162.

53. *SHY* shihuo 31/27b–28a; *CYZJ* jia 14/439–440.

54. *XNYL* 17/704; *CYZJ* jia 14/440; *SS* 184/4510.

55. For example, the fiscal intendants of Chengdu, Lizhou, and Zizhou Circuits had to provide annual subventions of 50,000, 10,000 and 30,000 lengths of silk respectively for the horse trade: *XNYL* 154/4883. By the turn of the century, prefectural sources of countertrade commodities had become an integral part of the horse trade, supplemented by THA cash and tea. See, for example, the description by Intendant Peng Ge in 1204: "The various prefectures regularly provide subventions of silver, tabby, damask, and pongee for the frontier horse trade, but the only source of currency is [700,000 strings a year] generated by the Tea and Horse Agency's sale of tea licenses": *SHY* bing 26/16b. For THA purchases of 4,429 ounces of silver annually in Daningjian at confiscatory prices, see *SHY* bing 23/22b.

56. Income, expenditure, and deficits for the Sichuan financial administration are as follows (all units in strings of cash):

Year	Income	Expenditure	Deficit
1134	33,420,000+	33,930,000+	510,000
1135	30,600,000+	40,000,000+	10,000,000
1136	—	32,760,000	—
1137	36,670,000+	38,280,000+	1,610,000+

Sources: XNYL 111/3517–3518; SS 374/11594.

Of these sums Generalissimo Wu Jie, the first of three members of the Wu family to command the Qinling defense system, received 19,500,000 strings in 1134 and 23,700,000 strings in 1135: XNYL 104/3314–3315; SS 174/4224. On the rise and fall of the Wu family, see Yamauchi Masahiro, "Nan Sō no Shisen ni okeru Chō Shun to Go Kei—sono seiryoku kōtai no katei o chūshin to shite," Shirin 44.1:98–125; and Ihara Hiroshi, "Nan Sō Shisen ni okeru Goshi no seiryoku—Go Gi no ranzen shi," in Aoyama Hakushi koki kinen Sōdaishi ronso, pp. 1–33.

57. Sichuanese salt taxes provided about 4,000,000 strings annually up to 1140, and about 3,000,000 strings annually thereafter. CYZJ jia 14/440. About the year 1130 wine taxes were worth 6,900,000 strings, and commutation fees for the levies on silk and homespun were worth 3,000,000 and 2,000,000 strings respectively. See Guo Zhengshong, "Nan Song zhongyang caizheng huobi suishou kaoban," p. 175.

58. Rice prices increased about five times from 1075 (1,200 cash per *dan*) to 1165 (6,000 cash per *dan*): Lü Tao, *Jingde ji* 1/2a–b; Wang Yingzhen, *Wending ji* 4/2a; silver was up 3.9 times from 1.4 strings (iron currency) per *liang* in 1076 to 5.5 strings (iron-based paper notes) in 1192: Lü Tao, *Jingde ji* 1/7a; SHY bing 23/22b–23a. Tabby silk was up about 3.3 times, from 1.5 strings in 1077 to somewhat under 5 strings (full) in 1159: Lü Tao, *Jingde ji* 1/2b; XNYL 174/5621. As further evidence of the drastic decline in profitability of the Southern Song Intendancy, it should also be noted that whereas TMA net surpluses during the New Policies were worth between 1.5 and 3 percent of the imperial government's cash income of 60,000,000 strings, during the Southern Song THA gross receipts, at ca. 2,000,000 strings, were worth only about 6 percent of the Sichuan provincial income of 30,000,000–36,000,000 strings during the 1130s.

59. CYZJ jia 14/440.

60. The 1121 ruling placed the THA chief below ordinary fiscal intendants as well as the unusually powerful Fiscal Intendant of Shaanxi, but above ordinary assistant fiscal intendants and judicial intendants. Superintendant status was revived in 1137, but by that time THA power had been significantly diminished by structural reorganization. For the status equivalents of the

Super-, Co-, and Assistant Intendants over time, see *SHY* zhiguan 43/47a, 52a–b, 65a, 90a–b, 101a–b, 104b–105a; *XCB* 341/2a; *XNYL* 108/3453.
61. *XNYL* 147/4650.
62. *SS* 361/11297-11311. Yang Dequan attempts to reassess Zhang's contribution to the Southern Song cause in "Zhang Jun shiji shuping," in Deng Guangming and Li Jiaju, eds., *Songshi yanjiu lunwen ji,* pp. 563–592.
63. The remaining two Sichuanese were Zhang Shen (Int. 1137–1139) and Feng Kangguo (Int. 1140–1142). Li Dai (Int.1136–1137) was the lone outsider in these early years. See *SS* 174/4223–4225.
64. On Qin Gui's career, see *SS* 473/13747–13765, Xu Ziming, *Song Zaifu,* zhuan 15–16; and Gong Wei-ai, "The Usurpation of Power by Ch'in Kuei through the Censorial Organ (1138–1155 A.D.)," in *Chinese Culture* 15.3:25–42.
65. Lo, "Circuits and Circuit Intendants," pp. 86–91.
66. On the viceroy, see *SS* 167/3957; and Lo, "Circuits and Circuit Intendants," pp. 99–103. During the first years of the Southern Song, according to Li Xinchuan, tea funds "belonged exclusively to the THA for the purchase of horses, and could not be used to meet the expenses of the Fiscal Intendant": *XNYL* 17/702. By 1143, however, the viceroy had begun to appropriate and redistribute THA funds: *XNYL* 148/4667. As Guo Zhengzhong notes in "Nan Song zhongyang caizheng," p. 175–176, Sichuan evolved into an autonomous fiscal zone that, though it paid almost no taxes to the capital, was required to meet annual expenses of about 35,000,000 strings on its own. Robert Hartwell sees the growth of powerful regional administrators during the Southern Song, particularly the viceroys and general supply commissioners, as a usurpation of central government functions ("Transformations," pp. 397–398); and Guo notes that in the case of Sichuan the court periodically pressed Sichuan to pay its taxes to the center. But given the extraordinary financial needs of Sichuan's militarized border, the northward diversion of Sichuan's tax payments appears as much a move towards administrative efficiency as towards regional usurpation.
67. The judicial intendants were Zhang Song (*SHY* zhiguan 41/113a); Zhang Deyuan (*SHY* xuanju 34/18a–b); Li Dacheng (*SHY* zhiguan 72/44a); and Wang Fei (*XNYL* 185/6090). The fiscal vice-intendants were Xu Yin (*XNYL* 174/5628–5629) and Wang Zhiwang (*XNYL* 179/5812). Fiscal supervisors included Zhao Kai (*XNYL* 18/742) and Jia Sicheng (*XNYL* 145/4563). The pacification commissioner was Feng Kangguo (*SHY* zhiguan 77/19a).
68. The five general supply commissioners were Fu Xingzhong (*XNYL* 167/5329); Tang Yungong (*XNYL* 167/5351); Xu Yin (*XNYL* 181/5899); Wang Zhiwang (*XNYL* 185/6096–6097); and Wang Ning (*SHY* zhiguan 74/11a).
   The two other men to succeed directly to another Sichuanese circuit post were Zhang Shen, to vice fiscal intendant (*XNYL* 130/4117; *Quan Shu yiwen*

zhi 55/6b); and Chao Gongwu, to Pacification Commissioner of Lizhou East Circuit (first divided in 1144 to circumscribe Wu Lin's power; see *CYZJ* yi 9/912–4) and concurrent Prefect of Xingyuanfu: *SHY* xuanju 34/20a.

69. The thirteen are Zhang Shen, Zhang Deyuan, Zhao Kai, Chao Gongwu, Zheng Ai, Jia Sicheng, Feng Kangguo, Fu Xingzhong, Xu Bi, Xu Yin, Wang Daguo, Wang Zhiwang, and Wu Zong. For sources, see Appendix C.

70. Hartwell, "Transformations," p. 400.

71. Smith, "State Power," p. 35.

72. Lo, "Circuits and Circuit Intendants," pp. 90–91.

73. For the committee and its deliberations, see *SHY* shihuo 63/13a–b; *XNYL* 176/5704–5705.

74. The sources for the five men are as follows: Xiao Zhen (*SS* 380/11724–11727); Tang Yungong (*XNYL* 167/5341, 169/5389–5391, 176/5704–5705; *SHY* zhiguan 40/12a; *SHY* xingfa 1/45a–b); Li Run (*SHY* shihuo 63/13a–b; *SHY* bing 24/37b–38a; *XNYL* 183/5993); Xu Yin (*SHY* shihuo 31/13a; *XNYL* 178/5777, 181/5899); Wang Zhiwang (*XNYL* 177/5720, 179/5812, 185/6032, 185/6096–6097).

75. *SHY* shihuo 31/12b–14a; *XNYL* 178/5777. According to Wang Zhiwang, Xu Yin had made the decision while still new in office, before he had fully grasped the implications of the eastern monopoly.

76. *SHY* bing 22/25a, which notes that Zhang was rewarded for meeting his horse-purchase quota.

77. Zhao was called back from retirement in 1139/2, while in his mid seventies, and allowed to resign once more in 1140: *XNYL* 126/4017, 135/4234.

78. *XCB* 104/20b; *SS* 198/4928, 4931; *SHY* zhiguan 43/106b–107a; *SHY* bing 22/24b. In Guangxi's Yongzhou market in the Southern Song, the vice-prefect was permitted to go outside the city to buy horses; but the prefect, presumably out of considerations of safety, was not: *SHY* bing 23/16a.

79. *SHY* zhiguan 43/11b, 115a–116a.

80. *SS* 167/3975. See also *SHY* zhiguan 43/109b–110a, 111a–b, 114b–115a. Up to 1165, save for a short hiatus in 1163 when selection temporarily reverted to the Ministry of Personnel, the THA controlled vice-prefectural appointments in Liizhou, Zhengzhou, Wenzhou, Nanpingjun, and Changningjun. In 1168 it got the rights to Jiezhou and Minzhou as well, but lost Minzhou in 1172 when it was decided that the *tongpan*'s chief responsibility in Minzhou was military preparedness; one of the Agency's four managing secretaries was instead set up as "concurrent vice-prefect for Danchang horse purchases." In 1179 a controversy ensued when the THA Intendant (Wu Zong) learned that the vice-prefect was still being rewarded for horse purchases even though he played no role in the operation, thereby damaging

morale; but the Minzhou *tongpan* was not completely removed from the horse-procurement bonus schedule until 1185: *SHY* bing 23/15a, 19a.

81. The Bureau of Military affairs assigned an official to check convoys in 1130 (*SHY* bing 24/41a–b); and in 1164 the Anterior Palace Command sent agents to check purchasing operations at the Danchang market (*SHY* bing 22/31a–b). In 1152 Wu Lin and Yang Zheng, chief military officers in Sichuan, took over the appointment of convoy masters *(guanya shichen)*, leaving selection of the convoy trail drivers *(qianma renbing)* to the THA (*SHY* zhiguan 43/107b). On the issue of incentives, in 1157 the Transmitter of Directives of the Bureau of Military Affairs set the incentive levels for convoys from Sichuan and Guangxi; in 1173 the central government revised all incentive schedules for Sichuan and Guangxi; and in 1194 the government altered the incentive system for horse purchases in Danchang and Liizhou (*SHY* bing 24/39a; *SHY* bing 25/41a–49a; *SHY* bing 23/23b). Not surprisingly, the Post-Reform Intendancy stands midway between the New Policies and Southern Song THA. Huang Lian encouraged other agencies to inform on TMA transgressions, which they had been prohibited from doing by orders of 1083 and 1085 (*SHY* zhiguan 43/70b); and critical decisions about the relative allocation of tea to the horse markets, grain trade, and consumer markets for cash sale were made by the Bureau of Military Affairs and the Secretariat and Department of Ministries in ways that ran counter to the expressed desires of the THA Intendants. But the Agency did retain the right to protect its basic capitalization from encroachment by other field bureaus, and its control over personnel on the whole remained intact: *SHY* zhiguan 43/82b, 94b–96b.

82. *CYZJ* jia 14/441; *SHY* bing 23/19a.

83. *SS* 167/3970.

84. *CYZJ* yi 14/1063–1065; *Liangchao gangmu beiyao* 8/481–483; *SS* 167/3970.

85. Lü Tao, *Jingde ji* 3/9b.

86. *SS* 183/4477; *SS* 184/4494. Saeki Tomi dates the first figure, 23,000,000 catties, to a survey taken by Lei Youzheng in 992 when he was Regulator of Tea and Salt for Jianghuai, Liangzhe, Jinghu, Fujian, and Guangnan: "Sōsho ni okeru cha no sembai seidko," p. 398. The 1055 figure was taken by government administrators as final evidence of the failure of the southeastern monopoly system. Part of the drastic loss since the late tenth century must have been due to extensive smuggling, and so I have not used the figure to compare household production in Table 6.

87. For household tea production by Song circuit, ca.1000 to 1165, see Smith, "Szechwan Tea Monopoly," Table 16, p. 478.

88. See William Rowe, *Hankow: Commerce and Society in a Chinese City, 1796–1889,* pp. 122–158. Tea production per household in China in the early twentieth century is as follows:

Province	Output, 1914–1918, in catties	Estimated Household Population	Production per Household, in catties
Shaanxi	1,000,000	2,000,000	0.5
Anhui	41,400,000	4,240,000	9.8
Zhejiang	43,600,000	3,840,000	11.35
Hubei	50,300,000	4,360,000	11.5
Hunan	230,000,000	5,980,000	38.5
Jiangxi	21,000,000	3,540,000	5.9
Fujian	18,100,000	2,780,000	6.5
Sichuan	23,000,000	9,540,000	2.4

Sources: Perkins, *Agricultural Development*, pp. 285, 212. I have divided his population figures for 1913 by individuals by 5 to get household estimates, following Ho Ping-ti, *Studies on the Population of China*, p. 56.

89. Su Che, *Luancheng ji* 36/7a.
90. Lü Tao, *Jingde ji* 1/6b–7a. Lü Tao gives an annual household production range for all of western Sichuan of 100–200 catties and 30,000–50,000 catties, but units at the upper end were clearly exceptional. According to Lü's description of the Pengkou riot, at the height of the season 300 families sold 60,000 catties of tea to the state, an average of 200 catties per household, in a single market day: *Jingde ji* 1/19a–b. Although we also learn from Lü that a cultivator could return to market with a lower grade of tea in about a week (see the case of Shi Guangyi below), 200 catties at least appears to be a likely lower limit for commercial household production. On this basis we can estimate that a maximum number of 150,000 households participated in the Sichuan and Hanzhong Basin tea industries, but the estimate cannot be confirmed.
91. Lü Tao, *Jingde ji* 1/12b–13a.
92. Lü Tao, *Jingde ji* 1/13a–b.
93. Lü Tao, *Jingde ji* 1/17b. At that time the ratio between iron and bronze coins was 2:1; it was changed to 1.5:1 in 1079: *XCB* 301/6a–b. One large cash was worth 10 small cash (*SHY* shihuo 11/8b–9a), and one *liang* of silver was worth 1,400 iron cash (presumably large): *Jingde ji* 1/7a.
94. Lü Tao, *Jingde ji* 1/7a, 21. Lü writes that although the twenty-seventh *jiaozi* issue was worth 960 cash on the market, the government valued it at 1,000 cash for the purpose of payments to cultivators; similarly although the twenty-sixth issue was worth 940 cash, the government valued it at 960 cash (p. 21a). New issues were printed every other year and were intended to be retired as the succeeding issue was released. Lü's observation is one of the earliest indications that the system had eased up, and that successive issues

circulated simultaneously, albeit at different prices. See Katō Shigeshi, *Shina keizaishi kōshō,* pp. 27–34.

95. Lü Tao, *Jingde ji* 1/6b–7a.

96. Lü Tao, *Jingde ji* 1/7b. Tea sales in Yongkang declined from 1,580,000 catties in 1074, to 1,410,000 catties in 1075 and 1,320,000 catties in 1076.

97. The number of participants has become confused. Lü Tao, *Jingde ji* 1/20a, has 5,000 individuals, with no mention of the *hu;* ibid., 11/2b, has 300 *hu* and 3,000 individuals. *XCB* 282/15b, quoting Lü, has 300 *hu* and 5,000 individuals.

98. Lü Tao, *Jingde ji* 1/19a–b. See also ibid., 11/21a–b; and *XCB* 282/15b.

99. Lü Tao *Jingde ji* 1/20b; *XCB* 282/15b–16a.

100. *XCB* 282/12b–13a. At this same time the Agency's first attempt to control the Jiezhou salt trade was beginning to sour, leading to Chief Intendant Liu Zuo's dismissal in 1077/7:*XCB* 283/9b.

101. Lü Tao, *Jingde ji* 1/23b; *SHY* shihuo 30/15b. Lü Tao estimated the most expensive of the late teas, i.e., those harvested after about July, at 30 cash per catty: *Jingde ji* 1/23b.

102. See Edwin Mansfield, *Microeconomics,* pp. 364–366; Paul Samuelson, *Economics,* pp. 482–483.

103. The problem was recorded as early as 984 in the southeastern monopoly, and was endemic ever after: *SHY* shihuo 30/1b.

104. *SHY* zhiguan 43/114a. According to the Intendant, shoots could be harvested in under two years. Ukers, vol. 1, p. 299, states that it takes three years for tea grown from seeds in the field to produce useful leaf.

105. Our information on the laborers in the tea industry is limited to, first, Lü Tao's description of the tea businesses of Mou Yuanji and Shi Guangyi, who hired workers at 60 cash per day plus food and could probably organize family members to take their place (*Jingde ji* 1/15b, 18a); and second, from the same county, Du Guangting's apocryphal tale of Zhang Shougui's tea garden during the Kingdom of Former Shu. Zhang hired over 100 male and female pickers who resided together during the harvest season. Obviously a tea estate as large as Zhang's would have had to keep its workers. But the largest garden owners were probably relatively immune to the price-cutting stratagems of the monopoly markets, because of their power and status, and may well have hired more workers and bought more land to profit from the new demand. On Zhang's plantation, see *Chongxiu Pengxian zhi* 11/9a–b.

106. *SHY* shihuo 30/15b; *XCB* 290/6b.

107. *Songdai Shuwen jicun* 54/2b.

108. *SHY* zhiguan 43/58b–59a, 80b. Tea-horse ratios are discussed in greater detail in Chapter Seven.

109. Liu Zhi, *Zhongsu ji* 5/13a.

110. Yang Tianhui's two inscriptions on the erection of new administrative ya-men by Huang Minyong, Intendant 1097–1098, are not in fact indict-ments, although they contain criticisms of clerks and clerical practices: "Duda chamasi xinjian yantang ji," and "Duda chamasi xinjian dating jiage ji," *Songdai Shuwen jicun* 26/6a–7b and 10a–11b. Li Xin's "Shang huangdi wan-yan shu," is an indictment, and a bitter one; see his *Kua'ao ji* 19/20a–b.

111. See *SHY* zhiguan 43/84a and Chapter Seven.

112. *SHY* shihuo 31/11a–b. Zhang was later made Prefect of Chengdu fu. A selection of his memorials is contained in *Songdai Shuwen jicun* 60/1a–11a.

113. If the composition of the 40 strings included transit taxes of about 3 strings (the figure for Dongxiang tea, the only figure we have); 9.3 strings for the merchant's license fee (as of 1157); and 2.3 strings for the cultivator's taxes (up to the year 1200); then the balance, the purchase-price payment to the cultivator, was about 25.4 strings per hundred-weight or 254 cash per catty. This excludes all hidden costs to the cultivator.

114. Because rice prices dropped owing to a shortage of iron cash during the 1080s, cultivators were not much worse off in 1085 than they had been in 1075, before the monopoly. The ratio of tea to rice prices was as follows:

Year	Tea per Catty	Rice per Dan	Ratio
1075	90 cash	1,200 cash	.07
1085	50 cash	800 cash	.06
1160	250 cash	6,000 cash	.04

Sources: Rice prices from Lü Tao, *Jingde ji* 1/2a–b, 3/10a; Wang Yingzhen, *Wen-ding ji* 4/2a.

115. Lü Tao, *Jingde ji* 1/8b–9a. As of 1083, an informer could be rewarded for uncovering as little as 1 catty of "contraband" tea: *SHY* shihuo 30/19a.

116. Li Xin, *Kua'ao ji* 19/20a–b.

117. *SHY* shihuo 30/19a.

118. *Songdai Shuwen jicun* 54/3a–b.

119. Zheng Jingyi, *Falü da cishu* vol. 1, p. 132–133, cites some of the basic classical sources on the five punishments. On the "heavy penalties" see Saeki Tomi, "Sōdai ni okeru juhō chibun ni tsuite," *Chūgokushi kenkyū* vol. 1, pp.458–487.

120. *SHY* shihuo 30/18b–19a; Lü Tao, *Jingde ji* 3/6a.

121. In addition to Saeki Tomi, *Chūgokushi kenkyū*, vol. 1, pp. 464–468, see *XCB* 344/2a–b.

122. *XCB* 476/2a. For the case of the commoner Zhao Shiheng, who sold 2,000 catties of fake Mingshan tea in Xizhou, see *XCB* 476/2a. Zhao was de-

ported to the custody of authorities in a prefecture neighboring the restricted tea region *(bianguan)*. This punishment was deemed to be more severe than the standard "heavy judgment for acts which ought not to be done" (but for which there was no fixed article of law)—*buyingwei zhongduanzui*. For the 1101 ruling, see *SHY* zhiguan 43/75b. The merchants referred to were probably employed as agents of the market officials.

123. *XNYL* 50/1724; *SHY* shihuo 32/27a–28b. On amnesties in general, see Shen Jiaben, "Shekao," in his *Shen Qiji xiansheng yishu,* vol. 1, pp. 230–358; and Brian McKnight, *The Quality of Mercy: Amnesties and Traditional Chinese Justice.*

124. *XNYL* 71/2307–2308.

125. *SHY* shihuo 31/3a. See Kracke, *Civil Service,* p. 170, on the interpretation of degree *(deng)* in a case such as this. The only explicit mention of the death penalty applied to tea smugglers that I have seen is for the merchant and captain of an ocean-going ship smuggling camphorated *la* tea by sea.

126. *SHY* shihuo 31/18a; *SHY* zhiguan 43/114a. Confiscation of property was a typical feature of the heavy laws. See Saeki Tomi, *Chūgokushi kenkyū,* vol. 1, p.465.

127. *SHY* shihuo 31/18a; *SHY* zhiguan 43/114a; *CYZJ* jia 14/441, 18/598.

128. *SHY* shihuo 31/15b.

129. Wang Yingzhen, *Wending ji* 4/2a; *SS* 34/642. According to Wang, rice prices jumped from 5 to 10 strings per *dan* in Kuizhou (p. 4a) and from about 6 to between 12 and 13 strings in Jianzhou (p. 2a).

130. *SHY* shihuo 3119a–b; *SHY* zhiguan 43/112b.

131. In the late 1160s, for example, Zhang Song had attempted to shore up sagging revenues by exporting extra amounts of Yongkang's "fine leaf tea" *(xicha)* in contravention of the usual proscriptions. In 1177 Yan Congshu indicted Zhang Song's relaxation of export controls as the cause of the tea glut in Danchang and successfully requested that export and smuggling restrictions be tightened. *Songdai Shuwen jicun* 61/784, *Huang Song zhongxing liangchao shengzheng* 55/2087.

132. *SHY* shihuo 31/28a–b.

133. *SHY* shihuo 30/19a.

134. Lü Tao, *Jingde ji* 3/6a.

135. *XNYL* 75/2391–2393. Zhang was attempting to counter critics who alleged that Zhao had inappropriately revised the smuggling codes.

136. *SHY* shihuo 31/3a. Tea prices are based on Wang Zhiwang's memorial of 1160: *SHY* shihuo 31/12b–14a.

137. *SHY* shihuo 31/18a; *SHY* zhiguan 43/114a.

138. For examples, see *SHY* zhiguan 43/74a–b, 107a–b; *SHY* zhiguan 48/124b–135a.

139. A limit was reached in 1012 when the Finance Commissioner, Ding Wei,

recommended to Emperor Zhenzong that family members be encouraged to inform on one another. The horrified Emperor responded that the idea violated all canons of morality, should not be uttered in court, and was not to be permitted: *SHY* shihuo 30/4a. But informing on fellow villagers had been encouraged from as early as 977 (ibid., 1b); and members of such tea-merchant groups as "associations of partners," "joint-capital partnerships," and "associations of members without joint capital" engaged in smuggling were incited to inform on their associates with promises of immunity and the right to the confiscated tea. They could also instruct family members to do the informing instead (to protect their own safety?), for which immunity and half the confiscated goods were the rewards. (See *SHY* xingfa 2/107a–b, for the year 1142.) Finally, the importance of bounties was explicitly acknowledged by the Intendant for Tea and Salt of Jinghu South Circuit (modern Hunan) in 1133, when the reserves of funds allocated for bounties had been depleted by campaigns to suppress bandits: "Suppressing illegal tea and salt sales," he memorialized, "depends completely on the use of bounties to encourage and exhort people to denounce and seize [violators]." *SHY* shihuo 32/29a–b; cf. 20b.

140. My impression of (early) Tang attitudes towards informants is based on Changsun Wuji's *Tanglü shuyi* of 653, which is replete with punishments and warnings for persons who bring incorrect charges against another (even where some accusations against some persons in the group are correct), or against members of their mourning group even if the charges are accurate. See especially zhuan 23 and 24, *"dousong,"* assaults and suits. I am not aware of a systematic study of the role of bounties and informants in Chinese law.

141. For example the 360 leaves of Mengding tea that were presented to the court annually: *Mingshanxian xinzhi* 4/9b–10a. Taxes could be paid with tea, and the supplementary trade tax *(touziqian)* had a commutation rate for such cases, but there does not appear to have been a specific tax on tea production.

142. Lü Tao, *Jingde ji* 3/9b–10a. Thus a merchant would have paid a maximum of about 32 cash per catty, or 3.2 strings per 100-catty unit. This is one-third to one-quarter the tax burden paid by the merchant during the Southern Song; but when inflation is taken into account, the amounts become comparable.

143. Lü Tao, *Jingde ji* 1/5a–b.

144. *WXTK* 4/55a–b.

145. *SHY* shihuo 30/22b. On the precedent, see *WXTK* 4/55a–b.

146. *CYZJ* jia 15/453; *WXTK* 4/55b. Fees collected from the tea trade went into a common pool that was distributed in varying proportions to the fiscal intendant and local government administrators, and to two general management funds, the *jingzhi* and *zongzhi* accounts. If I am correct in identi-

fying these two funds with the general business surtaxes known collectively as *jingzong zhi qian* put under the control of the regional commissioners of supply, then Sichuan's total burden came to 5,400,000 strings of cash, most of which went to meet military expenses in Sichuan and neighboring Huguang. See *SHY* shihuo 31/32b and Wei Liaoweng's epitaph for Li Fan, General Supply Master of Sichuan during the 1170s. *Chongjiao Heshan xiansheng daquan wenji* 78/641. Wei notes that during his term as Provisional Fiscal Intendant for Chengdu Circuit, Li Fan "provisionally managed" the Sichuan tea and horse trade. But there is no indication in any of the standard records that Li Fan ever formally served as THA Intendant, and so I have not included him among the Southern Song THA incumbents in Appendix B.

147. *SHY* shihuo 30/22b; *XNYL* 167/5326–5327. See also *Zhongguo lishi da cidian—Songshi zhuan*, p. 103. Su Che claimed that during the Yuanfeng period the tax was collected in kind, at the rate of 10 catties per hundred: *Luancheng ji* 36/7a.
148. Lü Tao, *Jingde ji* 1/16b; *SHY* shihuo 30/21a.
149. *SHY* shihuo 31/32b.
150. *SHY* shihuo 31/32a–b. For silks and hempen cloth, see *CYZJ* jia 14/418–421.
151. *SHY* shihuo 31/32a–b; *SS* 184/4510.
152. *SHY* shihuo 31/32b; *CYZJ* jia 15/458–459.
153. *SHY* shihuo 30/29a–30a.
154. On Sichuan, see *Songdai Shuwen jicun* 54/3a–b; *Zhongxing xiaoji* 4 in Saeki Tomi, *Sōdai chahō*, p. 667. In the original southeastern contract markets the *yuanhu* had to "come forth and acknowledge himself as a cultivator," at which point he would be registered by the government. Only registered cultivators were permitted to trade with merchants: *SHY* shihuo 30/32b, 40a–b. An entry for 1161 indicates that cultivators were categorized into grades, upper, middle, and lower; but the sources are frustratingly silent about the basis for grading, and we have no information at all on the upper, and presumably quite prosperous, garden owners: *SHY* shihuo 31/15a.
155. *XNYL* 175/5665–5666.
156. *SHY* shihuo 31/11a–b, 15a.
157. *SHY* shihuo 31/15a; *Huang Song zhongxing liangchao shengzheng* 55/2100–2102. The court ordered the THA to make the appropriate cuts and gave cultivators the right to report their grievances.
158. In 1086 Sima Guang argued that officials in the Ever-Normal Granary system should be judged by the efficiency of their disaster relief measures, and not according to the volume of rural "Green Sprouts" loans they issued and collected: *XCB* 374/11b–13a.
159. *Huang Song zhongxing liangchao shengzheng* 55/2100–2102.

160. *Huang Song zhongxing liangchao shengzheng* 57/2161–2162; *SHY* shihuo 31/25a–b.
161. *SHY* shihuo 31/25a–b. The tea cuts were worth 152,994 strings of cash in license and land-produce-fee quotas to the Intendancy.
162. *SHY* shihuo 31/27b–28a.
163. From the New Policies onward, an increasing portion of the empire's taxes, including its direct *liangshui* taxes, was collected in cash. By commuting payments in kind into cash, formally known as *zheqian,* financial officials could substantially increase their revenues by manipulating the commutation rates. This question is discussed by Wang Shengduo, pp. 40–42.
164. *SHY* shihuo 31/28a–b.
165. *SHY* shihuo 31/28a–b, and 30b–31a for the same text in 1191.
166. *SHY* shihuo 31/30b–31a.
167. *SHY* shihuo 31/33a. This amnesty may have applied to the entire empire, since no location is specified.
168. In 1190 160,000 strings in cultivators' taxes were permanently cut from the Agency's revenue quota. Five years later it was found necessary to transfer the tea-commutation fee of 927 strings from the Long'an cultivators to the prefectural and regional governments. This was followed in 1200 by two similar transfers: 5,042 strings of cash in supplementary trade taxes industry-wide were split equally between the judicial intendant and the THA; and the total industry assessment of 3,148 strings in the *chengti* surtax were wholly taken over by the Commissioner of Supply. At the same time the package of land-produce, broker, and market-usage fees was reduced from 2 strings 300 cash to 1 string 500 cash. This remission was worth a total of 104,943 strings. See *CYZJ* jia 14/440; *SHY* shihuo 31/32b.
169. On the Mongol assaults against Sichuan, see Hu Zhaoxi, "Luelun Nan Song monian Sichuan junmin kangji Menggu guizu de douzheng," in Deng Guangming and Cheng Yingliu, *Songshi yanjiu lunwen ji,* pp. 374–409.
170. *Xu zizhi tongjian* 179, in Saeki Tomi, *Sōdai chahō,* p. 898.
171. Total population of the Upper Yangzi declined from 2,721,911 households in 1173 to 2,590,092 households in 1223: *SHY* shihuo 69/77a; *WXTK* 11/117a.
172. From mid Tang to early Song the teas of Peng, Mian, Shu, Qiong, Ya, Mei, and Han were notable in varying degrees, and worthy of comparison with the teas of the southeast. (See Lu Yu, *Chajing,* xia 9b–10a; Yue Shi, *Taiping huanyu ji* 72/558, 73/565–566, 74/573, 75/581, 583, 77/592.) But only four Sichuanese teas were at all comparable to those in the southeast: the Zhaopo tea of Guanghan (Hanzhou), Shuinan tea of Hezhou, Baiya tea of Emei, and Mengding tea of Mingshan. Moreover, only very small amounts of these teas were produced (*CYZJ* jia 14/441). As symbolic evi-

dence of the degree to which Sichuan's tea industry remained wedded to the production of low-quality tea for the Tibetan trade, it is worth noting that when Huguang migrants began resettling Sichuan in the eighteenth century, rather than drink the tea of their adopted region they imported tea from Hunan and Hupei: *Baxian zhi* (1939) 4A/42b, cited by Robert Entenmann, "Migration and Settlement in Sichuan, 1644–1796," pp. 183–184.
173. Zhu Mu, *Fangyu shenglan* 56/1160.

7. The Limits of Bureaucratic Power in the Tea and Horse Trade

1. In practice most economies include a mix of command and market forces. In a useful overview of the possible relationships between state and economy Charles E. Lindblom identifies three methods of control: exchange, authority, and persuasion. See his *Politics and Markets*, pp. 12–32.
2. McNeill, pp. 5–7.
3. For depictions of Central Asian and Tibetan herdsmen, see the paintings reproduced in Zhang Anzhi, *Li Gonglin.* I have encountered no descriptions of tribal horse merchants in the frontier markets, but von Glahn cites and translates a description by Lu You of tribesmen gambling with dice in a famous Xuzhou temple that probably typifies Han impressions of the tribesmen: "While playing they shouted and guffawed, making sounds like the bellowing of wild beasts. Coiled sinuously on a felt mat, they looked exceedingly complacent. With their mallet hairstyles and barbarian faces they hardly seemed kin to men. They barely took notice of the Han around them. At this time the season had advanced to the middle of the fifth month, but all of them wore felt clothes on their backs which smelled so bad that you could not approach them": *Country of Streams and Grottoes,* p. 125.
4. *SHY* bing 22/10a; *SHY* zhiguan 43/60b–61a. Horse Purchase Intendant Guo Maoxun recommended that a feast be held every ten days.
5. *XCB* 381/22a. The bitter conflict between the Tea and Horse Agency and the Shaanxi Horse Purchase and Pastures Agency that prefaced the unification is taken up below.
6. *SHY* zhiguan 43/66a.
7. In Shaanxi the marketing year began in the eighth month and ran for a twelve-month cycle (*SHY* zhiguan 43/68a). In Liizhou, on the other hand, officials were instructed to keep the markets open only until the third month, to stem excessive purchases of the less valuable Sichuanese animals (ibid., 79b). During the Southern Song, the THA closed its Danchang and Fengtie markets in the fourth month, after which the Governor-General's office was allowed to begin its own purchase (*SHY* bing 23/6b).
8. From information provided by Su Che, we can infer that a convoy was made up of fifty men carrying 400 *jin* each, or 20,000 *jin* total. But in 1095 Lu

Shimin estimated a convoy at 30,000 *jin*. At these rates the minimum quota of 4,000,000 catties of tea to Western Shaanxi would require between 133 and 200 convoys. See Su Che, *Luancheng ji,* 36/8b; *SHY* shihuo 30/28a.

9. *SHY* shihuo 30/21a–b. It was Lu Shimin who transferred the responsibility for mustering porters to the local officiary.

10. Su Che, *Luancheng ji* 36/8b. Depot spurs were divided between densely traveled and dangerous stretches of roadway. In 1082, twenty-eight depots were established to help speed tea convoys along the 170-mile stretch between Qinzhou and Xizhou, at an average spacing of 6 miles that was very close to the standard 5.1 miles (15 *li*) cited by Su Che: *XCB* 326/16b; Su Che, *Luancheng ji* 36/8b. Depot networks were also set up between Chengdu and Lizhou, Xingyuanfu and Fengxiangfu, and one spur between Shangjinxian and modern Xi'an to move consumer tea from Jinzhou to Eastern Shaanxi (*SHY* shihuo 30/24b–25a). The tea-relay depot system continued to expand in the Post-Reform period. In 1094 Lu Shimin ordered "all major tea-transport roads" to establish additional permanently manned depots, in preference to the compulsory hiring (*hegu*) of commoners; and by 1101 eight depots had been opened on the southwest-to-northeast axis of Mianzhou, Sichuan's second largest prefecture and, because of its position at the junction of the Fu River and the Golden Ox Highway, a major transport center. See *SHY* zhiguan 43/76a–b; *SHY* shihuo 26b–28b.

11. Sue Che, *Luancheng ji* 36/8b.

12. *SHY* shihuo 30/25a–b.

13. *SHY* shihuo 30/25a.

14. Lü Tao, *Jingde ji* 3/4b.

15. *SHY* shihuo 30/25a–b, 27a–b. Tea-depot inspectors were almost certainly Sichuanese, since their reward for a successful term of office (no tea backlogs and less than 5 percent of their transport soldiers absconded) included not only a year's reduction before their *mokan* review, but also the privilege of indicating their preferences for a next assignment close to home—a typical feature of the eight-circuit appointment regulations. See also *SHY* zhiguan 43/98b–99a; *SHY* bing 23/2b–3a. Chengdu and Mianzhou contained inspectors' yamens; and inspectors were appointed to Yongxing, Fuyan, Huanqing, and probably Qinfeng circuits of Shaanxi as well. *SHY* zhiguan 43/76a–b; *SHY* shihuo 30/26b.

16. *SHY* shihuo 30/21b.

17. Baber, pp. 194–195.

18. See Joseph Needham and Wang Ling, *Mechanical Engineering,* pp. 260–262.

19. Su Che, *Luancheng ji* 36/8b.

20. *SHY* zhiguan 43/96b.

21. Su Che, *Luancheng ji* 36/8b.

22. Li Xin, "Shang Huangdi wanyan shu," *Kua'ao ji* 19/20b–21a.

23. Yuan Xingzong, *Jiuhua ji* 7/5a. For an example of government depot-soldiers in Hupei picking, processing, and openly selling tea to troops in transit in 1143, see *SHY* shihuo 31/7a–b.

24. The warehouses were located in Zhaohuaxian, Lizhou, and Shunzheng and Changjüxian, Xingzhou. In 1121 Intendant He Jian boasted that when he was managing supervisor of the Agency in 1113, "I . . . managed the hiring for transporting the tea-bales backed up along the way, and they all got to the frontier markets." Nonetheless he was dismissed at the end of the term. It was He who originally called attention to the backup 1113/7/27. He attributed it to regulations prohibiting the THA from exchanging Mingshan tea for anything but horses. But the next month his chief, Zhang Hui, sent up a long analysis of the problem that linked it equally to the sales restrictions, the exhaustion of conscript porters in Lizhou Circuit owing to famine, and insufficient incentives to the district magistrates and warehouse supervisors responsible for tea transport. The THA was denied the rights to sell surplus Mingshan tea or to disregard statutory requirements for minimum ranks when making appointments in the key transport districts (e.g., putting an executory-class official in an administrative-class post, a qualification often imposed even on irregular appointments); but it was given incentive privileges over the ten transport-related posts (albeit less generous than requested) indexed to the successful movement of 40,000 bales of tea annually. See *SHY* zhiguan 94b–99a.

25. *SHY* bing 22/25b.

26. *SHY* shihuo 36/31b.

27. See Yuan Xingzong, "Yi Guoma shu," *Jiuhua ji* 7/3a–6b.

28. *CYZJ* jia 18/596–599, "Chuan-Qin maima."

29. *CYZJ* jia 18/597.

30. *CYZJ* jia 18/597; *SHY* zhiguan 43/110b–111a. See also Gu Zuyu, *Dushi fangyu jiyao* 59/2605 and 60/2646.

31. Yuan Xingzong, Li Xinchuan, and Wu Yong accept the Wenzhou animals as war horses; and in the 1170s Wenzhou was officially transferred from the Chuan Branch to the Qin Branch: Yuan Xingzong, *Jiuhua ji* 7/4b; *CYZJ* jia 18/596; Wu Yong, *Helin ji* 37/20a–b. But Wenzhou horses were smaller than the Danchang and Fengtie animals, and were similar in kind to those bought in Sichuan. See Yu Yunwen, in *Lidai mingchen zouyi* 242/12a–13a; and Hua Yue, "Pingrong shice: mazheng," in *Cuiwei xiansheng beizheng lu* 1/27b.

32. For lists of early tribal suppliers, see, for example, *XCB* 43/14a and Sogabe Shizuo's gloss in "Sōdai no basei," p. 68. Presentations of tribute horses by political chieftains are routinely noted in the source materials on foreign relations and frontier management in the *Song huiyao, SS,* and the *WXTK;* but even these sources are silent on the question of how the chieftains them-

selves obtained the animals. And, in any event, by the New Policies era the number of tribute horses had dwindled to insignificance. During the tea and horse trade only one northern horse seller is identified precisely: Sabi, chieftain of the Gulezangkamu tribe of Deshun (mod. Ningxia, Longdexian). In 1077 Sabi and fourteen followers were arrested en route to the horse markets by the Deshun authorities, who suspected them of being spies, presumably for the Tanguts. Sabi was subsequently paid, but doubts that he was not a horse merchant persisted (*XCB* 284/16b–17a). In any event, the Deshun tribes preferred to trade for cash rather than tea (*SHY* zhiguan 43/55b).

Southern Song sources are no more helpful. The sources inform us that in 1133 General Wu Lin enticed the "thirty-eight small Tibetan tribes" into restarting the dormant horse trade with stocks of tea and silk: *XNYL* 66/2183; and we are told that Danchang and Fengtie were supplied once a year by the Tibetans of Lugan (otherwise unidentifiable), every month or two by the Tibetans of Taozhou (Gansu, Lintanxian), and every three or six months by the Tibetans of Diezhou (Gansu, Diebu). *SS* 184/4511; *SHY* zhiguan 43/111a.

33. The importance of roads and towns to the Tibetan polities is emphasized in *SS* 492, passim.

34. It was, of course, control of the trade routes that enriched Juesiluo and his tribe: *SS* 492/14161–14162. Further north, the Tanguts levied an ad valorem tax of 10 percent on Uighur trade caravans passing through Xi Xia lands, to be paid in only the finest goods; this was said to have embittered the Uighur merchants: Hong Hao, *Songmo jiwen* 1/5a; *SHY* fanyi 4/10a–b.

35. *SHY* zhiguan 43/59b. Each *fanguan* was to drum up between 500 and 1,000 head.

36. *XNYL* 66/2183.

37. *SHY* bing 17/30b; the same story is told in *SHY* li 62/69a.

38. For example, see *SHY* bing 22/10a, 26b; *SHY* bing 23/9a; *SHY* zhiguan 43/61a. For a memorial on the art of summoning horses in Guangxi, see *SHY* bing 22/18b–19a.

39. Hong Hao, *Songmo jiwen* 1/4b–5a; *SHY* fanyi 4/10a–b. Hong writes that "at the height of our dynasty some [Uighurs] lived in Qinchuan [i.e., the Longxi Basin lands of Shaanxi, Ningxia, and Gansu] as cooked households. When the Jurchen conquered Shaanxi, they fled to Yanshan and Gan, Liang, Gua, and Sha prefectures . . . [where they were] haltered and bridled to the Xi Xia." It is likely that at least some of the Northern Song Uighurs remained attached to the new Shaanxi territories controlled by the Southern Song. Hong's comments are based on his observations as a hostage of the Jurchen from 1129 to 1143. In 1113 THA Intendant Zhang Hui described the "gate households" as "cooked-household Tibetan tribesmen who serve as horse brokers *(zangkuai)*": *SHY* zhiguan 43/96a.

40. Initially the native retainer or Tibetan tribesman who brought in the greatest number of horses each month earned a prize of 1 length of silk, 1 silver dish, and 1 liang of silk thread. In 1082 Guo Maoxun raised the stakes by making every broker or tribal merchant who delivered 100 horses eligible for the monthly prize: *SHY* zhiguan 43/60b–61a. As of 1111, native brokers were allowed to purchase one tou (50 catties) of a tea varietal—Hanzhong's "four-varieties convoy-tea" (sisi gangcha)—just recently set aside for the herdsmen: *SHY* zhiguan 43/93a–b.

41. Yuan Xingzong, *Jiuhua ji* 7/5a.

42. *SHY* zhiguan 43/96a. In 1105 the Intendants specially ordered that brokers be prevented from undercutting a plan to divert extra tea to the horse merchants: *SHY* zhiguan 43/84b.

43. *SHY* zhiguan 43/54b.

44. In 1105 the Pacification Commissioner suggested the following procedure for meting out extra tea in Minzhou: "After the Tibetan guests drive their horses to market, differentiate between the good and the weak horses, and add tea accordingly. For the fine horses *(liangma)* add an extra 30 catties of tea [to the basic purchase price]; for the [ordinary] convoy horses *(gangma)* add 20 catties of tea," *SHY* zhiguan 43/84b.

45. Yuan Xingzong, *Jiuhua ji* 7/5a–b.

46. *SHY* bing 23/5b–6a.

47. In 1082, for instance, Guo Maoxun argued that by reducing the price of tea in relation to horses, "because [the horse merchants themselves] will earn profits on the sale of tea [to the tribes in the interior], horses will be brought to the market in droves": *SHY* zhiguan 43/60a. Some tea was sold off before the Tibetans left Song domains. An edict of 1155 noted that some horse merchants traded their tea to private agents for silk, which was easier to transport, and ordered the horse merchants to pay either tea or silk, according to the convenience of the horse merchants: *SHY* zhiguan 43/108a. And around 1170 Yuan Xingzong wrote that because some of the Tibetan tribesmen lack funds for travel expenses, "they use tea as money as of old. Up until now, the market officials would exchange some tea for cash, each time 'pumping up the value of the cash' [*chengti*, a technical term for efforts to preserve the value of an inflated currency] in order to increase the worth of [the Tibetans'] tea. But recently they have been unable to do this. If the value of tea [to the Tibetans] decreases, with what will we summon horses": *Jiuhua ji* 7/4b–5a.

48. *XCB* 381/23a. For a list of tea varieties and prices, see Table 13.

49. *SHY* zhiguan 43/87b–88a, 96a.

50. *XCB* 381/23a; *SHY* fanyi 4/16a. In 1078 the TMA was instructed to exempt Khotanese tea importers from paying taxes. It is likely that they purchased their tea with profits from the frankincense trade.

51. *SHY* zhiguan 43/87b–88a, 96a. The convoy teas included the "myriad springs," "great bamboo," and "auspicious gold" teas of Xingyuanfu and Xiang County tea of Yangzhou.
52. *XCB* 381/23a. Huang Lian describes the destination of the convoy teas quite precisely, but the place names can no longer be identified.
53. *SHY* zhiguan 43/59a.
54. *XNYL* 94/3034.
55. *SHY* shihuo 31/24b–25a.
56. The charge was made by Yan Cangshu in 1177, after Danchang tea had become "as cheap as mud." See *Shengzheng* 55/2086–2087.
57. Denunciations of Sichuanese horses abound. See, for example, Song Qi, *Jingwen ji* 29/7b; *SHY* bing 22/2a; *CYZJ* jia 18/597.
58. Von Glahn analyzes the complex interaction between native dwellers, Han colonists, and the Song state in Luzhou in *Country of Streams and Grottoes*. As he points out, expansion into the resource-rich southwest was as much a centerpiece of New Policies foreign policy as Wang Shao's expeditions in Qinghai. Both expansionist surges reflected Wang Anshi's conviction that the riches of the frontier must be exploited "as fuel for the engines of economic growth" (p. 104).
59. *SHY* bing 22/24a. Von Glahn, *Country of Streams and Grottoes,* p. 182, gives the passage a somewhat different reading. See pp. 181–187 for his discussion of the frontier trade in Luzhou.
60. Yu Yunwen's argument of circa 1170 was typical. See *Lidai mingchen zouyi* 242/12a–13a.
61. According to Fan Chengda, Military Commissioner of Sichuan circa 1170, a crescendo of Sichuanese voices rose up against the Liizhou horse trade while he was in office: *Lidai mingchen zouyi* 242/13b–14a. The THA chiefs, however, were as concerned about their bureaucratic empires as about the horse procurement. In 1104 Intendant Sun Aobian argued that a cut in Liizhou procurement quotas would not only fan Tibetan anti-government sentiments, but also deprive horse-market officials of their all-important annual bonuses: *SHY* zhiguan 43/81a–b.
62. This is the gravamen of Fan Chengda's argument, cited above. See also *SHY* bing 23/16b–17a, and the discussion of *liangma* purchases below.
63. Li Xinchuan, "Gengzi (1180) wu buluo zhi bian," in *CYZJ* yi 19/1197–1208.
64. See "Bingshen (1176) Qing Qiang zhi bian," *CYZJ* yi 19/1194–1197. The Blue Qiang earned their initial patent to trade in 1165 by staging vindictive raids after market officials turned their horses away. Prefect Yuwen Shaozhi was cashiered for the affair, and the vice-administrator Li Shanglao was sent out to mollify the tribes: *SHY* fanyi 5/59b–60a.
65. *CYZJ* yi 19/1198.

66. *CYZJ* yi 19/1199–1206. For a description of frontier defense institutions in southern Sichuan, see von Glahn, *Country of Streams and Grottoes,* pp. 39–48.

67. *CYZJ* yi 19/1206–1208. Sino-tribal violence might also turn in the other direction. In 1157, for instance, the Qiongbuchuan horse trader Yai Yu hired fifteen local conscripts to help him transport the payments he had earned for his and his prince's horses in Liizhou. As they approached the Liizhou-tribal border, about forty knife-wielding Chinese attacked and slaughtered Yai Yu and his band and stole his cash and goods. The prefectural authorities quickly captured the bandits, sentenced their leader Zhang Daer to fifteen canings with the heavy bamboo and banishment, and ordered the horse broker Yang Shi to make restitution. But the prefect and vice-prefect were nonetheless judged to have been negligent in maintaining good Sino-tribal relations, and were both cashiered: *SHY* fanyi 5/59a–b.

68. *WXTK* 160/1390. The official, Ding Du, is referring specifically to the number of horses the state needed to buy after suspending its pasturage system in 1028, but his figure can be used as an estimate of total replacement needs.

69. In 1047 Zhang Fangping estimated the full complement of cavalry mounts at 60,000 head (*XCB* 161/13a); but around 1060 Song Qi claimed that only 10 or 20 percent of the cavalrymen had horses: Song Qi, *Jingwen ji* 29/11a, "Yi Xiren zhazi." The state could claim far more than 6,000–12,000 head in its possession, but most of its horses fell below cavalry standards.

70. As Lo Jung-pang points out, some Southern Song "naval propagandists" dismissed the need for a cavalry at all. One Chen Ke, for example, memorialized that "our defenses today are the [Yangzi] River and the sea, so our weakness in mounted troops is no cause for concern." See "Emergence of China as a Sea Power," p. 502. On the administration and deployment of the Southern Song navy, see Sogabe Shizuo, "Nan Sō no suigun," in his *Sōdai seikeishi no kenkyū,* pp. 249–271.

71. This average excludes the 1204 quota, which Li Xinchuan deprecates as beyond reach: *CYZJ* jia 18/597. On the designated recipients of THA horses, see *CYZJ* jia 18/603–604 and Hua Yue, *Beizheng lu* 1/27a–b.

72. The most important sources on the Guangxi trade include: Zhou Qufei, *Lingwai daida* 5/5a–8b; *CYZJ* jia 18/599–602; and the material in *SHY* bing 22 and 23. For useful secondary coverage, see Sogabe Shizuo, "Sōdai no basei," pp. 128–133; and Huang Guanzhong "Nan Song shidai Yongzhou de Hengshan zhai," *Hanxue yanjiu* 3.2:507–534. Horse procurement in Guangxi was supervised by the regional Military Affairs Commissioner (*jinglue si*), and was directed primarily at the horses of Dali, near Lake Erhai in Yunnan. But most of the surrounding tribes and kingdoms participated, with some, such as Luodian and Ziqi, competing to act as brokers for the Dali herdsmen: Zhou Qufei, *Lingwai daida* 5/6a–7a; *Lidai mingchen zouyi* 242/11a–12a. Unlike the self-financing tea and horse trade, the Guangxi trade

was wholly financed externally, through yearly disbursements of provincial tax receipts, gold and silver, brocades from Chengdu, and 200,000–1,000,000 catties of salt from the Guangdong coast.

73. As the Jiankang Command did in 1204: *SHY* bing 23/25b–26a. On the average sizes and costs in silver of the horses bought in Guangxi, see *CYZJ* jia 18/600 and *SHY* bing 22/28a.

74. Convoys issued by the Southern Song horse markets may be represented as follows: in 1167 Sichuan (including Wenzhou) issued 80 convoys, Shaanxi issued 75.4 convoys (including a statutory quota of 720 or 14.4 convoys to the Sichuan Pacification Commission *{Xuanfusi}*, added to all the Shaanxi figures below), and Guangxi issued its statutory 30 convoys, for a total of 185.4 convoys. In 1170 the figures were 60 for Sichuan, 115.4 for Shaanxi, and 30 for Guangxi, at a total of 205.4 convoys. For the years 1197–1203 the annual figures were 90 for Sichuan, an average of 90.25 for Shaanxi, and 30 for Guangxi, for a total of 210.25 convoys. These figures unavoidably mix quotas and actual shipments. Sources for the Shaanxi and Sichuan figures are *SHY* bing 22/31a; *SHY* bing 23/1b–2a, 27a–b; *SHY* bing 25/29a; *SHY* bing 26/17a–b. In the case of Guangxi, Zhou Qufei claimed that the number of convoys shipped out from Guangxi was raised from 30 to 71 after 1160: *Lingwai daida* 5/6a. But the additions in fact represent emergency purchase orders, often issued in an effort to make up for previous shortages, and not an overall reliable increase in the number of yearly convoys. See *SHY* bing 23/4b–5a (1169), 6a–b (1171), and 8a (1172).

75. In the four years between 1163 and 1176, for example, the dispatches were short an average of 23 convoys (29 percent) a year out of Chengdu and 13.7 convoys (19 percent) out of Xingyuanfu: *SHY* bing 23/1b–2a.

76. See *CYZJ* jia 18/602–603; *SHY* bing 23/22a–b, 24b, 25a–b, 26b–27a, 28a.

77. *SHY* zhiguan 43/54a–b, 58b–59a.

78. *SHY* zhiguan 43/50b–51b.

79. *SHY* zhiguan 43/53b–54a; *XCB* 314/1b–2a.

80. Guo was made a Co-Intendant for Tea, but he could never gain real executive power in the Agency and was ousted from it in mid 1083 after Pu Zongmin and Lu Shimin complained that his interference threatened the enterprise's profits: see Chapter Five. Guo's most important statements are all gathered in *SHY* zhiguan 43, listed here in chronological order: 53b–56b (1081/7/9); 56b–58a (1081/9/21); 59a–61a (1082/2/18); 62b–63a (1083/6/7); 63b (1083/6/22). See in addition *XCB* 314/1b–2a (1081/7). Guo's position is very clearly analyzed by Umehara Kaoru, "Seito no uma," pp. 215–216.

81. *SHY* zhiguan 43/58b–59a.

82. *SHY* zhiguan 43/61b, 62a; *XCB* 334/12b–13b.

83. For application of the policy to Shaanxi markets, see *XCB* 335/15b. For its enactment in Wenzhou in 1085, see *SHY* zhiguan 43/68b–69b. Horse mar-

kets in Sichuan, under the control of a joint Chengdu-Lizhou Circuit Horse Purchase Commissioner, had to agree in addition to the payback procedures that "[additional disbursements of] tea that were not used could not be deducted [from their bill] and returned" (*SHY* zhiguan 43/69b–70a).

84. *SHY* zhiguan 43/62b–63a; *XCB* 355/15b.

85. *SHY* zhiguan 43/62b.

86. *SHY* zhiguan 43/67b–68b, 70a; *XCB* 359/18a–b, 381/22a.

87. A change in the official attitude towards horse procurement and the Intendancy was signaled in 1094, when the Bureau of Military Affairs retroactively rebuked the Yuanfeng Intendancy for having pursued profits and bonuses to the exclusion of horses: *SHY* zhiguan 43/71b.

88. *SHY* zhiguan 43/75b.

89. *SHY* zhiguan 43/75a–76a, 93b–94b. Zhang Hui insisted that the restrictions were the principal cause of the 3,800-ton Mingshan tea backlog of 1112–1113. See his policy review at *SHY* zhiguan 43/95a–96b.

90. *SHY* zhiguan 43/80a–b. Throughout I have translated Chinese horse measurements into hands, the standard measurement of height at the withers. One hand is equal to 4 inches. A horse of 12½ hands is, therefore, 50 inches at the withers.

91. Tong Guan's memorial of 1108 (*SHY* zhiguan 43/92a) documents the first use of the term *fanpao maima,* but it is fairly clear that the policy was initiated around 1103, as evidenced by the accelerated procurements in Sichuan (*SHY* zhiguan 43/79a–b, 83a), and the "doubling of the amount of tea" policy (see next note). On the *fanpao* universal purchase policy, see also ibid., 92b, 95a.

92. The *liangbeicha* policy was first mentioned by Sun Aobian in 1103, when he requested permission to cancel a planned trip to the capital in order to administer the new program (*SHY* zhiguan 43/79a–b). Increased shipments of tea began with Cheng Zhishao's recommendation that 3,000 to 5,000 bales of tea be shipped to the newly recovered Huangzhou for horse and grain procurement (ibid., 78a–b). In 1105 Minzhou Administrator Feng Huan was ordered to use an "additional" 30,000 bales of Mingshan tea to purchase an extra 10,000 head (ibid., 83b–85a); that same year Cheng Zhishao and Sun Aobian were commended for trading 50,000 bales of tea for 20,000 horses (*SHY* bing 24/28a–b).

93. In 1104/2 Liizhou officials were instructed to pay no more than half the value of a horse with tea—the *bancha* or "half-tea" measure—in order to save tea for the Shaanxi market; ten months later the measure had to be revoked, and the premiums added to re-engage the trade. See *SHY* zhiguan 43/76a–77a, 79b–82a, 83a.

94. *SHY* zhiguan 43/84a–b.

95. *SHY* zhiguan 43/90a, 93a–b. In 1107 Intendant Pang Yinsun memorialized that "the price of tea for the horse trade is set lower than other tea prices in

order to enrich the Tibetan [horse merchants] and summon forth horses for the nation" (90a).

96. *SHY* zhiguan 43/92a–b
97. *SHY* zhiguan 43/92b–93a (1111); 101b–102a (1122), and 102a–b (1123).
98. *SHY* zhiguan 43/99b–100a, 101b–102a, 102a–b; *SHY* bing 24/30b.
99. *SHY* zhiguan 43/108a. *XNYL* 154/4883 gives the figures on silk subventions to the THA. They are part of Li Xinchuan's standard enumeration of THA accounts, and though appended to an entry for 1145, are not dated by that entry. They are repeated for the Qiandao era (1165–1173) in *CYZJ* jia 18/596.
100. *SHY* bing 25/7b. This is close to Yuan Xingzong's estimate circa 1170 of 150 strings of cash (excluding brokerage fees) at the marketplace: Yuan Xingzong, *Jiuhua ji* 7/5a.
101. *SHY* bing 23/9b.
102. *Huang Song zhongxing liangchao shengzheng* 55/2086–2087.
103. *SHY* bing 22/31b.
104. *Lidai mingchen zouyi* 242/11a–b.
105. *SHY* bing 23/10a. The quotation is from a War Ministry memorial of 1173 citing complaints from all the armies in the field about the poor quality of the horses convoyed in from Danchang and Fengtie, Sichuan, and Guangxi. The problem of quality, in other words, was ubiquitous. The "long teeth" at issue refer to the incisors, which acquire a characteristic long and "bucked" appearance with age.
106. An order of 1167 (*SHY* bing 23/2a) from the Bureau of Military Affairs was typical: "Recently the western horses sent out [to the armies] have all been small and emaciated. Command the Tea and Horse Agency to purchase horses that are up to standard and tender-toothed and able to bear [a rider]. But they must not fall short of the annual quota." In 1168 Zhang Song attempted to ensure responsible procurement in Danchang by having the size of the horse and the name of its purchaser branded on the animal's neck. Although enacted, there is no information on the effects of the practice: *SHY* bing 23/2b.
107. In 1005, when the Song government enjoyed its greatest abundance of horses, the age limits for purchases of foreign horses were reduced from between 3 and 17 *sui* to between 4 and 13 *sui,* when the animals would have been at their peak strength (*SHY* bing 22/2a).
108. *SHY* bing 22/25b–25a. In fact, the court simply ordered the THA to "see if it can be done."
109. *SHY* bing 23/12a–b, 13b.
110. *SHY* bing 23/7b.
111. *SHY* bing 23/13b–14a.
112. *SHY* bing 23/20b–21a.

113. *SHY* bing 23/15b.
114. *SHY* bing 22/26a.
115. *SHY* bing 23/26a–b.
116. *Encyclopedia Americana,* vol. 14, p. 397. By American standards none of the horses of Central Asia would qualify as adult mounts. A review of Epstein, *Domestic Animals of China,* pp. 107–112, shows the animals of Qinghai and Gansu to range between 12½ and 13¼ hands; those of the Tibetan table-land from 12½ to 14 hands; and the horses of Xikang from 11 to 12¾ hands. All were well suited for mountain pack work, but Epstein does not comment on their qualifications as riding horses, the main interest of Song procurement officials. In reference to the horses of Mongolia, whose average height at the withers was only 12½ hands, Epstein cites a Western observer of 1930 that "there is no advantage in a Mongolian pony exceeding 13½ hands for racing" (p. 100).
117. *SHY* bing 23/3b–41.
118. *SHY* bing 23/16b–17a.
119. *SHY* bing 23/24b.
120. Hartwell, "Chinese Monetary Analysis."
121. Horse-market officials were prohibited from using copper coins as early as 981 (*SS* 198/4933; *SHY* bing 24/2a), but were allowed to pay 10 percent of the price of a horse with copper coins during the New Policies era: *SHY* zhiguan 43/54a–b). One hundred thousand *liang* of silver were allotted to the horse trade in 1055; and although the value was gradually replaced with silk and tea, silver remained a standard countertrade item for horses and grain even during the New Policies: *SS* 198/4935; *SHY* zhiguan 43/53b–56a.
122. *SHY* bing 22/29a, 31b–32a.
123. *SHY* bing 23/18a–b, 19a.
124. *Kuozhuang* was suspended from 1183 to 1185. The THA Intendant asked whether he was expected to buy the larger horses in the 1186 market season, since if so the Tibetan merchants would have to be informed before-hand: *SHY* bing 23/18a–b. In 1187 Emperor Xiaozong observed that the horses were no larger than regular animals and ordered the suspension continued. At the same time total silver expenditures were pegged to the pre-1169 level, probably 20,000 *liang* (ibid., 19a). That same year, the emperor remarked that it would be best gradually to diminish the use of silver, in order to bring the Tibetans around to a genuine "mutual trade" (ibid., 19a); the next year the *kuozhuang* policy was again suspended and the silver put in a discretionary fund, with officials prohibited from using the metal "recklessly." But in 1189 the order was watered down to a request for officials to "attempt a reduction in silver use" (ibid., 19b).
125. *SHY* bing 23/22a, 25a.

126. *Lidai mingchen zouyi* 242/13a; *Jin shi* 44/1005.
127. Hua Yue, "Pingrong shice: mazheng," in his *Cuiwei xiansheng beizheng lu* 1/27b.
128. We cannot, of course, estimate the number of horses foreign herdsmen withheld from market, but the government's attempt to buy mares is instructive. In 1171/2 Emperor Xiaozong inquired whether mares were hard to buy in Sichuan. Yu Yunwen replied in a memorial that they were in fact so plentiful in the western borderlands that the government could easily purchase 2,000 head annually. The Sichuan Governor-General was ordered to do so, but ten months later he replied that the command was impossible to fulfill: the herdsmen of Sichuan and Shaanxi saved their mares for breeding, and they simply would not sell them: *SHY* bing 23/6a–b, 7b–8a.
129. *Jin shi* 44/1005.
130. For examples, see *Songdai Shuwen jicun* 54/2b; *SHY* zhiguan 43/103b–104a, 104b–105a; *XNYL* 116/3664.
131. *Lidai mingchen zouyi* 242/10b.
132. On the Sino-Jurchen tea trade, see Katō Shigeshi "Sō to Kingoku to no boeki ni tsuite," and "Sō-Kin boeki ni okeru chasen oyobi kinu ni tsuite," in his *Shina keizaishi kōshō,* vol. 2, pp. 247–282, 284–304; Hok-lam Chan, "Tea Production and the Tea Trade under the Jurchen-Chin Dynasty"; and Quan Hansheng, "Song-Jin jian de zousi maoyi," in *Zhongguo jingjishi luncong,* vol. 2, p. 217.
133. *CYZJ* jia 14/441.
134. Wu Yong, "Hushi," *Helin ji* 37/20a–b.
135. Because of the easier terrain and shorter distances between market and front, convoy problems were much less pronounced during the Northern Song. There were apparently some difficulties; for in 1094 Lu Shimin temporarily reestablished a voluntary *quanma* policy, with horse merchants driving their own animals to the capital. Four years later Zeng Bu reported that under the *quanma* merchant-convoy system, deaths in transit amounted to less than 1 percent, in contrast with losses of 12 percent under the THA-run *gangma* convoy system. But the issue of horse transport in the north does not come up again until the Southern Song. See, in chronological order, *SHY* bing 22/13a; *SHY* zhiguan 43/72a–b; *XCB* 501/4a. The Liizhou-to-Shaanxi convoy was plagued by high mortality rates during the Northern as well as Southern Song, but the Liizhou horses were less essential in the earlier period. See *SHY* zhiguan 43/79b–82a; *Songdai Shuwen jicun* 54/2a–b. For information on the Guangxi convoys during the Southern Song, see Zhou Qufei, "Magang," in *Lingwai daida* 5/7b–8b; and Sogabe Shizuo, "Sōdai no basei," pp. 128–138.
136. *SHY* bing 23/18b–19a, 21a–22a; *SHY* bing 25/16a–b. Danchang and Fengjie were too crowded and poor in resources to host horses or drivers for

long periods of time, and officials never succeeded in establishing rest stations closer than Xingyuan.

137. Hua Yue, *Beizheng lu* 1/29b.

138. The Jurchen presence blocked the much easier Han River valley route through Junzhou: *CYZJ* jia 18/604; *SHY* bing 23/36a–b. Xie Chengxia surmises (p. 48) that iron horse shoes had possibly entered China by Tang or Song, and certainly by Ming. Jagchid Sechin and C. R. Bowden cite (p. 249, n. 12) Wang Guowei's conclusion that wooden horse shoes were known to the Chinese by Tang. But despite the availability of at least some horse-shoeing techniques, it appears that the THA bought and shipped out horses unshod. For distances and stages between points, see *SHY* bing 23/20a–b, 21b; *SHY* bing 25/8a, 24a–b, 28b–30b; Hua Yue, *Beizheng lu* 1/27a, 29b. The distance between Chengdu and the capital, Lin'an, was measured at 6,119 *li*, or about 2,000 miles; the distance from Xingyuan to Lin'an was estimated at 4,889 *li*, or about 1,600 miles.

139. In 1163 an anonymous official claimed that convoyers sent from Lin'an to Xingyuan to pick up horses made one round trip in two years, suggesting that they took at least one year to make the downriver drive: *SHY* bing 25/1b–2a. But according to Hua Yue the round trip from either Hangzhou to Xingyuan or Zhenjiang to Chengdu took half a year, implying that the horses were in transit for roughly three to four months: *Beizheng lu* 1/27a. The round trip from Chengdu to Hanyang, a distance of about 1,100 miles in 64 stages, took 120 days: *SHY* bing 25/29a.

140. In 1165 Hong Gua memorialized that "the roads of Kui, Gui, and Xia prefectures are dangerous and steep, and people still cannot travel them. The so-called 'gallery roads' are not to be compared with those of the western circuits [i.e., the roads through the Qinling Mountains], so how can horses travel over them?": *SHY* bing 23/31a–b. On the rise of Sichuan's Yangzi River corridor, see Smith, "Commerce, Agriculture, and Core Formation."

141. The major sources on the riverine transport experiment are Li Xinchuan, "Gangma shuilu lu," *CYZJ* jia 18/604–608; Wang Shipeng, "Kuizhou lun magang zhuang" and "Zai lun magang zhuang," in *Meixi ji* 4/7b–11b; and *SHY* bing 23/29a–37a. See also Sogabe Shizuo, "Sōdai no basei", pp. 120–127.

142. See Ouyang Xiu's "Xia zhou zhi Xiting ji," as cited by Yuan Xingzong in *Jiuhua ji* 7/6a.

143. *SHY* bing 25/19b; *SHY* bing 26/17b–18a. The celestial stems were used as brands, *jia* to *bing* for the Three Palace Commands, *ding* through *ren* for the Six Yangzi River Armies.

144. Crews were supposed to arrive and depart the city according to schedules. But weather, travel conditions, and the arrival of horses at the principal

markets were all stronger influences on the movement of crews. In 1192, for example, the Xingyuan Prefect called for strict adherence to the official schedules, after 36 crews from the capital all arrived in Xingyuan at one time, lolling about at Xingyuan's expense while waiting for their horses: *SHY* bing 26/4b–5a.

145. *SHY* bing 25/5b–6a, 19a–b, 22a.

146. *SHY* bing 23/27a–b; *SHY* bing 25/5b–6a, 22a.

147. *SHY* bing 25/22a.

148. There was a substantial corpus of veterinary literature available by Song times. Xie Chengxia lists 36 separate hippological texts, including veterinary, dating from classical (pre-Sui) periods that would have been available to Song administrators: *Zhongguo yangma shi,* pp. 56–58.

149. *SHY* zhiguan 43/116b–117a.

150. Hong Mai, "Ezhou gangma," *Yijian zhi* jing ji 7/1a–b.

151. *SHY* zhiguan 43/117a–b; *SHY* bing 25/51b–52a. The fate of the Chengdu Terminal convoys is not as clear, but by the end of the century, and possibly 1189, the Yangzi Commands all picked up their horses in Chengdu: *SHY* bing 23/19b–20a; Hua Yue, *Beizheng lu* 1/27a.

152. In 1175 what had been a ten-day rest stop at Hanyang was reduced to three days, while the drive from Jinzhou to Hanyang was slowed down by seven days: *SHY* bing 23/13a–b.

153. *SHY* bing 25/28b–31a; Hua Yue, *Beizheng lu* 1/27a.

154. Hua Yue, *Beizheng lu* 1/26b; *SHY* bing 23/20a–b; *SHY* bing 25/29a–b.

155. *SHY* bing 23/14a–b; *SHY* bing 25/19b–20b. Even the Yukang depot could accommodate just one convoy crew at a time.

156. The allotments per horse were generous: 8 *sheng* (6.9 quarts, equivalent to 13.8 pounds) of barley and 13 catties (16.9 pounds) of millet grass. Modern feeding guidelines are more parsimonious. For a horse in light use, experts recommend 0.5 to 1 pound of grain and 1.25 to 1.5 pounds of hay for every 100 pounds of body weight. Estimating Song horses at a median weight for ponies, ca. 700 pounds, yields maximum feed requirements of 7 pounds of grain and 10.5 pounds of hay daily: *Encyclopedia Americana,* vol. 14, p. 397.

157. *SHY* bing 24/40a–b; *SHY* bing 25/2a, 7b–8b.

158. Hua Yue, *Beizheng lu* 1/29b.

159. *SHY* bing 24/37a; *SHY* bing 25/11a.

160. Circuit-level agencies that provided some funding for the riverine transport experiment included the THA and the Governor-General in Sichuan (*SHY* bing 23/31a, 33a–35a), the Jingxi and Hubei fiscal intendancies and the Huguang Supply Master General (*SHY* bing 23/13a–b, 18b), and the Yangzi River Commands-General (*SHY* bing 23/20a–b). In addition, travel maintenance for the trail crews was covered by travel vouchers. Vouchers allowed the crews to be sent out without large sums of money, while providing local

depot administrators with receipts for theoretically regaining the funds spent on feeding the men from higher-level agencies: *SHY* bing 25/8a; *SHY* bing 26/4b–5a. An anonymous memorial of 1216 indicates that provisioning and funding responsibilities were entirely local: *SHY* bing 26/22a.

161. In 1156 the Bureau of Military Affairs accused the officers and clerks of the THA itself of stealing hay for their own use and letting the convoy horses starve: *SHY* zhiguan 43/109a.

162. *SHY* bing 24/35b–36a.

163. *SHY* bing 25/16a–b.

164. Between 1166 and 1173 the government created three new Intendants for Horse Convoy Relay Depots, staffed by servitors major. They were to supervise the Chengdu-Xingyuan, Xingyuan-Hanyang, and Hanyang-Hangzhou spurs: *SHY* zhiguan 43/117b–118b. In 1189 responsibility for the 100 depots between Danchang and Hangzhou was divided among the seven military commands-general, each of which appointed a "military supervisor" (*jiangguan*) for the job: *SHY* bing 23/19b–20a.

165. For examples of the possible dysfunctional consequences of incentive systems to the performance of a wide array of tasks, see Chapter Five. Note that when the "military supervisors" referred to above were charged with responsibility for the depots, they alone were tied to a system of rewards and fines. The local officials they were to supervise remained insulated from personal accountability by the multiplicity of their overall tasks.

166. In 1204 circuit financial administrators were ordered to prod the prefectures and counties into undertaking much-needed repairs of the relay depots and supplying fodder within a given length of time: *SHY* bing 23/26b. But Hua Yue's critique of ca. 1210, suffused with indignant accusations of collapsed bridges and plankways, dilapidated depot sheds, and starving horses, indicates that any improvements were short-lived.

167. Joe B. Frantz and Julian E. Choate, Jr., *The American Cowboy*, pp. 33–47.

168. Composition of the crews was fairly standard regardless of the particular despatch system in force, and changed little over time. See *SHY* zhiguan 43/107b; *SHY* bing 25/29a, 51b–52b; and on the Guangxi crews Zhou Qufei, *Lingwai daida* 5/7b.

169. At 50 men per crew, the Southern Song average of 203 convoys annually would require 10,150 men if every man worked one convoy.

170. In 1145 the War Ministry complained that during the Northern Song, "it only required the services of 110 foremen (*shichen*) to transport 20,000 horses [Nb.: a ratio of 3.6 convoys per foreman]. Now it takes the services of 58 foremen to drive only 58 convoys of western horses": *SHY* bing 24/36a–b. On the foreman's tasks, see *SHY* zhiguan 43/107b and Hua Yue, *Beizheng lu* 1/29a.

171. In 1159 Hong Cun complained that in Sichuan currently active officials of

high rank were employed as convoy foremen, and that the number of men receiving promotions in stipendiary office each year—"several tens"—was excessive. He requested that civil officials of grade 7B *(chengyilang)* and military officials of grade 8 *(wuyi daifu)* or above be prohibited from taking the post: *SHY* bing 24/40b.

172. *SHY* zhiguan 43/107b. The court ordered Wu Lin and Yang Jing instead of the THA to pick the foremen and to select "responsible men familiar with horses." In 1153 the Bureau of Military Affairs complained that all the convoys arriving at the capital from Sichuan still showed the disastrous influence of the THA foremen: *SHY* bing 24/37a. During the Hanyang transfer system, THA foremen were said to cause an unusually high number of deaths on their stretch of the relay; and in 1173 the Bureau of Military Affairs sent out seven Palace Command *(Sanya)* foremen directly to Xing-yuan to pick up their herds at the source, effectively ending the Hanyang relay system: *SHY* zhiguan 43/117a–b. Subsequently the foremen had to be sent all the way to Danchang with an advance team, to take over the short haul to Xingyuan from the Sichuanese foremen: *SHY* bing 25/51b–52b.

173. *SHY* bing 23/19b–20a. In 1190 the Bureau of Military Affairs reported that the convoy foremen for the short haul from Danchang to Xingyuan were chosen by the THA from among "servitors temporarily residing [in Danchang and Xingyuan] while awaiting vacancies": *SHY* bing 23/21a–22a.

174. Hua Yue, *Beizheng lu* 1/29b.

175. *SHY* bing 25/28b, 29b, 44b–45a; *SHY* bing 26/17b.

176. *SHY* bing 25/51b–52a. Sogabe Shizuo identifies the hundred households as minor tribes: "Sōdai no basei," p. 112. In 1173 an official of the Palace Command requested that the children be replaced with soldiers. But in 1190 the Bureau of Military Affairs reported that, because there were not enough soldiers for the Danchang short haul, the THA hired drivers from among the local bands of hooligans: *SHY* bing 23/21a.

177. *SHY* zhiguan 43/106a–b, 109a; *SHY* bing 23/19b–20a; *SHY* bing 25/5b.

178. *SHY* bing 25/1b, 29a, 44b. In 1204 THA Intendant Peng Ge reported that the number of *baizhi renbing* auxiliaries sent to augment the convoy troops had been halved from an original quota or 4,000 men: *SHY* bing 26/17b. The term *baizhi* denoted soldiers in menial service to civil and military officials: *Zhongguo lishi da cidian—Songshi* p. 98. The *wufeng jun* was originally stationed in coastal Chuzhou (Anhui, Huai'an County). On this and the other new semi-independent armies that proliferated from Emperor Xiaozong's reign onwards, see Wang Zengyu, *Songchao bingzhi chutan* pp. 187–192.

179. *SHY* bing 26/6a. Branding was supposed to make schemes of this sort

impossible, but Hua Yue charged that in any event the receiving officials rarely checked the brands: *Beizheng lu* 1/29a.

180. Hua Yue, *Beizheng lu* 1/27a.

181. *SHY* bing 26/22a–b.

182. Even when these drivers were placed under *Sanya* foremen, they found ways to steal provisions or injure the horses with their ignorance. On mixed crews, see *SHY* zhiguan 43/107b (1152); *SHY* bing 25/1b–2a (1163); *SHY* zhiguan 43/117a–b (1173).

183. *SHY* zhiguan 43/106a–b.

184. *SHY* bing 26/22a–b.

185. In 1170 Executive of the War Ministry Wang Zhiqi argued that the cheapest and most equitable system would put the transfer point at Xiangyang, because then the labor pool could be widened to include Jiangxi and Hubei, and the shorter convoy relays would enable each crew to make two trips yearly. Although never implemented, Wang's proposal is supported with valuable information on costs and manpower: *SHY* bing 25/28b–31a.

186. *SHY* bing 25/1b–2a.

187. *SHY* zhiguan 43/106a–b, 107b; *SHY* bing 24/37a.

188. *SHY* bing 24/37b, 39b–40a; *XNYL* 183/5992. See also *SHY* bing 22/31a–b; *SHY* bing 23/19b–20a, 21a–22a; *SHY* bing 25/51b, 52b.

189. *SHY* bing 25/5b–6a.

190. *SHY* bing 25/51b–52b; Hua Yue, *Beizheng lu* 1/27a. The Ezhou Command had picked up its own 15 convoys since the 1160s: *SHY* bing 25/29a. Sichuanese crews remained responsible for convoying brood mares and studs to the Ezhou command and a stock farm in Jingzhou, and they continued to participate in the Danchang short haul: *SHY* bing 23/19b–20a, 21a–22; *SHY* bing 25/43b–44a.

191. For example, in 1210 Hua Yue peevishly inquired why "the soldiers of the [Three Palace Commands] are not allowed to go directly to Danchang to pick up their horses themselves": *Beizheng lu* 1/27a–b. And in 1219 an anonymous official, drawing attention to a THA report that because Army-despatched crews were often late, Chengdu and Xingyuan corrals overflowed with horses waiting to be shipped out, recommended a return to the Hanyang-terminal transfer system, "abolished long ago": *SHY* bing 26/23a–b.

192. The complete schedule, including Guangxi crews, is at *SHY* bing 25/41a–50b.

193. *SHY* bing 25/41b–42a, 42b–43a, 43b–44a. To illustrate the system, if the entire convoy arrived safely, the foreman of a crew despatched from the capital for the run from Sichuan or Xingyuan to Hangzhou was promoted two grades; the foremen of crews sent from Zhenjiang, Jiankang (Nanjing), or Chizhou were rewarded one-third less generously—a promotion of one

grade and hastening of the promotional review by 1 year 8 months; foremen from army commands at Jiangzhou (Dehua, Jiangxi *sheng*) and east received half the Hangzhou foreman's reward—a promotion of one grade.

194. The commutation values for each grade promotion ranged between 20 and 30 strings of cash per grade, depending on the despatching unit. Staffmen making a second trip could double their promotions: *SHY* bing 25/42a–b, 43a–b, 44a.

195. *SHY* bing 25/44b–45a.

196. In 1163 military attachés *(jiangjiao)* received 1.5 *sheng* (1.25 quarts) of rice and 150 copper cash daily; drivers, who expended greater energy, received one *sheng* of rice more per day, but only 70 copper cash. (The minimum daily grain requirement of an adult male or female was estimated to be one *sheng* during the Song: Kinugawa Tsuyoshi, *Songdai wenguan fengji*, p. 91.) In Sichuan the copper-cash payments were commuted to iron coins or iron-backed paper notes at the current rate of 2 iron cash to 1 copper: *SHY* bing 25/2a. Two years later wages for the trail drivers were raised to 100 copper or 200 iron per diem: *SHY* bing 25/7b–8a.

197. It is not certain how rigorously the incentive schedule was maintained. In 1207 Hua Yue wrote that "among the horse-driving conscripts it is said, 'Even if the horse [arrives] fat, I have no expectation of a promotion; even if a horse dies, I am not held responsible' ": *(Beizheng lu* 1/27a.) But it is uncertain whether Hua's observation denotes a change in policy, a specific exemption for civilian conscripts as opposed to soldiers, or a deterioration of the system.

198. *SHY* bing 26/22b–23a.

199. In his landmark study of compliance in complex organizations, Etzioni (pp. 55–56) observes that the combination of coercive and utilitarian—i.e., material—means of eliciting compliance from lower participants is relatively rare. He cites the case of company towns where management could call on private or public police forces to force laborers to work at a given wage as one example. More typical combinations link coercive with normative controls, as in the case of combat units, and utilitarian with normative controls, as in the case of labor unions. It is the absence of a normative component—a mechanism for eliciting the moral commitment of the participants—that most hindered the Southern Song convoy operation.

200. The Northern Song *quanma* system essentially contracted delivery of its horses to the native traders, but by the Southern Song the practice appears to have lapsed.

201. See Wang Zengyu, *Songchao bingzhi chutan*, pp. 183–192.

202. On the Mongol campaigns in Sichuan, see Hu Zhaoxi, "Sichuan junmin kangji Menggu" and *Songmo Sichuan zhanzheng shiliao xuanbian;* and Chen Shisong, *Menggu ding Shu shigao*.

203. Hua Yue, "Yu qi," *Beizheng lu* 1/7b–8a. Hua's own answer was to use light, mobile carts equipped with incendiary devices.

204. McNeill, p. 39. The following observations are based on McNeill and on Elvin, *Pattern,* who between them synthesize the research on Song military technology by Yoshida Mitsukuni, Lo Jung-pang, Joseph Needham, and others.

205. For the Mongol conquest of north and south China, see H. Desmond Martin, *The Rise of Chingis Khan and his Conquest of North China,* and David Morgan, *The Mongols.* The sophistication of Mongol military tactics, including their use of boats along the Yangzi, can be seen in Francis Woodman Cleaves, "The Biography of Bayan of the Barin in the Yuan Shih," *Harvard Journal of Asiatic Studies* 19:185–303.

CONCLUSION

1. Wang Zengyu, "Wang Anshi bianfa jianlun," *Zhongguo shehui kexue* 3:149–150.

2. Wang Anshi made his claim in a debate with Sima Guang before the emperor in 1068. The issue of engrossers is not raised in this exchange, but can be inferred from Wang's many other references to the *jianbing* problem. Sima Guang utterly rejected the idea that the state could take more resources out of the economy without leaving the people with less: "The wealth and goods produced by heaven and earth is limited to a given amount and no more. If it is not among the people, then it is in [the hands of] the commonweal"— where, Sima elsewhere insists, it will be squandered. The debate is reported in Sima Guang, "Erying zoudui," *Sima wenzhenggong chuanjia ji* 42/543–545.

3. The first quotation is by the New Policies opponent Wang Yansou, caustically invoking the typical justification used by New Policies advocates for enlarging the scope of state monopolies: *XCB* 360/6a–b. The second quotation is by the Sichuanese critic of THA Intendant Han Qiu's *raocha* bonus, Zhang Shen: *SHY* shihuo 31/11a.

4. *SHY* shihuo 4/16a–17a; Smith, "State Power."

5. Ouyang Xiu, "Tong jinsi shangshu," in *Ouyang wenzhonggong ji* 5/85–86; cited in Wang Shengduo, "Songdai caizheng," p. 52.

6. By "merchant liturgies" Mann means, following Max Weber, local elites (in this case merchant elites) "called upon to perform important public services in the state's behalf, at their own expense": *Local Merchants and the Chinese Bureaucracy, 1750–1950,* pp. 12–13. Mann distinguishes between three models of tax collection: liturgical tax management, in which taxation is managed by elite groups; tax-farming; and bureaucratic tax collection. I think that Mann is correct in viewing the rise of "liturgical" tax collection during the Song as a response to diminishing returns to centralized bureaucratic tax

strategies, but that she overemphasizes the extent to which it replaced bureaucratic methods; see esp. pp. 30–36. As Wang argues, and as I have tried to show in this study, "liturgical" and bureaucratic strategies of commercial control coexisted side by side during the Song.

7. Wang Shengduo, "Sondai caizheng," pp. 47–53.

8. See Elvin, *Pattern,* pp. 203–234.

9. Hartwell analyses evidence on economic decline prior to the fall of the Southern Song in terms of a model of regional cycles of development and decline in "Transformations," pp. 365–394.

10. Data on economic vitality and comparative well-being during the Southern Song is of course complex, contradictory, and geographically diverse. For evidence on rural poverty, see Liang Gengyao, *Nan Song de nongcun jingji;* and Richard von Glahn, "Community and Welfare: Chu Hsi's Community Granary in Theory and Practice." On commercial disruption, see, for example, Saeki Tomi, "Sōdai chagun ni tsuite," in his *Chūgokushi kenkyū,* vol. 1, pp. 409–420, which narrates the rise of tea-bandit armies in response to the dislocation of the Middle Yangzi tea economy in the late twelfth century.

11. The Song economy was by no means alone in succumbing to the suffocating policies of a state stretched to the limit by the costs of defense. For a provocative analysis of the relationship between military expenditures and the rise and fall of nations in a global historical context, see Paul Kennedy, *The Rise and Fall of the Great Powers: Economic Change and Military Conflict from 1500 to 2000.*

12. See, for example, Ramon Myers, "Some Issues on Economic Organization during the Ming and Ch'ing Periods," *Ch'ing-shih wen-t'i* 3.2:77–97; Thomas Metzger, "On the Historical Roots of Economic Modernization in China: The Increasing Differentiation of the Economy from the Polity during Late Ming and Early Ch'ing Times," in Chi-ming Hou and Tzong-shian Yu, eds., *Conference on Modern Chinese Economic History,* pp. 33–44; and Harriet Zurndorfer, "Chinese Merchants and Commerce in Sixteenth Century China," in W. L. Idema, ed., *Leyden Studies in Sinology,* pp. 75–86. Peter Perdue discusses this literature in the Introduction to his *Exhausting the Earth: State and Peasant in Hunan, 1500–1850.*

13. See Rueschemeyer and Evans, "The State and Economic Transformation."

14. Ray Huang, *Taxation,* p. 321.

15. Marianne Bastid, "The Structure of the Financial Institutions of the State in the Late Qing," in Stuart R. Schram, ed., *The Scope of State Power in China,* p. 67.

16. Frances V. Moulder, *Japan, China, and the Modern World Economy,* p.48.

17. Moulder, pp. 49–50.

18. G. William Skinner has offered a very convincing and influential explanation of the long-term withdrawal of the state from the economy in late imperial

China. Skinner argues that given the limited administrative capacity of any premodern agrarian state, as China's population increased eight-fold over the course of the imperial era, "a unified empire could be maintained on into the late imperial era only by systematically reducing the scope of basic-level administrative functions and countenancing a decline in the effectiveness of bureaucratic government within local systems." Following the work of Twitchett on the collapse of regulated markets in the Tang, Skinner postulates "a long-term trend beginning in the [Tang] whereby the degree of official involvement in local affairs—not only in marketing and commerce but also in social regulation . . . and administration itself—steadily declined, a retrenchment forced by the growing scale of empire." See his "Urban Development in Imperial China," in G. William Skinner, ed., *The City in Late Imperial China,* pp. 19–24. Skinner's view is echoed by Madeleine Zelin in her assessment of the failure of Yongzheng's rationalizing fiscal reforms of the eighteenth century: *The Magistrate's Tael,* pp. 303–308.

19. Hartwell, "Transformations," pp. 416, 421–422.

20. Hymes, chs. 3, 8, and Conclusion, esp. pp. 117, 212.

21. These issues are explored by the contributors to the forthcoming conference volume on Song statecraft edited by Robert Hymes and Conrad Schirokauer.

22. See Mark Elvin, "The Last Thousand Years of Chinese History: Changing Patterns in Land Tenure," *Modern Asian Studies* 4.2:97–114; Hilary J. Beattie, *Land and Lineage in China: A Study of T'ung-ch'eng County, Anhwei, in the Ming and Ch'ing Dynasties;* and Mi Chu Wiens, "Lord and Peasant: The Sixteenth to Eighteenth Centuries," *Modern China* 6.1:3–40.

23. Chaffee, Table 5, p. 27; Ho Ping-ti, *The Ladder of Success in Imperial China: Aspects of Social Mobility,* 1368–1911, ch. 3.

24. See Ho, *Ladder of Success,* ch. 4.

25. For examples of elites nullifying state-strengthening reforms, see, for example, Ray Huang, *1587, A Year of No Significance;* and Susan Mann, *Local Merchants.* This same theme is explored from a comparative perspective by Theda Skocpol in *States and Social Revolutions* and Barrington Moore in *Social Origins of Dictatorship and Democracy.*

Abbreviations Used in the Bibliography

SBBY   *Sibu beiyao* 四部備要 collectanea. Shanghai and Taipei, Zhonghua shuju.

SBCK   *Sibu congkan* 四部叢刊 collectanea. Shanghai and Taipei, Shangwu yinshuguan.

SKQSZB   *Siku quanshu zhenben* 四庫全書珍本 collectanea. Shanghai and Taipei, Shangwu yinshuguan.

Bibliography

Aoyama Sadao 青山定雄. *Tō Sō jidai no kōtsū to chishi chizu no kenkyū* 唐宋時代 の交通と地誌地図の研究. Tokyo, Yoshikawa Kobunkan, 1963.

Araki Toshikazu 荒木敏一. *"Nan Sō no ruishōshi"* 南宋の類省試, *Shirin* 44.6: 28–37 (1962).

Ardant, Gabriel. "Financial Policy and Economic Infrastructure of Modern States and Nations," in Charles Tilly, ed., *The Formation of National States in Western Europe*. Princeton, Princeton University Press, 1975.

Baber, E. Colborne. *Travels and Researches in Western China*. Reprint of the 1882 ed.; Taipei, Ch'eng Wen Publishing Co., 1971.

Backus, Charles. *The Nan-chao Kingdom and T'ang China's Southwestern Frontier*. Cambridge, University Press, 1981.

Bastid, Marianne "The Structure of the Financial Institutions of the State in the Late Qing," in Stuart R. Schram, ed., *The Scope of State Power in China*. New York, Chinese University Press and St. Martin's Press, 1985.

Beattie, Hilary J. *Land and Lineage in China: A Study of T'ung-ch'eng County, Anhwei, in the Ming and Ch'ing Dynasties*. Cambridge, Cambridge University Press, 1979.

Bielenstein, Hans. "The Census of China during the Period 2–742 A.D.," *Bulletin of the Museum of Far Eastern Antiquities* 19: 125–263 (1947).

Bo Juyi 白居易. *Bo Juyi xuanji* 白居易選集. Shanghai, Gujie chubanshe, 1980.

Bol, Peter. "Principles of Unity: On the Political Visions of Ssu-ma Kuang (1019–1086) and Wang An-shih (1021–1086)," prepared for the Conference on Sung Dynasty Statecraft in Thought and Action sponsored by the American Council of Learned Societies and the Social Science Research Council, Scottsdale, Arizona, 1986.

Braudel, Fernand. *Capitalism and Material Life, 1400–1800*. New York, Harper and Row, 1973.

Braun, Rudolf. "Taxation, Sociopolitical Structure, and State-Building: Great Britain and Brandenburg-Prussia," in Charles Tilly, ed., *The Formation of National States in Western Europe*. Princeton, Princeton University Press, 1975.

Bray, Francesca. *Agriculture*, pt. 2 of *Biology and Biological Technology*, vol. 6 of Joseph Needham, gen. ed., *Science and Civilisation in China*. Cambridge, Cambridge University Press, 1984.

Bretschneider, E. *Mediaeval Researches from Eastern Asiatic Sources*. 2 vols. Reprint of 1888 ed.; New York, Barnes and Noble, 1967.

Cai Shangxiang 蔡上翔. *Wang jinggong nianpu kaolue* 王荊公年譜考略. Shanghai, Shanghai renmin chubanshe, 1959.

Cao Xuequan 曹學佺. *Shuzhong guangji* 蜀中廣記. *SKQSZB* ed.

Chaffee, John W. *The Thorny Gates of Learning in Sung China*. Cambridge, Cambridge University Press, 1985.

Chan, Hok-lam. "Tea Production and the Tea Trade under the Jurchen-Chin Dynasty," in Wolfgang Bauer, ed., *Studia Sino-Mongolica*. Wiesbaden, Franz Steiner, 1979.

Chang Fu-jui. *Les Fonctionnaires des Song: Index des Titres*. Paris, Mouton, 1962.

Chang Qu 常璩. *Huayang guozhi* 華陽國志. *SBBY* ed.

Changsun Wuji 長孫無忌. *Tang lü shuyi* 唐律疏議. Taipei, Taiwan Shangwu yinshuguan, 1969.

Chao Yuezhi 晁說之. *Songshan wenji* 嵩山文集. *SBCK* ed.

Chen Jun 陳均. *Huangchao biannian gangmu beiyao* 皇朝編年綱目備要. *Jingjiatang congshu* 靜嘉堂叢書, ed. Taipei, Chengwen chubanshe, 1966.

Chen Shisong 陳世松. *Menggu ding Shu shigao* 蒙古定蜀史稿. Chengdu, Sichuan sheng shehui kexue yuan chubanshe, 1985.

Chen Zhen 陳振. "Lun baoma fa" 論保馬法, in Deng Guangming and Cheng Yingliu, eds, *Songshi yanjiu lunwen ji* (q.v.).

Chen Zi'ang 陳子昂. *Xinjiao Chen Zi'ang ji* 新校陳子昂集. Taipei, Shijie shuju, 1964.

Chen Zugui 陳祖槼 and Zhu Zizhen 朱自振, eds. *Zhongguo chaye lishiziliao xuanji* 中國茶葉歷史資料選集. Beijing, Nongye chubanshe, 1981.

Cheng Guangyu 程光裕. "Cha yu Tang-Song sixiangjie de guanxi" 茶與唐宋思想界的関係, in *Songshi yanjiu ji* 宋史研究集, vol. 3. Taipei, 1966.

——. "Songdai chashu kaolue" 宋代茶書考略, in *Songshi yanjiu ji*, vol. 8, Taipei, 1976.

Cheng Minsheng 程民生. "Lun Bei Song caizheng de tedian yu jipin jiaxiang" 論北宋財政的特点与积贫的假象, *Zhongguoshi yanjiu* 3: 27–40 (1984).

Chengdu wenlei 成都文類. *SKQSZB* ed.

Chongxiu Pengxian zhi 重修彭縣志. 1878 ed.

Ch'ü T'ung-tsu. *Han Social Structure*. Seattle, University of Washington Press, 1972.

Clark, Hugh. "Consolidation on the South China Frontier: The Development of Ch'uan-chou, 699–1126." PhD diss., University of Pennsylvania, 1981.

Cleaves, Francis Woodman. "The Biography of Bayan of the Barin in the Yuan Shih," *Harvard Journal of Asiatic Studies* 19: 185–303 (1956).

Creel, Herrlee G. "The Role of the Horse in Chinese History," in his *What is Taoism? and Other Studies in Chinese Cultural History*. Chicago, University of Chicago Press, 1970.

Cressey, George B. *China's Geographic Foundations*. New York, McGraw Hill, 1934.

Dai Yixuan 戴裔煊. *Songdai chaoyan zhidu yanjiu* 宋代鈔鹽制度研究. Shanghai, Shangwu yinshuguan, 1957.

Dalby, Michael T. "Court Politics in Late T'ang Times," in Denis Twitchett, ed., *The Cambridge History of China*, vol. 3: *Sui and T'ang China, 589–906, Part I*. Cambridge, Cambridge University Press, 1979.

Dayi xianzhi 大邑縣志. 1929.

Deng Guangming 鄧廣銘. "Wang Anshi dui Bei Song bingzhi de gaige cuoshi ji qi shexiang" 王安石對北宋兵制的改革措施及其設想, in Deng Guangming and Cheng Yingliu, eds., *Songshi yanjiu lunwen ji* (q.v.).

—— and Cheng Yingliu 保應鐐, eds. *Songshi yanjiu lunwen ji* 宋史研究論文集. Shanghai, Shanghai gujie chubanshe, 1982.

—— and Li Jiaju 酈家駒, eds. *Songshi yanjiu lunwen ji* 宋史研究論文集. Henan, Henan renmin chubanshe, 1984.

—— and Xu Gui 徐規, eds. *Songshi yanjiu lunwen ji* 宋史研究論文集. Hangzhou, Zhejiang renmin chubanshe, 1987.

Deutsch, Karl. *Nationalism and Social Communication*. New York, John Wiley and Sons and MIT Press, 1953.

Du Fu 杜甫. *Du Gongbu shiji* 杜工部詩集. Hong Kong, Zhonghua shuju, 1972.

Ebrey, Patricia Buckley. *The Aristocratic Families of Early Imperial China: A Case Study of the Po-ling Ts'ui Family*. Cambridge, Cambridge University Press, 1978.

——. "The Dynamics of Elite Domination in Sung China," *Harvard Journal of Asiatic Studies* 48.2: 493–519 (1988).

Elvin, Mark. "The Last Thousand Years of Chinese History: Changing Patterns in Land Tenure," *Modern Asian Studies* 4.2: 97–114 (1970).

——. *The Pattern of the Chinese Past*. Stanford, Stanford University Press, 1973.

The Encyclopedia Americana. International Edition, Danbury, Connecticut, Grolier International, 1981.

Enoki Kazuo 榎一雄. "Ō Sei no Kasei keiryaku ni tsuite" 王韶の熙河經略 について, *Mōko gakuhō* 1: 87–168 (1940).

Entenmann, Robert. "Migration and Settlement in Sichuan, 1644–1796." PhD dissertation, Harvard University, 1982.

Epstein, H. *Domestic Animals of China*. London, Commonwealth Agricultural Bureaux, 1969.

Essin, Emil. "The Horse in Turkic Art," *Central Asiatic Journal* 10: 167–227 (1965).

Etzioni, Amitai. *A Comparative Analysis of Complex Organizations*. New York, The Free Press, 1975.

Fairbank, John King. "Varieties of the Chinese Military Experience," in Frank Kierman and John K. Fairbank, eds., *Chinese Ways in Warfare*. Cambridge, Harvard University Press, 1974.

Fan Zhen 范鎮. *Dongzhai jishi* 東齊紀事. *Shoushange congshu* 守山閣叢書 ed. 1899.

Fei Zhu 費著. "Shizu pu" 氏族譜, in *Quan Shu yiwen zhi* (q.v.).

Feng Yan 封演. *Fengshi wenjian ji* 封氏聞見記. *Xuejin taoyuan* 學津討原 ed. Taipei, 1965.

Feuerwerker, Albert. "The State and the Economy in Late Imperial China." Unpublished manuscript, 1983.

Fletcher, Joseph. "Ch'ing Inner Asia c. 1800," in John K. Fairbank, ed., *The Cambridge History of China*, vol. 10, *Late Ch'ing, 1800–1911, Part I*. Cambridge, Cambridge University Press, 1978.

Franke, Herbert. "Siege and Defense of Towns in Medieval China," in Frank Kierman and John K. Fairbank, eds., *Chinese Ways in Warfare*. Cambridge, Harvard University Press, 1974.

——, ed. *Sung Biographies*. Wiesbaden, Steiner, 1976.

Frantz, Joe B., and Julian E. Choate, Jr. *The American Cowboy*. Norman, University of Oklahoma Press, 1955.

Freedman, Maurice. "The Politics of an Old State: A View from a Chinese Lineage," in *The Study of Chinese Society: Essays by Maurice Freedman*. Stanford, Stanford University Press, 1979.

Freeman, Michael. "Lo-yang and the Opposition to Wang An-shih: The Rise of Confucian Conservatism, 1068–1086." PhD dissertation, Yale University, 1973.

Gale, Essen M., tr. *Discourses on Salt and Iron*. Reprint of the 1931 ed.; Taipei, Ch'eng Wen Publishing Co., 1973.

Gernet, Jacques. *Daily Life in China on the Eve of the Mongol Invasion*. New York, Macmillan, 1962.

Ginsburg, Norton Sydney, ed. *The Pattern of Asia.* Englewood Cliffs, N.J., Prentice Hall, 1958.

Golas, Peter. "Rural China in the Song," *Journal of Asian Studies* 39.2: 291–325 (1980).

Gong Wei-ai. "The Usurpation of Power by Ch'in Kuei through the Censorial Organ (1138–1155 A.D.)," *Chinese Culture* 15.3: 25–42 (1974).

Grigg, D. B. *The Agricultural Systems of the World.* Cambridge, Cambridge University Press, 1974.

Gu Zuyu 顧祖禹. *Dushi fangyu jiyao* 讀史方輿紀要. Taipei, Letian chubanshe, 1973.

Guo Yundao 郭允蹈. *Shu jian* 蜀鑑. Taipei, Taiwan Shangwu yinshuguan, 1973.

Guo Zhengzhong 郭正忠. "Nan Song zhongyang caizheng huobi suishou kaoban" 南宋中央財政货币岁收考辨, in Zhongguo shehuikexueyuan lishi yanjiusuo, comp., *Song-Liao-Jin shi luncong* 宋辽金史论丛. Beijing, Zhonghua shuju, 1985.

——. "Songdai Jiechi yanchan kaoxi" 宋代解池盐产考析, in Deng Guangming and Li Jiaju, eds., *Songshi yanjiu lunwen ji* (q.v.).

Haeger, John Winthrop. "1126–27: Political Crisis and the Integrity of Culture," in John Winthrop Haeger, ed., *Crisis and Prosperity in Sung China.* Tucson, University of Arizona, 1975.

Hanzhou zhi 漢州志. 1817.

Hartwell, Robert M. *A Guide to Sources of Chinese Economic History* A.D. 618–1368. Chicago, The Committee on Far Eastern Civilizations, University of Chicago, 1964.

——. "Markets, Technology, and the Structure of Enterprise in the Development of the Eleventh-Century Chinese Iron and Steel Industry," *Journal of Economic History* 26.9: 29–58 (1966).

——. "A Cycle of Economic Change in Imperial China: Coal and Iron in Northeast China," *Journal of the Economic and Social History of the Orient* 10: 103–159 (1967).

——. "The Evolution of the Northern Sung Monetary System, A.D. 960–1025," *Journal of the American Oriental Society* 87: 280–289 (1967).

——. "Classical Chinese Monetary Analysis and Economic Policy in T'ang–Northern Sung China," *Transactions of the International Conference of Orientalists in Japan,* No. 13 (1968).

——. "Financial Expertise, Examinations, and the Formulation of Economic Policy in Northern Sung China," *Journal of Asian Studies* 30: 281–314 (1971).

——. "Demographic, Political, and Social Transformations of China, 750–1550," *Harvard Journal of Asiatic Studies* 42.2: 365–442 (1982).

Hasegawa Yoshio. "Trends in Postwar Japanese Studies on Sung History: A Bibliographical Introduction," *Acta Asiatica* 50.95–120 (1986).

He Guangyuan 何光遠. *Jianjie lu* 鑒戒錄 Facsimile of the *Xuejin taoyuan* ed. Taipei, 1965.

Herrmann, Albert. *An Historical Atlas of China.* Chicago, Aldine, 1966.

Higashi Ichio 東一雄. *Ō Anseki shimpō no kenkyū* 王安石新法の研究. Tokyo, Kazama shobō, 1970.

———. *Ō Anseki jiten* 王安石事典. Tokyo, Kokusho kankōkai, 1980.

Hino Kaisaburo. "Government Monopoly on Salt in T'ang in the Period before the Enforcement of the Liang Shui Fa," *Memoirs of the Research Department of the Toyo Bunko* 22.1–56 (1963).

Hirth, Friedrich, and W. W. Rockhill. *Chau Ju-kua: His Work on the Chinese and Arab Trade in the Twelfth and Thirteenth Centuries, entitled Chu-fan-chi.* Reprint of the 1911 ed.; Taipei, 1967.

Hisayuki Miyakawa, "An Outline of the Naitō Hypothesis and its Effects on Japanese Studies of China," *Far Eastern Quarterly* 14: 533–552 (1954–1955).

Ho Ping-ti. "Early-ripening Rice in Chinese History," *Economic History Review* (2nd Series) 9: 200–218 (1956–1957).

———. *Studies on the Population of China.* Cambridge, Harvard University Press, 1959.

———. *The Ladder of Success in Imperial China: Aspects of Social Mobility,* 1368–1911. New York, John Wiley and Sons, 1964.

Hoffman, Helmut. *Tibet: A Handbook.* Bloomington, Indiana University Asian Studies Research Institute, 1975.

Holland, Stuart. *The State as Entrepreneur.* London, Weidenfeld and Nicolson, 1972.

Hong Hao 洪皓. *Songmo jiwen* 松漠紀聞. *SKQSZB* ed.

Hong Mai 洪邁. *Yijian zhi* 夷堅志. Facsimile of the 1927 Shanghai Shangwu yinshuguan ed.; Kyoto, Chūbun shuppansha, 1975.

Hosie, Alexander. *Three Years in Western China.* Reprint of the 1897 ed.; Taipei, Ch'eng Wen Publishing Co., 1972.

Hu Zhaoxi 胡昭曦. "Luelun Nan Song monian Sichuan junmin kangji Menggu guizu de douzheng" 略论南宋末年四川军民抗击蒙古贵族的斗争, in Deng Guangming and Cheng Yingliu, eds., *Songshi yanjiu lunwen ji* (q.v.).

———. *Songmo Sichuan zhanzheng shiliao xuanbian* 宋末四川战争史料选编. Chengdu, Sichuan renmin chubanshe, 1984.

Hua Shan 華山. "Cong chaye jingji kan Songdai shehui" 从茶叶经济看宋代社会, in *Song-Liao-Jin shehui jingji luncong* 宋辽金社会经济论丛, 2nd collection. Hong Kong, Chongwen shudian, 1973.

Hua Yue 華岳. *Cuiwei xiansheng beizheng lu* 翠微先生北征錄. Facsimile of the

1920 *Guichi xianzhe yishu* 貴池先哲遺書 ed., Liu Shiheng 劉世珩, comp. Taipei, Yiwen yinshuguan.

Huang Kuanzhong 黃寬重. "Nan Song shidai Yongzhou de Hengshanzhai" 南宋時代邕州的横山寨, *Hanxue yanjiu* 3.2: 507–534 (1985).

Huang Nailong 黃乃隆. *Wang Anshi bianfade caijing zhengce shuping* 王安石变法的财经政策述評. Taizhong, Zhongxing University, 1968.

Huang, Ray. *Taxation and Governmental Finance in Sixteenth-Century Ming China.* Cambridge, Cambridge University Press, 1974.

———. *1587, A Year of No Significance.* New Haven, Yale University Press, 1982.

Huang Song zhongxing liangchao shengzheng 皇宋中興兩朝聖政. *Songshi ziliao cuibian* 宋史資料萃編, 1st series. Taipei, Wenhai chubanshe, 1967.

Huang Tingjian 黃庭堅. *Yuzhang xiansheng wenji* 豫章先生文集. *SBCK* ed.

Huang Xiufu 黃休復. *Maoting kehua* 茅亭客活. *Shuoku* 說庫 ed. Taipei, Xinxing shuju, 1963.

Hymes, Robert P. *Statesmen and Gentlemen: The Elite of Fu-chou, Chiang-hsi, in Northern and Southern Sung.* Cambridge, Cambridge University Press, 1986.

Ihara Hiroshi 伊原弘. "Nan Sō Shisen ni okeru Goshi no seiryaku—Go Gi no ranzen shi" 南宋四川における呉氏の勢力—呉曦の乱前史, in *Aoyama Hakushi koki kinen Sōdaishi ronsō* 青山博士古稀記念宋代史論叢. Tokyo, Shōshin shobō, 1974.

———. "Nan Sō Shisen ni okeru teikyo shihin—Seitofuro Shishuro o chūshin to shite" 南宋四川における定居士人—成都府路、梓川路を中心として, *Tōhōgaku* 54: 47–62 (1977).

Iwasaki Tsutomu 岩崎力. "Seiryōfu Hanrashi seiken shimatsu kō 西涼府潘羅支政権始末考, *Tōhōgaku* 47: 25–41 (1974).

———. "Sōkajō Kakushira seiken no seikaku to kōhai" 宗哥城唃厮囉政権の性格と興廃, *Ajiashi kenkyū* 2: 1–28 (1978).

Jagchid Sechin 札奇斯欽. *Beiya youmu minzu yu zhongyuan nongye minzu jian de heping zhanzheng yu maoyi guanxi* 北亞遊牧民族與中原農業民族間的和平戰争與貿易関係. Taipei, Zhengzhong shuju, 1973.

——— and C. R. Bowden, "Some Notes on the Horse Policy of the Mongol Dynasty," *Central Asiatic Journal* 10: 246–268 (1965).

Jia Daquan 賈大泉. *Songdai Sichuan jingji shulun* 宋代四川经济述论. Chengdu, Sichuansheng shehuikexueyuan chubanshe, 1985.

Jiang Fucong 蔣復璁. "Shanyuan zhi meng de yanjiu" 澶淵之盟的研究, *Songshi yanjiu ji*, vol. 2. Taipei, 1964.

Jiang Wanfang 蔣晚芳 et al. *Zhongguo mingcha* 中国名茶. Hangzhou, Zhejiang renmin chubanshe, 1979.

Jin shi 金史, compiled by Tuo Tuo 脱脱 et al. Beijing, Zhonghua shuju, 1975.

Jiu Tang shu 舊唐書, compiled by Liu Xu 劉昫. Facsimile of the 1739 ed. Taipei, Xinwenfeng chuban gongsi.

Johnson, Chalmers A. *Peasant Nationalism and Communist Power: The Emergence of Revolutionary China, 1937–1945.* Stanford, Stanford University Press, 1962.

Johnson, David. "The Last Years of a Great Clan: The Li Family of Chao Chün in Late T'ang and Early Sung," *Harvard Journal of Asiatic Studies* 37.1: 5–102 (1977).

——. *The Medieval Chinese Oligarchy.* Boulder, Westview Press, 1977.

Ju Qingyuan 鞠清遠. "Tang-Song shidai Sichuan de canshi" 唐宋時代四川的蠶市, *Shihuo* 3.6: 28–34 (1936).

Kanei Yukitada 金井之忠. "Tō no empō" 唐の塩法, *Bunka* 5.5: 9–45 (1938).

——. "Tō no chahō" 唐の茶法, *Bunka* 5.8: 35–53 (1938).

Katō Shigeshi 加藤繁. *Tō Sō jidai ni okeru kingin no kenkyū* 唐宋時代における金銀の研究. Tokyo, Tōyō bunko, 1926.

——. "On the Hang or Associations of Merchants in China," *Memoirs of the Research Department of the Toyo Bunko* 8: 45–83 (1936).

——. *Shina keizaishi kōshō* 支那経済史考証. 2 vols., Tokyo, Tōyō bunko, 1952–1953.

——. *Tang-Song shidai zhi jinyin yanjiu* 唐宋時代之金銀研究. Taipei, Xinwenfeng chuban gongsi, 1974.

——. *Zhongguo jingjishi kaozheng* 中国経済史考証. Taipei, Huashi chubanshe, 1976.

Kawahara Yoshirō 河原由郎. *Hoku Sōki tochi shoyū no mondai to shōgyō shihon* 北宋斯土地所有の問題と商業資本. Fukuoka, Nishi Nihon gakujutsu shuppansha, 1964.

Kawakami Koichi 河上光一. "Sōdai Shisen no kakuchahō" 宋代の権茶法, *Shigaku zasshi* 71.11: 1–25 (1962).

——. "Sōdai Shisen ni okeru kakuchahō no kaishi" 宋代四川における権茶法の開始, *Tōhōgaku* 23: 65–78 (1962).

——. "Sōdai kaien no seisangaku ni tsuite" 宋代解塩の生産額について, *Tōhōgaku* 50: 66–78 (1975).

Kennedy, Paul. *The Rise and Fall of the Great Powers: Economic Change and Military Conflict from 1500 to 2000.* New York, Random House, 1987.

Kingdon-Ward, F. "Tibet as a Grazing Land," *Geographical Journal* 110: 60–75 (1947).

Kinugawa Tsuyoshi 衣川強. *Songdai wenguan fengji zhidu* 宋代文官俸給制度. Zheng Liangsheng, tr. Taipei, Taiwan Shangwu yinshuguan, 1977. Translations of "Sōdai no hōkyū ni tsuite—bunjin kanryō o chūshin to shite" 宋代の俸給について—文人官僚を中心として, *Tōhō gakuhō* 41 (1970);

and "Kanryō to hōkyū ni tsuite, zokkō" 官僚と俸給について, 續考, *Tōhō gakuhō* 42 (1971).

Kong Pingzhong 孔平仲. *Chaosan ji* 朝散集. Yuzhang congshu 豫章叢書 ed. Nanchang, 1915–1920.

Kracke, Edward A., Jr. *Civil Service in Early Sung China.* Cambridge, Harvard University Press, 1953.

———. *Translations of Sung Civil Service Titles.* Paris, École Pratique des Hautes Études 1957.

Kurihara Masuo 栗原益男. "Tōmatsu no dogōteki zaichi seiryoku ni tsuite— Shisen no I Kunsei no baai" 唐末の土豪在地勢力について—四川の韋君靖の場合, *Rekishigaku kenkyū* 243: 1–14 (1960).

Kwanten, Luc. "Chio-ssu-lo (997–1065): A Tibetan Ally of the Northern Sung," *Rocznik Orientalistyczny* 39: 92–106 (1977).

———. *Imperial Nomads.* Philadelphia, University of Pennsylvania Press, 1979.

Kychanov, E. I. "Les guerres entre les Sung du Nord et le Hsi Hsia," in Françoise Aubin, ed., *Études Song in Memoriam Étienne Balázs.* Sér. I, no. 2. The Hague, 1971.

LaPalombara, Joseph. "An Overview of Bureaucracy and Political Development," in Joseph LaPalombara, ed., *Bureaucracy and Political Development.* Princeton, Princeton University Press, 1963.

Lattimore, Owen. *Inner Asian Frontiers of China.* 3rd ed. Boston, Beacon Press, 1962.

Laufer, Berthold. *Sino-Iranica.* Reprint of the 1919 ed.; Taipei, Ch'eng Wen Publishing Co., 1978.

Lee, Robert H. G. "Frontier Politics in the Southwestern Sino-Tibetan Borderland during the Ch'ing Dynasty," in Joshua A. Fogel and William T. Rowe, eds., *Perspectives on a Changing China.* Boulder, Westview Press, 1979.

Levy, Howard. "The Family Background of Yang Kuei-fei," *Sinologica* 5.2: 101–118 (1961).

Lewis, Eugene. *Public Entrepreneurship: Toward a Theory of Bureaucratic Political Behavior.* Bloomington, Indiana University Press, 1980.

Li Fang 李昉. *Taiping yulan* 太平御覽. Facsimile of the Japanese copy of a Southern Song ed. Tainan, Minglun chubanshe, 1975.

Li Jifu 李吉甫. *Yuanhe junxian tuzhi* 元和郡縣圖志. Facsimile of the (Qing) *Jifu congshu* ed. Kyoto, Chūbun shuppansha.

Li Shi 李石. *Fangzhou ji* 方舟集. *SKQSZB* ed.

Li Shizhen 李時珍. *Bencao gangmu* 本草綱目 *Guoxue mingzhu zhenben huikan* ed. Taipei, Dingwen shuju, 1973.

Li Tao 李燾. *Xu zizhi tongjian changbian* 續資治通鑑長編. Taipei, Shijie shuju, 1974.

Li Xin 李新. *Kua'ao ji* 跨鼇集. *SKQSZB* ed.

Li Xinchuan 李心傳. *Jianyan yilai chaoye zaji* 建炎以來朝野雜集. *Songshi ziliao cuibian*, 1st series, facsimile of the *Shiyuan congshu* 適園叢書 ed. Taipei, Wenhai chubanshe, 1967.

——. *Jianyan yilai xinian yaolu* 建炎以來繫年要錄. *Songshi ziliao cuibian*, 2nd series, facsimile of the 1900 *Guangya shuju* ed. Taipei, Wenhai chubanshe, 1968.

Li You 李攸. *Songchao shishi* 宋朝事實. *Wuyingdian juzhenbanshu* 武英殿聚珍版書 ed.

Li Zhi 李真. *Huang Song shichao gangyao* 皇宋十朝綱要. *Songshi ziliao cuibian*, 1st series, facsimile of the *Shiyuan congshu* 適園叢書 ed. Taipei, Wenhai chubanshe, 1967.

Liang Gengyao 梁庚堯. *Nan Song de nongcun jingji* 南宋的農村經濟. Taipei, Lianjing chuban shiye gongsi, 1984.

Liangchao gangmu beiyao 兩朝綱目備要. *Songshi ziliao cuibian*, 1st series, facsimile of the *Shiyuan congshu* 適園叢書 ed. Taipei, Wenhai chubanshe, 1967.

Liao Longsheng 廖隆盛. "Bei Song dui Tubo de zhengce" 北宋對土著的政策, *Songshi yanjiu ji*, vol. 10. Taipei, 1978.

Liao shi 遼史, compiled by Tuo Tuo 脫脫 et al. Beijing, Zhonghua shuju, 1974.

Libu tiaofa 吏部條法, in *Yongle dadian* 永樂大典, zhuan 14620–14629. Beijing, Zhonghua shuju, 1960.

Lidai mingchen zouyi 歷代名臣奏議. Punctuated facsimile of a Ming ed. Taipei, Xuesheng shuju, 1964.

Lin Ruihan 林瑞翰. "Songdai guanzhi tanwei" 宋代官制探微, *Songshi yanjiu ji*, vol. 9. Taipei, 1977.

——. "Songdai bianjun zhi mashi ji ma zhi gangyun" 宋代邊郡之馬市及馬之綱運, *Songshi yanjiu ji*, vol. 11. Taipei, 1979.

——. "Bei Song zhi bianfang" 北宋之邊防, *Songshi yanjiu ji*, vol. 13. Taipei, 1981.

——. "Songdai bingzhi chutan" 宋代兵制初探 *Songshi yanjiu ji*, vol. 12. Taipei, 1980.

Lindblom, Charles E. *Politics and Markets*. New York, Basic Books, 1977.

Little, Archibald John. *Through the Yang-tse Gorges*. Reprint of 1898 ed; Taipei, Ch'eng Wen Publishing Co., 1972.

Liu, James T. C. *Reform in Sung China*. Cambridge, Harvard University Press, 1959.

——. "An Early Sung Reformer: Fan Chung-yen," in John K. Fairbank, ed., *Chinese Thought and Institutions*. Chicago, University of Chicago Press, 1957.

——. "Polo and Cultural Change: From T'ang to Sung China," *Harvard Journal of Asiatic Studies* 45.1: 203–224 (1985).

Liu Ts'ui-jung. *Trade on the Han River and its Impact on Economic Development, c. 1800–1911*. Taipei, Institute of Economics, Academia Sinica, 1980.

Liu Zhi 劉摯. *Zhongsu ji* 忠肅集. Wuyingdian juzhenbanshu ed.

Lo Jung-pang. "The Emergence of China as a Sea Power during the Late Sung and Early Yuan Periods," *Far Eastern Quarterly* 14: 484–503 (1955).

——. "Maritime Commerce and its Relationship to the Sung Navy," *Journal of the Economic and Social History of the Orient* 12: 57–107 (1969).

Lo, Winston W. "Circuits and Circuit Intendants in the Territorial Administration of Sung China," *Monumenta Serica* 31: 39–107 (1974–1975).

——. *Szechwan in Sung China: A Case Study in the Political Integration of the Chinese Empire*. Taipei, The University of Chinese Culture, 1982.

——. *An Introduction to the Civil Service of Sung China: With Emphasis on its Personnel Administration*. Honolulu, University of Hawaii Press, 1987.

Loewe, Michael. "The Campaigns of Han Wu-ti," in Frank Kierman and John K. Fairbank, eds., *Chinese Ways in Warfare*. Cambridge, Harvard University Press, 1974.

Lou Yue 樓鑰. *Gongwei ji* 攻媿集. Wuyingdian juzhenbanshu ed.

Lu Tingcan 陸廷燦. *Xu chajing* 續茶經 *SKQSZB* ed.

Lu Xinyuan 陸心源. *Songshi yi* 宋史翼 *Songshi ziliao cuibian*, 1st series, facsimile of the *Shiyuan congshu* 適園叢書 ed. Taipei, Wenhai chubanshe, 1967.

Lu Yaoyu 陸耀遹. *Jinshi xubian* 金石續編. *Piling Lushi Shuangbaiyantang kanben* 毗陵陸氏雙白燕堂刊本 ed. 1874.

Lu You 陸游. *Lu Fang Weng quanji* 陸放翁全集. *SBBY* ed.

Lu Yu 陸羽. *Chajing* 茶經. Facsimile of the (Song) *Baichuan xuehai* 百川學海 ed. Kyoto, Chubun shuppansha, 1979.

Lu Zhen 陸振. *Jiuguo zhi* 九國志. *Guoxue jiben congshu* ed. Shanghai, Shangwu yinshuguan, 1937.

Lü Tao 呂陶. *Jingde ji* 淨德集. *SKQSZB* ed.

Lü Yihao 呂頤浩. *Zhongmu ji* 忠穆集 *SKQSZB* ed.

Ma Duanlin 馬端臨. *Wenxian tongkao* 文獻通考. *Shitong* 十通 ed. Taipei, Xinxing shuju, 1963.

Maeda Masana 前田正名. *Kasei no rekishi chirigaku teki kenkyū* 河西の歴史地理学的研究. Tokyo, Yoshigawa kōbunkan, 1964.

Mann, Susan. *Local Merchants and the Chinese Bureaucracy, 1750–1950*. Stanford, Stanford University Press, 1987.

Mansfield, Edwin. *Microeconomics*. 2nd ed. New York, Norton, 1975.

Martin, H. Desmond. *The Rise of Chingis Khan and His Conquest of North China*. Baltimore, Johns Hopkins Press, 1950.

Matsui Shuichi 松井秀一. "Tōdai zenhanki no Shisen—ritsuryōsei shihai to gōzokusō to no kankei o chūshin to shite" 唐代前半期の四川―律令支配と豪族層との関係を中心として, *Shigaku zasshi* 71.9: 1–37 (1962).

——. "Tōdai kōhanki no Shisen—kanryō shihai to dogōsō no shutsugen o chūshin to shite" 唐代後半期の四川—官僚支配と土豪層の出現を中心として, *Shigaku zasshi* 73.10: 46–88 (1964).

McKnight, Brian E. *Village and Bureaucracy in Southern Sung China*. Chicago, University of Chicago Press, 1971.

——. "Fiscal Privileges and the Social Order in Sung China," in John Winthrop Haeger, ed., *Crisis and Prosperity in Sung China*. Tucson, University of Arizona Press, 1975.

——. *The Quality of Mercy: Amnesties and Traditional Chinese Justice*. Honolulu, University of Hawaii Press, 1981.

McNeill, William H. *The Pursuit of Power: Technology, Armed Force, and Society since A.D. 1000*. Chicago, University of Chicago Press, 1982.

Metzger, Thomas A. *The Internal Organization of the Ch'ing Bureaucracy*. Cambridge, Harvard University Press, 1973.

——. "On the Historical Roots of Economic Modernization in China: The Increasing Differentiation of the Economy from the Polity during the Late Ming and Early Ch'ing Times," in Chi-ming Hou and Tzong-shian Yu, eds., *Conference on Modern Chinese Economic History*. Taipei, Institute of Economics, Academia Sinica, 1977.

Ming huidian 明會典. Guoxue jiben congshu ed. Taipei, Taiwan Shangwu yinshuguan, 1968.

Ming shi 明史. Beijing, Zhonghua shuju ed, 1974.

Mingshanxian xinzhi 名山縣新志. 1930.

Miyazaki Ichisada 宮崎市定. *Godai Sōsho no tsūka mondai* 五代宋初の通貨問題. Kyoto, Hoshino shoten, 1943.

——. "Ō Anseki no rishi gōitsu saku—sōhō o chūshin to shite" 王安石の吏士合一策—倉法を中心として, in his *Ajiashi kenkyū* アジア史研究, vol. 1. Kyoto, Dōhōsha, 1957.

——. "Sōdai kansei josetsu" 宋代官制序説, intro. to Saeki Tomi, *Sōshi shokkanshi sakuin*. Kyoto, Dōhōsha, 1974.

Miyazawa Tomoyuki 宮沢知之. "Sōdai no gajin" 宋代の牙人, *Tōyōshi kenkyū* 39.1: 1–34 (1980).

Moore, Barrington. *Social Origins of Dictatorship and Democracy*. Boston, Beacon Press, 1966.

Morgan, David. *The Mongols*. Oxford, Basil Blackwell, 1986.

Morita Kenji 森田憲司. "Seito shizokufu shōko" 成都氏族譜小考, *Tōyōshi kenkyū* 36.3: 101–127 (1977).

Moriya Takeshi 守屋毅. *Ocha no kita michi* お茶のきた道. Tokyo, Nippon hosō chubankyōkai, 1981.

Morizumi Toshinao 森主利直. "Nan Sō Shisen no taiteki ni tsuite" 南宋四川の對糴について, *Shisen* 10: 105–141 (1935).

Moulder, Frances V. *Japan, China, and the Modern World Economy*. Cambridge, Cambridge University Press, 1977.

Murong Yanfeng 慕容彥逢. *Liwentang ji* 摛文堂集. Facsimile of the 1899 *Changzhou xianzhe yishu* 常州先哲遺書 ed. Taipei, 1972.

Myers, Ramon. "Some Issues on Economic Organization during the Ming and Ch'ing Periods," *Ch'ing-shih wen-t'i* 3.2: 77–97 (1975).

Needham, Joseph and Wang Ling. *Mechanical Engineering*, pt. 2 of *Physics and Physical Technology*, vol. 4 of Joseph Needham, gen. ed., *Science and Civilisation in China*. Cambridge, Cambridge University Press, 1970.

——, Wang Ling, and Lu Gwei-djen. *Civil Engineering and Nautics*, pt. 3 of *Physics and Physical Technology*, vol. 4 of Joseph Needham, gen. ed., *Science and Civilisation in China*. Cambridge, Cambridge University Press, 1971.

Niida Noboru 仁井田陞. *Chūgoku hōseishi kenkyū: tochihō, torihikihō* 中国法制史研究: 土地法, 取引法. Rev. ed. Tokyo, Tōkyō daigaku, 1981.

Nunome Chōfū 布目潮渢 and Nakamura Takashi 中村喬, eds. *Chūgoku no chasho* 中国の茶書. Tōyō bunko publications No. 289. Tokyo, Heibonsha, 1976.

Ouyang Xiu 歐陽修. *Ouyang wenzhonggong ji* 歐陽文忠公集. *Guoxue jiben congshu* ed. Taipei, Taiwan Shangwu yinshuguan, 1967.

——. *Tang shu* 唐書. Facsimile of the Wuyingdian juzhenbanshu ed. Taipei, Yiwen yinshuguan.

——. *Guitian lu* 歸田錄. Beijing, Zhonghua shuju, 1981.

Peng Xinwei 彭信威. *Zhongguo huobi shi* 中國貨幣史. Shanghai, Shanghai renmin chubanshe, 1958.

Peng Yuanrui 彭元瑞. *Wudai shi jizhu* 五代史記注. Facsimile of the 1828 ed. Taipei, Yiwen yinshuguan.

Perdue, Peter C. *Exhausting the Earth: State and Peasant in Hunan, 1500–1850*. Cambridge, Council on East Asian Studies, Harvard University, 1987.

Perkins, Dwight H. *Agricultural Development in China, 1368–1968*. Chicago, Aldine, 1969.

Petech, Luciano. "Tibetan Relations with Sung China and with the Mongols," in Morris Rossabi, ed., *China Among Equals*. Berkeley, University of California Press, 1983.

Peterson, Charles. "Corruption Unmasked: Yuan Chen's Investigations in Szechwan," *Asia Major* (n.s.) 18: 34–78 (1973).

——. "Court and Province in Mid- and Late-T'ang," in Denis Twitchett, ed. *The Cambridge History of China*, vol. 3: *Sui and T'ang China, 589–906, Part I*. Cambridge, Cambridge University Press, 1979.

Qi Xia 漆侠. *Wang Anshi bianfa* 王安石变法. 2nd ed. Shanghai, Shanghai renmin chubanshe, 1979.

Qingyuan tiaofa shilei 慶元條法事類. Facsimile of the Tokyo Seikadō bunku ed. Tokyo, Koten kenkyūkai, 1968.

Quan Hansheng 全漢昇. *Zhongguo jingjishi luncong* 中國經濟史論叢. 2 vols. Hong Kong, Xinya yanjiusuo chuban, 1972.

———. *Zhongguo jingjishi yanjiu* 中國經濟史研究. 3 vols. Hong Kong, Xinya yanjiusuo chuban, 1976.

Quan Shu yiwen zhi 全蜀藝文志. 1889 *Yuyushan fang* 雨餘山房 ed.

Radnitzky, Gerard, and Peter Bernholz, eds. *Economic Imperialism: The Economic Approach Applied Outside the Field of Economics.* New York, Paragon House Publishers, 1987.

Read, Bernard. *Chinese Materia Medica: Turtle and Shellfish Drugs; Avian Drugs; A Compendium of Minerals and Stones used in Chinese Medicine from the Pen Ts'ao Kang Mu.* Taipei, Southern Materials Center, 1977.

Riggs, Fred W. "Prismatic Society and Financial Administration," *Administrative Science Quarterly* 5: 1–46 (1960).

Rossabi, Morris. "The Tea and Horse Trade with Inner Asia during the Ming," *Journal of Asian History* 4: 136–168 (1970).

———, ed. *China Among Equals: The Middle Kingdom and its Neighbors, 10th–14th Centuries.* Berkeley, University of California Press, 1983.

Rowe, William T. *Hankow: Commerce and Society in a Chinese City, 1796–1889.* Stanford, Stanford University Press, 1984.

———. "Approaches to Modern Chinese Social History," in Olivier Zunz, ed., *Reliving the Past: The Worlds of Social History.* Chapel Hill, The University of North Carolina Press, 1985.

Rueschemeyer, Dietrich, and Peter B. Evans. "The State and Economic Transformations: Toward an Analysis of the Conditions Underlying Effective Intervention," in Peter B. Evans, Dietrich Rueschemeyer, and Theda Skocpol, eds., *Bringing the State Back In.* Cambridge, Cambridge University Press, 1985.

Saeki Tomi 佐伯富. *Sōdai chahō kenkyū shiryō* 宋代茶法研究資料. Kyoto, Tōhō bunka kenkyūjo, 1941.

———. *Chūgoku shi kenkyū* 中国史研究. 3 vols. Kyoto, Dōhōsha 1969–1977.

———. "Sōsho ni okeru cha no sembai seido" 宋初における茶の專賣制度, in his *Chūgokushi kenkyū*, vol. 1 (1969).

———. *Sōshi shokkanshi sakuin* 宋史職官志索引. Kyoto Dōhōsha, 1974.

———. "Cha to rekishi" 茶と歷史, in his *Chūgokushi kenkyū*, vol. 3 (1977).

Samuelson, Paul. *Economics.* 5th ed. Tokyo, McGraw-Hill, 1961.

Sariti, Anthony William. "Monarchy, Bureaucracy and Absolutism in the

Political Thought of Ssu-ma Kuang," *Journal of Asian Studies* 32.1: 53–76 (1972).

Satake Yasuhiko 佐竹靖彦. "Sōdai Shisen Kishūro no minzoku mondai to tochi shoyū mondai" 宋代四川夔川路の民族問題と土地所有問題, *Shirin* 50: 801–828 (1967) and 51: 44–74 (1968).

——. "Tō Sō henkakuki ni okeru Shisen Seitofuro chiiki shakai no henbō ni tsuite" 唐宋変革期における四川成都府路地域社会の変貌について, *Tōyōshi kenkyū* 35.2: 103–136 (1976).

——. "Tōdai Shisen chiiki shakai no henbō to sono tokushitsu" 唐代四川地域社会の変貌とその特質, *Tōyōshi kenkyū* 44.2: 1–39 (1985).

Saunders, J. J. *The History of the Mongol Conquests.* New York, Barnes and Noble, 1971.

Schafer, Edward H. *The Golden Peaches of Samarkand.* Berkeley, University of California Press, 1963.

——. "T'ang" in K. C. Chang, ed., *Food in Chinese Culture.* New Haven, Yale University Press, 1977.

Schumpeter, Joseph. "The Crisis of the Tax State," in Alan T. Peacock, Ralph Turvey, Wolfgang F. Stoper and Elizabeth Henderson, eds., *International Economic Papers: Translations Prepared for the International Economic Association*, vol. 4 (1954).

——. *The Theory of Economic Development.* New York, Oxford University Press, 1961.

Schwartz, Benjamin I. "The Chinese Perception of World Order, Past and Present," in John K. Fairbank, ed., *The Chinese World Order: Traditional China's Foreign Relations.* Cambridge, Harvard University Press, 1968.

Serruys, Henry. *Sino-Mongol Relations during the Ming*, vol. 3: *Trade Relations: The Horse Fairs (1400–1600).* Bruxelles, Institut Belge des Hautes Etudes Chinoises, 1975.

Shaanxi tongzhi 陝西通志. 1735.

Shen Gua 沈括. *Mengqi bitan jiaozheng* 夢溪筆談校証. 2 vols. Taipei, Shijie shuju, 1965.

Shen Jiaben 沈家本. *Shen Qiji xiansheng yishu* 沈寄簃先生遺書. 2 vols. Taipei, Wenhai chubanshe, 1967.

Shiba Yoshinobu 斯波義信. *Sōdai shōgyōshi kenkyū* 宋代商業史研究. Tokyo, Kazama shobo, 1968.

——. *Commerce and Society in Sung China.* Extended summary of *Sōdai shōgyōshi kenkyū* by Mark Elvin. Ann Arbor, Center for Chinese Studies, University of Michigan, 1970.

——. "Sōdai shiteki seido no enkaku" 宋代市糴制度の沿革, in *Aoyama Hakushi koki kinen Sōdaishi ronsō* 青山博士古稀記念宋代史論叢. Tokyo, Shōshin shobō, 1974.

——. "Urbanization and the Development of Markets in the Lower Yangtze

Valley," in John Winthrop Haeger, ed., *Crisis and Prosperity in Sung China*. Tucson, University of Arizona, 1975.

Shimasue Kazuyasu 島居一康. "Ō shōha Ri jun no ran no seikaku—Sōdai Shisen no jinushi tenosei tono kanren ni oite" 王小波、李順の乱の性格 —宋代四川の地主佃戸制との関連において, *Tōyōshi kenkyū* 29.1: 1–30 (1970).

Sichuan chaye 四川茶叶. Chengdu, Sichuan renmin chubanshe, 1977.

Sichuan tongzhi 四川通志. 1816.

Sichuan zongzhi 四川總志. 1619.

Sima Guang 司馬光. *Sima wenzhenggong chuanjia ji* 司馬文正公傳家集. *Guoxue jiben congshu* ed. Shanghai, Shangwu yinshuguan, 1937.

——. *Zizhi tongjian* 資治通鑑. Beijing, Zhonghua shuju, 1956.

Sima Qian 司馬遷. *Shi ji* 史記. Beijing, Zhonghua shuju, 1964.

Skinner, G. William. "Cities and the Hierarchy of Local Systems," in G. William Skinner, ed., *The City in Late Imperial China*. Stanford, Stanford University Press, 1977.

——. "Urban Development in Imperial China," in G. William Skinner, ed., *The City in Late Imperial China*. Stanford, Stanford University Press, 1977.

Skocpol, Theda. *States and Social Revolutions*. Cambridge, Cambridge University Press, 1979.

——. "Bringing the State Back In: Strategies of Analysis in Current Research," in Peter B. Evans, Dietrich Rueschemeyer, and Theda Skocpol, eds., *Bringing the State Back In*. Cambridge, Cambridge University Press, 1985.

Smith, Paul J. "Interest Groups, Ideology, and Economic Policy-making: The Northern Sung Debates over the Southeastern Tea Monopoly," prepared for the Regional Conference, Association for Asian Studies on the Pacific Coast, Eugene, Oregon, 1977.

——. "State Power and Economic Activism during the New Policies, 1068–1085: The Tea and Horse Trade and the 'Green Sprouts' Loan Policy," prepared for the Conference on Sung Dynasty Statecraft in Thought and Action, sponsored by the American Council of Learned Societies and the Social Science Research Council, Scottsdale, Arizona, January 1986.

——. "Taxing Heaven's Storehouse: The Szechwan Tea Monopoly and the Tsinghai Horse Trade, 1074–1224." PhD dissertation, University of Pennsylvania, 1983.

——. "Commerce, Agriculture, and Core Formation in the Upper Yangzi, 2 A.D. to 1948," *Late Imperical China* 9.1: 1–78 (1988).

Sogabe Shizuo 曽我部静雄. *Sōdai zaiseishi* 宋代財政史. Tokyo, Seikatsusha, 1941.

——. *Sōdai seikeishi no kenkyū* 宋代経済史の研究. Tokyo, Yoshigawa kobunkan, 1974.

——. "Nan Sō no suigun" 南宋の水軍, in his *Sōdai seikeishi no kenkyū*.

——. "Sōdai no basei" 宋代の馬政, in his *Sōdai seikeishi no kenkyū*.

Somers, Robert. "The End of the T'ang," in Denis Twitchett, ed., *The Cambridge History of China*, vol. 3: *Sui and T'ang China 589–906, Part I*. Cambridge, Cambridge University Press, 1979.

Song huiyao jiben 宋會要輯本. Taipei, Shijie shuju, 1964.

Song Qi 宋祁. *Jingwen ji* 景文集. Wuyingdian juzhenbanshu ed.

Song shi 宋史, compiled by Tuo Tuo 脫脫 et al. Beijing, Zhonghua shuju, 1977.

Song Xi 宋晞. "Songdai de shangshui gang" 宋代的商稅綱, *Songshi yanjiu ji*, vol. 3. Taipei, 1966.

——. "Bei Song shangshui zai guojizhong de diwei yu jianshui guan" 北宋商稅在國計中的地位與監稅官, *Songshi yanjiu ji*, vol. 5. Taipei, 1970.

——. "Bei Song shangren de ruzhong bianliang" 北宋商人的入中邊糧, *Songshi yanjiu ji*, vol. 6. Taipei, 1971.

Songdai Shuwen jicun 宋代蜀文輯存. Compiled by Fu Zengxiang 傅增湘. Facsimile of the 1943 edition. Taipei, Xinwengeng chuban gongsi, 1974.

Songren chuanji ziliao suoyin 宋人傳記資料索引. Compiled by Chang Bide 昌彼得, Wang Deyi 王德毅 et al. Taipei, Dingwen shuju, 1974–1976.

Songshi jishi benmo 宋史紀事本末. Compiled by Chen Bangzhan 陳邦瞻. Beijing, Zhonghua shuju, 1977.

Sowerby, Alexander. "The Horse and Other Beasts of Burden in China," *China Journal of Science and the Arts* 26: 282–287 (1937).

Stuart, G. A. *Chinese Materia Medica: Vegetable Kingdom*. Reprint of 1911 ed., Taipei, Southern Materials Center, 1976.

Su Che 蘇轍. *Luancheng ji* 欒城集. *SBBY* ed.

Su Shi 蘇軾. *Su Dongbo ji* 蘇東坡集. *Guoxue jiben congshu* ed. Taipei, Taiwan Shangwu yinshuguan, 1967.

Su Xun 蘇洵. *Jiayou ji* 嘉祐集. *SBCK* ed.

Sudō Yoshiyuki 周藤吉之. *Sōdai kanryōsei to daitochi shoyū* 宋代官僚制と大土地所有. Tokyo, Nippon Hyōronsha, 1950.

——. *Sōdai keizaishi kenkyū* 宋代経済史研究. Tokyo, Tōkyō daigaku shuppankai, 1962.

——. *Sōdaishi kenkyū* 宋代史研究. Tokyo, Tōyō bunko, 1969.

——. *Tō Sō shakai keizaishi kenkyū* 唐宋社会経済史研究. Tokyo, Tōkyō daigaku shuppansha, 1975.

——. "Sōdai Shisen no tenko sei—saikin no kenkyū o yonde" 宋代四川の佃戸制—最近の研究を讀んで, in his *Tō Sō shakai keizaishi kenkyū* (q.v.).

Sui shu 隋書. Facsimile of the 1739 ed. Taipei, Xinwenfeng chuban gongsi, 1975.

Suzuki, Chusei. "China's Relations with Inner Asia: The Hsiung-nu, Tibet," in J. K. Fairbank, ed., *The Chinese World Order*. Cambridge, Harvard University Press, 1968.

Tan Kyōji 丹喬二. "Sōsho no shōen ni tsuite: Seitofu Gōshoku koku setsudoshi Ten Kinzen no shoryō o chūshin to shite" 宋初の莊園について：成都府後蜀国節度使田欽全の所有を中心として, *Shichō* 87: 1–25 (1964).
——. "Sōsho Shisen no Ō Shōha Ri Jun no ran ni tsuite—Tō Sō henkaku no ichi mondai" 宋初四川の王小波・李順の乱について—唐宋変革の一問題, *Tōyōgaku* 61.3: 67–102 (1980).
Tang guoshibu deng bazhong 唐國史補等八種. Taipei, Shijie shuju, 1978.
Tang xinxiu bencao 唐新修本草. Hefei, Anhui kexuezhishu chubanshe, 1981.
Tang shu 唐書. Compiled by Ouyang Xiu and Song Qi. Taipei, Yiwen yinshuguan.
Tani Mitsutaka 谷光隆. "Mindai chaba bōeki no kenkyū" 明代茶馬貿易の研究, parts 1 and 2, *Shirin* 49.5: 733–751 and 49.6: 861–879 (1966).
——. *Mindai basei no kenkyū* 明代馬政の研究. Kyoto, Tōyōshi kenkyūkai, 1972.
Tao, Jing-shen. *The Jurchen in Twelfth-Century China*. Seattle, University of Washington Press, 1976.
Terada Takanobu 寺田隆信. *Sansei shōnin no kenkyū* 山西商人の研究. Kyoto, Tōyōshi kenkyūkai, 1972.
Thompson, James D. *Organizations in Action: Social Science Bases of Administrative Theory*. New York, McGraw Hill, 1967.
Tietze, Klaus-Peter. *Ssuch'uan vom 7. bis 10. Jahrhundert: Untersuchungen zur fruhen Geschichte einer chinesischen Provinz*. Wiesbaden, Steiner, 1980.
Twitchett, Denis. "The Salt Commissioners after the Rebellion of An Lushan," *Asia Major* (n.s.) 4.1: 60–89 (1954).
——. "Monastic Estates in T'ang China," *Asia Major* (n.s.) 5.2: 123–146 (1956).
——. "Provincial Autonomy and Central Finance in Late T'ang," *Asia Major* (n.s.) 11.11: 211–232 (1965).
——. "Merchant, Trade, and Government in Late T'ang," *Asia Major* (n.s.) 14.1: 63–95 (1968).
——. *Financial Administration under the T'ang Dynasty*. 2nd ed. Cambridge, Cambridge University Press, 1970.
——. "The Composition of the T'ang Ruling Class: New Evidence from Tunhuang," in Arthur F. Wright and Denis Twitchett, eds., *Perspectives on the T'ang*. New Haven, Yale University Press, 1973.
——. "Hsuan-tsung," in Denis Twitchett, ed., *The Cambridge History of China*, vol. 3: *Sui and T'ang China 589–906, Part I*. Cambridge, Cambridge University Press, 1979.

Uchigawa Kyūhei 内河久平. "Nan Sō sōryō kō" 南宋総領考, *Shicho* 78–79: 1–26 (1962).

Ukers, William. *All About Tea*. 2 vols. New York, The Tea and Coffee Trade Journal, 1935.

Umehara Kaoru 梅原郁 "Sōdai chahō no ichi kōsatsu" 宋代茶法の一考察. *Shirin* 55.1 (1972).

———. "Seitō no uma to Shisen no cha" 青唐の馬と四川の茶, *Tōhō gakuhō* 45: 195–244 (1973).

———. "Sōsho no kirokuhan to sono shūhen—Sōdai kansei no rikai no tame ni" 宋初の寄録官とその周辺—宋代官制の理解のために, *Tōhō gakuhō* 48: 135–182 (1975).

———. *Sōdai kanryō seido kenkyū* 宋代官僚制度研究. Kyoto, Dōhōsha, 1985.

———. "Civil and Military Officials in the Sung: the *Chi-lu-kuan* System," *Acta Asiatica* 50: 1–30 (1986).

Vittinghoff, Helmolt. *Proskription and Intrige gegen Yuan-yu-Parteiganger: Ein Beitrag Zu den Kontroversen nach den Reformen des Wang An-shih*. Bern, Herbert Lang, 1975.

von Glahn, Richard. "Community and Welfare: Chu Hsi's Community Granary in Theory and Practice," prepared for the Conference on Sung Dynasty Statecraft in Thought and Action sponsored by the American Council of Learned Societies and the Social Science Research Council, Scottsdale, Arizona, 1986.

———. *The Country of Streams and Grottoes: Expansion, Settlement, and the Civilizing of the Sichuan Frontier in Song Times*. Cambridge, Council on East Asian Studies, Harvard University, 1987.

Wang Anshi 王安石. *Wang Linchuan quanji* 王臨川全集. Taipei, Shijie shuju, 1966.

Wang Cun 王存. *Yuanfeng jiuyu zhi* 元豐九域志. Indexed facsimile of the 1784 ed. Kyoto, Chūbun shuppansha, 1976.

Wang Gungwu. "The Rhetoric of a Lesser Empire: Early Sung Relations with Its Neighbors," In Morris Rossabi, ed. *China Among Equals* (q.v.).

Wang Shengduo 汪圣铎. "Songdai caizheng yu shangpin jingji fajan" 宋代财政与商品经济发展, in Deng Guangming and Li Jiaju, eds. *Songshi yanjiu lunwen ji* (q.v.).

Wang Shipeng 王十朋. *Meixi shiji* 梅谿詩集. *SKQSZB* ed.

Wang Xiaobo Li Shun qiyi ziliao huibian 王小波・李順起義資料汇编. Chengdu, Sichuan renmin chubanshe, 1978.

Wang Yeh-chien. *Land Taxation in Imperial China, 1750–1911*. Cambridge, Harvard University Press, 1973.

Wang Yingzhen 汪應辰. *Wending ji* 文定集. Wuyingdian juzhenbanshu ed.

Wang Zengyu 王曾瑜. "Wang Anshi bianfa jianlun" 王安石变法简论, *Zhongguo shehui kexue* 3: 131–154 (1980).

——. *Songchao bingzhi chutan* 宋朝兵制初探. Beijing, Zhonghua shuju, 1983.

Wang Zhiwang 王之望. *Hanbin ji* 漢濱集. *Hubei xianzheng yishu* 湖北先正遺書 ed., 1923.

Wang Zhen 王禎. *Nong shu* 農書. Wuyingdian juzhenbanshu ed.

Weber, Max. *General Economic History*. Frank K. Knight, tr. New York, Collier, 1961.

——. *Economy and Society*. New York, Bedminster Press, 1968.

Wechsler, Howard. "Tai-tsung the Consolidator," in Denis Twitchett, ed., *The Cambridge History of China*, vol 3: *Sui and T'ang China, 589–906, Part 1*. Cambridge, Cambridge University Press, 1979.

Wei Liaoweng 魏了翁. *Chongjiao Heshan xiansheng daquan wenji* 重校鶴山先生大全文集. *SBCK* ed.

Welsch, Roger L. ed. *Mister, You Got Yourself a Horse: Tales of Old-time Horse Trading*. Lincoln, University of Nebraska Press, 1981.

Wen Tong 文同. *Danyuan ji* 丹淵集. *SBCK* ed.

Wenjiang xianzhi 溫江縣志. 1921.

Wiens, Mi Chu. "Lord and Peasant: The Sixteenth to Eighteenth Centuries," *Modern China* 6.1: 3–40 (1980).

Williamson, H. R. *Wang An-shih, Chinese Statesman and Educationalist of the Sung Dynasty*. 2 vols. London, Arthur Probsthain, 1935–1937.

Wittfogel, Karl, and Feng Chia-sheng. *History of Chinese Society: Liao (907–1125)*. Philadelphia, American Philosophical Society, 1949.

Wong Hon-chiu. "Government Expenditure in Northern Sung China (960–1127)." PhD diss. University of Pennsylvania, 1975.

Worthy, Edmund H. "The Founding of Sung China, 950–1000: Integrative Changes in Military and Political Institutions." PhD dissertation, Princeton University, 1975.

——. "Regional Control in the Southern Sung Salt Administration," in John Winthrop Haeger, ed., *Crisis and Prosperity in Sung China*. Tucson, University of Arizona Press, 1975.

Wu Renchen 吳任臣. *Shiguo chunqiu* 十國春秋. 1793 *Haiyu Zhoushi Ciyige jiaokanben* 海虞周氏此宜閣校刊本 ed.

Wu Shu 吳淑. *Shilei fu* 事類賦. 1764 *Xishan Huashi Jianguangge kanben* 錫山華氏劍光閣刊本 ed.

Wu Tai 吳泰. "Xining-Yuanfeng xinfa sanlun" 熙寧、元豐新法散論. Zhongguo shehuikexueyuan lishi yanjiusuo, comp., *Song-Liao-Jin shi luncong*. Beijing, Zhonghua shuju, 1985.

Wu Tianchi 吳天墀. *Xi Xia shigao* 西夏史稿. Chengdu, Sichuan renmin chubanshe, 1981.

——. "Juesiluo yu Hehuang Tubo" 唃厮罗与河湟吐蕃, in Deng Guang-ming and Li Jiaju, eds., *Songshi yanjiu lunwen ji* (q.v.)

Wu Tingxie 吳廷燮. "Tang fangzhen nianbiao" 唐方鎮年表, in *Ershiwushi bubian* 二十五史補編. Shanghai, Kaiming shudian, 1936.

Wu Yong 吳泳. *Helin ji* 鶴林集. *SKQSZB* ed.

Wu Zeng 吳曾. *Nenggaizhai manlu* 能改齋漫錄. Shanghai, Shanghai gujie chubanshe, 1979.

Xie Chengxia 謝成俠. *Zhongguo yangma shi* 中国養馬史. Beijing, Kexue chubanshe, 1959.

Xinxiu bencao 新修本草. Taipei, Guoli Zhongguo yiyao yanjiusuo, 1963.

Xiong Fan 熊蕃. *Xuanhe beiyuan gongcha lu* 宣和北苑貢茶錄. Reprint of the Yuan Shuofu 說郛 ed. Shanghai, Shanghai yinshuguan, 1937.

Xu Cishu 許次紓. *Chashu* 茶疏. Facsimile of the *Baoyantang biji* 寶顏堂秘笈 ed. Taipei, 1965.

Xu Mengxin 徐夢辛. *Sanchao beimeng huibian* 三朝北盟會編. Facsimile of the 1878 ed. Taipei, Wenhai chubanshe, 1977.

Xu Ziming 徐自明. *Song zaifu biannianlu jiaobu* 宋宰輔編年錄校補. Beijing, Zhonghua shuju, 1986.

Xu zizhi tongjian changbian: shibu 續資治通鑑長編拾補. Compiled by Qin Xiangye 秦緗業 et al. Reconstructed chapters interspersed throughout Li Tao, *Xu zhizhi tongjian changbian* (q.v.).

Yamauchi Masahiro 山内正博. "Nan Sō no Shisen ni okeru Chō Shun to Go Kei—sono seiryoku kōtai no katei o chūshin to shite" 南宋の四川におけ る張浚と吳玠—その勢力交替の過程を中心として, *Shirin* 44.1: 98–125 (1961).

Yang, C. K. "Some Characteristics of Chinese Bureaucratic Behavior," in David Nivison and Arthur Wright, eds., *Confucianism in Action*. Stanford, Stanford University Press, 1959.

Yang Dequan 楊德泉, "Zhang Jun shiji shuping" 張浚事迹述評, in Deng Guangming and Li Jiaju, eds., *Songshi yanjiu lunwen ju* (q.v.).

Yang Lien-sheng. *Money and Credit in China*. Cambridge, Harvard University Press, 1952.

——. *Studies in Chinese Institutional History*. Cambridge, Harvard University Press, 1961.

——. "Historical Notes on the Chinese World Order," In John K. Fairbank, ed., *The Chinese World Order: Traditional China's Foreign Relations*. Cambridge, Harvard University Press, 1968.

Yang Zhongliang 楊仲良. *Zizhi tongjian changbian jishi benmo* 資治通鑑長編紀事本末. *Songshi ziliao cuibian*, 2nd series. Taipei, Wenhai chubanshe, 1967.

Yano Jinnichi 矢野仁一. "Cha no rekishi ni tsuite" 茶の歴史について, in his *Kindai Shina no seiji oyobi bunka* 近代支那の政治及文化. Tokyo, Idea Shoin, 1926.

Yetts, W. Perceval. "The Horse: A Factor in Early Chinese History," *Eurasia Septentrionalis Antiqua* 9: 231–255 (1934).

Yoshida Mitsukuni 吉田光邦. "Sō-Gen no gunji gijutsu" 宋元の軍事技術, in Yabuuchi Kiyoshi 藪内清, ed., *Sō-Gen jidai no kagaku gijutsu shi* 宋元時代の科学技術史. Kyoto, 1967.

Yu Chou 虞儔. *Zunbaitang ji* 尊白堂集. *SKQSZB* ed.

Yü Ying-shih. *Trade and Expansion in Han China*. Berkeley, University of California Press, 1967.

——. "Han," in K. C. Chang, ed., *Food in Chinese Culture*. New Haven, Yale University Press, 1977.

Yuan shi 元史, compiled by Song Lian 宋濂 et al. Beijing, Zhonghua shuju, 1976.

Yuan Xingzong 員興宗. *Jiuhua ji* 九華集 *SKQSZB* ed.

Yuan Zhen 元稹. *Yuanshi changqing ji* 元氏長慶集. *SBCK* ed.

Yue Shi 樂史. *Taiping huanyu ji* 太平寰宇記. Facsimile of the 1793 ed. Taipei, Wenhai chubanshe.

Yuki Tōru 幸徹. "Hoku Sō jidai no seiji ni okeru kantōkan no haichi jōtai ni tsuite" 北宋時代の盛時における監當官の配置状態について. *Tōyōshi kenkyū* 23.2: 166–190 (1964).

Zelin, Madeleine. *The Magistrate's Tael*. Berkeley, The University of California Press, 1984.

Zeng Gong 曾鞏. *Longping ji* 隆平集. *Songshi ziliao cuibian*, 1st series. Taipei, Wenhai chubanshe, 1967.

Zhang Anzhi 張安治. *Li Gonglin* 李公麟. Beijing, Renmin meishu chubanshe, 1979.

Zhang Fangping 張方平. *Lequan ji* 樂全集. *SKQSZB* ed.

Zhang Tangying 張唐英. *Shu taowu* 蜀檮杌. Facsimile of the Ming *Lidai xiaoshi* ed. Taipei, Taiwan Shangwu yinshuguan, 1979.

Zhang Xiaomei 張肖梅. *Sichuan jingji cankao ziliao* 四川经济參考資料. Shanghai, Zhongguo guominjingji yanjiusuo, 1939.

Zhang Yinlin 張蔭麟. "Songchu Sichuan Wang Xiaobo–Li Shun zhi luan" 宋初四川王小波・李順之乱 *Songshi yanjiu ji*, vol. 1. Taipei, 1958.

Zhao Ruli 趙汝礪. *Beiyuan bielu* 北苑別錄. Reprint of the Yuan Shuofu 說郛 ed. Shanghai, Shanghai yinshuguan, 1937.

Zhao Tiehan 趙鐵寒. "Yan-Yun shiliu zhou de dili fenxi" 燕雲十六州的地理分析, *Songshi yanjiu ji*, vol. 3 Taipei, 1966.

Zhao Wannian 趙萬年. *Xiangyang shouchenglu* 襄陽守城錄. *Bijixiaoshuo daguan* 筆記小記大觀 ed.

Zheng Jingyi 鄭競毅, ed. *Falü da cishu* 法律大辭典. 2nd ed. Taipei, Taiwan Shangwu yinshuguan, 1972.

Zhongguo lishi da cidian: Songshi zhuan 中國歷史大辭典：宋史卷. Shanghai, Shanghai Cishu chubanshe, 1984.

Zhongguo tongshi 中国通史. Beijing, Renmin chubanshe.

Zhou Bodi 周伯棣. *Zhongguo caizheng shi* 中国财政史. Shanghai, Shanghai renmin chubanshe, 1981.

Zhou Hui 周煇. *Qingbo zazhi* 清波雜志. *SBCK* ed.

Zhou Linzhi 周麟之. *Hailing ji* 海陵集. *SKQSZB* ed.

Zhou Qufei 周去非. *Lingwai daida* 嶺外代答. *Zhibuzuzhai congshu* 知不足齋叢書 ed. Taipei, 1966.

Zhu Jiayuan 朱家源 and Wang Zengyu. "Songdai de guanhu" 宋代的官戶, in Deng Guangming and Cheng Yingliu, eds. *Songshi yanjiu lunwen ji* (q.v.).

Zhu Mu 祝穆. *Fangyu shenglan* 方輿勝覽. Taipei, Wenhai chubanshe, 1981.

Zhu Ruixi 朱瑞熙. "Songdai shangren de shehui diwei jiqi lishi zuoyong" 宋代商人的社会地位及其历史作用, *Lishi yanjiu* 2: 127–143 (1986).

Zhu Zhongsheng 朱重聖. *Bei Song cha zhi shengchan yu jingying* 北宋茶之生產與經營. Taipei, Taiwan xuesheng shuju, 1985.

Zurndorfer, Harriet. "Chinese Merchants and Commerce in Sixteenth Century China," in W. L. Idema, ed., *Leyden Studies in Sinology*. Leiden, E. J. Brill, 1981.

Glossary

Characters for all the terms and many of the persons cited in the text and notes are provided below. The names of persons referred to for purely illustrative purposes are not glossed. Characters for all the Intendants will be found in Appendix C; characters for authors and works cited are provided in the Bibliography.

anfusi 安撫司

baitu 白土
baizhi renbing 白直人兵
balu xinfa 八路新法
banchapu bingshi 般茶鋪兵士
banchapu junren 般茶鋪軍人
bansibuwei 判司簿尉
bao (guarantee or guarantee group) 保
bao (tea package) 包
bao (low earthen wall) 堡
baojia 保甲
baoma 保馬
baren 罷任
benqian 本錢
benwu lixu zhi tu 本務吏胥之徒
bi 箆
bianguan 編管
bianyi chuzhi 便宜黜陟
bianzhuan 變轉
bianzhuan xianqian 變轉見錢
bingji 兵級

bingtuancha 餅團茶
bingxiao 兵校
bomaicha duchang 博賣茶都場
boyisi 博易司
buli shangfa 不理賞罰
buyi changzhi jubi 不依常制舉辟
buyingwei zhongduanzui 不應為重斷罪
buzhi 不職

Cai Jing 蔡京
canpu 贊普
caocha 草茶
caozeren 草澤人
cha 茶
chaben 茶本
chachang jianguan 茶場監官
chachangsi 茶場司
chaci 茶詞
chaiqian 差遣
chake zhegu 茶課折估
chakou 茶寇
chami 茶米

Chang Gong 常珙
changyin 長引
changzhutian 常住田
chaoqinglang 朝請郎
chapu (tea shop) 茶鋪
Chapu 茶譜 (Monograph on tea, by
　　Mao Wenxi 毛文錫)
chayin 茶引
chazang 茶駔
Chen Si 陳嗣
Chen Xiliang 陳希亮
cheng 程
chengfenglang 承奉郎
chengmai 承買
chengti 稱提
chengtiqian 稱提錢
chengwulang 承務郎
chengyilang 承議郎
chengzhilang 承直郎
chengzi 秤子
chezi dipu 車子遞鋪
chimai 斥賣
chongti 衝替
chou 紬
choujiang 酬獎
choushang gefa 酬賞格法
chuan 串
Chuancha jindi 川茶禁地
Chuansi 川司
cuifa gangyunguan 催發綱運官

da 大
dai 袋
daique 待闕
dan 石
Dang Yuanji 党元吉
daxiao shichen 大小使臣
deng 等
deti 得替
dianli 典吏
dianmeng 佃甿
didang fa 抵當法

digonglang 廸工郎
dima 遞馬
Ding Weiqing 丁惟清
dingqian 定錢
Dongzhan 董氈
dousong 鬭訟
duansong 短送
duanyin 短引
duda 都大
duda tiju chamasi 都大提舉茶馬司
duguan langzhong 都官郎中
duidimi 對糴米
duimai 對賣
duishu jiaoyi 對數交易
dujian 都監
dutongsi 都統司

eben 額本

Fan Bailu 范百祿
Fan Chunren 范純仁
Fan Zhen 范鎮
Fang La 方臘
Fanguan 蕃官
Fanke 蕃客
fanpao maima 泛拋買馬
Fanshang 蕃商
fanshui 翻稅
fanzhen 蕃鎮
fei liancai heben er jiuji tonghang
　　非連財合本而糾集同行
feiqian 飛錢
fengzhuang 封樁
fuguo qiangbing 富國強兵
fuzai 負載

gaiguan 改官
ganban gongshi 幹辦公事
gandang gongshi 幹當公事
gang 綱
gangcha 綱茶
gangchang jianguan 綱場監官

gangguan 綱官
gangma 綱馬
gangyuan 綱院
gong 公
gongjia 公家
gongli 公吏
gongren 公人
goudang gongshi 勾當公事
goudang guan 勾當官
guan tianxia 冠天下
guan'gan wenzi 管幹文字
guancha 官茶
guancha difen 官茶地方
guangou 管勾
Guangya 廣雅
guanhu 官戶
guanpin 官品
guanshu xu zi bizhi 官屬許自辟置
Guanwai zhujun 關外諸軍
guanxi 關係
guanya shichen 管押使臣
guanyin 關引
gumasi 估司馬
Guo Fu 郭輔
Guo Renwo 郭仁渥
Guo Zigao 郭子皐
guoma 國馬
guoshui 過稅
guqianren 估欠人

Han Qi 韓琦
hang 行
hangshang 行商
hangyi 行役
hao 媷
haocha 耗茶
haomin xiali 豪民黠吏
haoyou 豪右
He Liang 何亮
hegu 和雇
heisha 黑殺
hemai 和買

heshi 合市
hetongchang 合同場
hetongchang maiyinsuo 合同場買
     引所
hu 戶
Hu Yuanzhi 胡元質
hubu shilang 戶部侍郎
hui 彗
huizi 會子
huma 戶馬
huofanbing 火蕃餅
huotou 火頭
hushi 互市

jiabian 家便
jian 煎
jianbing 兼并
jianbing haojia 兼并豪家
jiancha maima 減茶買馬
jiandang 監當
jiandangguan 監當官
jiangguan 將官
jiangjiao 將校
Jiangshang zhujun 江上諸軍
jiangshilang 將仕郎
jianguan 監官
jianli 監理
jianmu 監牧
jianna 監納
Jiannzhou 簡州
jiansheng qian 減省錢
jiantie 簡帖
jiaohu 腳戶
jiaozi 交子
jiatou 甲頭
jidi muma 給地牧馬
jie 界
jiebao jieqing 結保借請
jiebao sheqing 結保賒請
jiedushi 節度使
jiluguan 寄祿官
jimi 羈縻

jimima 羈縻馬
Jin 金
jin (catty) 斤
jin (now) 今
jindi 禁地
jingchaoguan 京朝官
jingliqian 淨利錢
jingluesi 經略司
jingzhi 經制
jingzongzhi qian 經總制錢
jinshi 進士
jiuhe huoban 糾合火伴
jizhu chajia 積貯茶家
ju 舉
juan 娟
Juesiluo 唃廝囉
juhe 舉劾
julian 聚歛
junbei chaishi 準備差使
jundian 軍典
junshu 均輸
juntian 均田
juting zhijia 居停之家

kao 考
kefan chuancha 客販川茶
kehu 客戶
keli changwufa 課利場務法
keshang 客商
kua 銙
kuai 儈
kucheng 庫秤
kuomai 括買
kuozhuang ma 闊壯馬
kuzi 庫子

la cha 臘(腊)茶
lantou 攔頭
li (clerk) 吏
li (profit) 利
Li Cha 李察
Li Deming 李德明

Li Fan 李蕃
Li Jiqian 李繼遷 李继迁
Li Lizun 李立遵
Li Shun 李順
Li Yuanhao 李元昊
liancai heben 連財合本
liang 兩
liangbeicha 兩倍茶
liangma 艮馬
liangshui 兩稅
liangshuifa 兩稅法
liangxi ma 艮細馬
Liangzhou 涼州
Liao 遼
liao 料
libu 吏部
licai 理財
Liizhou 黎州
Lingzhou 靈州
liu 六
Liugu 六谷
liuneiquan 流內銓
Liupan Shan 六盤山
liuwai chushen 流外出身
Lizhou 利州
longnao 龍腦
Lu Deming 陸德明
lüling 律令
lushi canjun 錄事參軍

mai gangcha buji 買綱茶簿藉
maichachang jianguan 賣茶場監官
maima Fanbu 賣馬蕃部
maipu 買撲
maipu jiufangren 買撲酒坊人
maipuren 買撲人
majian 馬監
maocha 毛茶
maoqian wuhuo 貿遷物貨
mashe 馬社
mayi 馬驛
mazheng 馬政

menfa 門閥
Meng Chang 孟昶
Meng Zhixiang 孟知祥
menhu 門戶
mianyi 免役
min bujia fu er guoyong rao 民不加
　賦而國用饒
ming 茗
mingci gaoxia 名次高下
mocha 末茶
mokan 磨勘
Mou Yuanji 牟元吉
Muzheng 木征
muzhiguan 募職官

namingchang 納名場
neidi 內地
neishu 內屬

panghu 旁戶
panguan 判官
pian 片
pingrongce sanbian 平戎策三篇
pochan 破產
poge 破格
Pu Zongmeng 蒲宗孟
puhu 鋪戶

qian Fan 淺蕃
qian Fan shuhu 淺蕃熟戶
Qian Neng 阡能
qianma bingshi 牽馬兵士
qianma renbing 牽馬人兵
qigangchang 起綱場
Qin Gui 秦檜
qingmeng 請盟
qingmiaocha 青苗茶
qingmiaofa 青苗法
Qingtang 青唐
qingtanzhong 清壇衆
qingzhong 輕重
Qinsi 秦司

qiu huanglao yecha 秋黃老葉茶
qizhang 耆長
quan 券
quanfu 泉府
quanma 券馬
quechasi 榷茶司
quehuowu 榷貨務

raocha 饒茶
ren 任
ruzhong 入中
ruzhongfa 入中法

san 散
sanban shichen 三班使臣
sancha 散茶
Sanya 三衙
shan licaizhe 善理財者
shanchang shisan 山場十三
shangfa 賞罰
Shangguan Jun 上官均
shanshi 善士
shanze 山澤
she 社
sheguan 攝官
sheng Fan 生蕃
shengcai zhi dao 生財之道
shengma 省馬
shenguanyuan 審官院
Shenzong 神宗
sheyin yuanmian 赦蔭原免
shi 士
Shi Guangyi 石光義
shibiao 誓表
shicha 食茶
shichachang 食茶場
shichen 使臣
shidafu 士大夫
shili 市利
shiliqian 市利錢
shima zhi chu 市馬之處
shiyi 市易

shiyiwu 市易務
shoufen zhi ren 熟分之人
shu Fan 熟蕃
shubu 屬部
shuhu 熟戶
shuimo mocha 水磨末茶
shuinan 水南
si 私
sise gangcha 四色綱茶

tanya 彈壓
Tian Lingzi 田令孜
Tian Qinquan 田欽全
tianfu 天府
tidian xingyu 提點刑獄
tiemai 貼賣
tiesi jundian 貼司軍典
tiju chamasi 提舉茶馬司
tiju maima jianmusi 提舉買馬監牧司
tingta zhijia 停塌之家
tingzang 停藏
tong jianguan 同監官
Tong Jun 桐君
tong zhuguan 同主管
tongpan 通判
tongrong bianzhuan 通融變轉
tongshang 通商
tongshang difen 通商地方
touzi 頭子
touziqian 頭子錢
tu 茶
tuan 團
Tubo 土蕃
tuchan 土產
tuding 土丁
tuhao 土豪
tuhao dazu 土豪大族
tuo 駝
tuocha 駝茶

wancha 晚茶

Wang Bao 王褒
Wang Jian 王建
Wang Jun 王均
Wang Shao 王韶
Wang Xiaobo 王小波
Wang Yan 王衍
wei 尉
Wei Jizong 魏繼宗
Wei Junqing 韋君靖
weiqian 違欠
wu buluo 五部落
wu chushen 無出身
Wu Jie 吳玠
Wu Shimeng 吳師孟
Wu Shu 吳淑
Wu Xi 吳曦
wufengjun 武鋒軍
wuling maimai tongkuai, wuzhi fangzhi qianben 務令買賣通快,無致防滯錢本
wuxing 五刑
wuyi daifu 武翼大夫

xi 席
Xi Xia 西夏
xian 獻
xianghao 鄉豪
xiangjun 廂軍
xiangli 鄉例
xianling 縣令
xianpai 先牌
xianqian 見錢
Xianyu Shen 鮮于侁
Xianyu Zhongtong 鮮于仲通
xiao guanya 小管押
xiao jiangjiao 小將校
xicha 細茶
xinfa 新法
xingshi banbu 形勢版簿
xingshihu 形勢戶
xu'e 虛額
xuanchai 選差

xuandelang 宣德郎
xuanfusi 宣撫司
xuanren 選人
Xue Xiang 薛向
xuguan 序官
xun liangzi 循兩資
xunjian 巡檢
xunxia bancha shichen 巡轄般茶
　使臣
xunxia chapu shichen 巡轄茶鋪使臣
xunxia madipu 巡轄馬遞鋪
xunzi 循資
xunzhuo sicha shichen 巡捉私茶
　使臣

yabaoren 牙保人
yacha 芽茶
yajiao 牙校
yakuai 牙儈
yama shichen 押馬使臣
yama zhi fuyi 押馬之夫役
Yan Cangshu 閻蒼舒
Yan Li 嚴礪
Yan Wu 嚴武
Yan Zhen 嚴震
Yang Tianhui 楊天惠
yangao cha 研膏茶
yaqian 衙前
yaren 牙人
yi jingli wei e 以淨利爲額
Yi Yi zhi Yi 以夷制夷
yicheng 驛程
yijun 義軍
yin 蔭
yinbu 蔭補
yiquan 驛券
yishou 醫獸
you chushen 有出身
youdong 游冬
Yu Yunwen 虞允文
Yuan 元

yuan Fan 遠蕃
Yuanfeng jiufa 元豐舊法
yuanguan jiuyi zhi fa 遠官就移之法
yuanhu 園戶

zangkuai 駔儈
zaocha 早茶
Zhang Jun 張浚
Zhang Pu 張溥
Zhang Qixian 張齊賢
Zhang Wansui 張萬歲
Zhang Yong 張詠
zhanma 戰馬
zhanshe chaiqian yici 占射差遣一次
zhaoma zhi chu 招馬之處
zhaoyou boma 招誘博馬
zheqian 折錢
Zhezong 哲宗
zhicai 治財
zhilinglu 知令錄
zhishe 指射
zhiyihu 職役戶
zhizhishi 制置使
zhongduan zui 重斷罪
zhongjia 中價
Zhou Biaoquan 周表權
Zhou Renmei 周仁美
Zhou Yin 周尹
zhuandian 專典
zhuanguan 轉官
zhuanyunshi 轉運使
zhuotongjing 卓筒井
zhushui 住稅
zhuzuo zuolang 著作佐郎
Ziizhou 資州
Zongge 宗哥
zongling 總領
zongzhi 總制
zoujian 奏薦
zouju 奏舉

Index

Senior level status (*jingchaoguan*), 158

Seniority rank, 185–186

Service auxiliaries (*baizhi renbing*), 296

Service personnel, 161

Shaanxi, 21, 30, 37–49 *passim*, 73, 74–75, 76, 103, 106, 123–150 *passim*, 153, 155, 156, 160, 161, 179, 187–219 *passim*, 228, 231, 243–285 *passim*, 293; horse markets of, 44, 228, 251, 254, 255, 259, 263, 266, 268, 276, 279, 284, 285; and horse procurement, 39, 258, 269–270, 273; and tea monopoly, 139–150, 217, 226

Shaanxi Horse Purchase Bureau, 269–272

Shandong, 103, 149

Shangfa (rewards and punishments), 177

Shaoxing era (1130–1162), 202

Shazhou, 26

Shen Gua, 97, 170

Shengma (field-administered horse policy), 34, 35

Shenzong, Emperor (1068–1085): and New Policies, 9, 38, 42, 124, 125, 150, 170, 192, 195, 310; and THA, 108, 127, 159, 162; and Wang Anshi, 111, 113, 116

Shi Chuwen, 88, 89

Shi Duanchen, 97

Shi Guangyi, 65, 66, 220, 222, 226

Shiba Yoshinobu, 72

Shicha (consumer-tea) markets, 138, 139, 184

Shichachang (retail tea markets), 138, 139, 161, 184

Shifang County, 98

Shiyiwu. See State trade bureaus

Shop households (*puhu*), 66–67

Shouning Monastery, 97

Shu. *See* Former Shu; Later Shu

Shuhu ("cooked" tribes), 27, 43, 257

Shuzhou, 61, 96, 97, 98, 134

Sichuan, 9–10, 44, 46–47, 287–297 *passim*, 303, 306–307, 312; agriculture, 50–51; commodities trade, 39–41, 44, 45–46, 51; horses, 26, 249, 255, 261–263, 266, 268, 276, 277, 279–280, 281, 282, 285; *jinshi* holders, 101–104; magnate society of, 80–87; silk industry, 41, 46; tea culture, 51–58; tea cultivators, 63–68; tea industry and the THA, 217–245; tea manufacture, 60–63; tea merchants, 69–76; tea monopoly, 52, 69, 188, 195, 232, 235, 268, 306, 308; tea monopsony, 132–139, 200, 217; topography, 49–50

Sichuan Branch (THA), 261–263

"Sichuan-tea restricted zone" (*Chuancha jindi*), 139

Sichuanese: horse drivers, 297–298; in TMA and THA, 130–131, 164–165

Silk industry, 41, 46, 73, 74, 90, 175–176, 276

Silver currency, 276, 277, 281, 282

Sima Guang, 112, 113, 117, 128, 193, 239

Sino-Jurchen war (1119–1127), 10, 14, 71, 192, 198, 200, 203, 255

Sino-Tibetan mutual trade and defense alliance, 28–30, 31

Sise gangcha ("four-varieties convoy-tea"), 134, 260

Six Valleys (*Liugu*) federation, 26, 27, 31, 36

Skinner, G. William, 49

Skocpol, Theda, 315

Smuggling laws (tea), 229–235

Sogabe Shizuo, 8

Song Administrative Digest, 58

Song dynasty (960–1279), 2, 3, 7, 79, 88, 111, 114, 132, 141, 177, 183, 198, 235, 236, 239, 249–268 *passim*, 277–285 *passim*, 294, 302–314 *passim;* economic activism and military vulnerability, 6–8; fiscal regulation of tea, 55–58; horse breeding, 16, 20–23, 259; horse procurement, 23–27, 248, 259; horse procurement, 23–27, 248, 262; horse supply crisis, 17–26, 304; rebellion and political mobilization, 93–108; trade alliance with Tibetan federation, 28–30, 31; wartime economy, 8

Song History, 27, 114, 159, 196

Song Qi, 17

Song Taizu, 4, 89

Songpan, 198, 255, 261

South China, 4, 51, 102, 200, 306

Southeast China, 3, 197

Southeastern tea: commercial structure, 70–73; competition with Sichuanese tea, 57–58, 143, 147, 192–198, 227, 243; development of, 52–56; government regulation of, 55–58, 69–70, 74, 149–150, 156, 180; manufacturing methods, 58–61; output, 219

Southern Tang, 57

Speculators, 68, 94, 95

State Trade Act (*shiyifa*), 44, 71, 193; as anti-engrosser measure, 115

右一匹元祐二年十二月廿三日於左天駟監楝中秦

馬好頭赤九歲四尺六寸

天馬登歌頌而今哈
薩及布魯歲市為
常年論等愛烏罕
又達於彼馬高七尺
有八寸五馬之高不
足稱于異牽來敬
以進肯之天閑師
備那末如上馴調
弓順玆今老矣迄
古希那以普年騺
枝迅展因自愧且
同悌石火光陰速
誠作
甲辰新正之月
澥尾